drawnandquarterly.com

ISBN 978-1-77046-399-8
First edition: June 2020
Second printing: April 2021
Printed in China
10 9 8 7 6 5 4 3 2

Cataloguing data available from Library and Archives Canada.

Published in the USA by Drawn & Quarterly, a client publisher of Farrar, Straus
and Giroux. Published in Canada by Drawn & Quarterly, a client publisher of
Raincoast Books. Published in the United Kingdom by Drawn & Quarterly, a
client publisher of Publishers Group UK.

 Drawn & Quarterly acknowledges the support of the
Government of Canada and the Canada Council for the
Arts for our publishing program.

Drawn & Quarterly reconnaît l'aide financière du gouvernement du Québec
par l'entremise de la Société de développement des entreprises culturelles
(SODEC) pour nos activités d'édition. Gouvernement du Québec—Programme
de crédit d'impôt pour l'édition de livres—Gestion SODEC.

Wendy
Master of Art

Walter Scott

Drawn & Quarterly

Somewhere
in Berlin...

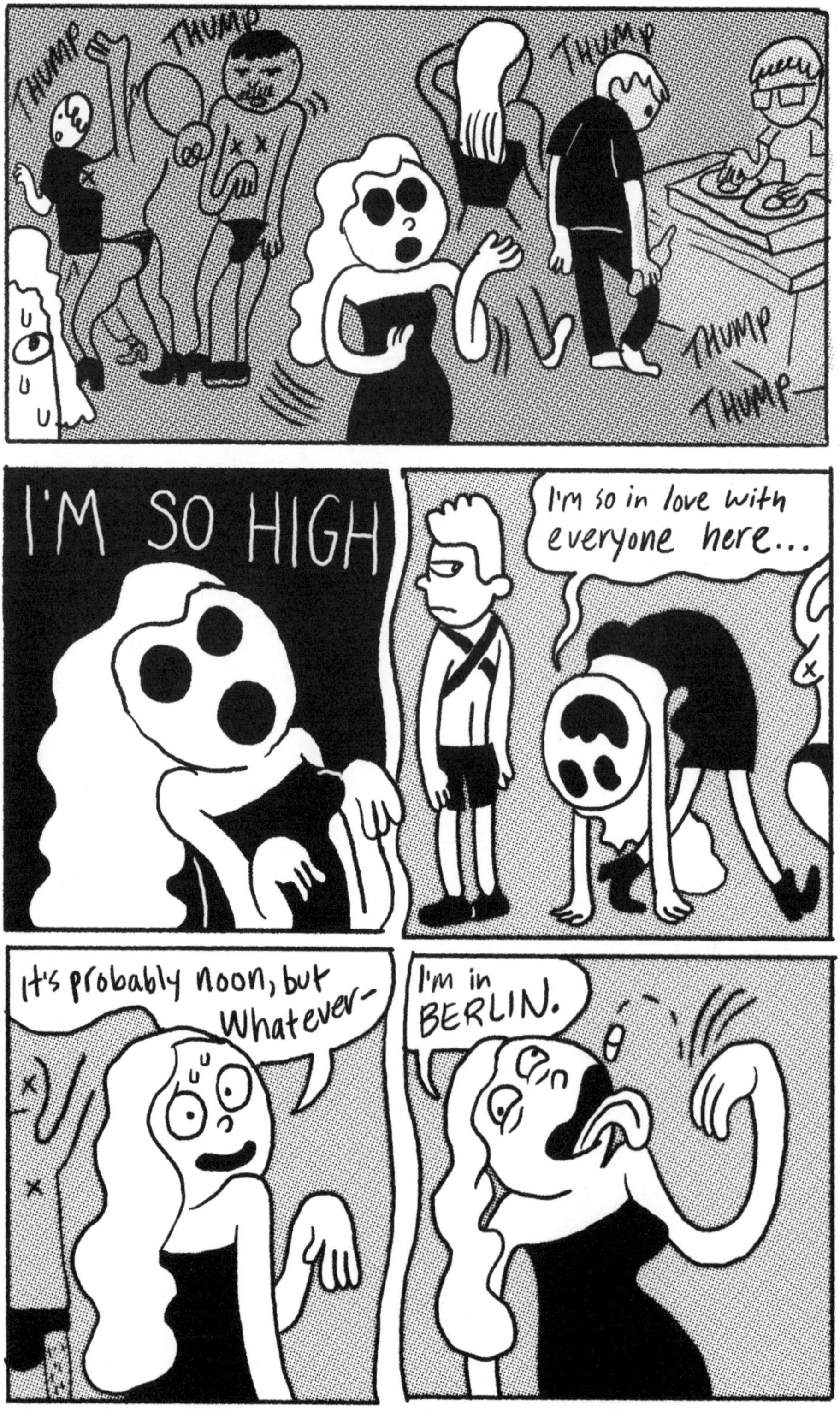
THUMP
THUMP
THUMP
THUMP
THUMP
THUMP
I'M SO HIGH
I'm so in love with everyone here...
It's probably noon, but Whatever-
I'm in BERLIN.

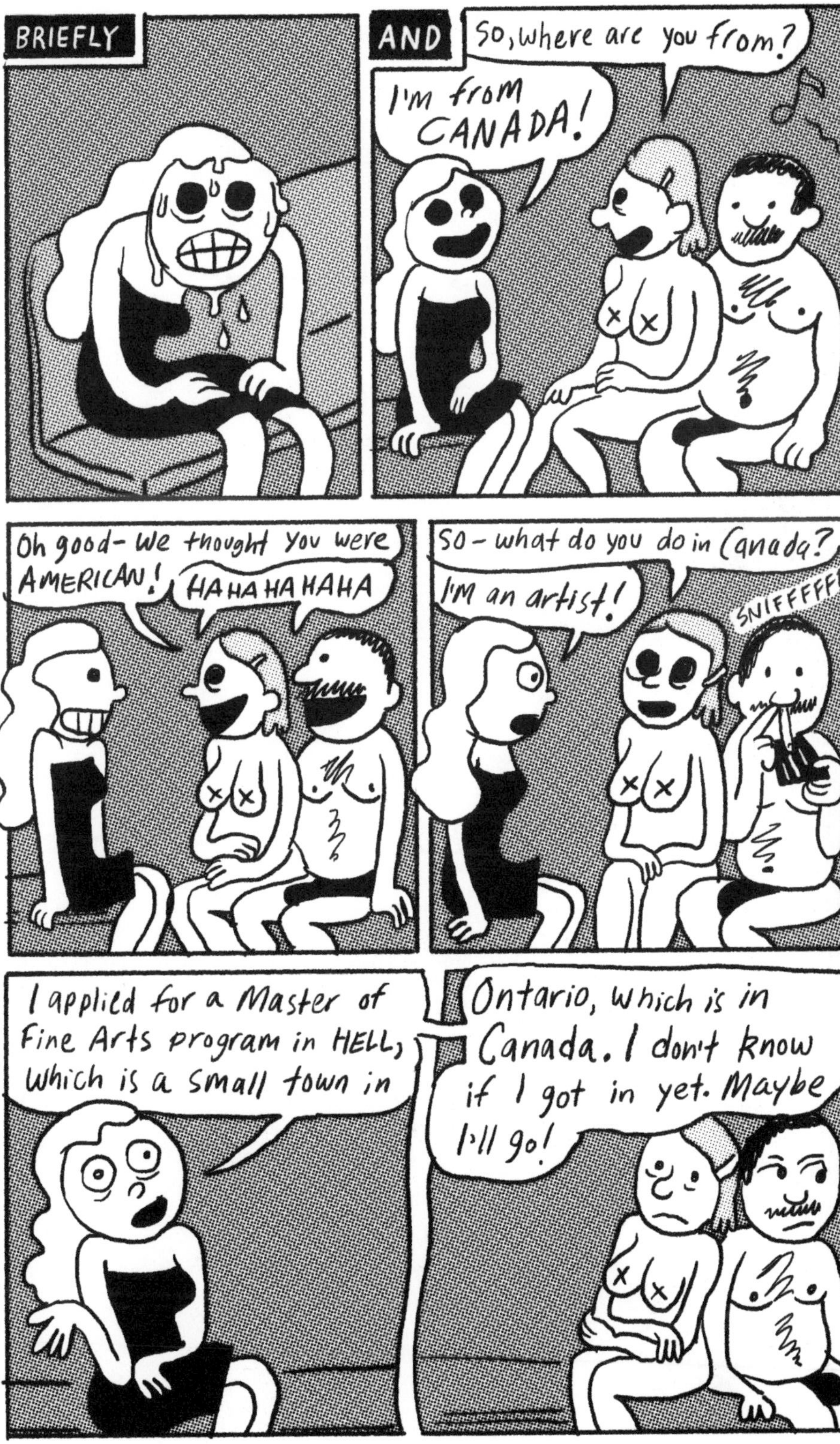
BRIEFLY
AND
So, where are you from?
I'm from CANADA!
Oh good- We thought you were AMERICAN!
HAHAHAHAHAHA
SO- what do you do in Canada?
I'm an artist!
SNIFFFFFF
I applied for a Master of Fine Arts program in HELL, which is a small town in
Ontario, which is in Canada. I don't know if I got in yet. Maybe I'll go!

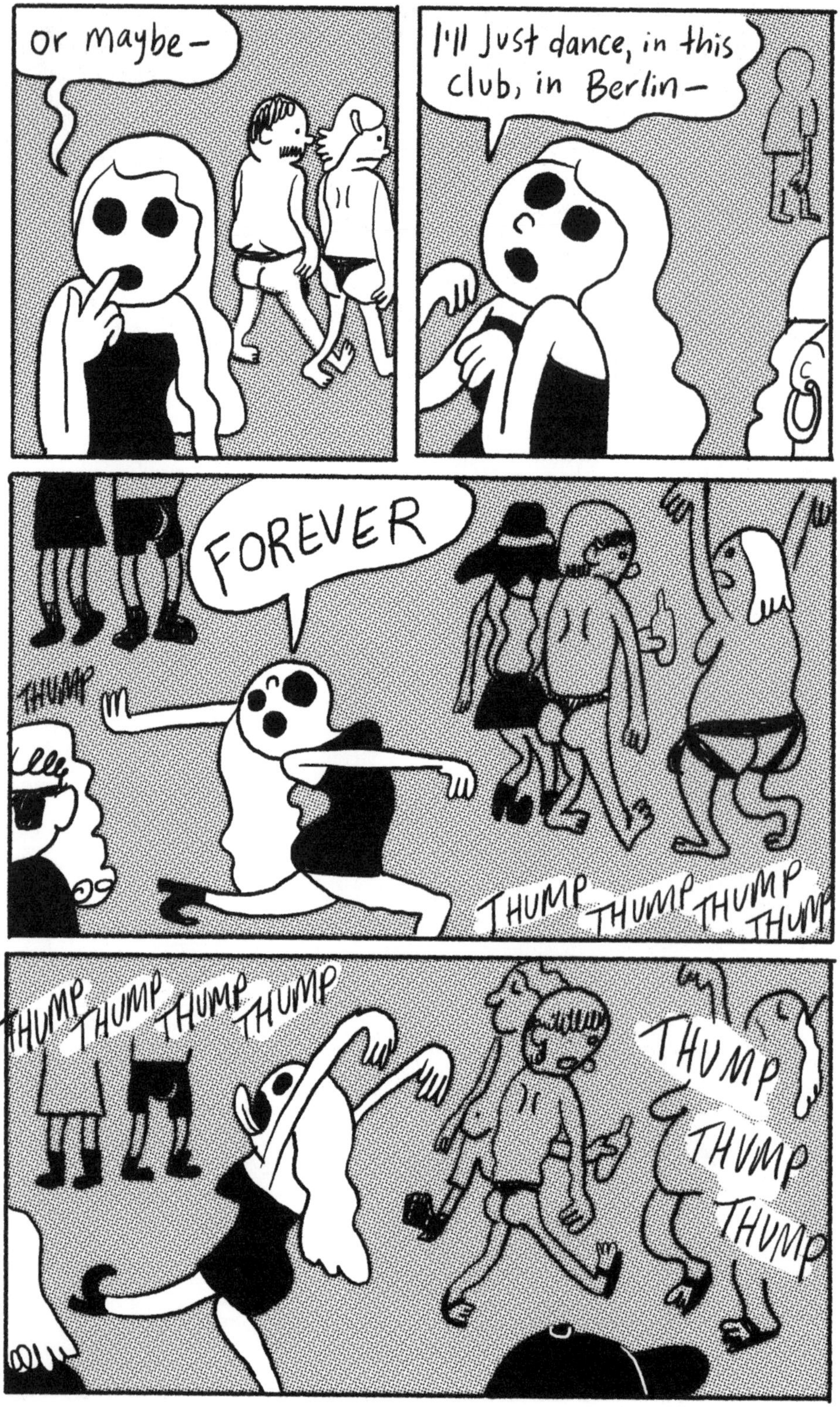
or maybe-
I'll Just dance, in this club, in Berlin-
FOREVER
THUMP
THUMP THUMP THUMP THUMP
THUMP THUMP THUMP THUMP
THUMP THUMP THUMP

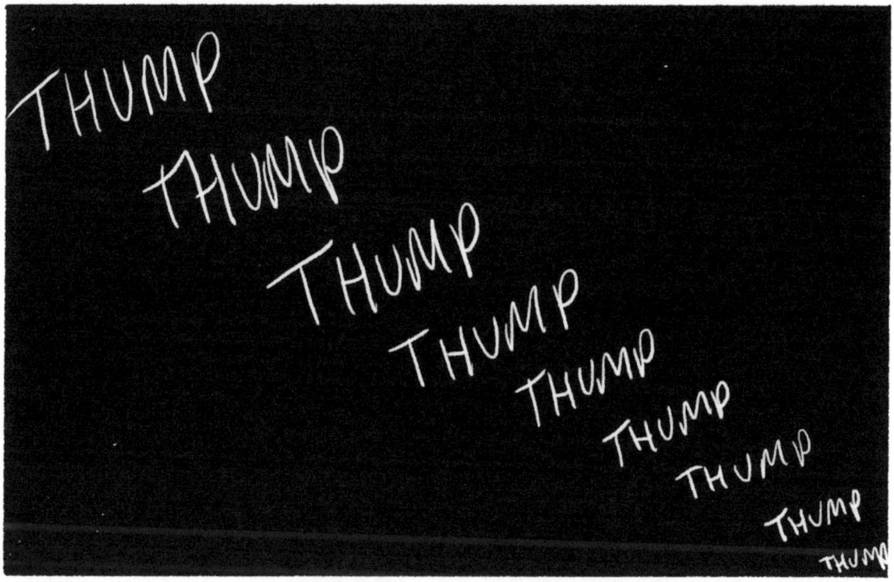
THUMP
THUMP
THUMP
THUMP
THUMP
THUMP
THUMP
THUMP

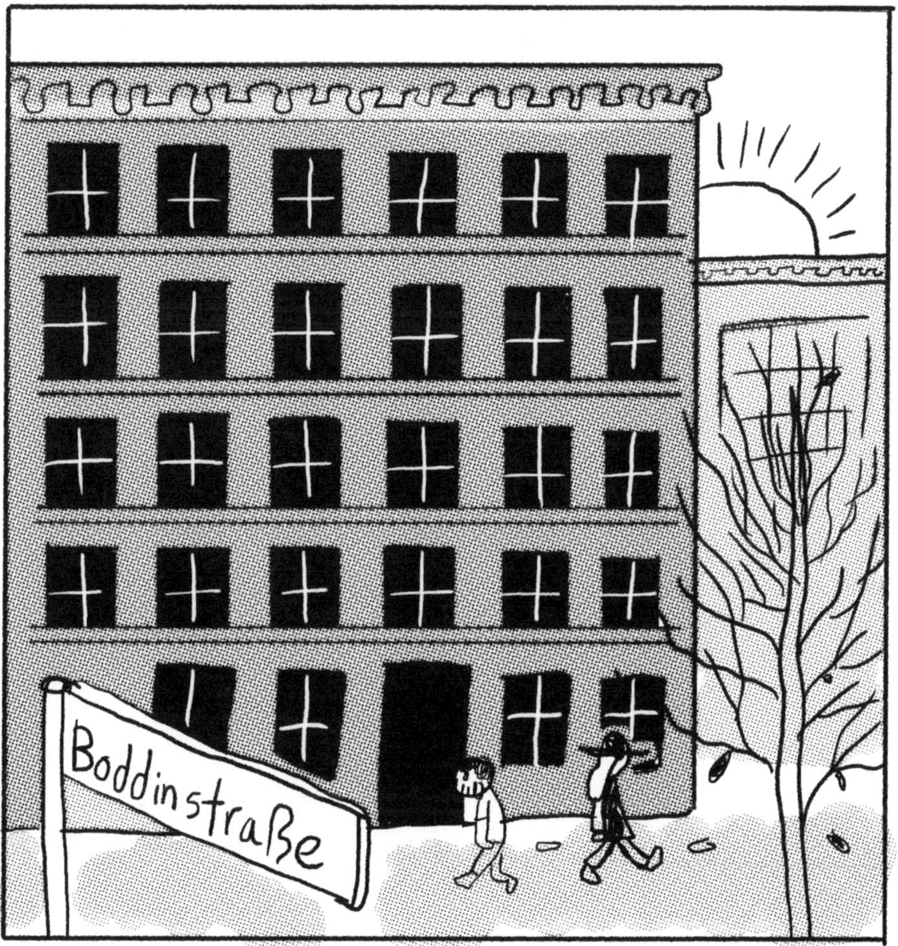
Boddinstraße

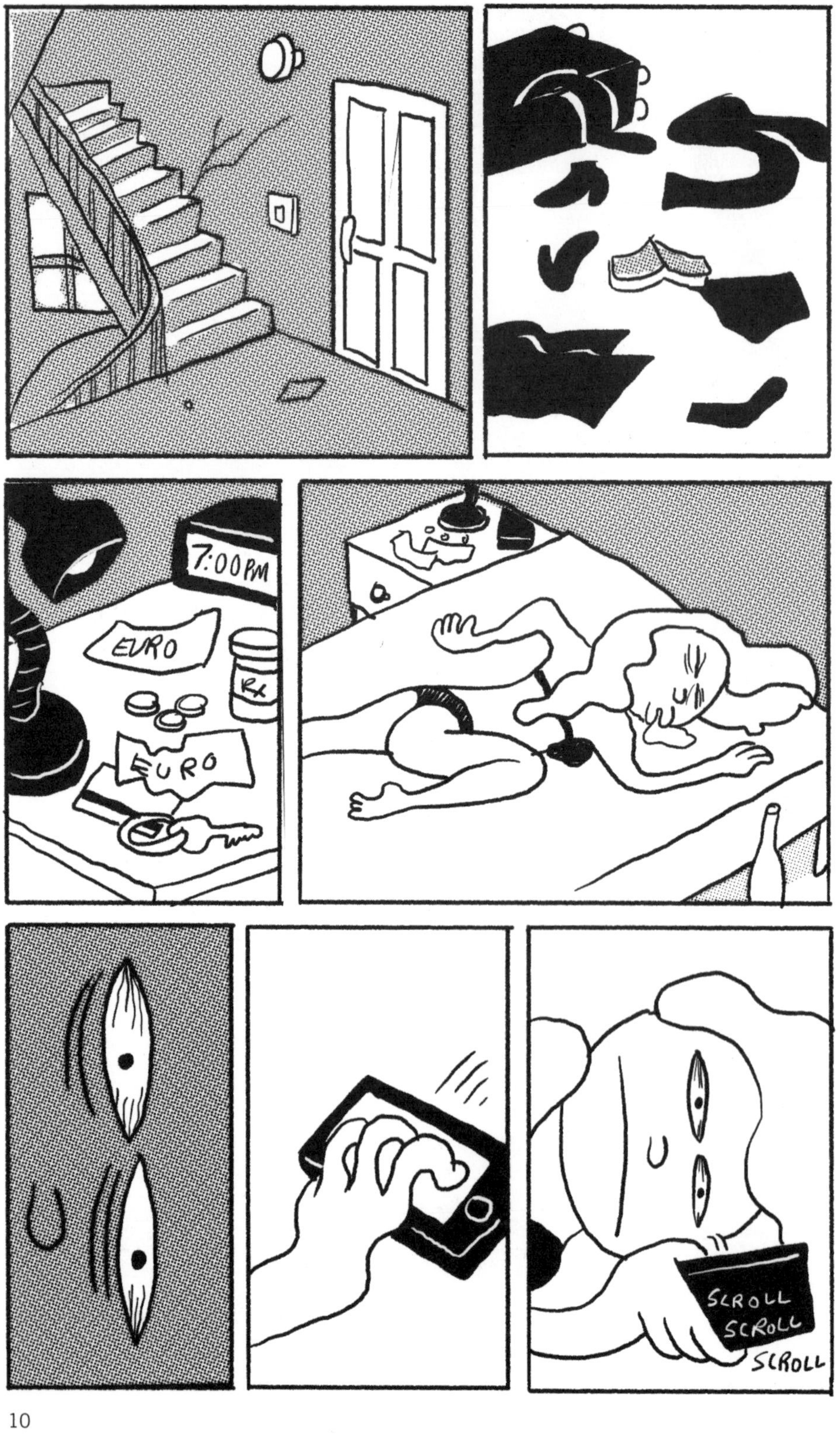
7:00PM
EURO
Rx
EURO
SCROLL
SCROLL
SCROLL

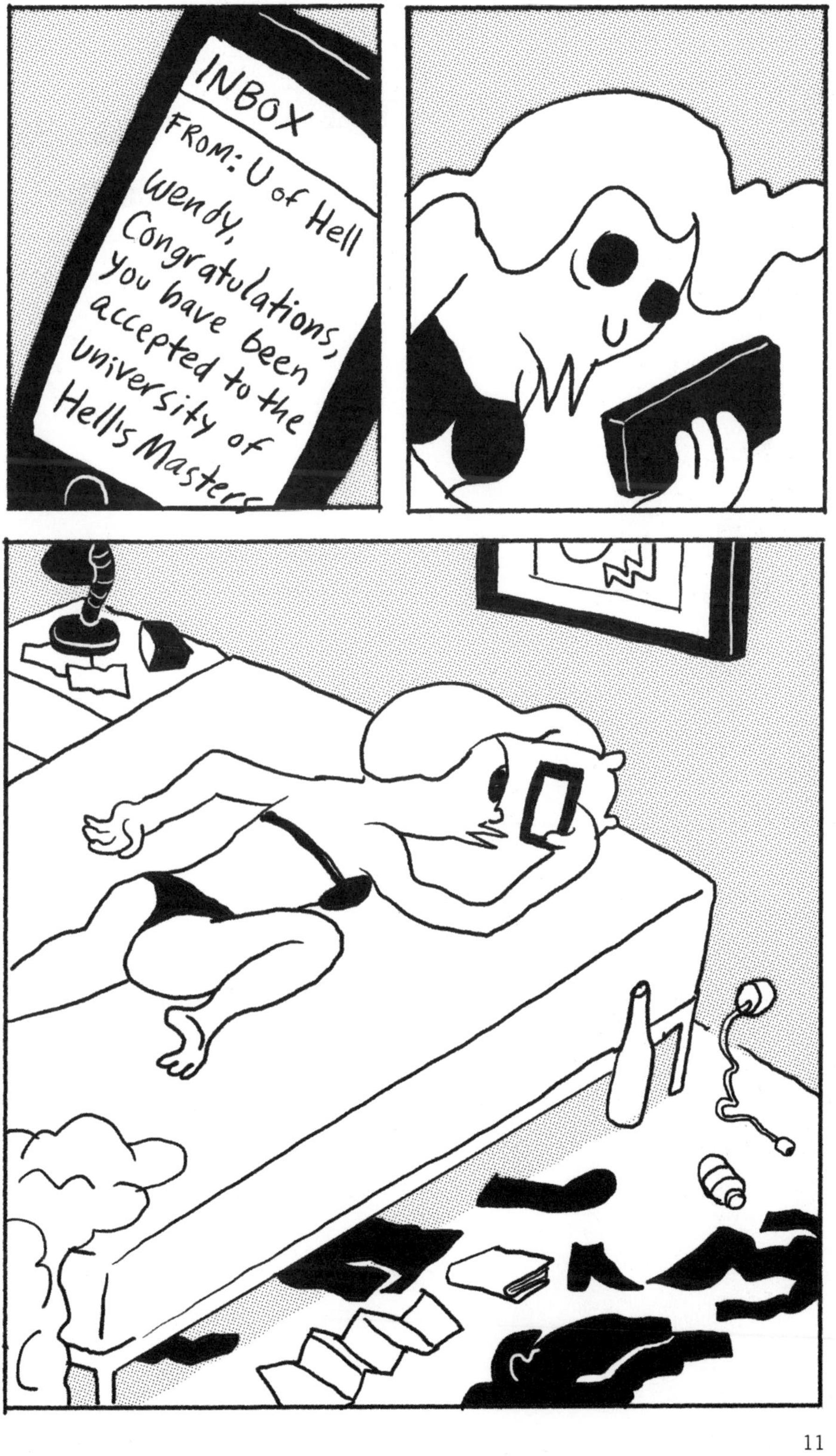
INBOX
FROM: U of Hell
Wendy,
Congratulations,
you have been
accepted to the
University of
Hell's Masters

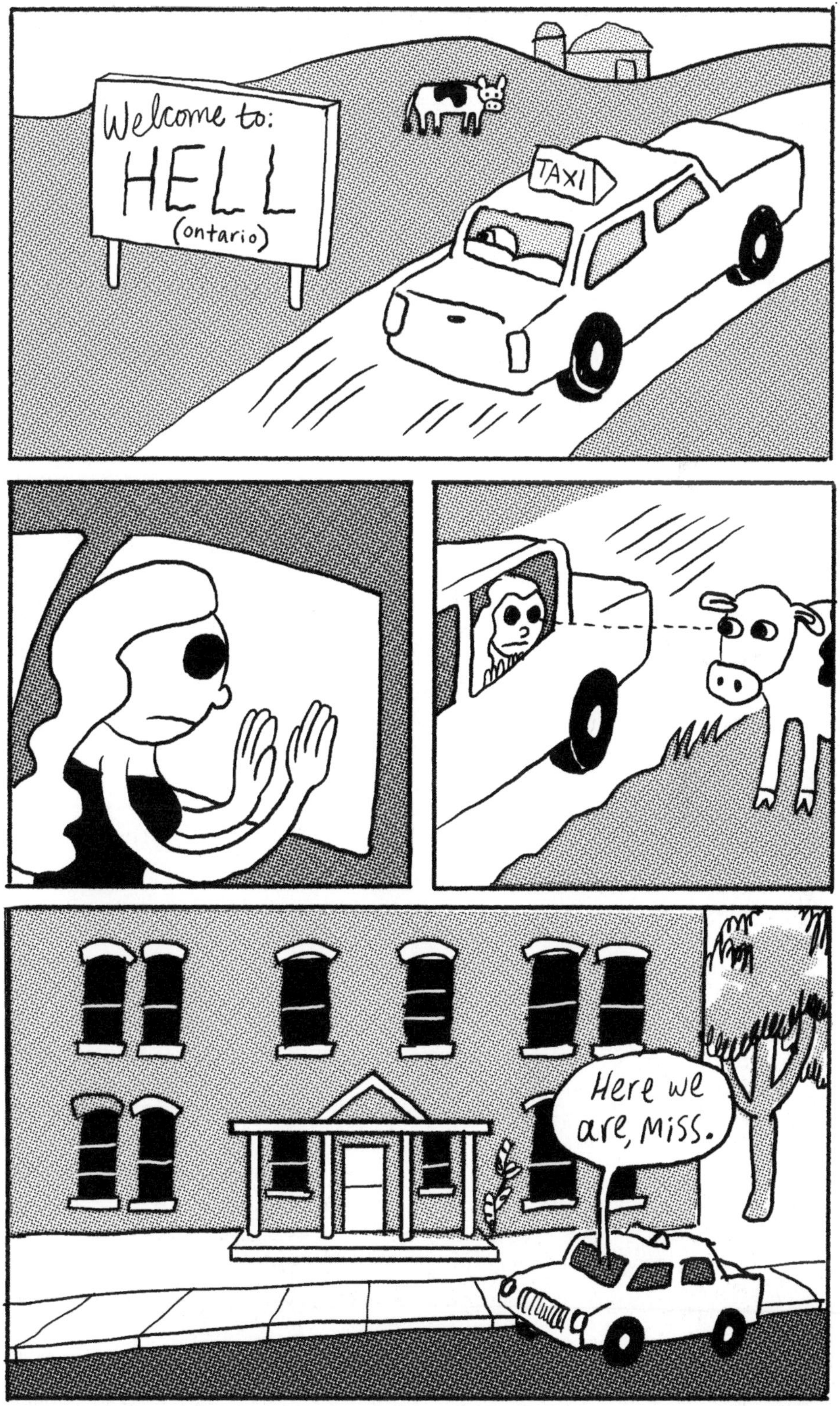
Welcome to:
HELL
(ontario)
TAXI
Here we are, Miss.

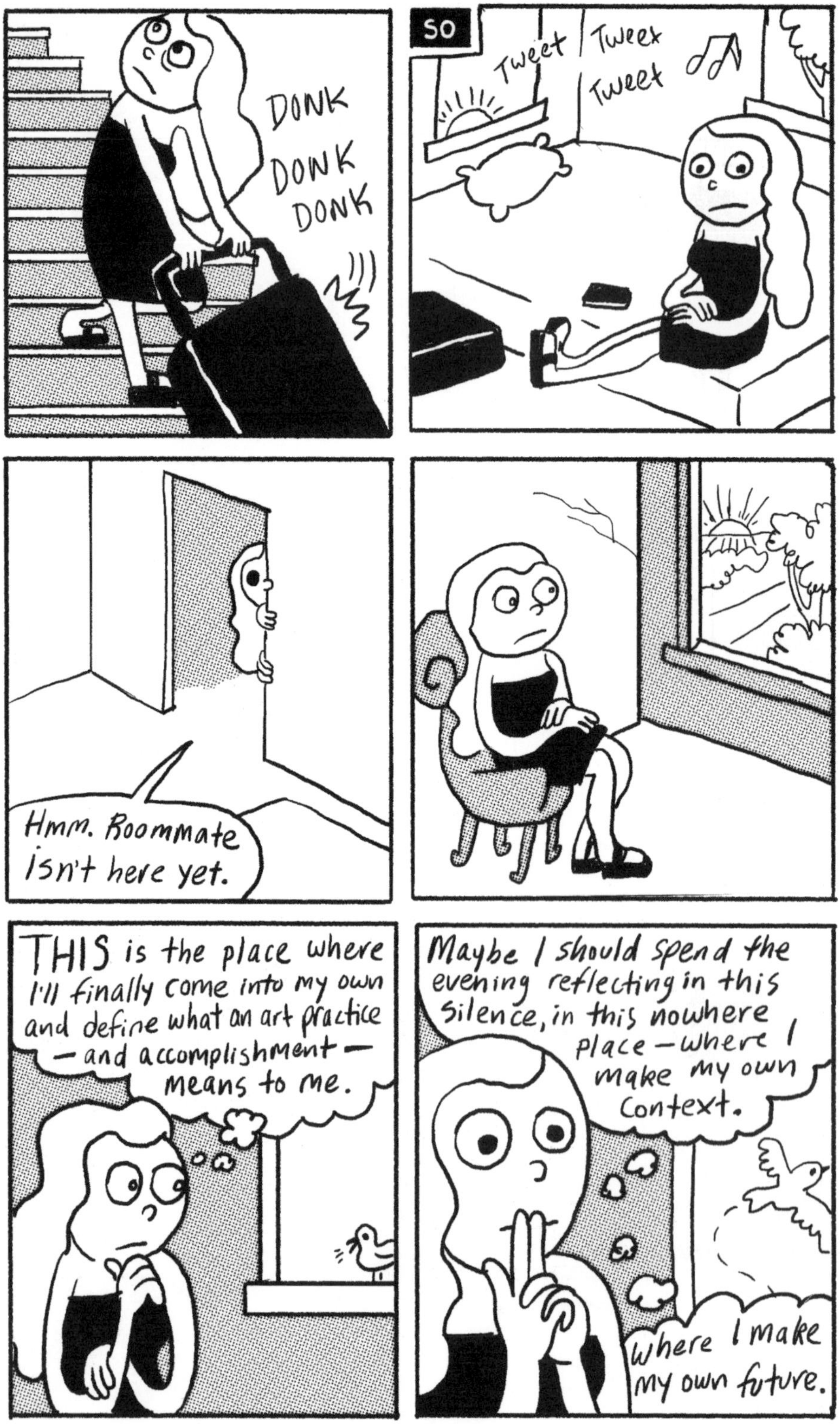
DONK
DONK
DONK
SO
Tweet
Tweet
Tweet
Hmm. Roommate isn't here yet.
THIS is the place where I'll finally come into my own and define what an art practice —and accomplishment— means to me.
Maybe I should spend the evening reflecting in this silence, in this nowhere place—where I make my own context.
Where I make my own future.

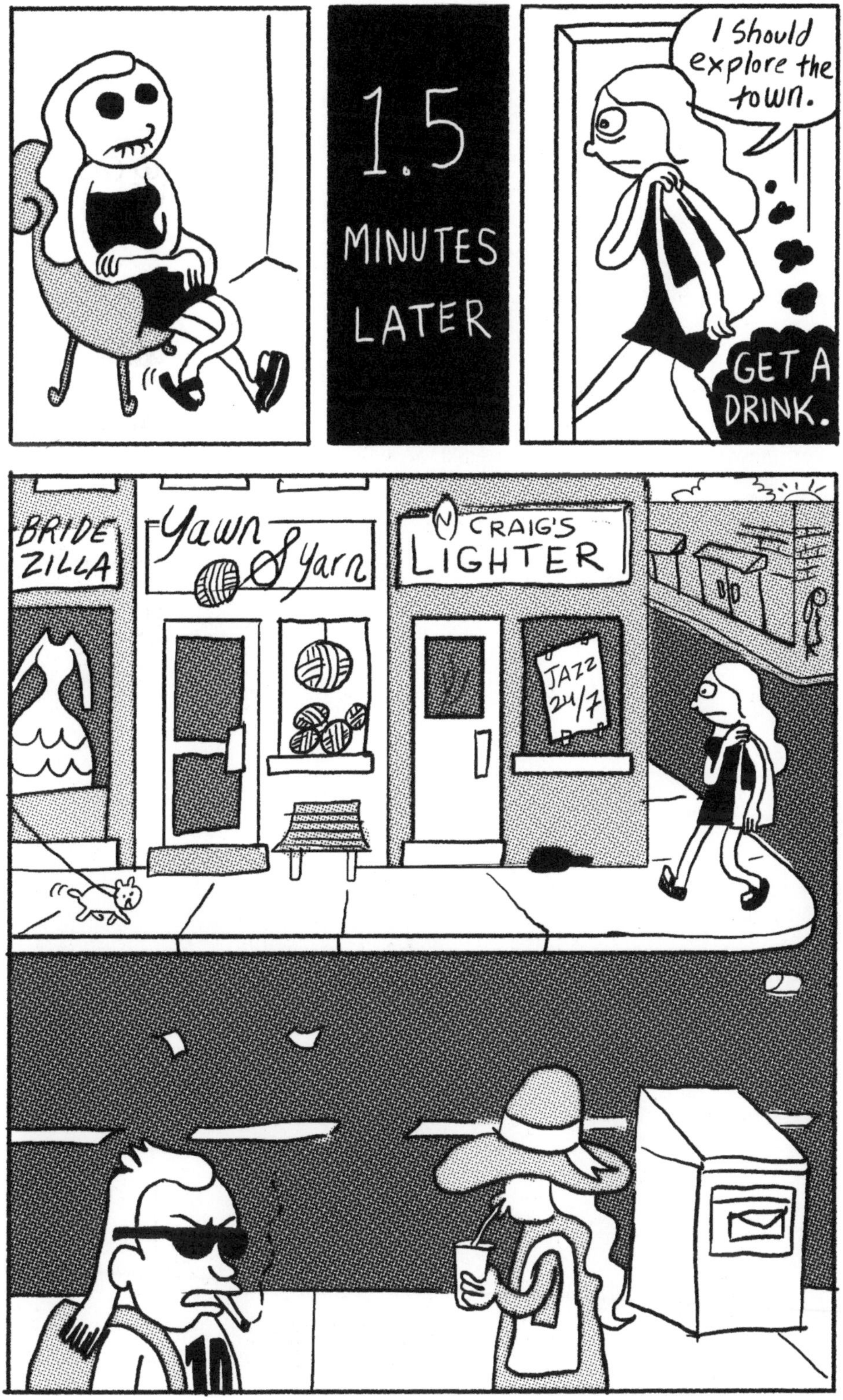
1.5 MINUTES LATER
I should explore the town.
GET A DRINK.
BRIDE ZILLA
Yawn & Yarn
CRAIG'S LIGHTER
JAZZ 24/7

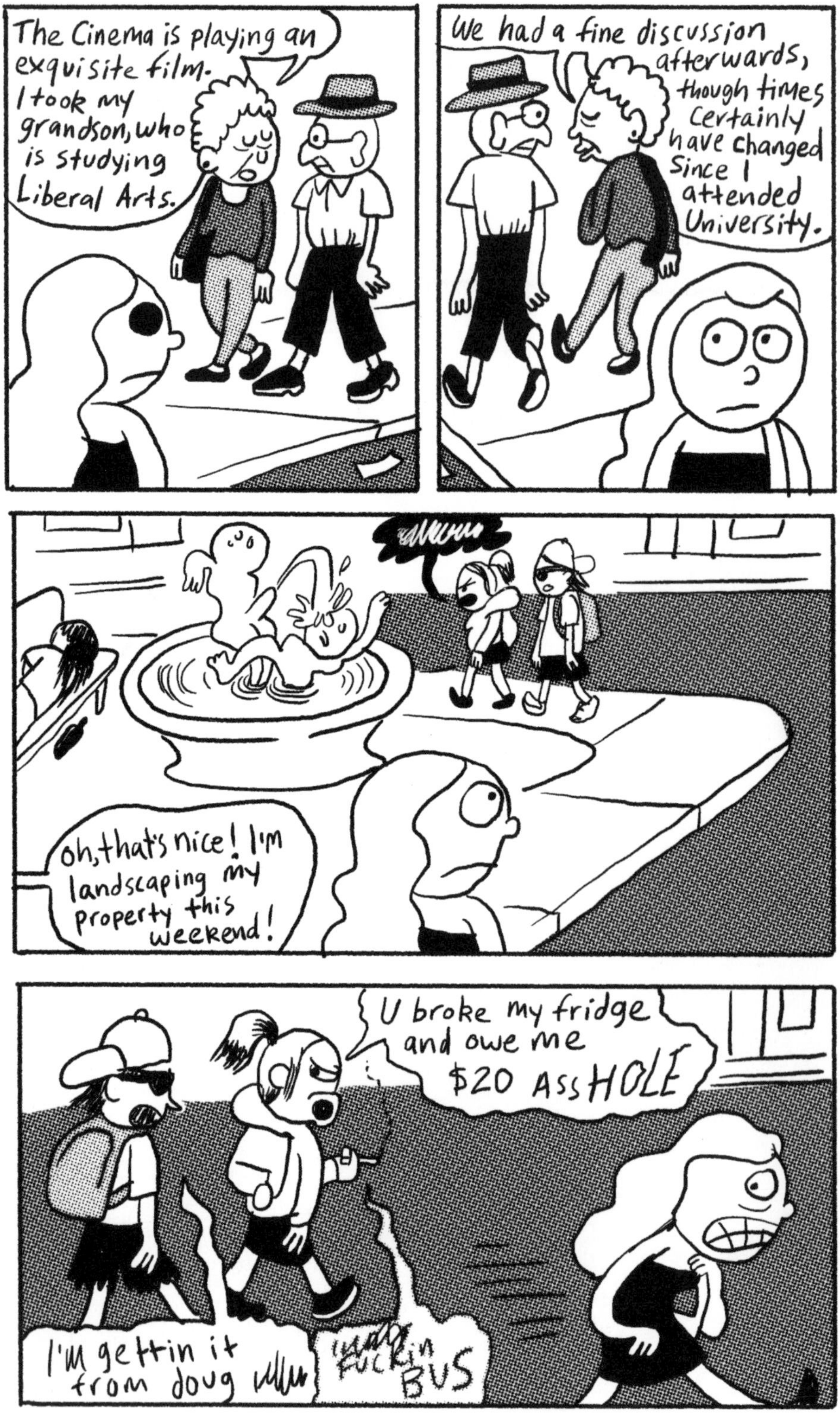
The Cinema is playing an exquisite film. I took my grandson, who is studying Liberal Arts.
We had a fine discussion afterwards, though times certainly have changed since I attended University.
oh, that's nice! I'm landscaping my property this weekend!
U broke my fridge and owe me $20 ASSHOLE
I'm gettin it from doug
FUCKin BUS

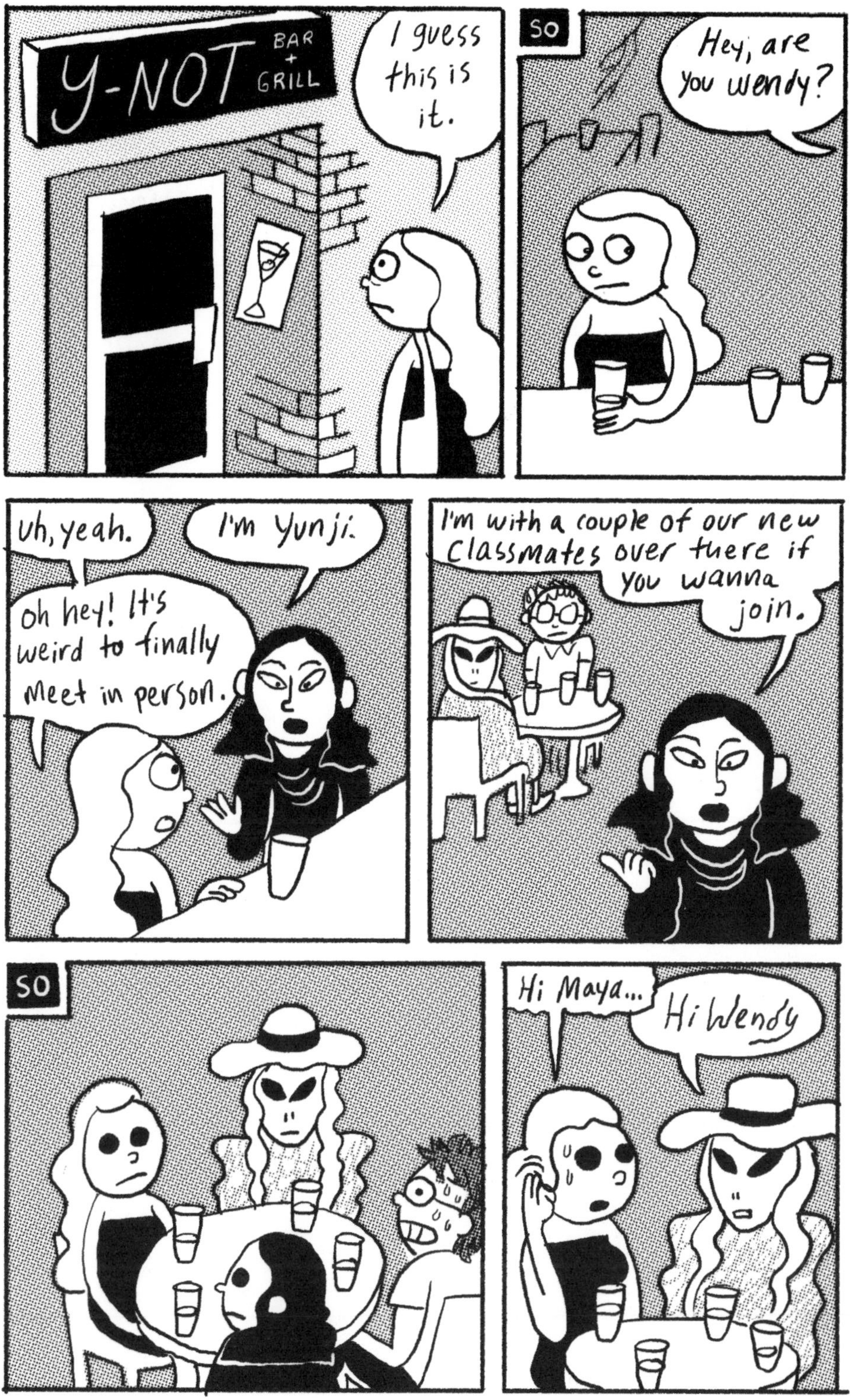
Y-NOT BAR + GRILL
I guess this is it.
SO
Hey, are you Wendy?
Uh, yeah.
I'm Yunji.
Oh hey! It's weird to finally meet in person.
I'm with a couple of our new classmates over there if you wanna join.
SO
Hi Maya...
Hi Wendy

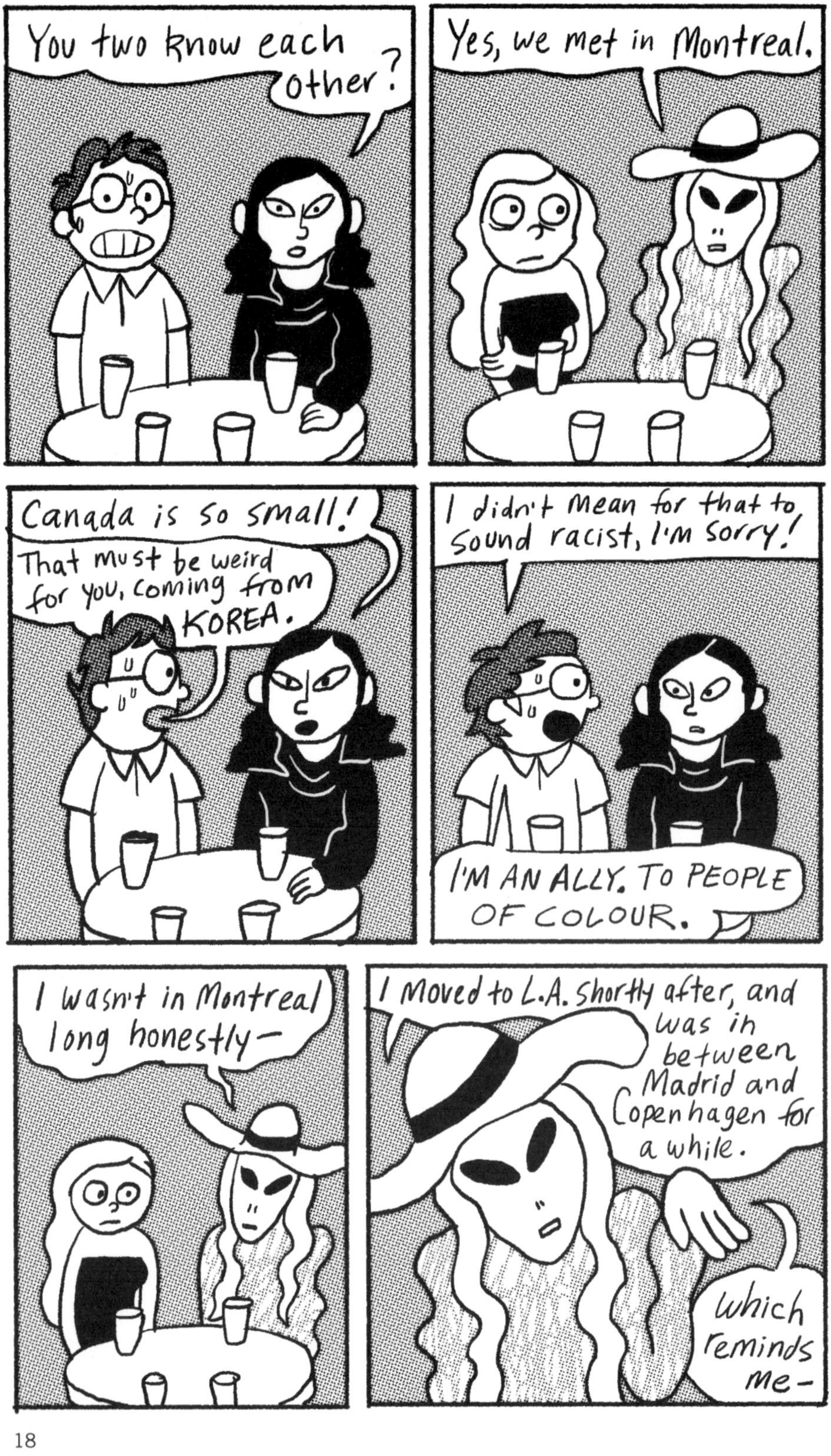
You two know each other?
Yes, we met in Montreal.
Canada is so small!
That must be weird for you, coming from KOREA.
I didn't mean for that to sound racist, I'm sorry!
I'M AN ALLY. TO PEOPLE OF COLOUR.
I wasn't in Montreal long honestly—
I Moved to L.A. shortly after, and was in between Madrid and Copenhagen for a while.
Which reminds me—

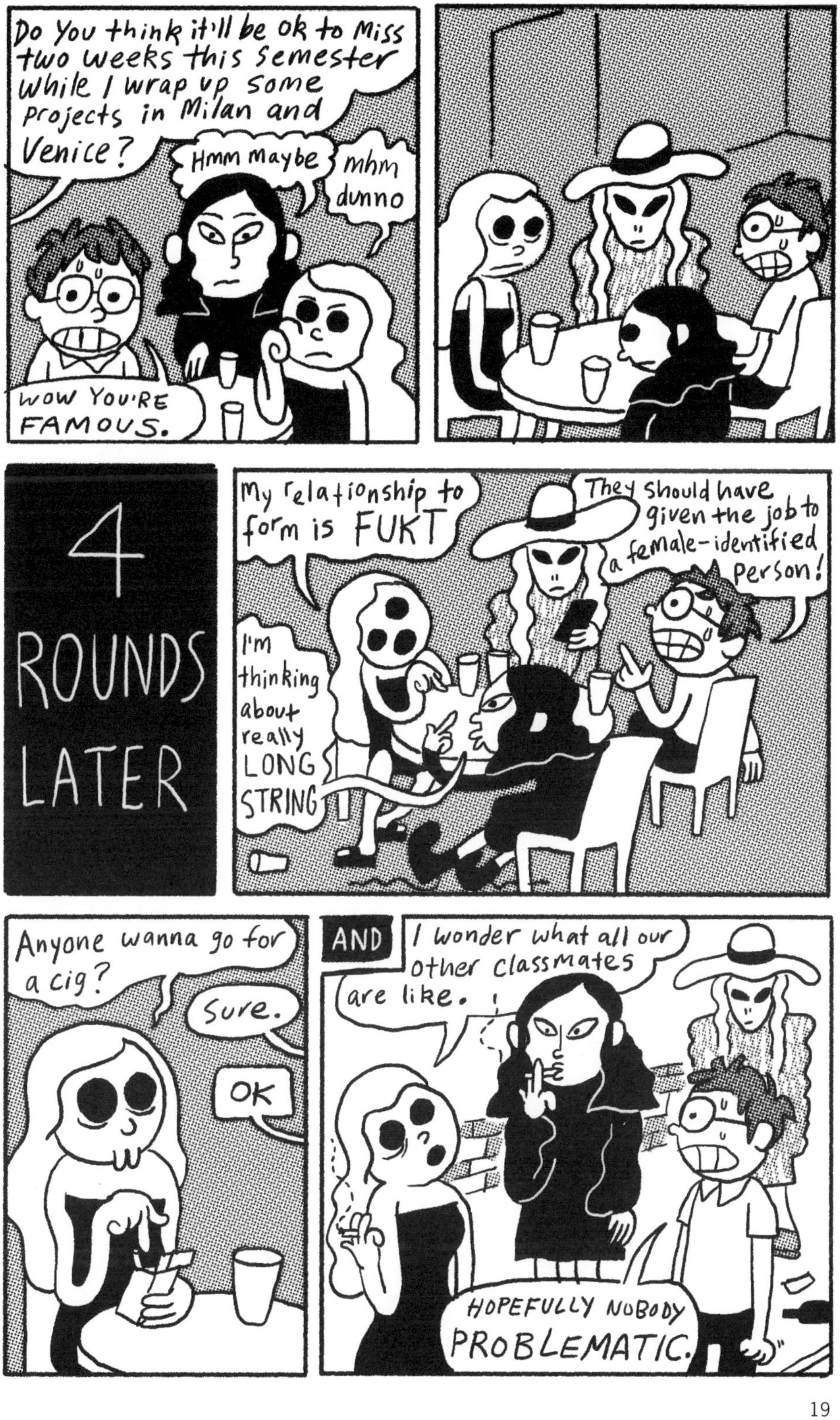
Do you think it'll be ok to miss two weeks this semester while I wrap up some projects in Milan and Venice?
Hmm maybe
mhm dunno
WOW YOU'RE FAMOUS.
4 ROUNDS LATER
My relationship to form is FUKT
They should have given the job to a female-identified person!
I'm thinking about really LONG STRING
Anyone wanna go for a cig?
Sure.
OK
AND
I wonder what all our other classmates are like.
HOPEFULLY NOBODY PROBLEMATIC.

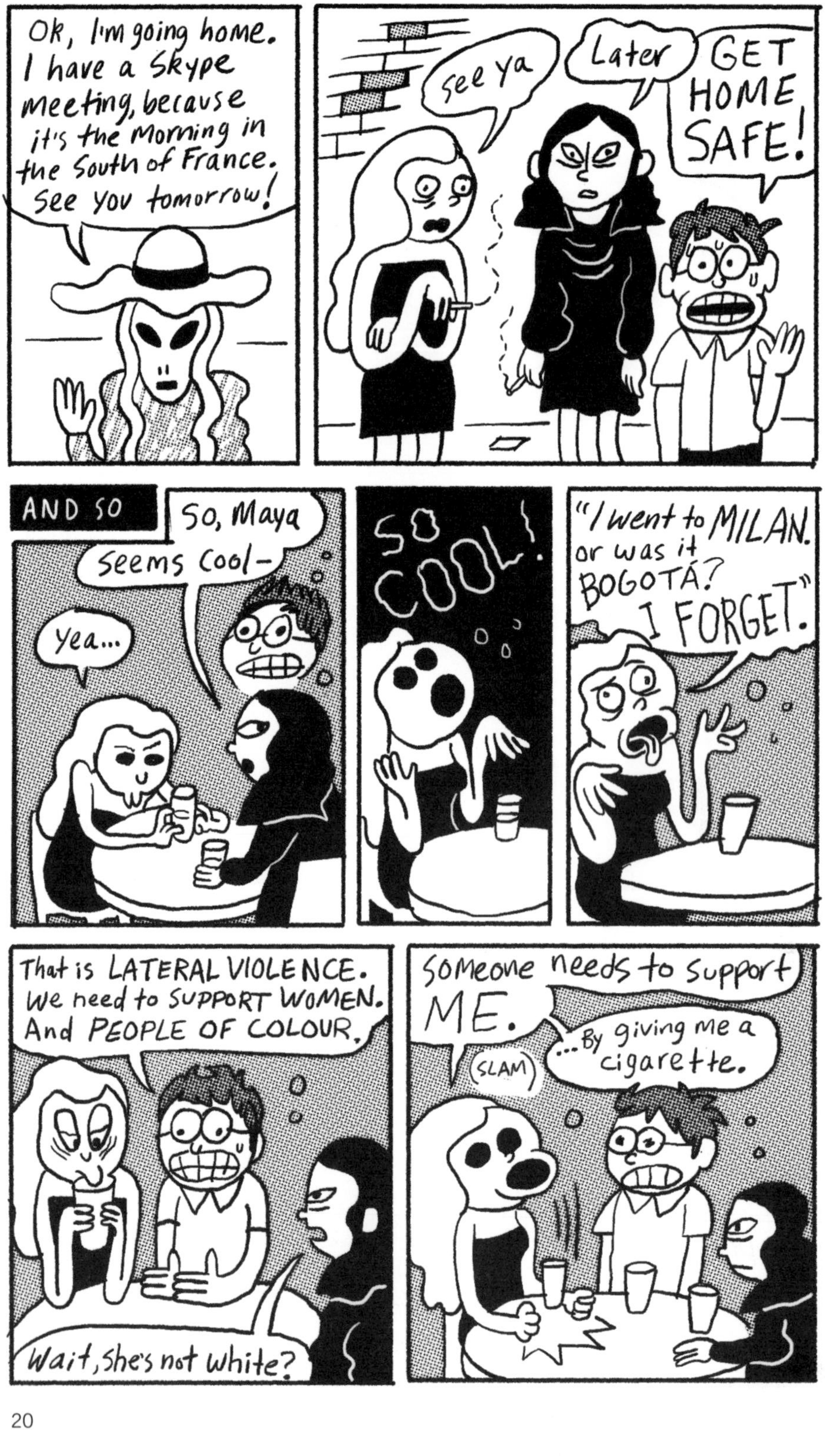
Ok, I'm going home. I have a Skype meeting, because it's the Morning in the South of France. See you tomorrow!
See ya
Later
GET HOME SAFE!
AND SO
So, Maya seems cool-
yea...
SO COOL!
"I went to MILAN. or was it BOGOTÁ? I FORGET."
That is LATERAL VIOLENCE. We need to SUPPORT WOMEN. And PEOPLE OF COLOUR.
Wait, She's not white?
Someone needs to support ME.
(SLAM)
...By giving me a cigarette.

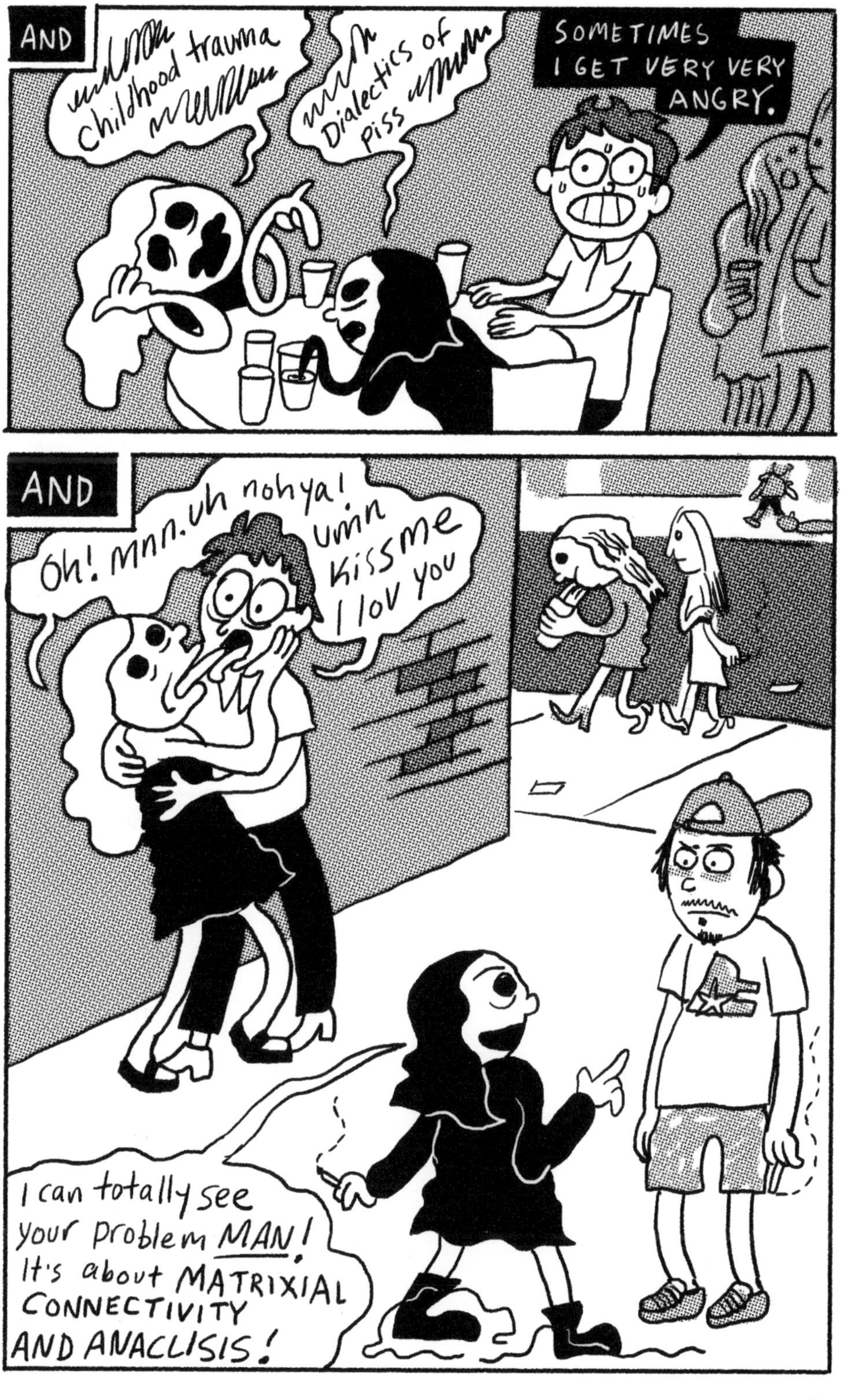
AND
childhood trauma
Dialectics of piss
SOMETIMES I GET VERY VERY ANGRY.
AND
Oh! Mnn.uh nohya! umn kiss me I lov you
I can totally see your problem MAN! It's about MATRIXIAL CONNECTIVITY AND ANACLISIS!

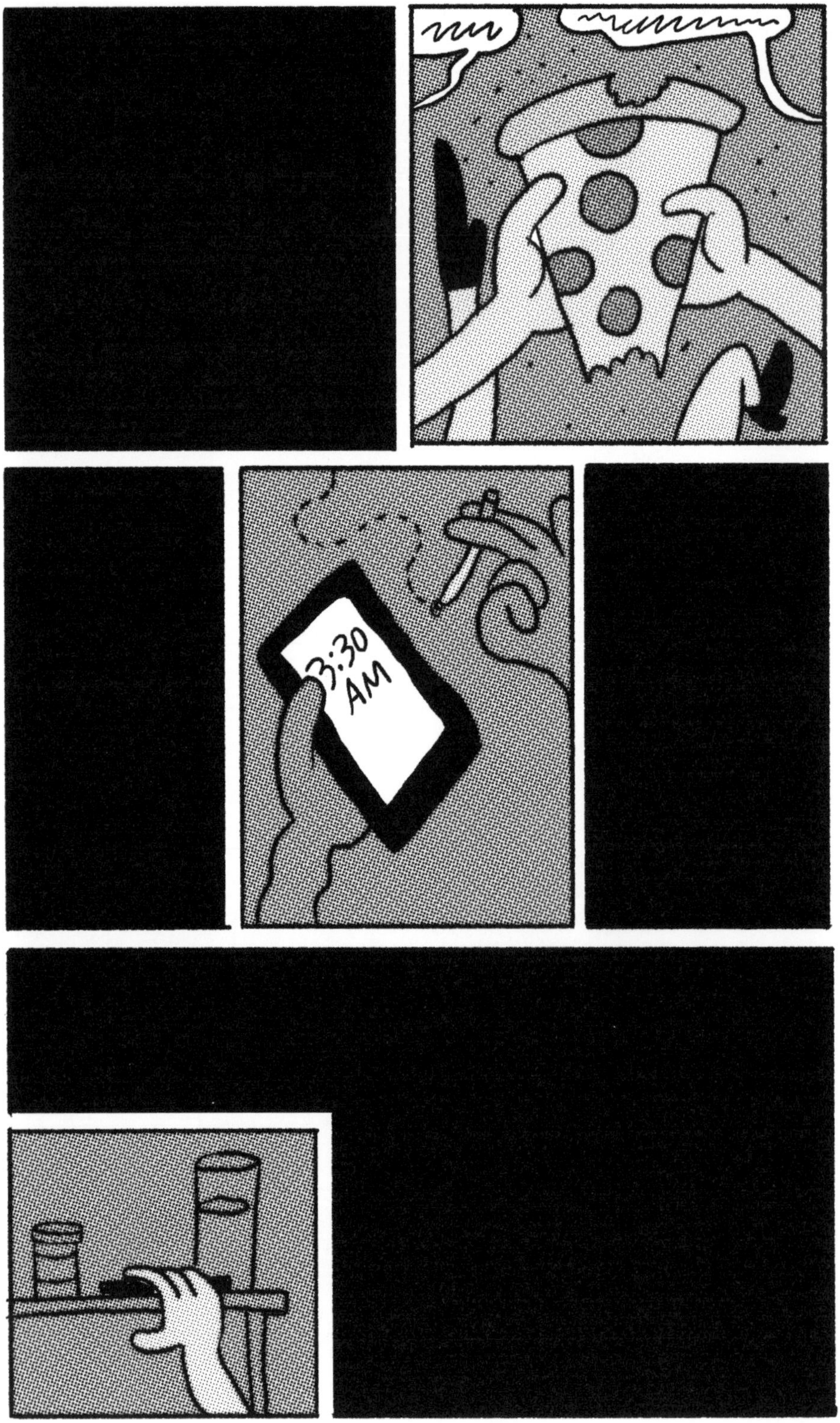
3:30
AM

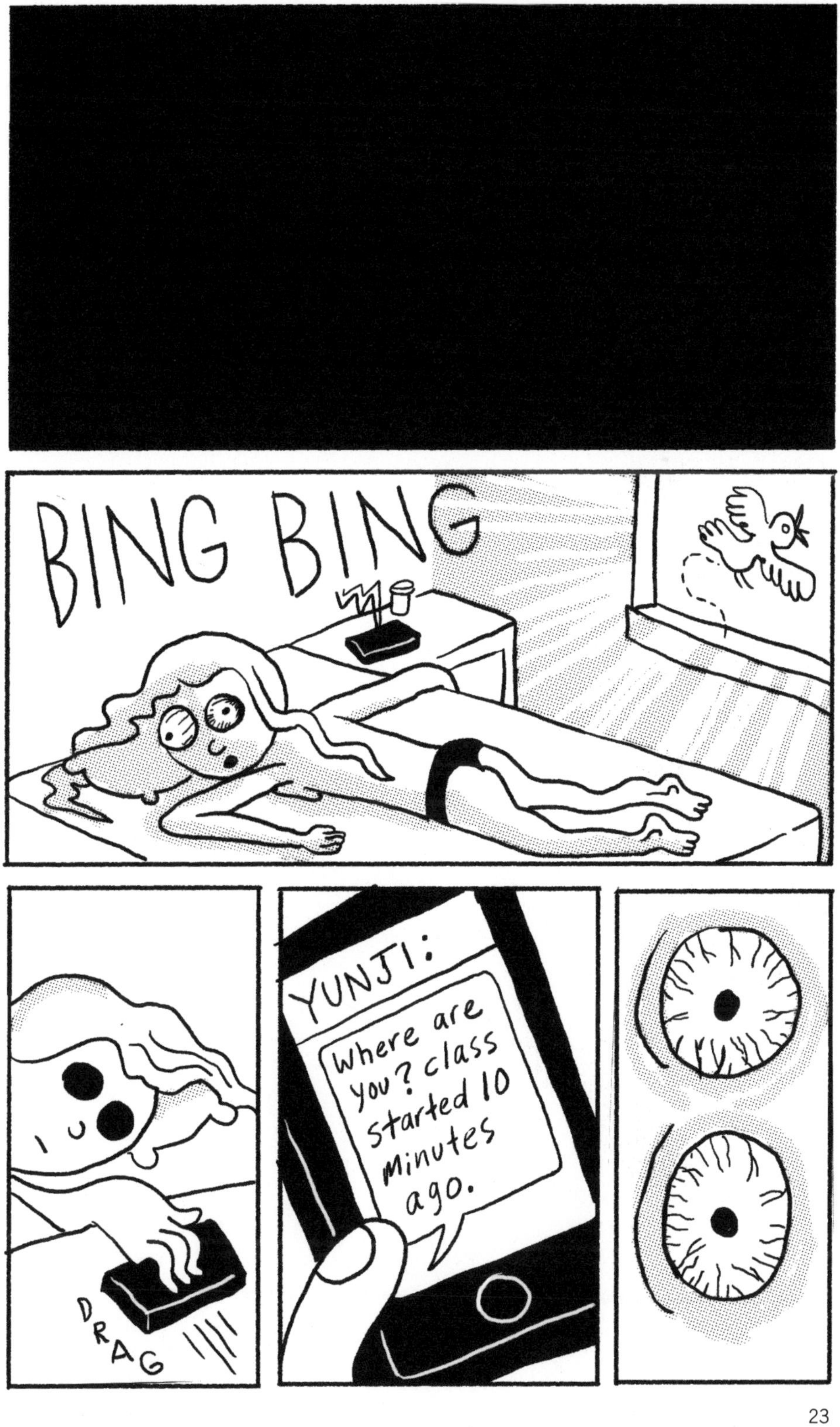
BING BING
DRAG
YUNJI:
Where are you? class started 10 minutes ago.

Wendy

Master

of

Art

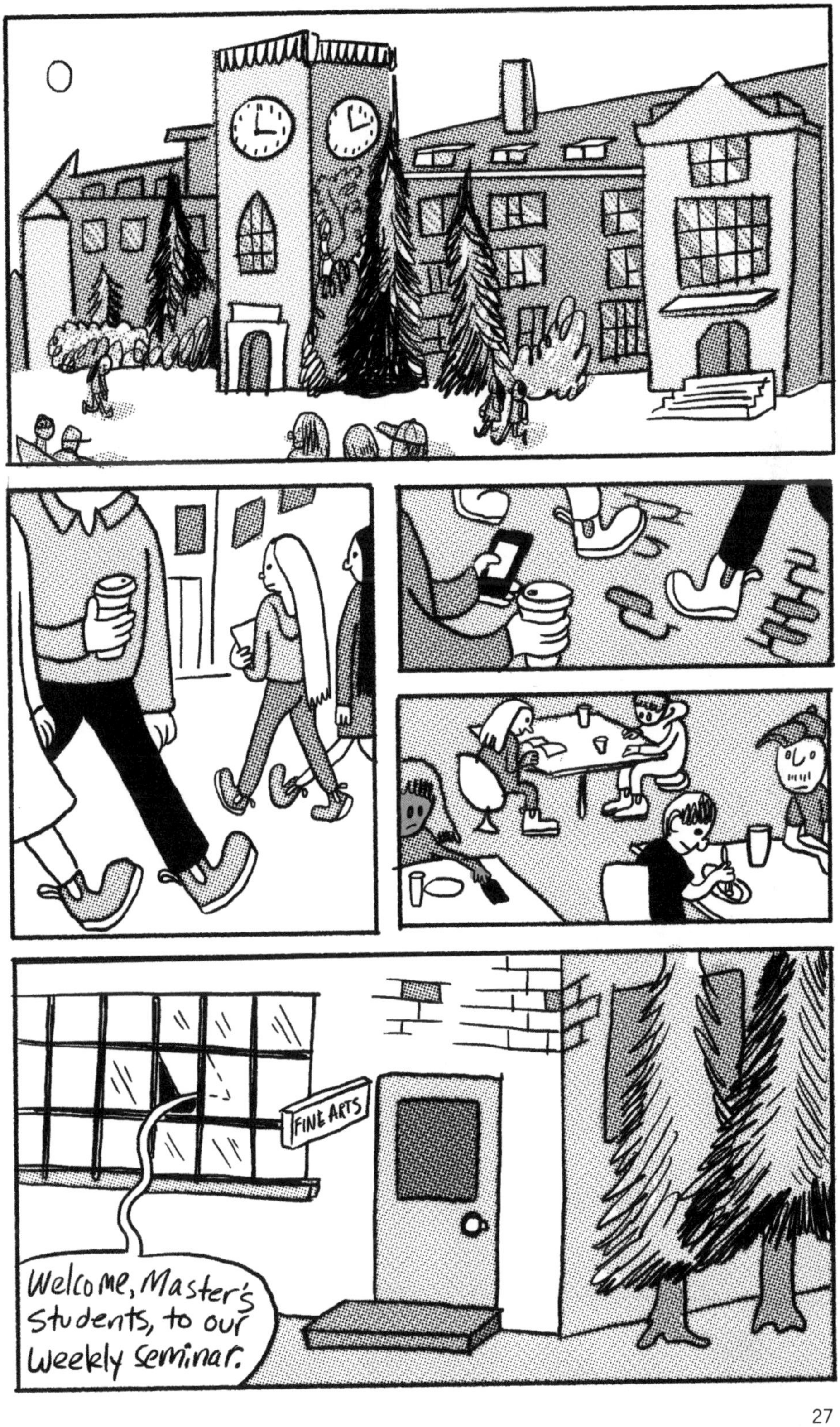
FINE ARTS
Welcome, Master's students, to our weekly seminar.

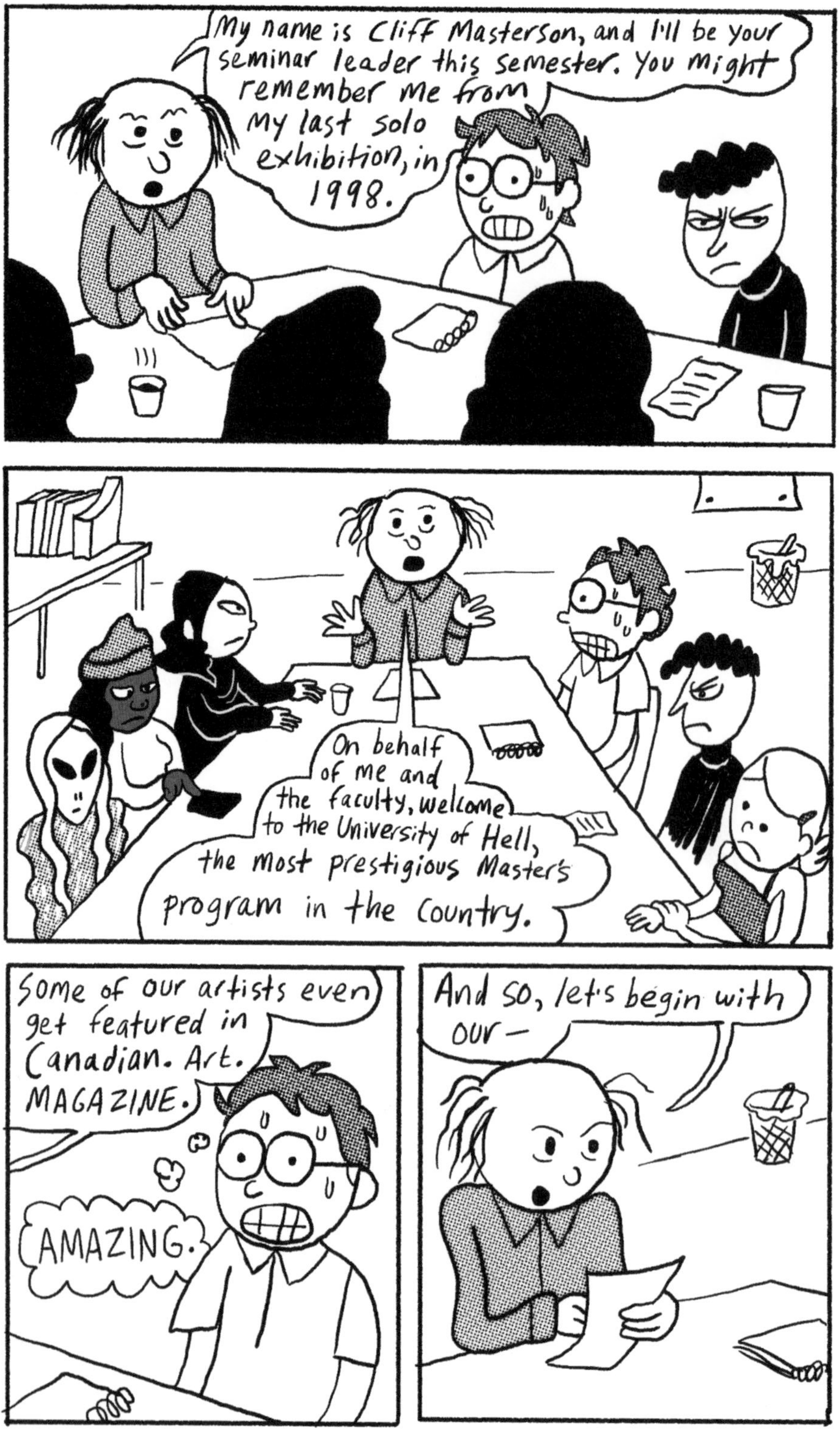
My name is Cliff Masterson, and I'll be your seminar leader this semester. You might remember me from my last solo exhibition, in 1998.
On behalf of me and the faculty, welcome to the University of Hell, the most prestigious Master's program in the Country.
Some of our artists even get featured in Canadian. Art. MAGAZINE.
AMAZING.
And so, let's begin with our—

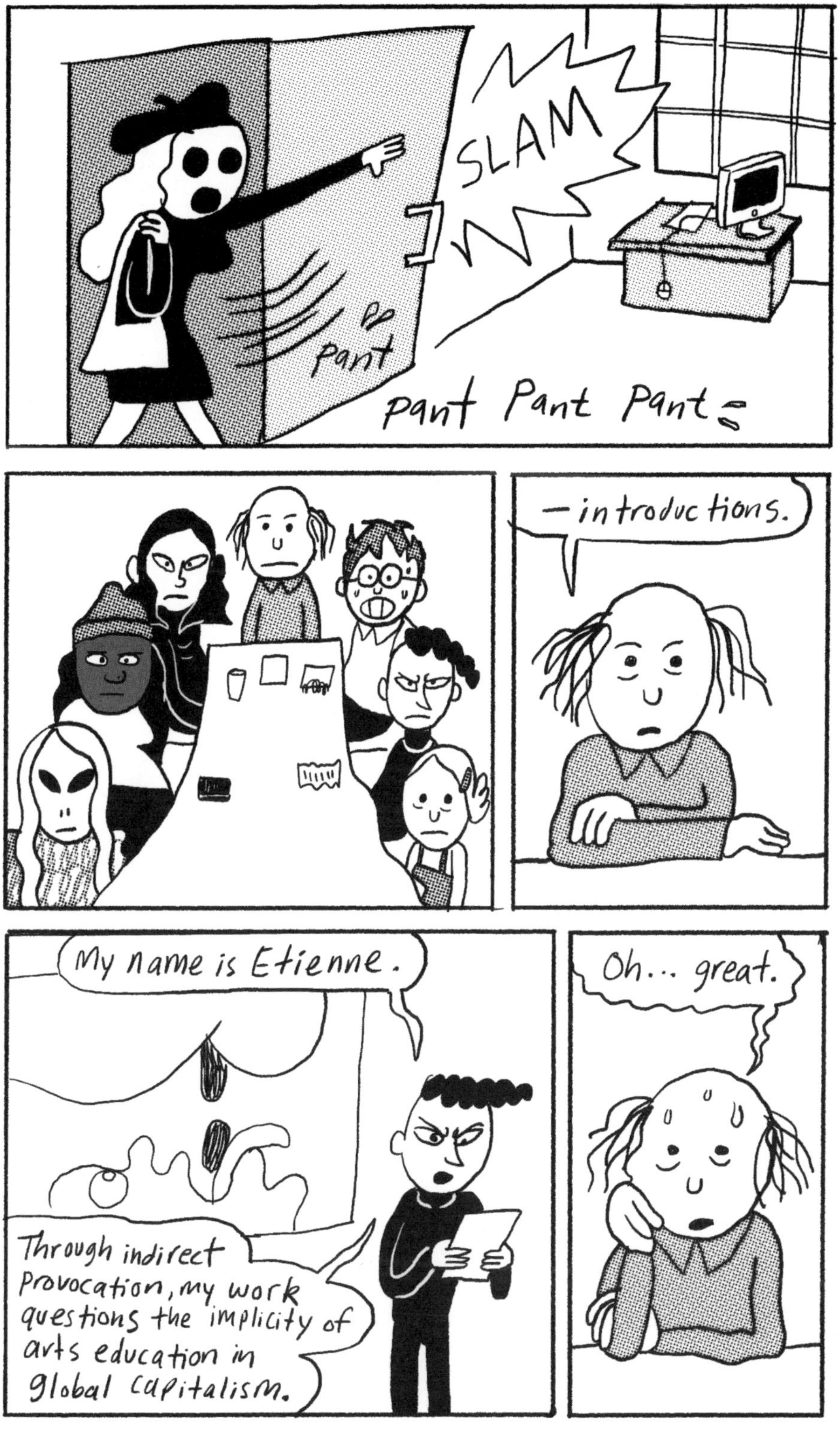
SLAM
pant
pant Pant Pant
—introductions.
My name is Etienne.
Through indirect provocation, my work questions the implicity of arts education in global capitalism.
Oh... great.

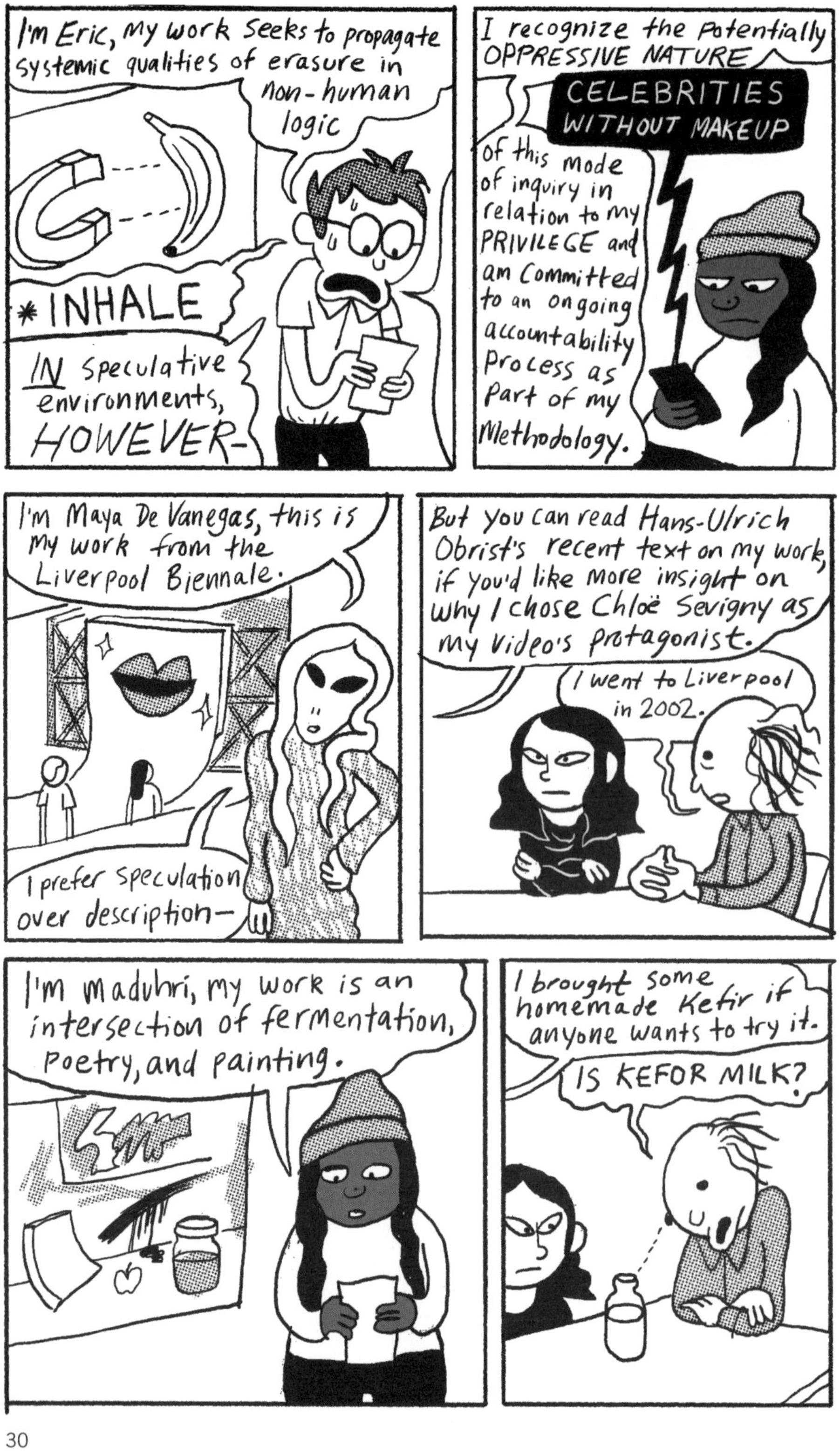
I'm Eric, my work seeks to propagate systemic qualities of erasure in non-human logic
*INHALE
IN speculative environments, HOWEVER-
I recognize the potentially OPPRESSIVE NATURE
CELEBRITIES WITHOUT MAKEUP
of this mode of inquiry in relation to my PRIVILEGE and am committed to an ongoing accountability process as part of my Methodology.
I'm Maya De Vanegas, this is my work from the Liverpool Biennale.
I prefer speculation over description-
But you can read Hans-Ulrich Obrist's recent text on my work, if you'd like more insight on why I chose Chloë Sevigny as my video's protagonist.
I went to Liverpool in 2002.
I'm madurhi, my work is an intersection of fermentation, poetry, and painting.
I brought some homemade kefir if anyone wants to try it.
IS KEFOR MILK?

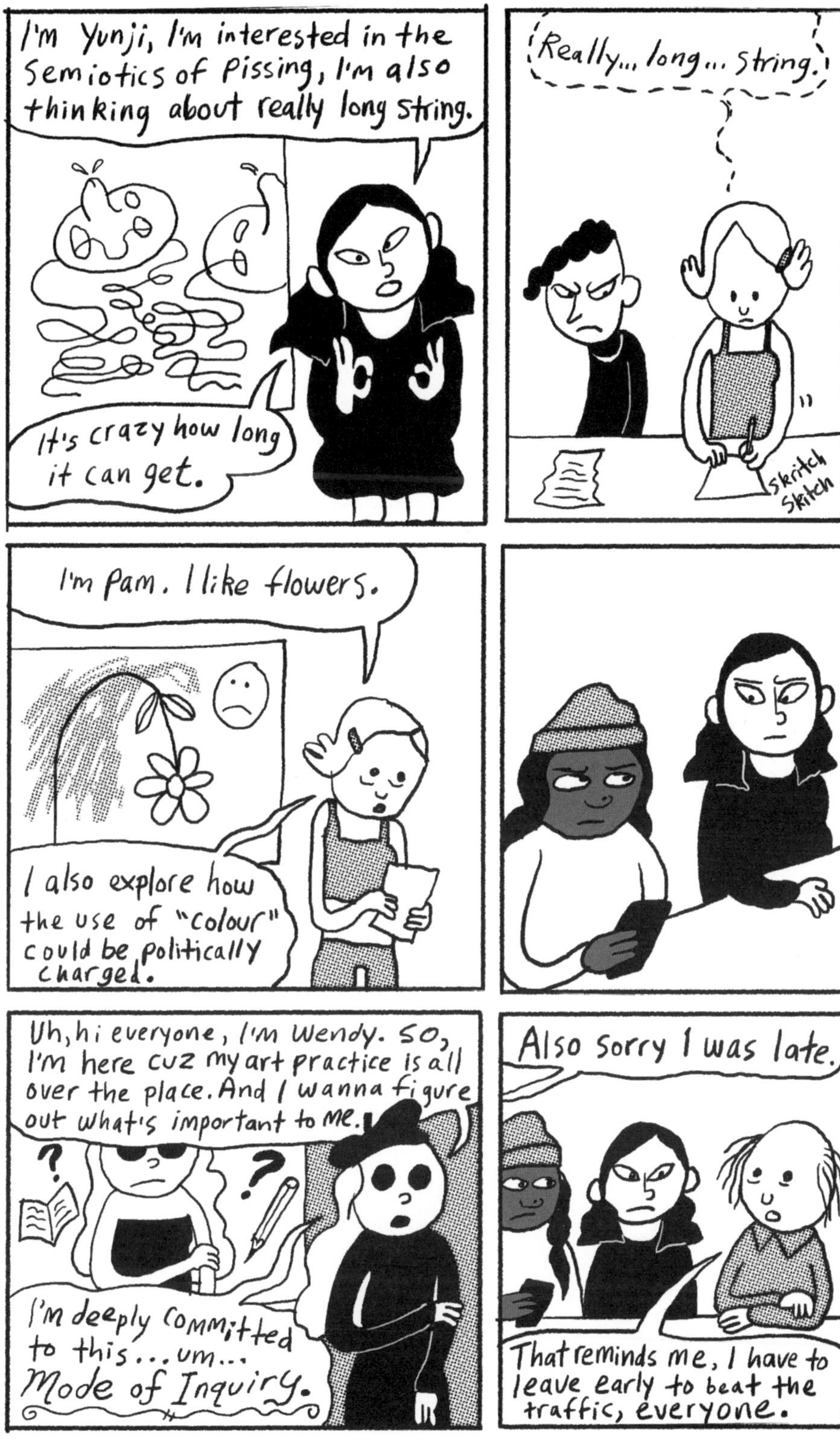

I'm Yunji, I'm interested in the semiotics of pissing, I'm also thinking about really long string.
It's crazy how long it can get.
Really... long... string.
Skritch
Skitch
I'm Pam. I like flowers.
I also explore how the use of "colour" could be politically charged.
Uh, hi everyone, I'm Wendy. So, I'm here cuz my art practice is all over the place. And I wanna figure out what's important to me.
I'm deeply committed to this... um... Mode of Inquiry.
Also sorry I was late.
That reminds me, I have to leave early to beat the traffic, everyone.

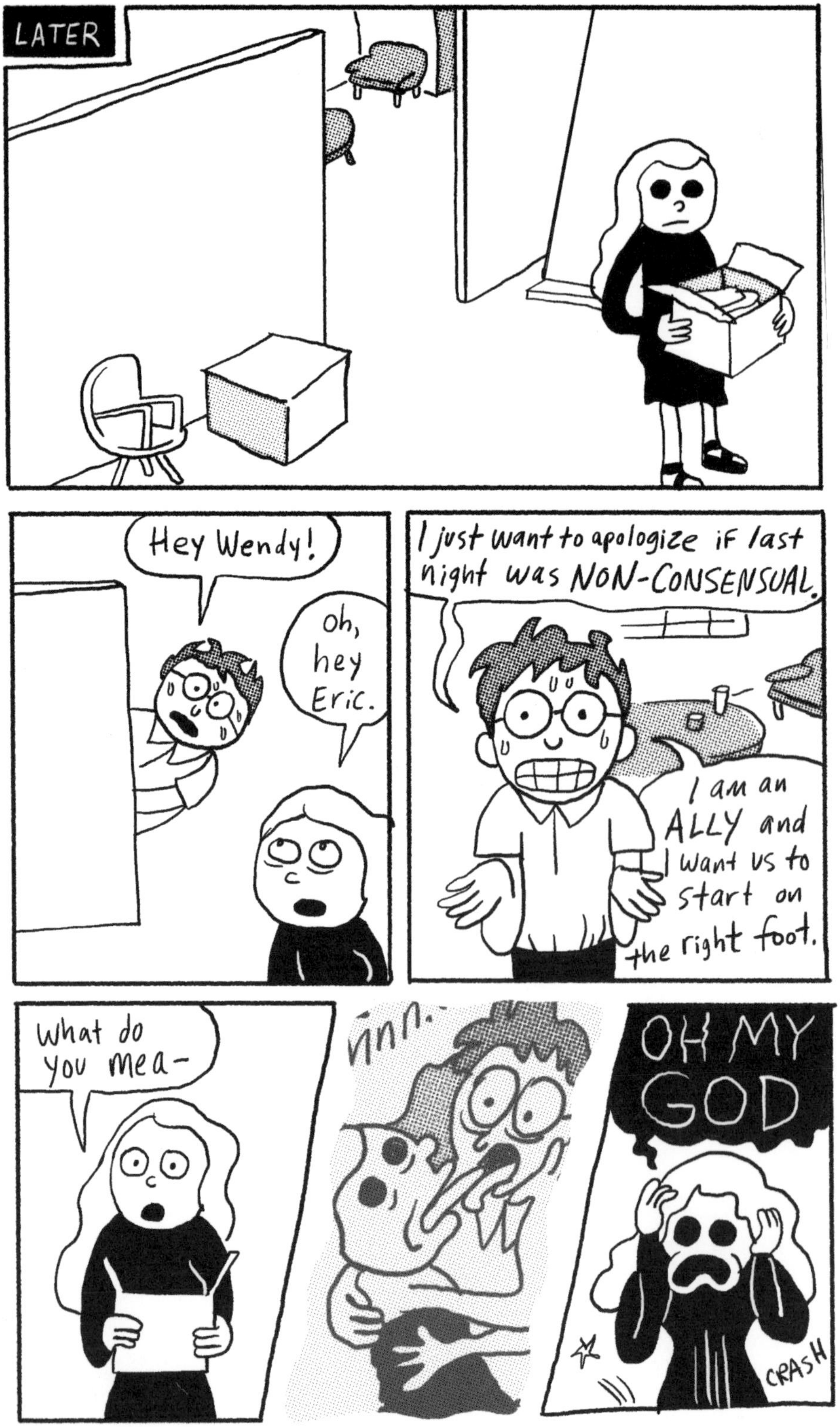
LATER
Hey Wendy!
Oh, hey Eric.
I just want to apologize if last night was NON-CONSENSUAL.
I am an ALLY and I want us to start on the right foot.
What do you mea-
nnn.
OH MY GOD
CRASH

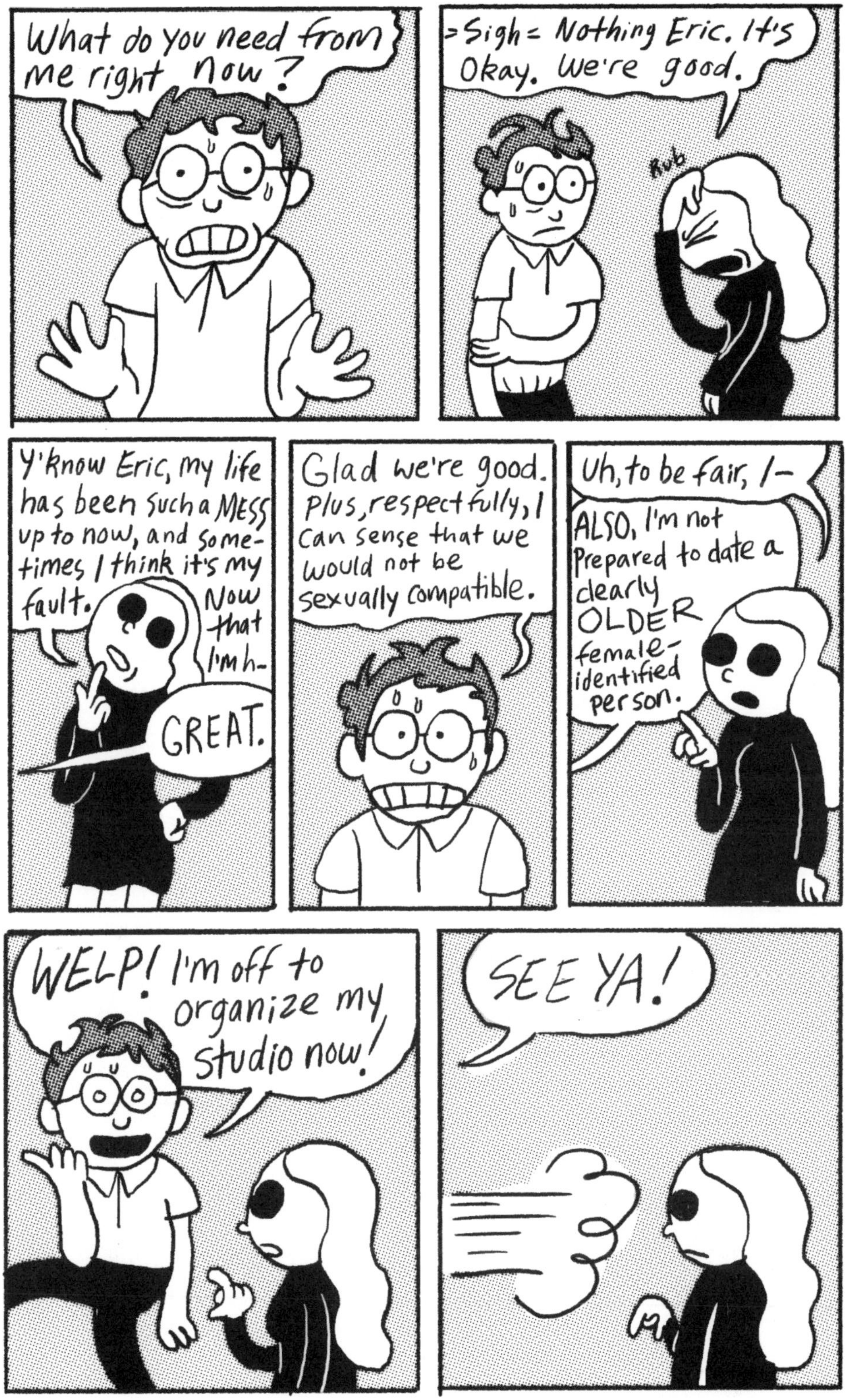
What do you need from me right now?
=Sigh= Nothing Eric. It's Okay. We're good.
Rub
Y'know Eric, my life has been such a MESS up to now, and sometimes I think it's my fault. Now that I'm h-
GREAT.
Glad we're good. Plus, respectfully, I can sense that we would not be sexually compatible.
Uh, to be fair, I-
ALSO, I'm not prepared to date a clearly OLDER female-identified person.
WELP! I'm off to organize my studio now!
SEE YA!

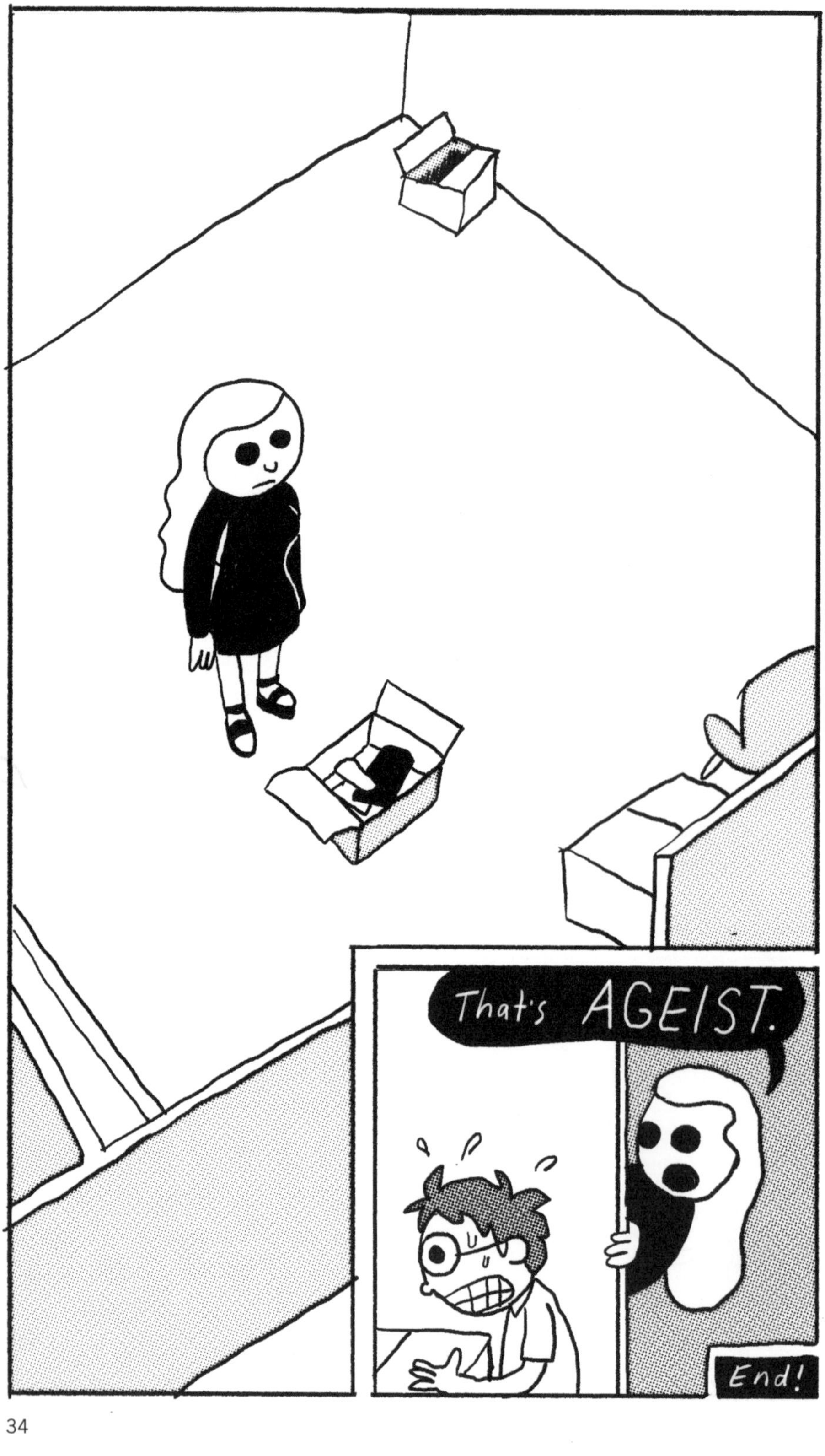
That's AGEIST.
End!

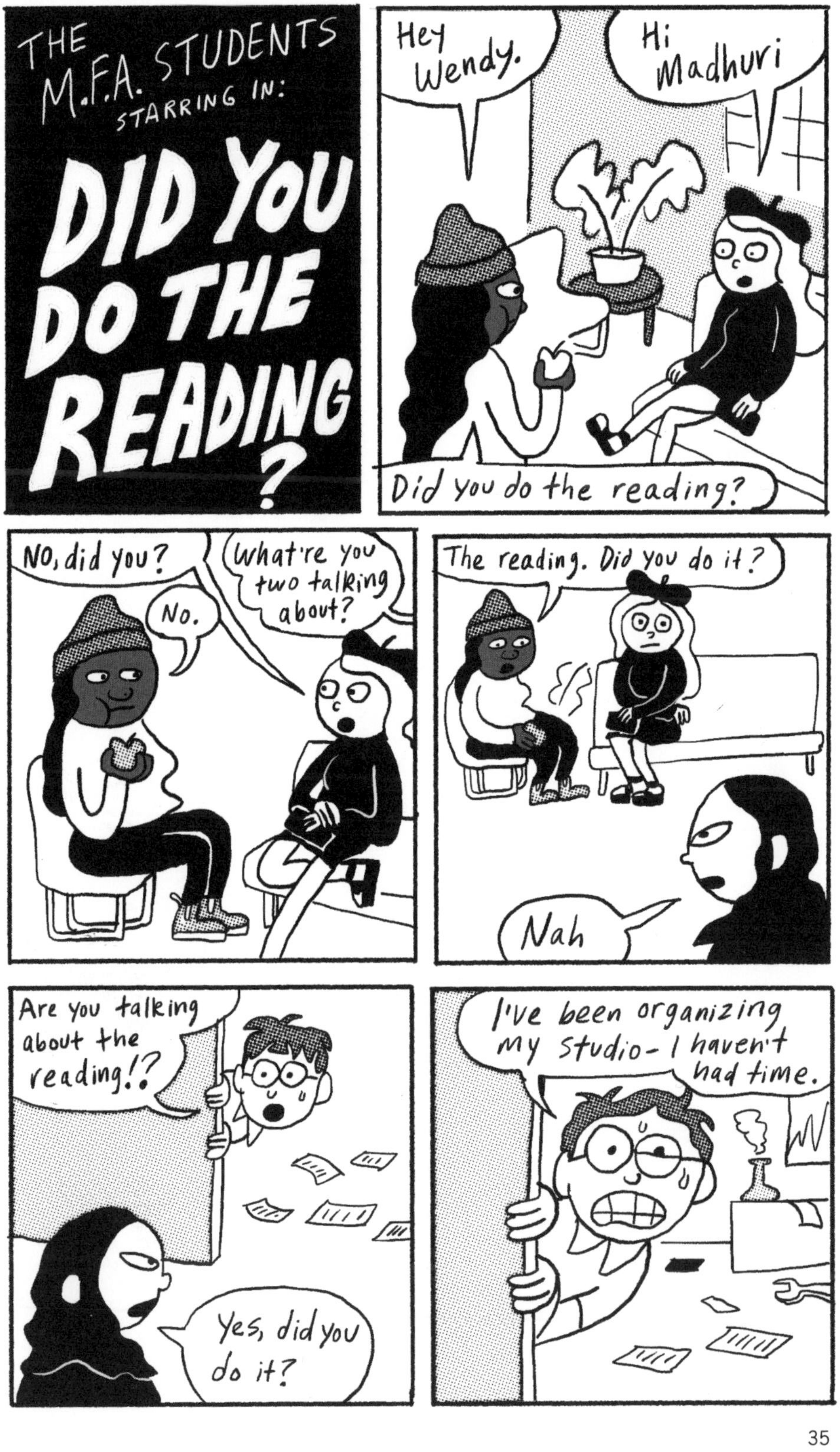
THE M.F.A. STUDENTS
STARRING IN:
DID YOU DO THE READING?
Hey Wendy.
Hi Madhuri
Did you do the reading?
No, did you?
No.
What're you two talking about?
The reading. Did you do it?
Nah
Are you talking about the reading!?
Yes, did you do it?
I've been organizing my studio- I haven't had time.

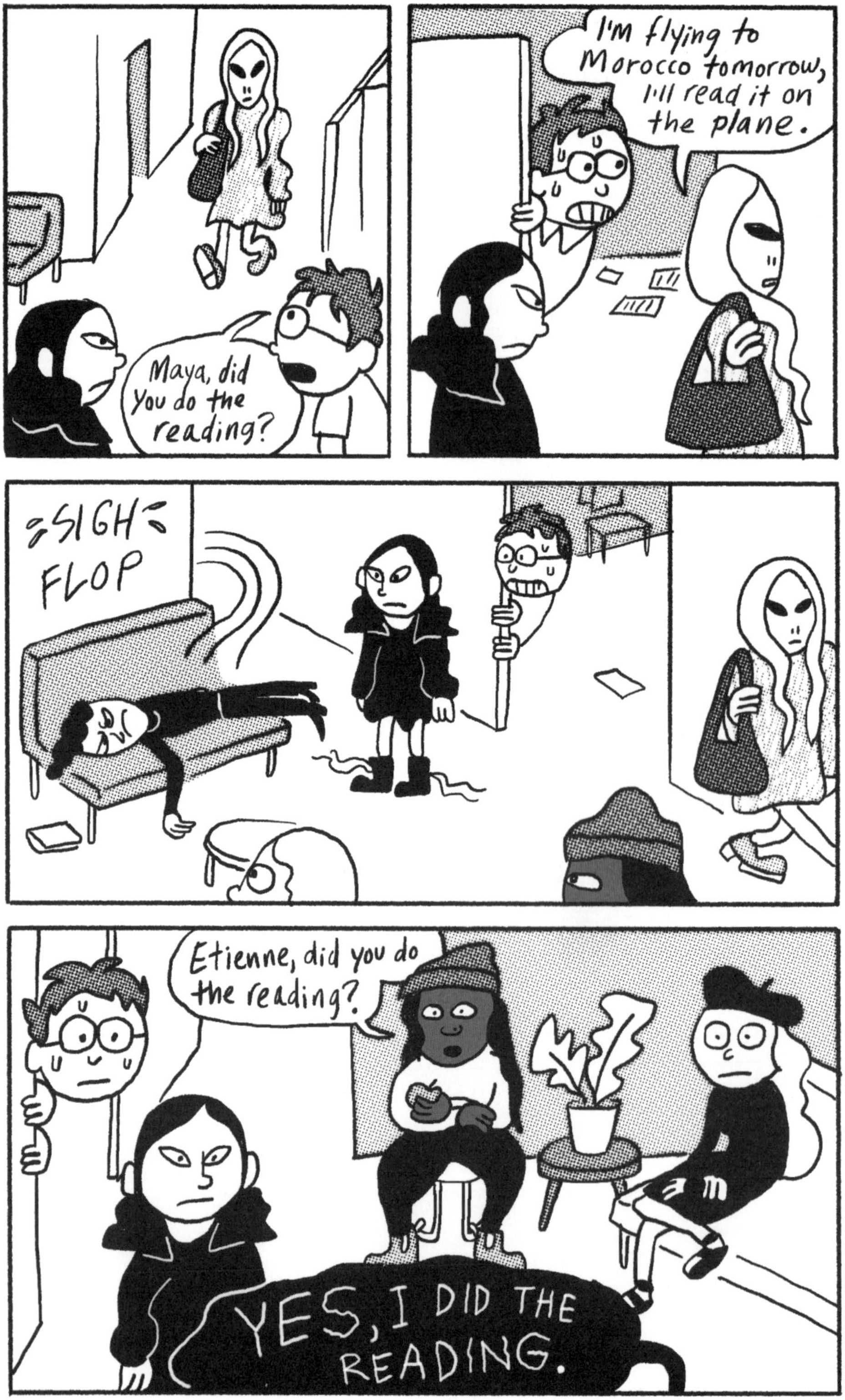
Maya, did you do the reading?
I'm flying to Morocco tomorrow, I'll read it on the plane.
SIGH
FLOP
Etienne, did you do the reading?
YES, I DID THE READING.

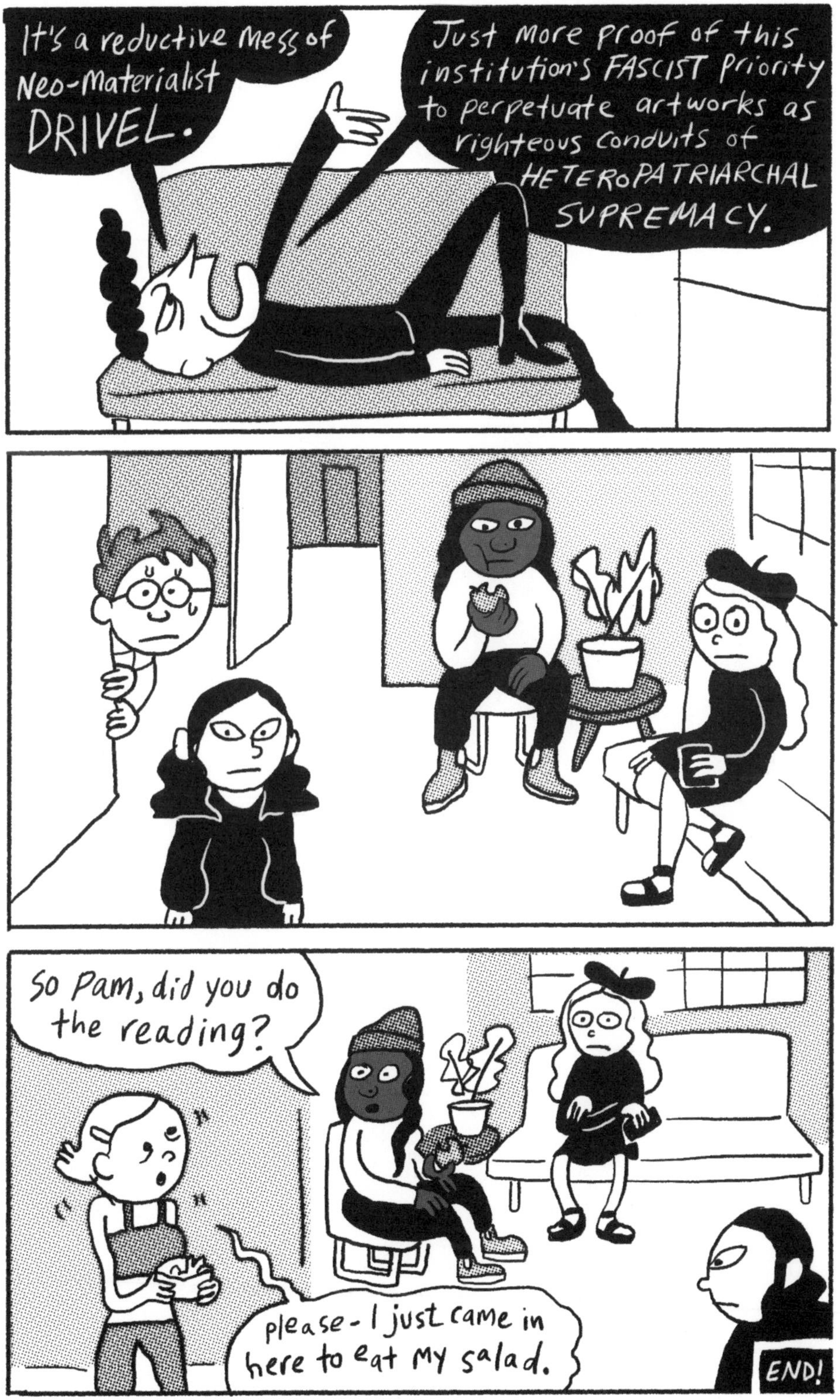
It's a reductive mess of Neo-Materialist DRIVEL.
Just more proof of this institution's FASCIST priority to perpetuate artworks as righteous conduits of HETEROPATRIARCHAL SUPREMACY.
So Pam, did you do the reading?
please - I just came in here to eat my salad.
END!

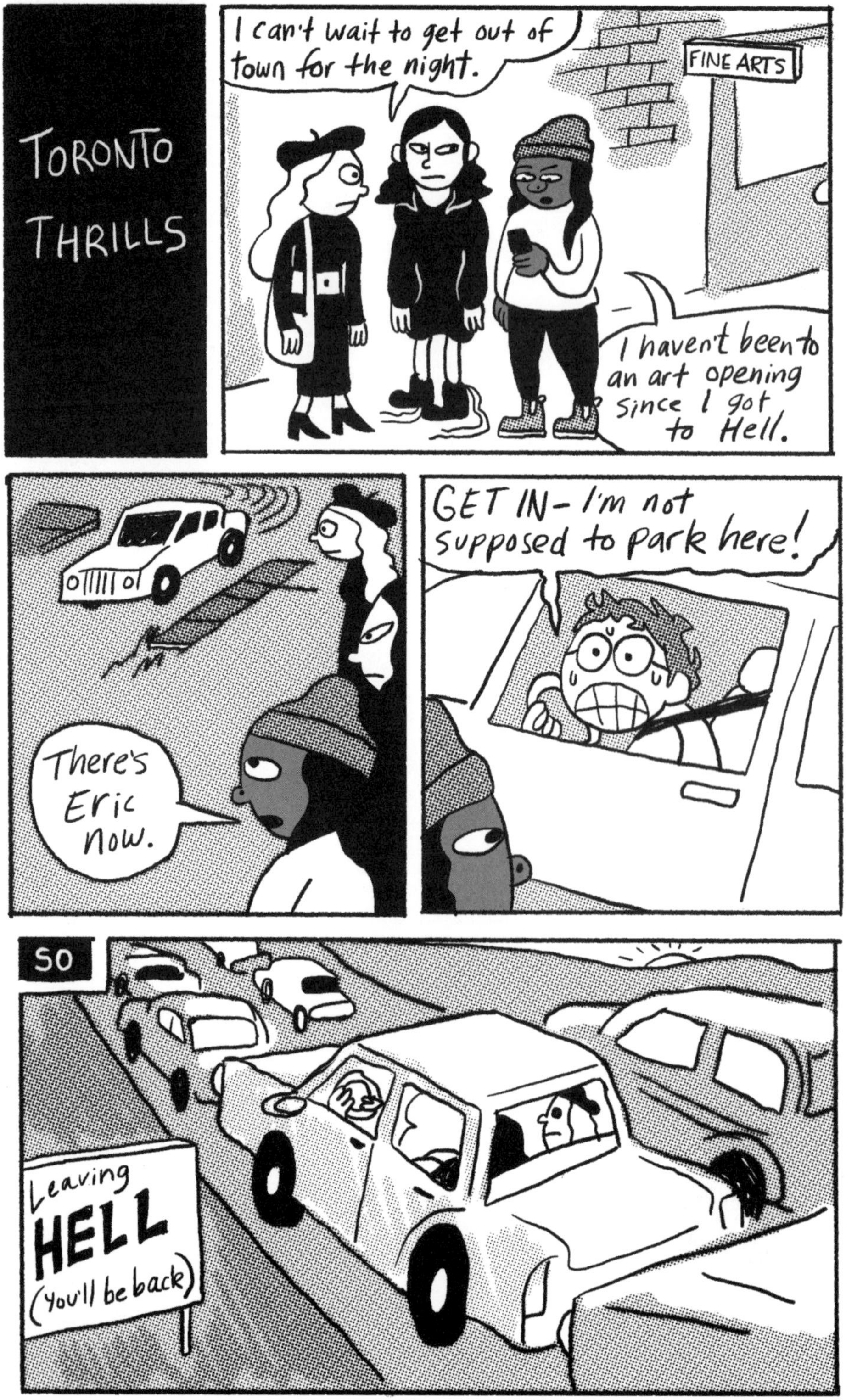
TORONTO THRILLS
I can't wait to get out of town for the night.
FINE ARTS
I haven't been to an art opening since I got to Hell.
There's Eric now.
GET IN– I'm not supposed to park here!
SO
Leaving HELL (You'll be back)

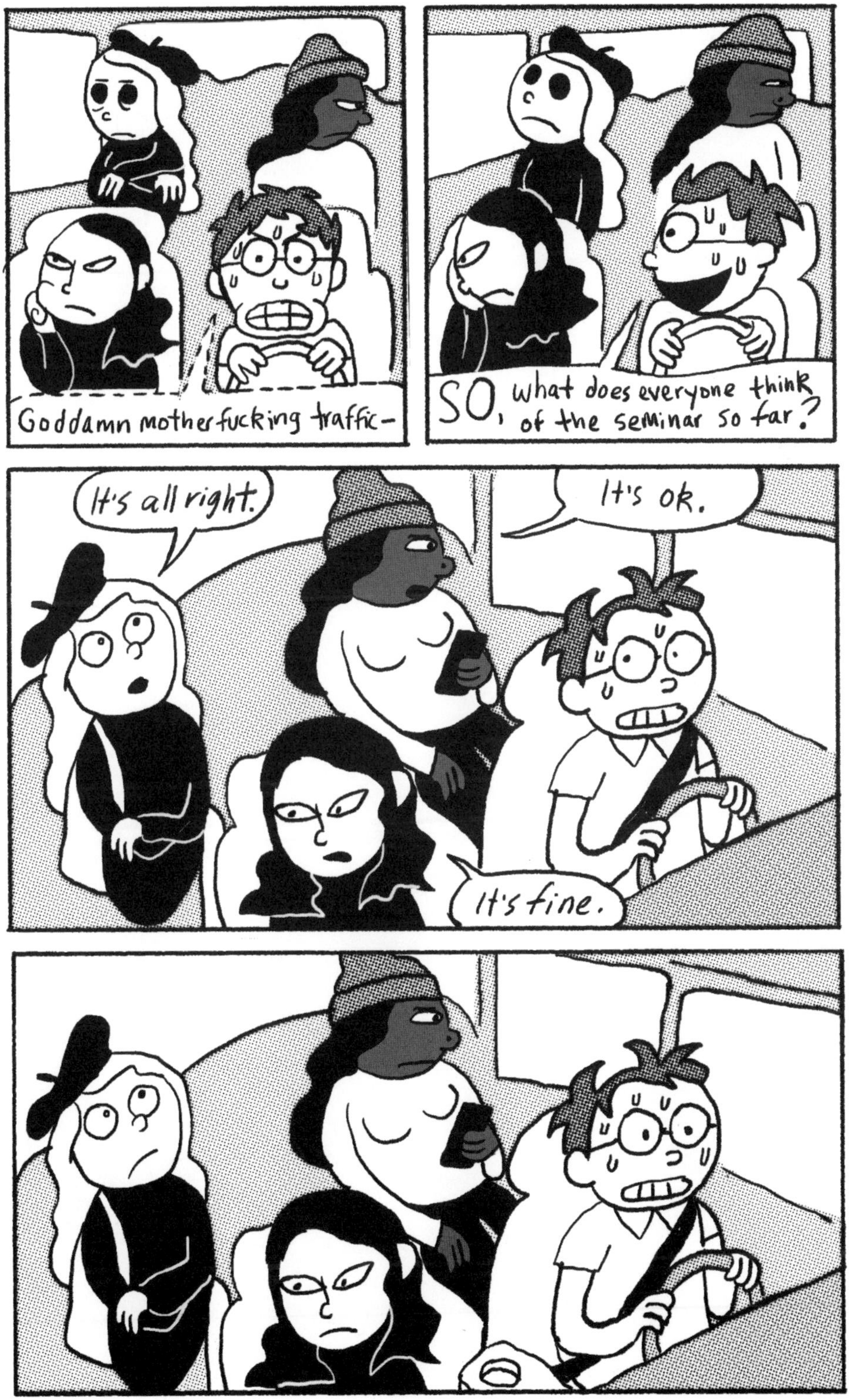
Goddamn motherfucking traffic-
SO, what does everyone think of the seminar so far?
It's all right.
It's ok.
It's fine.

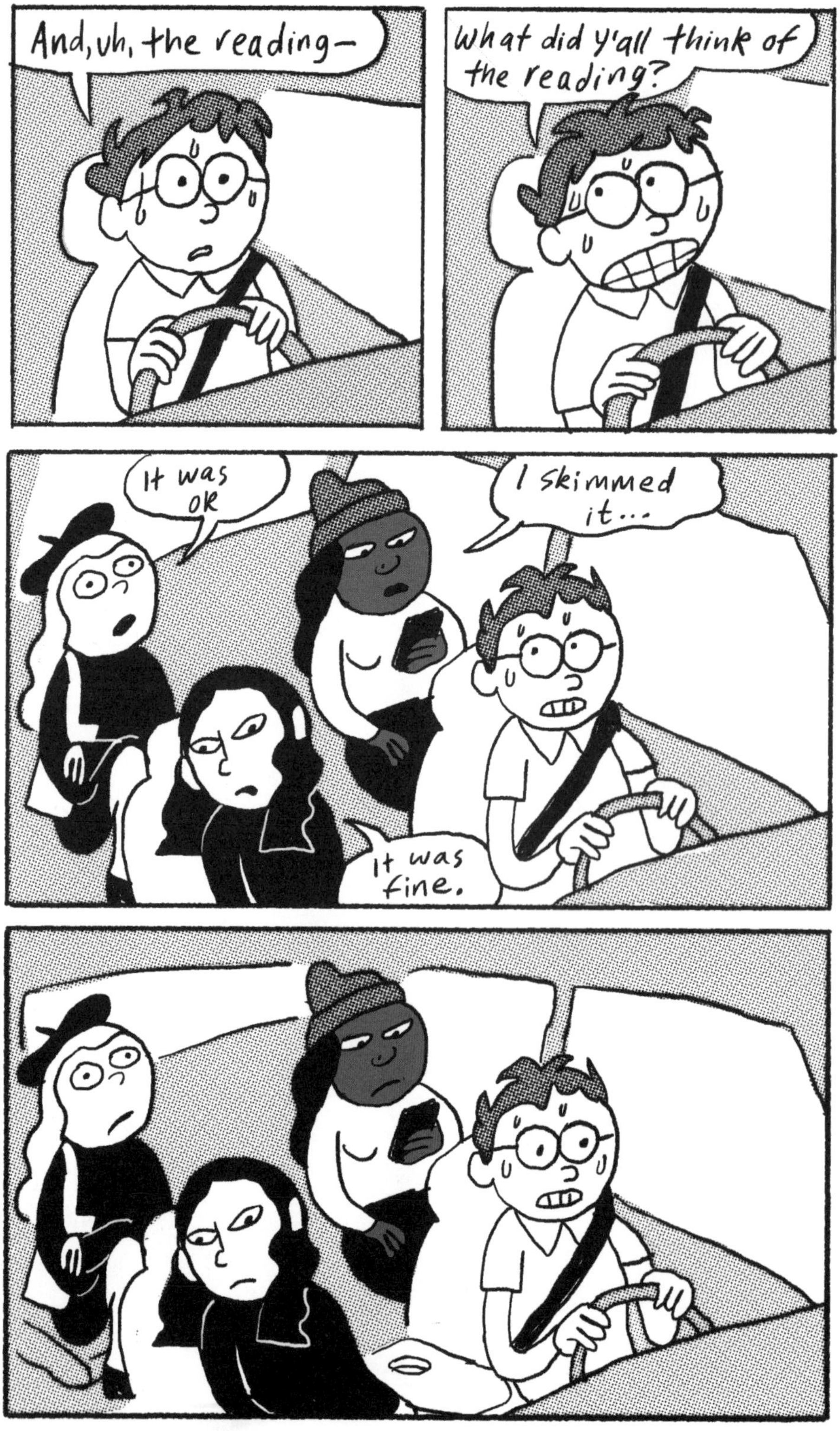
And, uh, the reading—
What did y'all think of the reading?
It was OK
I skimmed it...
It was fine.

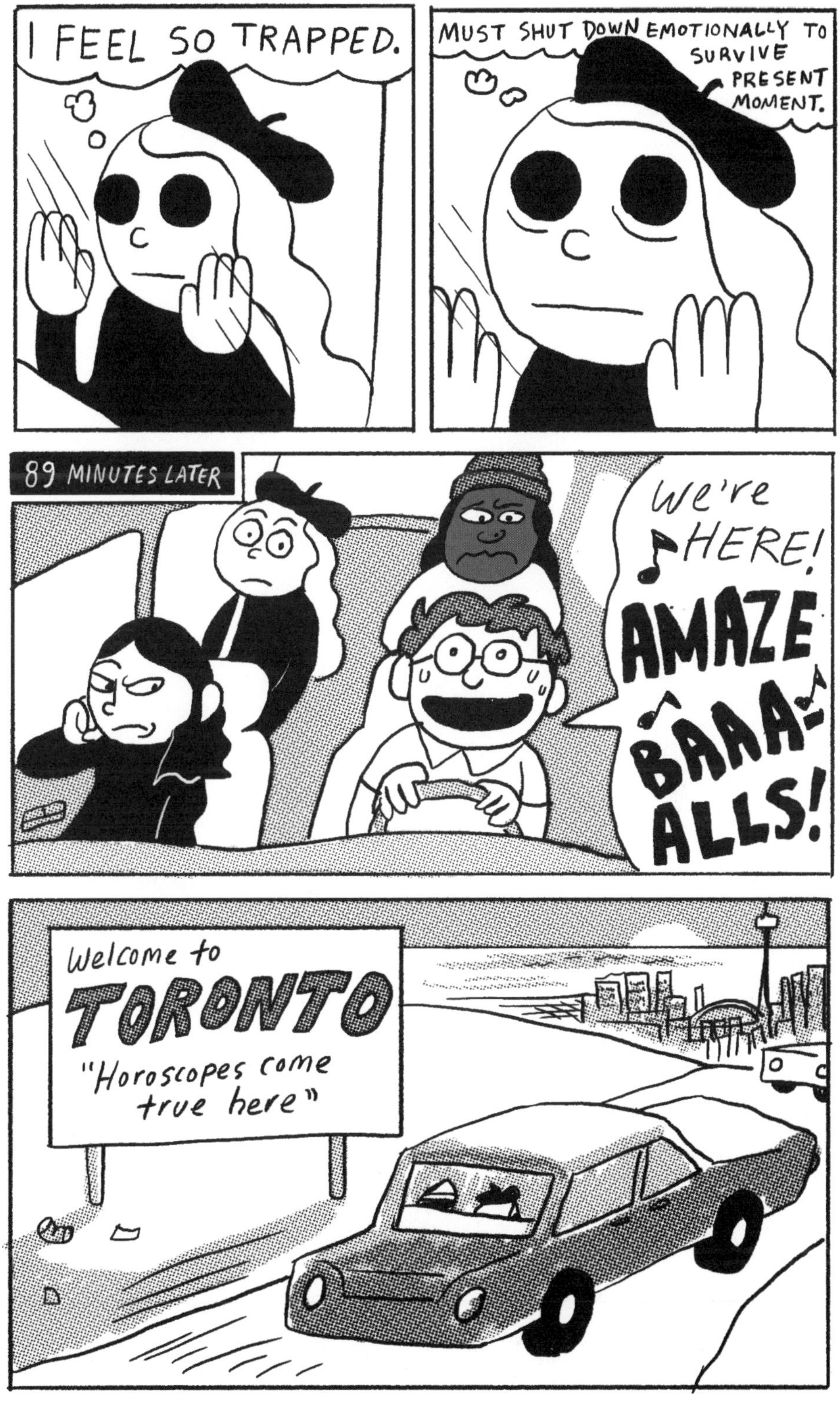
I FEEL SO TRAPPED.
MUST SHUT DOWN EMOTIONALLY TO SURVIVE PRESENT MOMENT.
89 MINUTES LATER
We're HERE! AMAZE BAAA-ALLS!
Welcome to TORONTO "Horoscopes come true here"

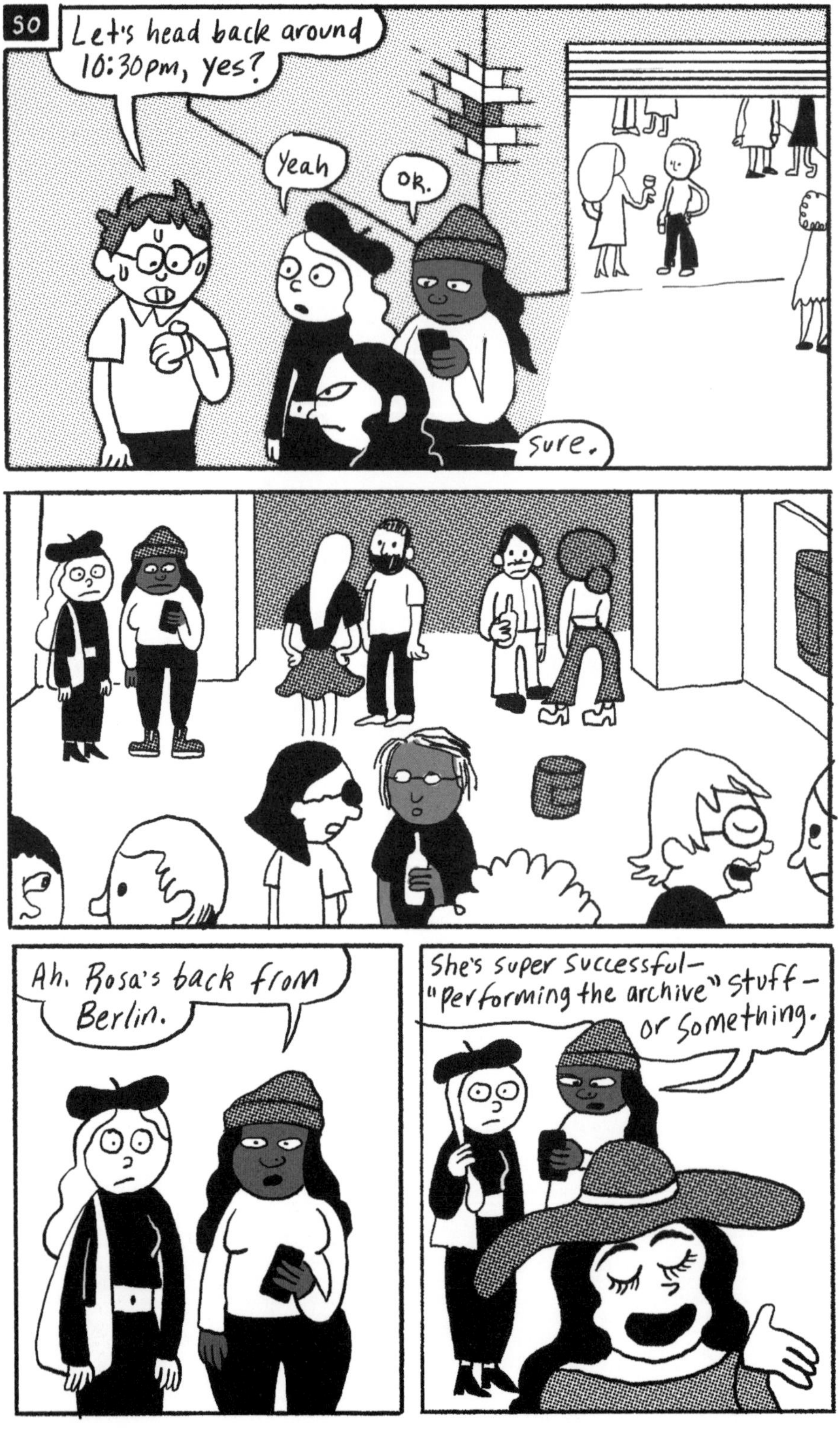
50
Let's head back around 10:30pm, yes?
Yeah
ok.
sure.
Ah. Rosa's back from Berlin.
She's super successful— "performing the archive" stuff — or something.

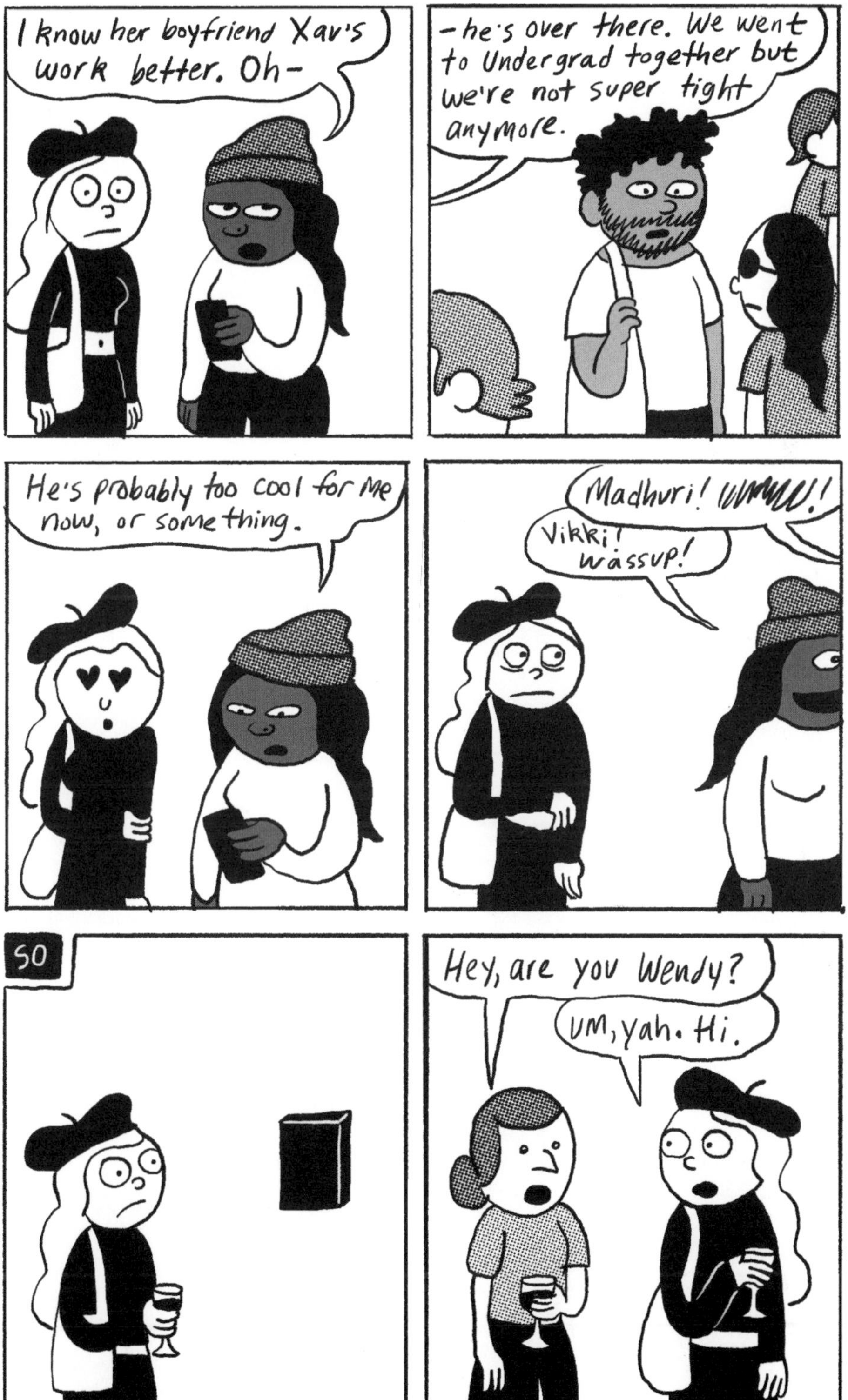
I know her boyfriend Xav's work better. Oh-
-he's over there. We went to Undergrad together but we're not super tight anymore.
He's probably too cool for me now, or something.
Madhuri!
Vikki! wassup!
SO
Hey, are you Wendy?
Um, yah. Hi.

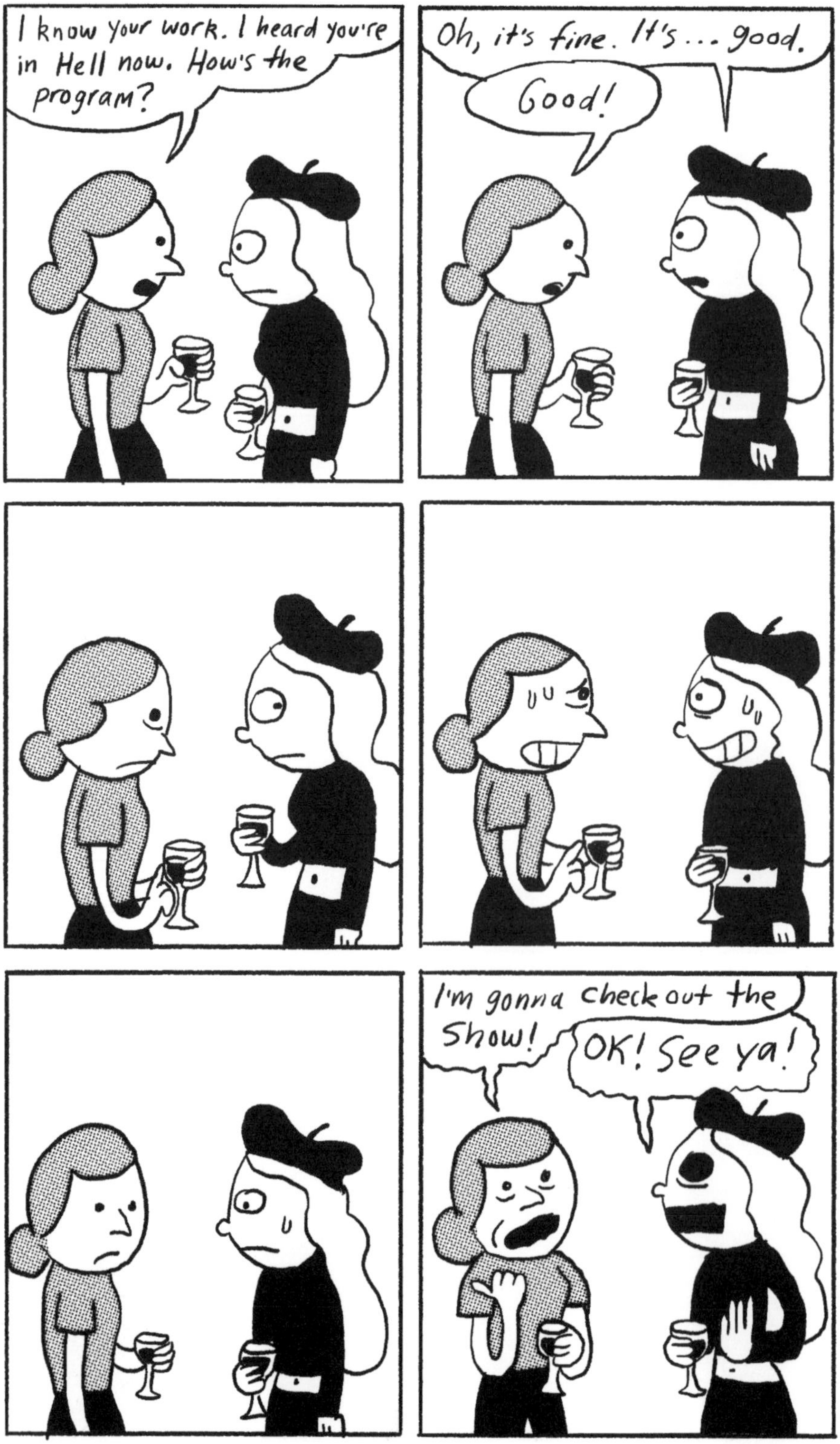
I know your work. I heard you're in Hell now. How's the program?
Oh, it's fine. It's... good.
Good!
I'm gonna check out the Show!
OK! See ya!

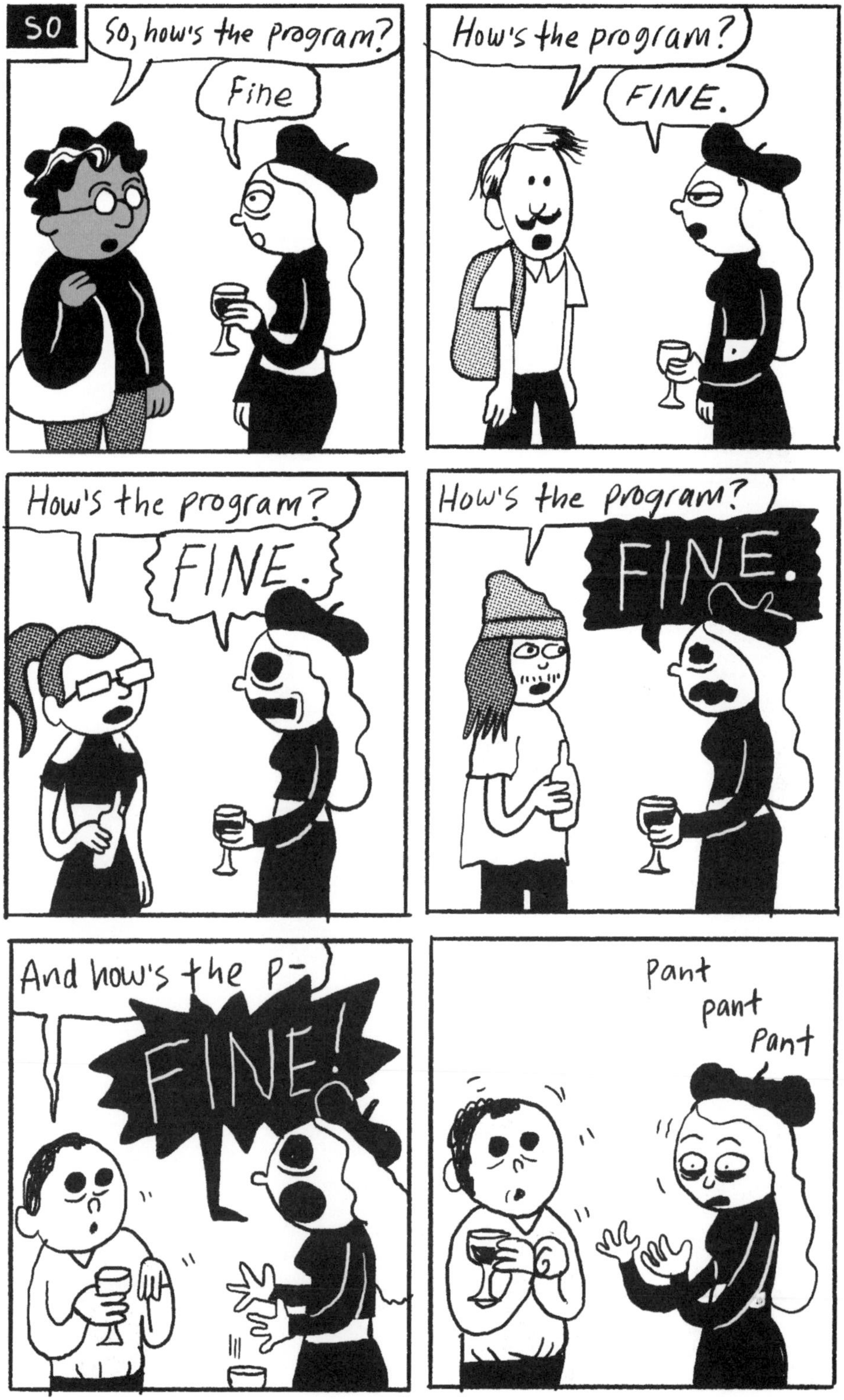
SO
So, how's the program?
Fine
How's the program?
FINE.
How's the program?
FINE.
How's the program?
FINE.
And how's the P-
FINE!
Pant
pant
Pant

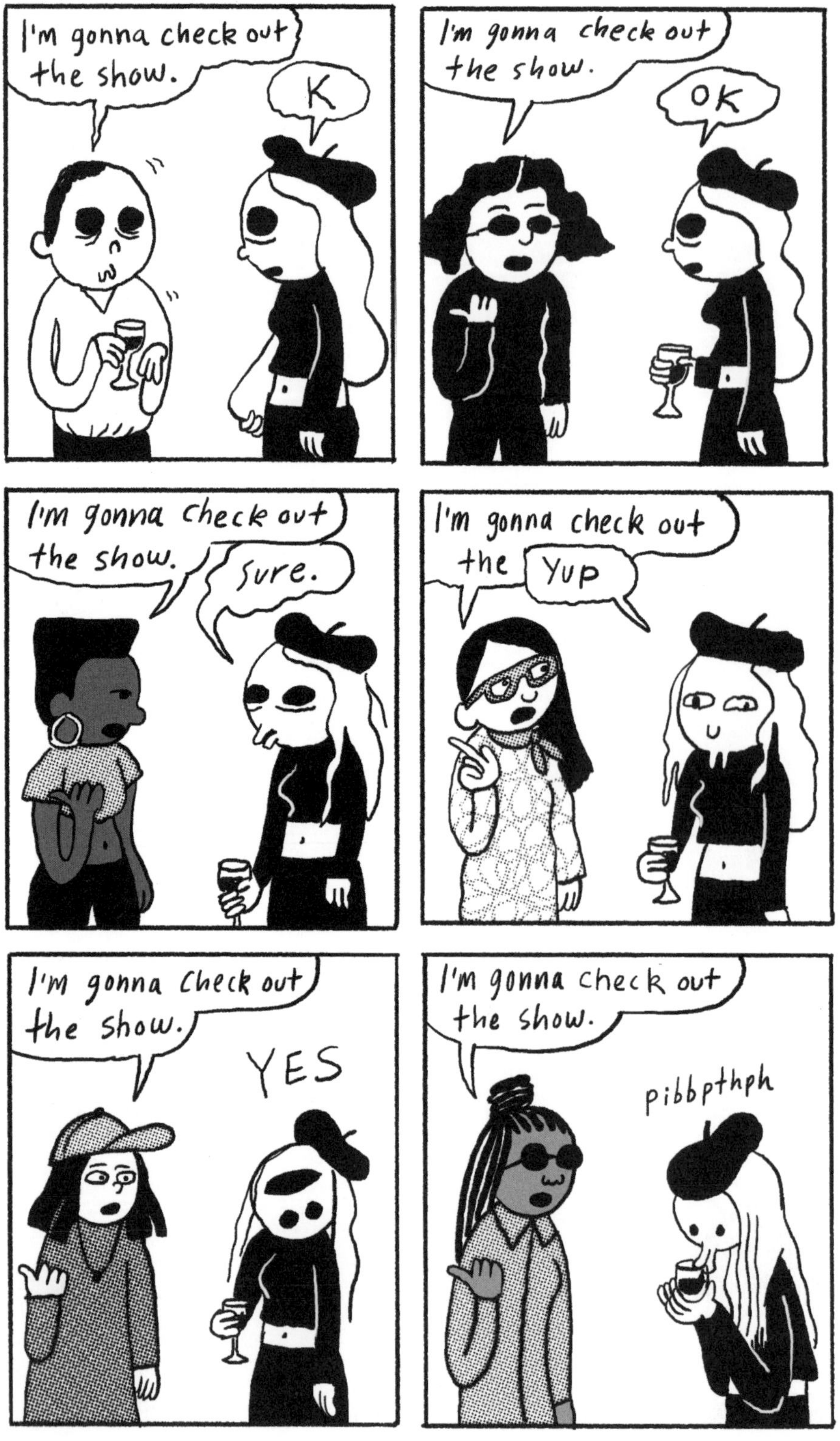
I'm gonna check out the show.
K
I'm gonna check out the show.
OK
I'm gonna check out the show.
Sure.
I'm gonna check out the
YUP
I'm gonna check out the show.
YES
I'm gonna check out the show.
pibbpthph

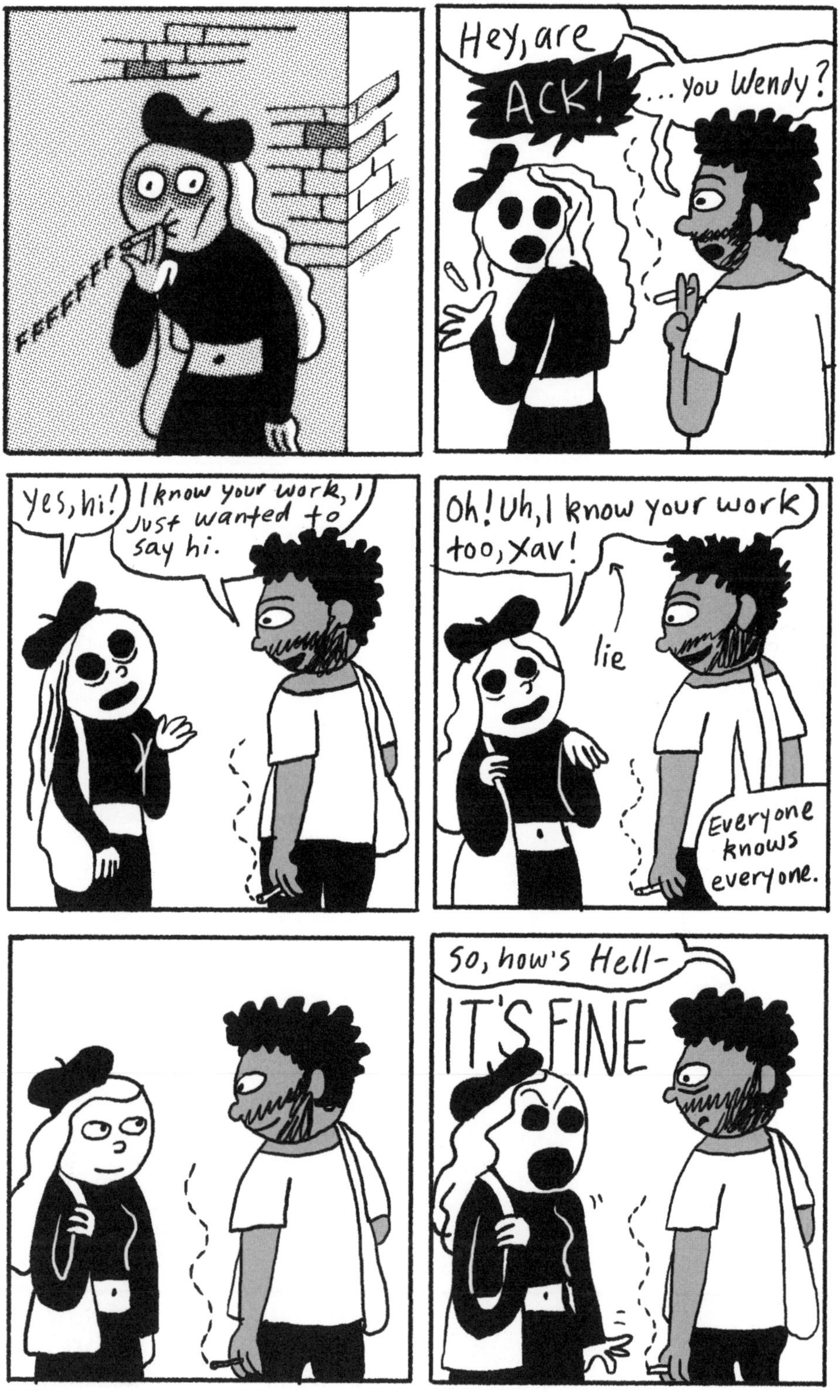
FFFFFFF
Hey, are
ACK!
...you Wendy?
Yes, hi!
I know your work, I just wanted to say hi.
Oh! Uh, I know your work too, Xav!
lie
Everyone knows everyone.
So, how's Hell-
IT'S FINE

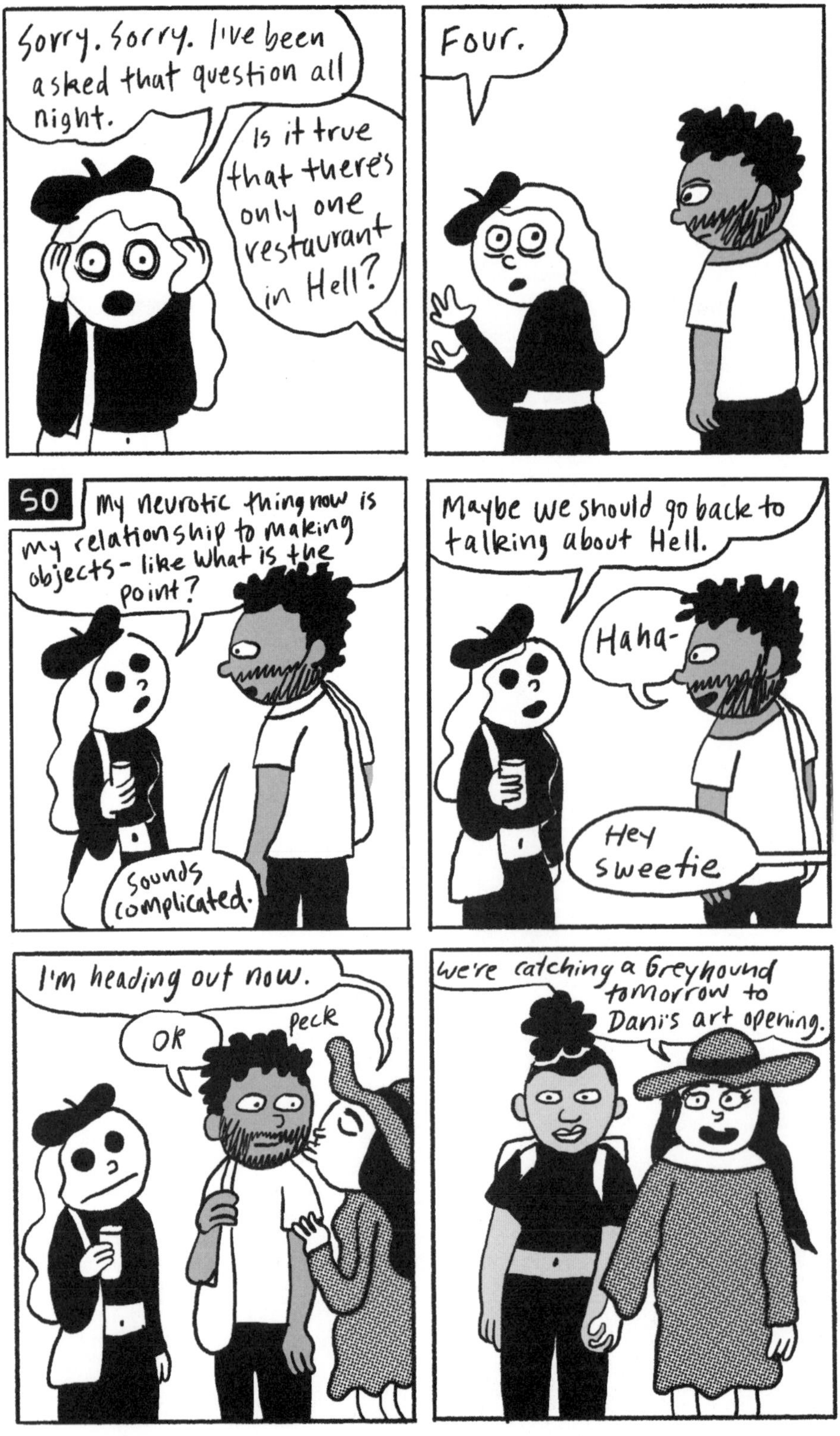
Sorry. Sorry. I've been asked that question all night.
Is it true that there's only one restaurant in Hell?
Four.
SO
My neurotic thing now is my relationship to making objects - like what is the point?
Sounds complicated.
Maybe we should go back to talking about Hell.
Haha-
Hey sweetie
I'm heading out now.
OK
peck
We're catching a Greyhound tomorrow to Dani's art opening.

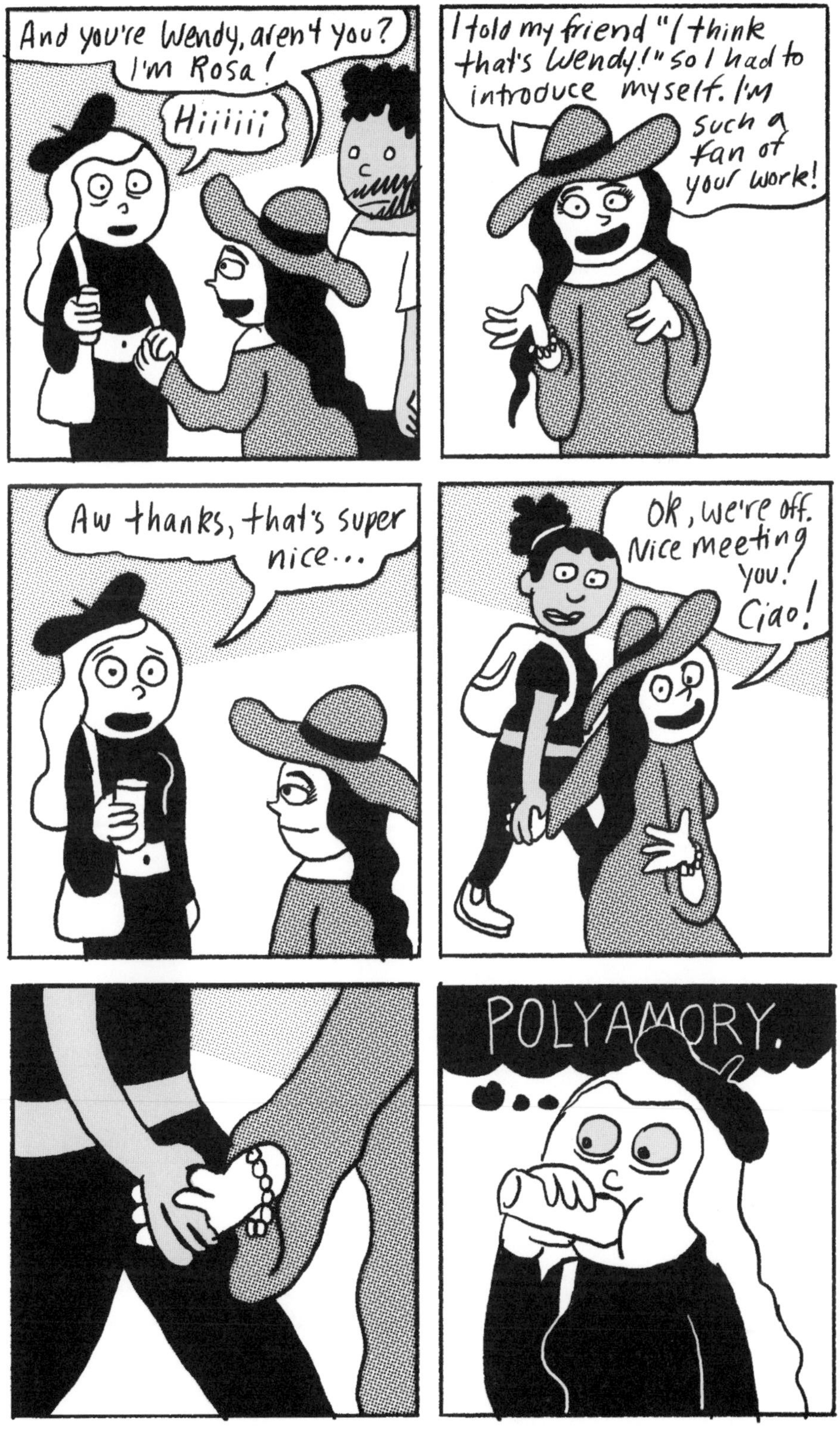
And you're Wendy, aren't you? I'm Rosa!
Hiiiiii
I told my friend "I think that's Wendy!" so I had to introduce myself. I'm such a fan of your work!
Aw thanks, that's super nice...
OK, we're off. Nice meeting you! Ciao!
POLYAMORY.

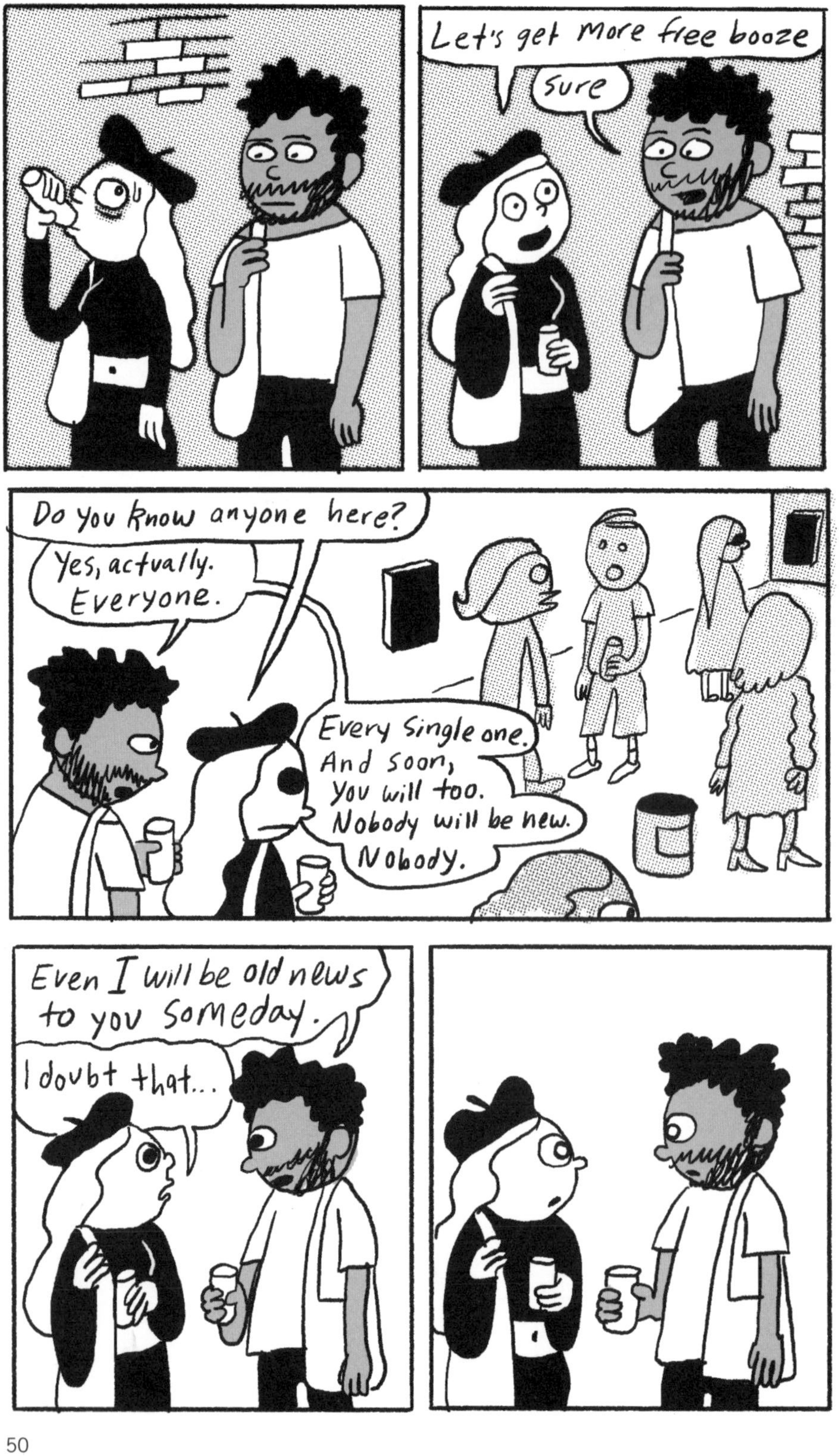
Let's get more free booze
Sure
Do you know anyone here?
Yes, actually. Everyone.
Every single one. And soon, you will too. Nobody will be new. Nobody.
Even I will be old news to you someday.
I doubt that...

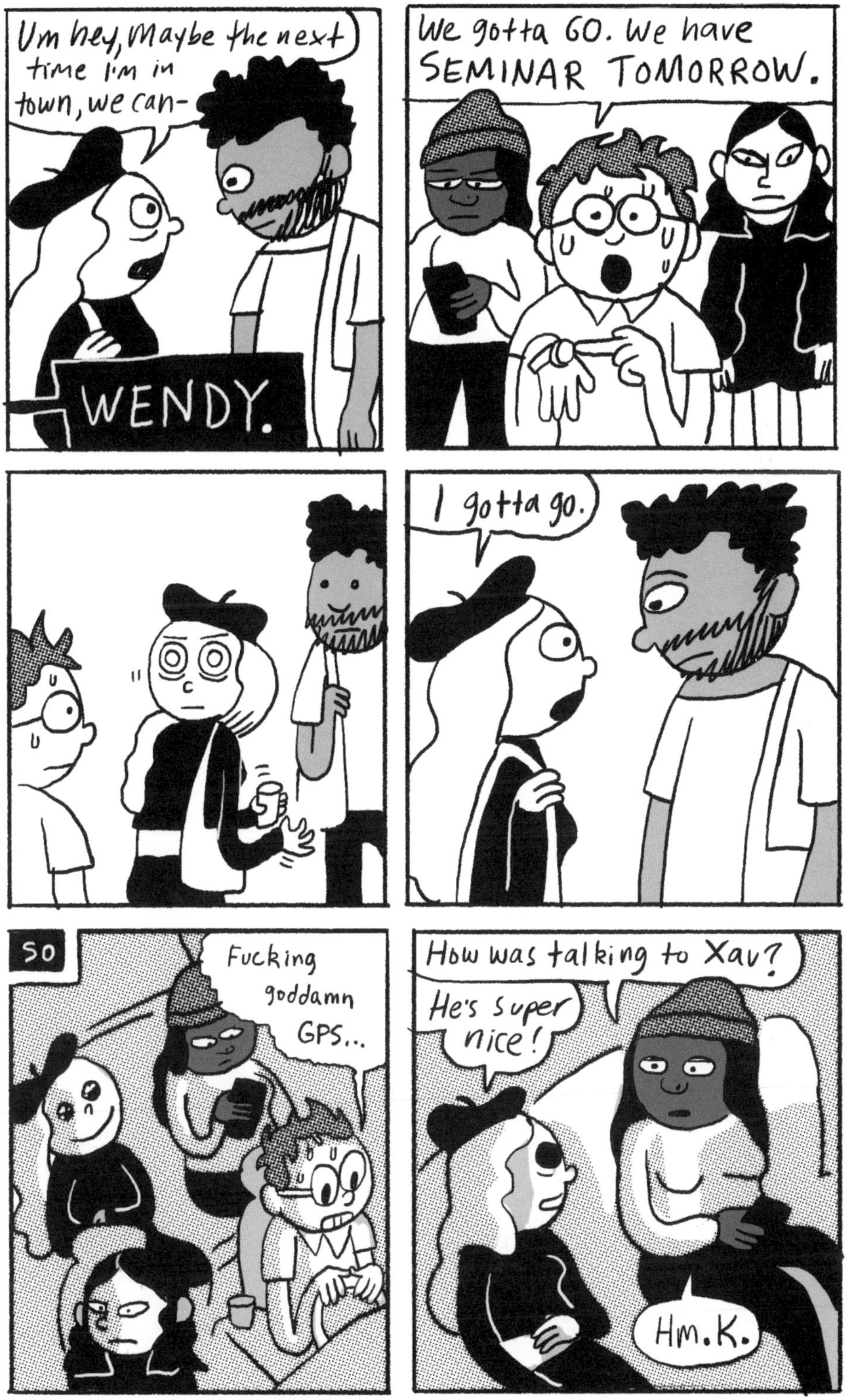
Um hey, maybe the next time I'm in town, we can-
WENDY.
We gotta GO. We have SEMINAR TOMORROW.
I gotta go.
SO
Fucking goddamn GPS...
How was talking to Xav?
He's super nice!
Hm.K.

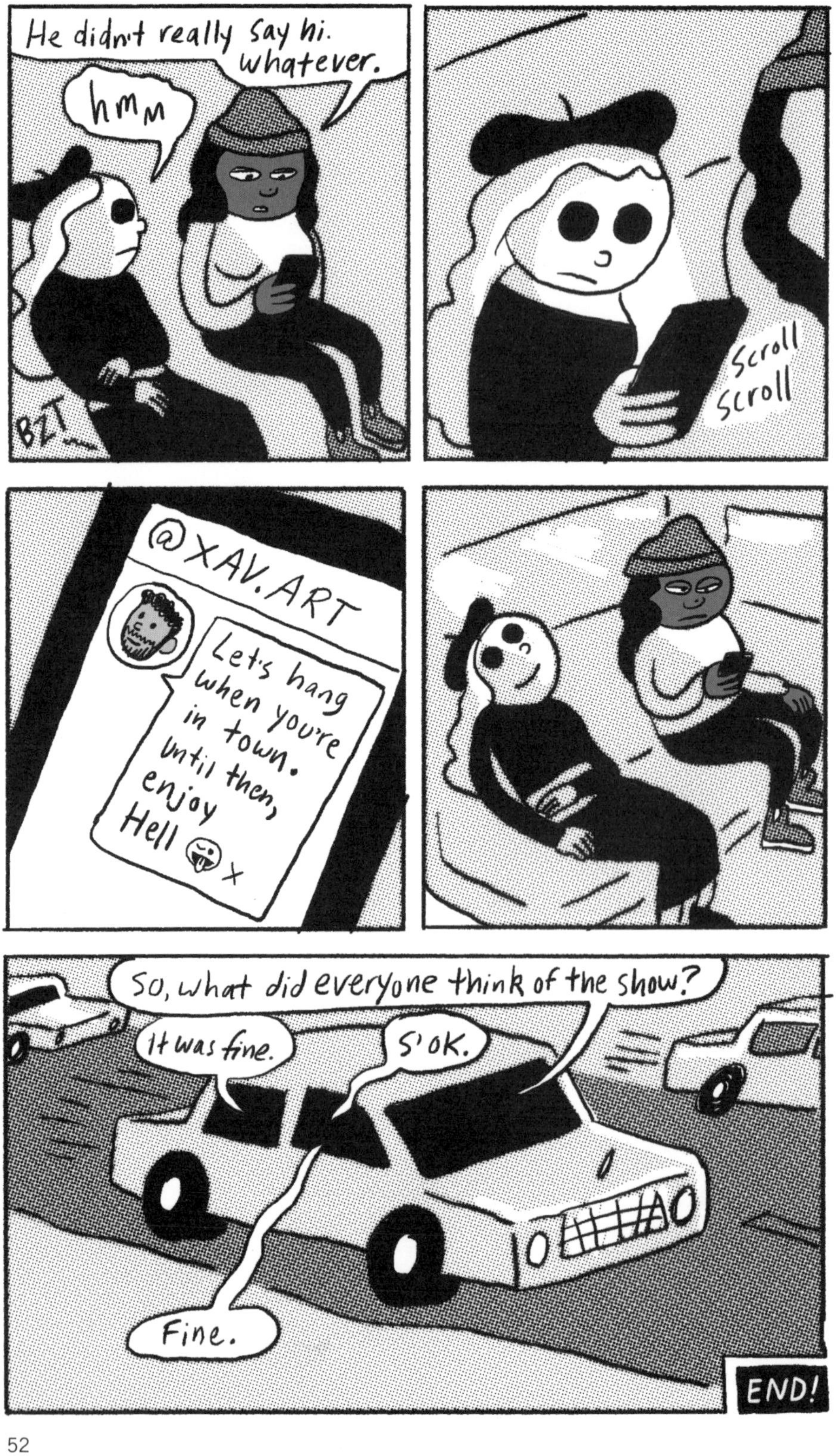
He didn't really say hi. whatever.
hmm
BZT
Scroll scroll
@XAV.ART
Let's hang when you're in town. Until then, enjoy Hell x
So, what did everyone think of the show?
It was fine.
S'ok.
Fine.
END!

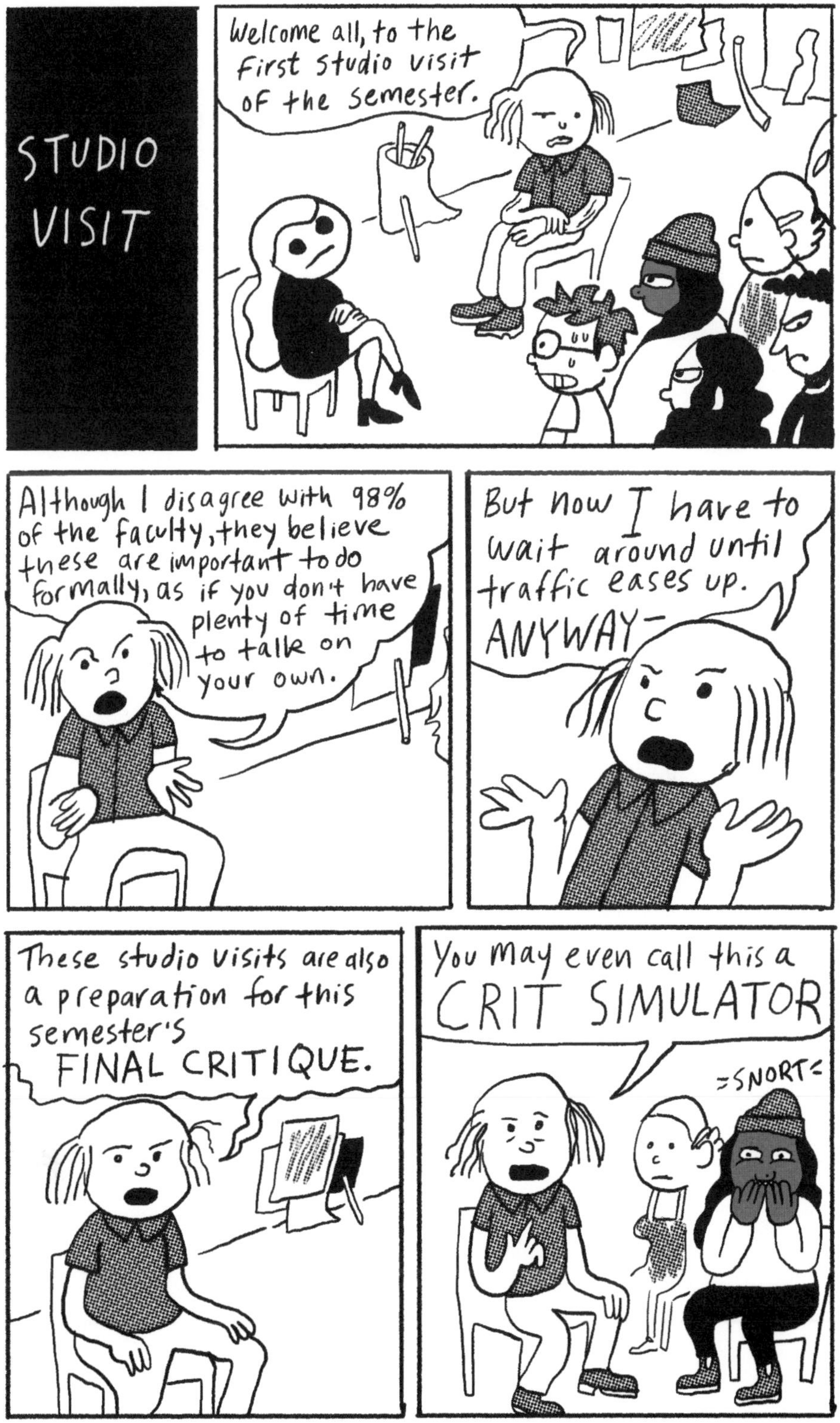
STUDIO VISIT
Welcome all, to the first studio visit of the semester.
Although I disagree with 98% of the faculty, they believe these are important to do formally, as if you don't have plenty of time to talk on your own.
But now I have to wait around until traffic eases up. ANYWAY—
These studio visits are also a preparation for this semester's FINAL CRITIQUE.
You may even call this a CRIT SIMULATOR
=SNORT=

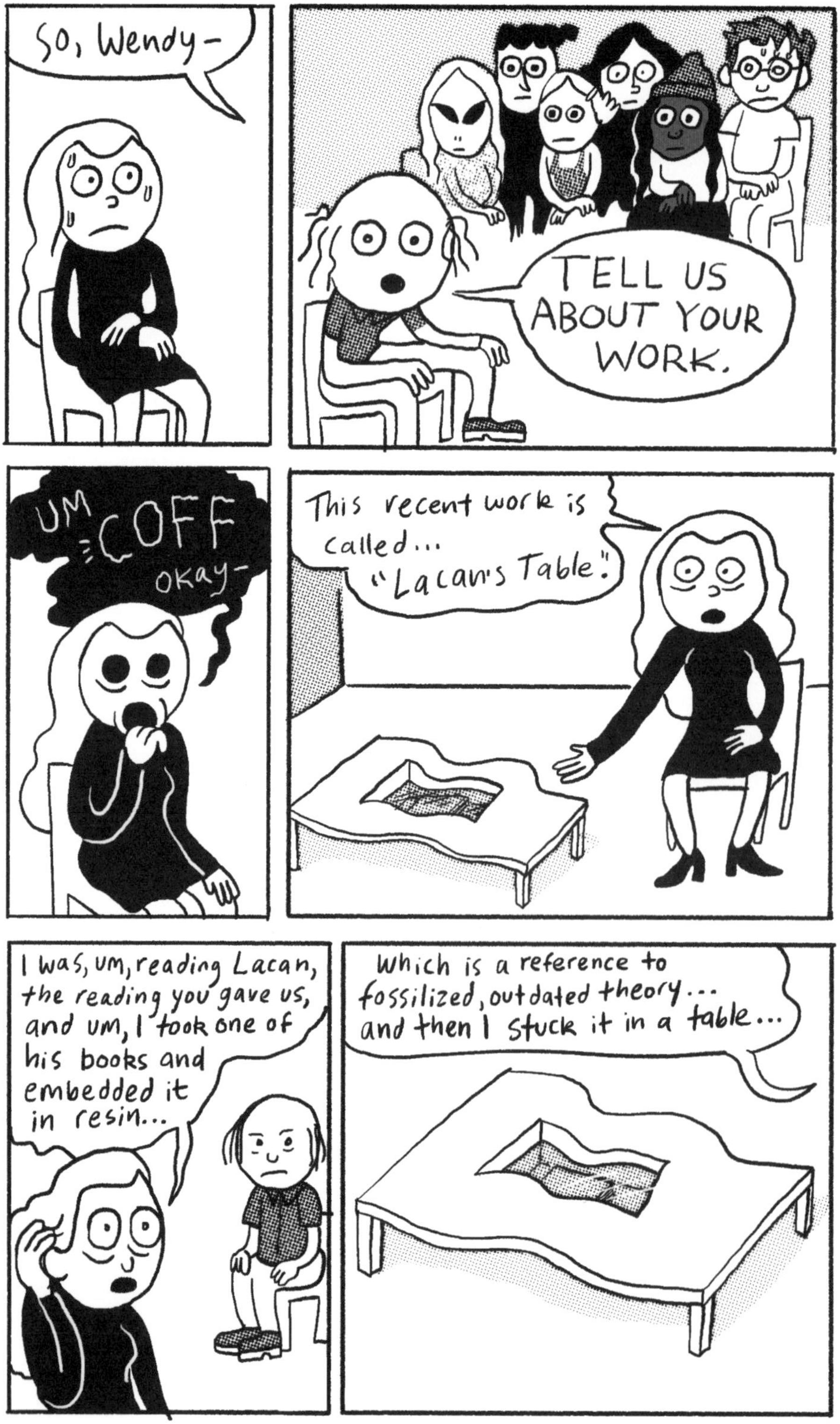

So, Wendy-
TELL US ABOUT YOUR WORK.
UM COFF okay-
This recent work is called... "Lacan's Table"!
I was, um, reading Lacan, the reading you gave us, and um, I took one of his books and embedded it in resin...
Which is a reference to fossilized, outdated theory... and then I stuck it in a table...

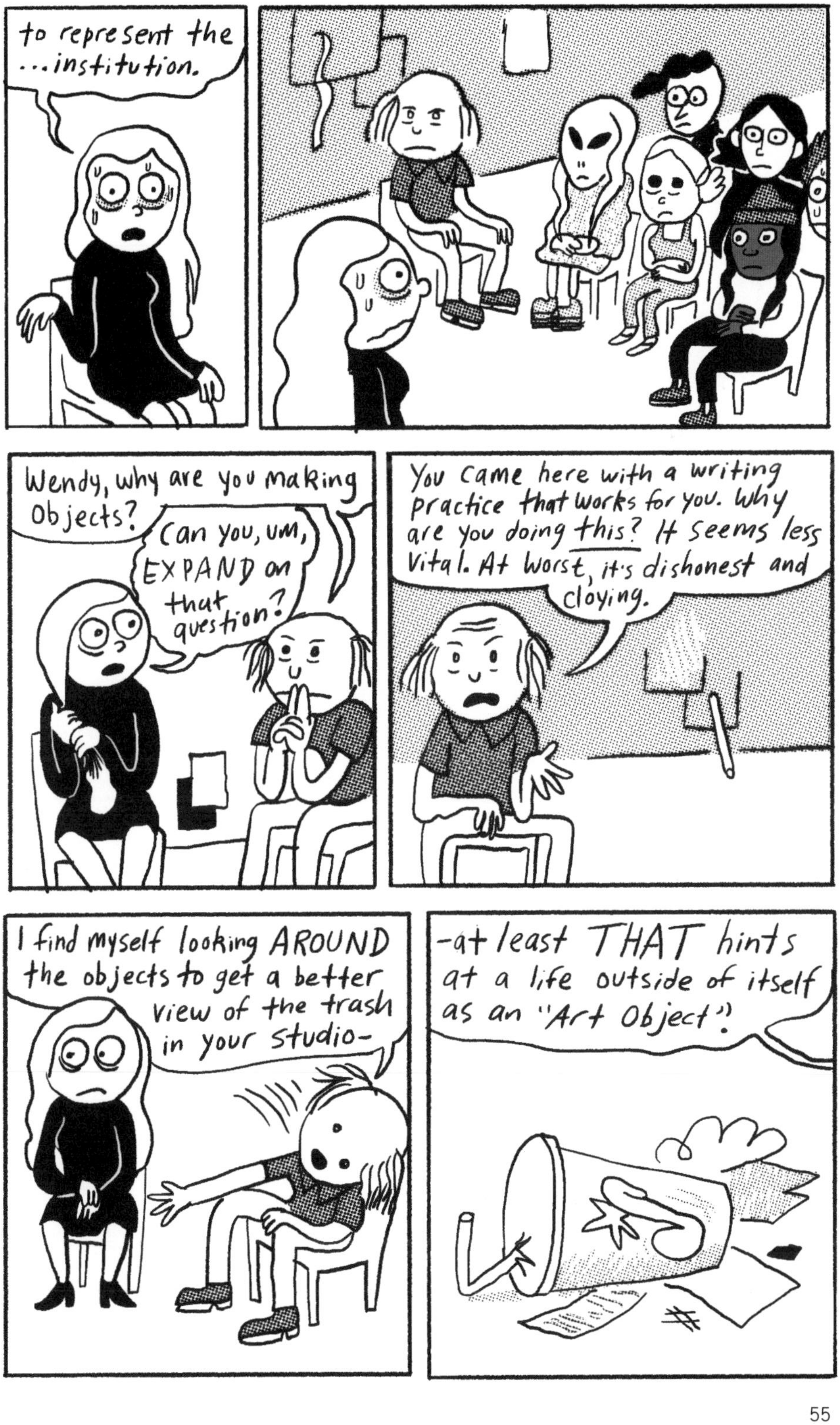
to represent the ...institution.
Wendy, why are you making Objects?
Can you, um, EXPAND on that question?
You came here with a writing practice that works for you. Why are you doing this? It seems less Vital. At worst, it's dishonest and cloying.
I find myself looking AROUND the objects to get a better view of the trash in your studio-
-at least THAT hints at a life outside of itself as an "Art Object".

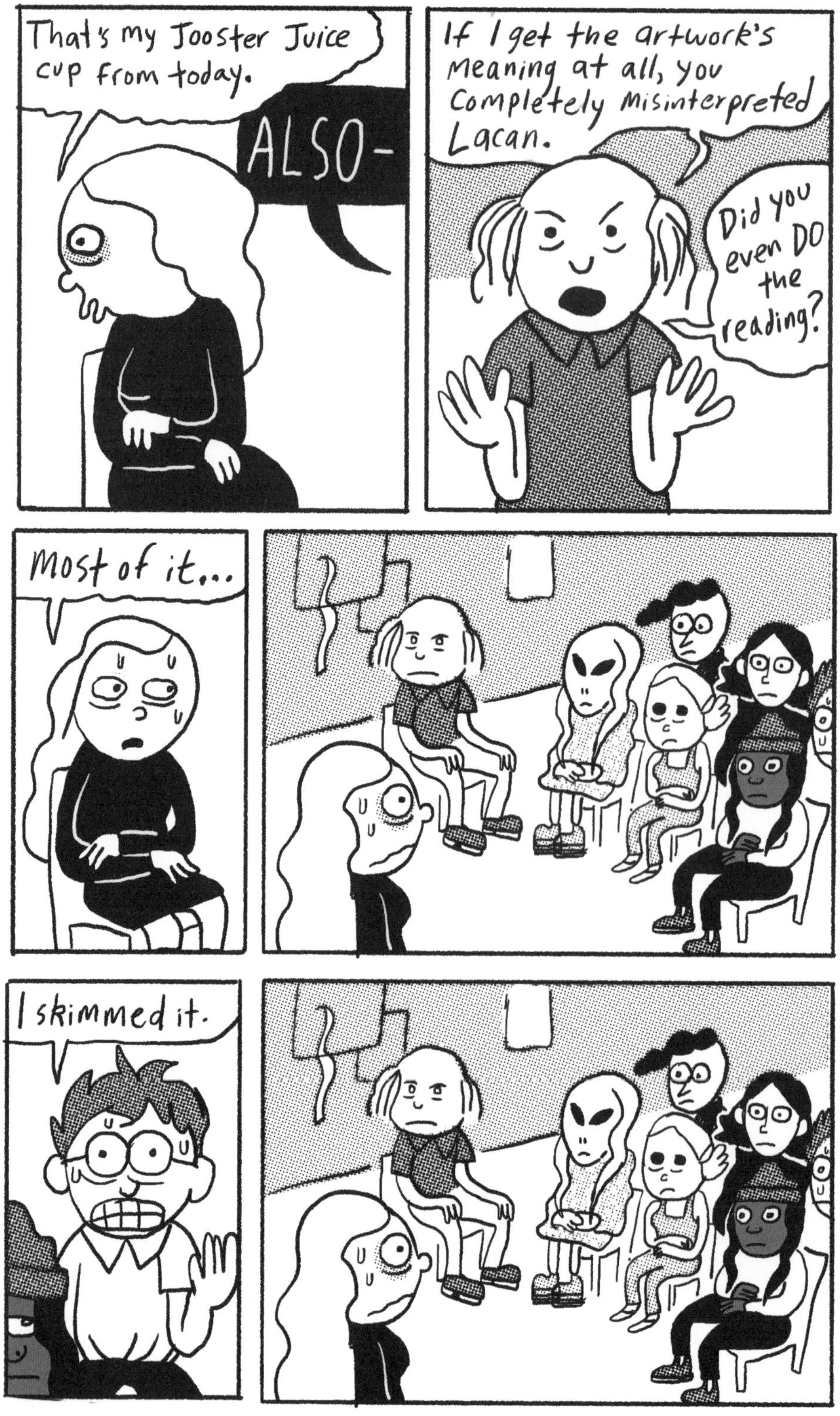
That's my Jooster Juice cup from today.
ALSO-
If I get the artwork's meaning at all, you completely misinterpreted Lacan.
Did you even DO the reading?
Most of it...
I skimmed it.

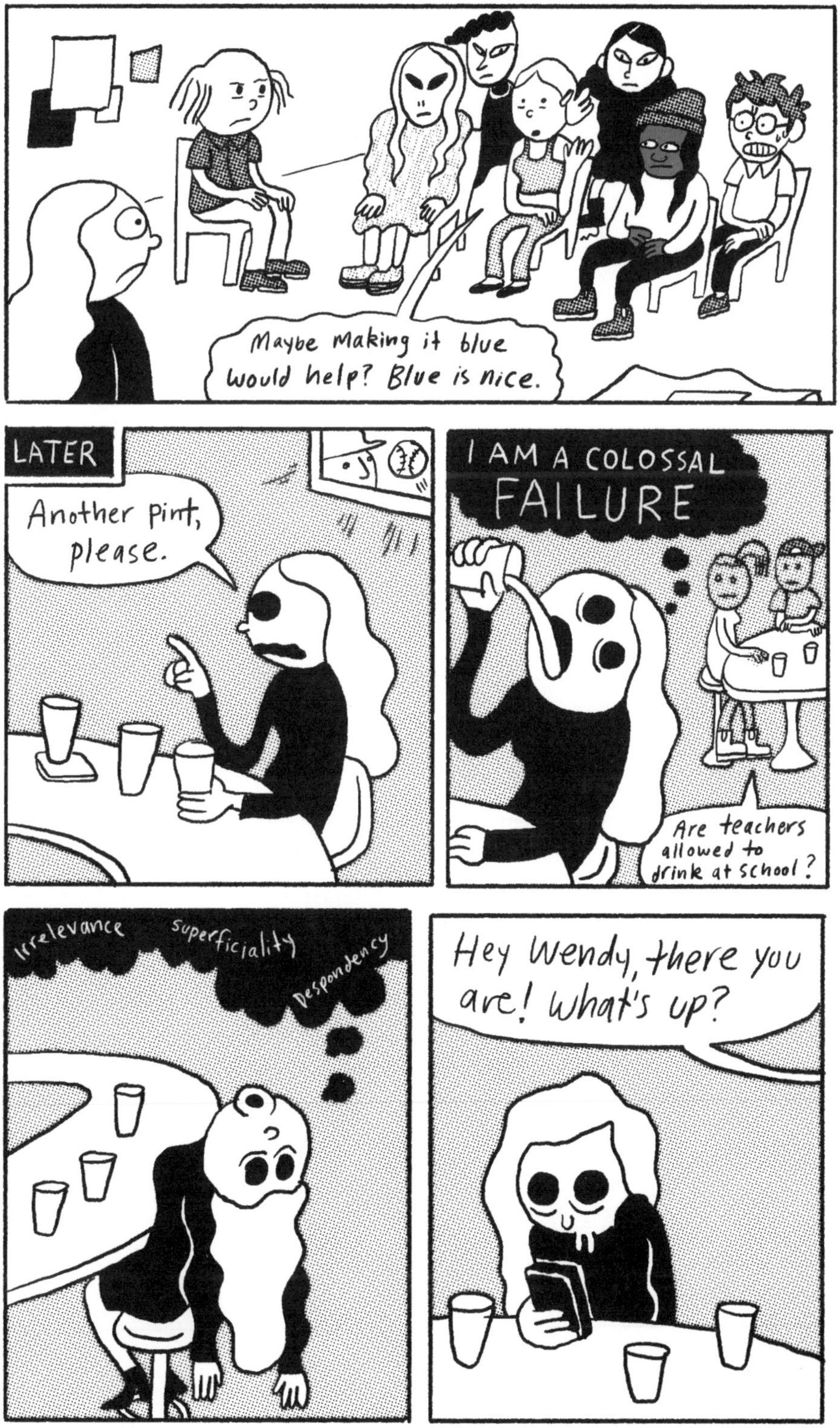
Maybe making it blue
would help? Blue is nice.
LATER
Another pint, please.
I AM A COLOSSAL FAILURE
Are teachers allowed to drink at school?
irrelevance
superficiality
despondency
Hey Wendy, there you are! What's up?

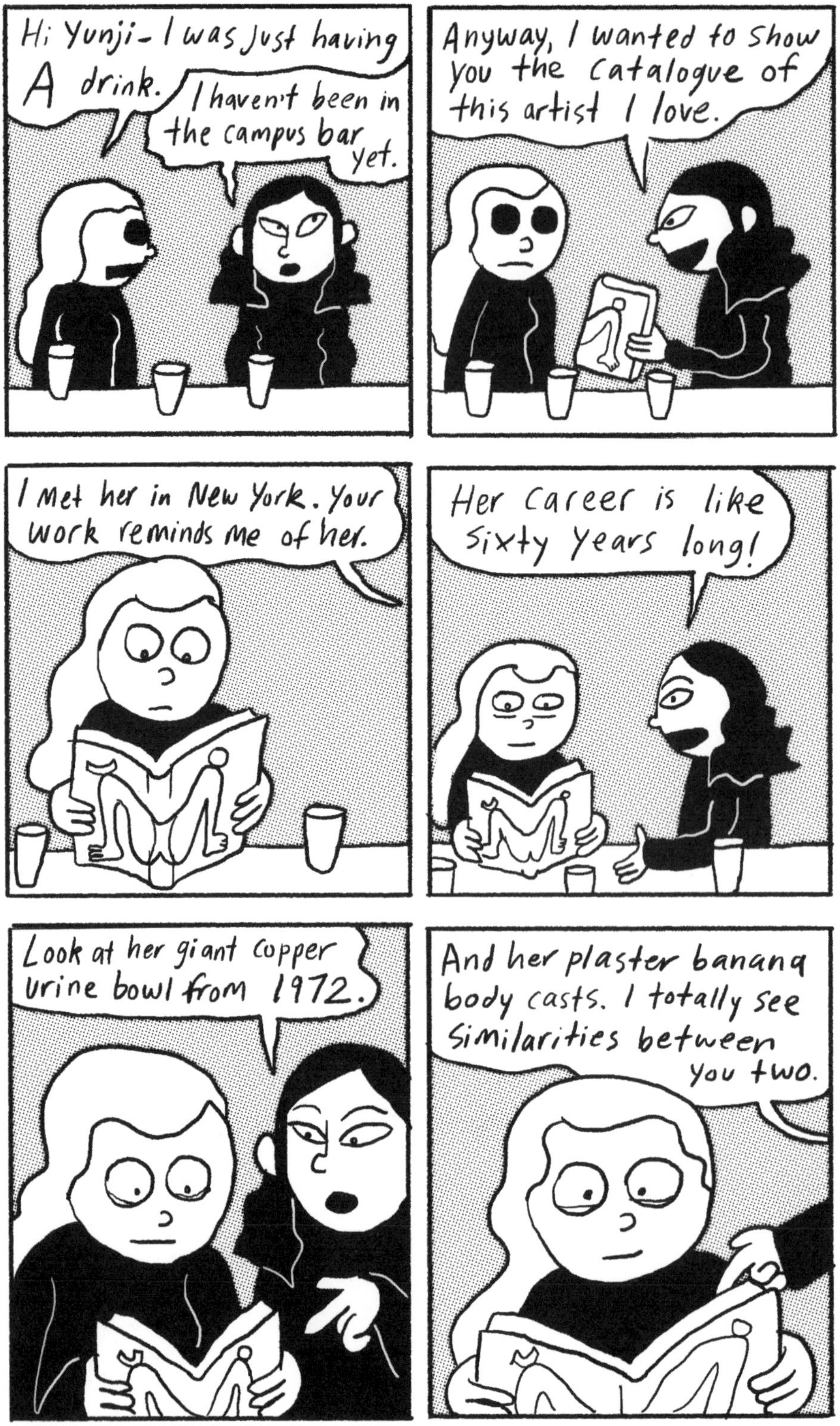
Hi Yunji - I was just having A drink.
I haven't been in the campus bar yet.
Anyway, I wanted to show you the catalogue of this artist I love.
I met her in New York. Your work reminds me of her.
Her career is like sixty years long!
Look at her giant copper urine bowl from 1972.
And her plaster banana body casts. I totally see similarities between you two.

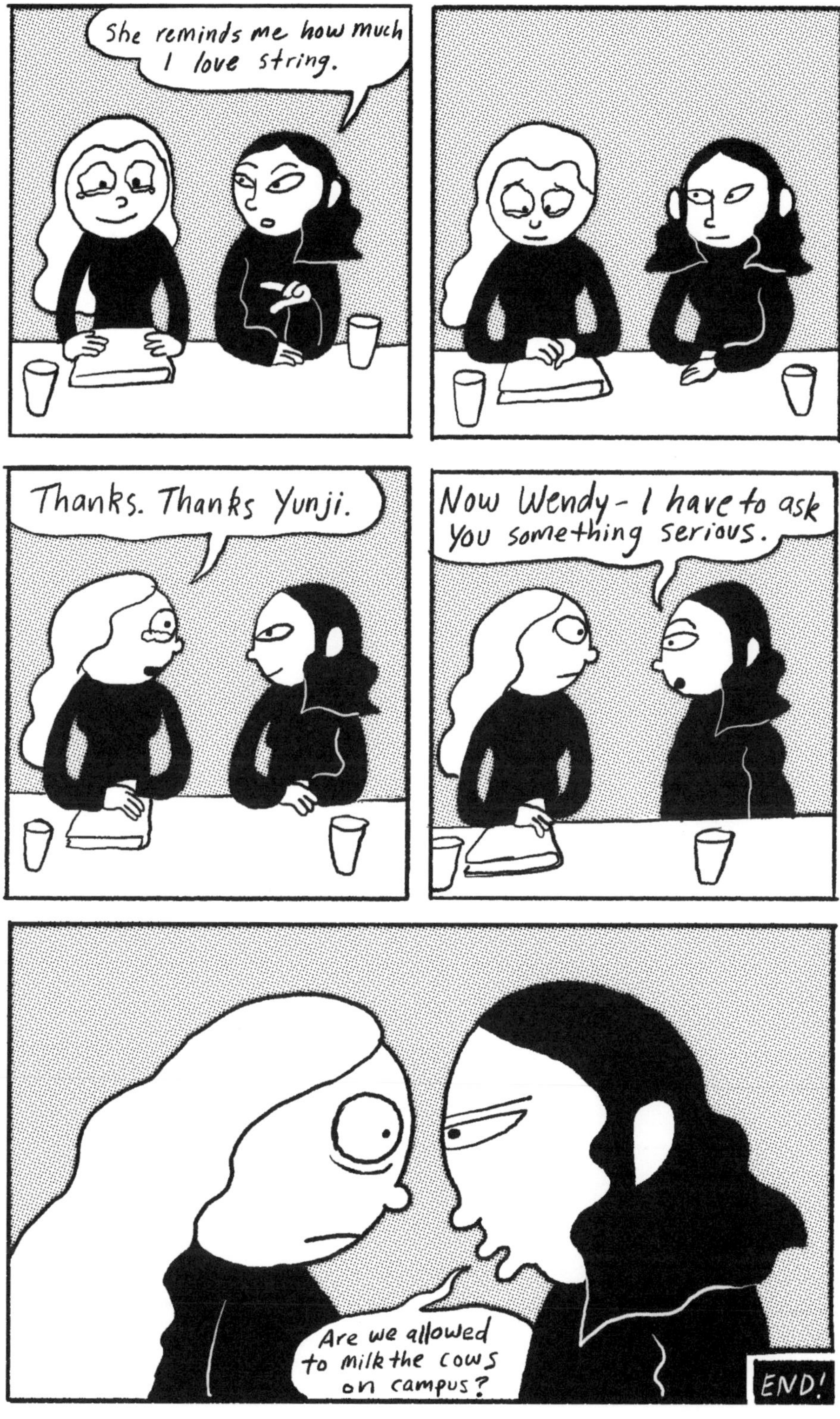
She reminds me how much I love string.
Thanks. Thanks Yunji.
Now Wendy - I have to ask you something serious.
Are we allowed to milk the cows on campus?
END!

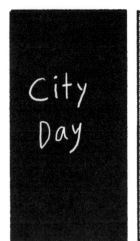

City
Day

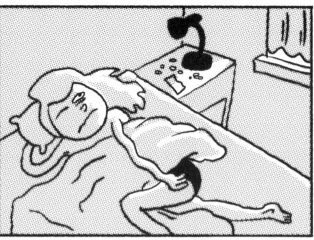

Hi Xav, I'm coming into town today to look at art, if you wanna meet up. SEND

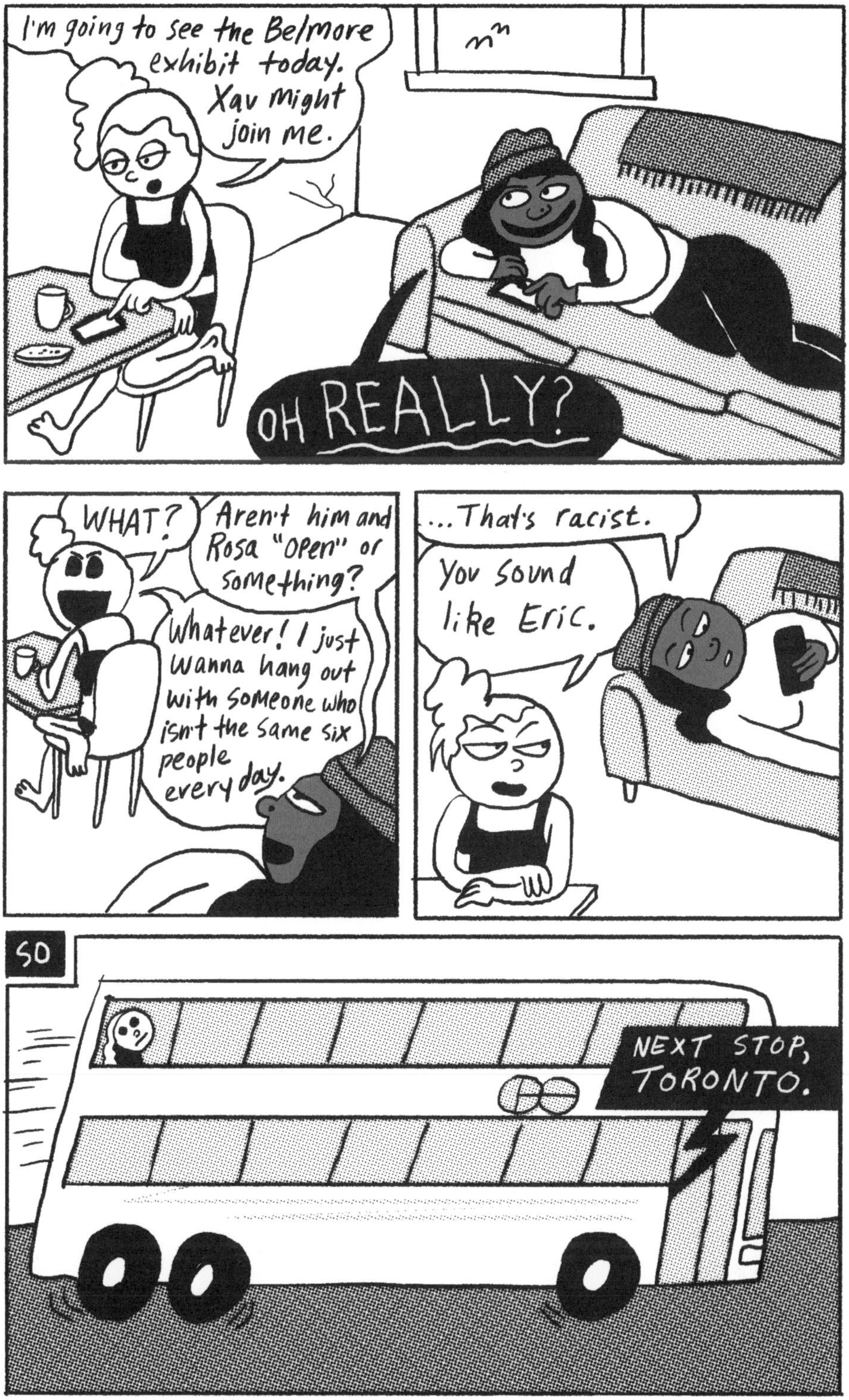
I'm going to see the Belmore exhibit today. Xav might join me.
OH REALLY?
WHAT?
Aren't him and Rosa "open" or something?
Whatever! I just wanna hang out with someone who isn't the same six people every day.
...That's racist.
You sound like Eric.
SO
NEXT STOP, TORONTO.

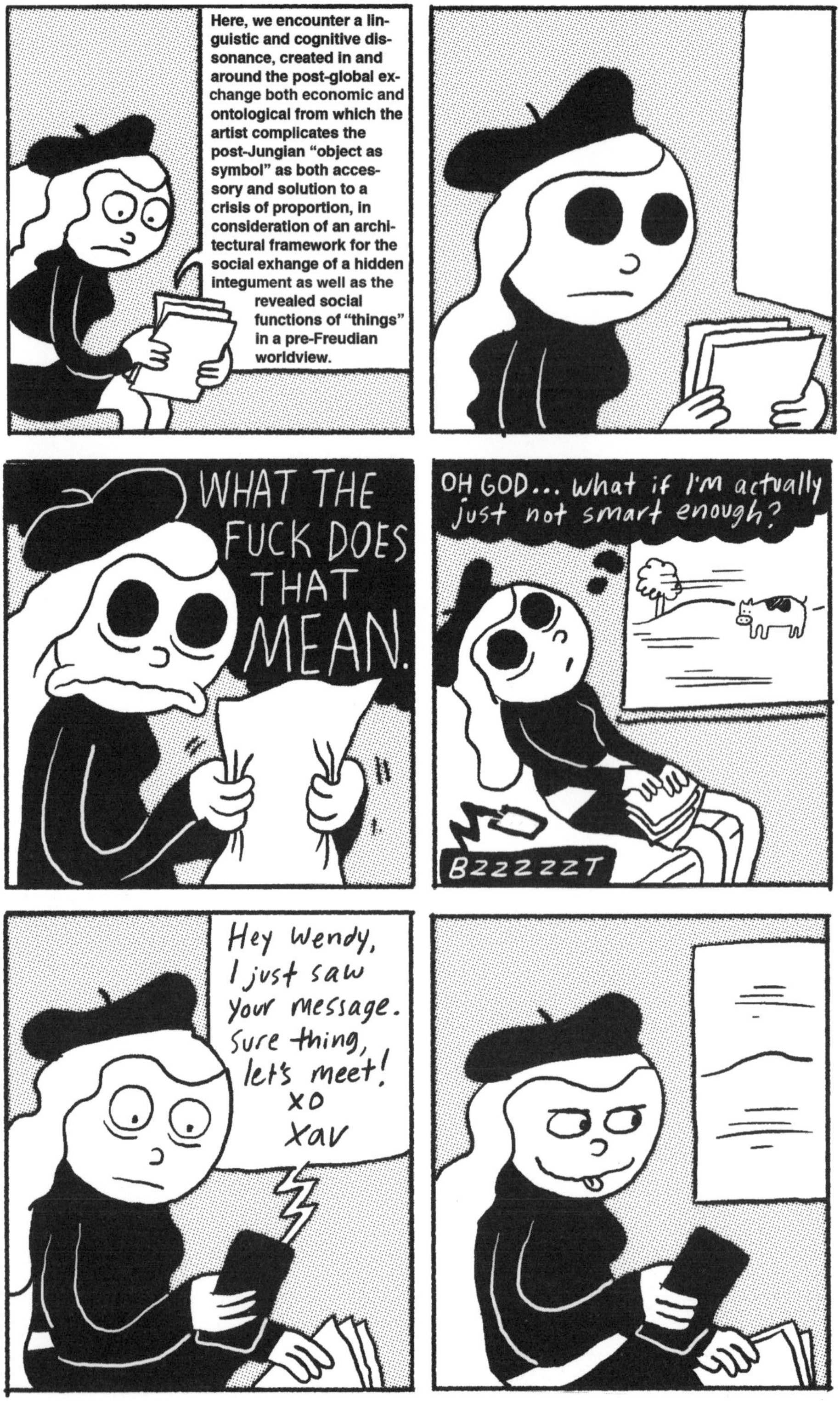
Here, we encounter a linguistic and cognitive dissonance, created in and around the post-global exchange both economic and ontological from which the artist complicates the post-Jungian "object as symbol" as both accessory and solution to a crisis of proportion, in consideration of an architectural framework for the social exhange of a hidden integument as well as the revealed social functions of "things" in a pre-Freudian worldview.
WHAT THE FUCK DOES THAT MEAN.
OH GOD... what if I'm actually just not smart enough?
BZZZZZT
Hey Wendy, I just saw your message. Sure thing, let's meet! XO Xav

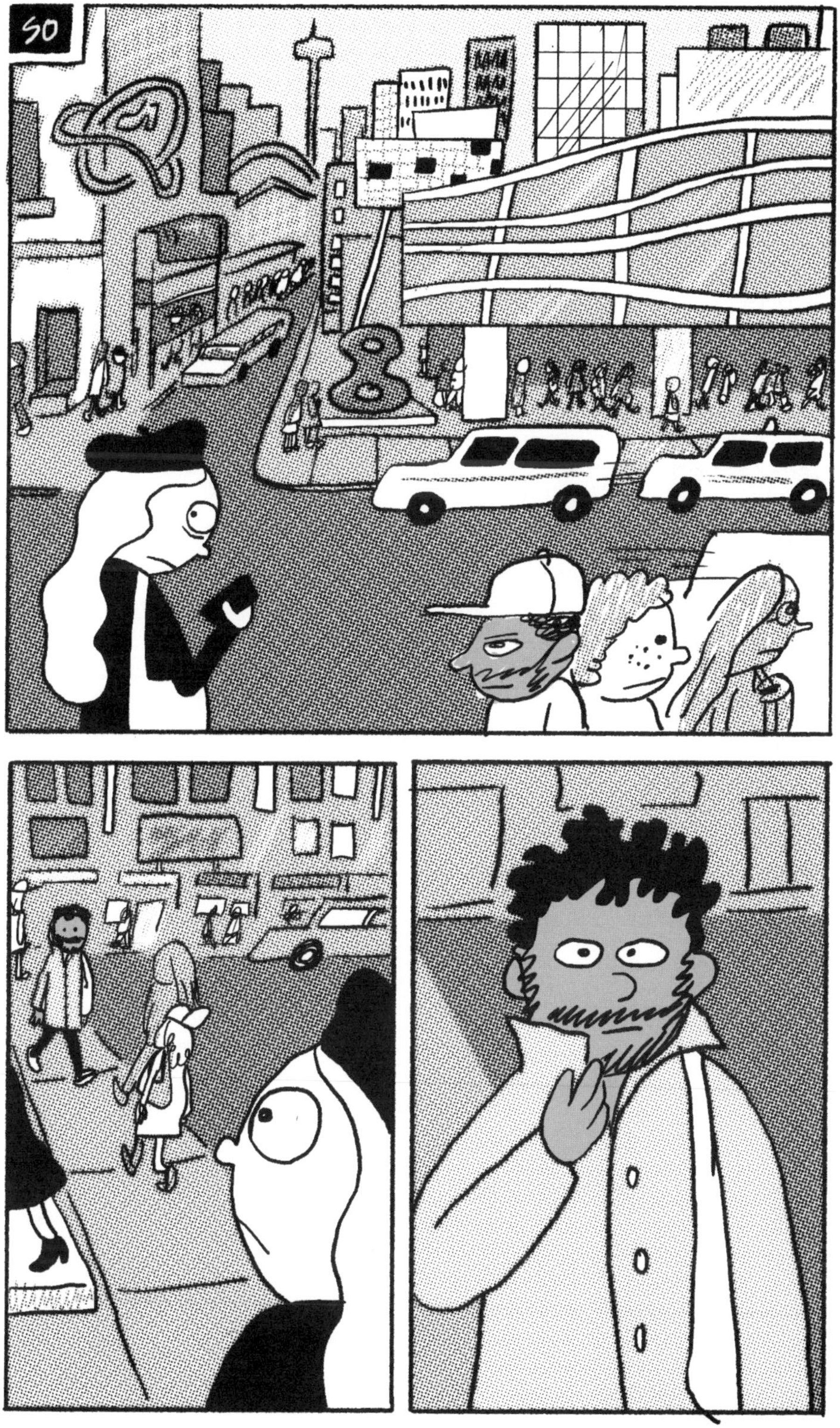
SO

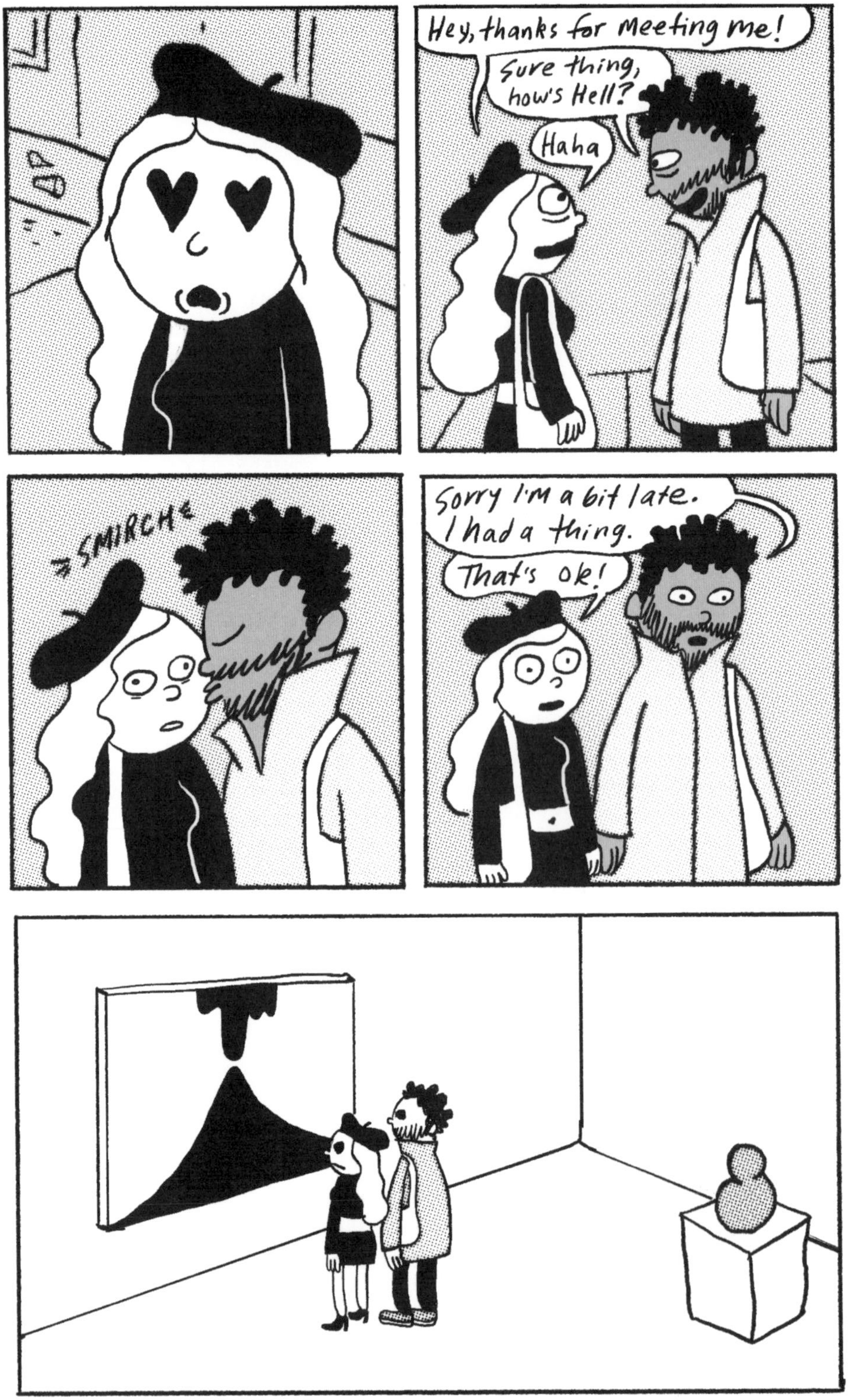
Hey, thanks for meeting me!
Sure thing, how's Hell?
Haha
SMIRCH
Sorry I'm a bit late. I had a thing.
That's ok!

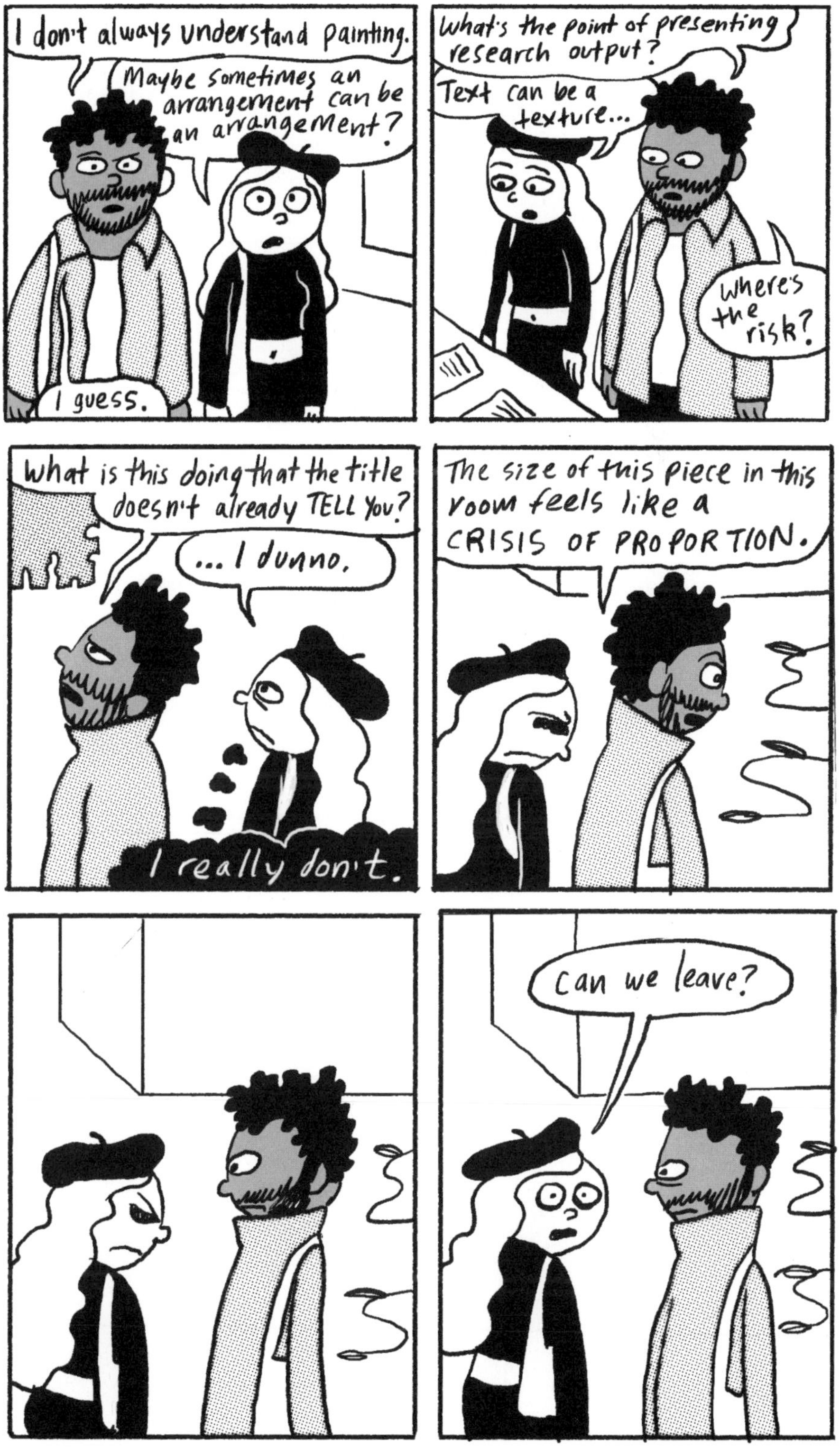
I don't always understand painting.
Maybe sometimes an arrangement can be an arrangement?
I guess.
What's the point of presenting research output?
Text can be a texture...
Where's the risk?
What is this doing that the title doesn't already TELL You?
...I dunno.
I really don't.
The size of this piece in this room feels like a CRISIS OF PROPORTION.
Can we leave?

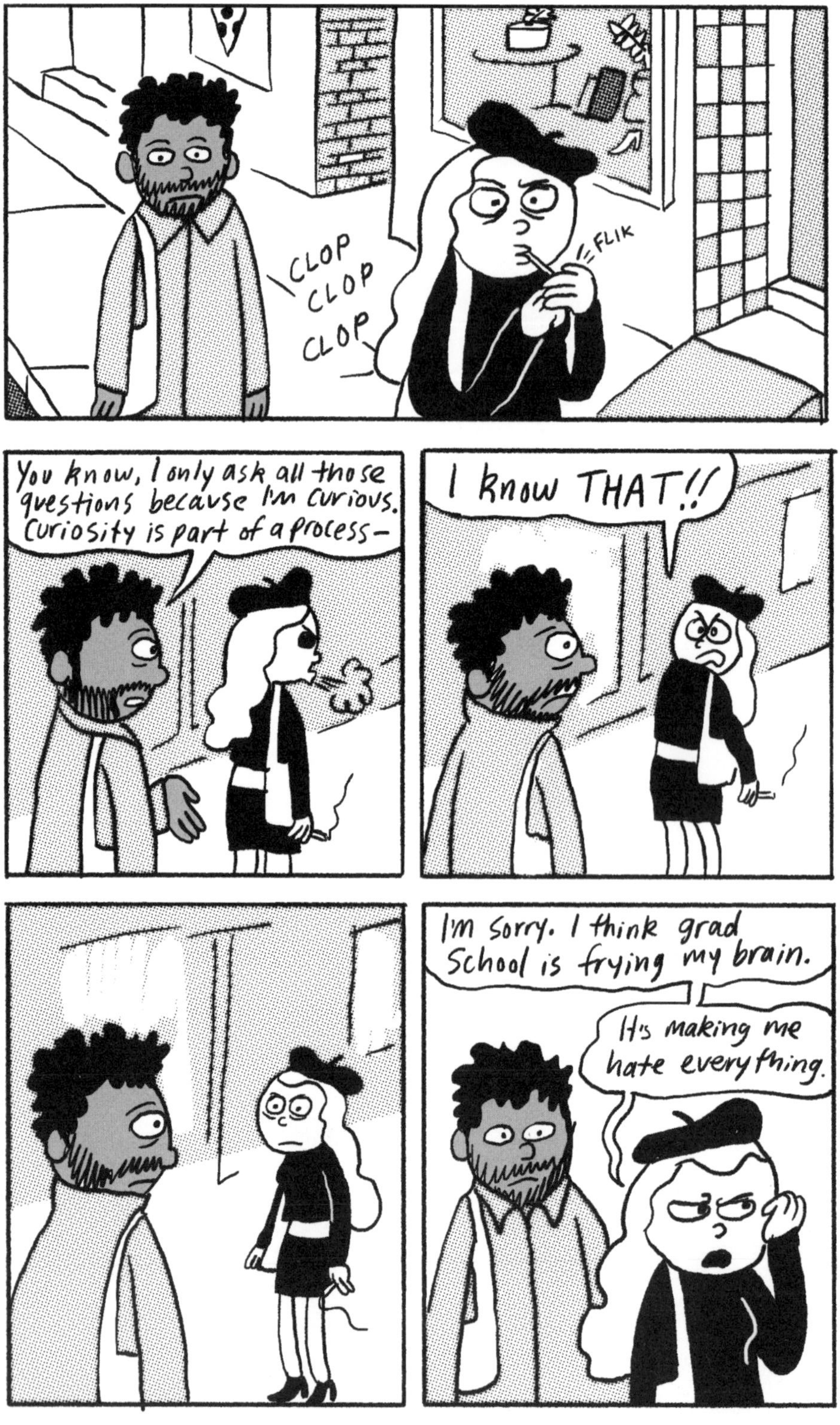
CLOP
CLOP
CLOP
FLIK
You know, I only ask all those questions because I'm curious. Curiosity is part of a process—
I know THAT!!
I'm sorry. I think grad school is frying my brain.
It's making me hate everything.

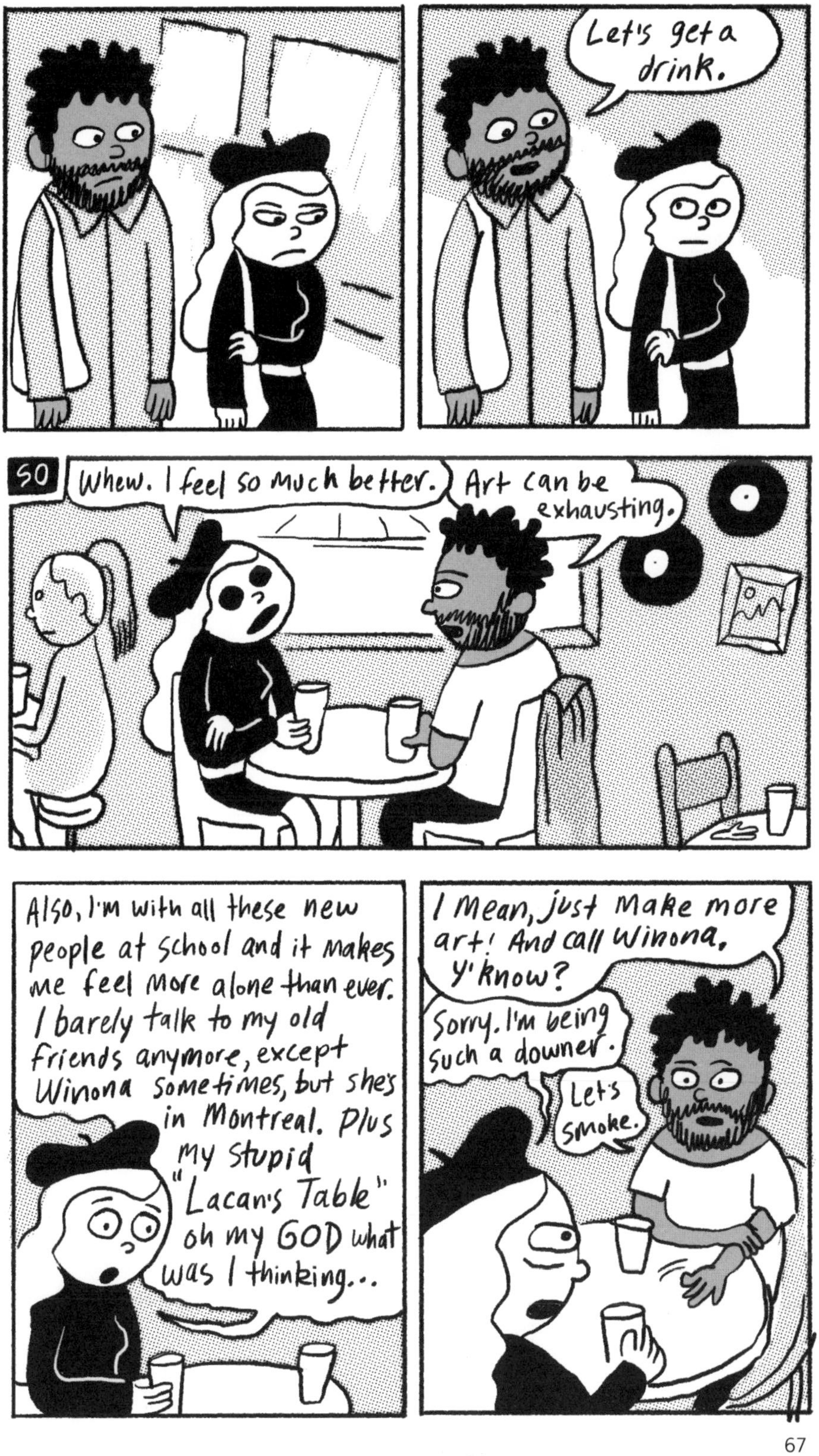
Let's get a drink.
SO
Whew. I feel so much better.
Art can be exhausting.
Also, I'm with all these new people at school and it makes me feel more alone than ever. I barely talk to my old friends anymore, except Winona sometimes, but she's in Montreal. Plus my stupid "Lacan's Table" oh my GOD what was I thinking...
I mean, just make more art! And call Winona, y'know?
Sorry. I'm being such a downer.
Let's smoke.

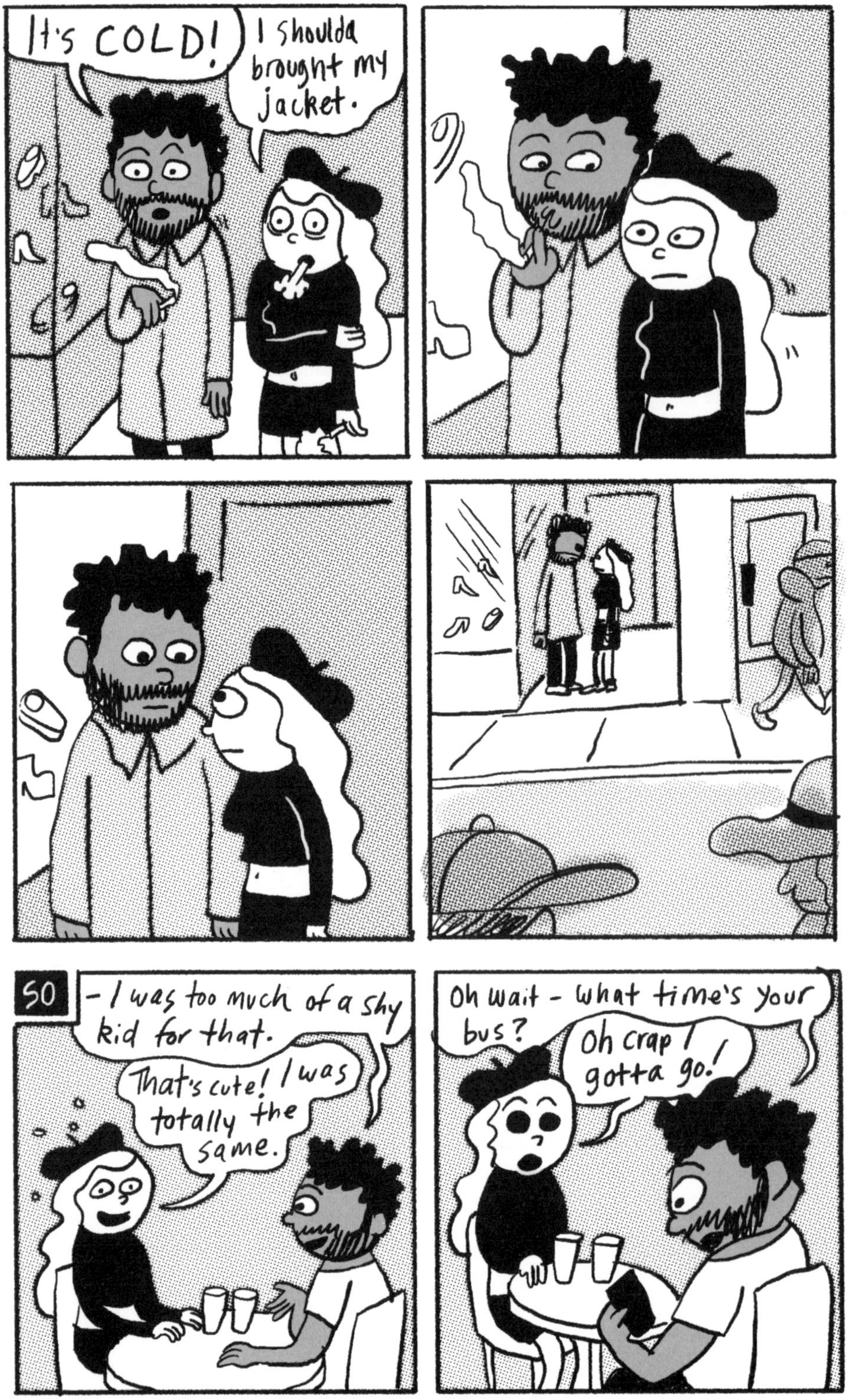
It's COLD!
I shoulda brought my jacket.
SO
- I was too much of a shy kid for that.
That's cute! I was totally the same.
Oh wait - what time's your bus?
Oh crap I gotta go!

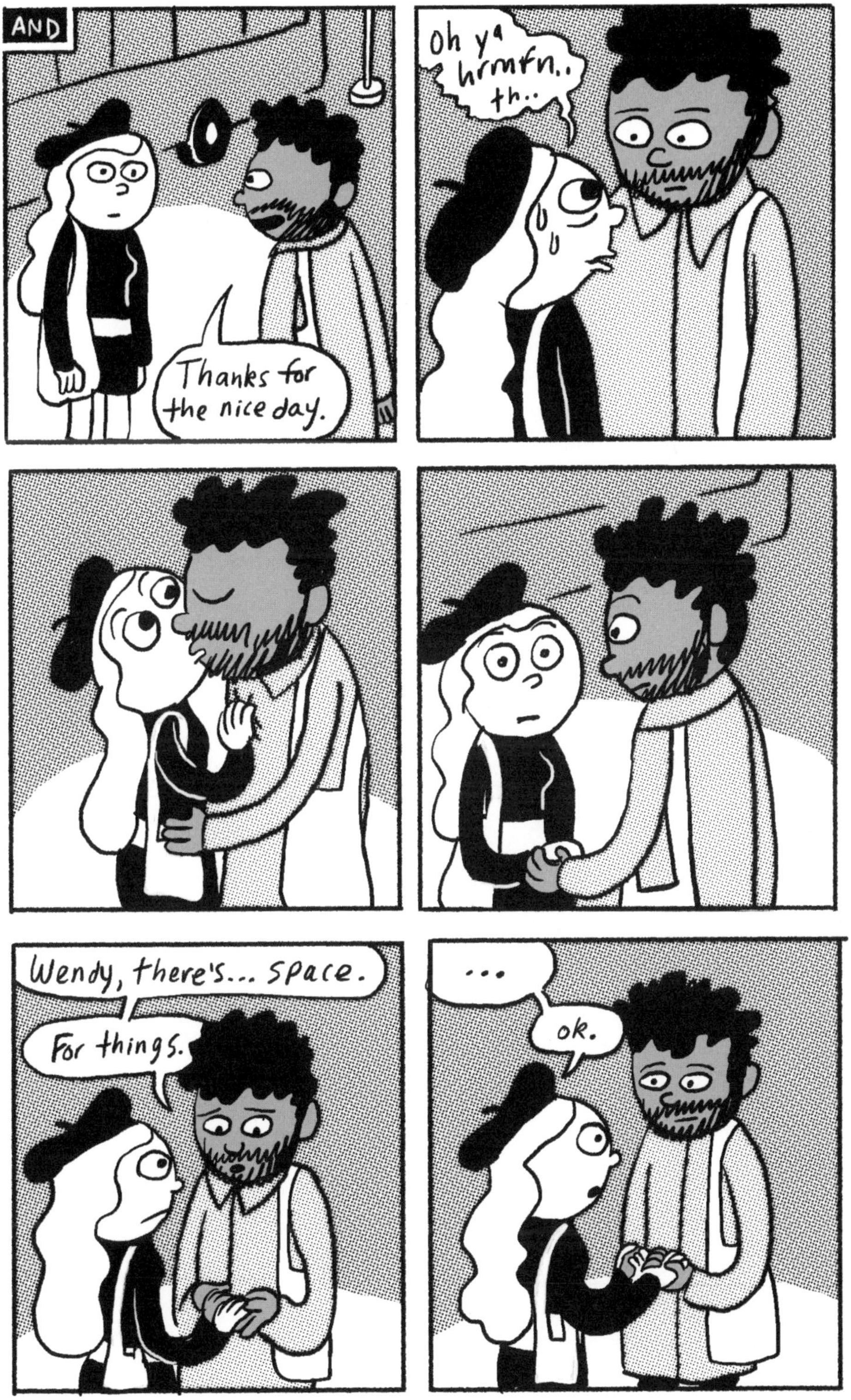
AND
Thanks for the nice day.
Oh ya hrmfn.. th..
Wendy, there's... space.
For things.
...
ok.

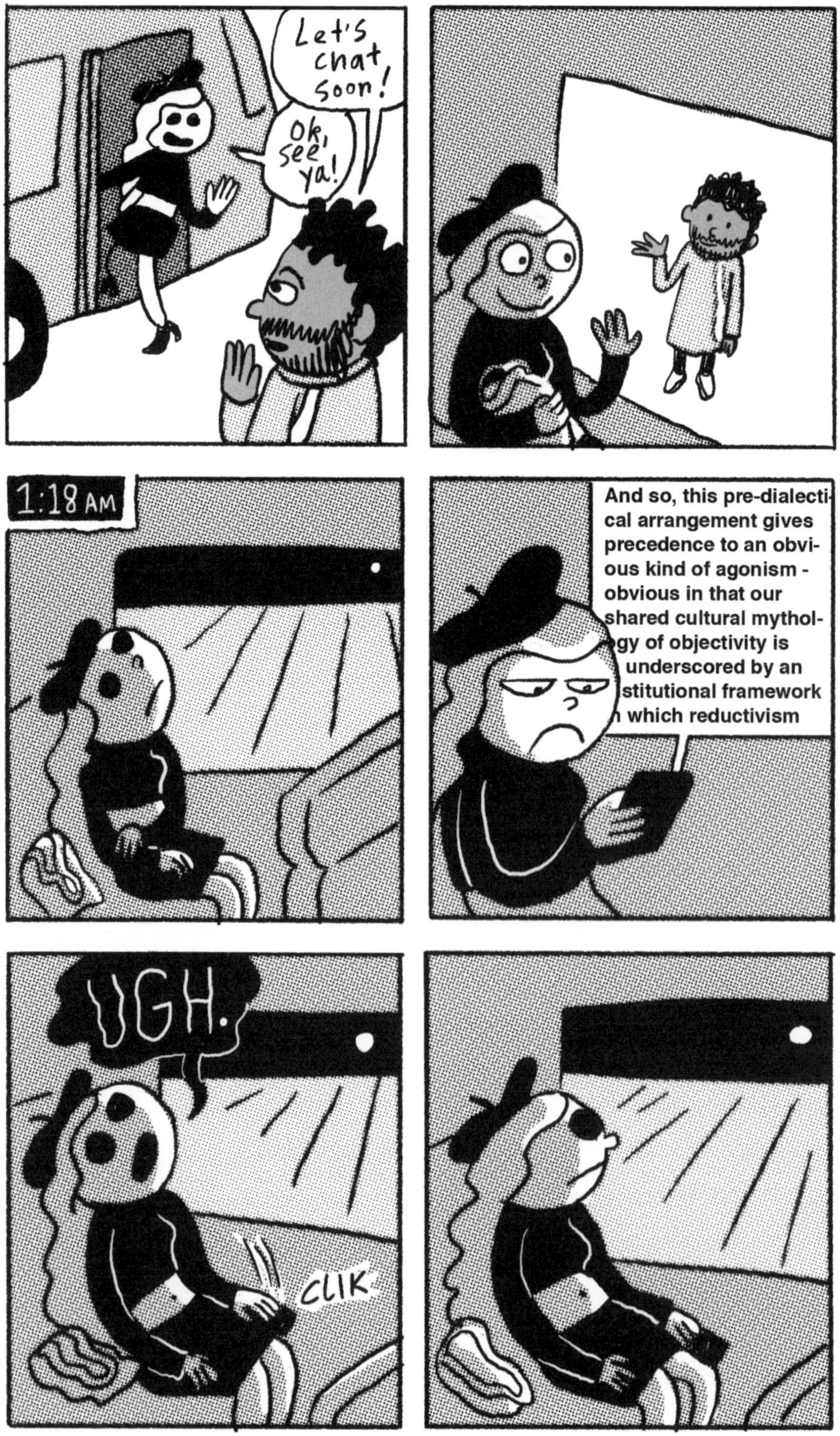
Let's chat soon!
Ok, see ya!
1:18 AM
And so, this pre-dialecti-
cal arrangement gives
precedence to an obvi-
ous kind of agonism -
obvious in that our
shared cultural mythol-
gy of objectivity is
underscored by an
stitutional framework
which reductivism
UGH.
CLIK

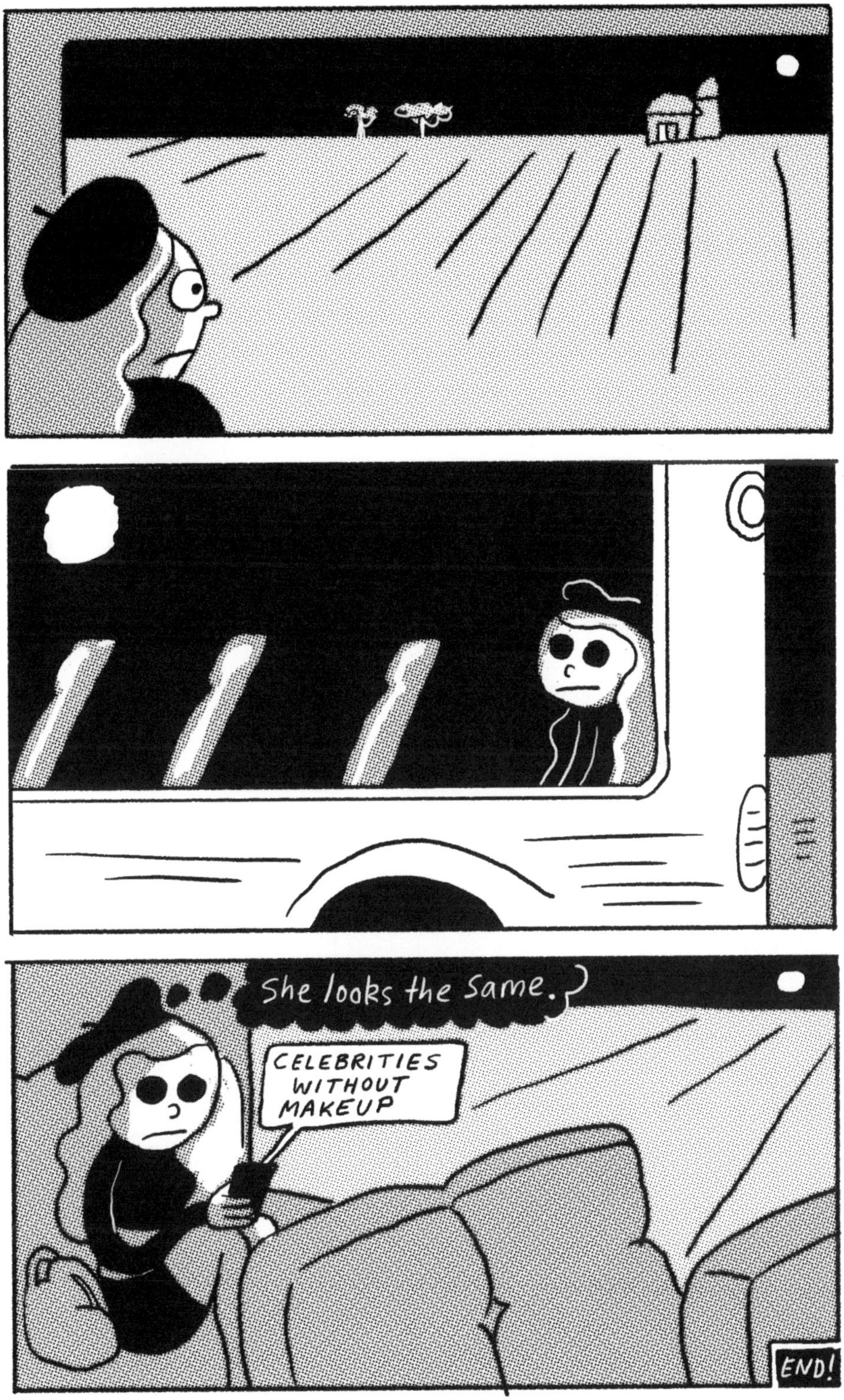
She looks the same.
CELEBRITIES WITHOUT MAKEUP
END!

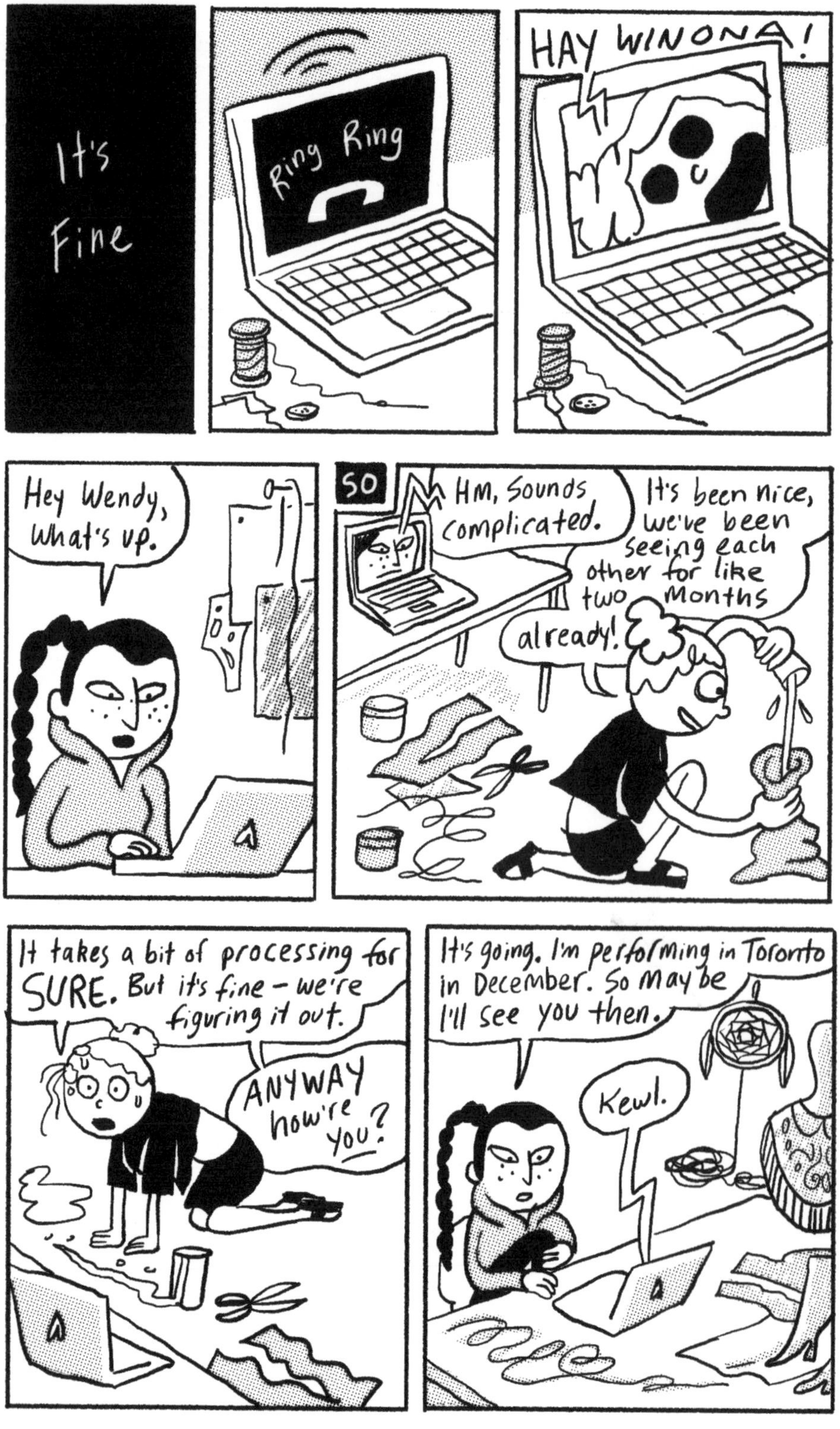
It's Fine
Ring Ring
HAY WINONA!
Hey Wendy, what's up.
SO
HM, Sounds complicated.
It's been nice, we've been seeing each other for like two Months
already!
It takes a bit of processing for SURE. But it's fine - we're figuring it out.
ANYWAY how're YOU?
It's going. I'm performing in Toronto in December. So May be I'll see you then.
Kewl.

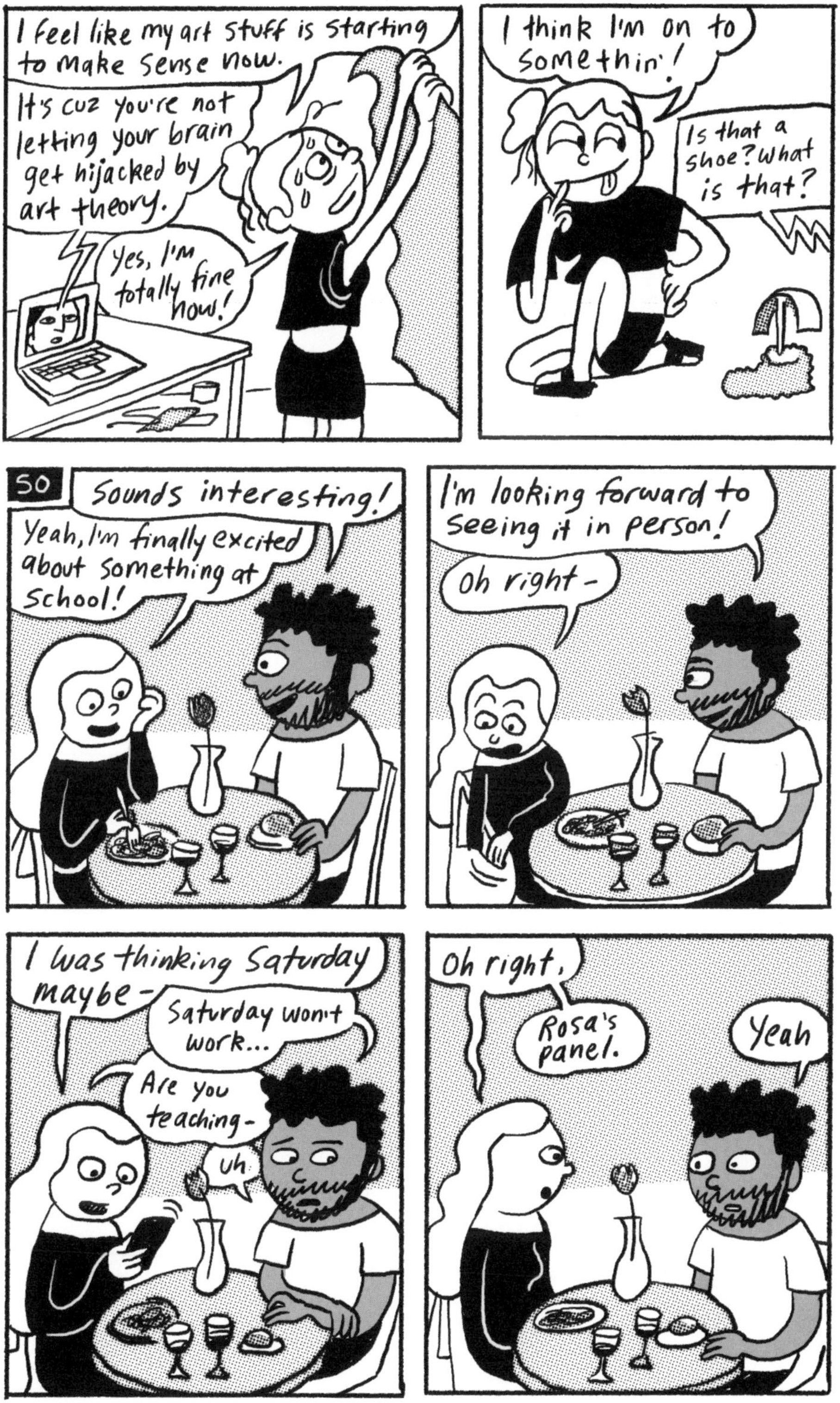
I feel like my art stuff is starting to make sense now.
It's cuz you're not letting your brain get hijacked by art theory.
Yes, I'm totally fine now!
I think I'm on to somethin'!
Is that a shoe? What is that?
SO
Sounds interesting!
Yeah, I'm finally excited about something at school!
I'm looking forward to seeing it in person!
Oh right -
I was thinking Saturday maybe -
Saturday won't work...
Are you teaching -
Uh
Oh right,
Rosa's panel.
Yeah

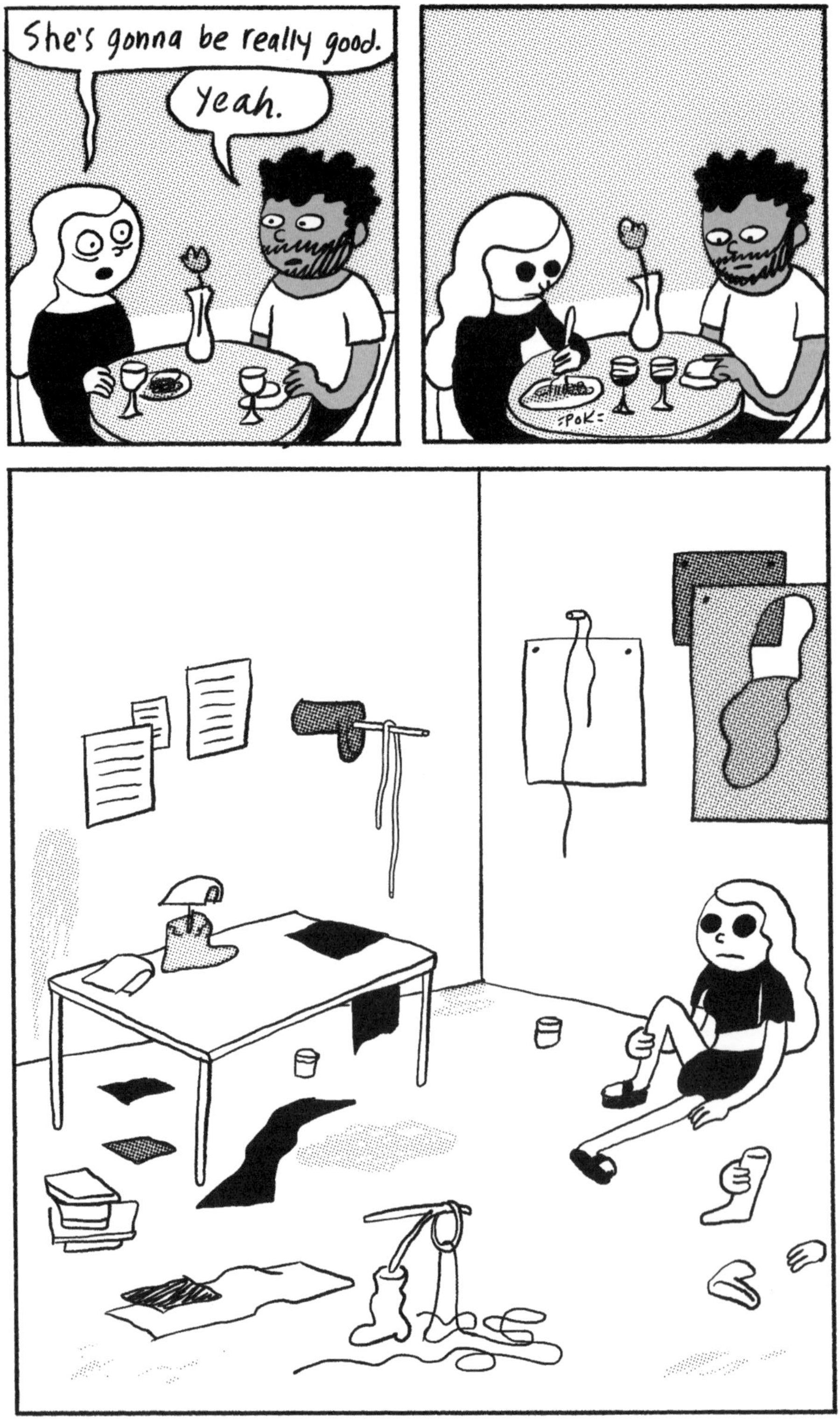
She's gonna be really good.
Yeah.
POK

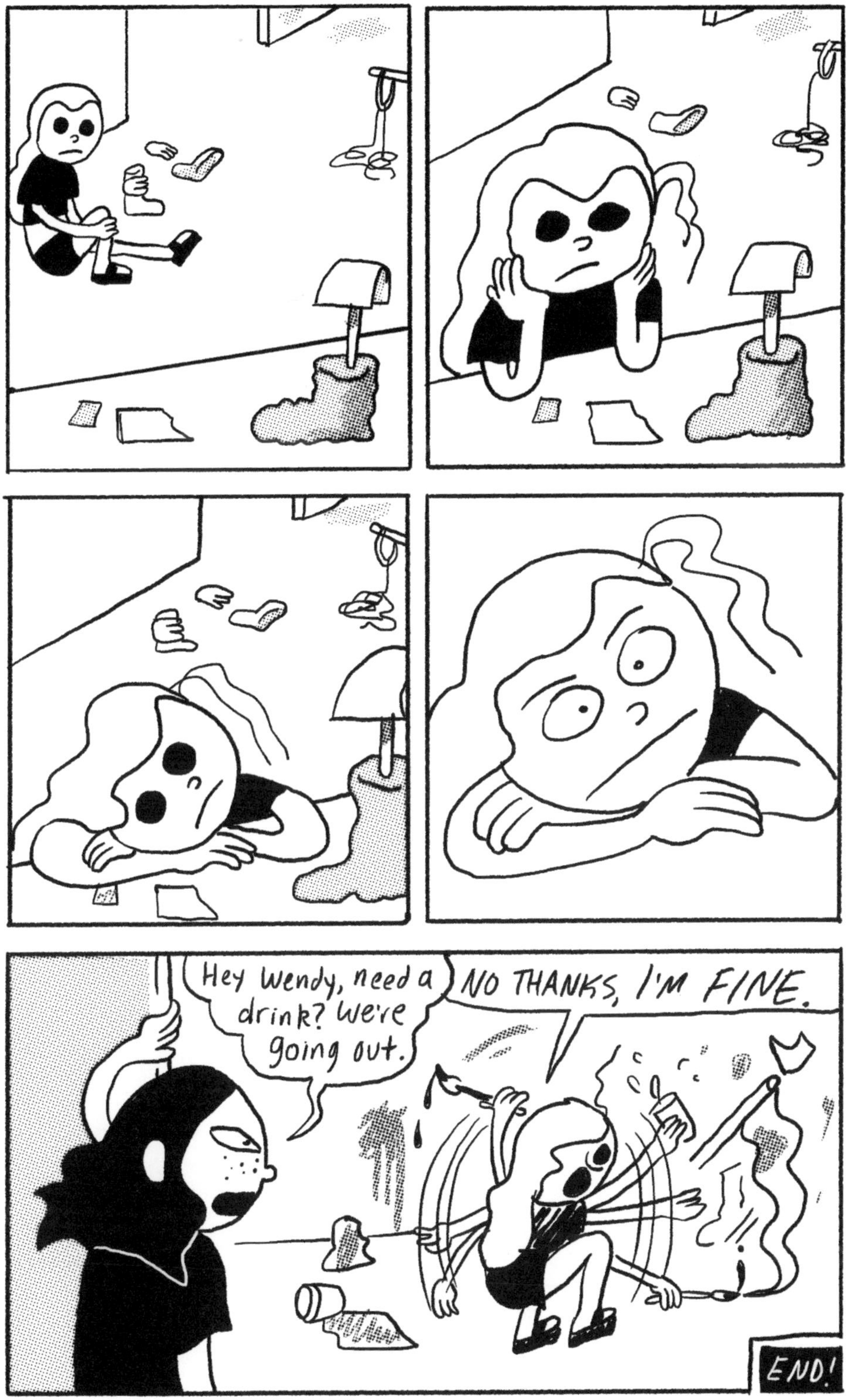

Hey Wendy, need a drink? We're going out.
NO THANKS, I'M FINE.
END!

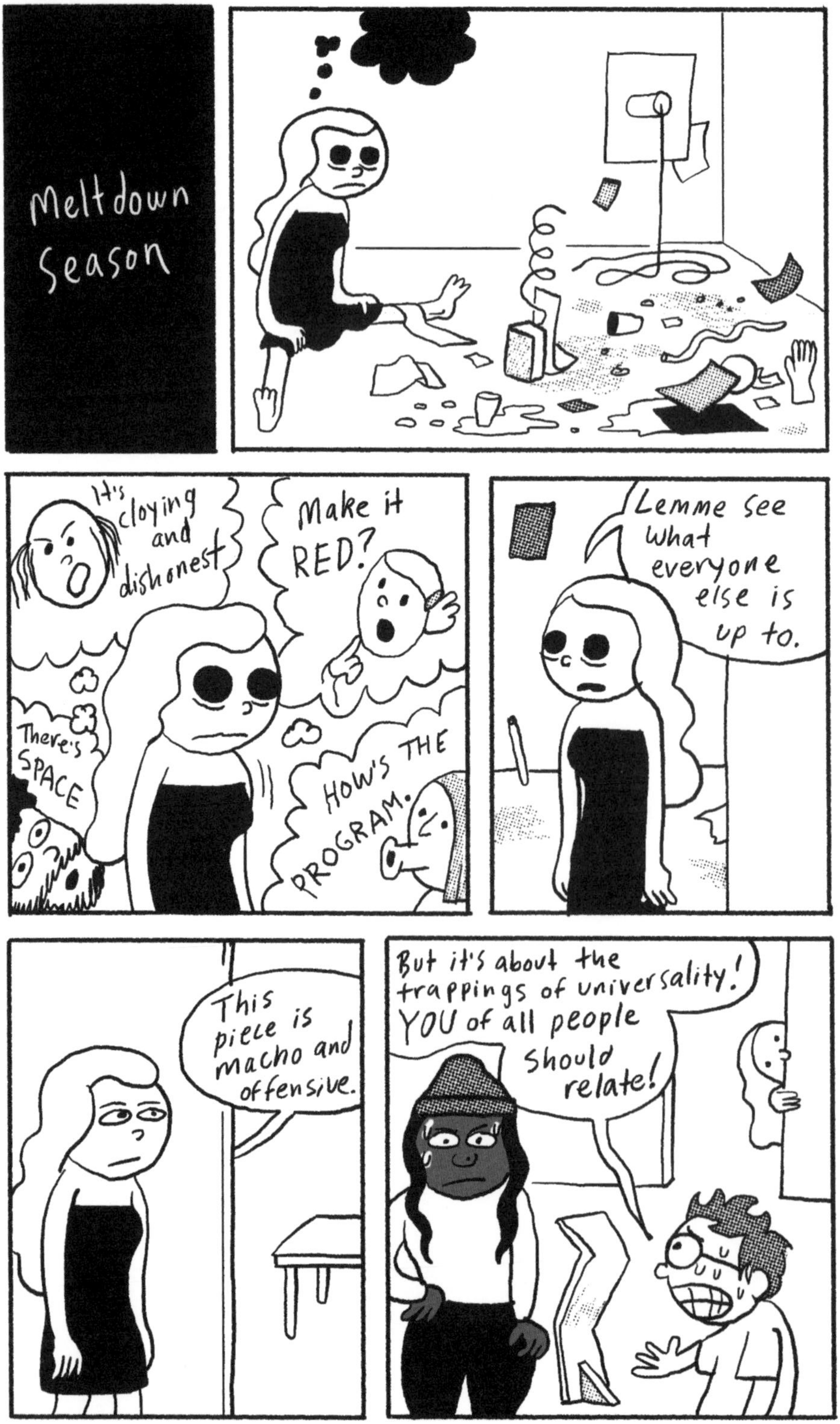
Meltdown Season
It's cloying and dishonest
Make it RED?
There's SPACE
HOW'S THE PROGRAM.
Lemme see what everyone else is up to.
This piece is macho and offensive.
But it's about the trappings of universality! YOU of all people should relate!

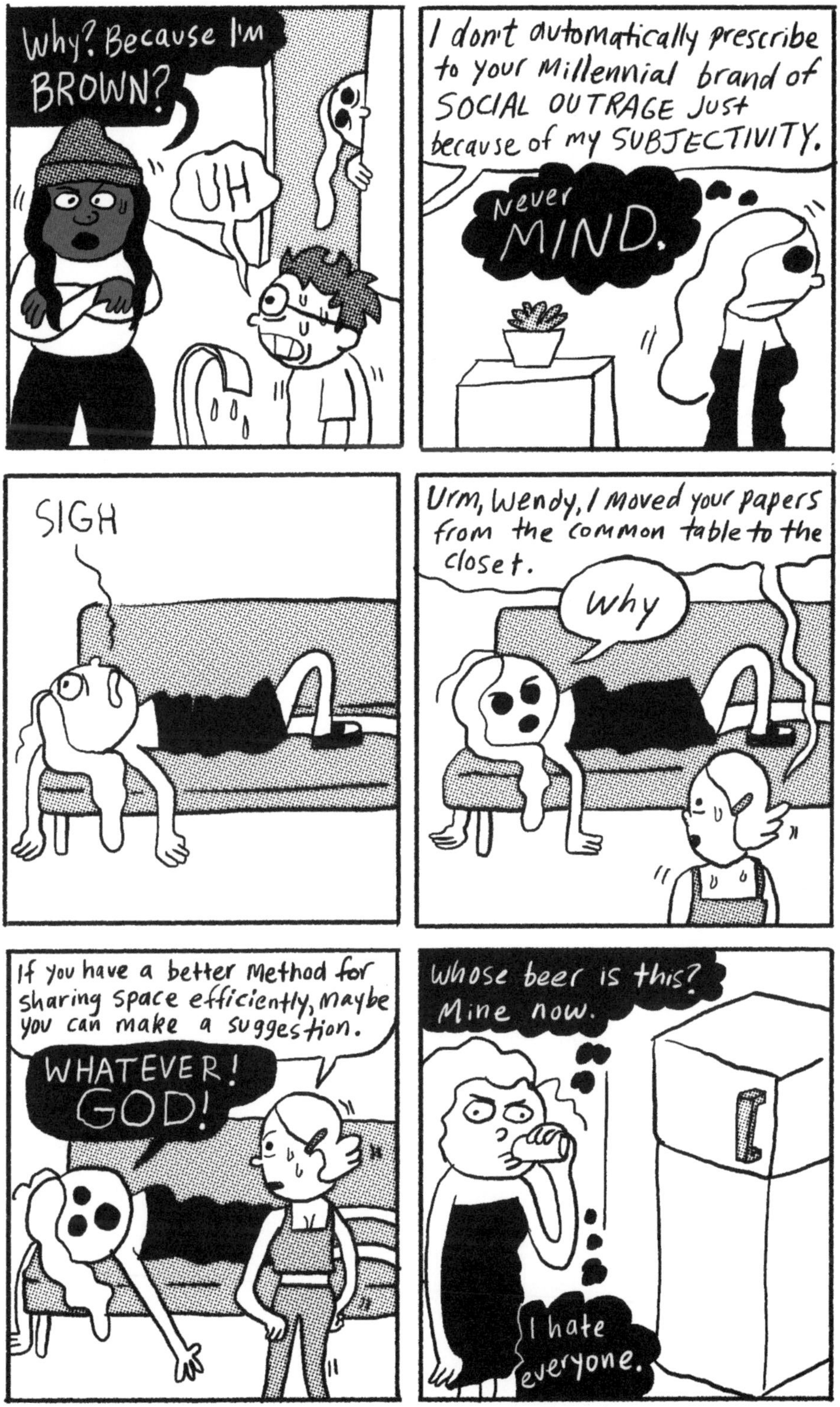
Why? Because I'm BROWN?
UH
I don't automatically prescribe to your Millennial brand of SOCIAL OUTRAGE just because of my SUBJECTIVITY.
Never MIND.
SIGH
Urm, Wendy, I moved your papers from the common table to the closet.
why
If you have a better method for sharing space efficiently, maybe you can make a suggestion.
WHATEVER! GOD!
Whose beer is this? Mine now.
I hate everyone.

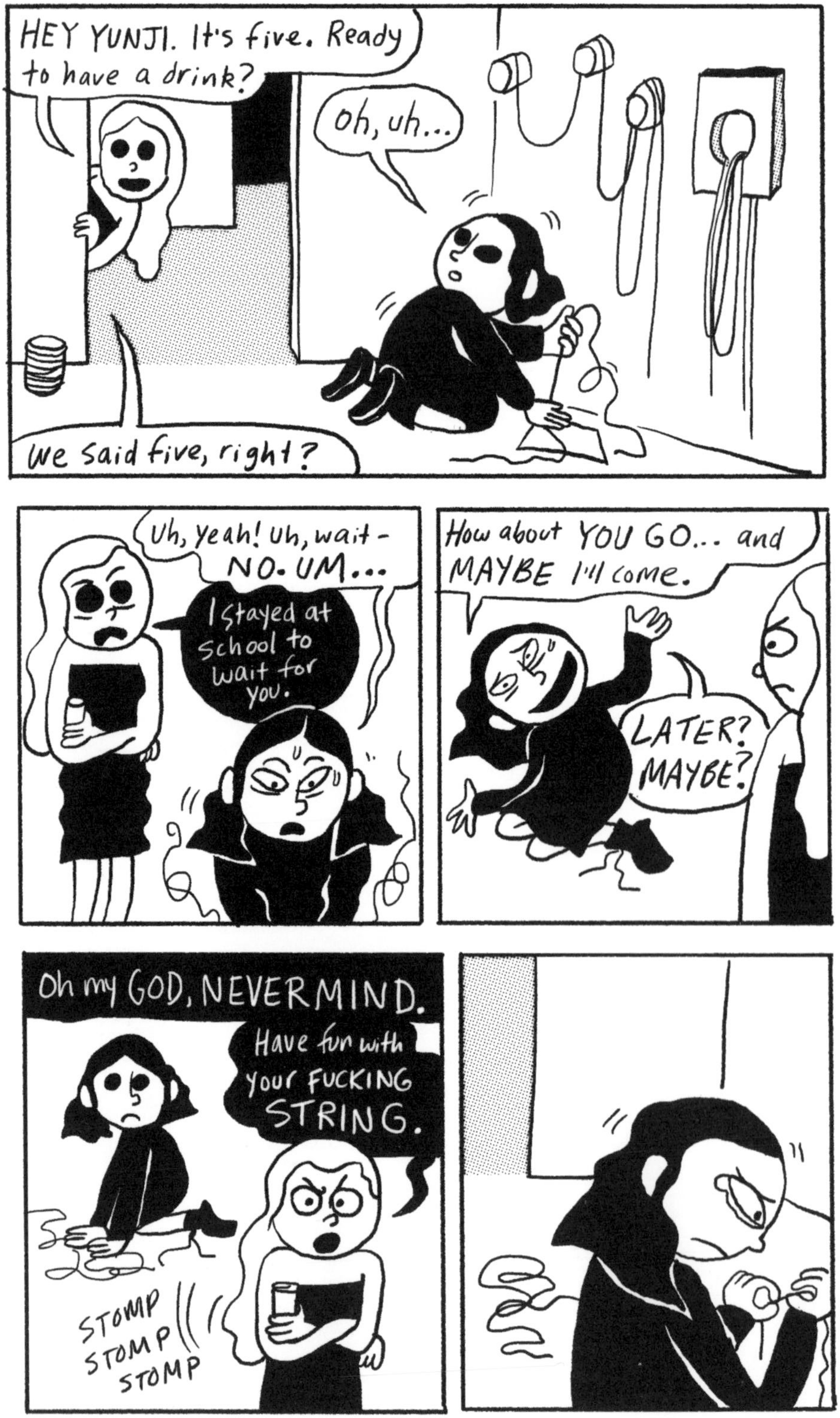
HEY YUNJI. It's five. Ready to have a drink?
Oh, uh...
We said five, right?
Uh, yeah! Uh, wait- NO. UM...
I stayed at school to wait for you.
How about YOU GO... and MAYBE I'll come.
LATER? MAYBE?
Oh my GOD, NEVERMIND.
Have fun with your FUCKING STRING.
STOMP STOMP STOMP

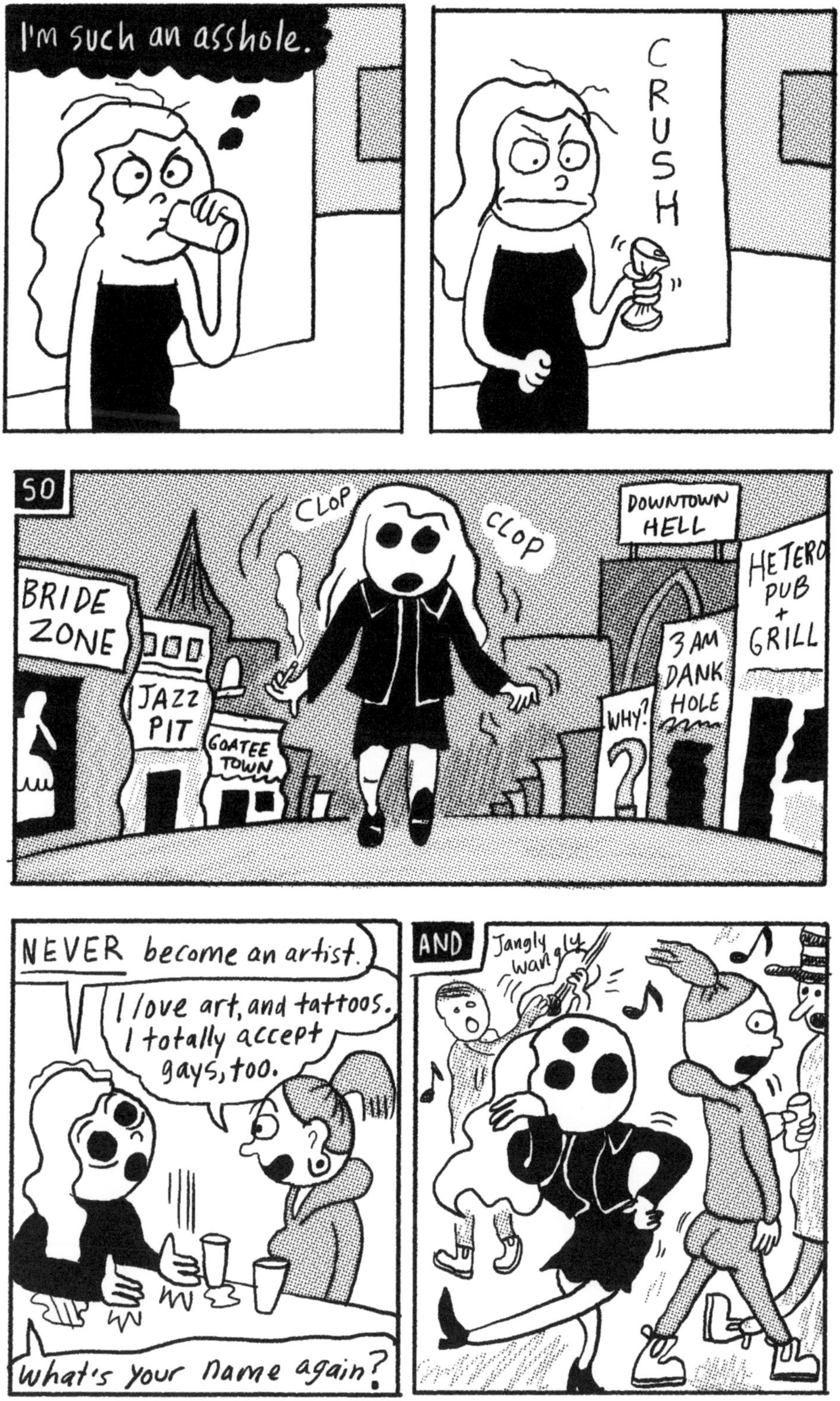

I'm such an asshole.
CRUSH
SO
CLOP
CLOP
DOWNTOWN HELL
BRIDE ZONE
JAZZ PIT
GOATEE TOWN
WHY?
3 AM DANK HOLE
HETERO PUB + GRILL
NEVER become an artist.
I love art, and tattoos. I totally accept gays, too.
What's your name again?
AND
Jangly wangly

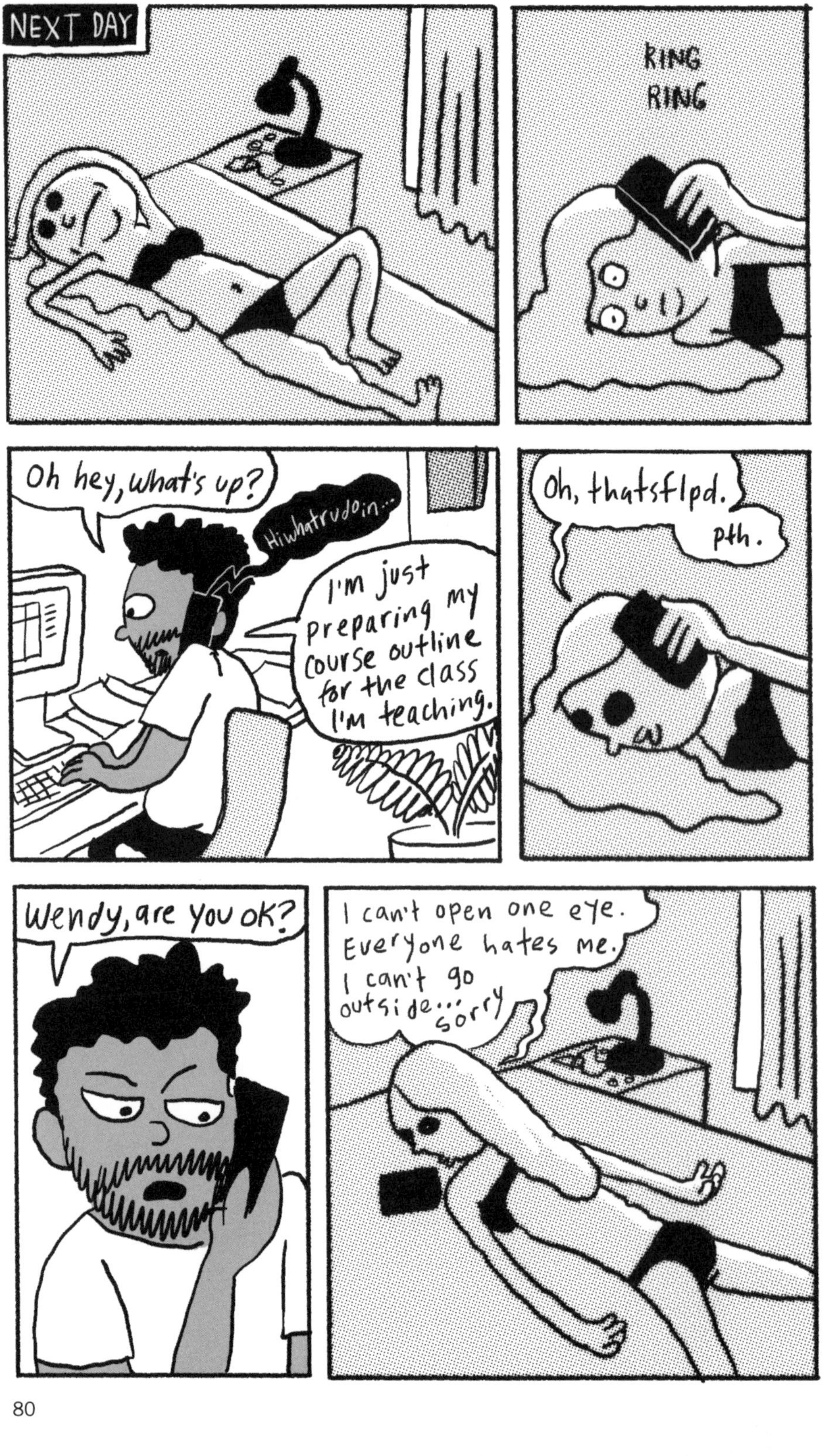
NEXT DAY
RING
RING
Oh hey, what's up?
Hiwhatrudoin...
I'm just preparing my course outline for the class I'm teaching.
Oh, thatsflpd.
pth.
Wendy, are you OK?
I can't open one eye.
Everyone hates me.
I can't go outside... sorry

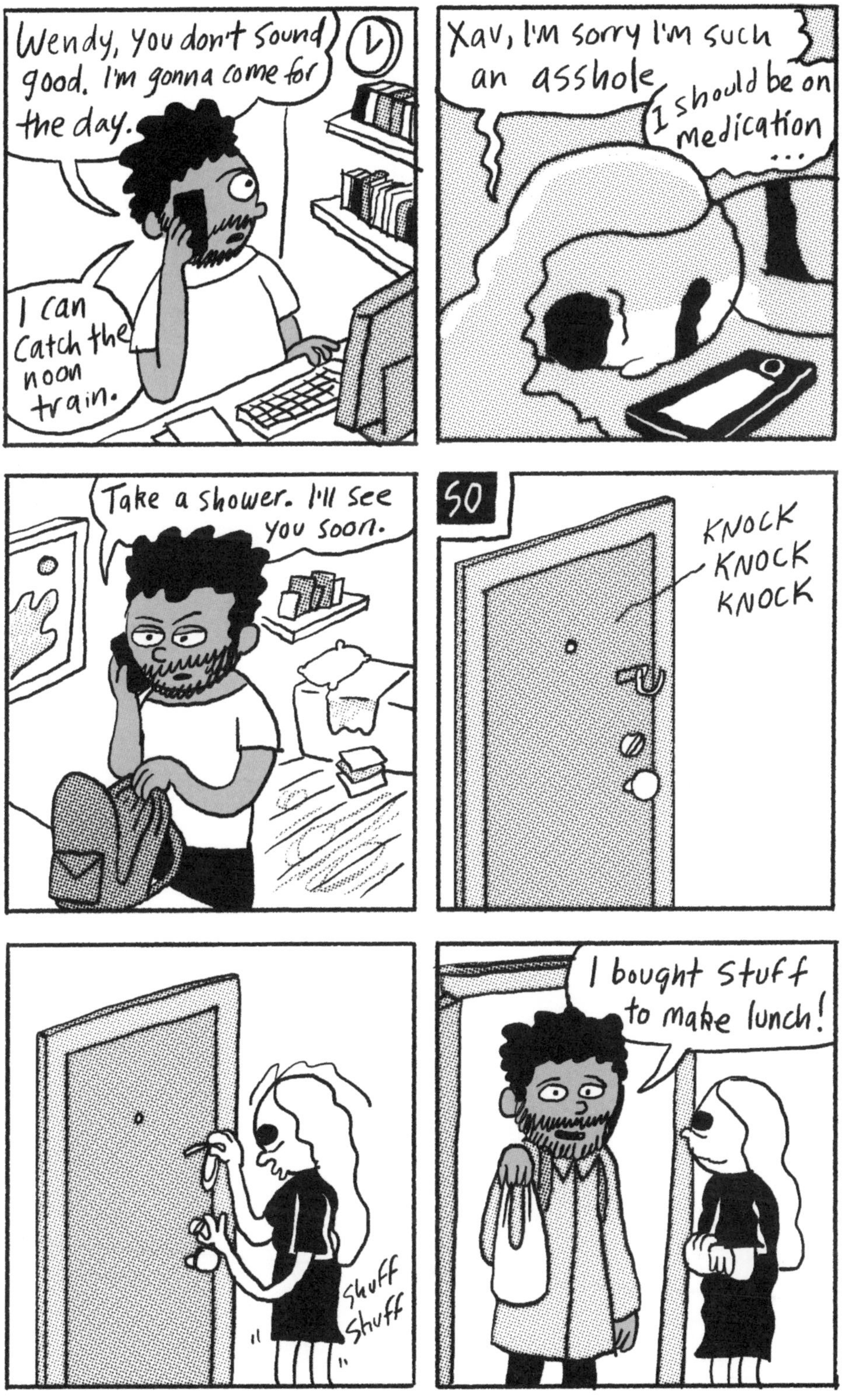
Wendy, you don't sound good. I'm gonna come for the day.
I can catch the noon train.
Xav, I'm sorry I'm such an asshole
I should be on medication ...
Take a shower. I'll see you soon.
SO
KNOCK KNOCK KNOCK
Shuff Shuff
I bought stuff to make lunch!

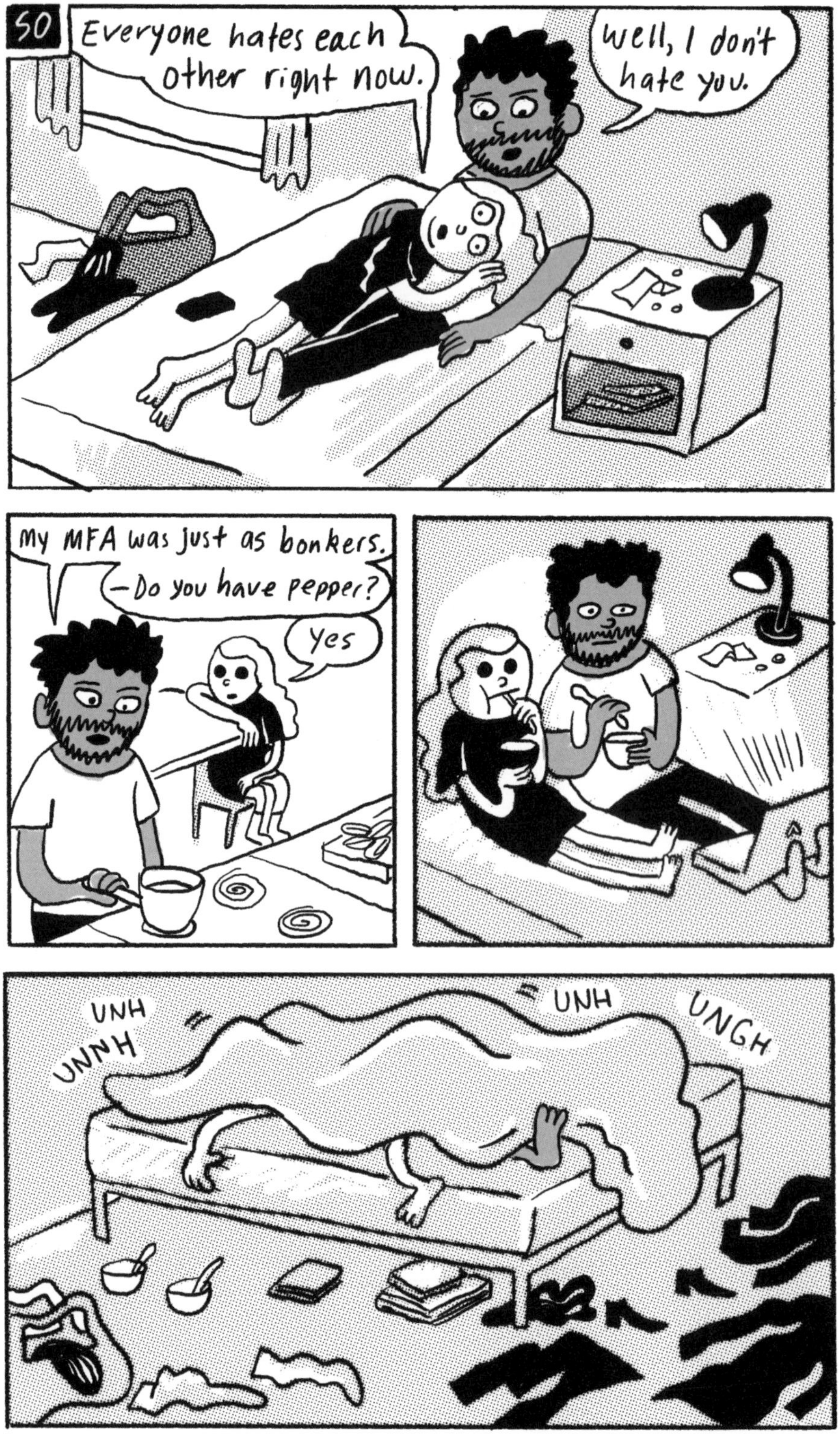

50
Everyone hates each other right now.
Well, I don't hate you.
My MFA was just as bonkers.
—Do you have pepper?
Yes
UNH
UNNH
UNH
UNGH

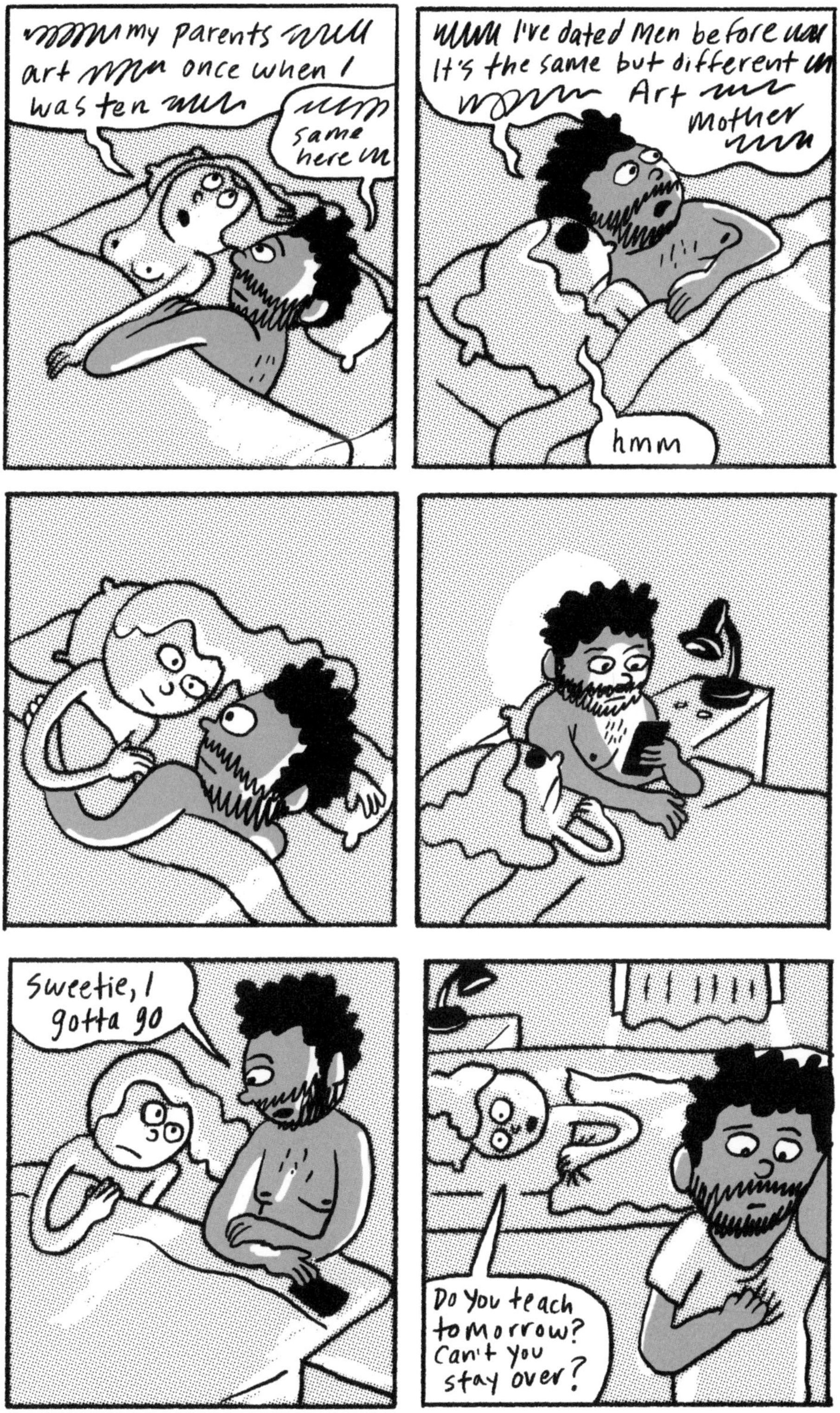

my parents art once when I was ten
same here
I've dated men before It's the same but different Art Mother
hmm
Sweetie, I gotta go
Do you teach tomorrow? Can't you stay over?

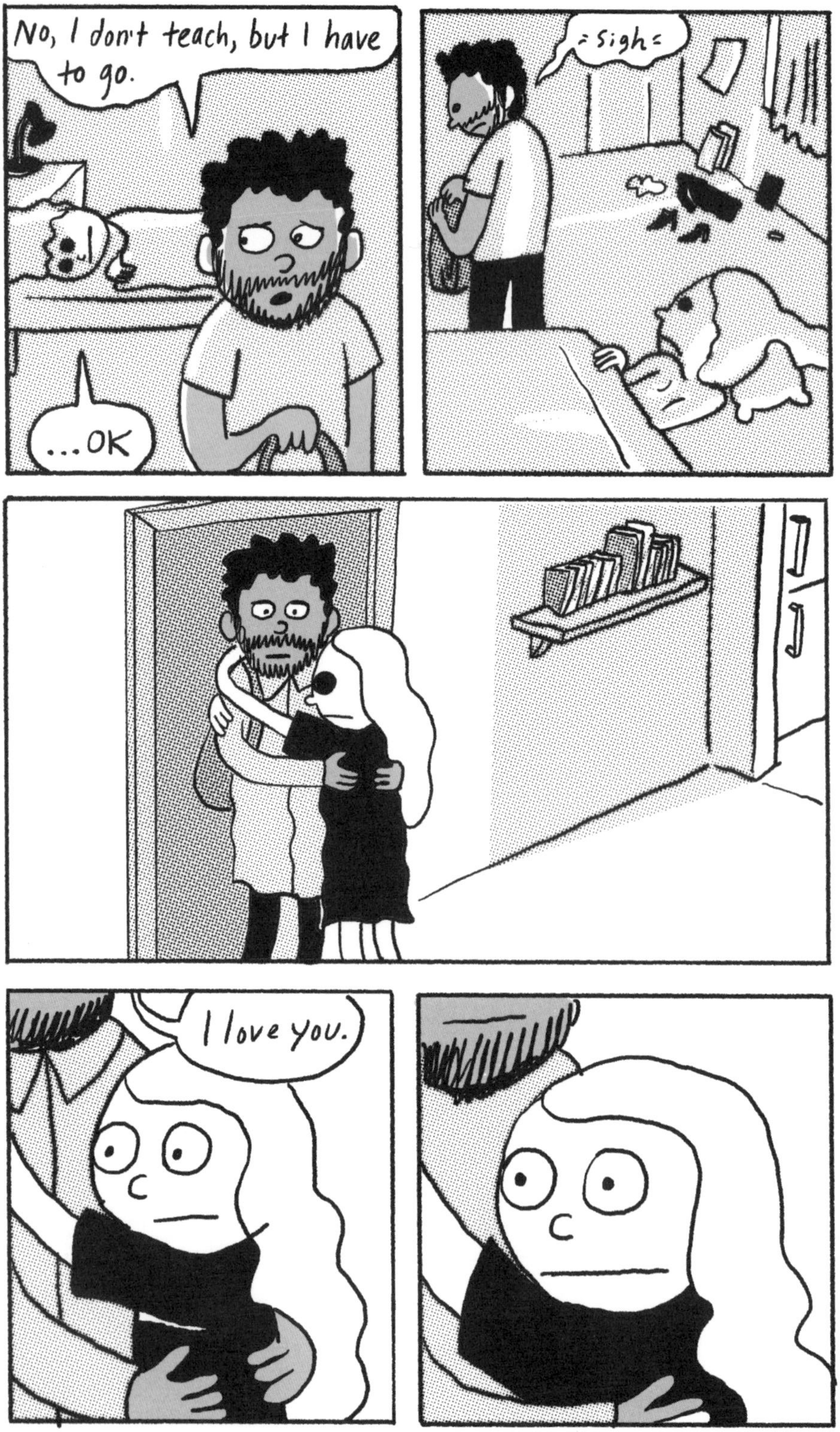
No, I don't teach, but I have to go.
...OK
=Sigh=
I love you.

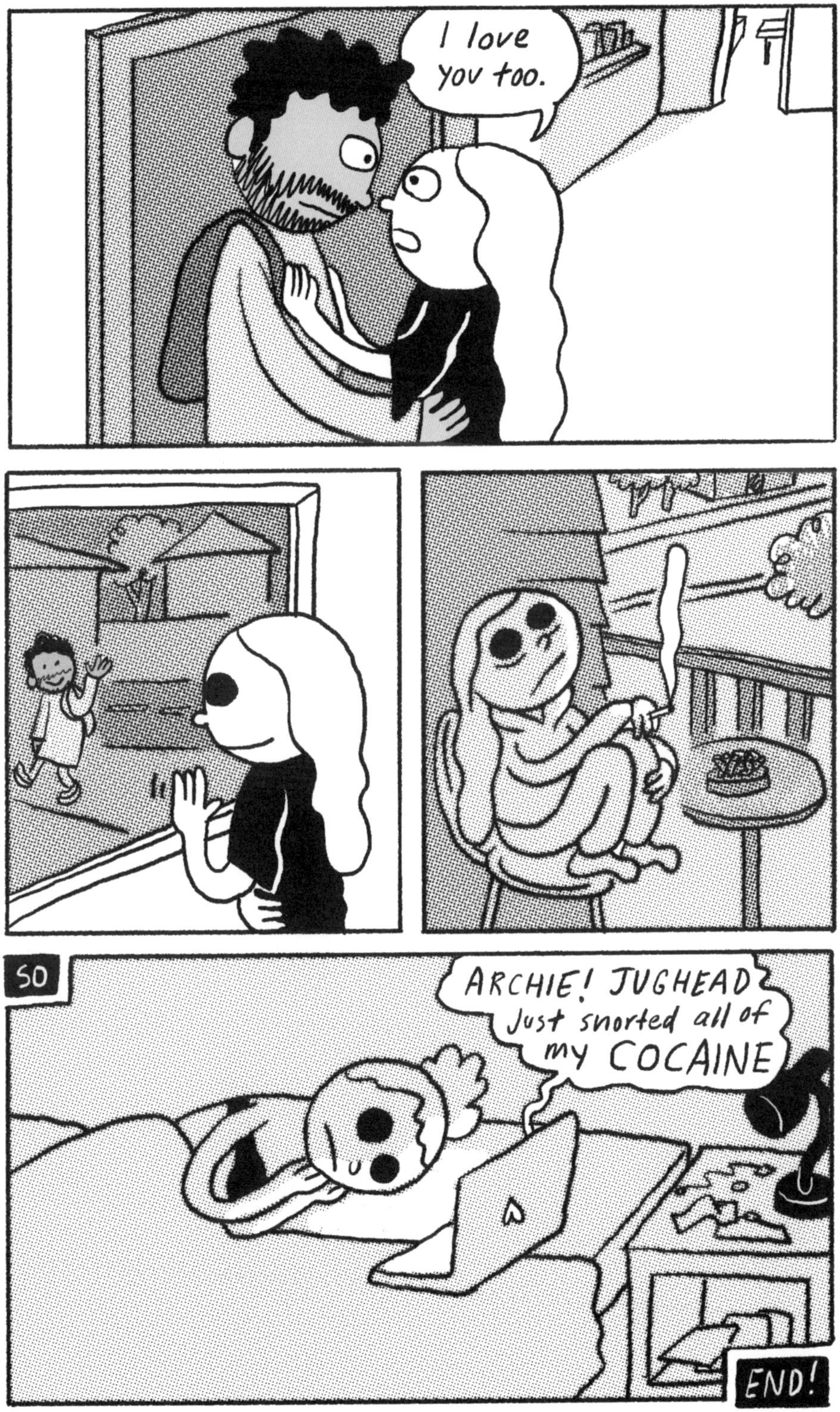
I love you too.
SO
ARCHIE! JUGHEAD Just snorted all of my COCAINE
END!

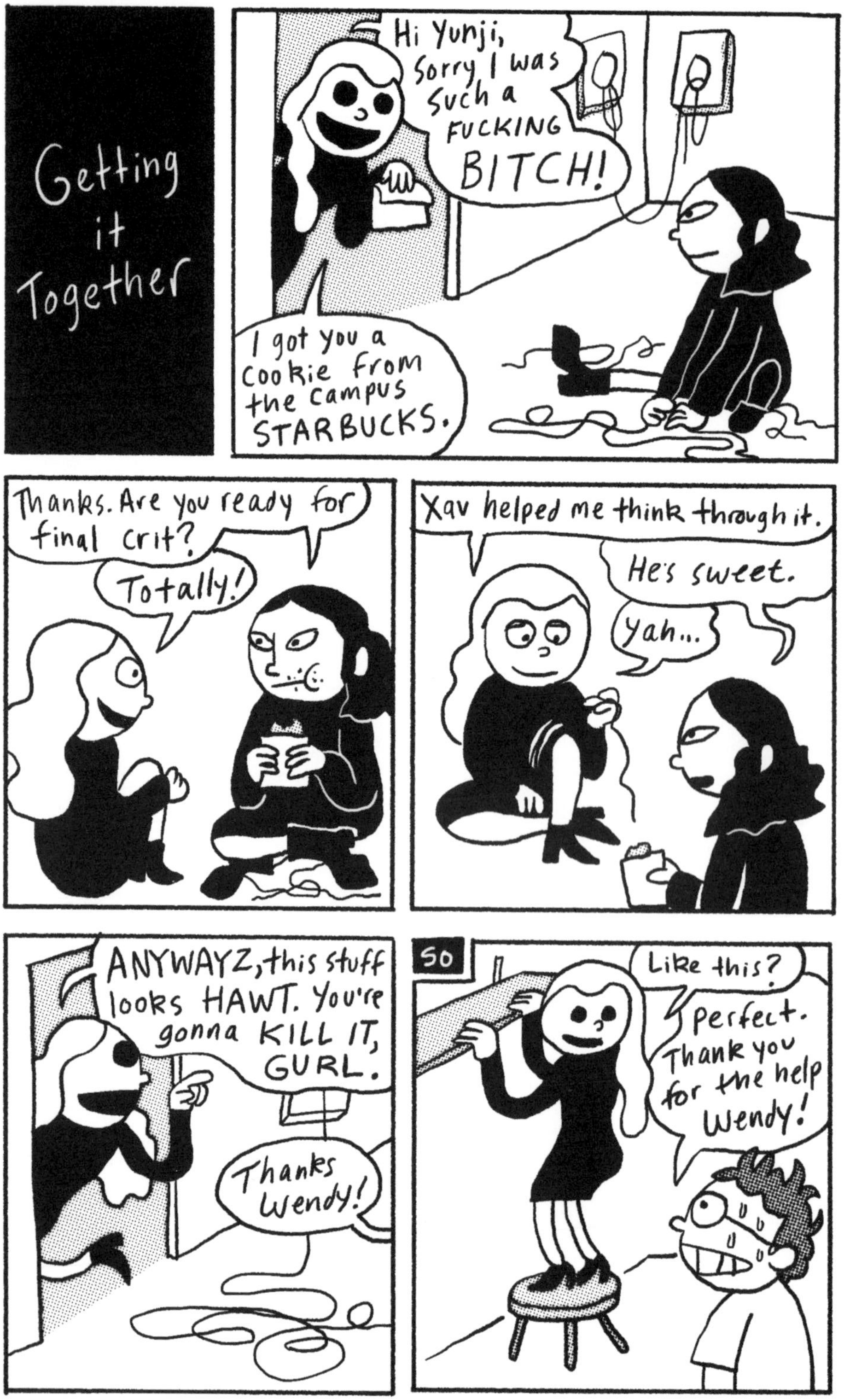
Getting it Together
Hi Yunji, Sorry I was such a FUCKING BITCH!
I got you a cookie from the campus STARBUCKS.
Thanks. Are you ready for final crit?
Totally!
Xav helped me think through it.
He's sweet.
yah...
ANYWAYZ, this stuff looks HAWT. You're gonna KILL IT, GURL.
Thanks Wendy!
SO
Like this?
Perfect. Thank you for the help Wendy!

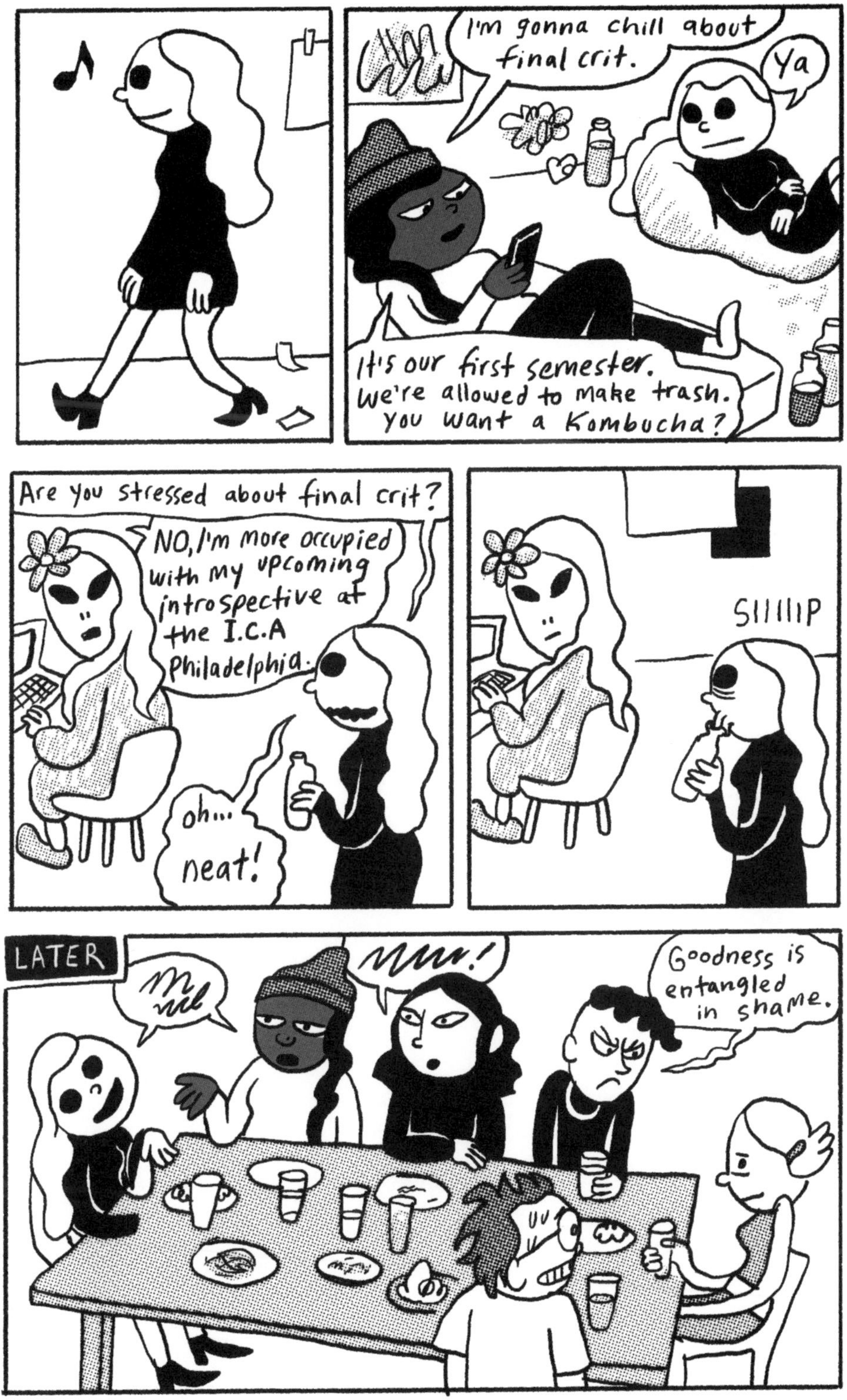
I'm gonna chill about final crit.
Ya
It's our first semester. We're allowed to make trash. You want a Kombucha?
Are you stressed about final crit?
NO, I'm more occupied with my upcoming introspective at the I.C.A Philadelphia.
oh... neat!
SIIIIIP
LATER
Goodness is entangled in shame.

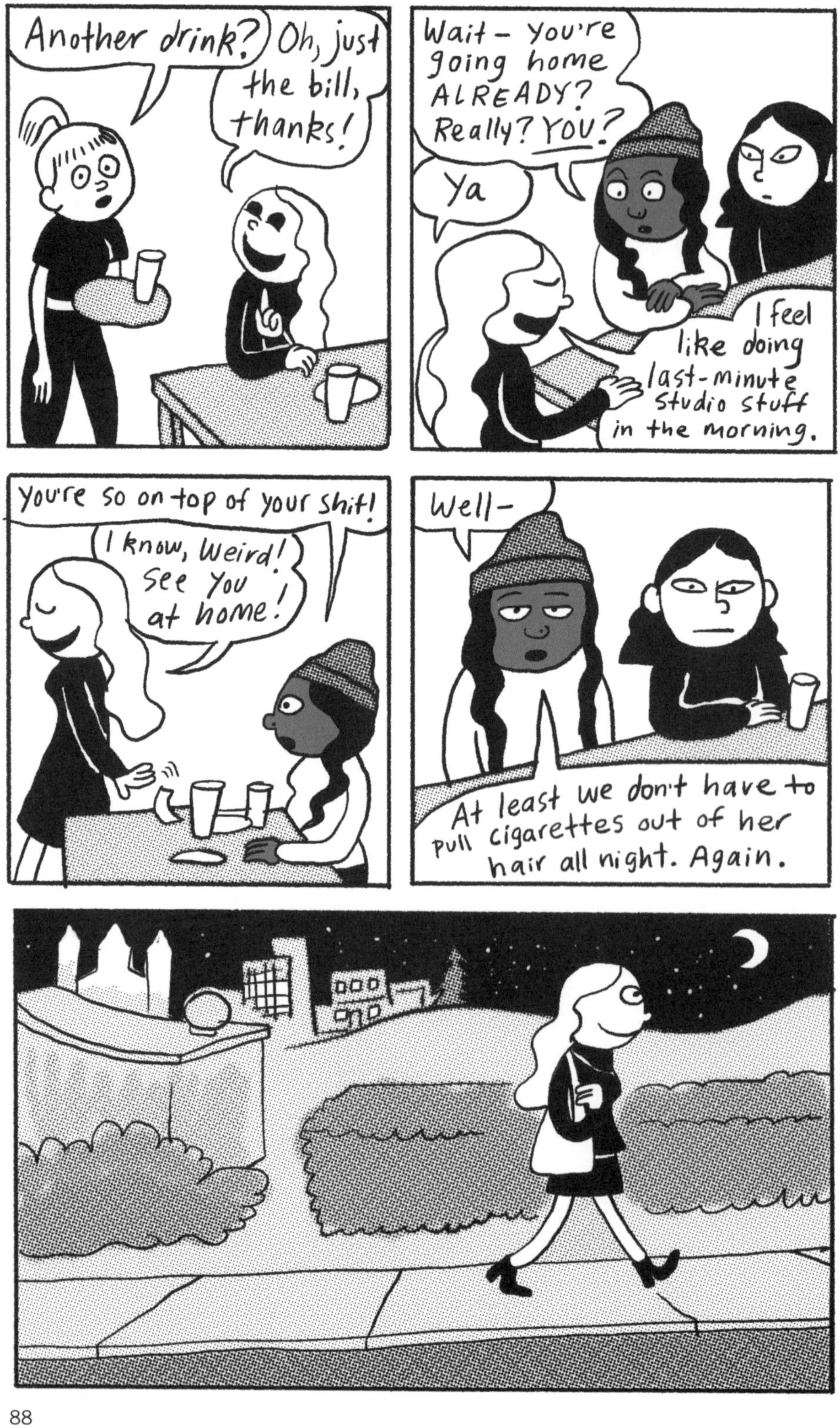
Another drink?
Oh, just the bill, thanks!
Wait- You're going home ALREADY? Really? YOU?
Ya
I feel like doing last-minute studio stuff in the morning.
You're so on top of your shit!
I know, Weird! See You at home!
Well-
At least we don't have to pull cigarettes out of her hair all night. Again.

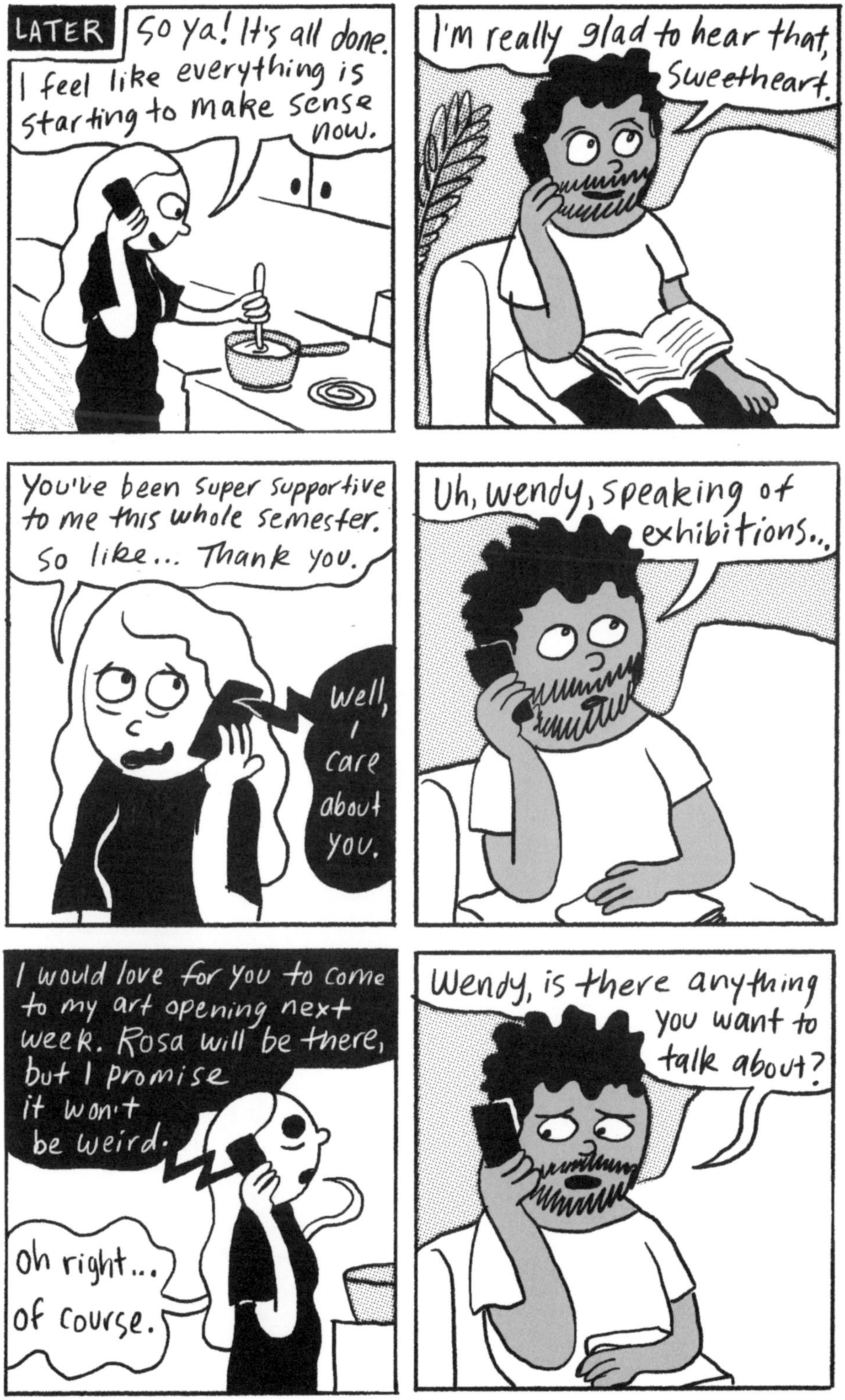
LATER
So ya! It's all done. I feel like everything is starting to make sense now.
I'm really glad to hear that, Sweetheart.
You've been super supportive to me this whole semester. So like... Thank you.
Well, I care about you.
Uh, wendy, speaking of exhibitions...
I would love for you to come to my art opening next week. Rosa will be there, but I promise it won't be weird.
Oh right... of course.
Wendy, is there anything you want to talk about?

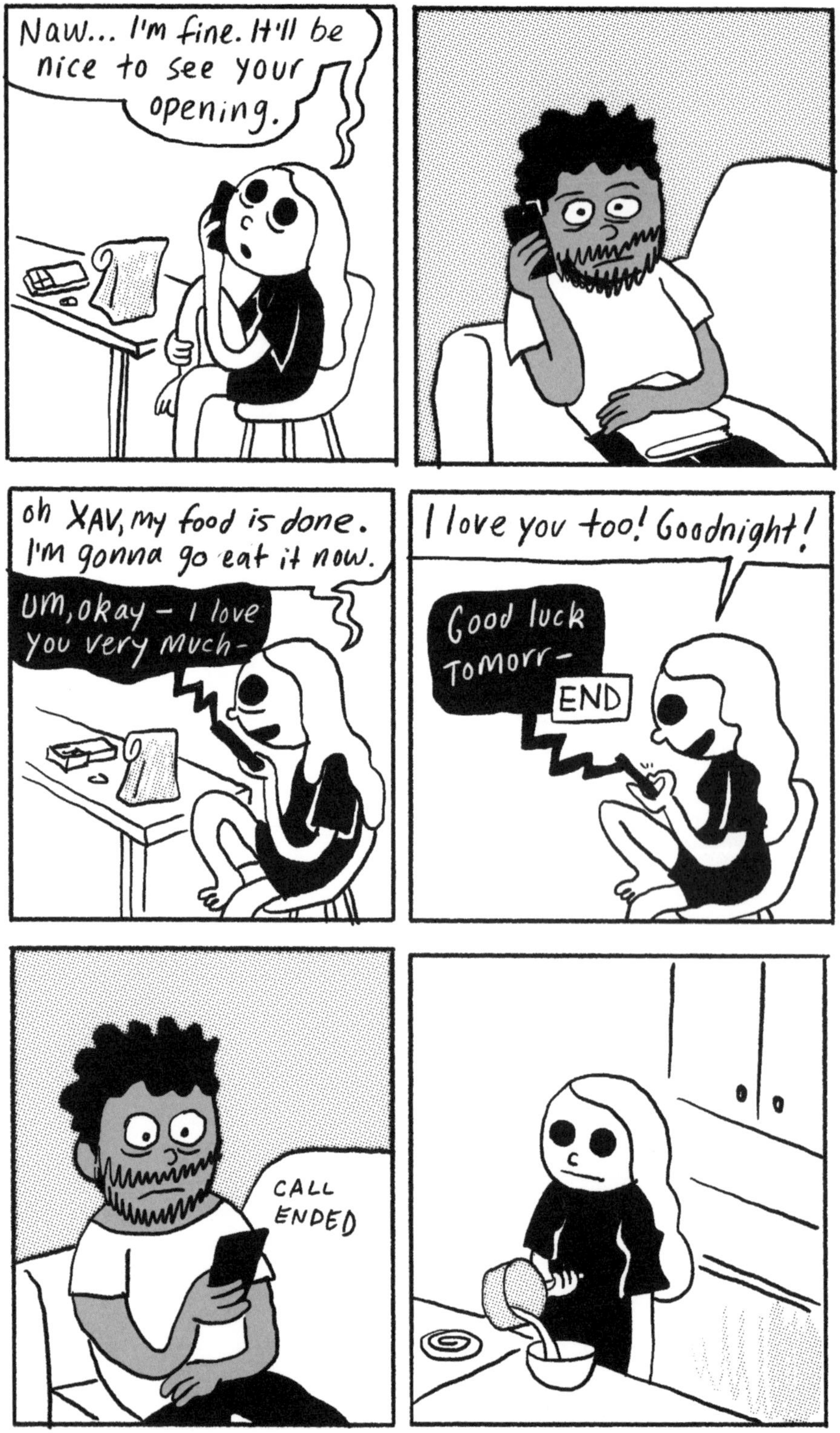
Naw... I'm fine. It'll be nice to see your opening.
oh XAV, my food is done. I'm gonna go eat it now.
Um, okay - I love you very much-
I love you too! Goodnight!
Good luck Tomorr-
END
CALL ENDED

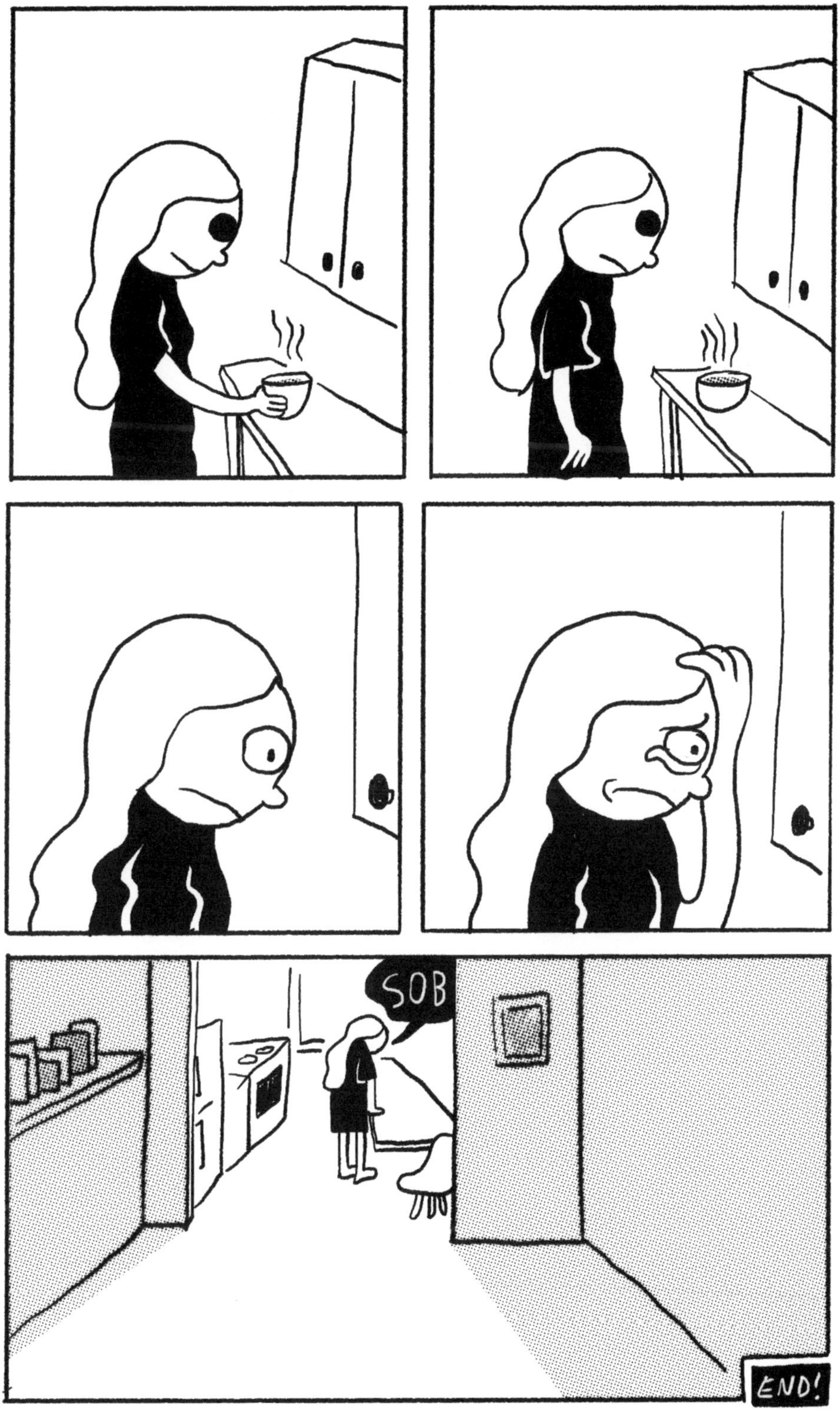
SOB
END!

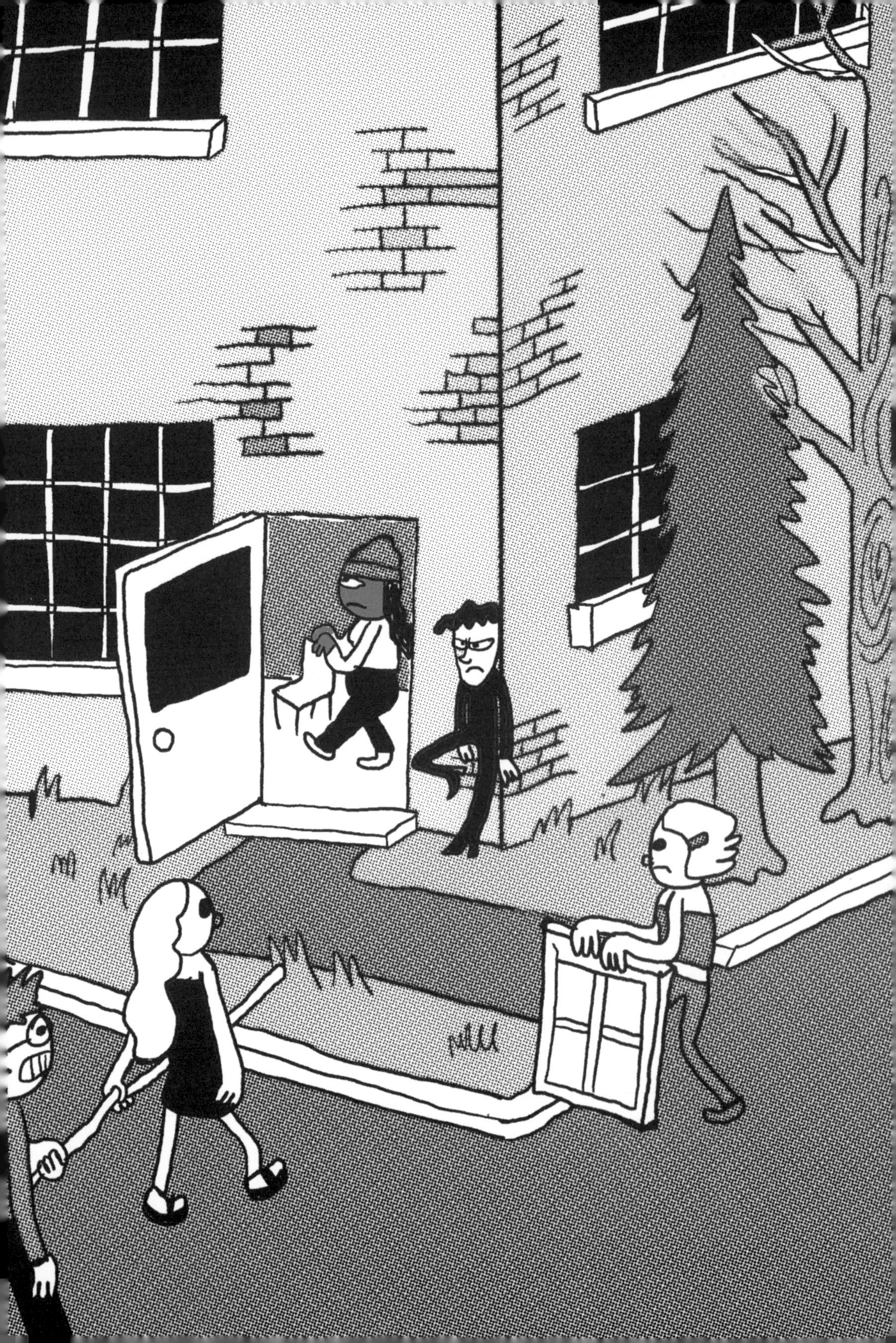

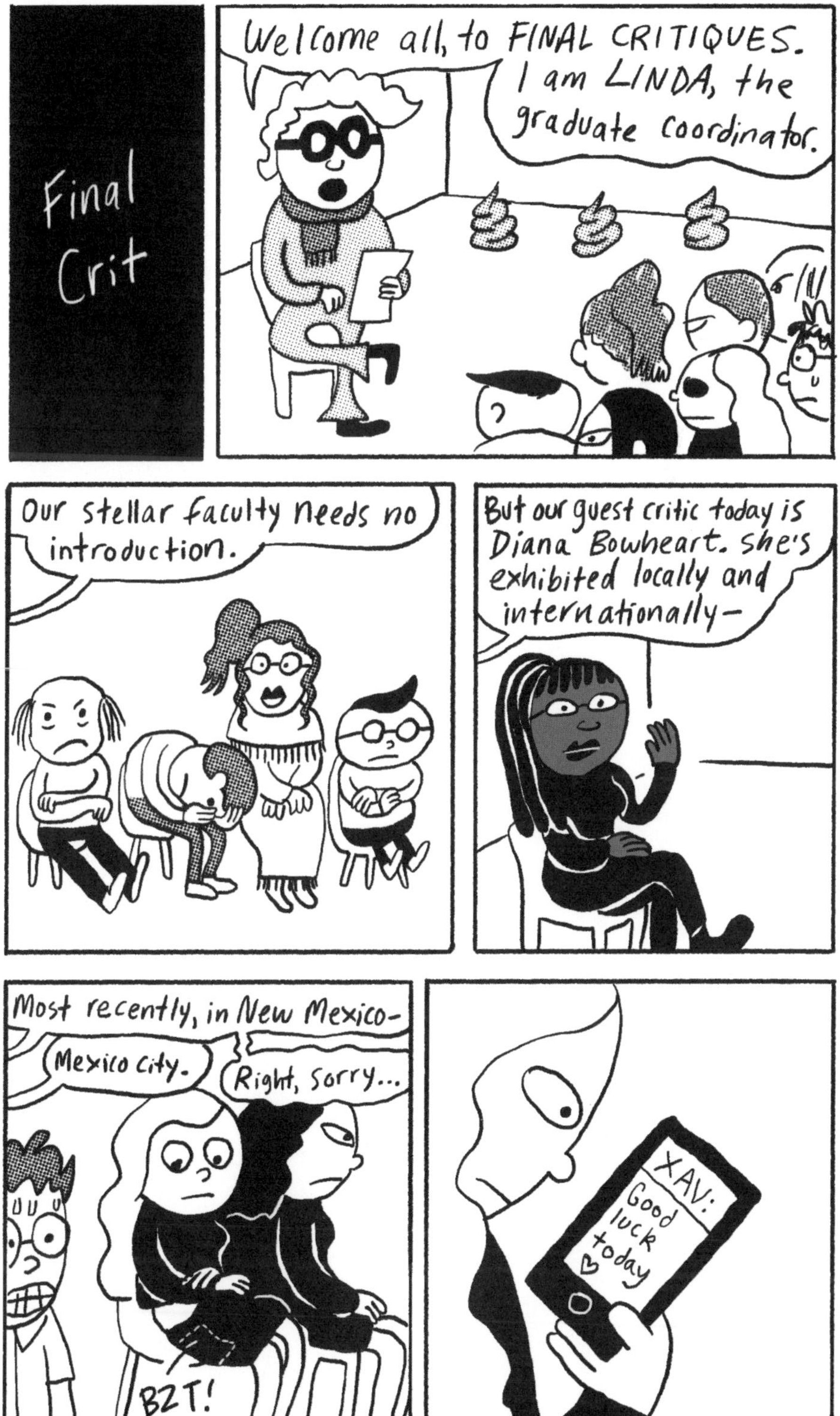
Final Crit
Welcome all, to FINAL CRITIQUES.
I am LINDA, the graduate coordinator.
Our stellar faculty needs no introduction.
But our guest critic today is Diana Bowheart. She's exhibited locally and internationally—
Most recently, in New Mexico-
Mexico City.
Right, sorry...
BZT!
XAV:
Good luck today

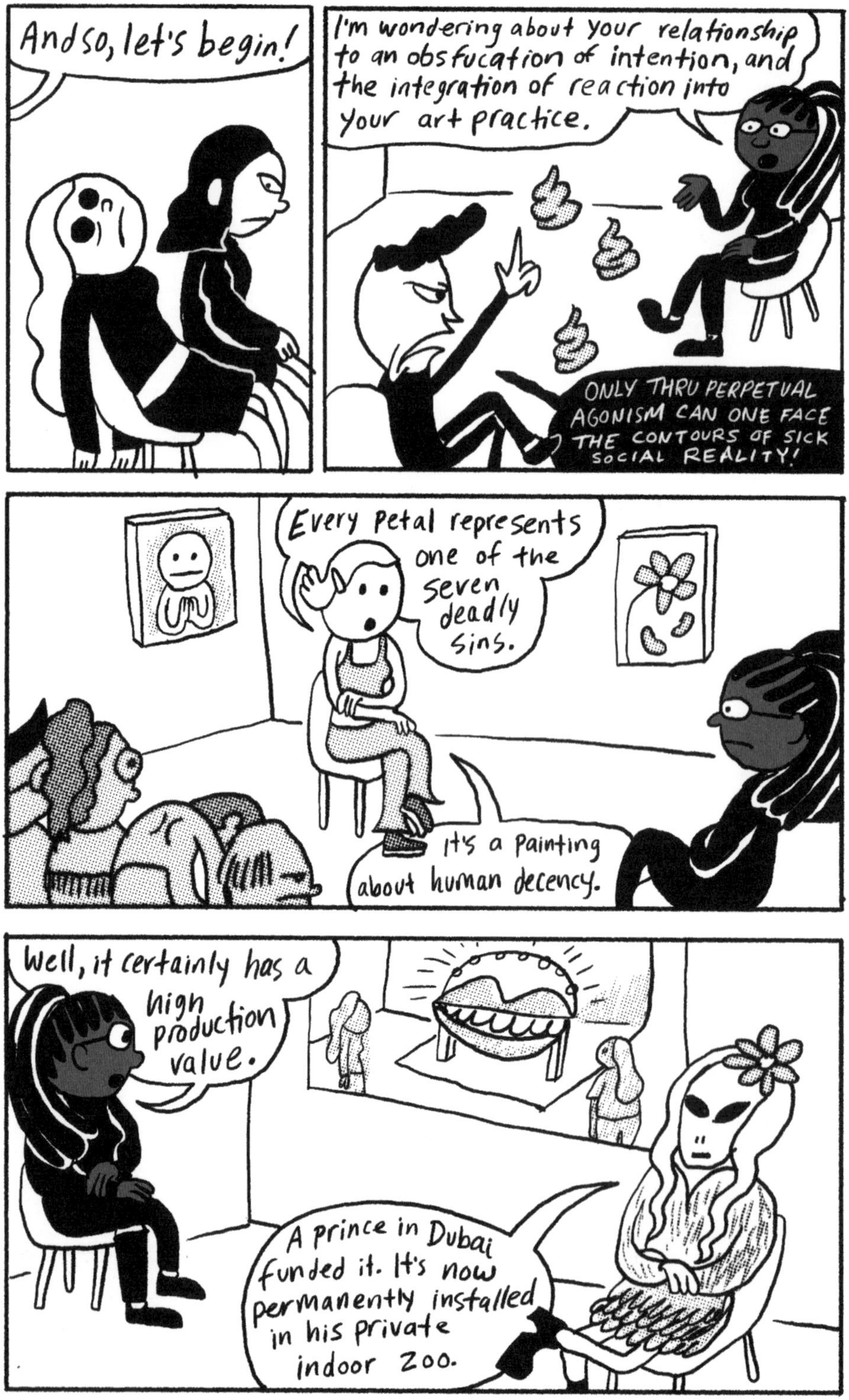

And so, let's begin!
I'm wondering about your relationship to an obsfucation of intention, and the integration of reaction into your art practice.
ONLY THRU PERPETUAL AGONISM CAN ONE FACE THE CONTOURS OF SICK SOCIAL REALITY!
Every petal represents one of the seven deadly sins.
It's a painting about human decency.
Well, it certainly has a high production value.
A prince in Dubai funded it. It's now permanently installed in his private indoor zoo.

Is the creative process a kind of fermentation for you?
Paintings begin to rot once they're done. Poems grow insidiously. So each are in relation to mold.
OK. Can you explain to me, in plain language, what you do again?
NO, BECAUSE SPEAKING IN REDUCTIVE TERMS RISKS AN UNDERINTERPRETATION WHICH CAN BREED DOGMA AND HENCEFORTH, WHITE SUPREMACY
If you place all of the bacteria currently living in one human in a line, they can go to the moon and back one thousand times.
Huh. I didn't know that.

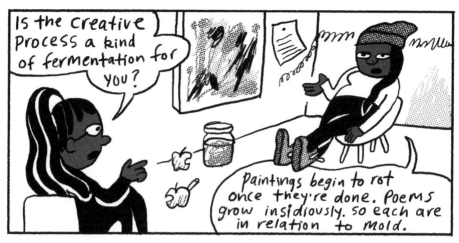

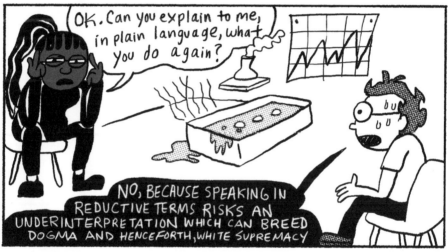

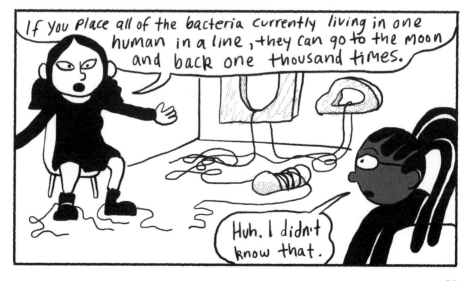

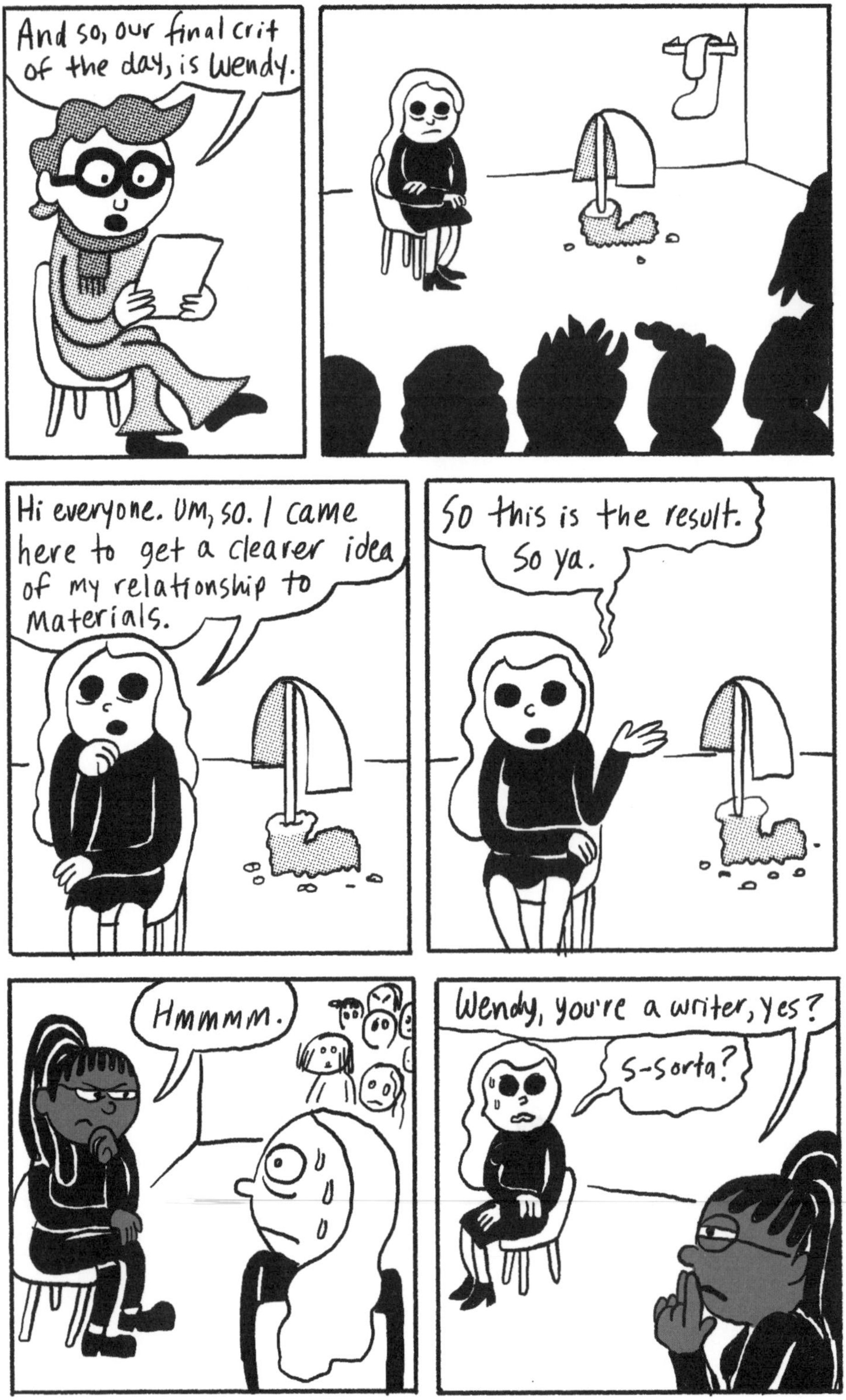
And so, our final crit of the day, is Wendy.
Hi everyone. Um, so. I came here to get a clearer idea of my relationship to Materials.
So this is the result.
So ya.
Hmmmm.
Wendy, you're a writer, yes?
S-sorta?

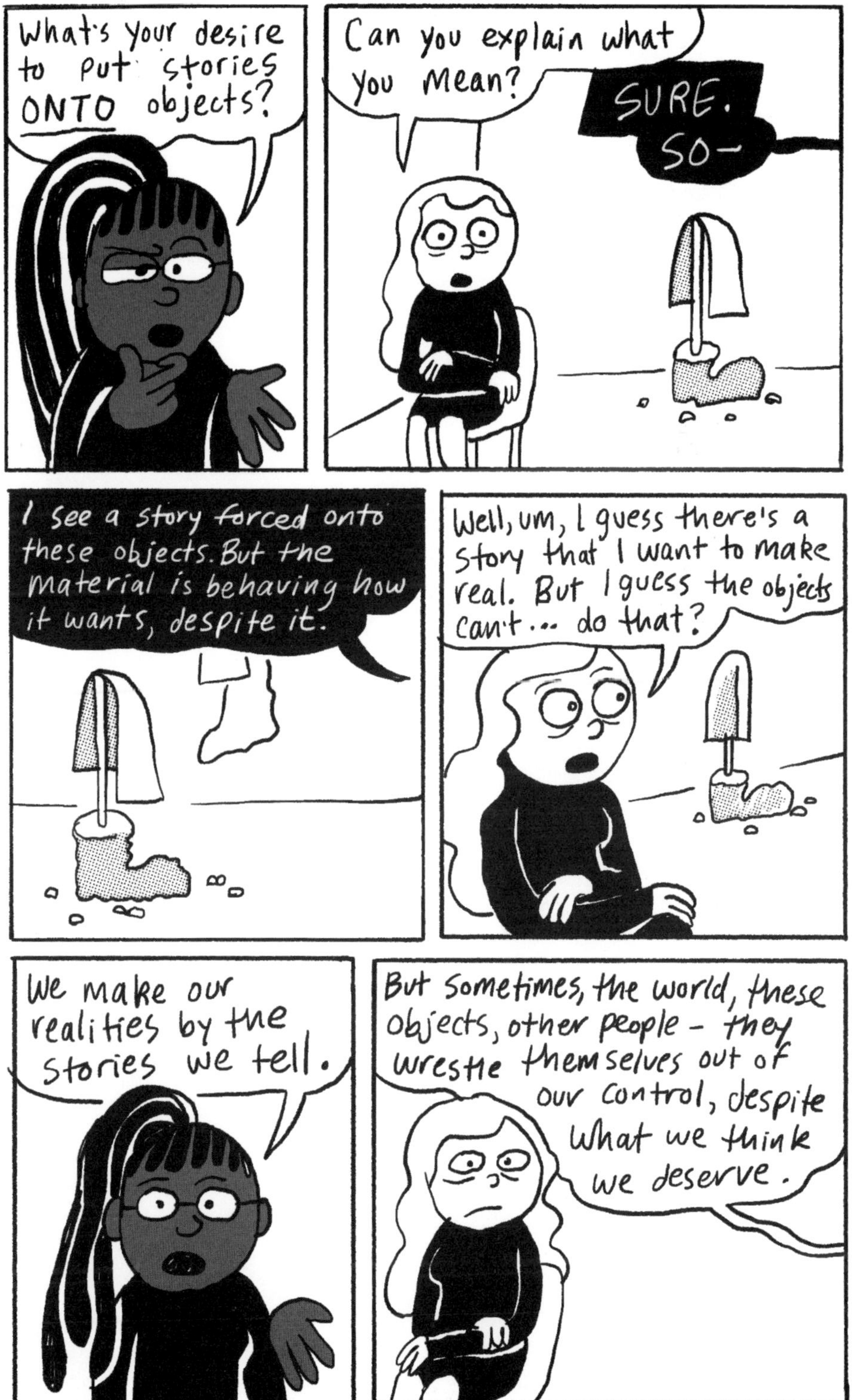
What's your desire to put stories ONTO objects?
Can you explain what you mean?
SURE. SO—
I see a story forced onto these objects. But the material is behaving how it wants, despite it.
Well, um, I guess there's a story that I want to make real. But I guess the objects can't... do that?
We make our realities by the stories we tell.
But sometimes, the world, these objects, other people - they wrestle themselves out of our control, despite what we think we deserve.

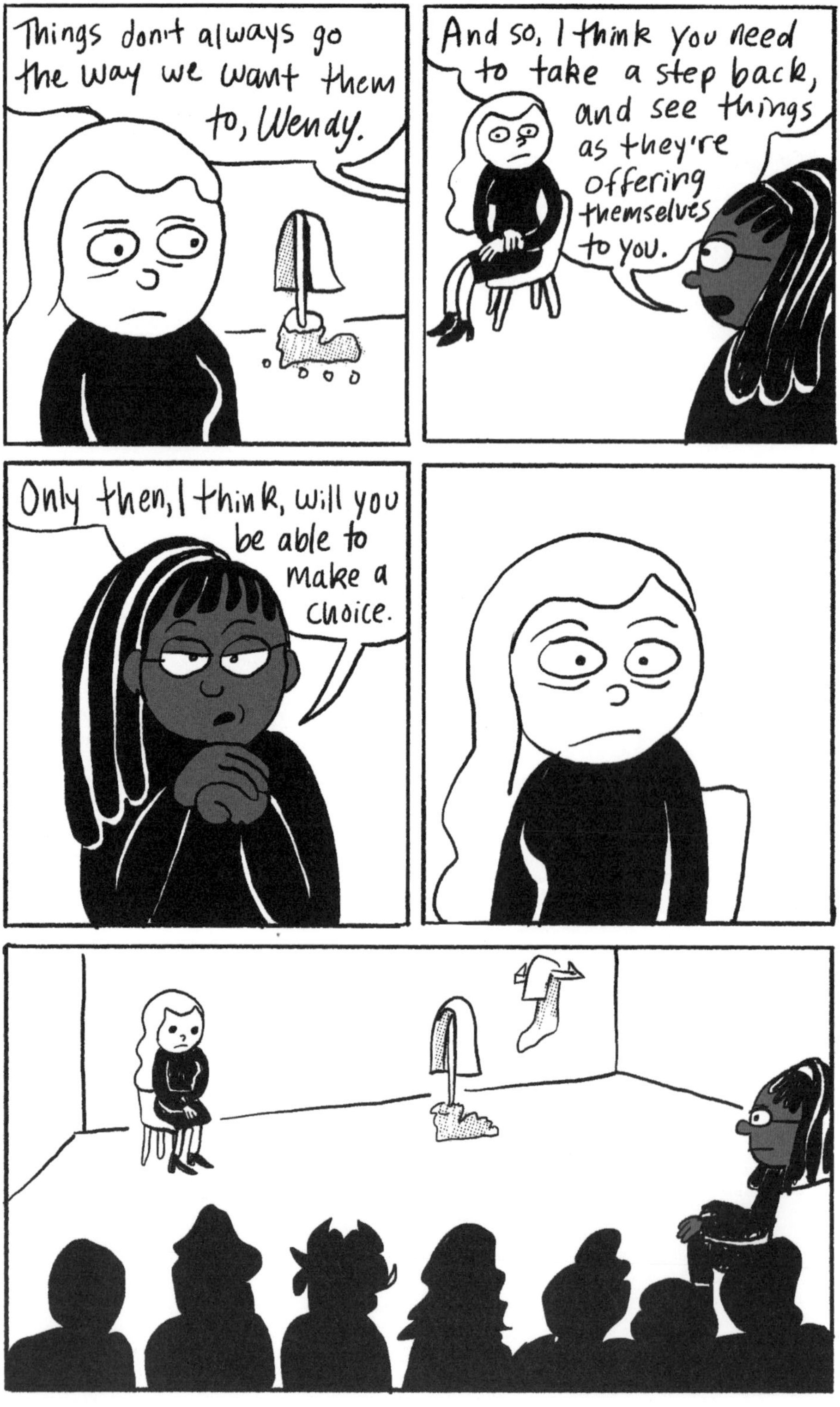
Things don't always go the way we want them to, Wendy.
And so, I think you need to take a step back, and see things as they're offering themselves to you.
Only then, I think, will you be able to make a choice.

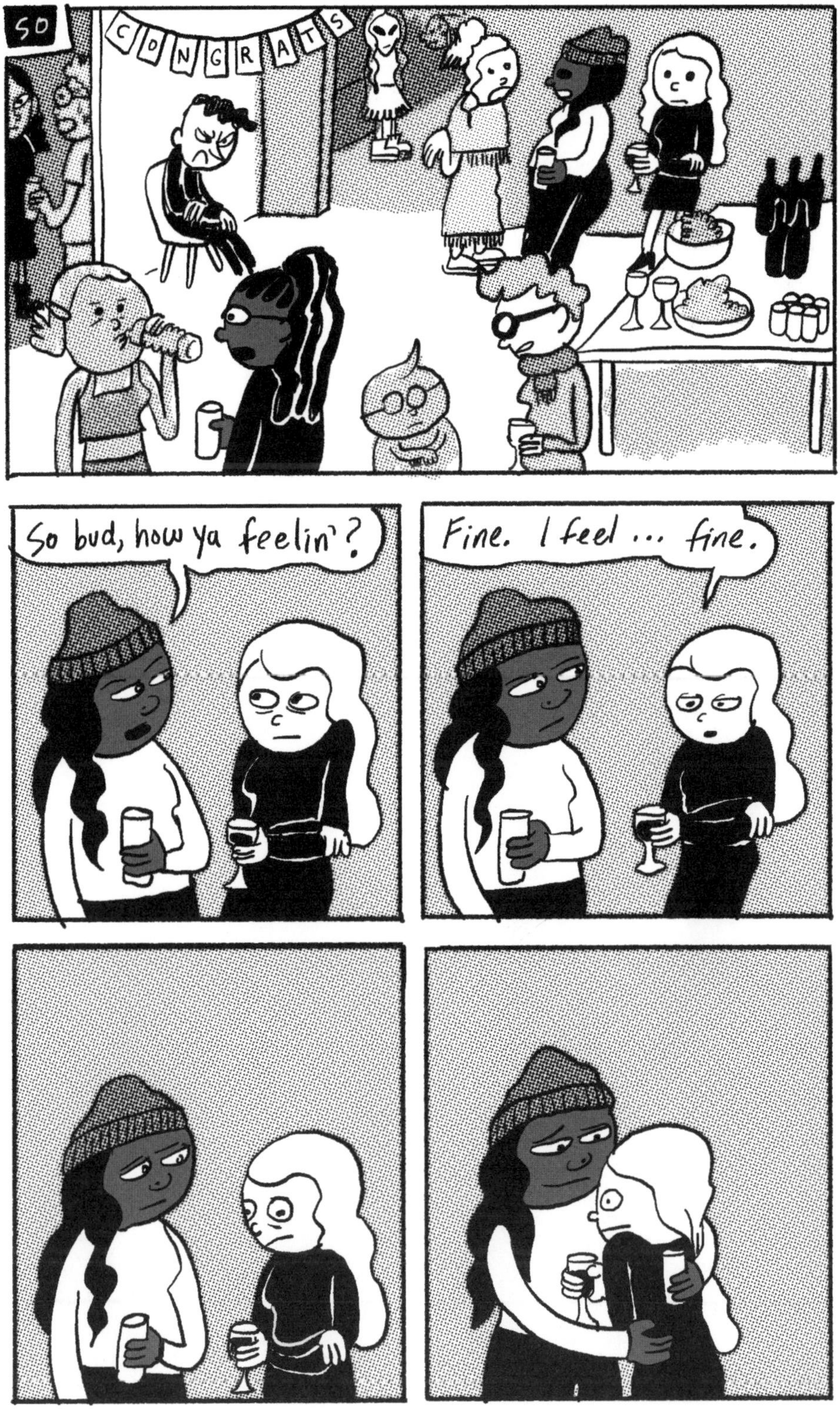
SO
CONGRATS
So bud, how ya feelin'?
Fine. I feel ... fine.

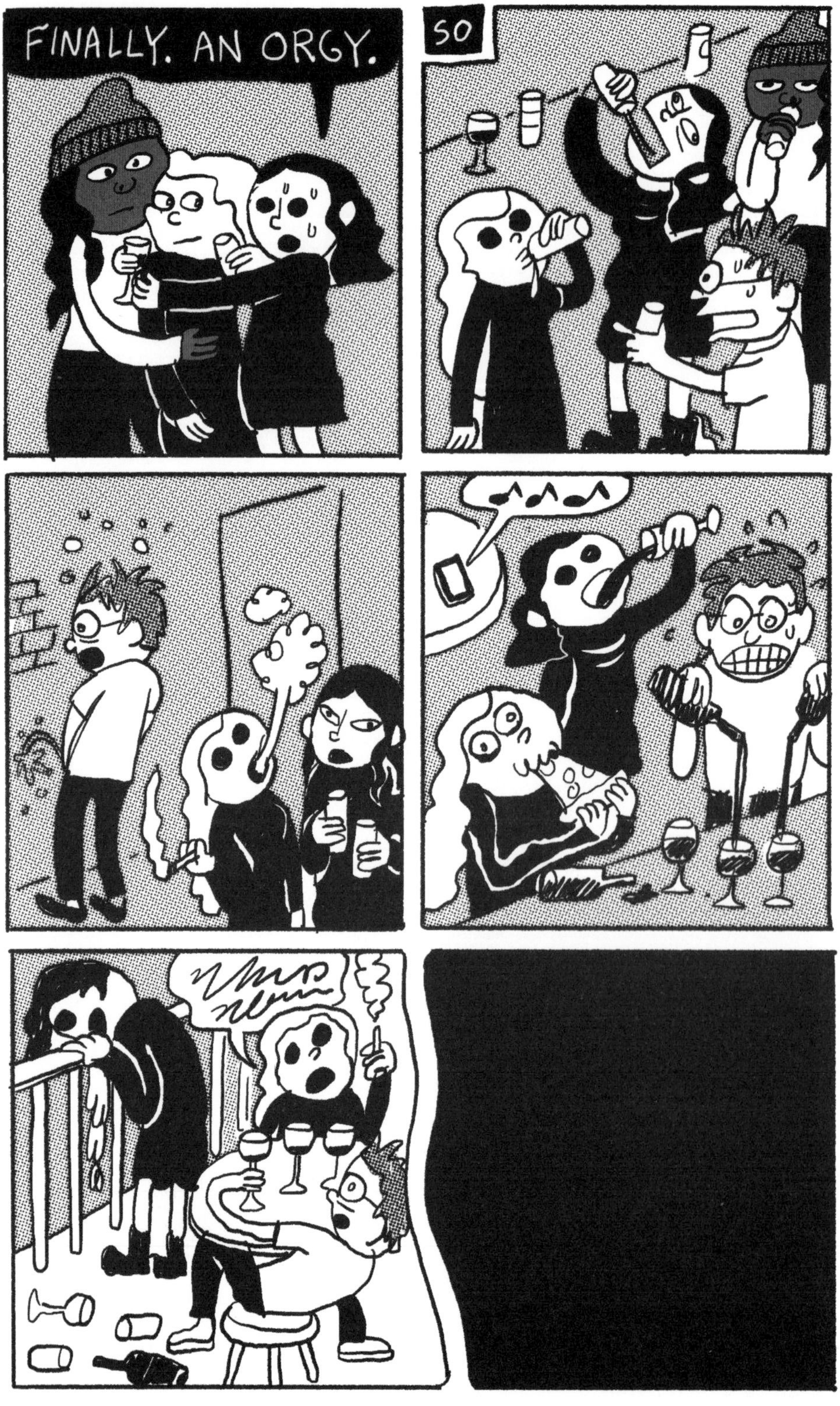
FINALLY. AN ORGY.
SO

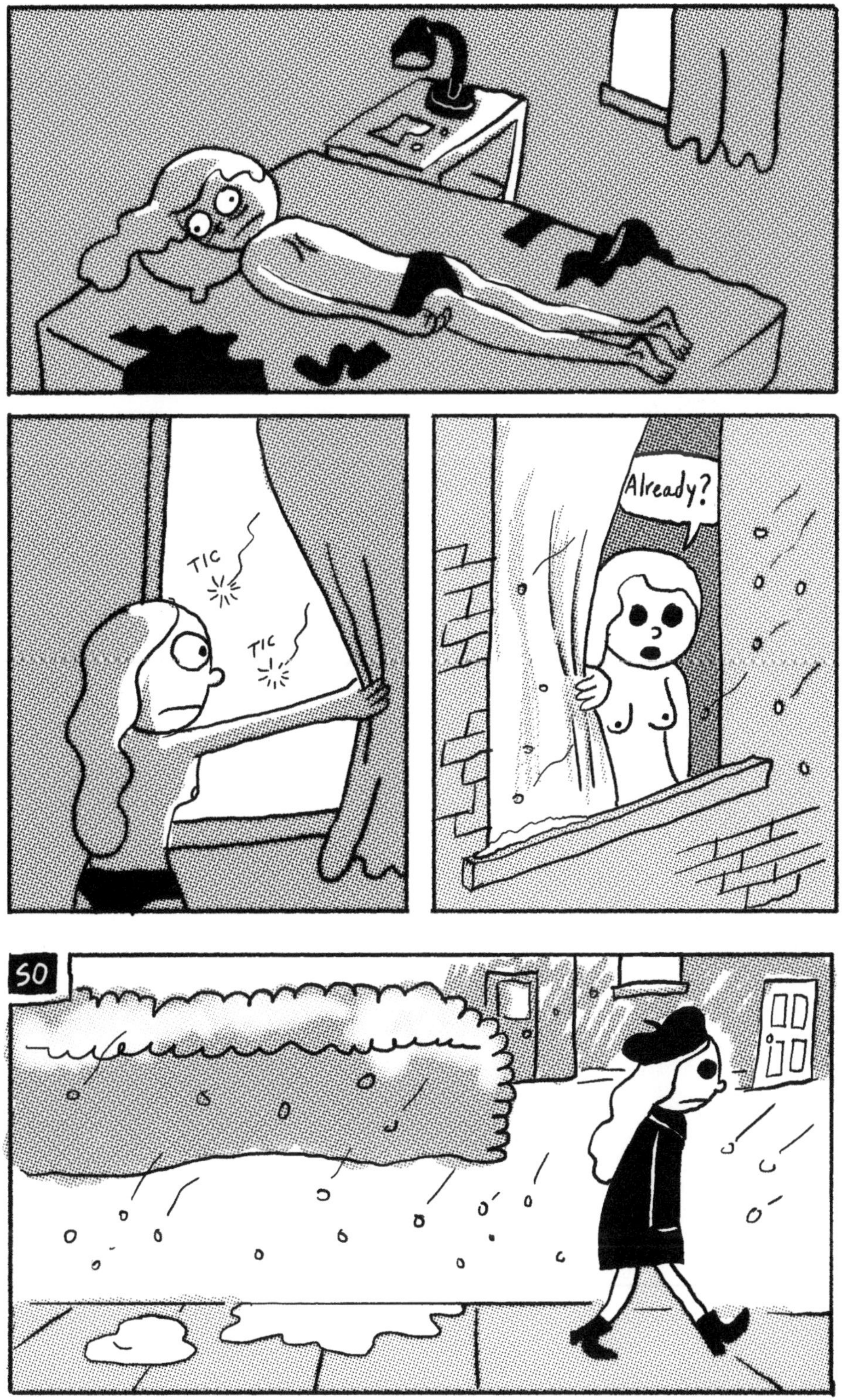
TIC
TIC
Already?
SO

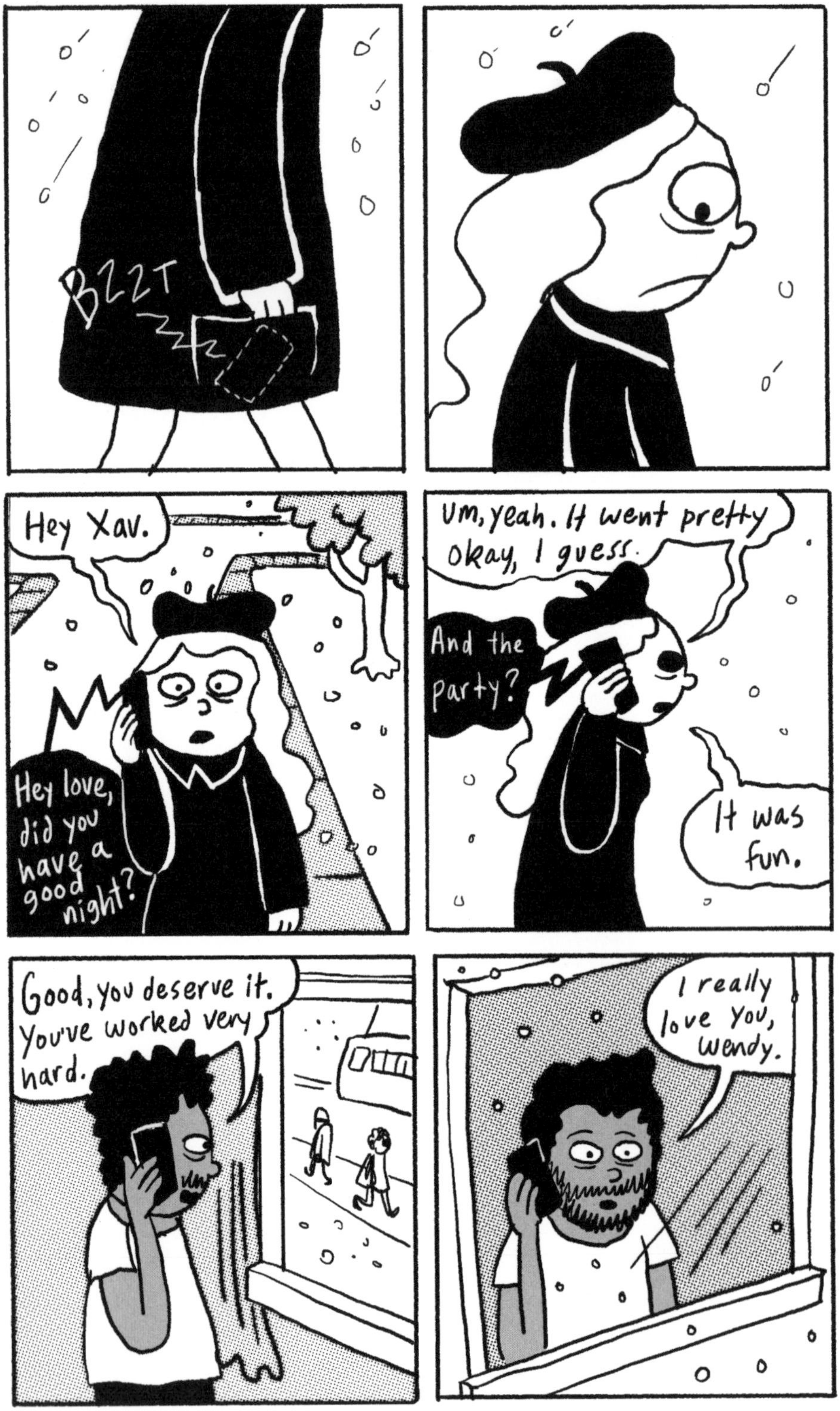
BZZT
Hey Xav.
Hey love, did you have a good night?
Um, yeah. It went pretty okay, I guess.
And the party?
It was fun.
Good, you deserve it. You've worked very hard.
I really love you, Wendy.

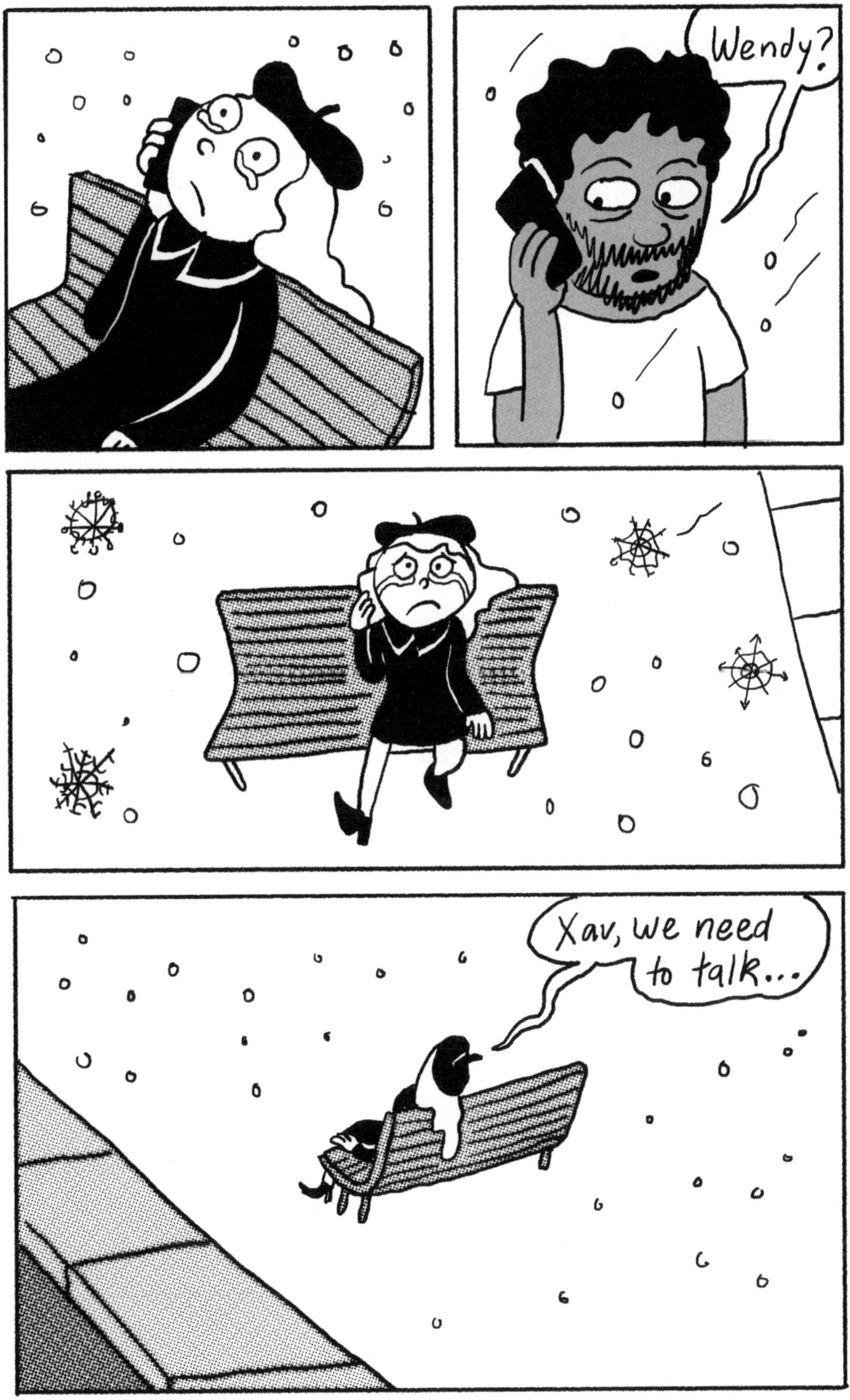
Wendy?
Xav, we need to talk...

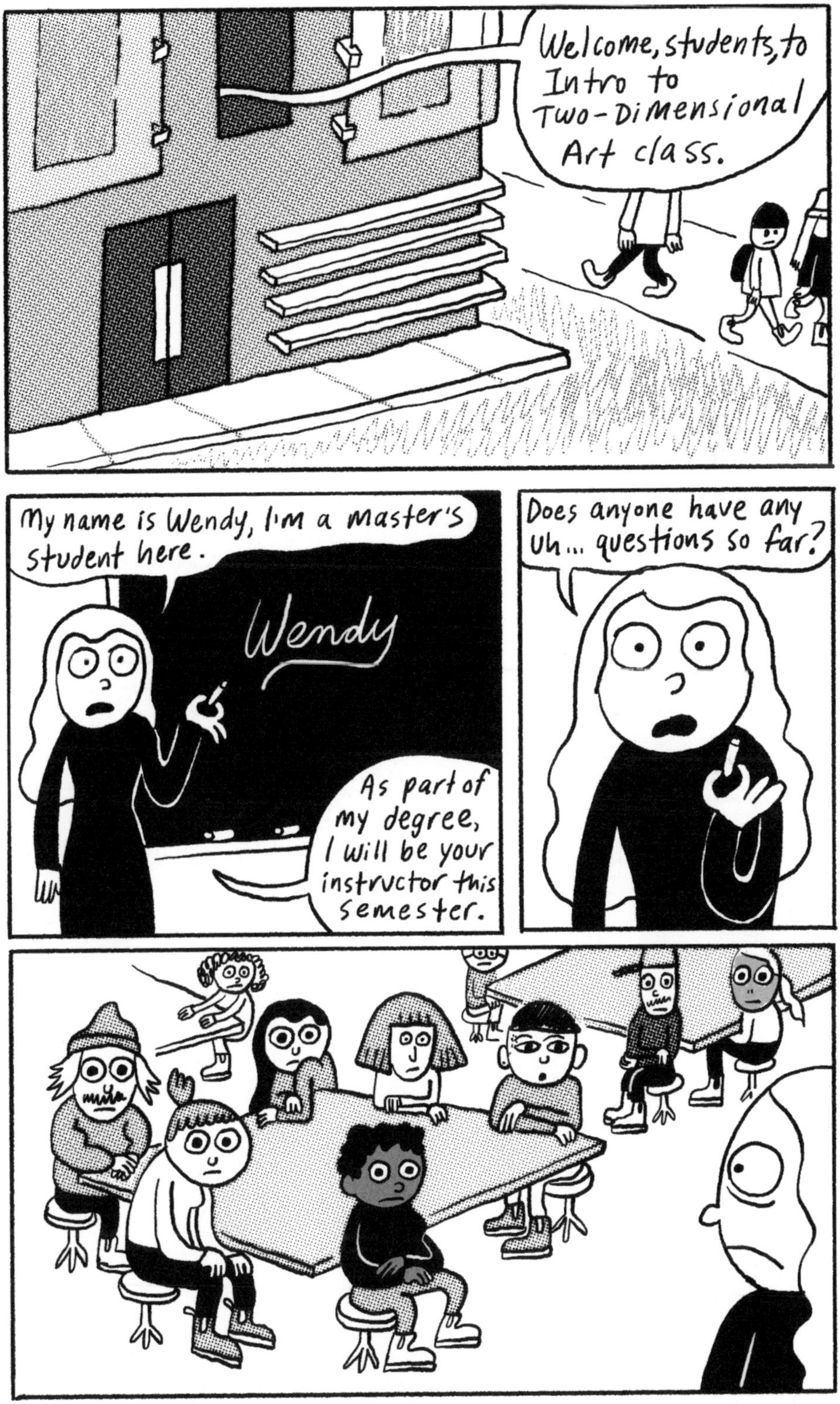
Welcome, students, to Intro to Two-Dimensional Art class.
My name is Wendy, I'm a master's student here.
Wendy
As part of my degree, I will be your instructor this semester.
Does anyone have any uh... questions so far?

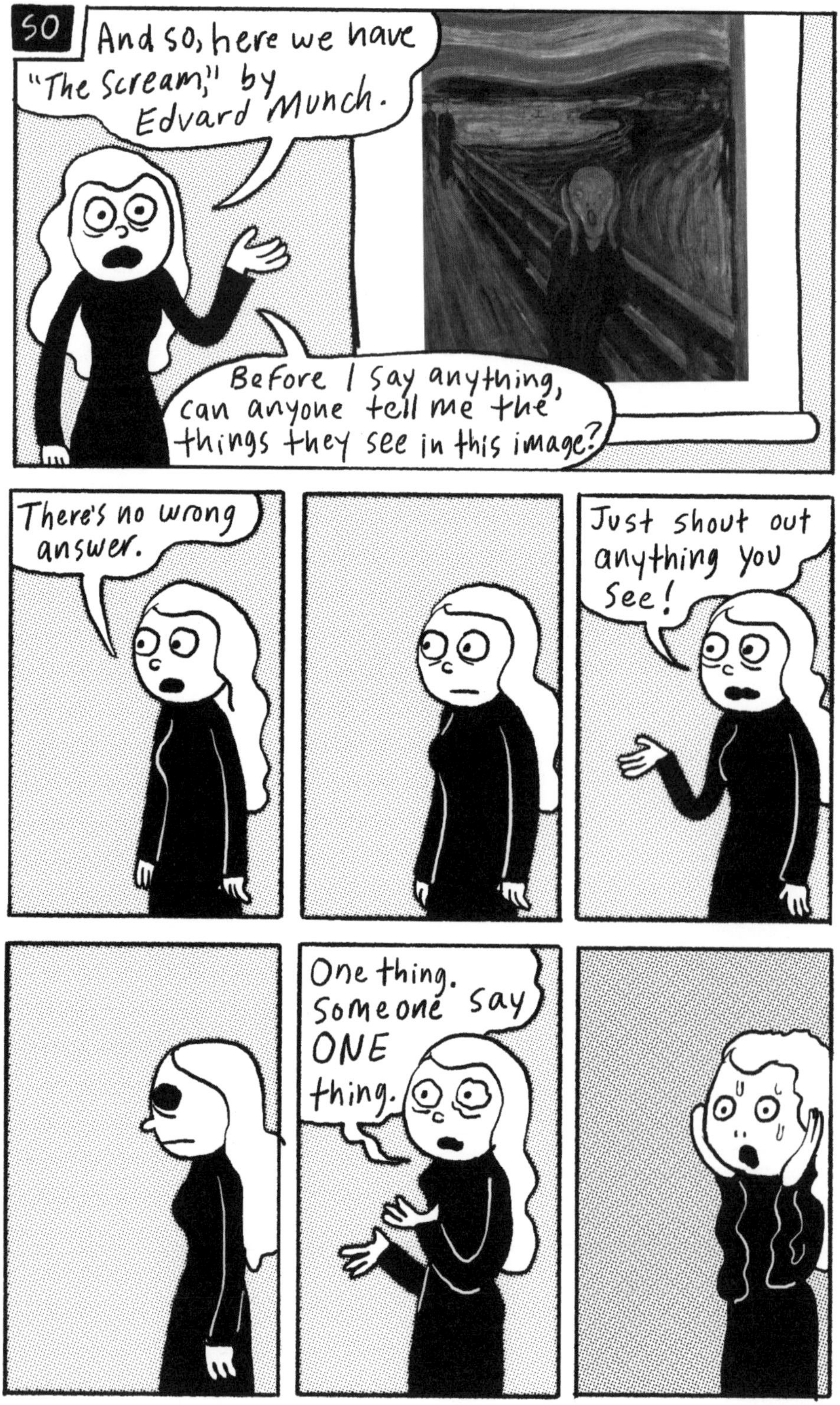
SO
And so, here we have "The Scream," by Edvard Munch.
Before I say anything, can anyone tell me the things they see in this image?
There's no wrong answer.
Just shout out anything you see!
One thing. Someone say ONE thing.

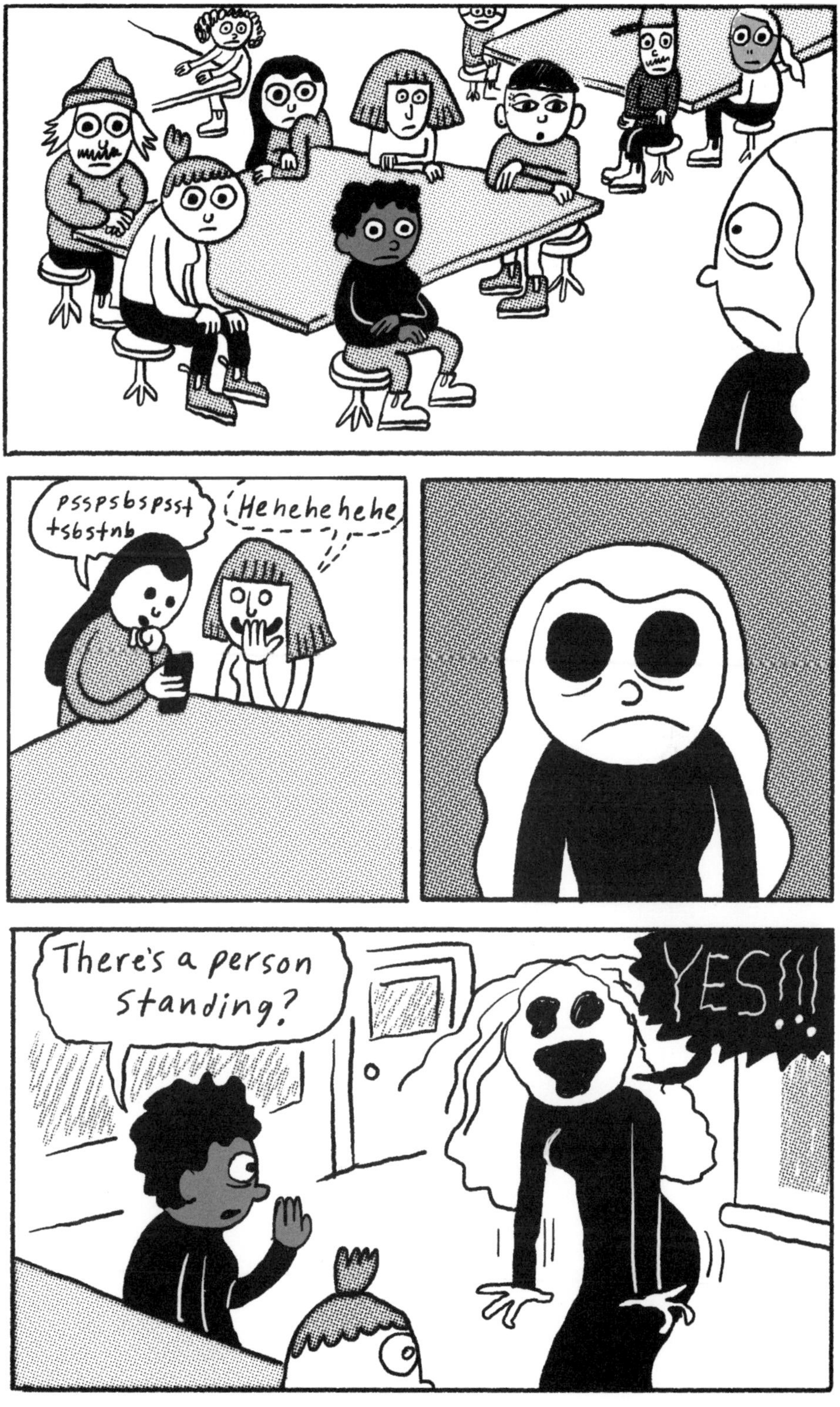
pssps bspsst tsbstnb
Hehehehehe
There's a person standing?
YES!!!

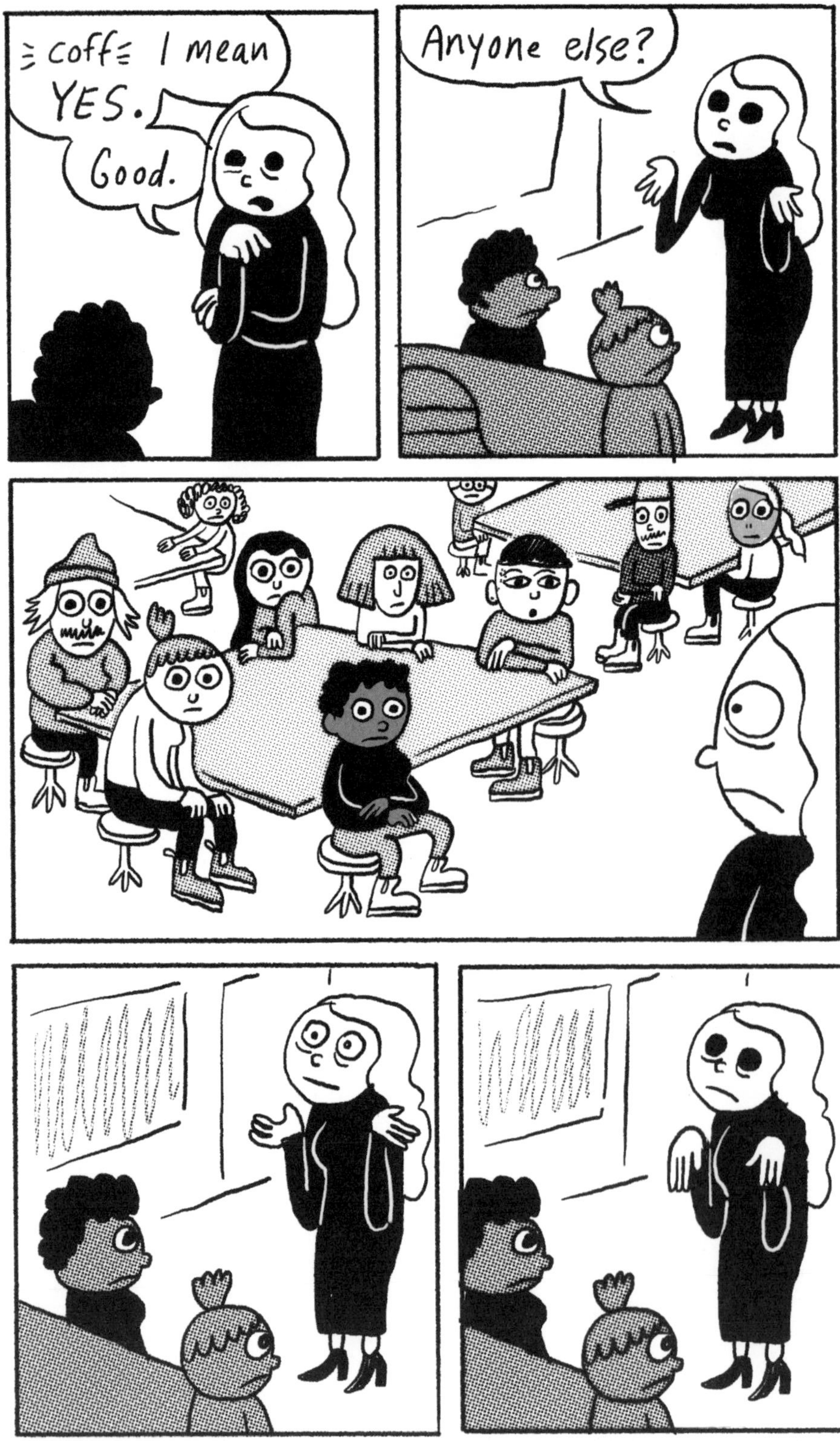

≡coff≡ I mean YES. Good.
Anyone else?

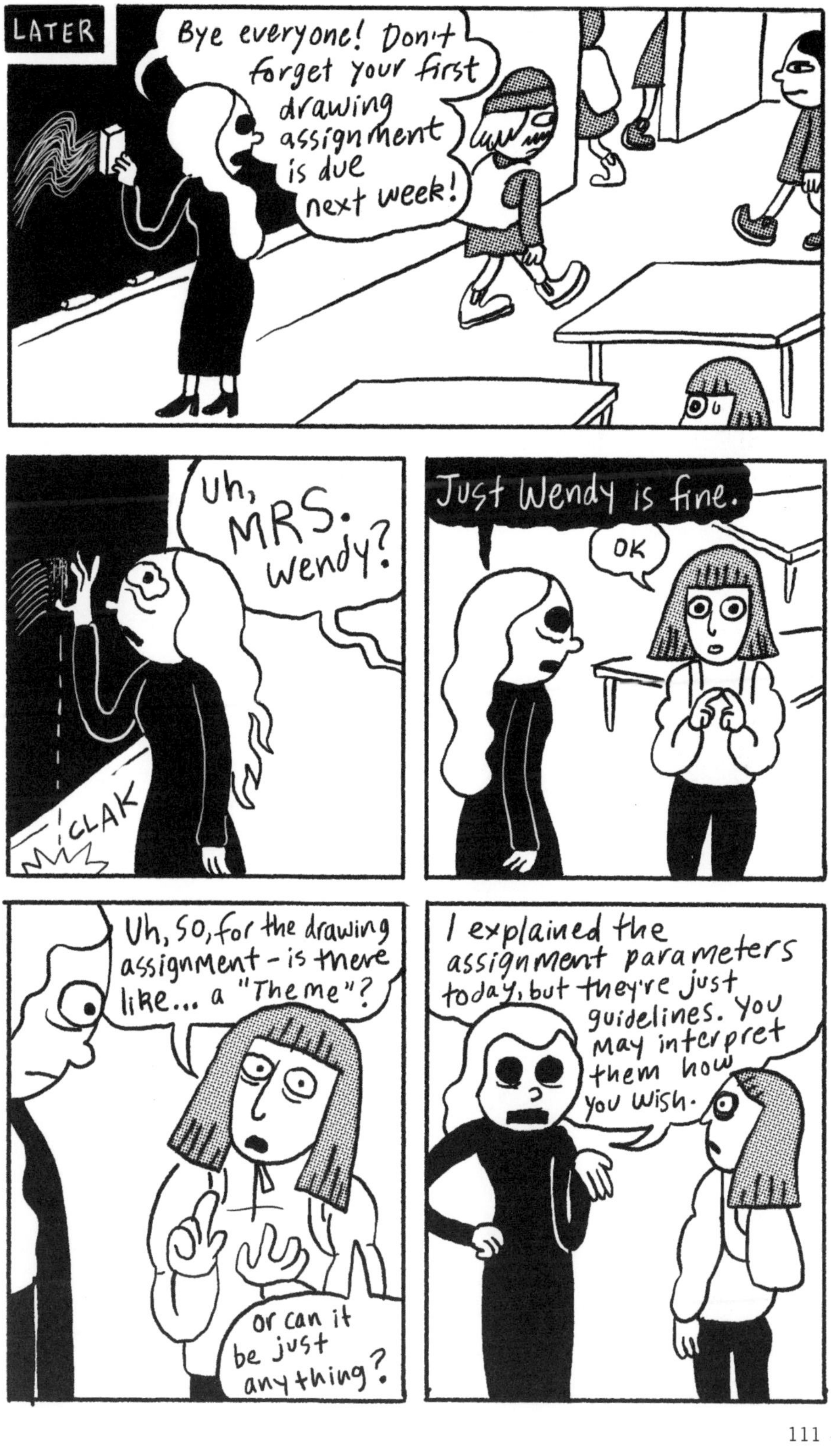
LATER
Bye everyone! Don't forget your first drawing assignment is due next week!
Uh, MRS. wendy?
CLAK
Just Wendy is fine.
OK
Uh, so, for the drawing assignment - is there like... a "Theme"?
or can it be just anything?
I explained the assignment parameters today, but they're just guidelines. You may interpret them how you wish.

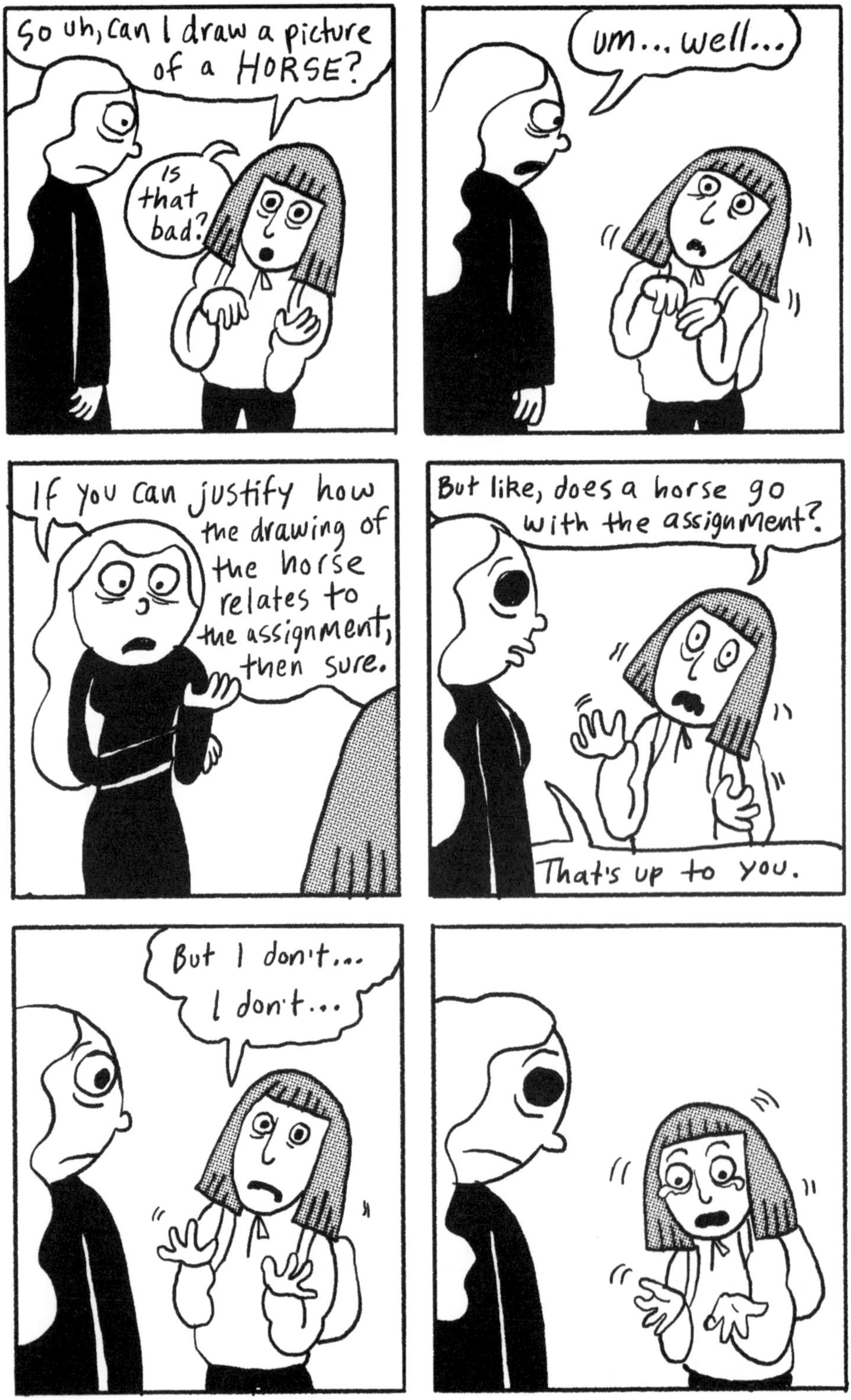
So uh, can I draw a picture of a HORSE?
Is that bad?
um... well...
If you can justify how the drawing of the horse relates to the assignment, then sure.
But like, does a horse go with the assignment?
That's up to you.
But I don't... I don't...

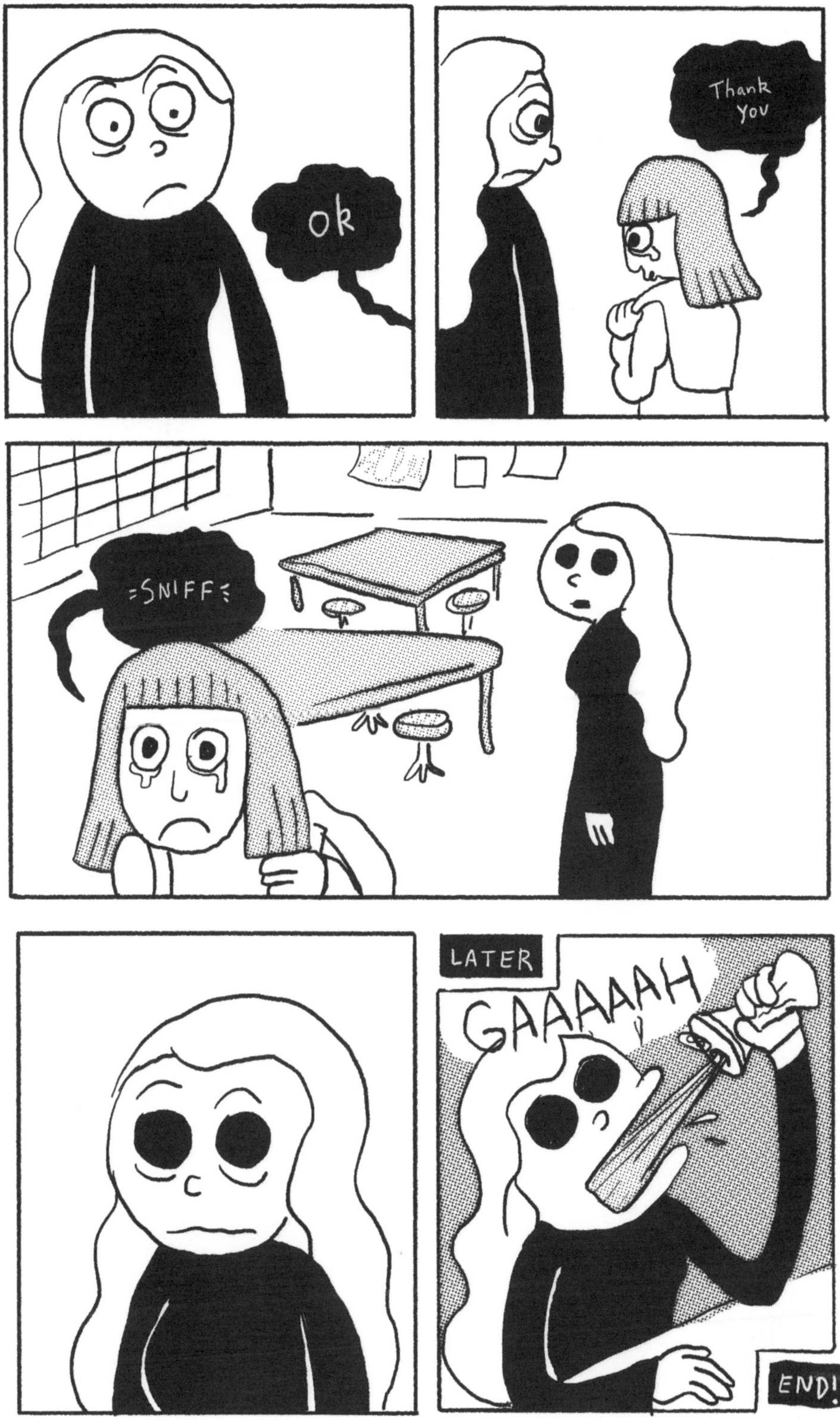
ok
Thank you
=SNIFF=
LATER
GAAAAAH
END!

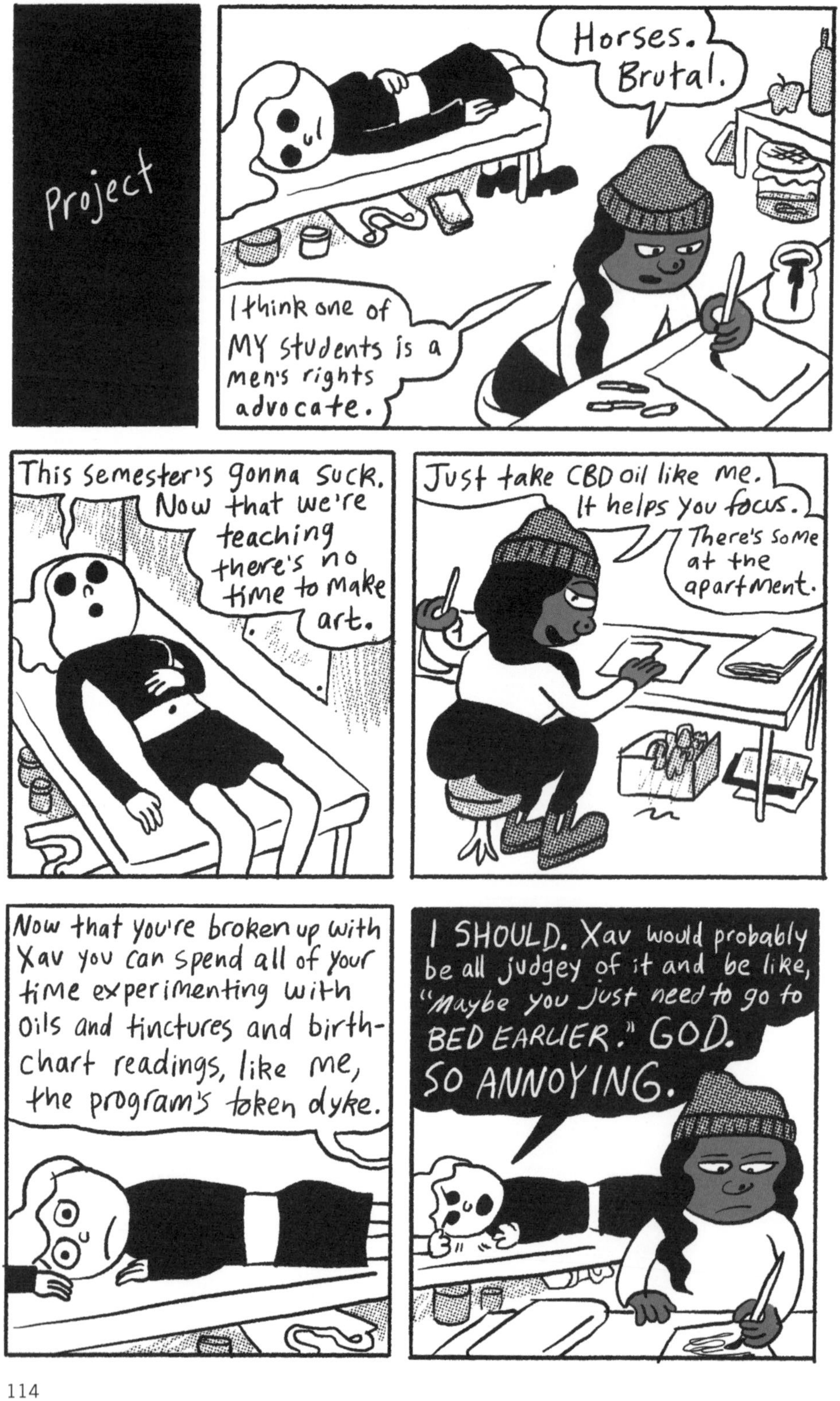
Project
Horses. Brutal.
I think one of MY students is a men's rights advocate.
This semester's gonna suck. Now that we're teaching there's no time to make art.
Just take CBD oil like me. It helps you focus.
There's some at the apartment.
Now that you're broken up with Xav you can spend all of your time experimenting with oils and tinctures and birth-chart readings, like me, the program's token dyke.
I SHOULD. Xav would probably be all judgey of it and be like, "Maybe you just need to go to BED EARLIER." GOD. SO ANNOYING.

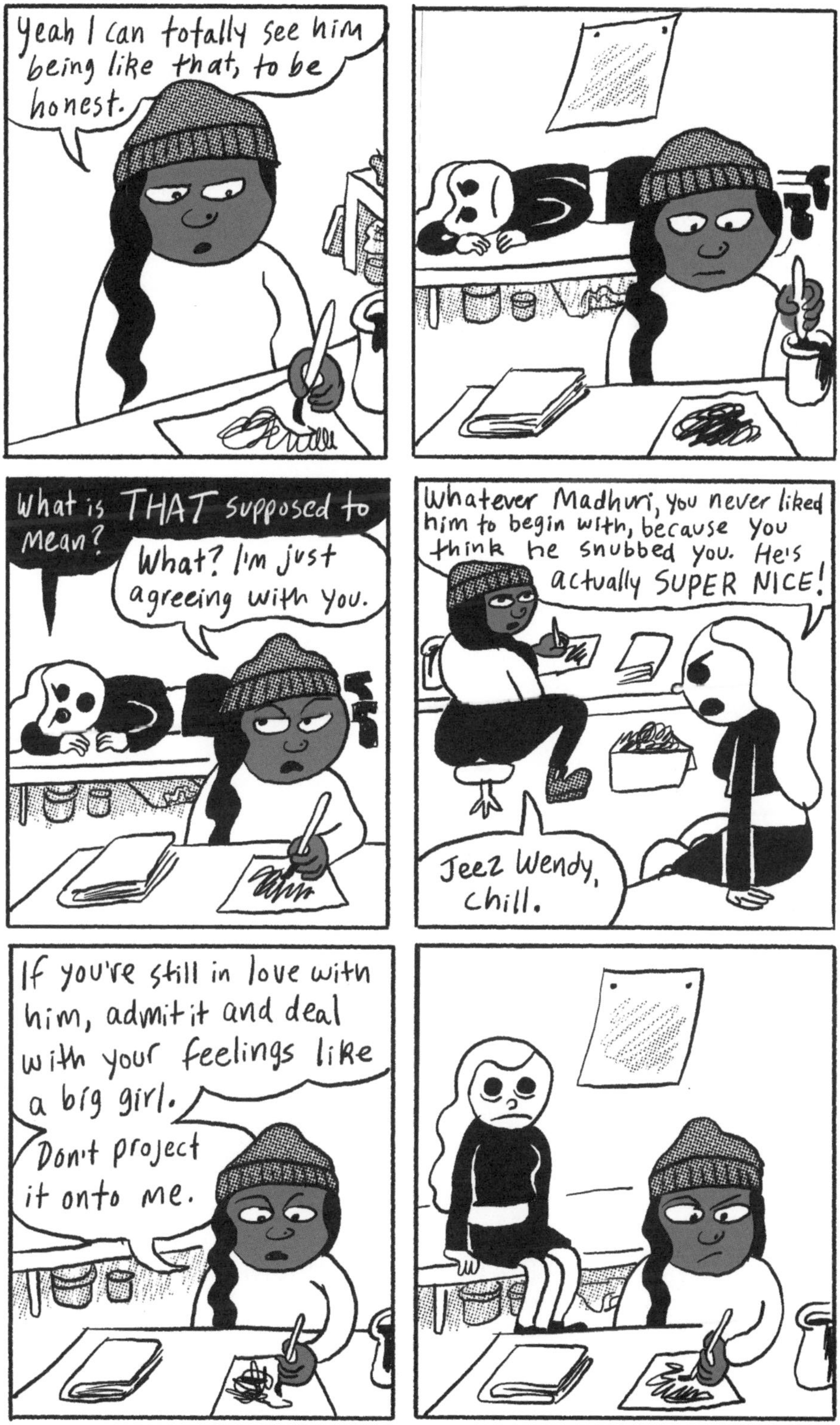
Yeah I can totally see him being like that, to be honest.
What is THAT supposed to mean?
What? I'm just agreeing with you.
Whatever Madhuri, you never liked him to begin with, because you think he snubbed you. He's actually SUPER NICE!
Jeez Wendy, chill.
If you're still in love with him, admit it and deal with your feelings like a big girl.
Don't project it onto me.

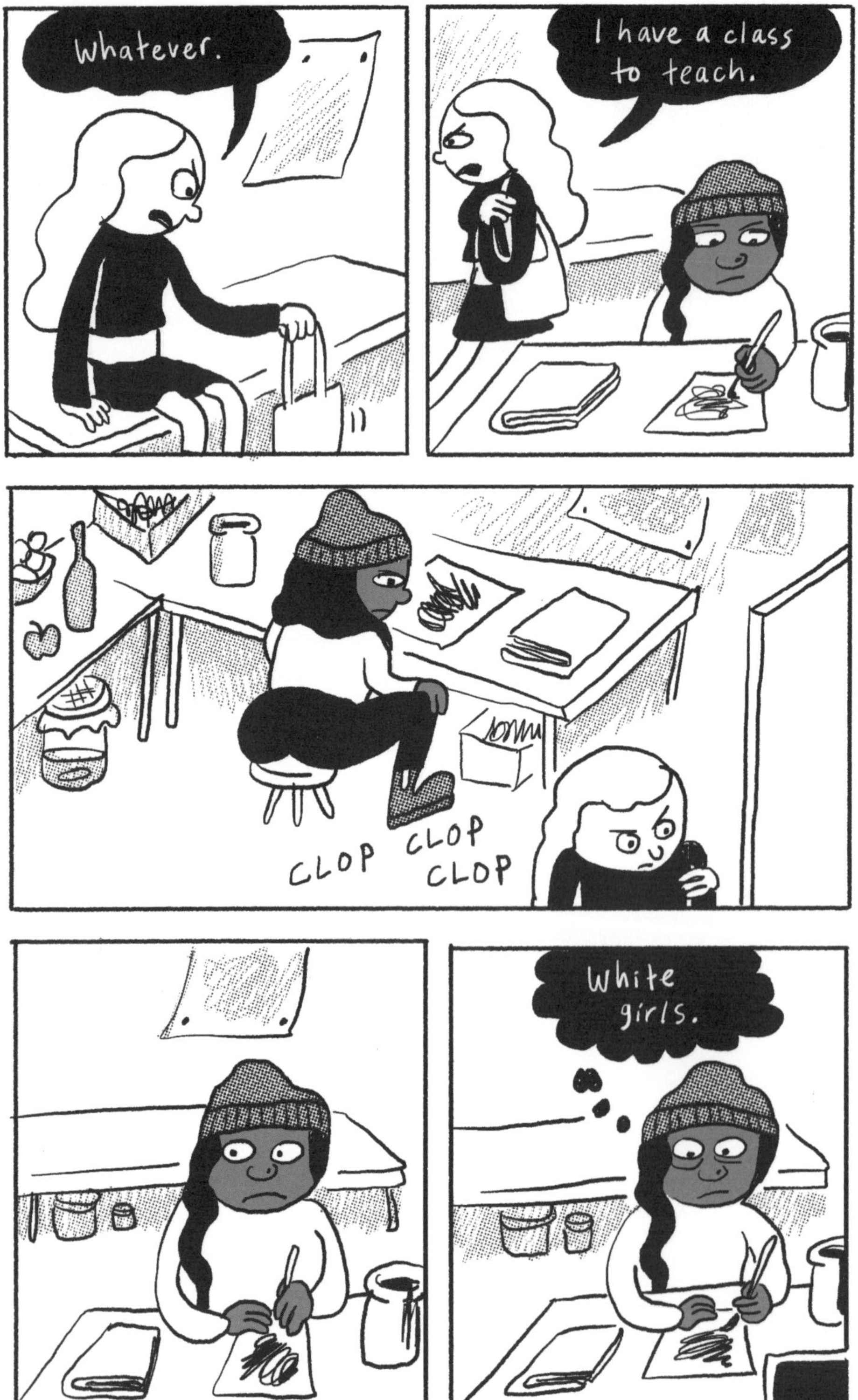
Whatever.
I have a class to teach.
CLOP CLOP CLOP CLOP
White girls.

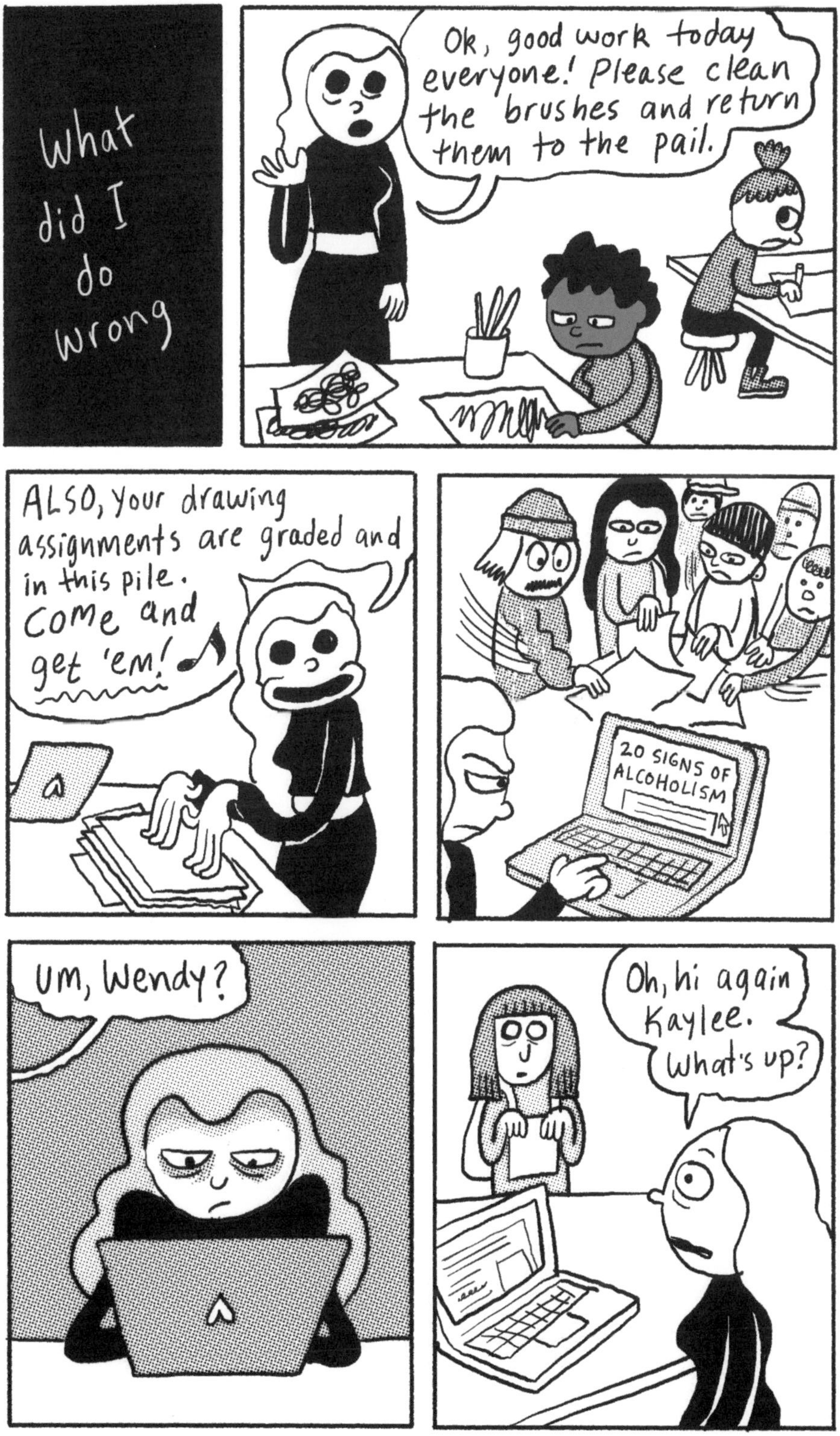
What did I do wrong
Ok, good work today everyone! Please clean the brushes and return them to the pail.
ALSO, your drawing assignments are graded and in this pile. Come and get 'em!
20 SIGNS OF ALCOHOLISM
Um, Wendy?
Oh, hi again Kaylee. What's up?

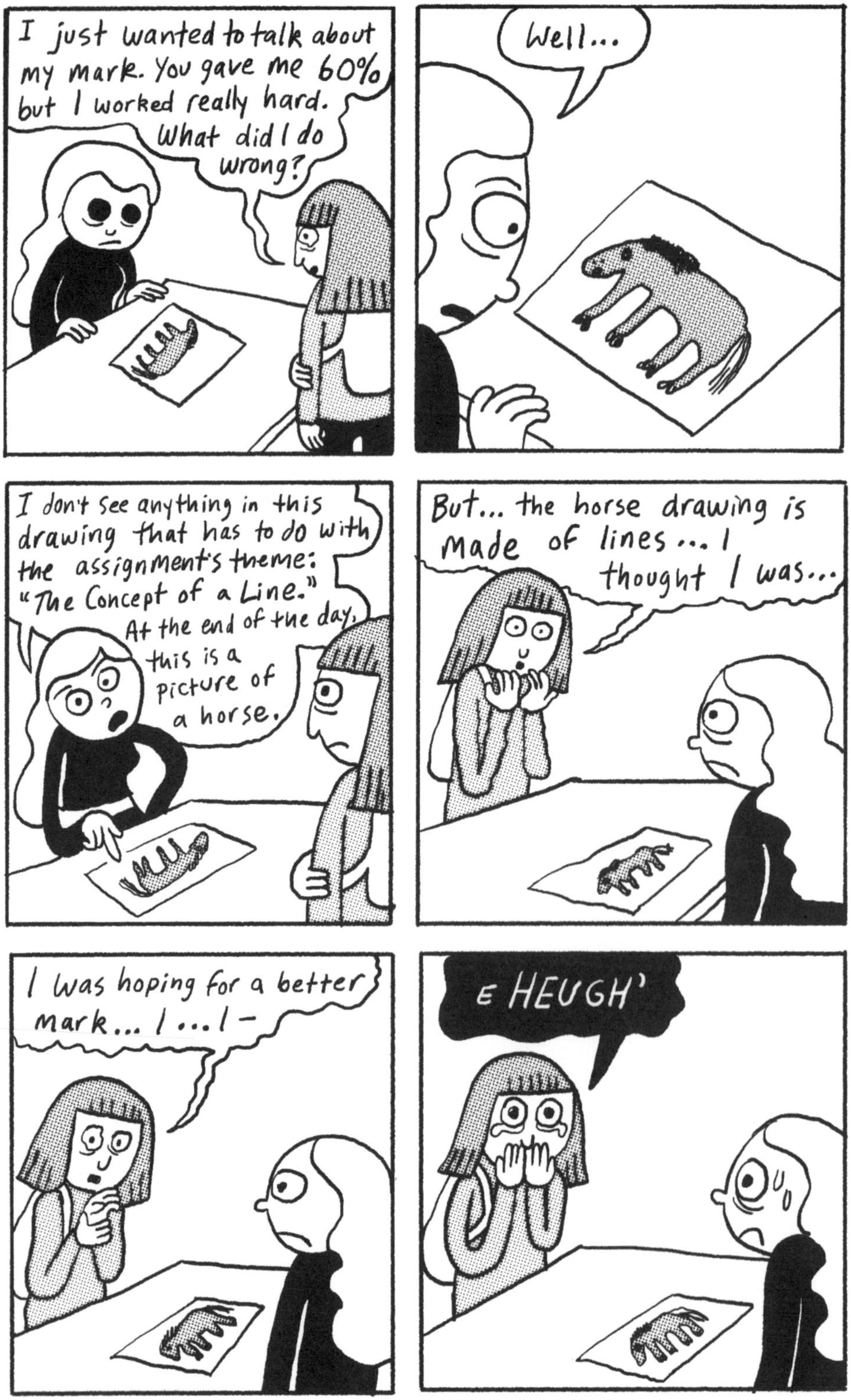
I just wanted to talk about my mark. You gave me 60% but I worked really hard.
What did I do wrong?
Well...
I don't see anything in this drawing that has to do with the assignment's theme: "The Concept of a Line."
At the end of the day, this is a picture of a horse.
But... the horse drawing is made of lines... I thought I was...
I was hoping for a better mark... I ... I–
E HEUGH'

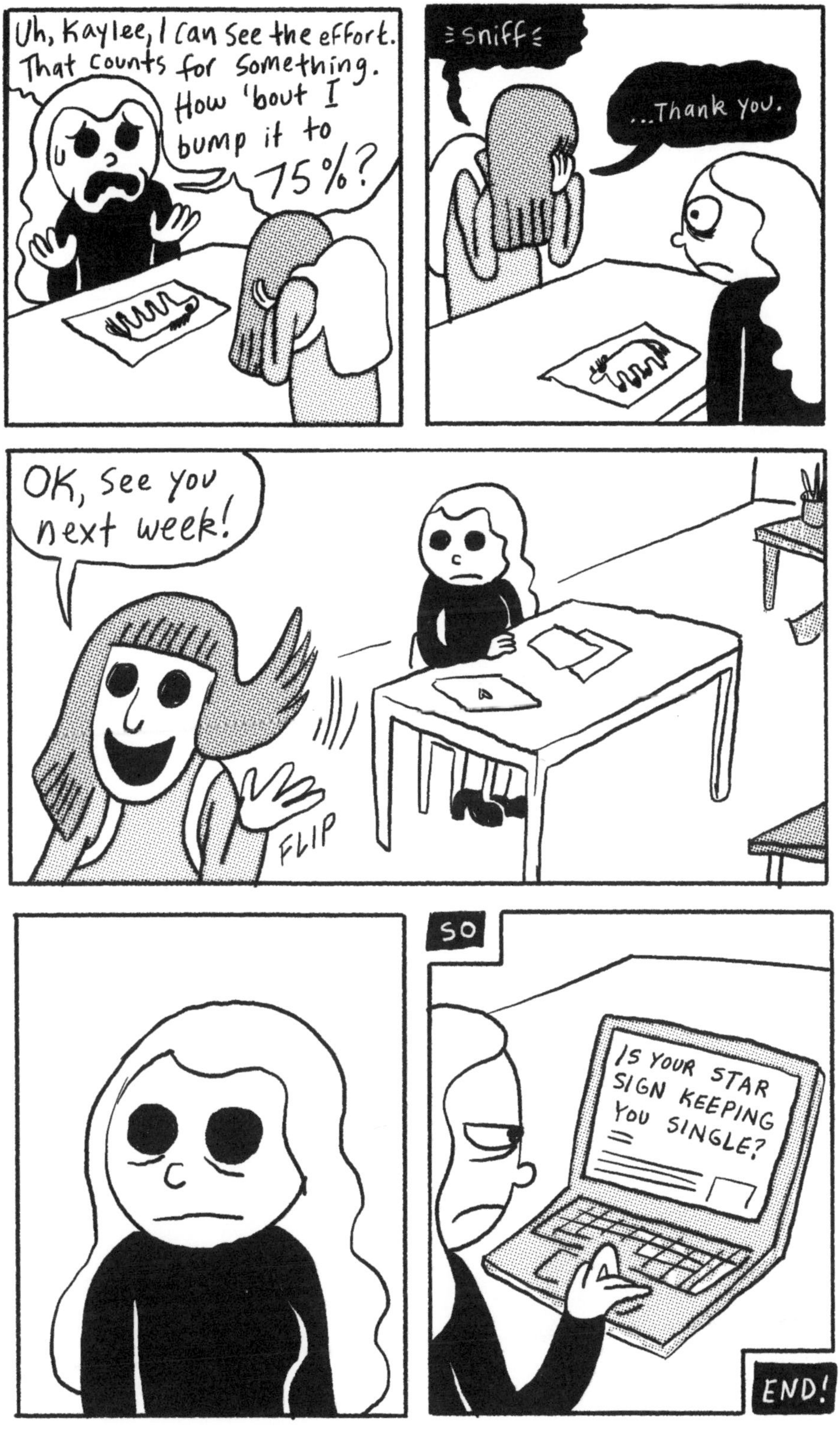
Uh, Kaylee, I can see the effort. That counts for something. How 'bout I bump it to 75%?
Sniff
...Thank you.
OK, see you next week!
FLIP
SO
IS YOUR STAR SIGN KEEPING YOU SINGLE?
END!

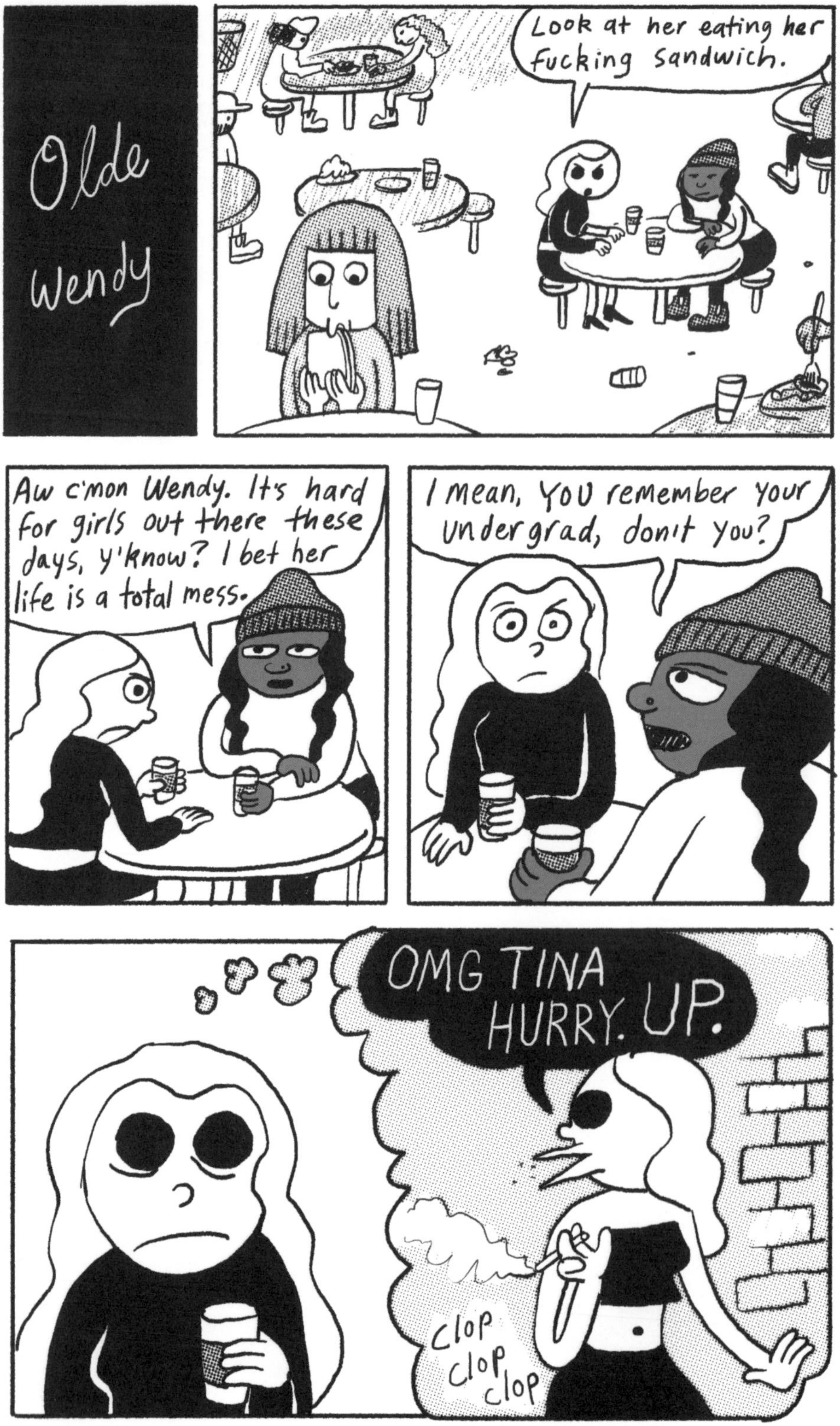
Olde Wendy
Look at her eating her fucking sandwich.
Aw c'mon Wendy. It's hard for girls out there these days, y'know? I bet her life is a total mess.
I mean, YOU remember your undergrad, don't you?
OMG TINA HURRY. UP.
clop clop clop

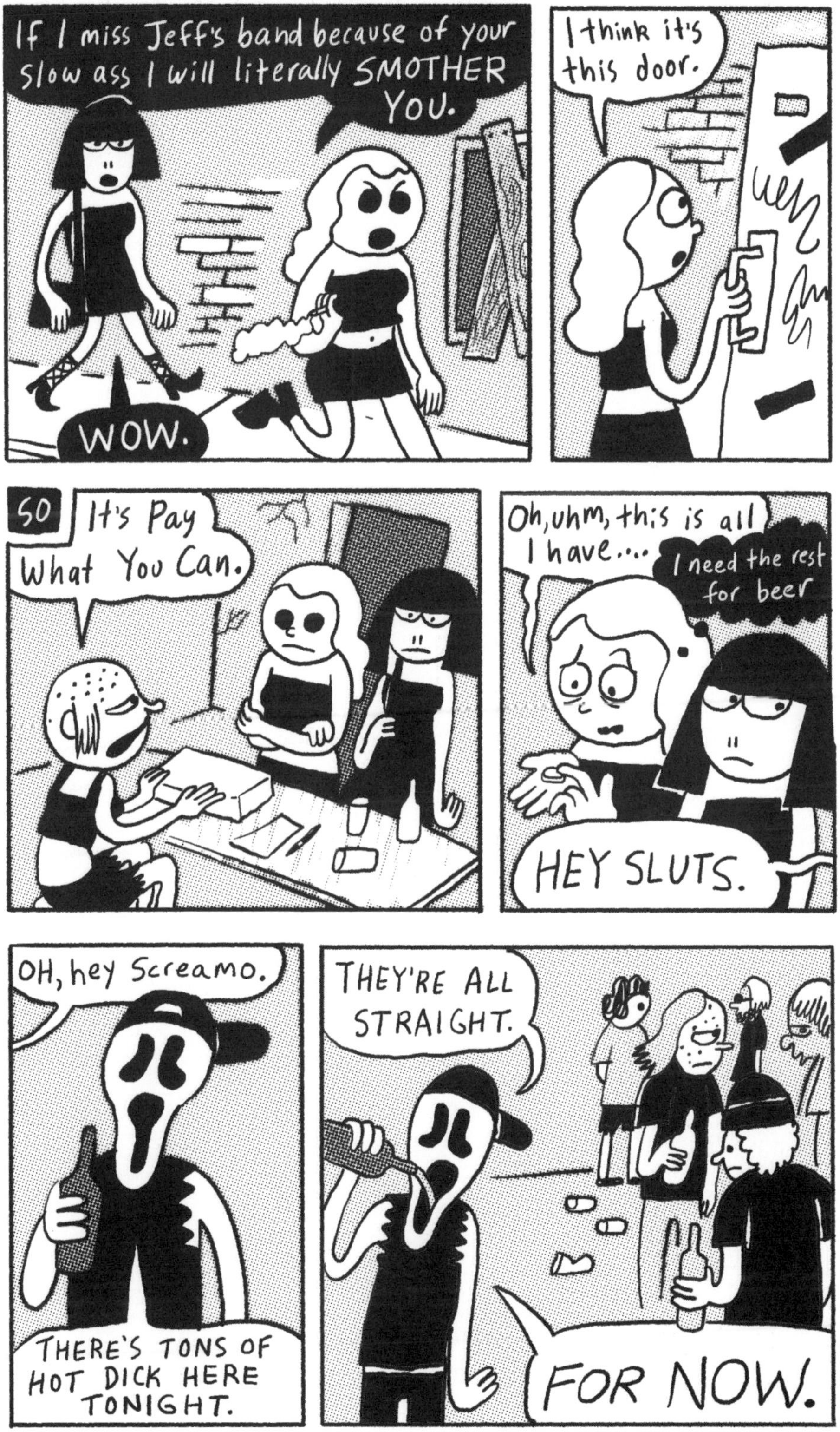
If I miss Jeff's band because of your slow ass I will literally SMOTHER YOU.
WOW.
I think it's this door.
SO
It's Pay What You Can.
Oh, uhm, this is all I have....
I need the rest for beer
HEY SLUTS.
OH, hey Screamo.
THERE'S TONS OF HOT DICK HERE TONIGHT.
THEY'RE ALL STRAIGHT.
FOR NOW.

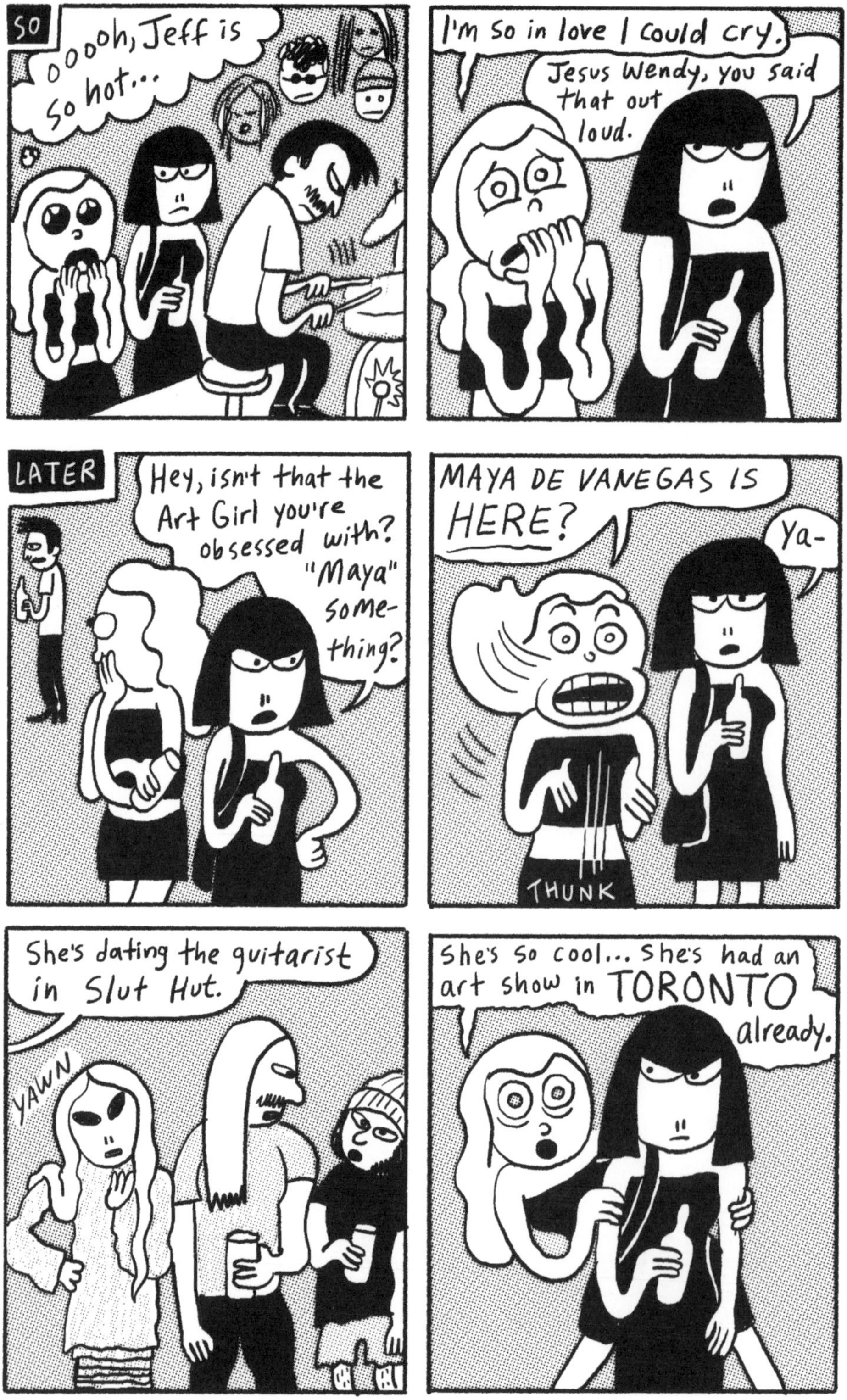
SO
oooooh, Jeff is so hot...
I'm so in love I could cry.
Jesus Wendy, you said that out loud.
LATER
Hey, isn't that the Art Girl you're obsessed with? "Maya" something?
MAYA DE VANEGAS IS HERE?
Ya-
THUNK
She's dating the guitarist in Slut Hut.
YAWN
She's so cool... She's had an art show in TORONTO already.

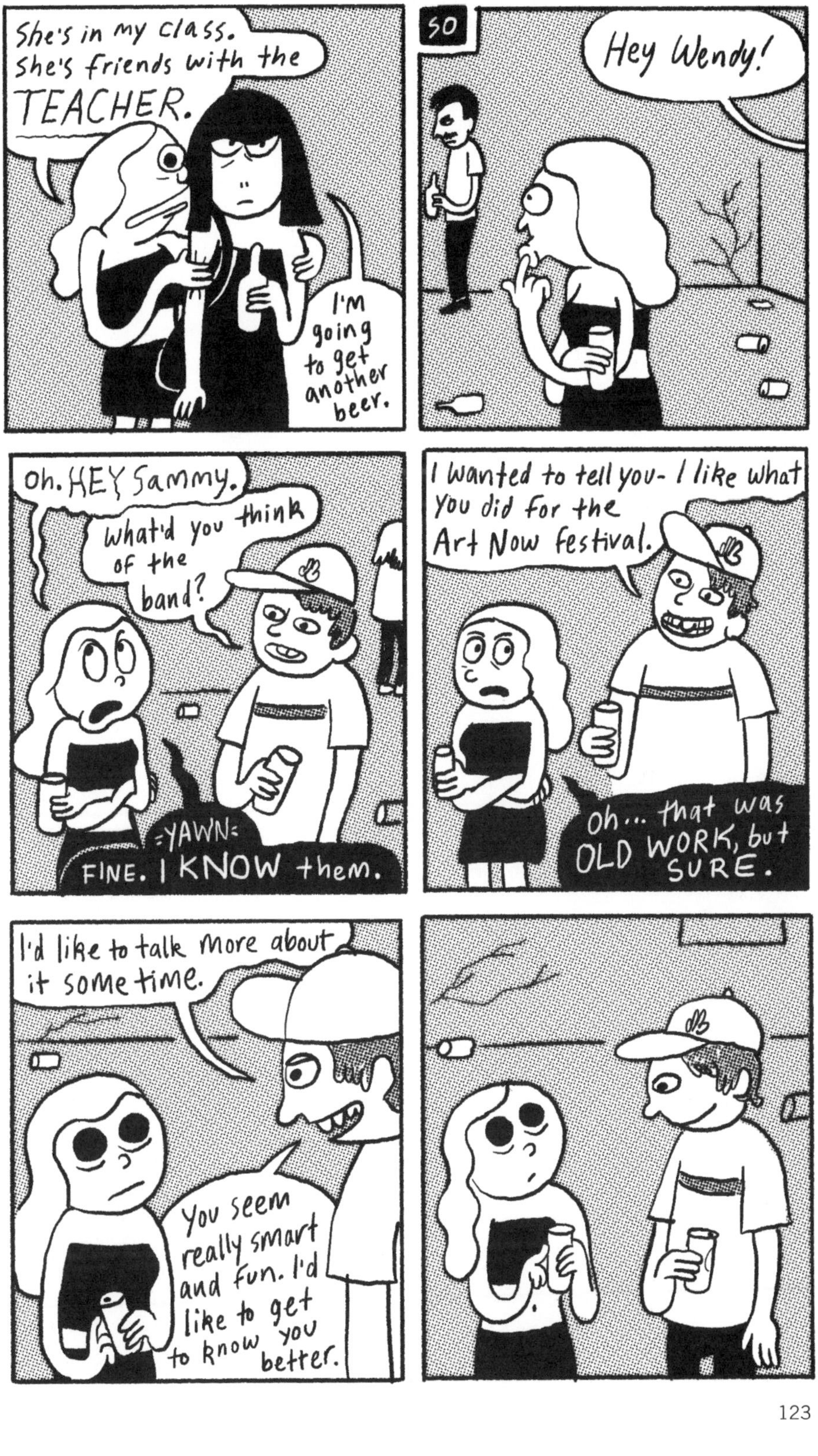

She's in my class. She's friends with the TEACHER.
I'm going to get another beer.
SO
Hey Wendy!
Oh. HEY Sammy.
What'd you think of the band?
=YAWN=
FINE. I KNOW them.
I wanted to tell you- I like what you did for the Art Now festival.
Oh... that was OLD WORK, but SURE.
I'd like to talk more about it some time.
You seem really smart and fun. I'd like to get to know you better.

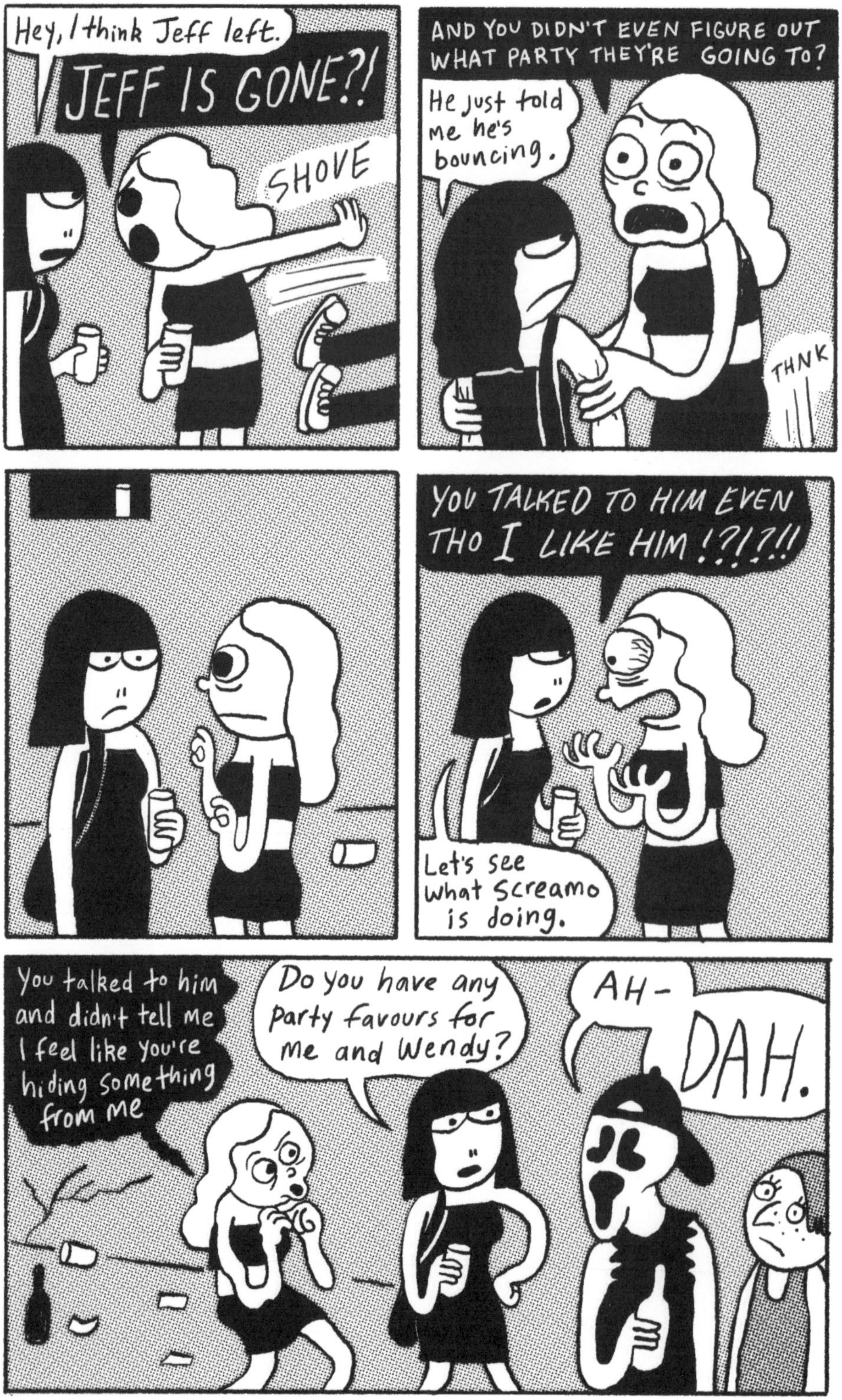
Hey, I think Jeff left.
JEFF IS GONE?!
SHOVE
AND YOU DIDN'T EVEN FIGURE OUT WHAT PARTY THEY'RE GOING TO?
He just told me he's bouncing.
THNK
YOU TALKED TO HIM EVEN THO I LIKE HIM!?!?!!
Let's see what Screamo is doing.
You talked to him and didn't tell me I feel like you're hiding something from me
Do you have any party favours for me and Wendy?
AH-
DAH.

SO
Tina I'm sorry, You're my best friend. When I met You I could tell it was meant to be.
AW THANX BABE *SNIFF*
Screamo, Can't you tell how Much we love each other?
YES BABY. HOLD STILL.
BZZ
I just wanna give You a hug!
AW.
ON MY WAY JEFF!
SEND
LATER
I'm suprised Tina left early, she's usually down to party.
WE, HOWEVER-
ARE GOING TO GET REKT.
SO
Bye, Wendy!
Tree planting opened my eyes.
YEAH
HM!
SHK!

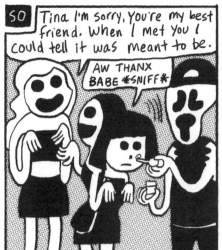

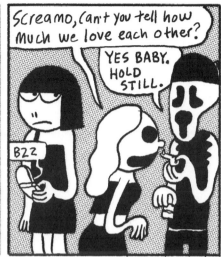

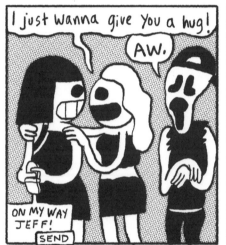

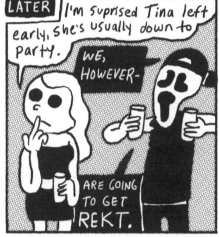

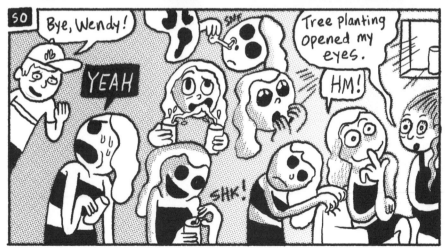

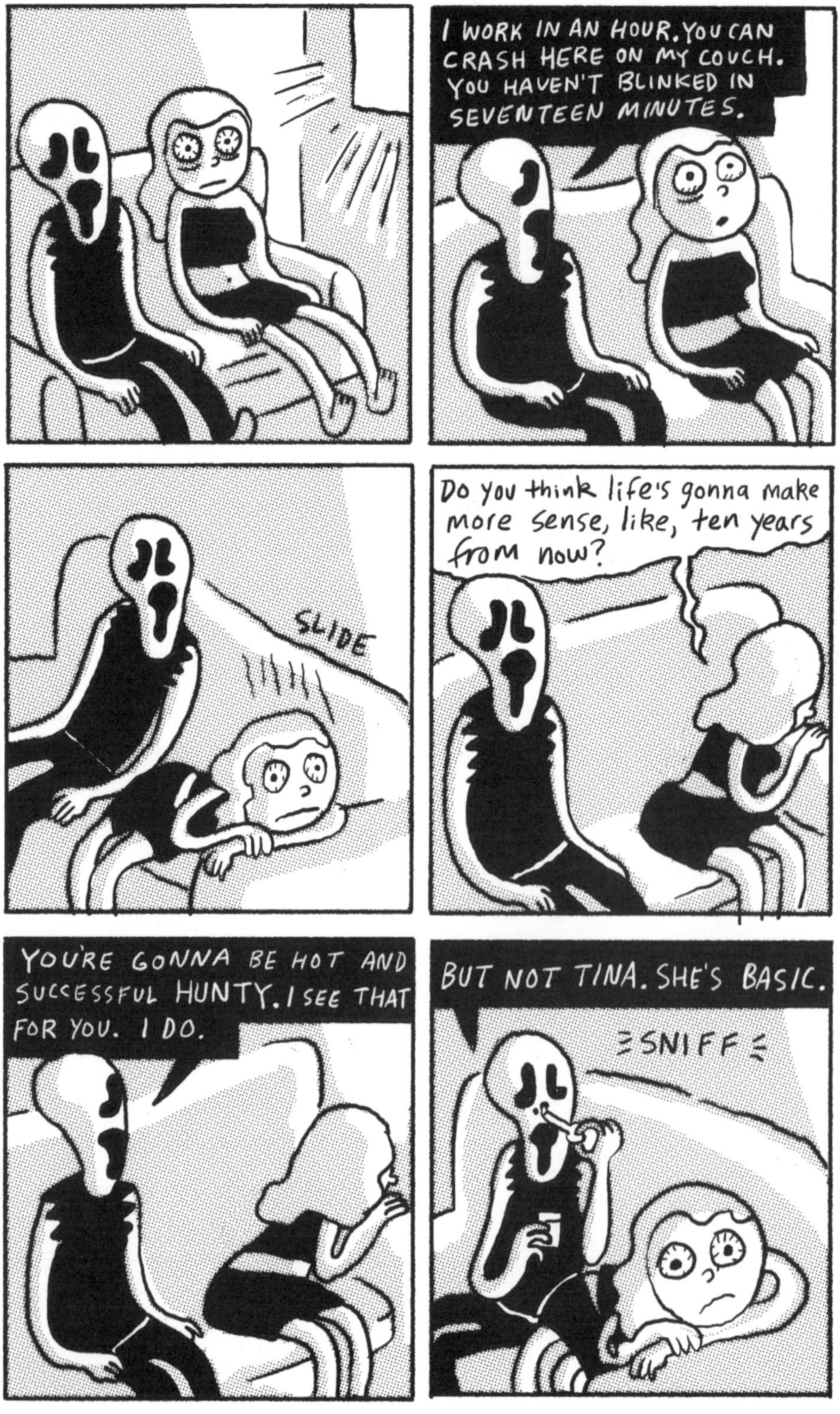

I WORK IN AN HOUR. YOU CAN CRASH HERE ON MY COUCH. YOU HAVEN'T BLINKED IN SEVENTEEN MINUTES.
SLIDE
Do you think life's gonna make more sense, like, ten years from now?
YOU'RE GONNA BE HOT AND SUCCESSFUL HUNTY. I SEE THAT FOR YOU. I DO.
BUT NOT TINA. SHE'S BASIC.
SNIFF

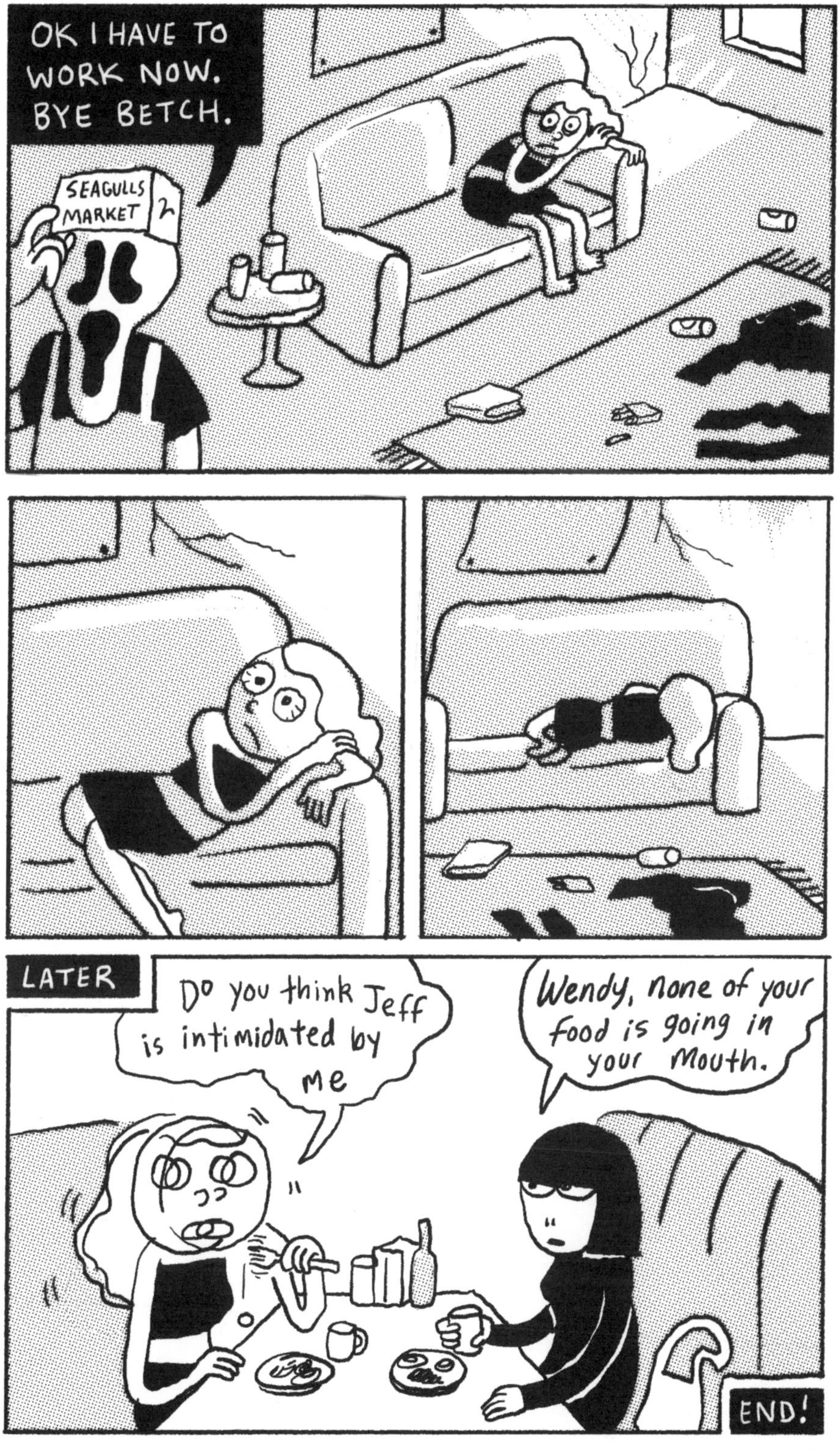

OK I HAVE TO WORK NOW. BYE BETCH.
SEAGULLS MARKET 2
LATER
Do you think Jeff is intimidated by me
Wendy, none of your food is going in your Mouth.
END!

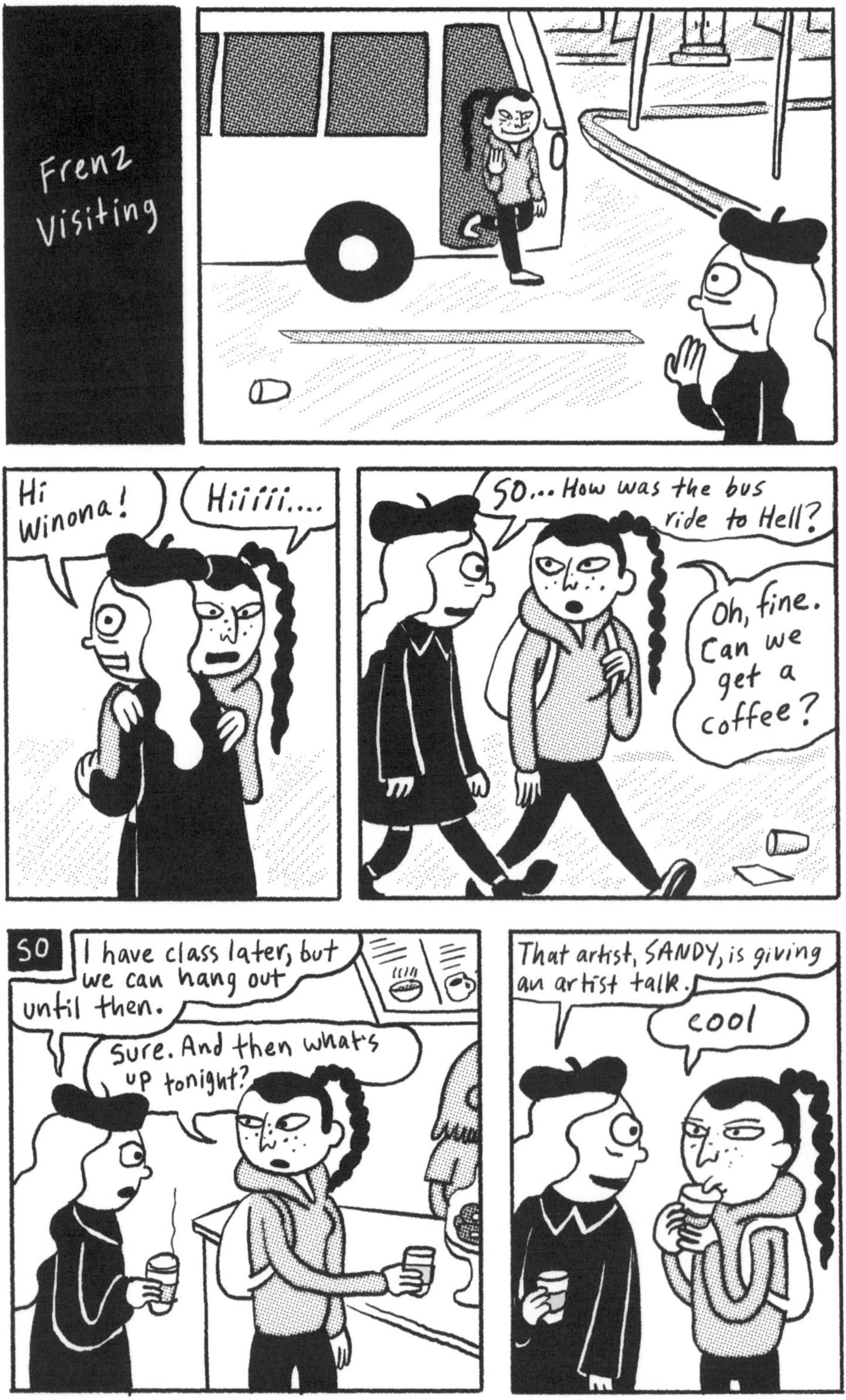

Frenz Visiting
Hi Winona!
Hiiiii....
SO... How was the bus ride to Hell?
Oh, fine. Can we get a coffee?
SO
I have class later, but we can hang out until then.
Sure. And then what's up tonight?
That artist, SANDY, is giving an artist talk.
cool

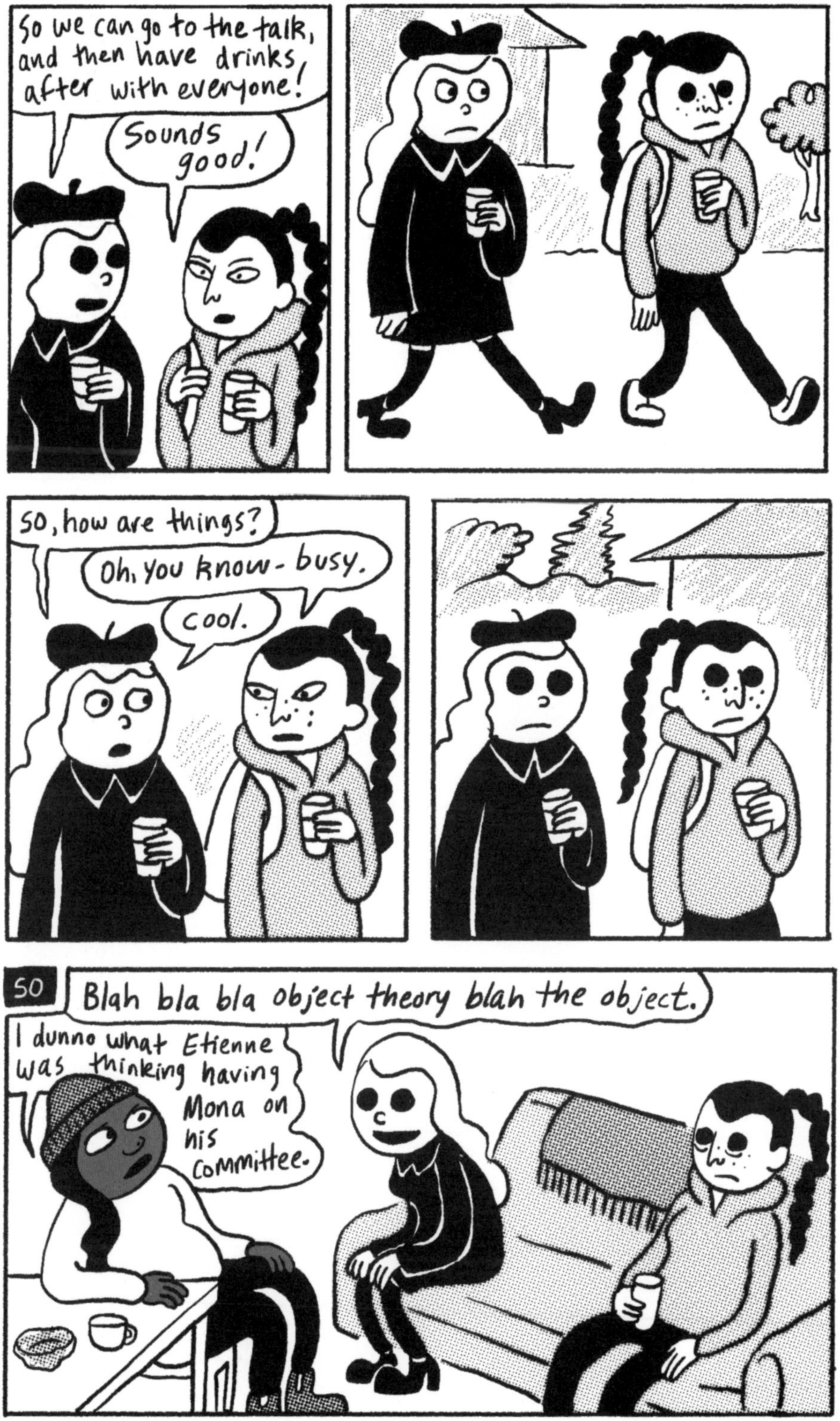
So we can go to the talk, and then have drinks after with everyone!
Sounds good!
So, how are things?
Oh, you know - busy.
Cool.
SO
Blah bla bla object theory blah the object.
I dunno what Etienne was thinking having Mona on his committee.

COF
Oh, Sorry. Our classmate Etienne put Mona on his committee even tho their relationship to the theory of objects is RADICALLY DIFFERENT.
SO different.
Uh yeah... so weird!
RIGHT?
ANYWAY YA, So Mona and that seminar where th
YA
materials.
uneasy relationship to form
END!

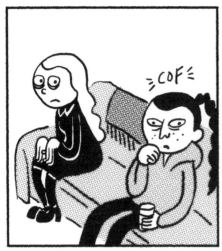

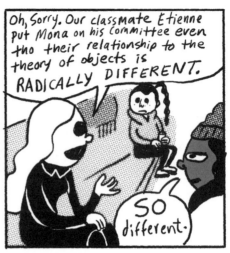

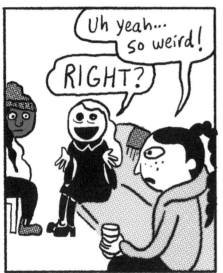

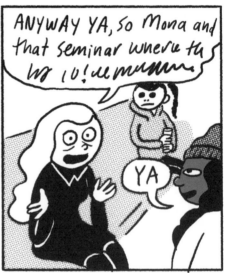

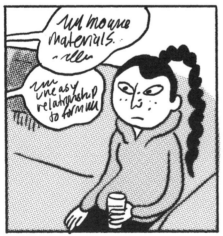

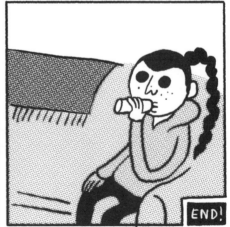

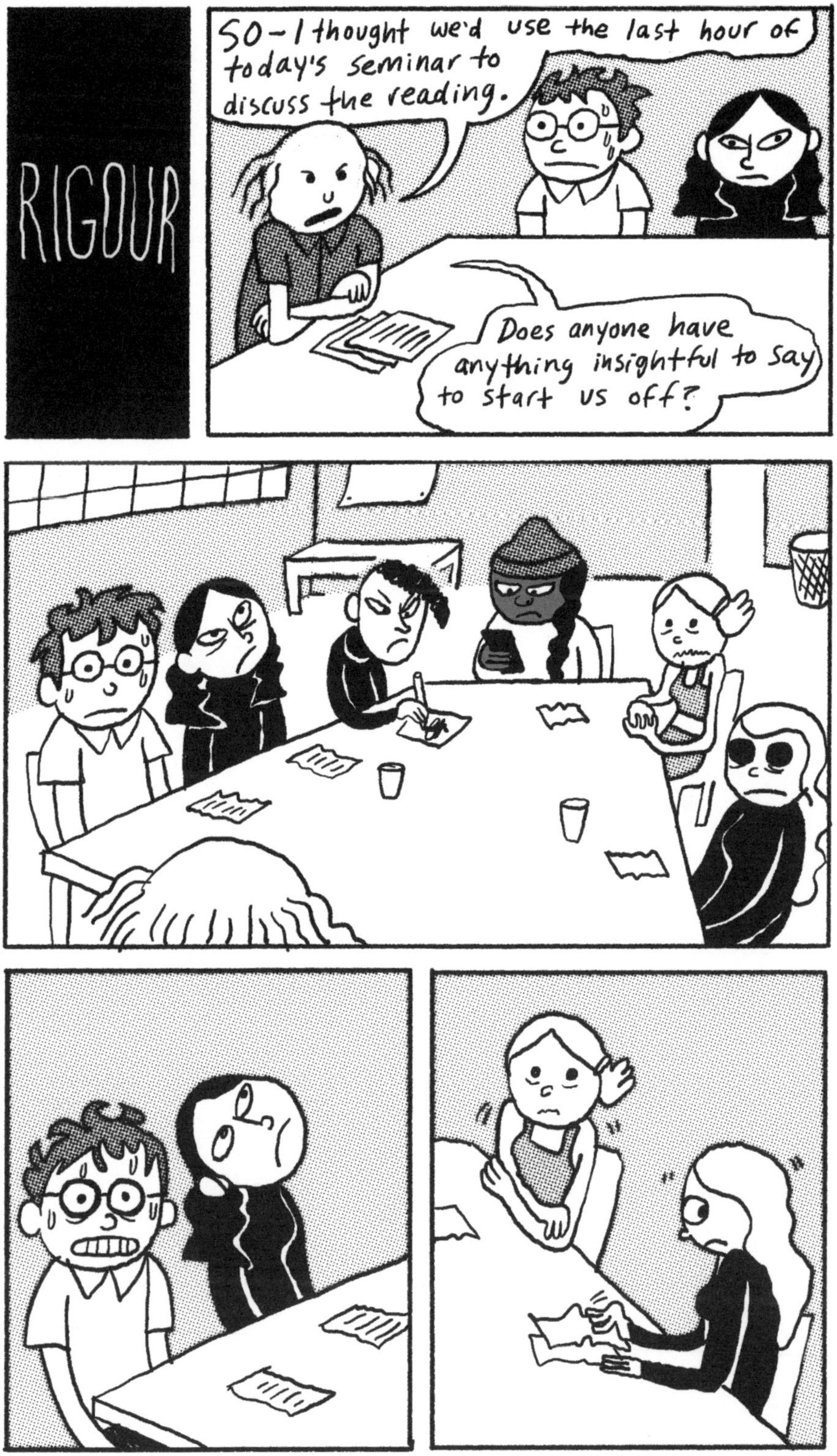
RIGOUR
SO - I thought we'd use the last hour of today's seminar to discuss the reading.
Does anyone have anything insightful to say to start us off?

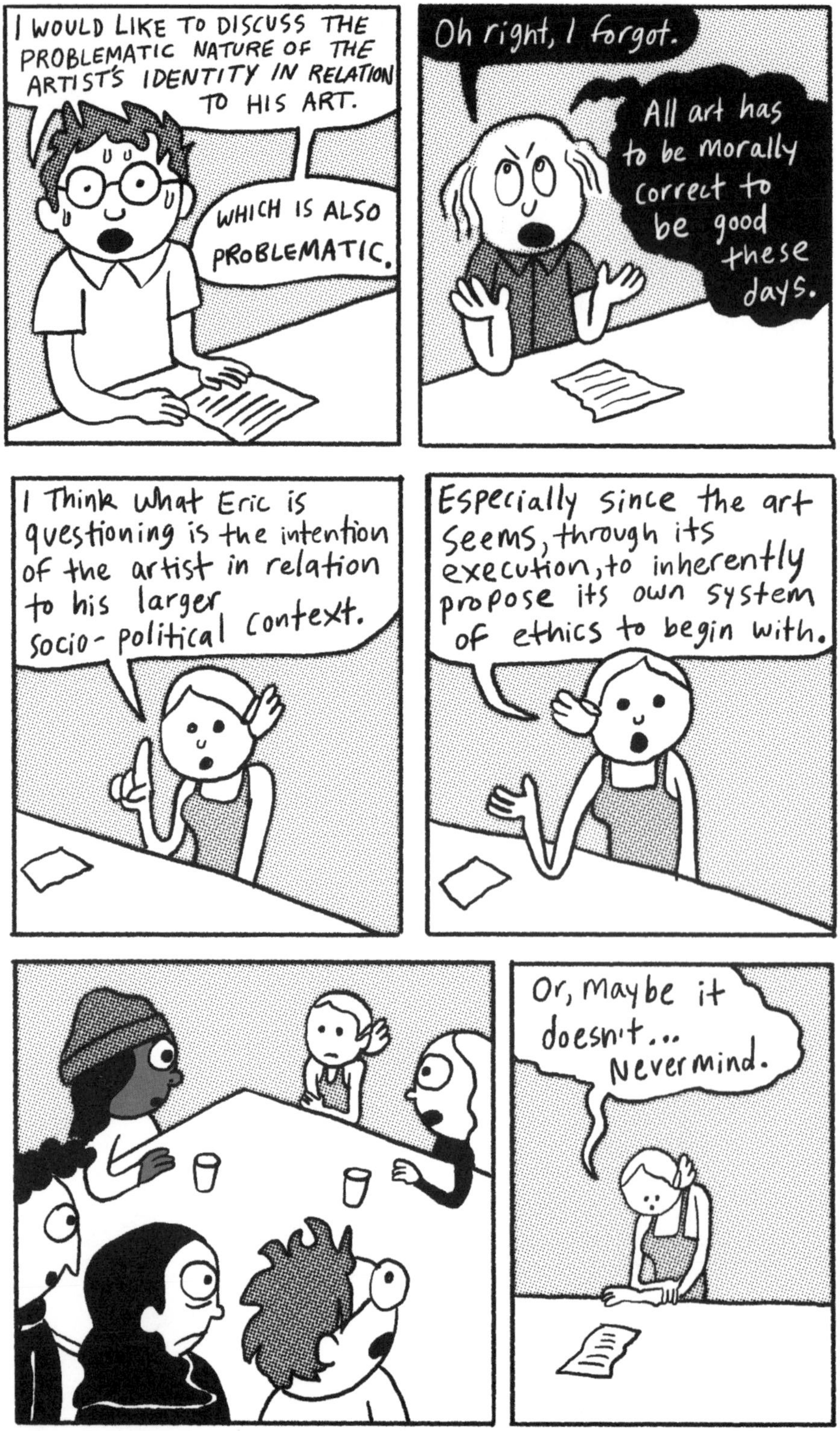
I WOULD LIKE TO DISCUSS THE PROBLEMATIC NATURE OF THE ARTIST'S IDENTITY IN RELATION TO HIS ART.
WHICH IS ALSO PROBLEMATIC.
Oh right, I forgot.
All art has to be morally correct to be good these days.
I Think what Eric is questioning is the intention of the artist in relation to his larger socio-political context.
Especially since the art seems, through its execution, to inherently propose its own system of ethics to begin with.
Or, maybe it doesn't... Nevermind.

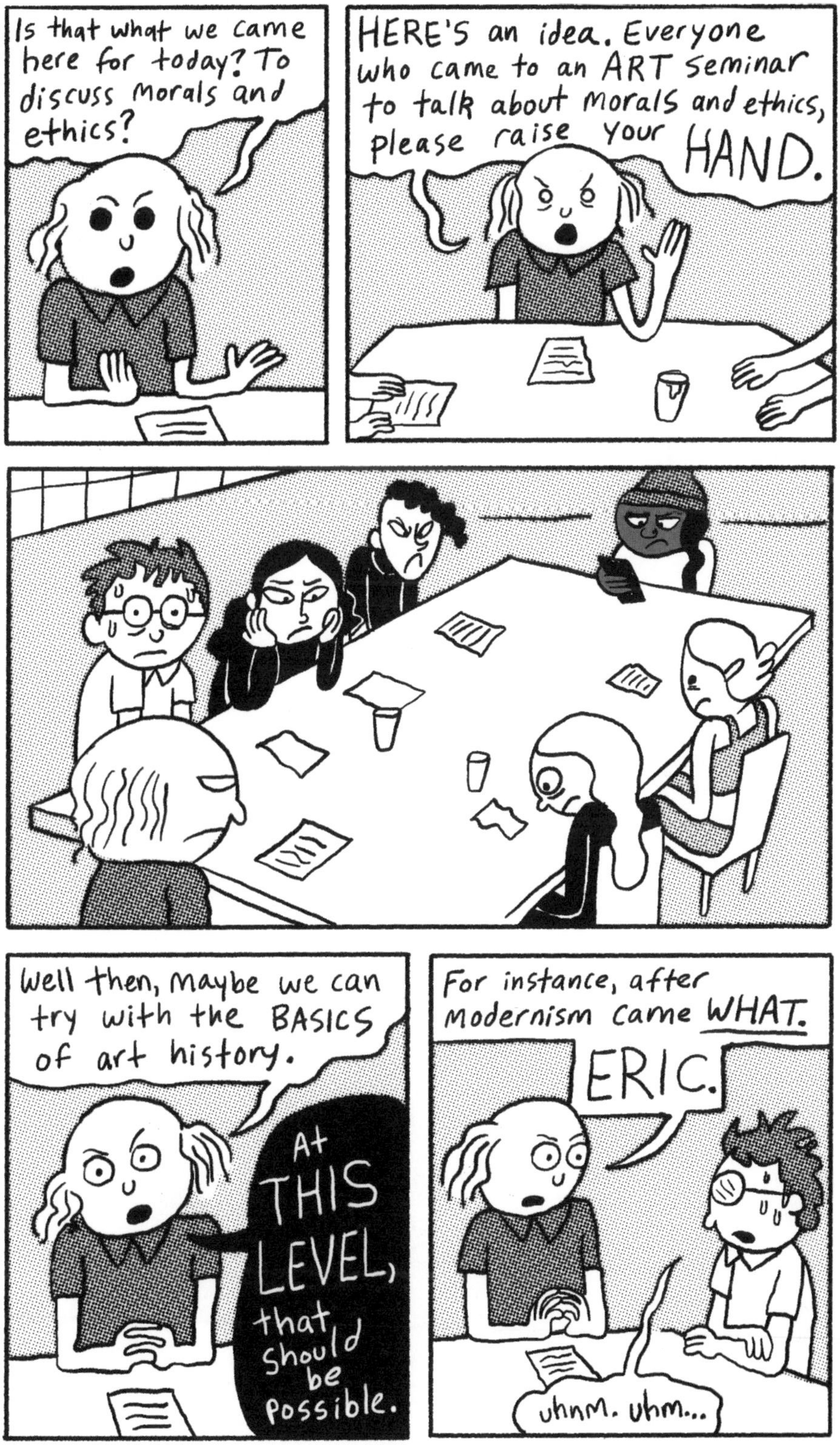
Is that what we came here for today? To discuss morals and ethics?
HERE'S an idea. Everyone who came to an ART seminar to talk about morals and ethics, please raise your HAND.
Well then, maybe we can try with the BASICS of art history.
At THIS LEVEL, that should be possible.
For instance, after modernism came WHAT.
ERIC.
uhnm. uhm...

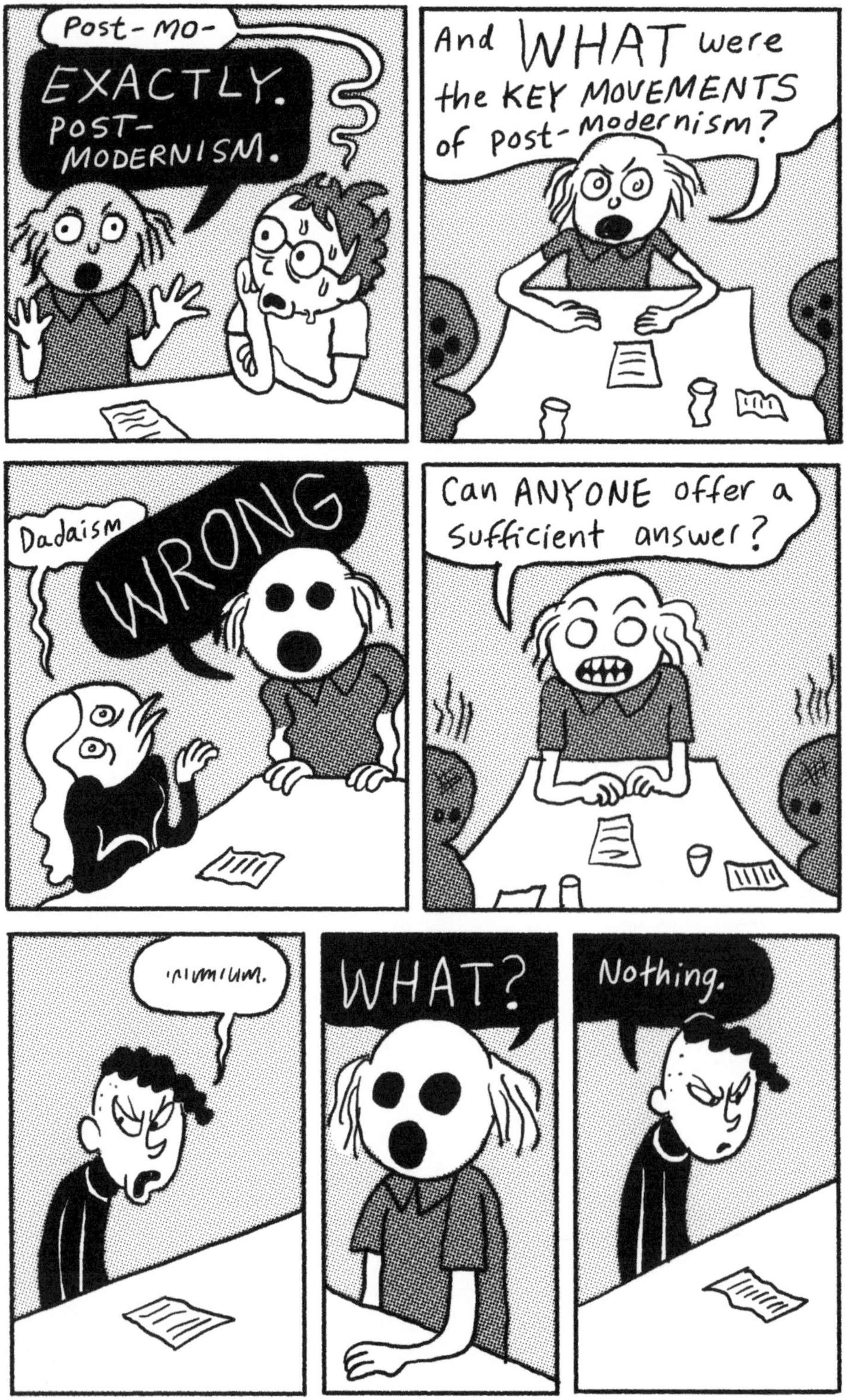
Post-mo-
EXACTLY. POST-MODERNISM.
And WHAT were the KEY MOVEMENTS of post-Modernism?
Dadaism
WRONG
Can ANYONE offer a sufficient answer?
WHAT?
Nothing.

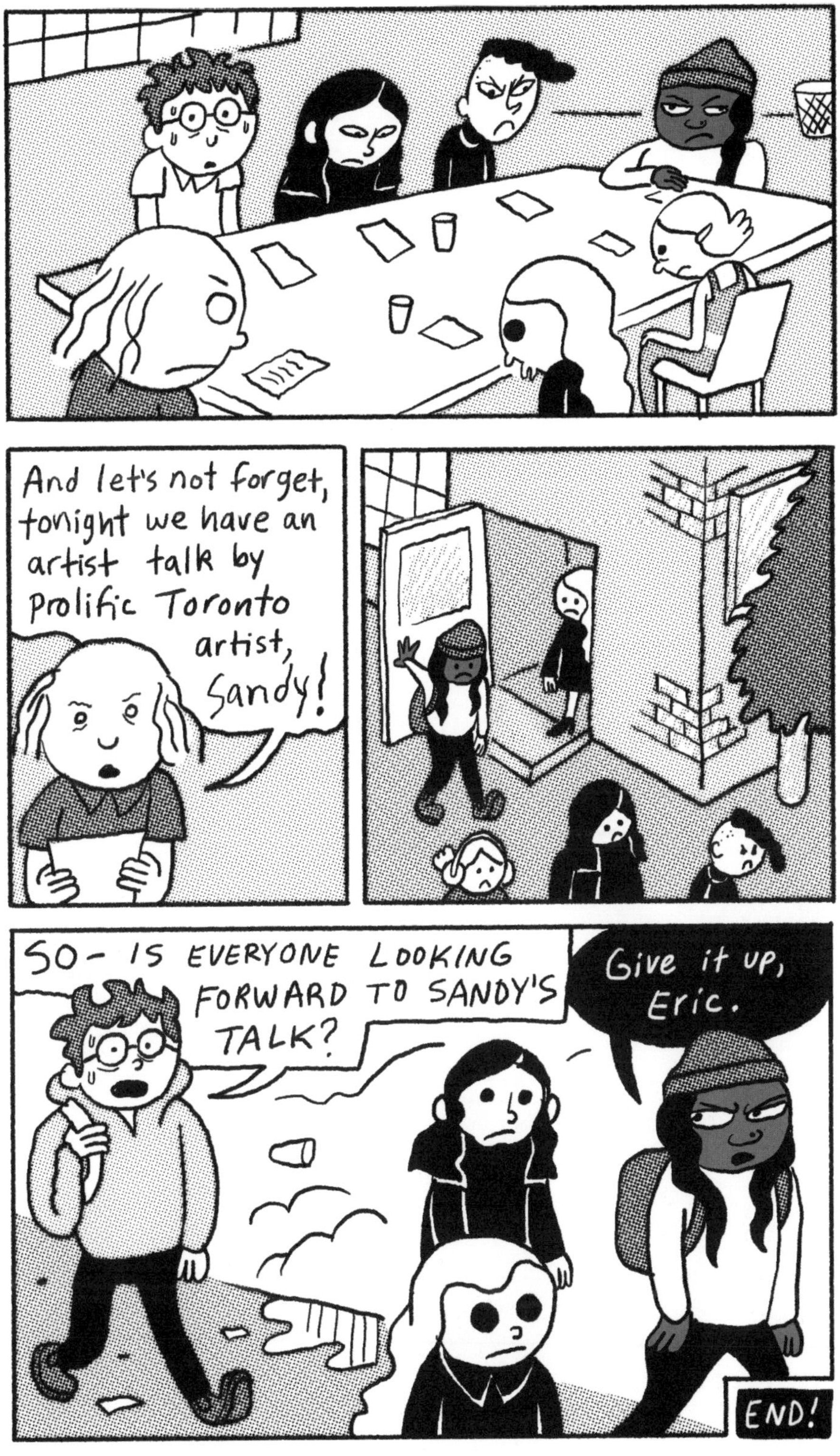
And let's not forget, tonight we have an artist talk by prolific Toronto artist, Sandy!
SO- IS EVERYONE LOOKING FORWARD TO SANDY'S TALK?
Give it up, Eric.
END!

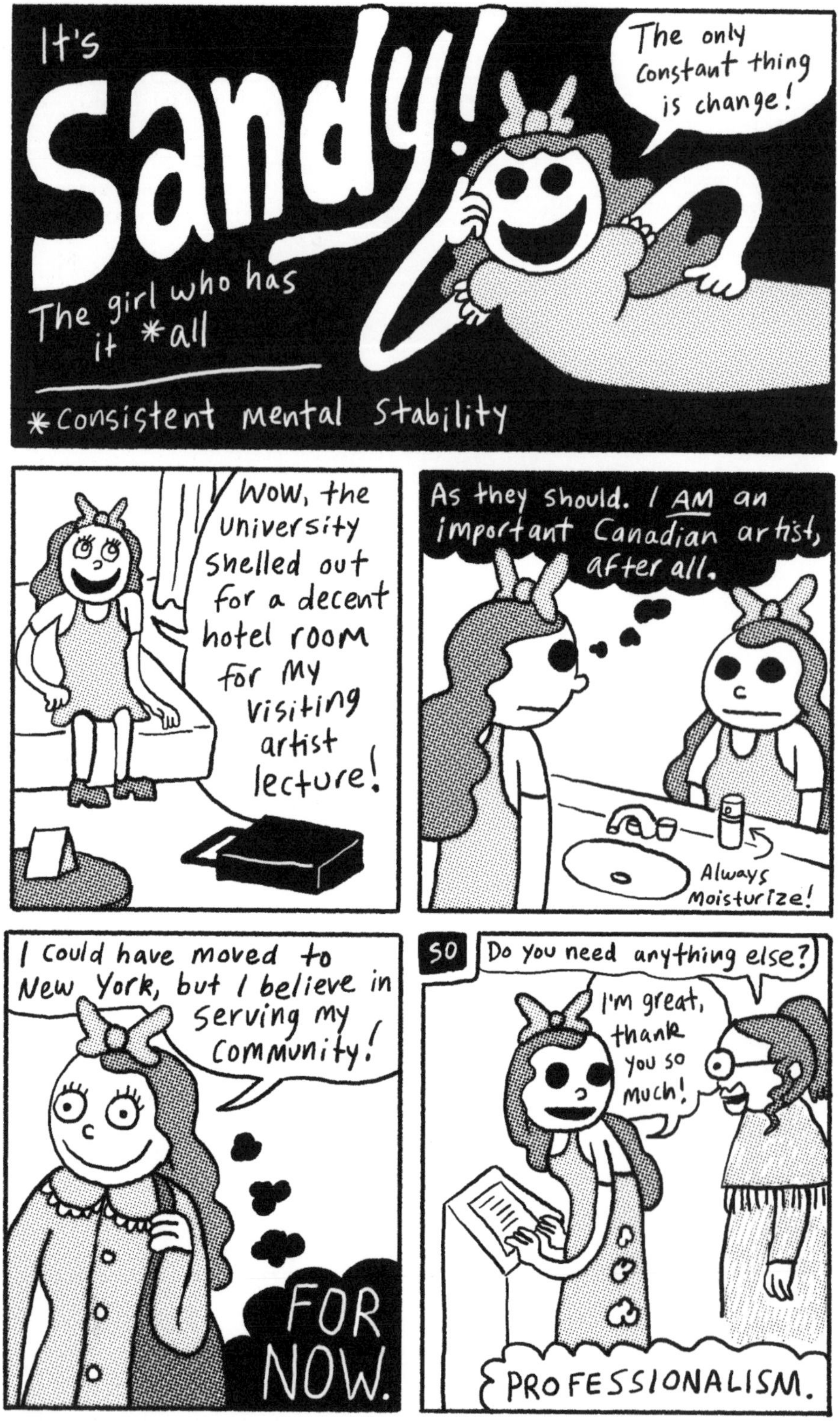

It's Sandy!
The only constant thing is change!
The girl who has it *all
*consistent mental stability
Wow, the university shelled out for a decent hotel room for my visiting artist lecture!
As they should. I AM an important Canadian artist, after all.
Always moisturize!
I could have moved to New York, but I believe in serving my community!
FOR NOW.
SO
Do you need anything else?
I'm great, thank you so much!
PROFESSIONALISM.

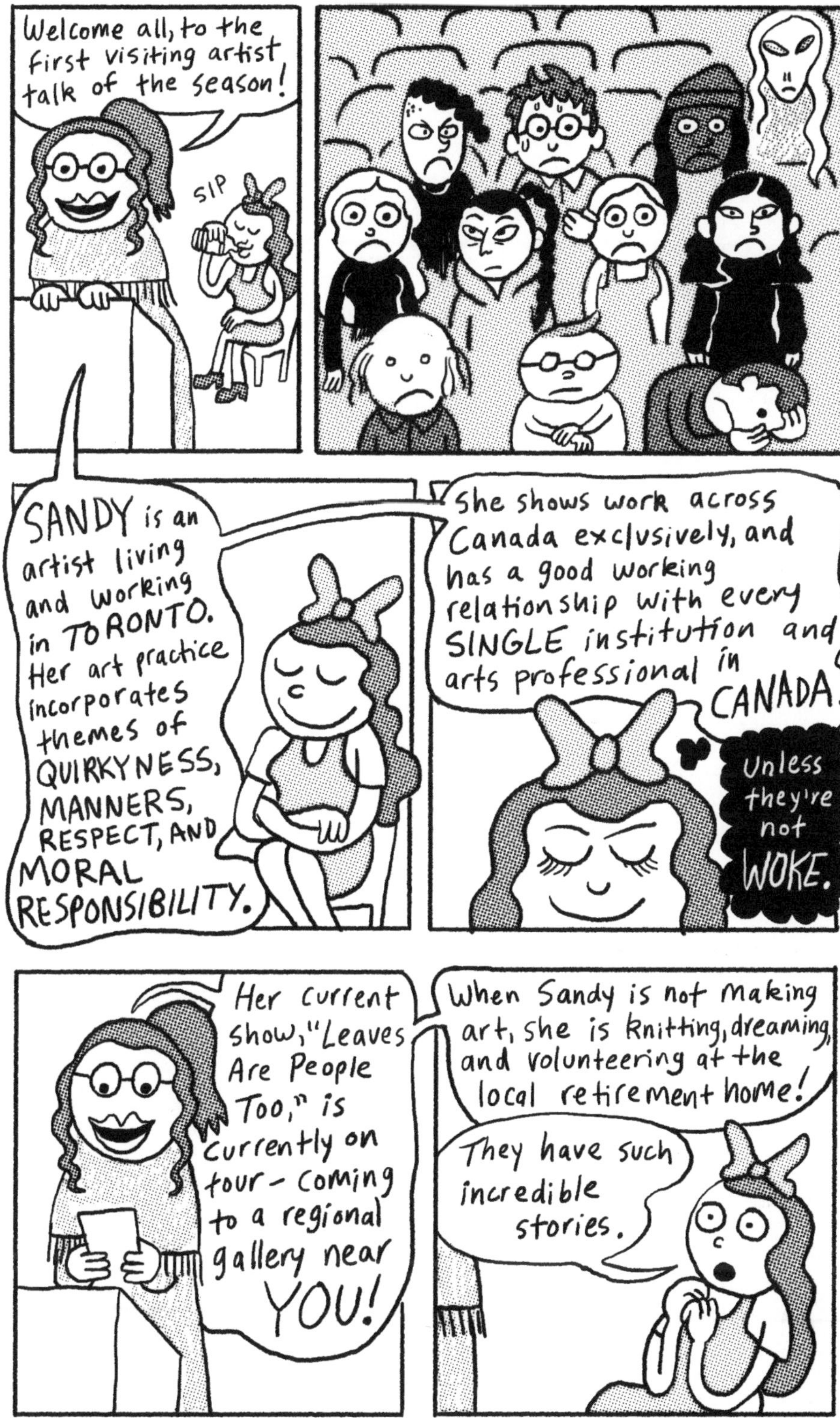
Welcome all, to the first visiting artist talk of the season!
SIP
SANDY is an artist living and working in TORONTO. Her art practice incorporates themes of QUIRKYNESS, MANNERS, RESPECT, AND MORAL RESPONSIBILITY.
She shows work across Canada exclusively, and has a good working relationship with every SINGLE institution and arts professional in CANADA.
Unless they're not WOKE.
Her current show, "Leaves Are People Too," is currently on tour - coming to a regional gallery near YOU!
When Sandy is not making art, she is knitting, dreaming, and volunteering at the local retirement home!
They have such incredible stories.

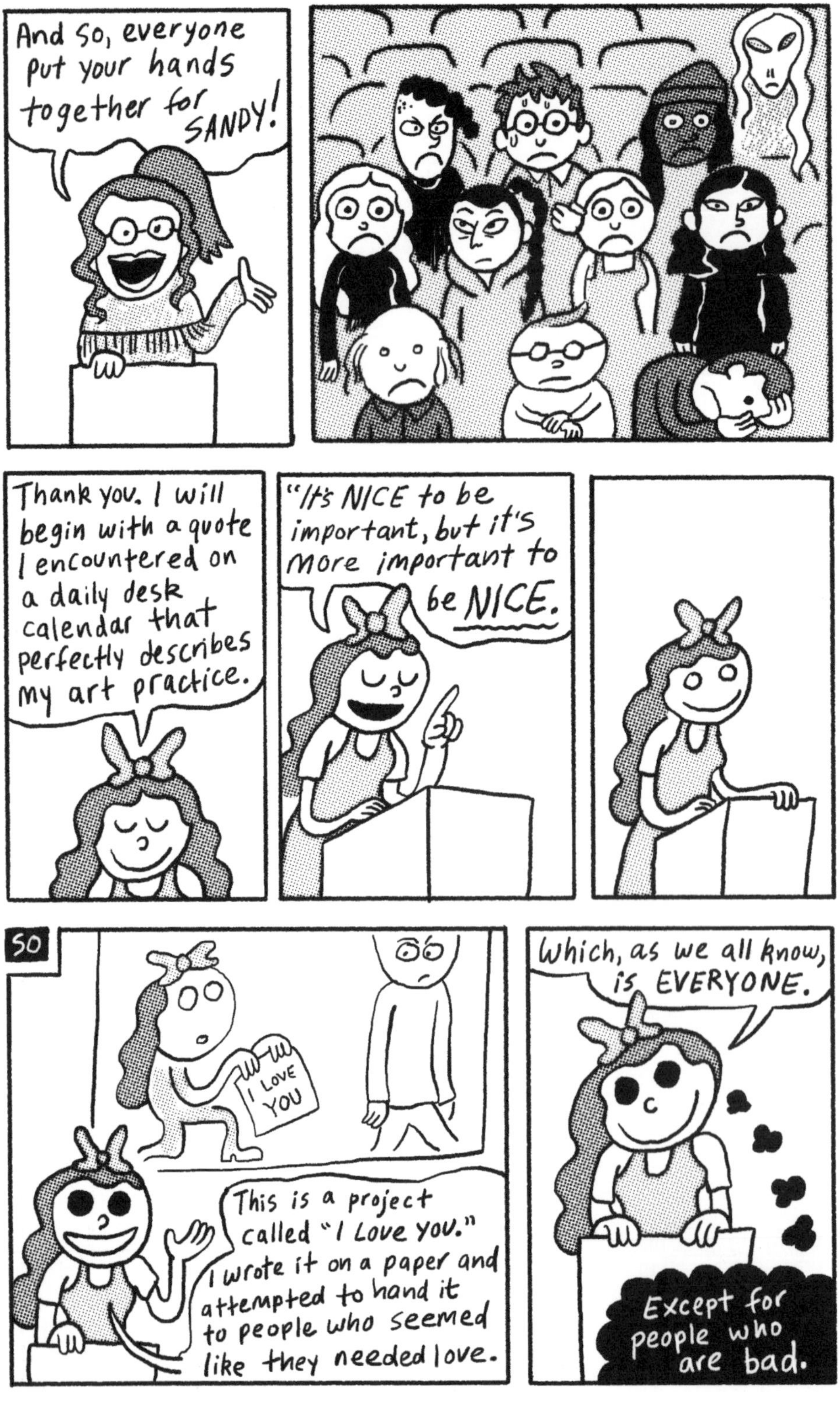
And so, everyone put your hands together for SANDY!
Thank you. I will begin with a quote I encountered on a daily desk calendar that perfectly describes my art practice.
"It's NICE to be important, but it's more important to be NICE.
50
I LOVE YOU
This is a project called "I Love You." I wrote it on a paper and attempted to hand it to people who seemed like they needed love.
Which, as we all know, is EVERYONE.
Except for people who are bad.

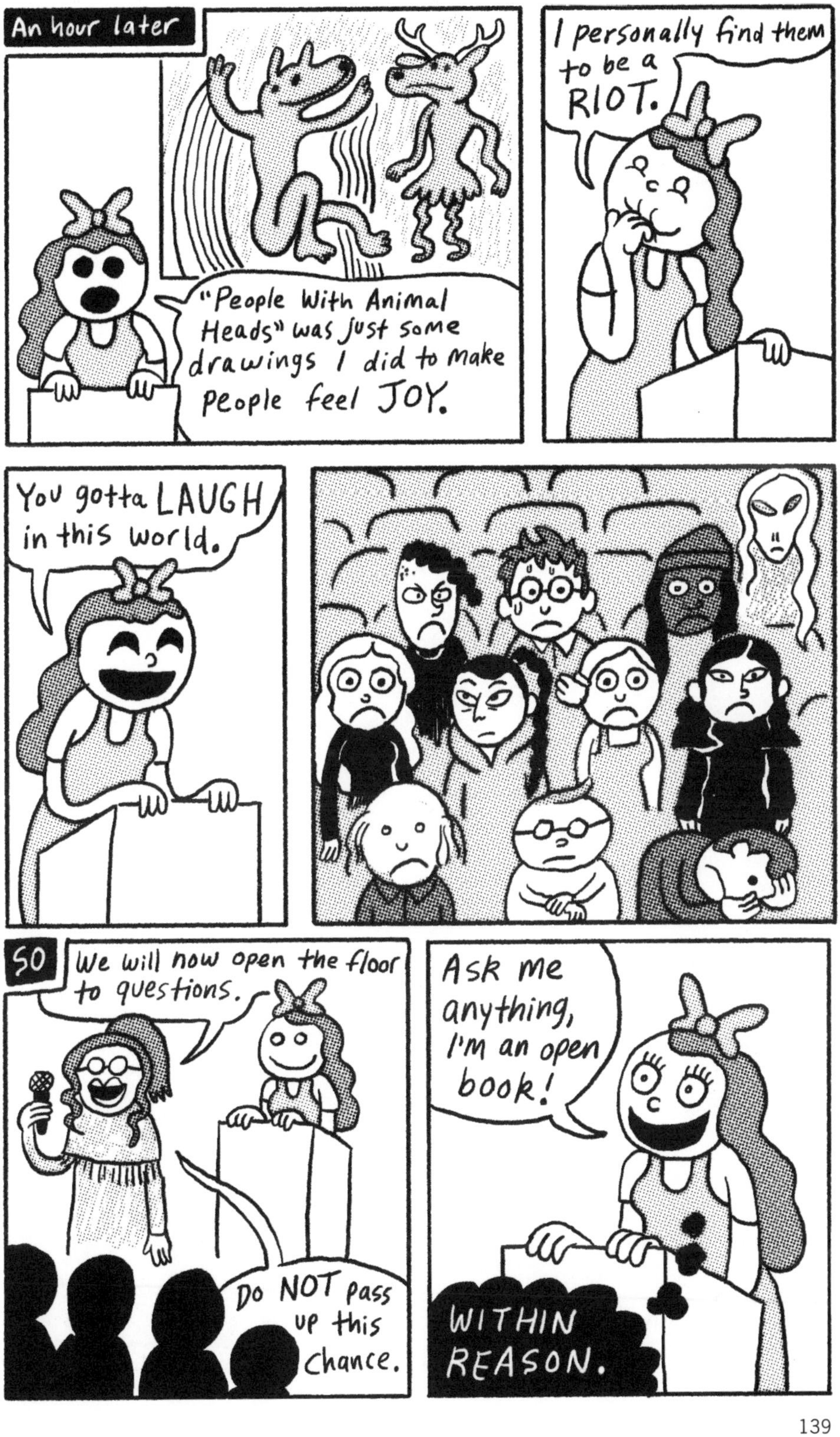
An hour later
"People With Animal Heads" was just some drawings I did to make people feel JOY.
I personally find them to be a RIOT.
You gotta LAUGH in this world.
SO
We will now open the floor to questions.
Do NOT pass up this chance.
Ask me anything, I'm an open book!
WITHIN REASON.

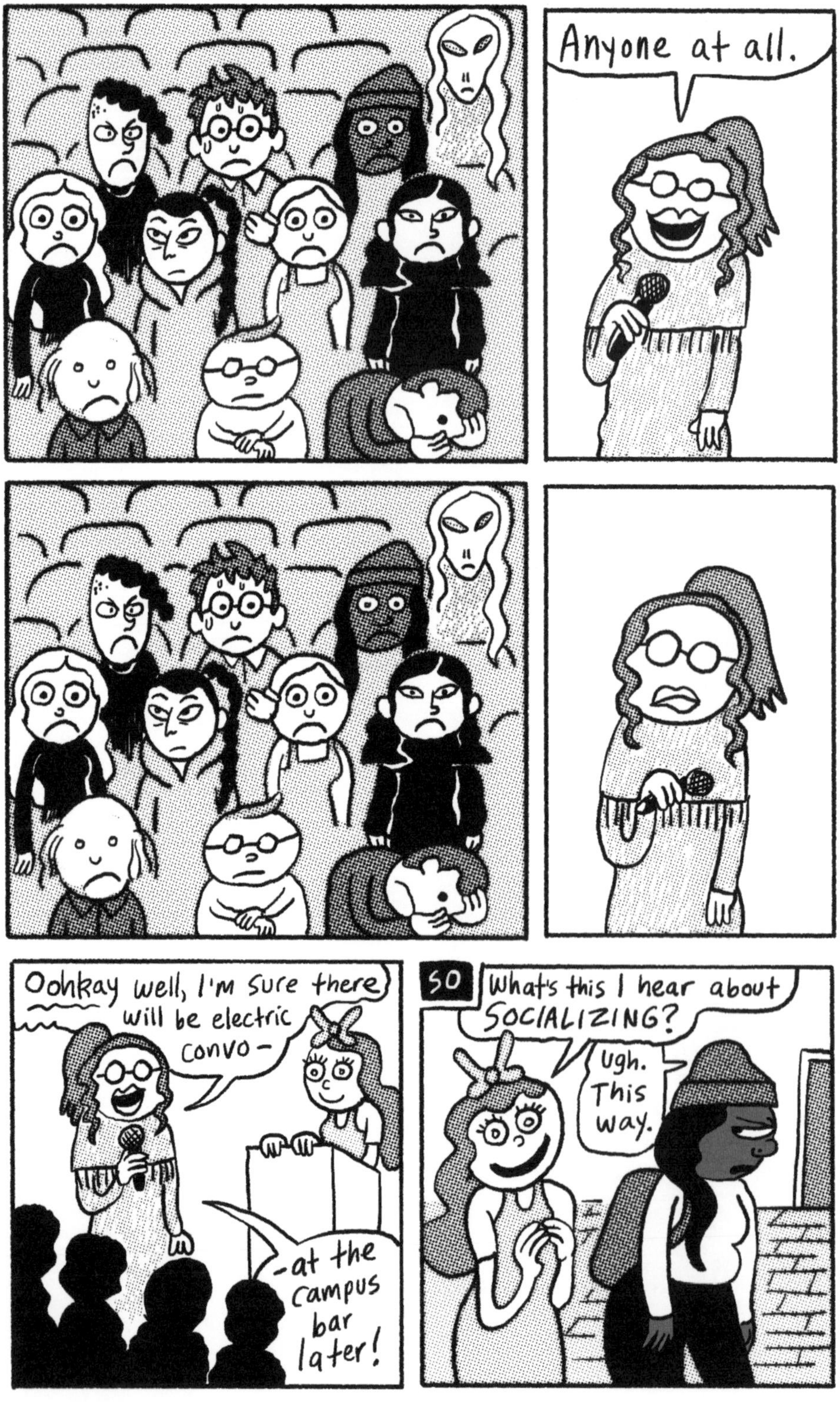
Anyone at all.
Oohkay well, I'm sure there will be electric convo-
-at the campus bar later!
SO
What's this I hear about SOCIALIZING?
Ugh. This way.

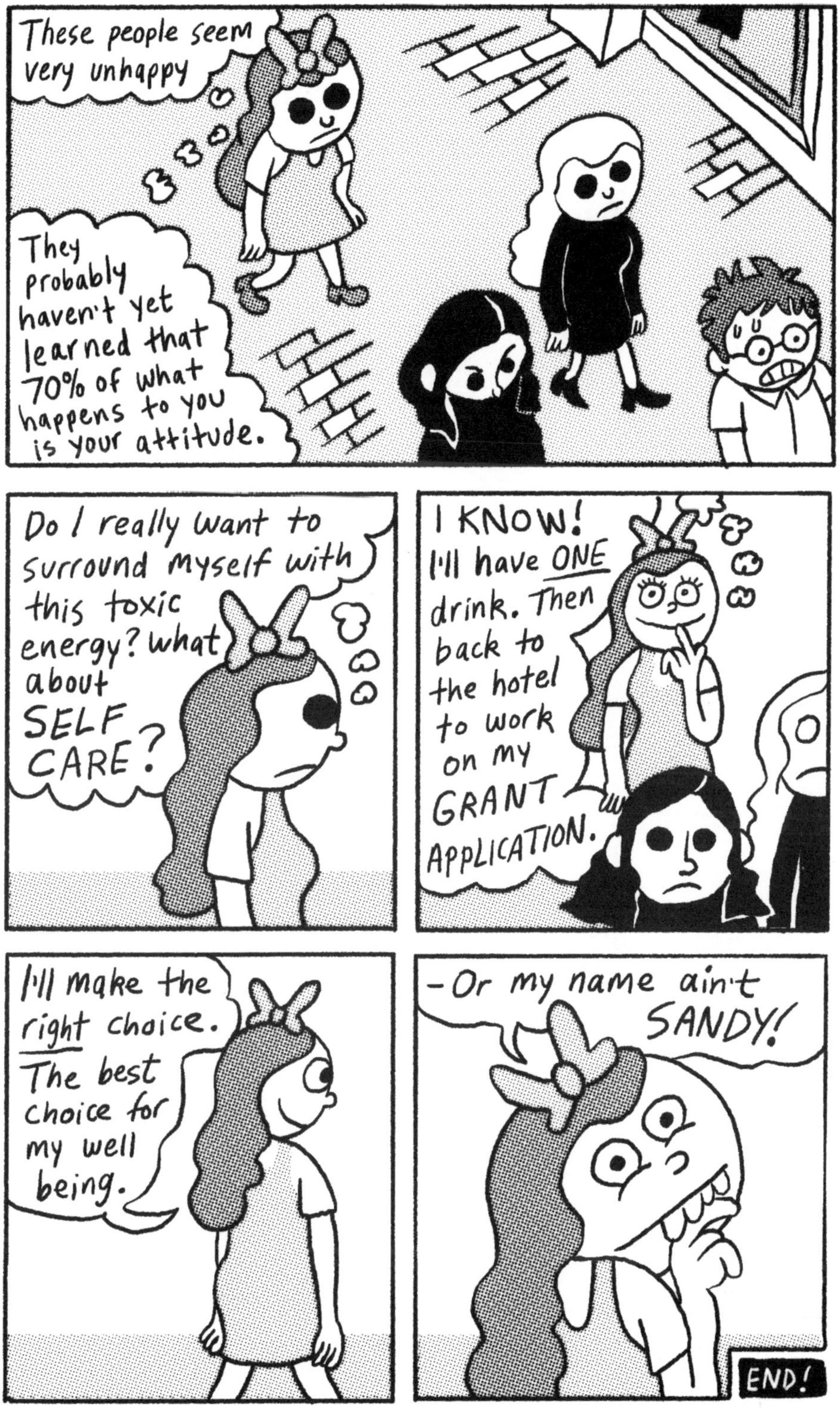
These people seem very unhappy
They probably haven't yet learned that 70% of what happens to you is your attitude.
Do I really want to surround myself with this toxic energy? what about SELF CARE?
I KNOW! I'll have ONE drink. Then back to the hotel to work on my GRANT APPLICATION.
I'll make the right choice. The best choice for my well being.
-Or my name ain't SANDY!
END!

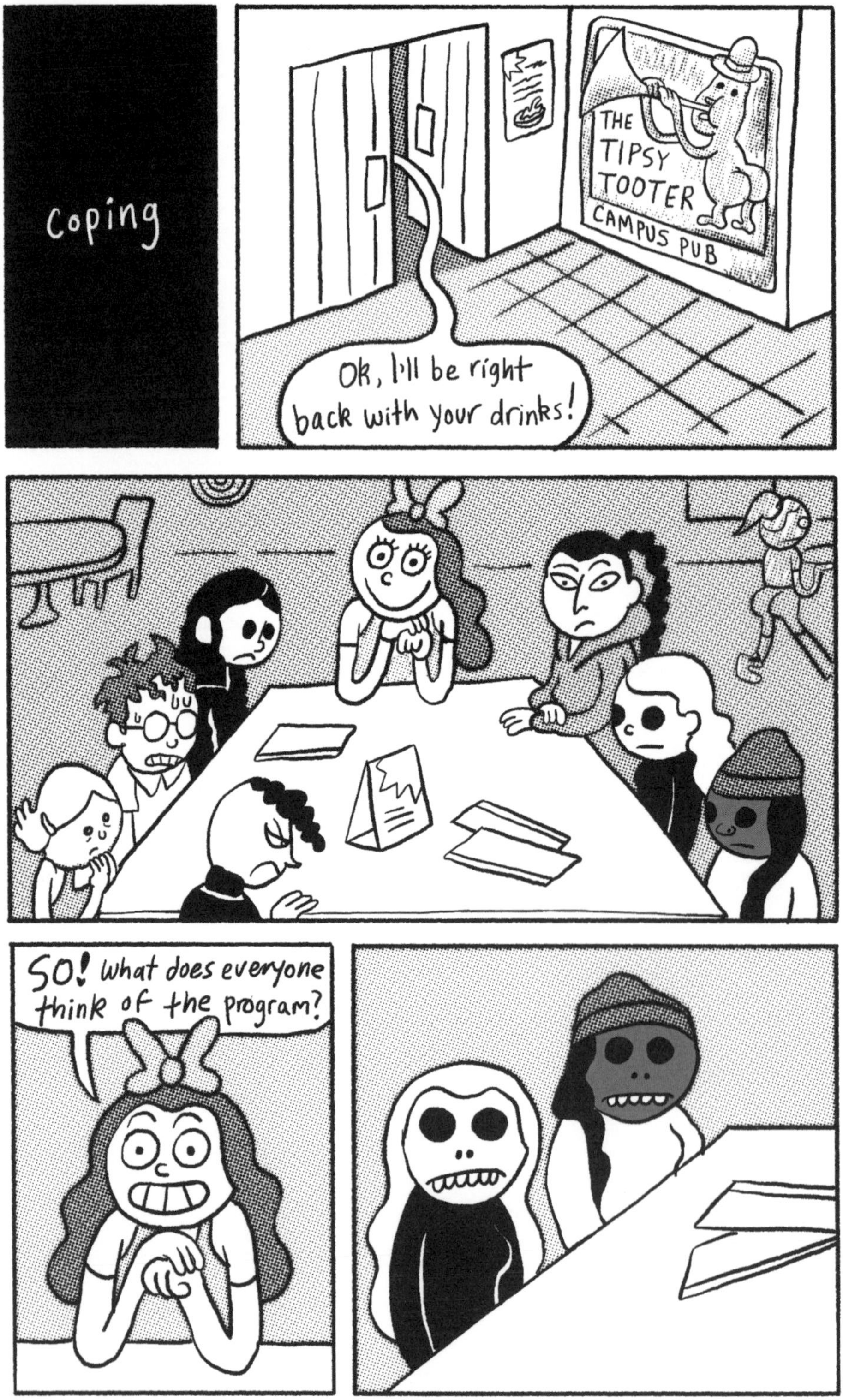
Coping
THE TIPSY TOOTER CAMPUS PUB
Ok, I'll be right back with your drinks!
SO! What does everyone think of the program?

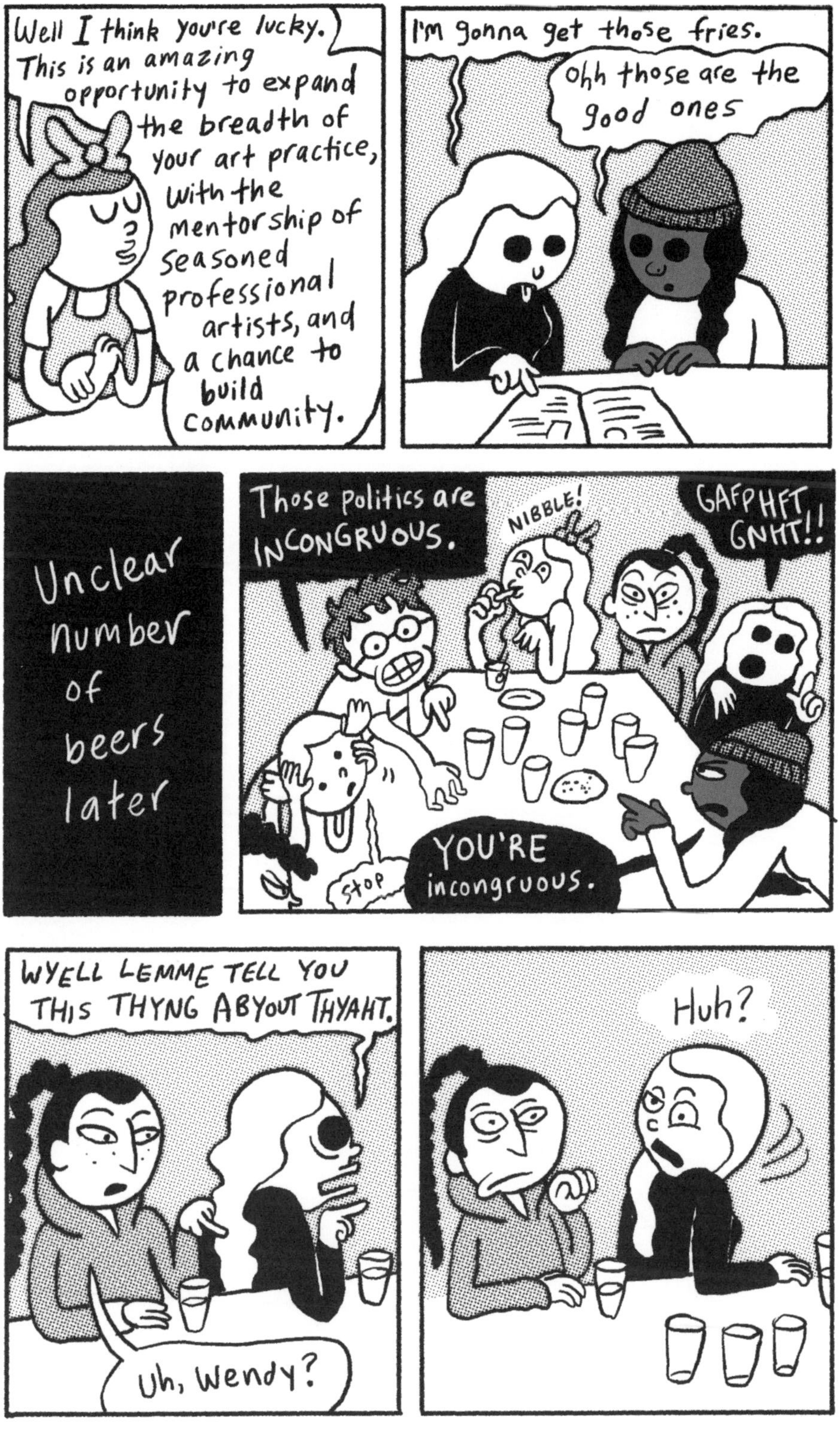
Well I think you're lucky. This is an amazing opportunity to expand the breadth of your art practice, with the mentorship of seasoned professional artists, and a chance to build community.
I'm gonna get those fries.
Ohh those are the good ones
Unclear number of beers later
Those politics are INCONGRUOUS.
NIBBLE!
GAFPHFT GNHT!!
stop
YOU'RE incongruous.
WYELL LEMME TELL YOU THIS THYNG ABYOUT THYAHT.
Uh, Wendy?
Huh?

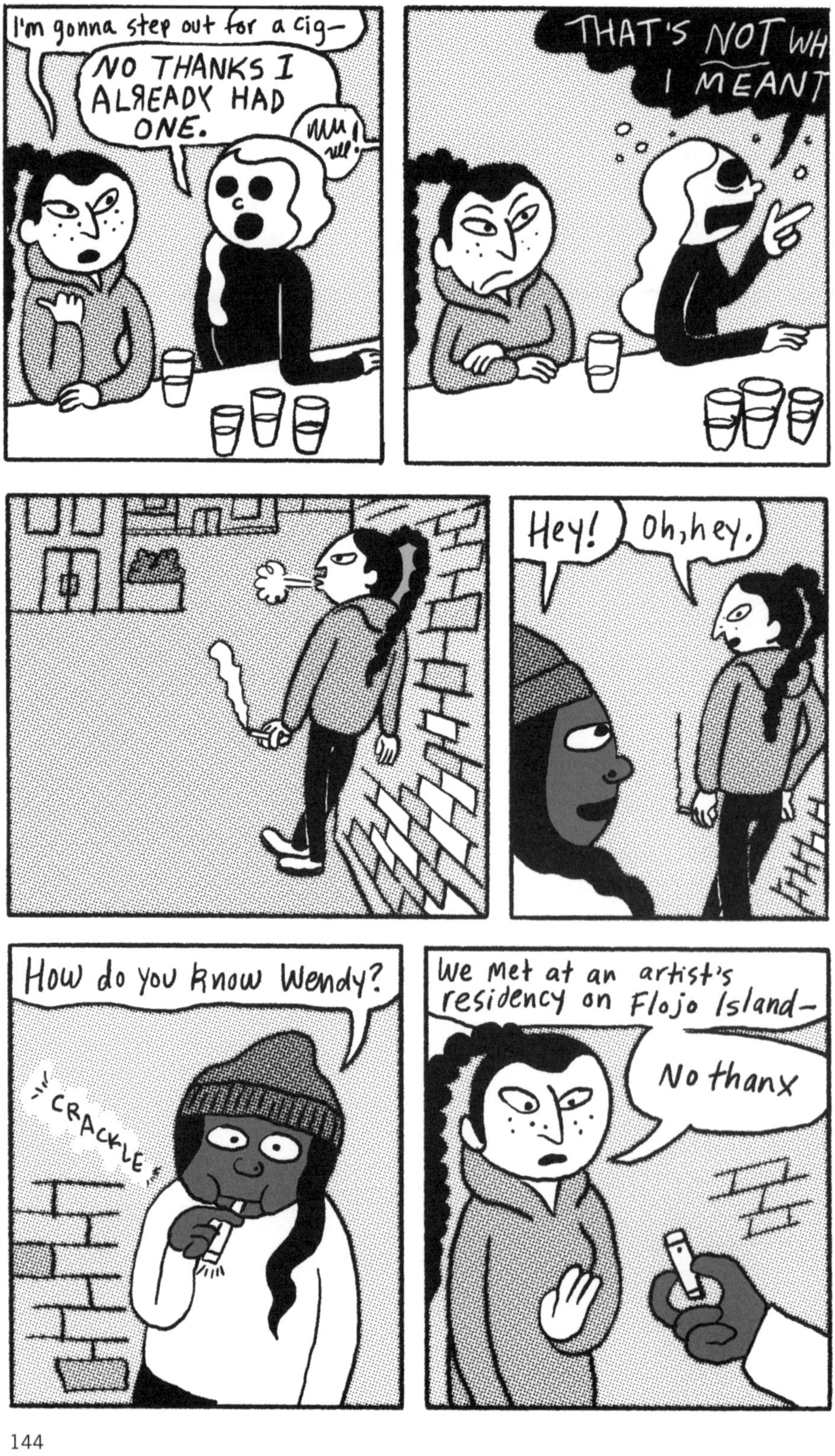
I'm gonna step out for a cig—
NO THANKS I ALREADY HAD ONE.
THAT'S NOT WH
I MEANT
Hey!
Oh, hey.
How do you know Wendy?
CRACKLE
We met at an artist's residency on Flojo Island—
No thanx

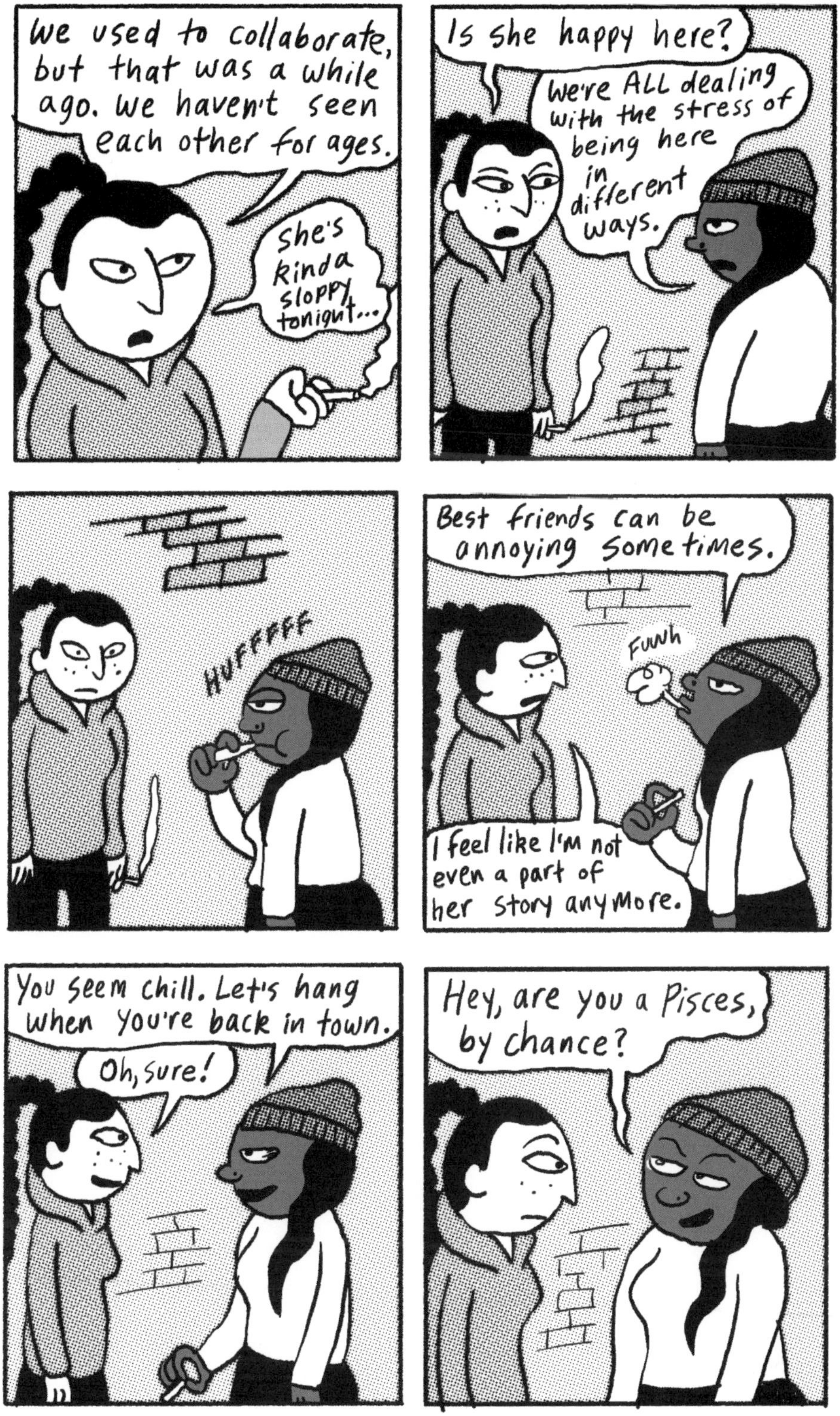

We used to collaborate, but that was a while ago. We haven't seen each other for ages.
She's kinda sloppy tonight...
Is she happy here?
We're ALL dealing with the stress of being here in different ways.
HUFFFFF
Best friends can be annoying sometimes.
Fuuh
I feel like I'm not even a part of her story anymore.
You seem chill. Let's hang when you're back in town.
Oh, sure!
Hey, are you a Pisces, by chance?

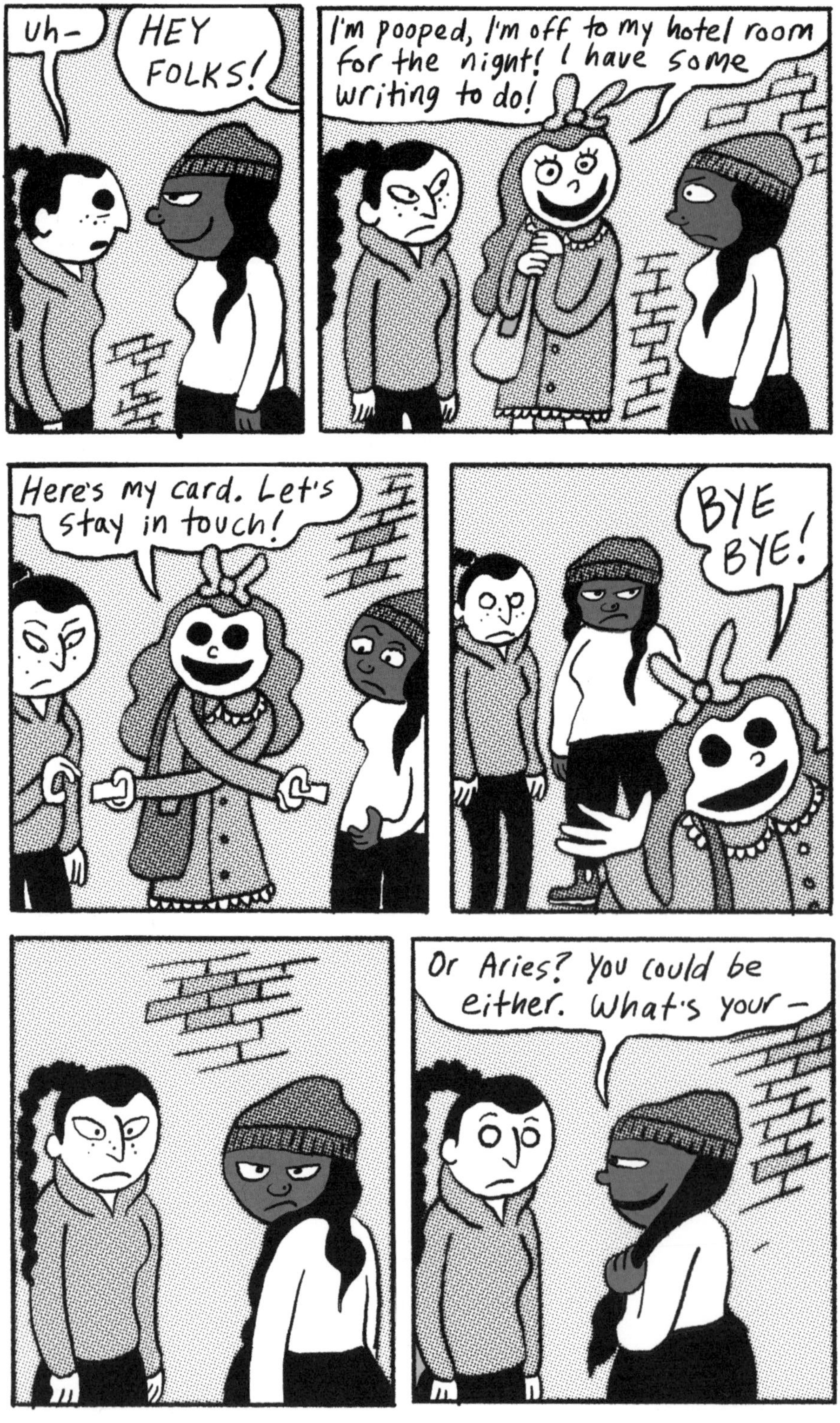
Uh-
HEY FOLKS!
I'm pooped, I'm off to my hotel room for the night! I have some writing to do!
Here's my card. Let's stay in touch!
BYE BYE!
Or Aries? You could be either. What's your-

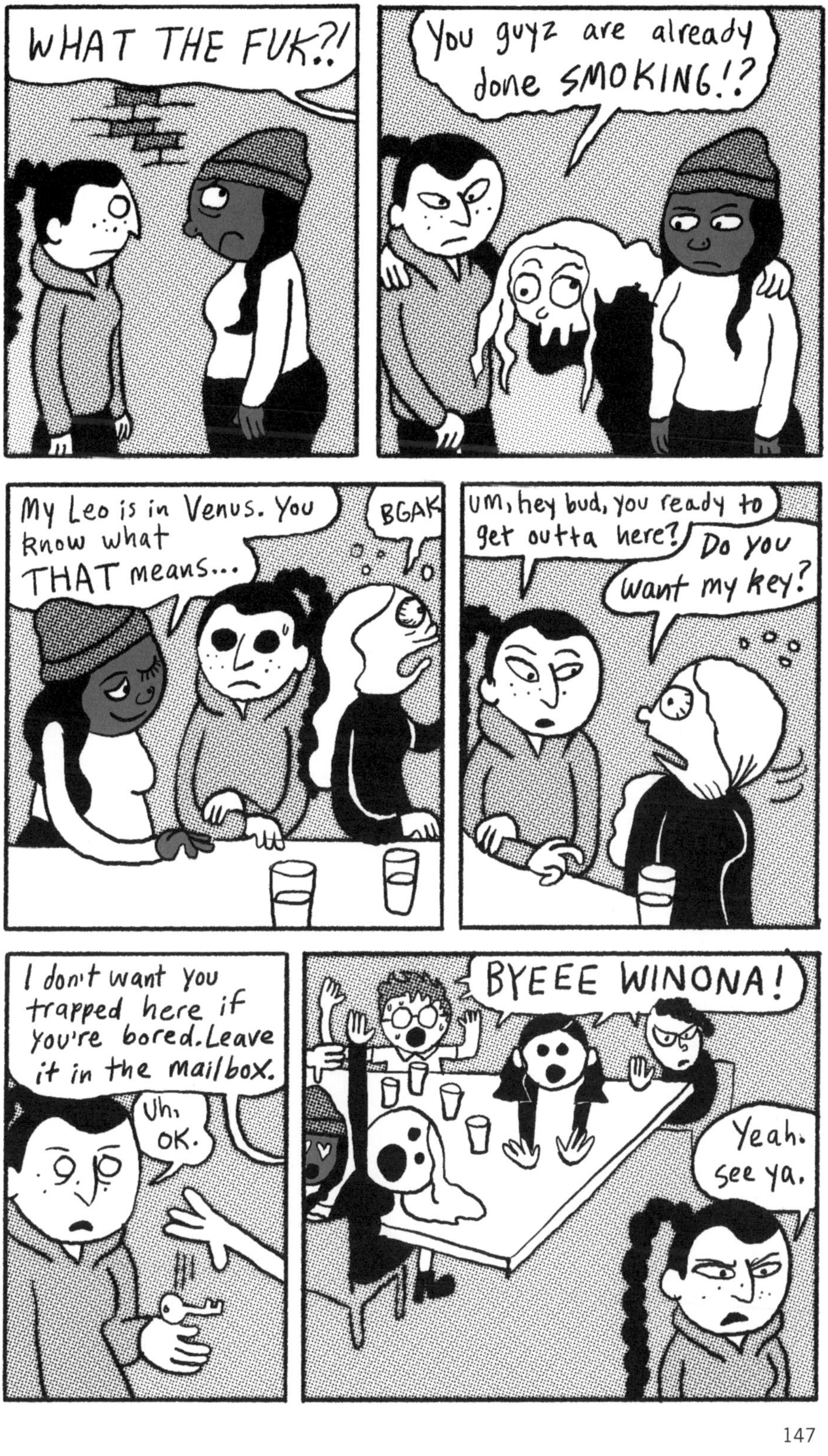
WHAT THE FUK?!
You guyz are already done SMOKING!?
My Leo is in Venus. You know what THAT means...
BGAK
Um, hey bud, you ready to get outta here?
Do you want my key?
I don't want you trapped here if you're bored. Leave it in the mailbox.
Uh, OK.
BYEEE WINONA!
Yeah. see ya.

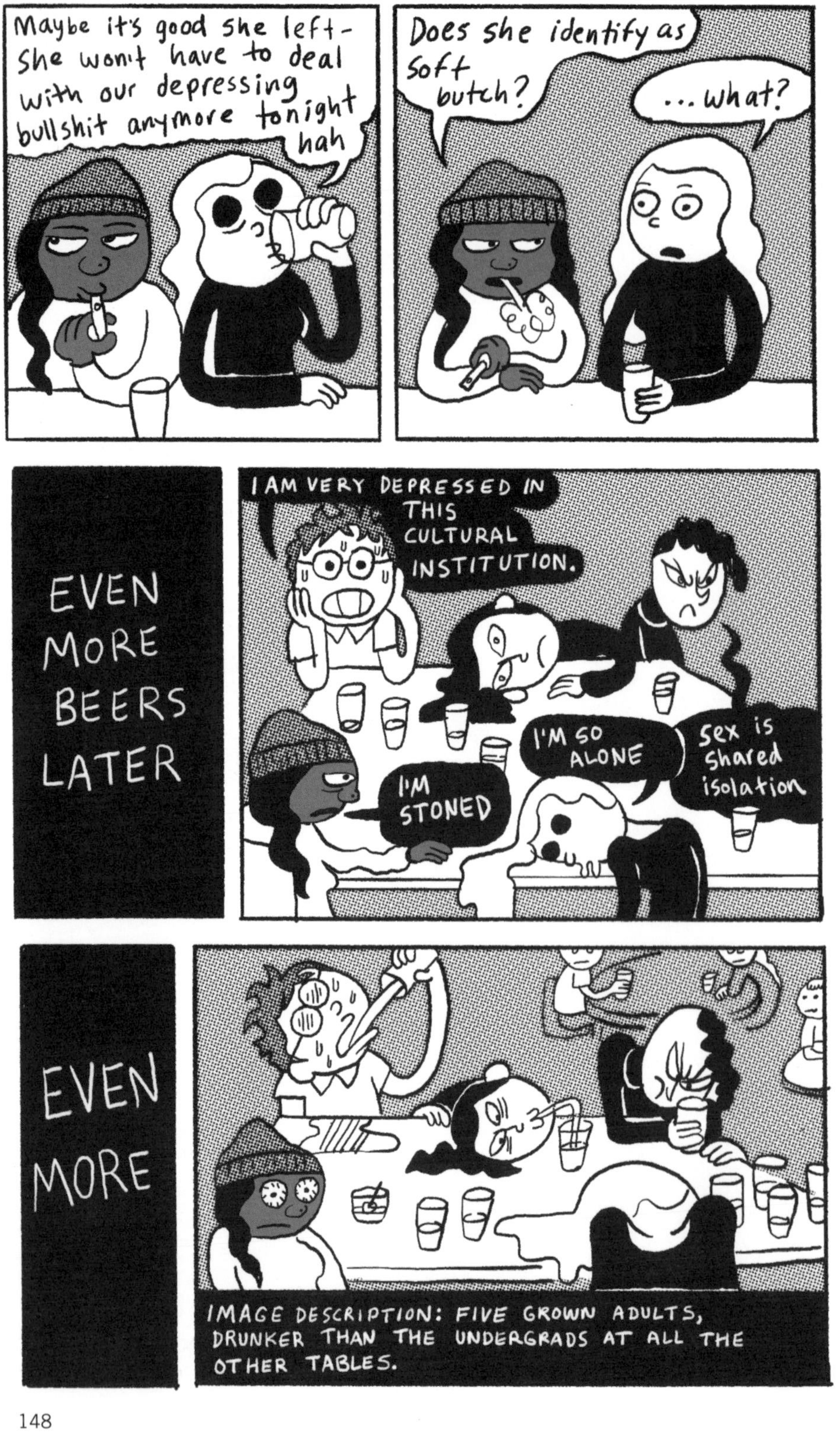
Maybe it's good she left- she won't have to deal with our depressing bullshit anymore tonight hah
Does she identify as soft butch?
...what?
EVEN MORE BEERS LATER
I AM VERY DEPRESSED IN THIS CULTURAL INSTITUTION.
I'M SO ALONE
sex is shared isolation
I'M STONED
EVEN MORE
IMAGE DESCRIPTION: FIVE GROWN ADULTS, DRUNKER THAN THE UNDERGRADS AT ALL THE OTHER TABLES.

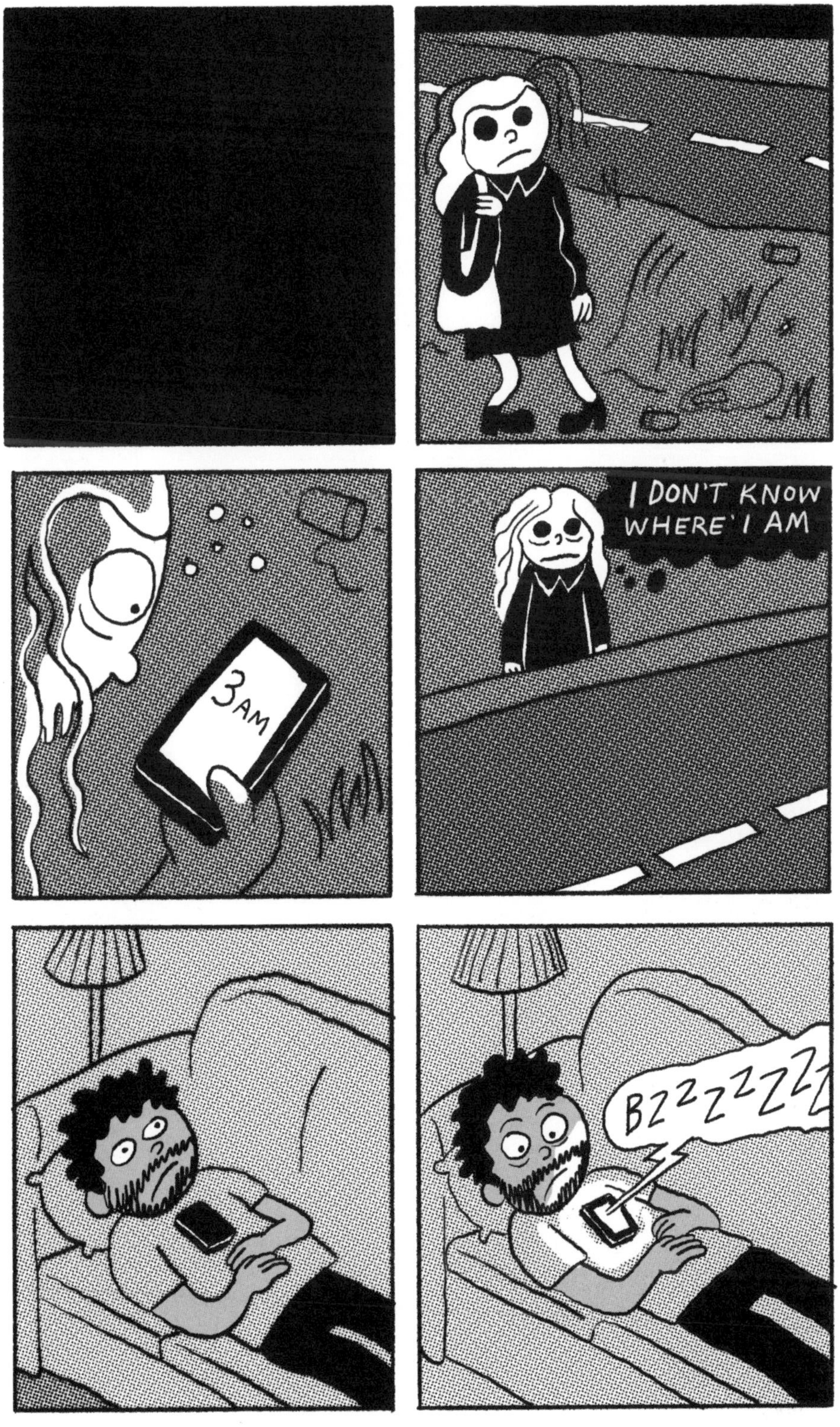
I DON'T KNOW WHERE I AM
3AM
BZZZZZZZ

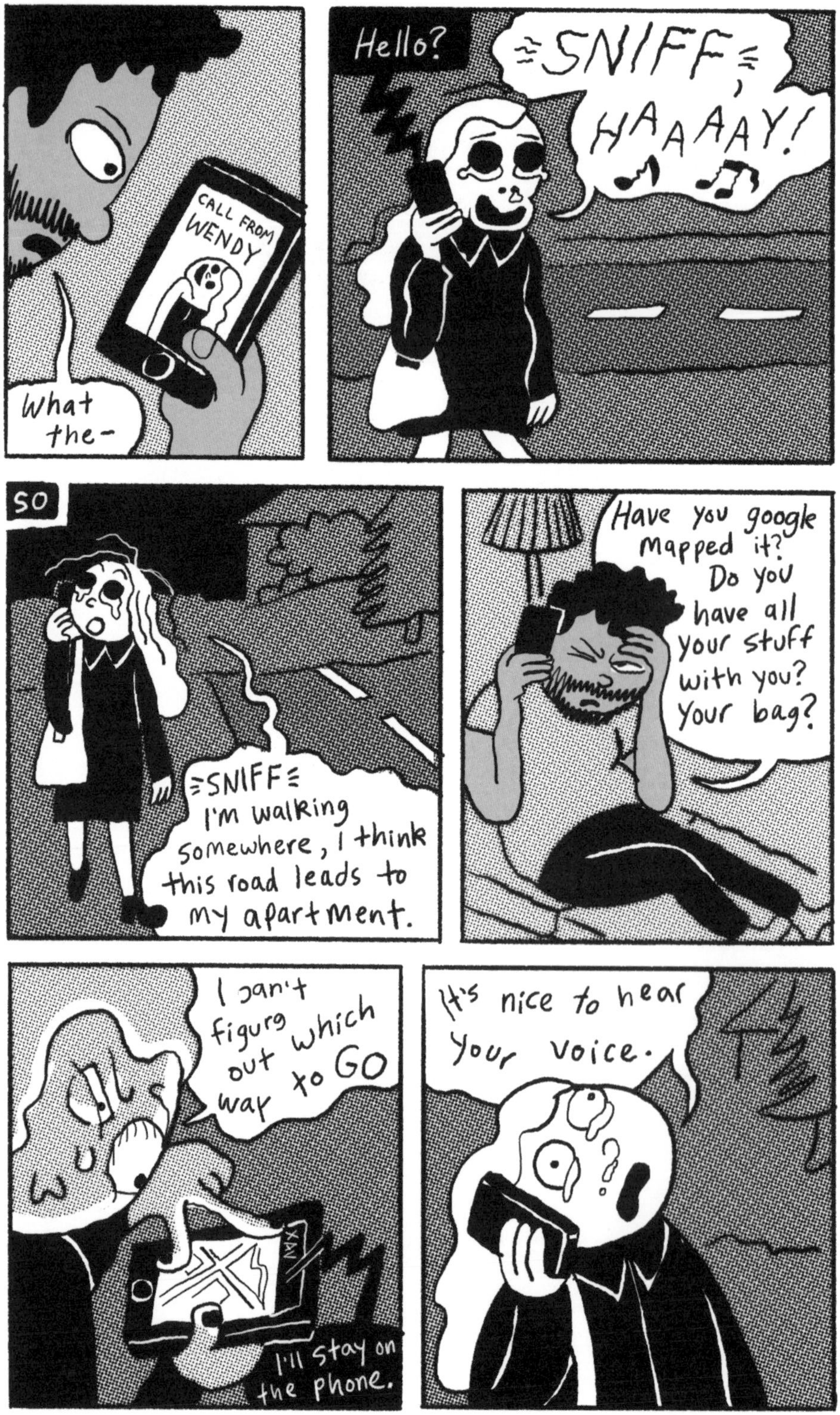
CALL FROM WENDY
What the-
Hello?
SNIFF, HAAAAY!
SO
SNIFF I'm walking somewhere, I think this road leads to my apartment.
Have you google mapped it? Do you have all your stuff with you? Your bag?
I can't figure out which way to GO
I'll stay on the phone.
It's nice to hear your voice.

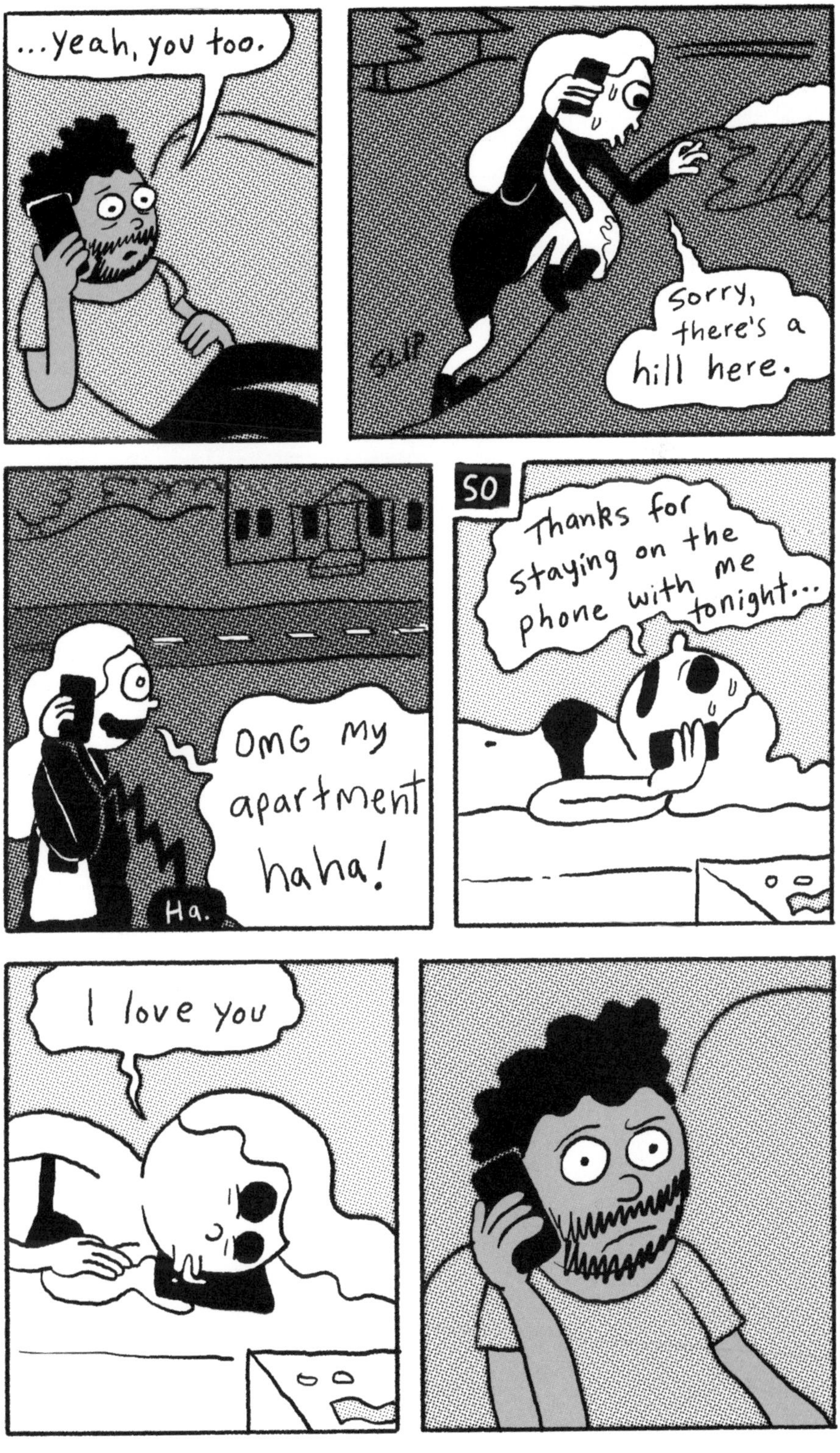
...yeah, you too.
SLIP
Sorry, there's a hill here.
OMG my apartment haha!
Ha.
SO
Thanks for staying on the phone with me tonight...
I love you

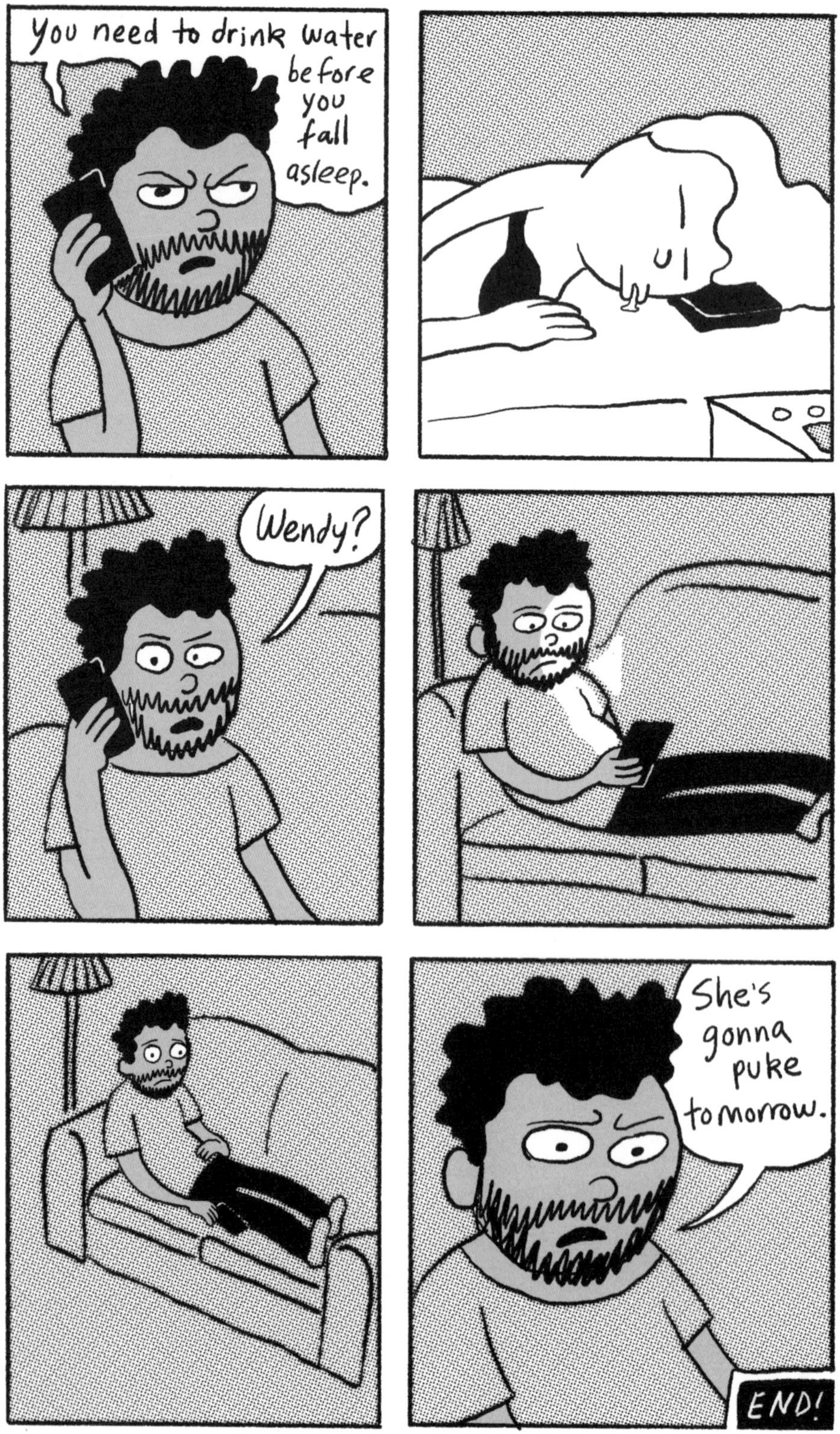
You need to drink water before you fall asleep.
Wendy?
She's gonna puke tomorrow.
END!

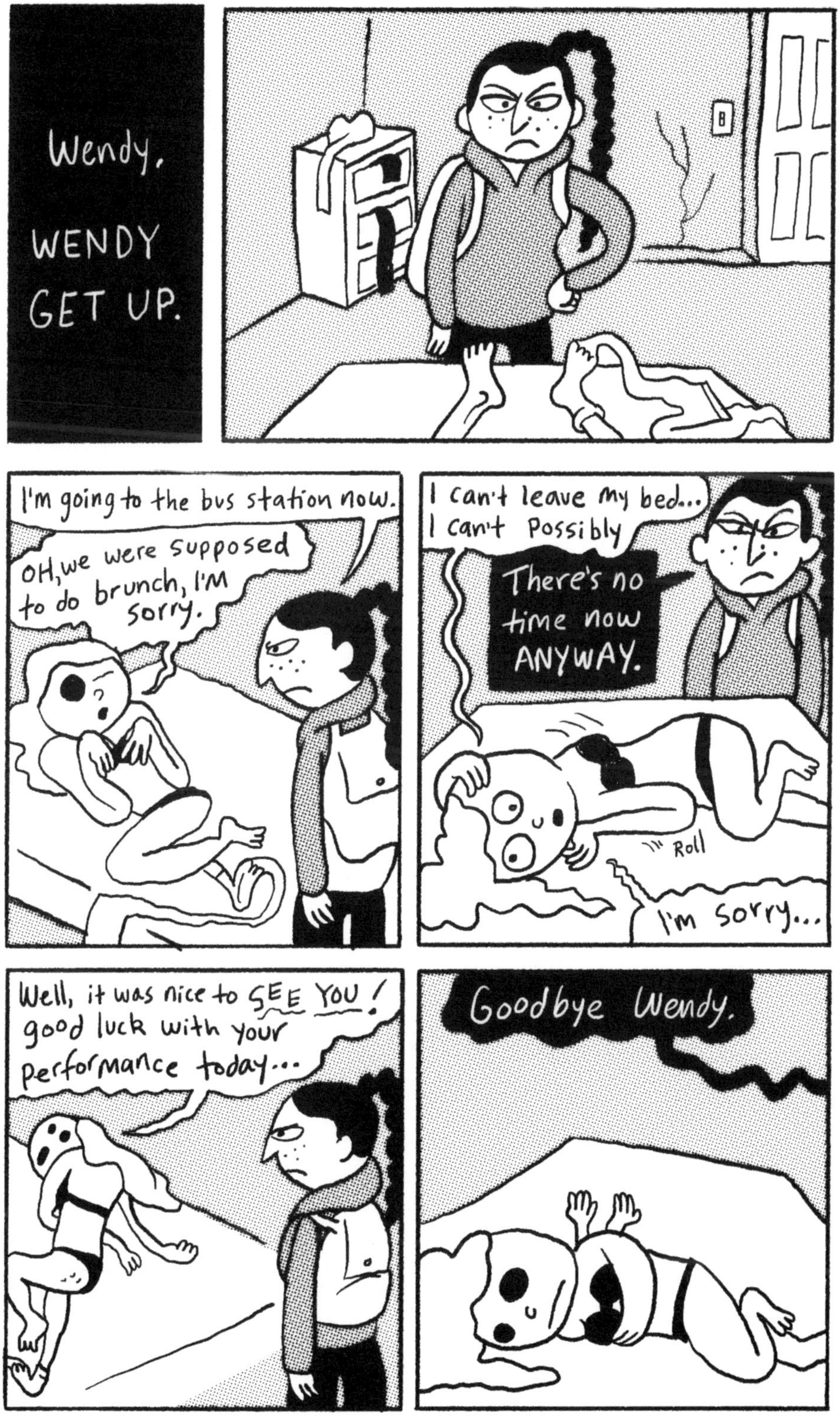
Wendy.
WENDY
GET UP.
I'm going to the bus station now.
OH, we were supposed to do brunch, I'M sorry.
I can't leave my bed... I can't possibly
There's no time now ANYWAY.
Roll
I'm sorry...
Well, it was nice to SEE YOU! good luck with your performance today...
Goodbye Wendy.

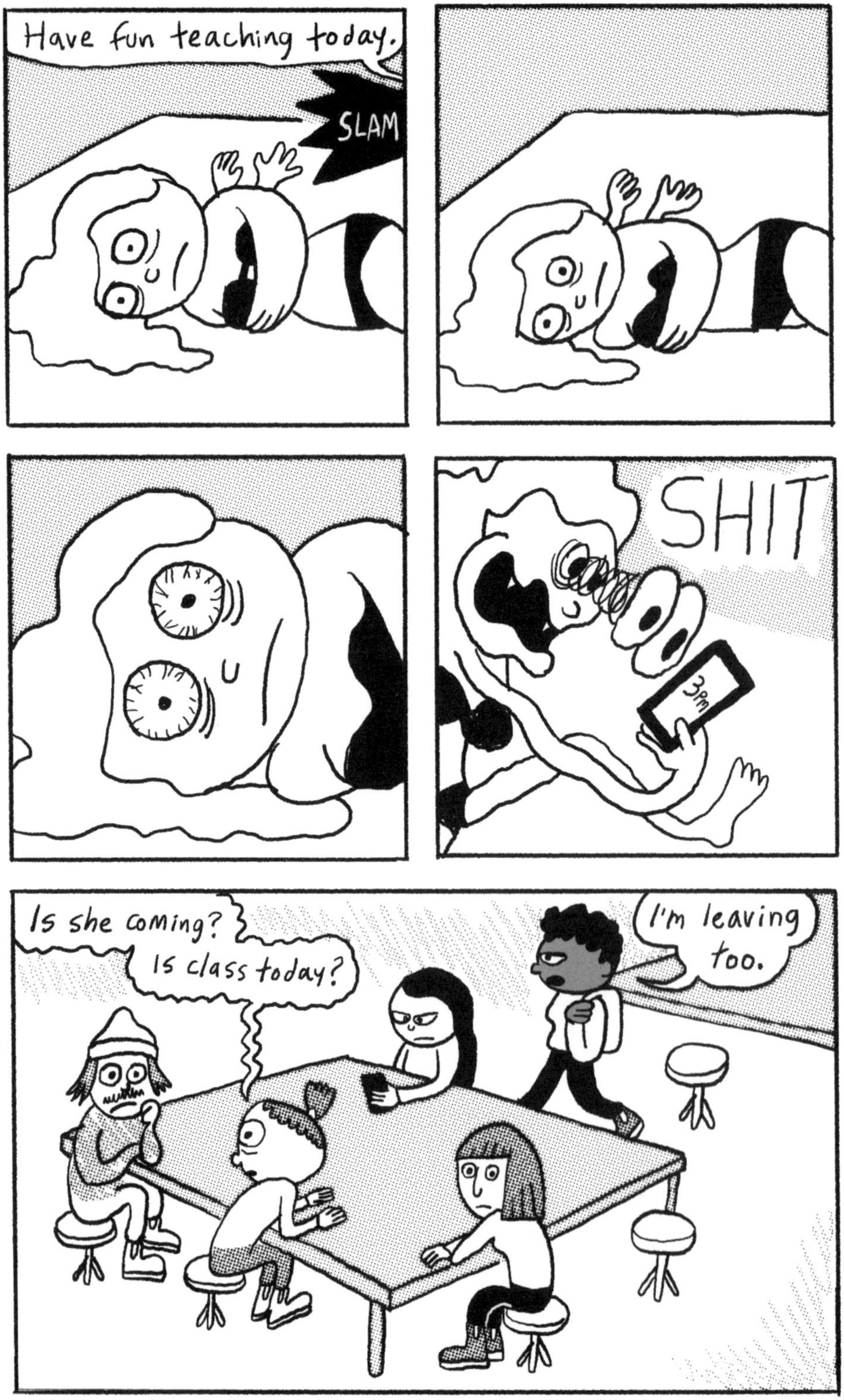
Have fun teaching today.
SLAM
SHIT
3PM
Is she coming?
Is class today?
I'm leaving too.

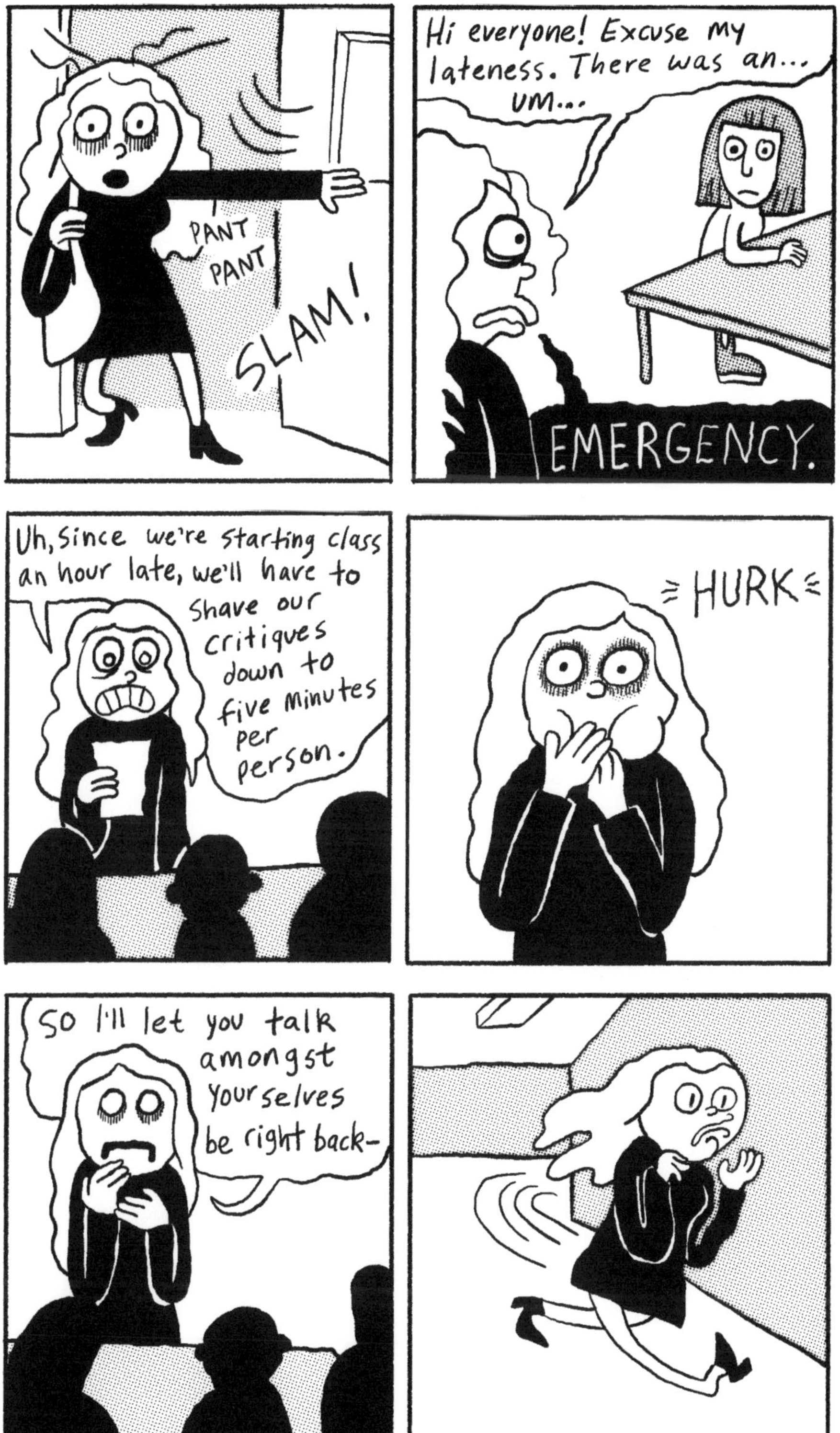
PANT
PANT
SLAM!
Hi everyone! Excuse my lateness. There was an... UM...
EMERGENCY.
Uh, Since we're starting class an hour late, we'll have to shave our critiques down to five minutes per person.
HURK
So I'll let you talk amongst yourselves be right back-

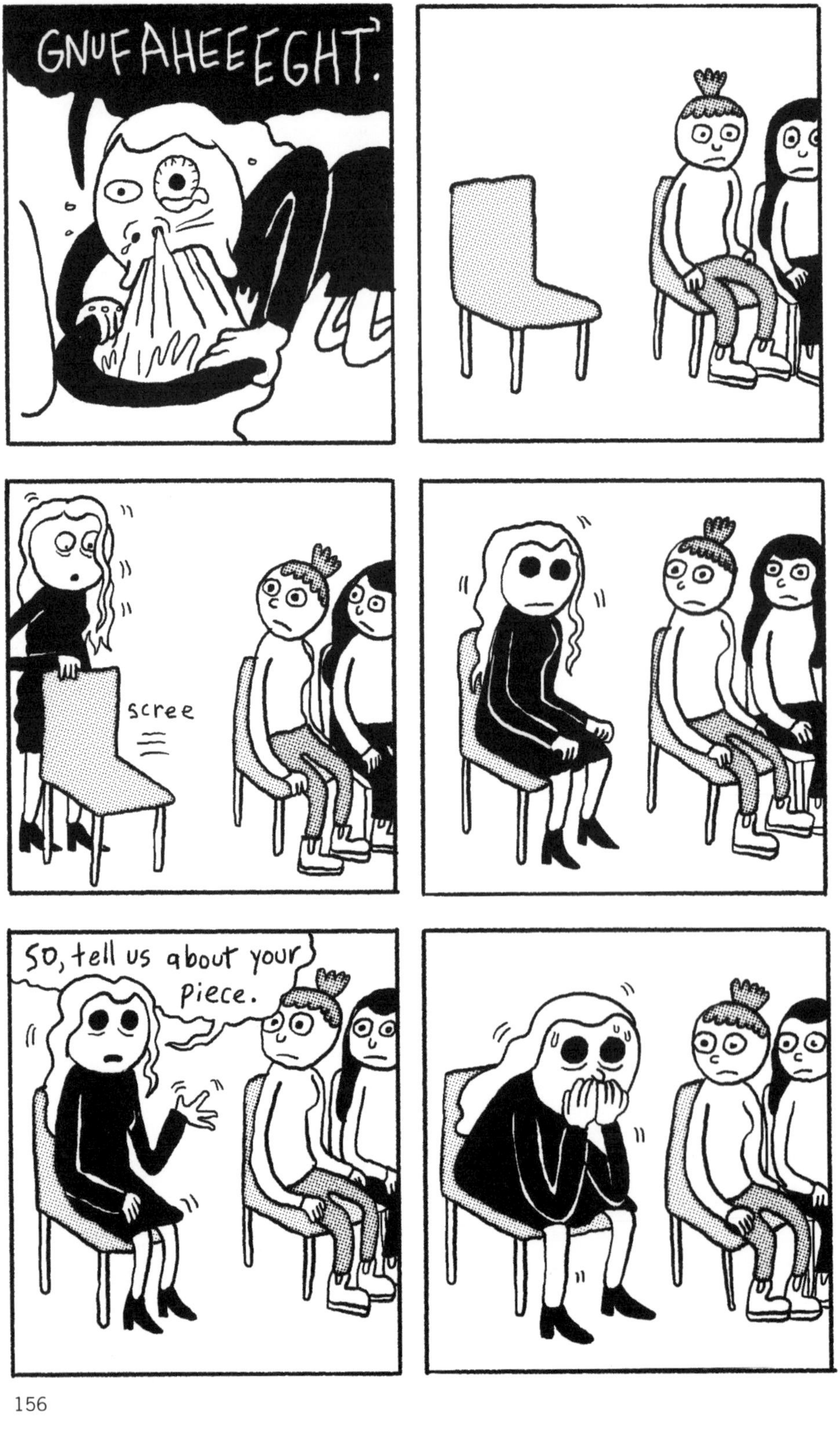
GNUFAHEEEEGHT!
scree
SO, tell us about your piece.

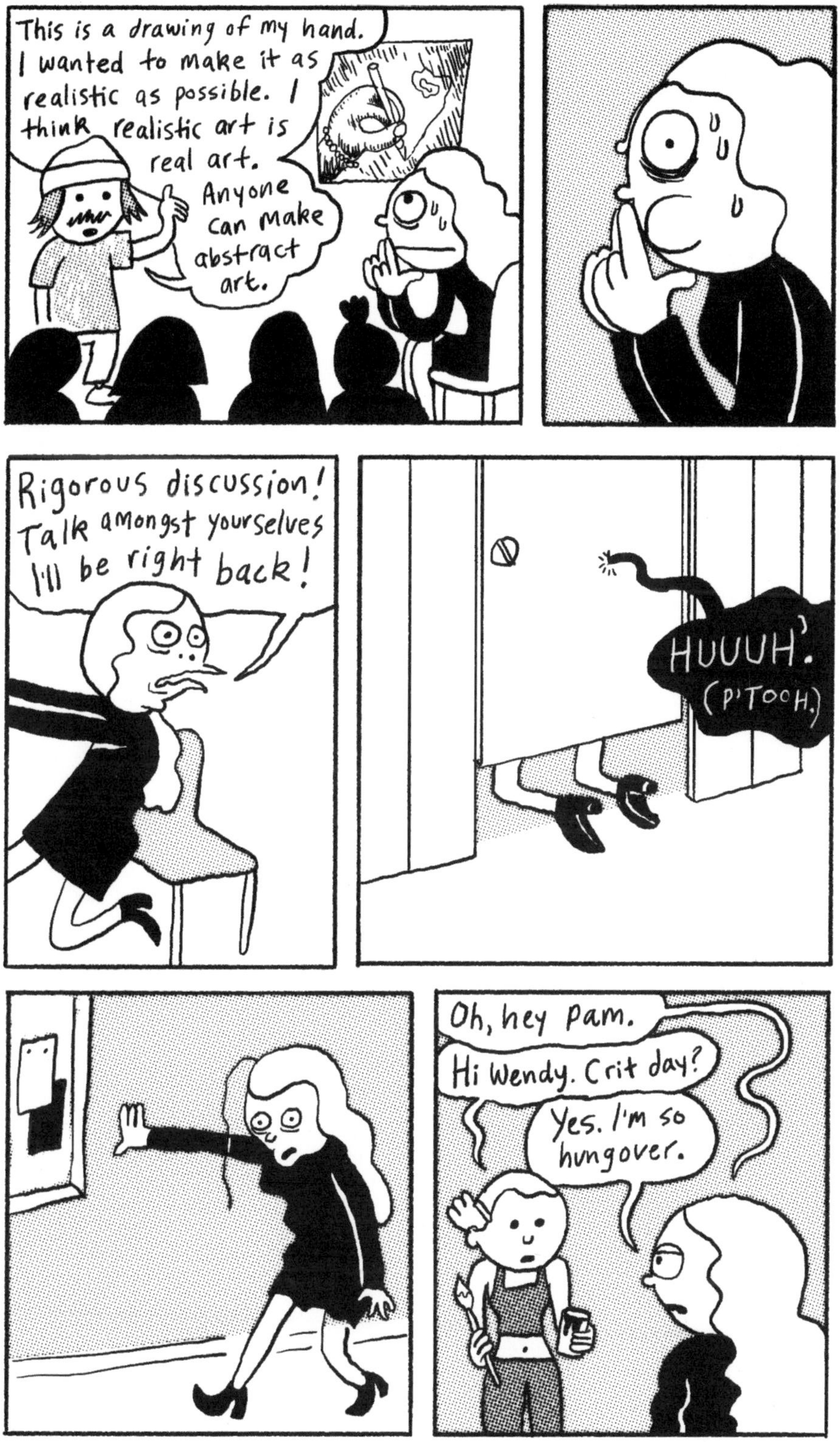
This is a drawing of my hand. I wanted to make it as realistic as possible. I think realistic art is real art.
Anyone can make abstract art.
Rigorous discussion! Talk amongst yourselves I'll be right back!
HUUUH!
(P'TOOH.)
Oh, hey pam.
Hi Wendy. Crit day?
Yes. I'm so hungover.

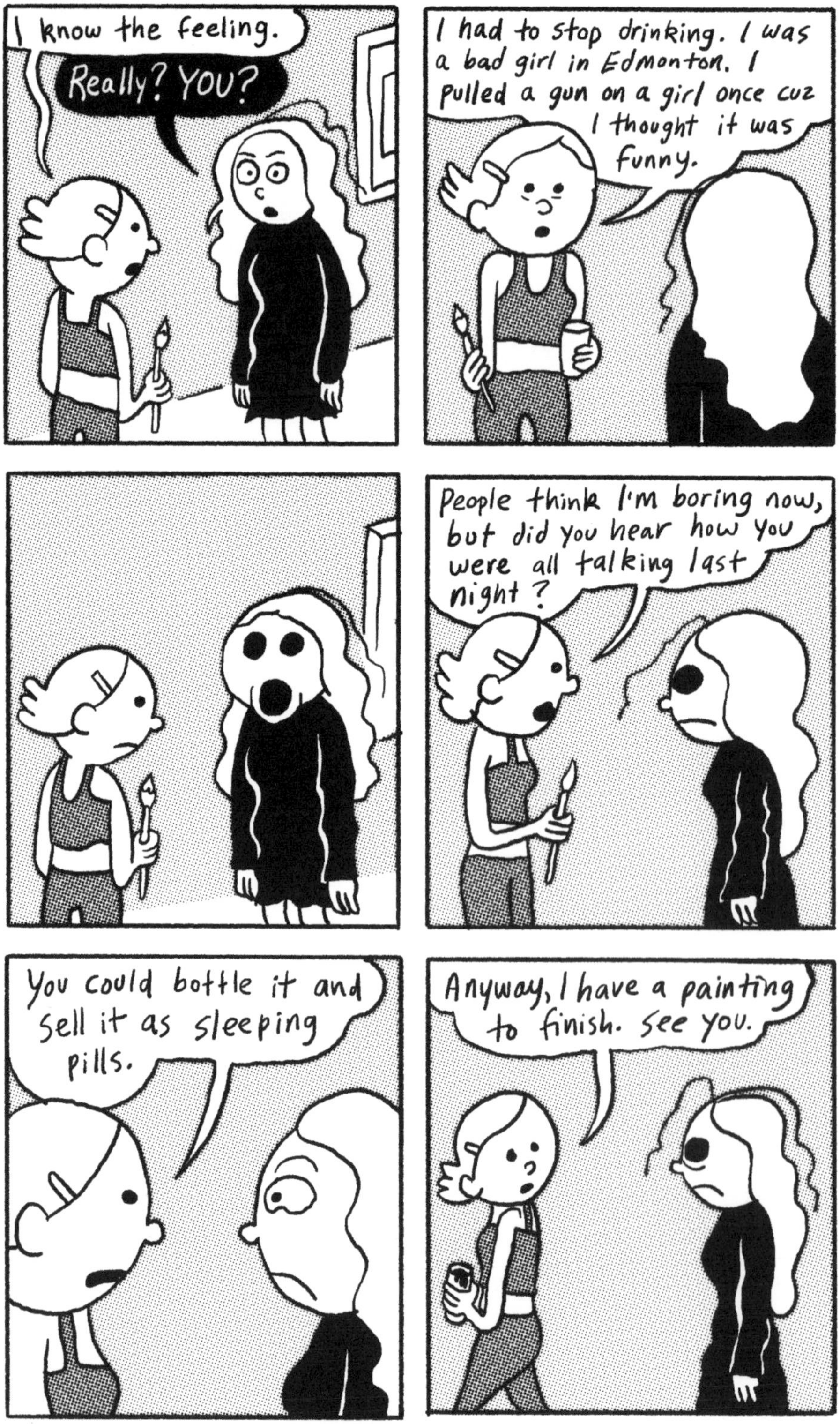
I know the feeling.
Really? YOU?
I had to stop drinking. I was a bad girl in Edmonton. I pulled a gun on a girl once cuz I thought it was funny.
People think I'm boring now, but did you hear how you were all talking last night?
You could bottle it and sell it as sleeping pills.
Anyway, I have a painting to finish. See you.

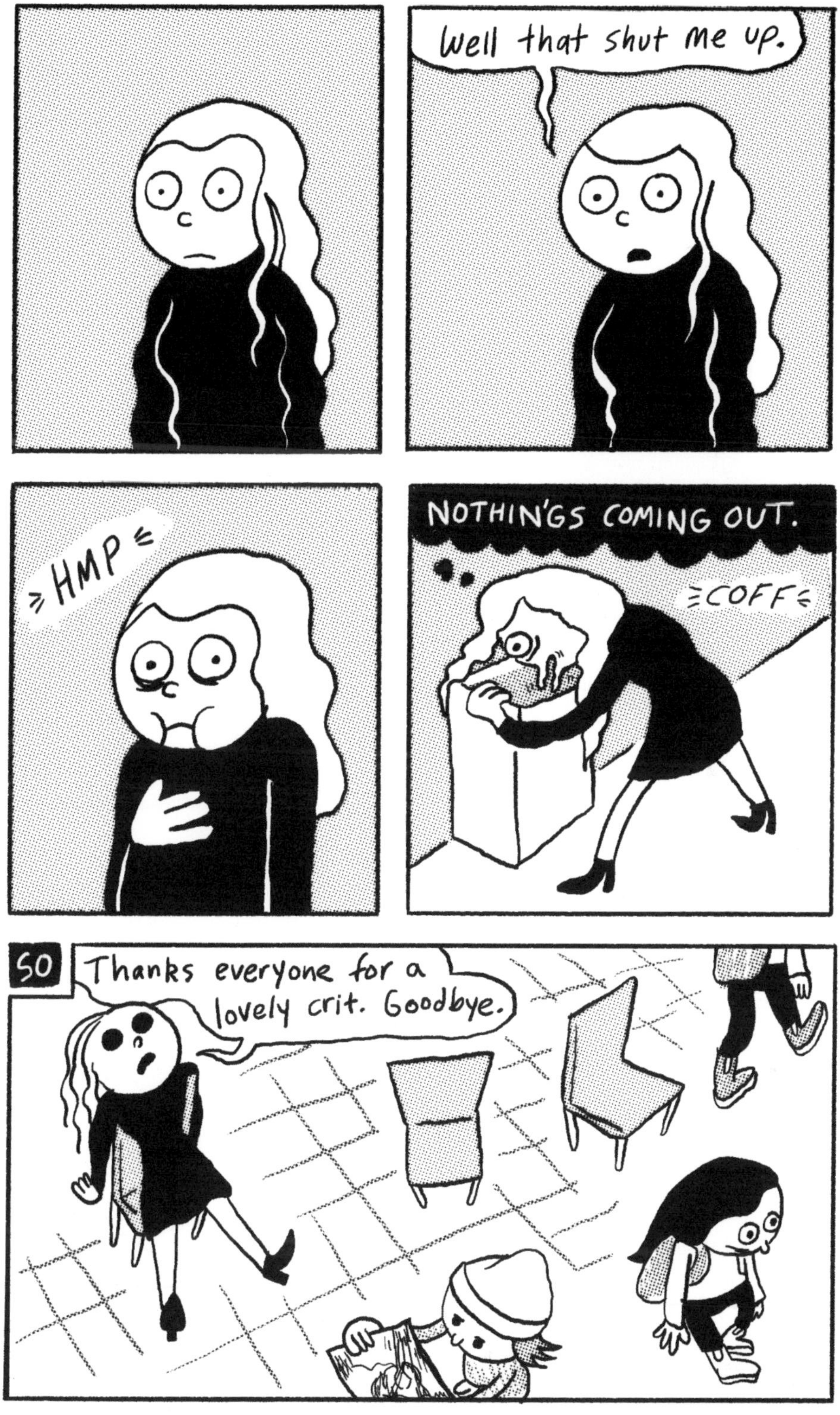
Well that shut me up.
HMP
NOTHING'S COMING OUT.
COFF
SO
Thanks everyone for a lovely crit. Goodbye.

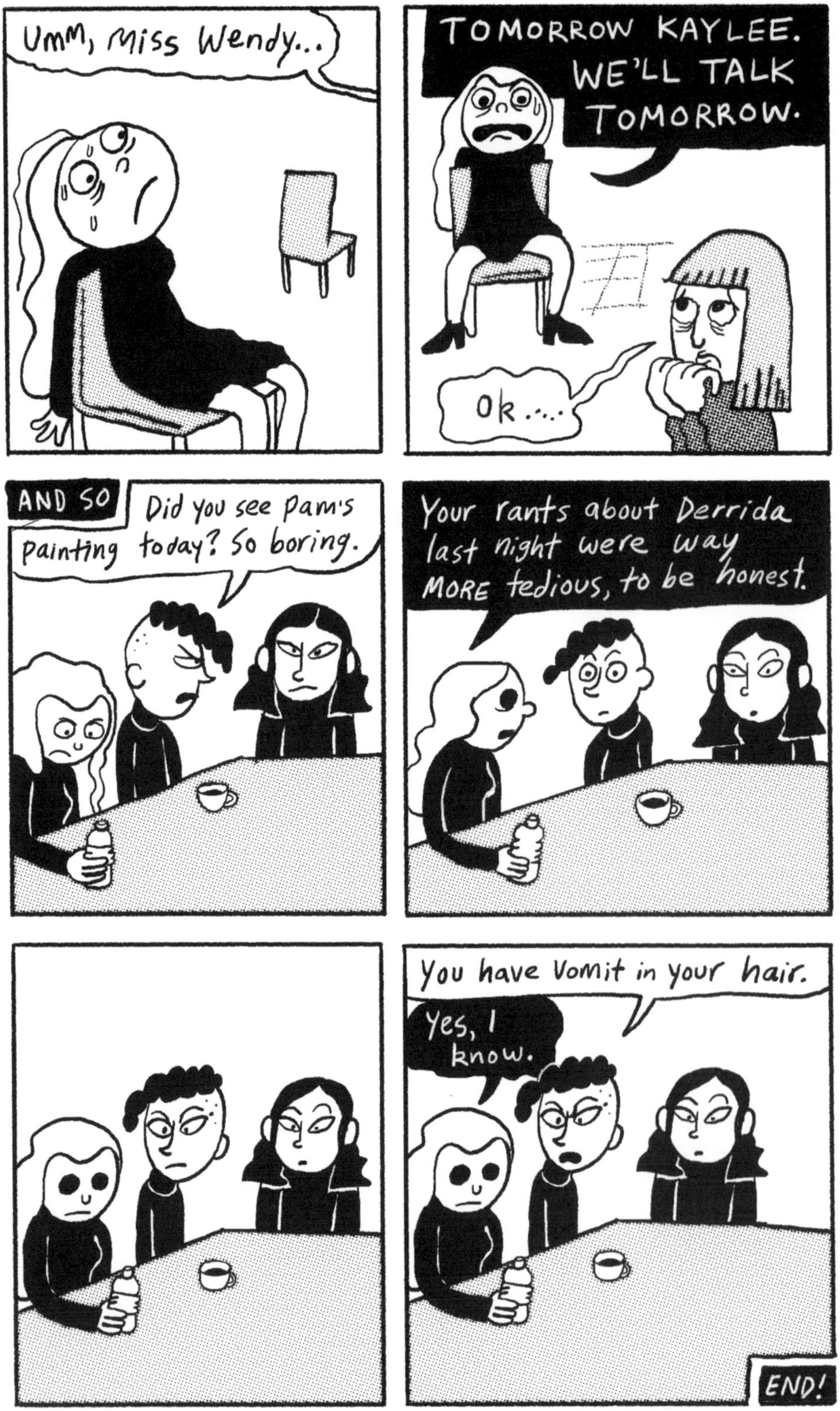
Umm, Miss Wendy...
TOMORROW KAYLEE. WE'LL TALK TOMORROW.
Ok.....
AND SO
Did you see Pam's painting today? So boring.
Your rants about Derrida last night were way MORE tedious, to be honest.
You have vomit in your hair.
Yes, I know.
END!

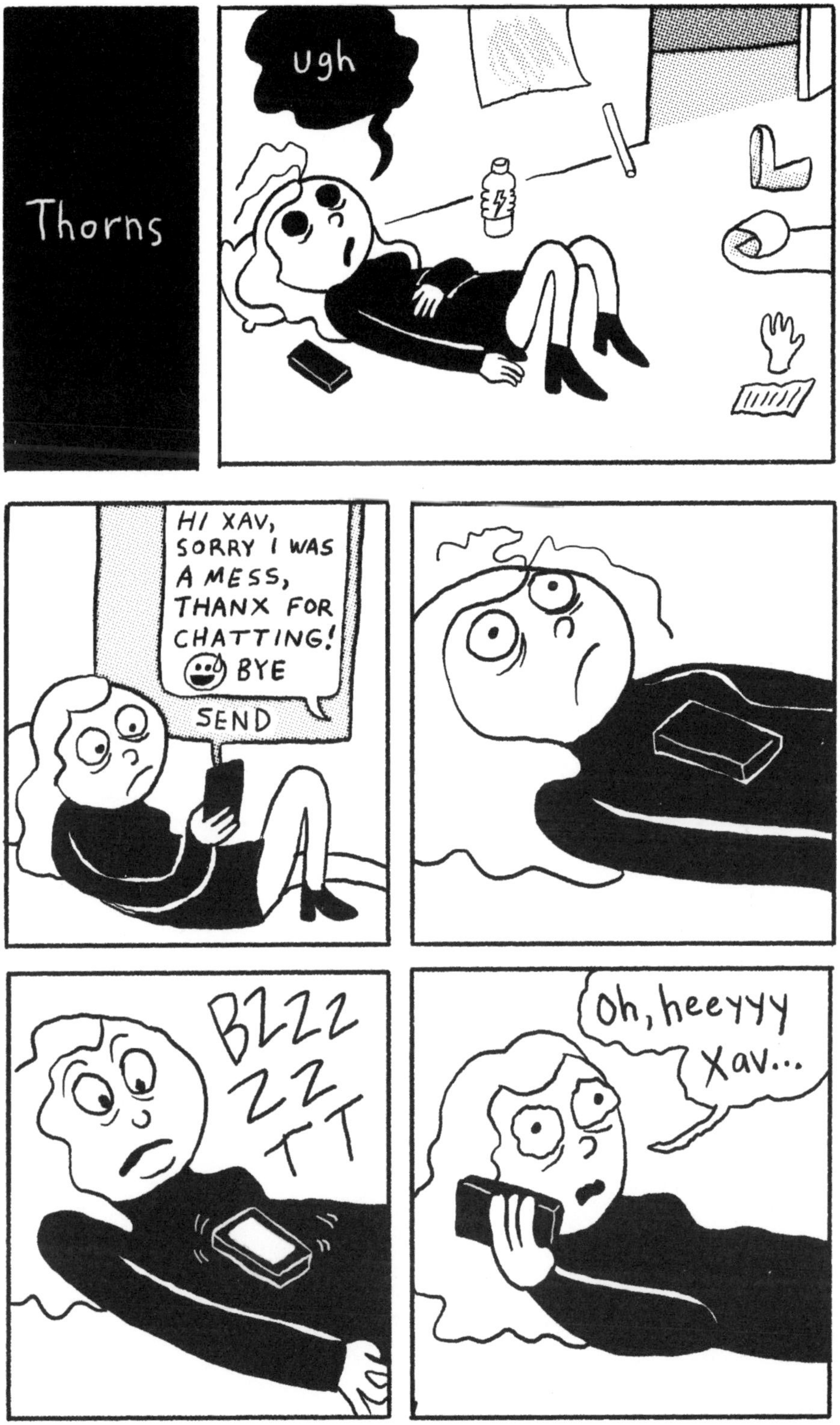
Thorns
ugh
HI XAV, SORRY I WAS A MESS, THANX FOR CHATTING! BYE
SEND
BZZZ ZZ TT
Oh, heeyyy Xav...

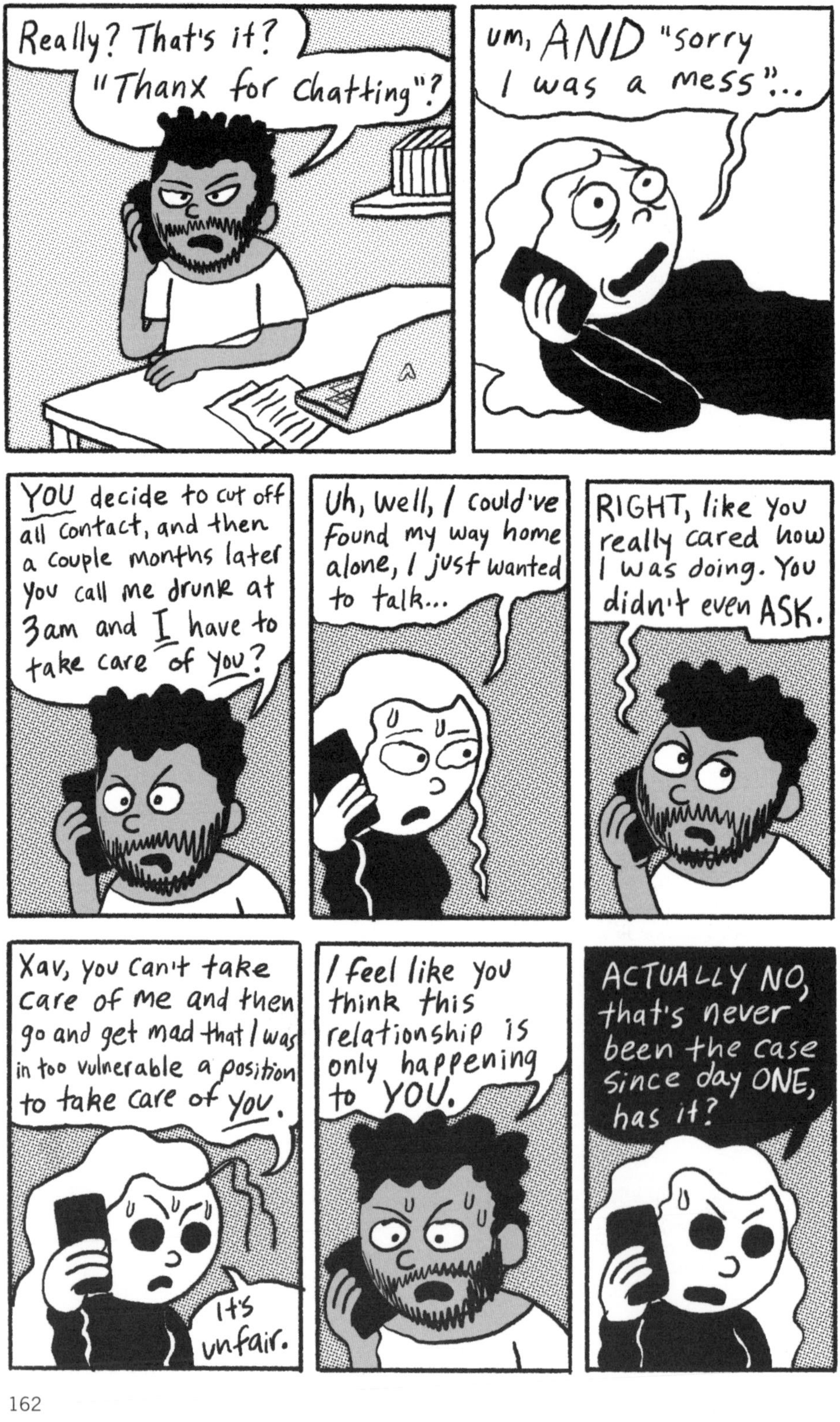
Really? That's it? "Thanx for Chatting"?
um, AND "sorry I was a mess"...
YOU decide to cut off all contact, and then a couple months later you call me drunk at 3am and I have to take care of you?
Uh, well, I could've found my way home alone, I just wanted to talk...
RIGHT, like you really cared how I was doing. You didn't even ASK.
Xav, you can't take care of me and then go and get mad that I was in too vulnerable a position to take care of you.
It's unfair.
I feel like you think this relationship is only happening to YOU.
ACTUALLY NO, that's never been the case since day ONE, has it?

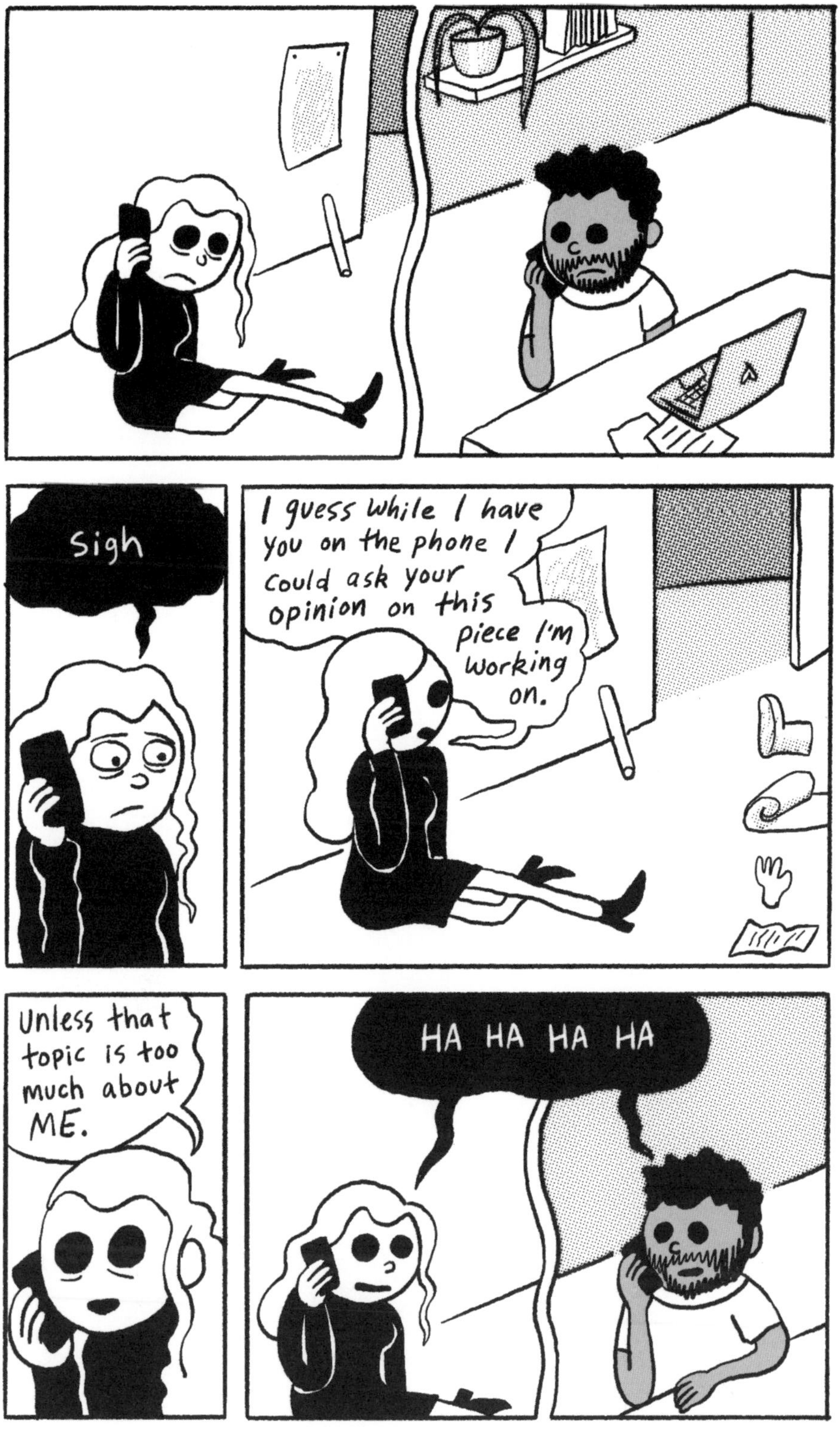
Sigh
I guess while I have you on the phone I could ask your opinion on this piece I'm working on.
Unless that topic is too much about ME.
HA HA HA HA

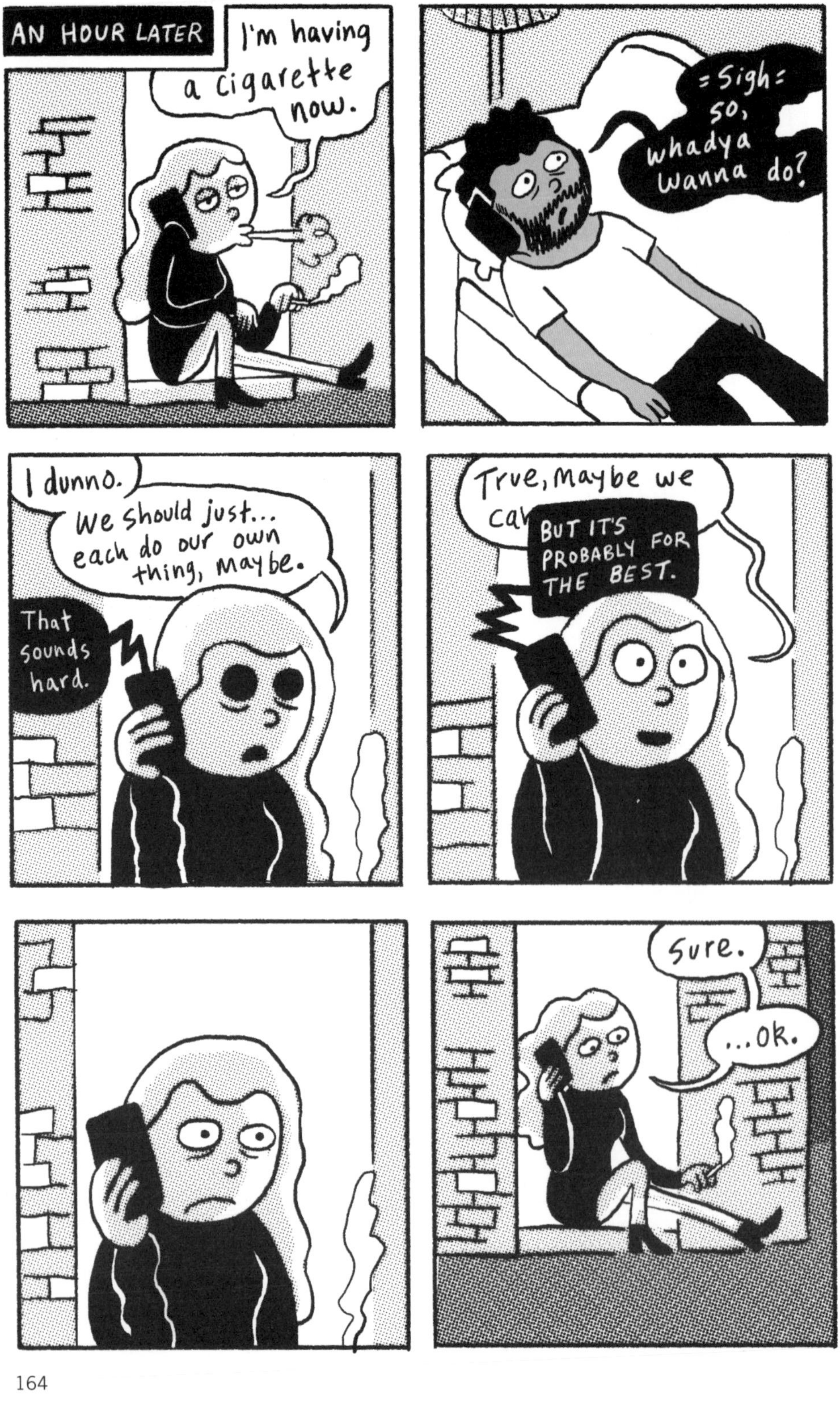
AN HOUR LATER
I'm having a cigarette now.
=Sigh= so, whadya wanna do?
I dunno.
We should just... each do our own thing, maybe.
That sounds hard.
True, maybe we ca
BUT IT'S PROBABLY FOR THE BEST.
Sure.
...ok.

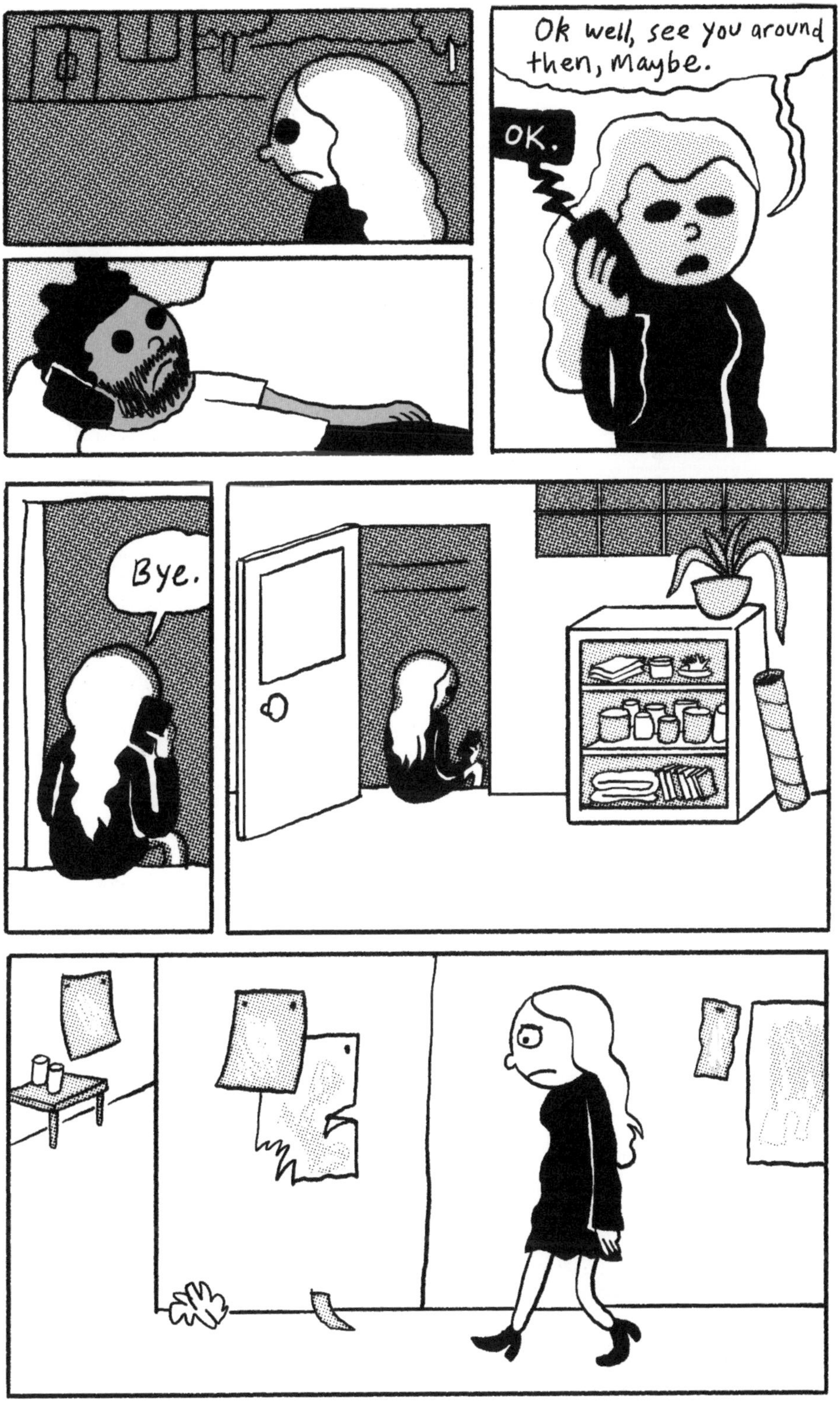
Ok well, see you around then, Maybe.
OK.
Bye.

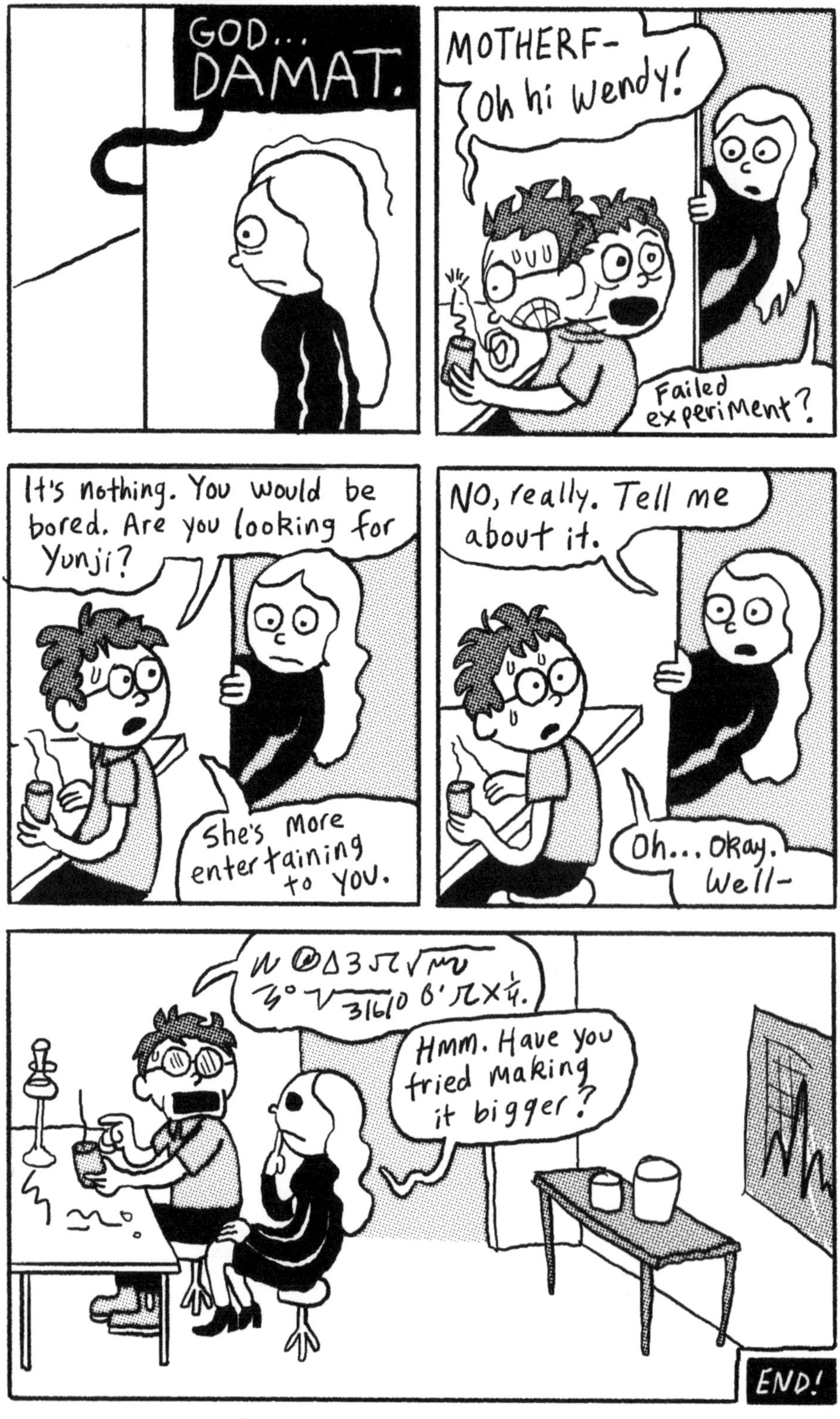
GOD...
DAMAT.
MOTHERF-
Oh hi Wendy!
Failed experiment?
It's nothing. You would be bored. Are you looking for Yunji?
She's more entertaining to you.
NO, really. Tell me about it.
Oh... Okay. Well-
Hmm. Have you fried making it bigger?
END!

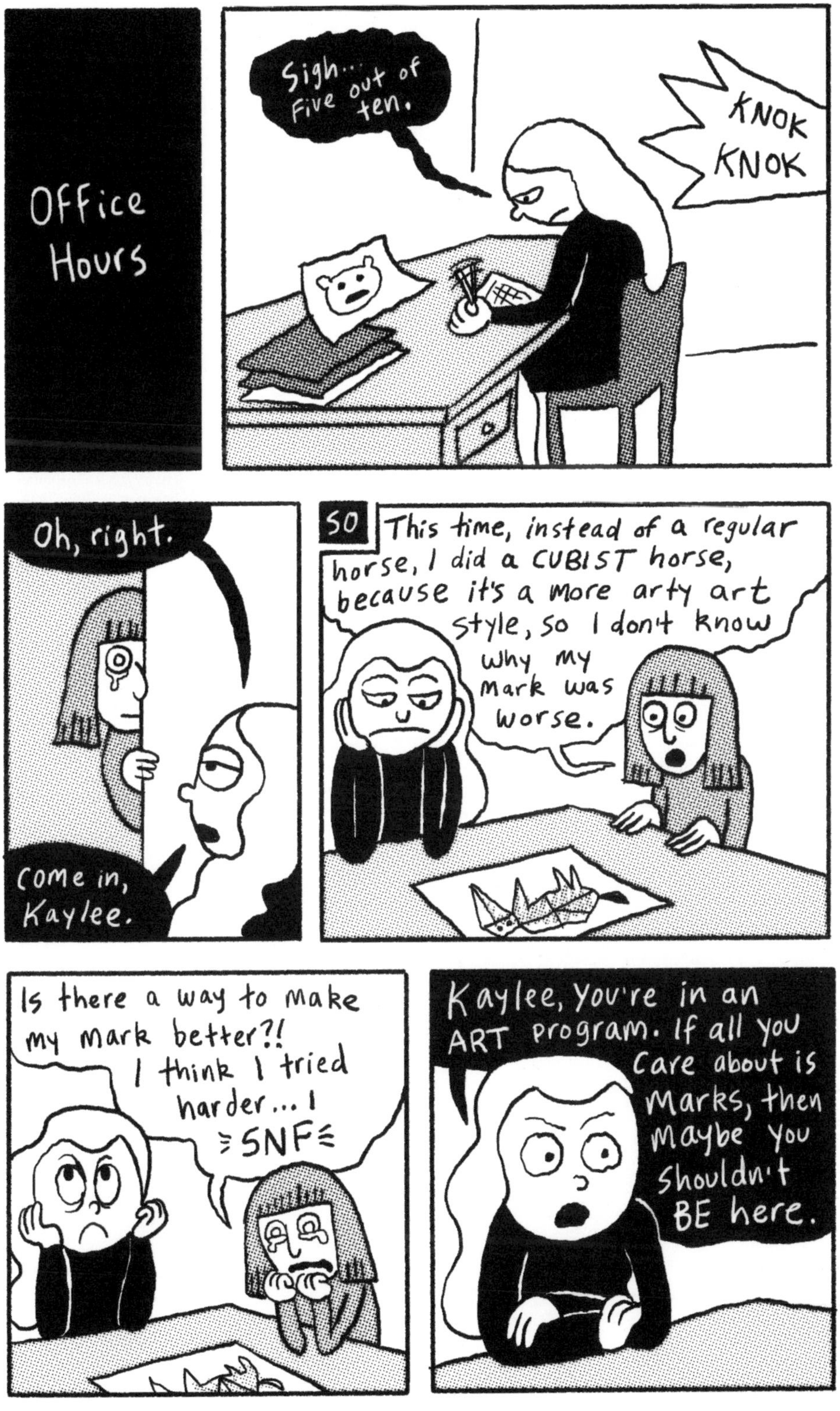
Office Hours
Sigh... Five out of ten.
KNOK KNOK
Oh, right.
Come in, Kaylee.
SO
This time, instead of a regular horse, I did a CUBIST horse, because it's a more arty art style, so I don't know why my mark was worse.
Is there a way to make my mark better?! I think I tried harder... I
SNF
Kaylee, you're in an ART program. If all you care about is marks, then maybe you shouldn't BE here.

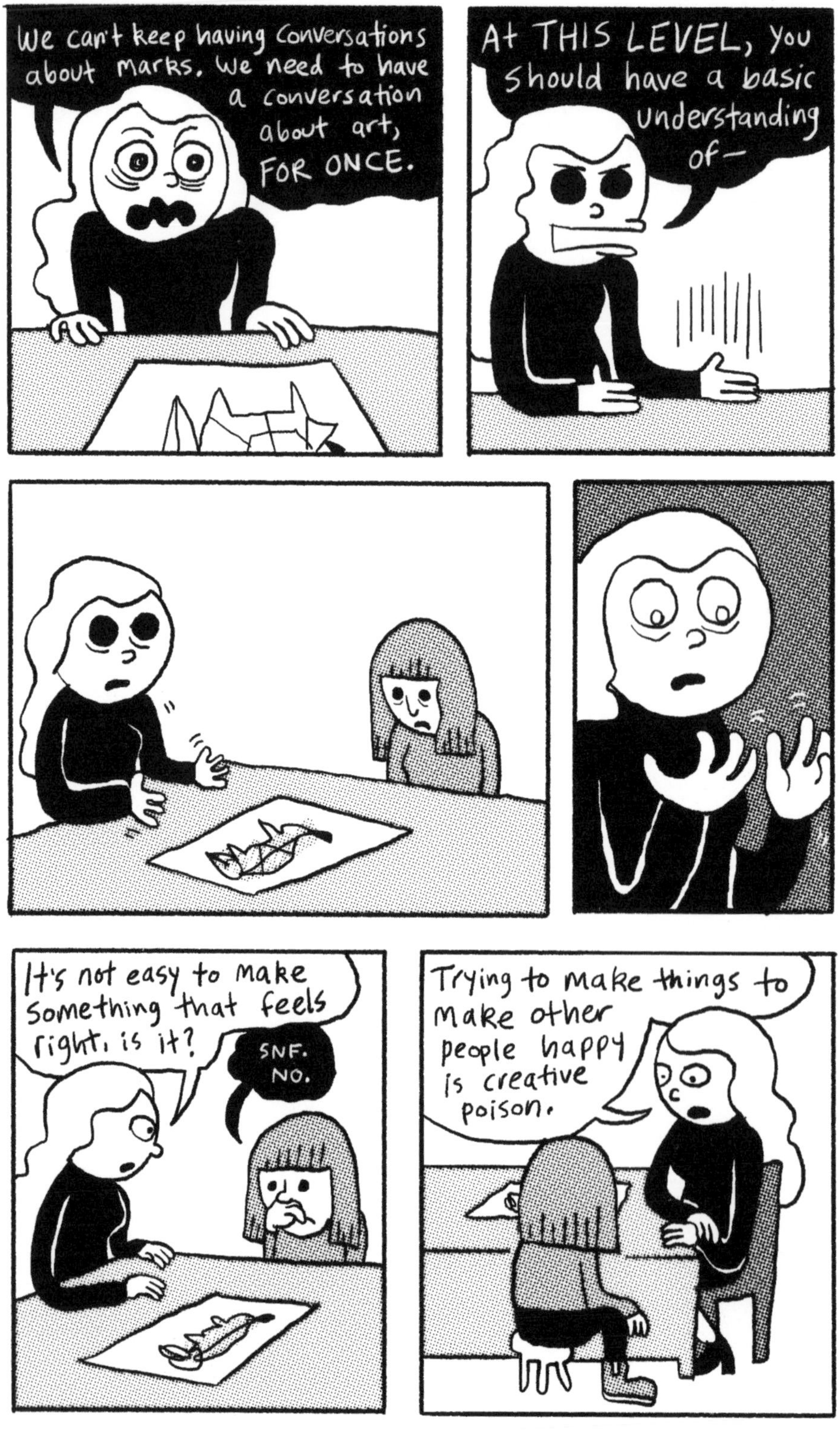
We can't keep having conversations about marks. We need to have a conversation about art, FOR ONCE.
At THIS LEVEL, you should have a basic understanding of—
It's not easy to make something that feels right, is it?
SNF. NO.
Trying to make things to make other people happy is creative poison.

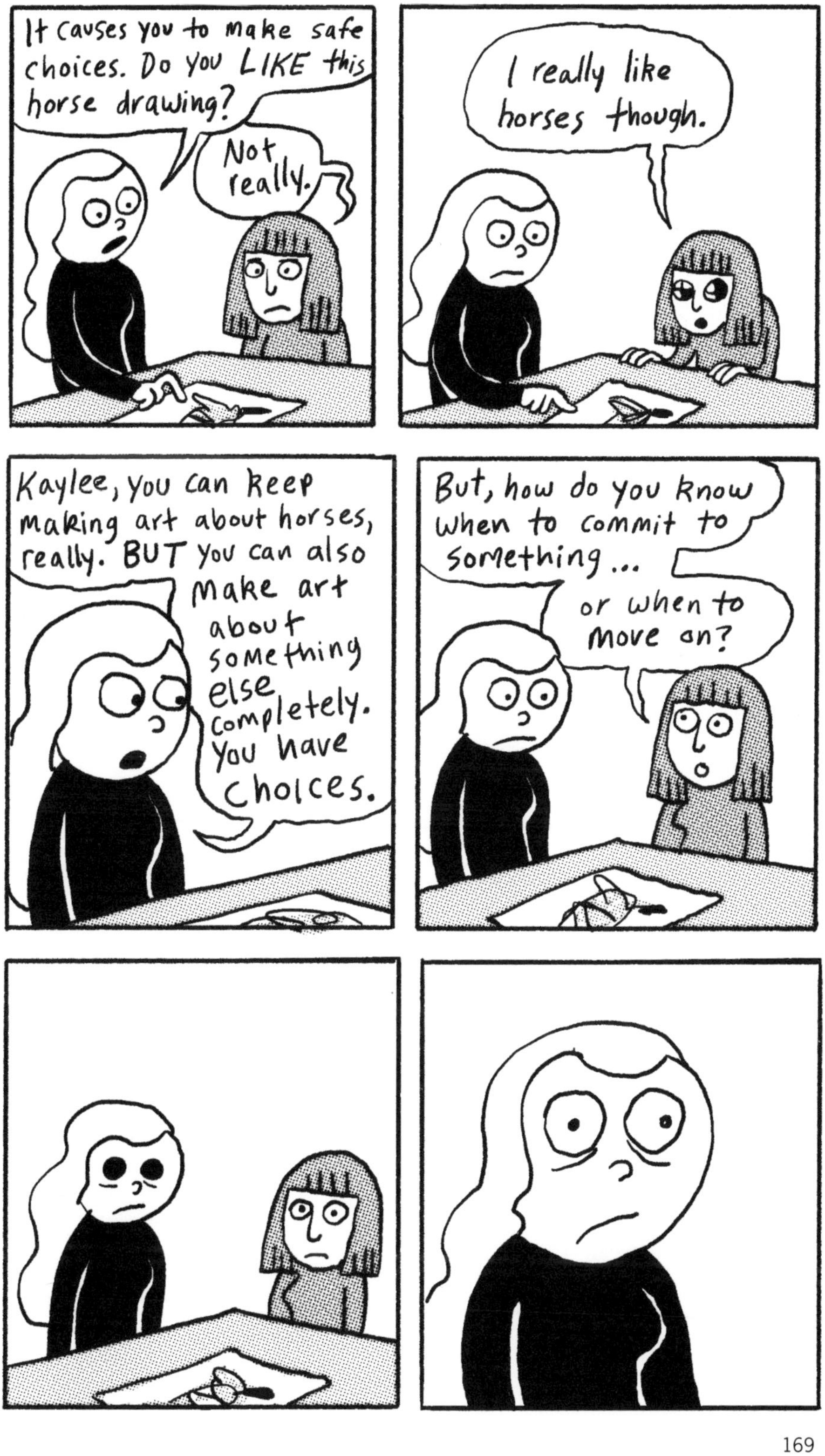

It causes you to make safe choices. Do you LIKE this horse drawing?
Not really.
I really like horses though.
Kaylee, you can keep making art about horses, really. BUT you can also make art about something else completely. You have choices.
But, how do you know when to commit to something...
or when to move on?

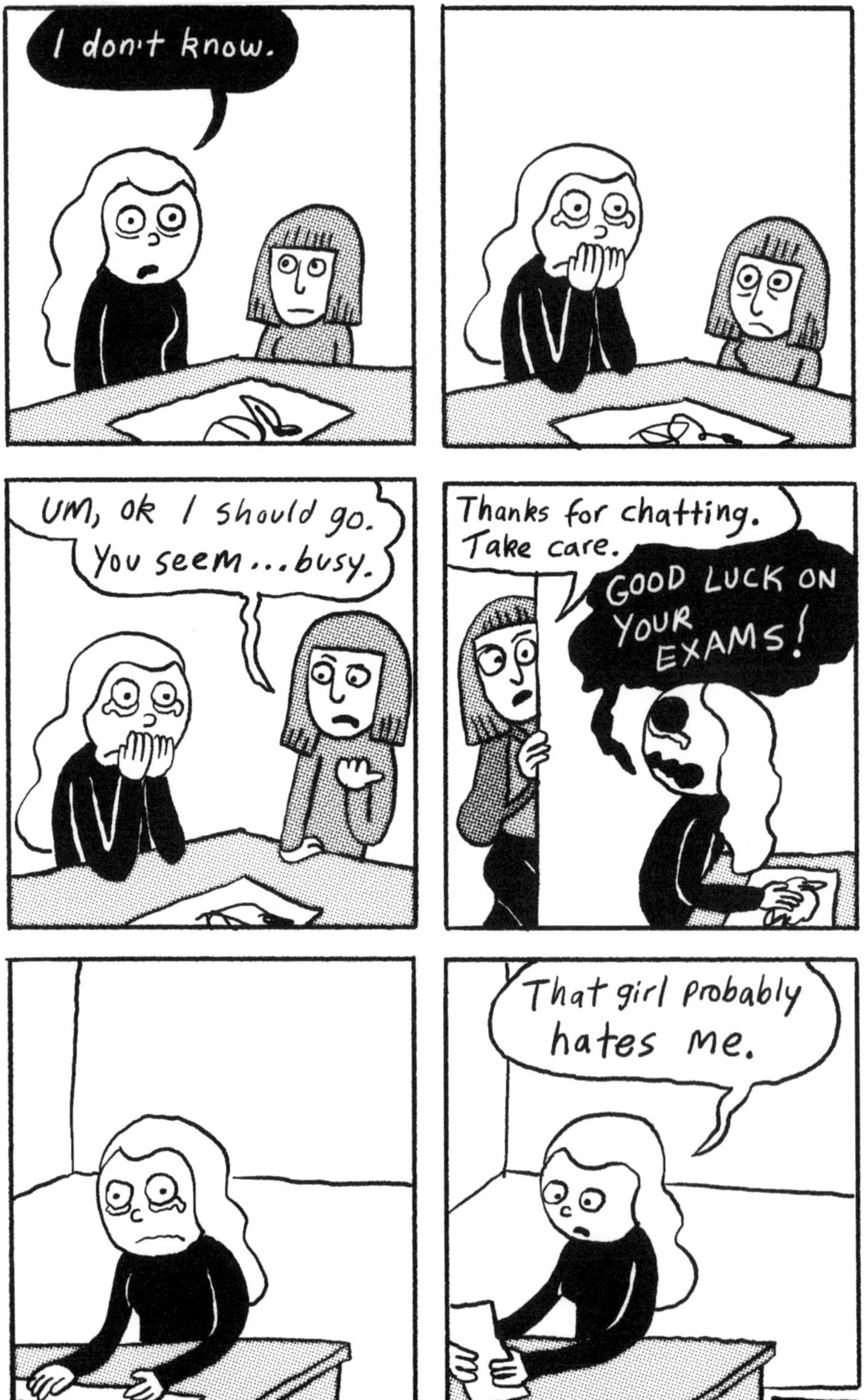
I don't know.
UM, ok I should go. You seem...busy.
Thanks for chatting. Take care.
GOOD LUCK ON YOUR EXAMS!
That girl probably hates me.
END!

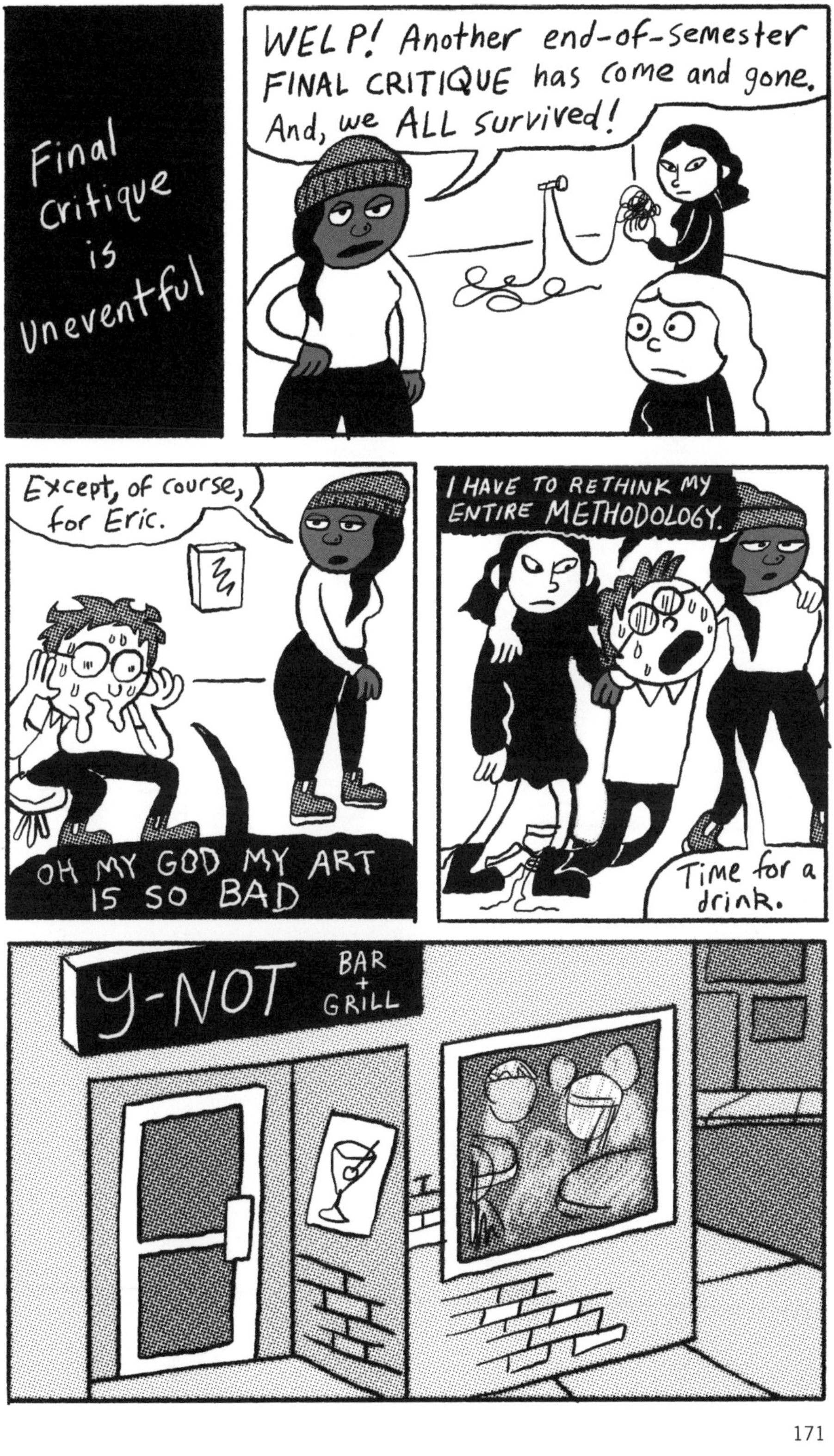
Final Critique is Uneventful
WELP! Another end-of-semester FINAL CRITIQUE has come and gone. And, we ALL survived!
Except, of course, for Eric.
OH MY GOD MY ART IS SO BAD
I HAVE TO RETHINK MY ENTIRE METHODOLOGY.
Time for a drink.
Y-NOT BAR + GRILL

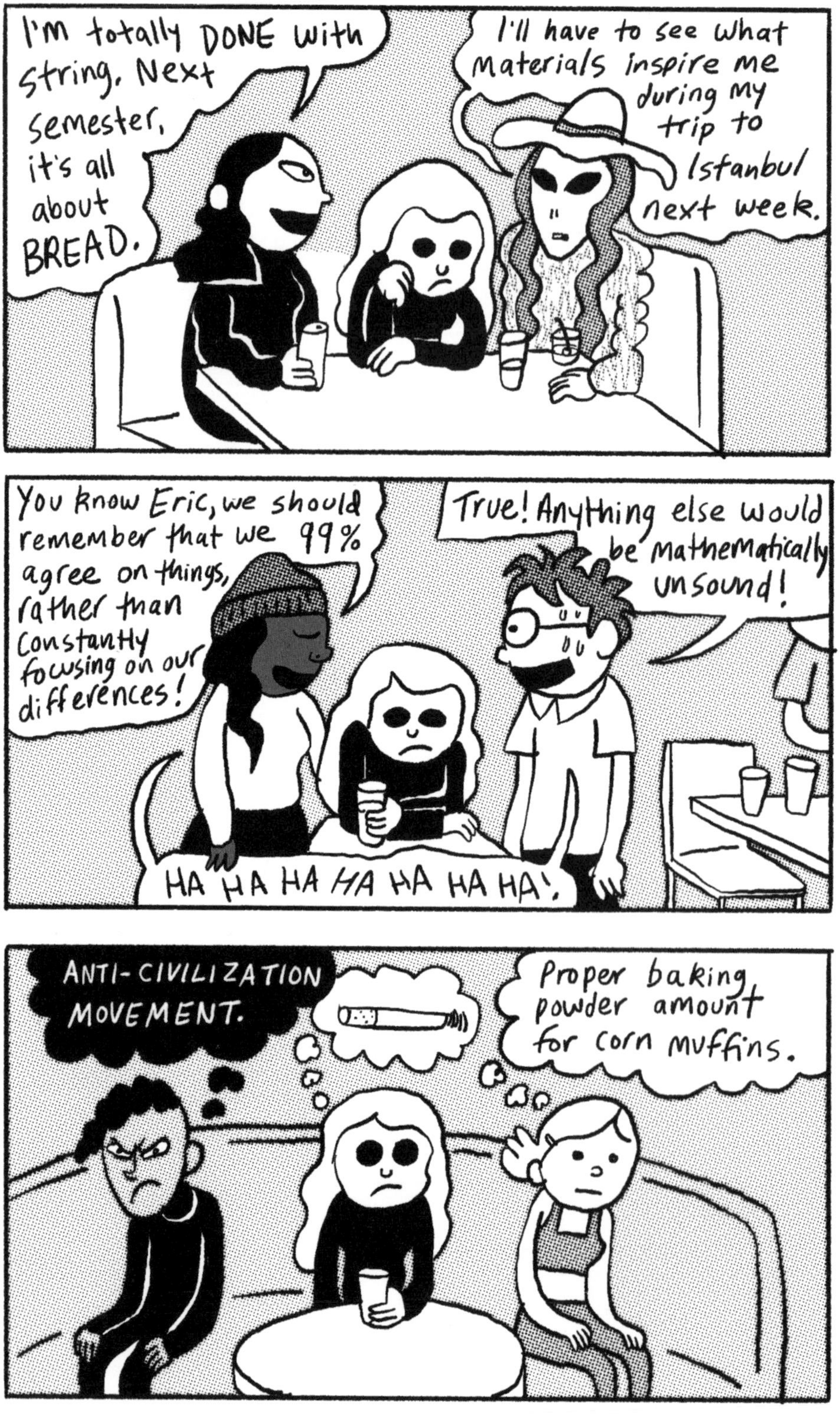
I'm totally DONE with string. Next semester, it's all about BREAD.
I'll have to see what materials inspire me during my trip to Istanbul next week.
You know Eric, we should remember that we 99% agree on things, rather than constantly focusing on our differences!
True! Anything else would be mathematically unsound!
HA HA HA HA HA HA HA!
ANTI-CIVILIZATION MOVEMENT.
Proper baking powder amount for corn muffins.

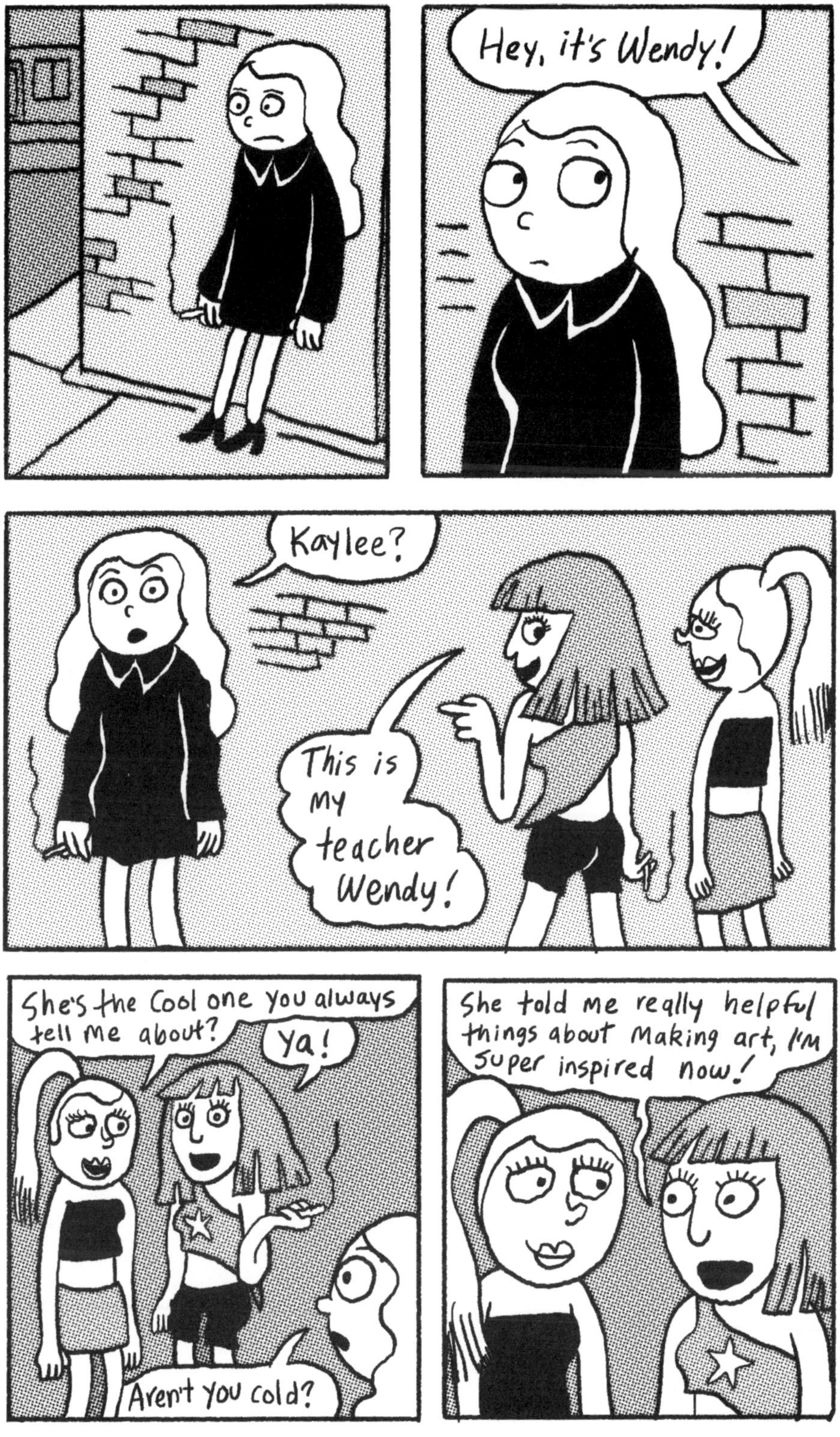
Hey, it's Wendy!
Kaylee?
This is my teacher Wendy!
She's the cool one you always tell me about?
Ya!
Aren't you cold?
She told me really helpful things about making art, I'm super inspired now!

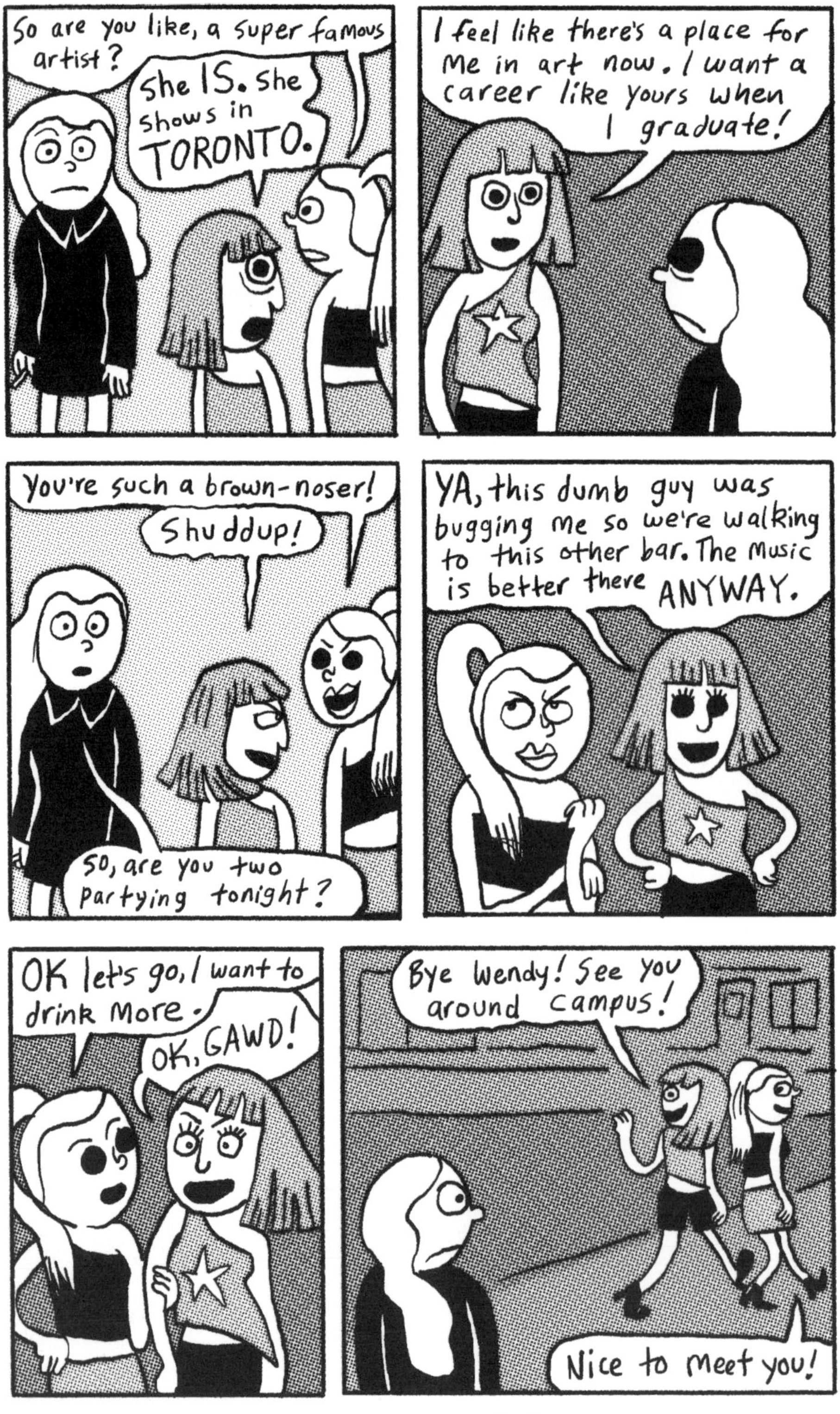
So are you like, a super famous artist?
She IS. She shows in TORONTO.
I feel like there's a place for me in art now. I want a career like yours when I graduate!
You're such a brown-noser!
Shuddup!
So, are you two partying tonight?
YA, this dumb guy was bugging me so we're walking to this other bar. The music is better there ANYWAY.
OK let's go, I want to drink more.
OK, GAWD!
Bye Wendy! See you around campus!
Nice to meet you!

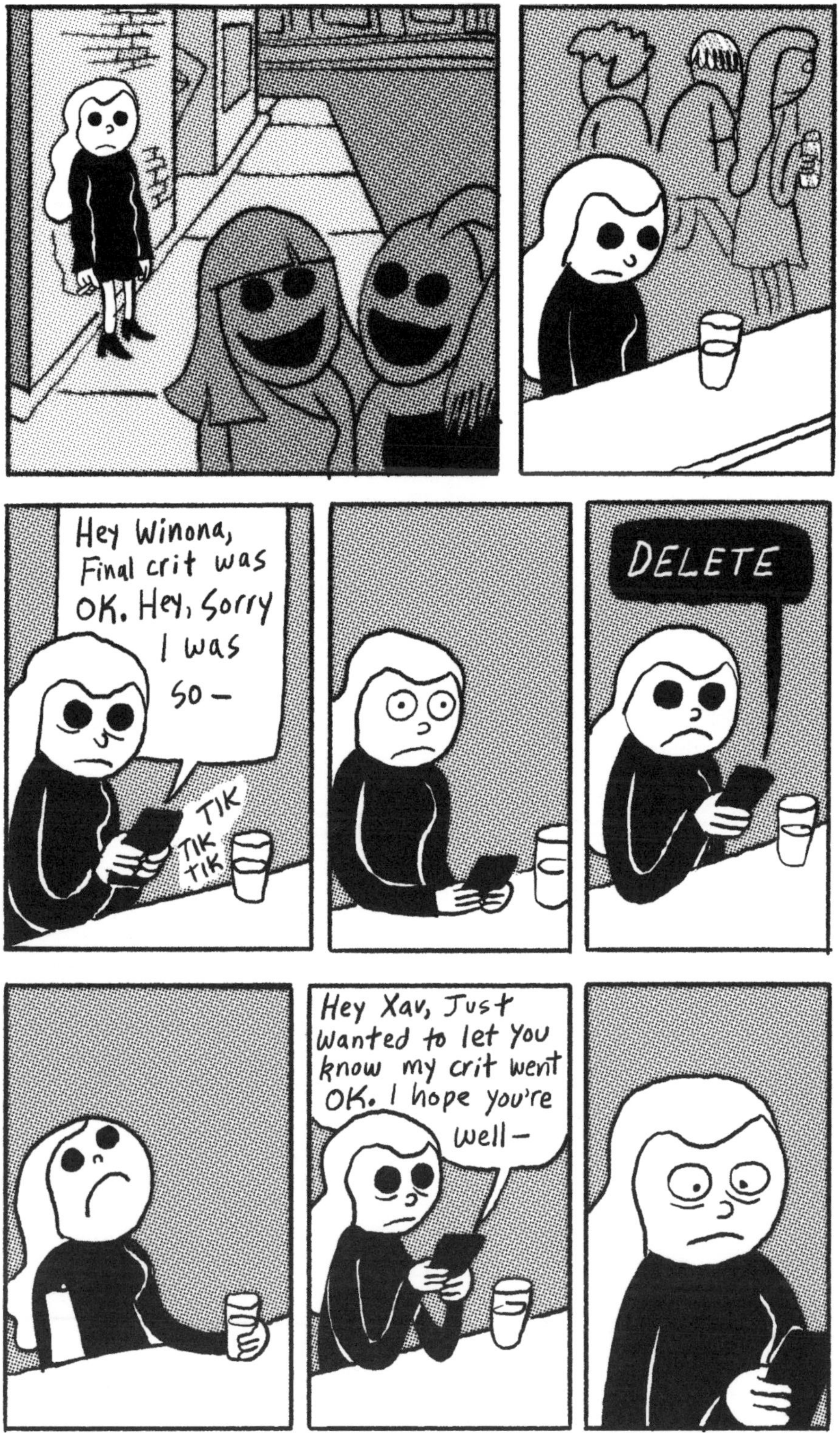
Hey Winona, Final crit was OK. Hey, Sorry I was so—
TIK TIK TIK
DELETE
Hey Xav, Just wanted to let you know my crit went OK. I hope you're well—

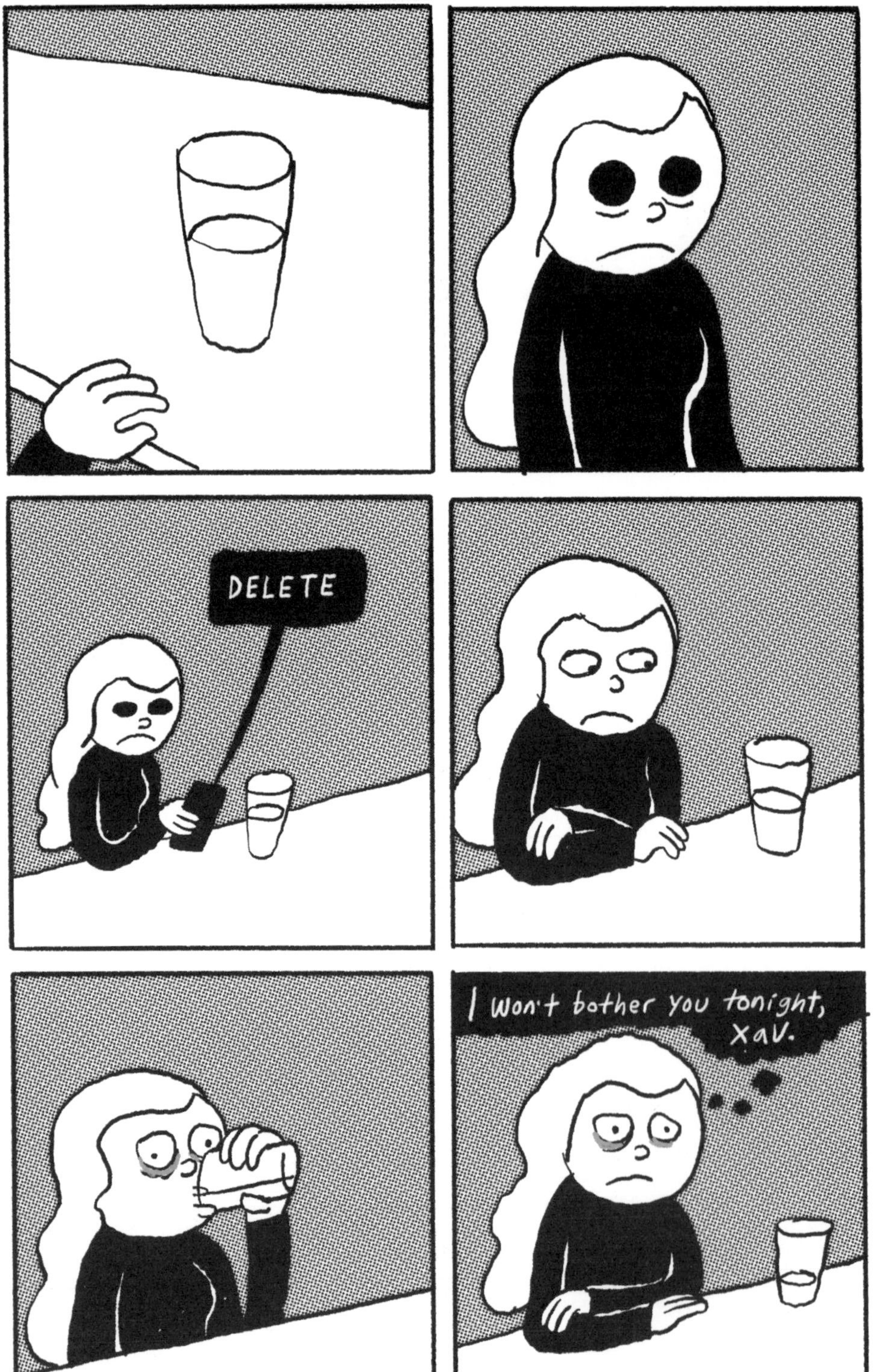
DELETE
I won't bother you tonight, Xav.

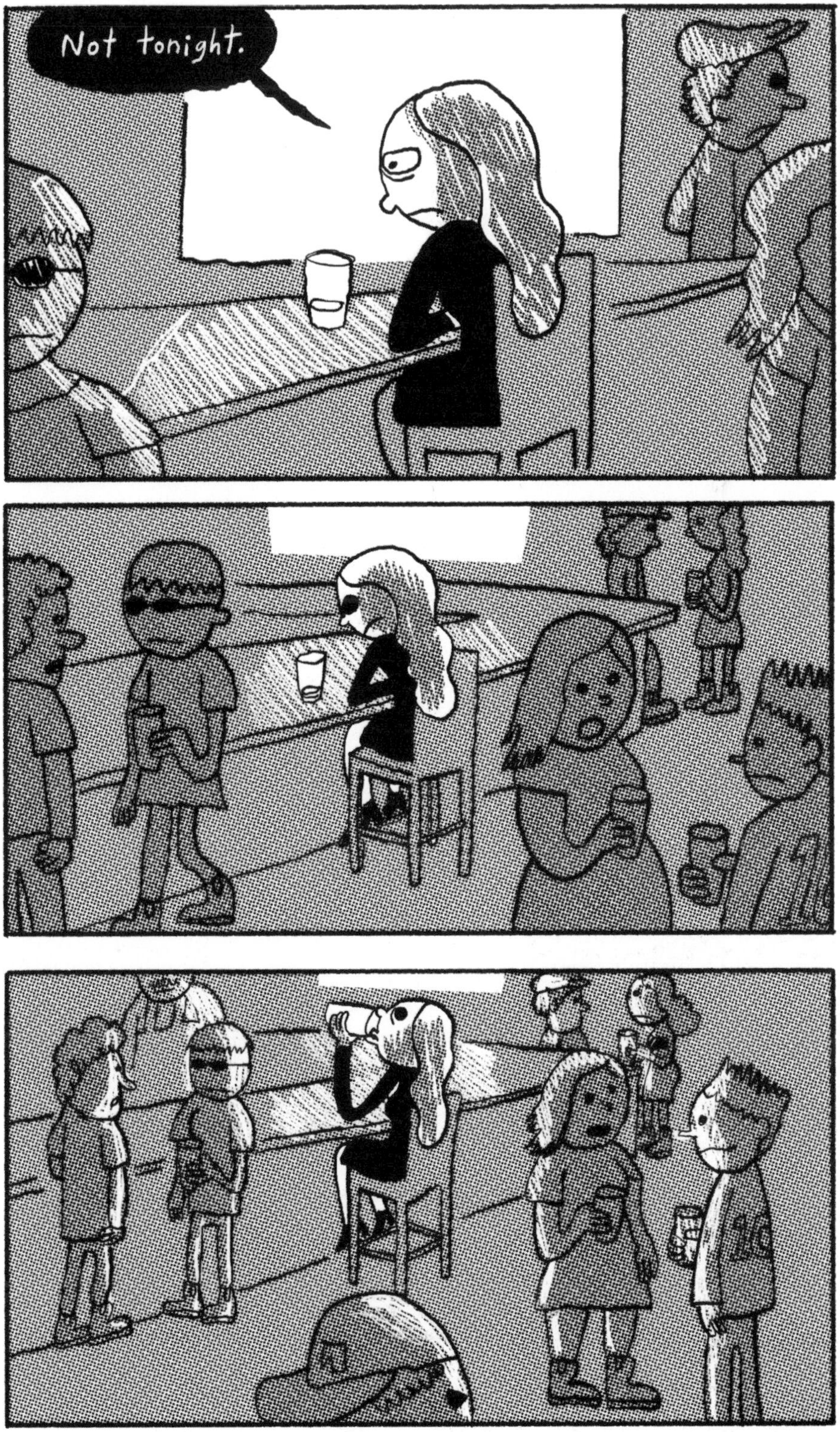
Not tonight.

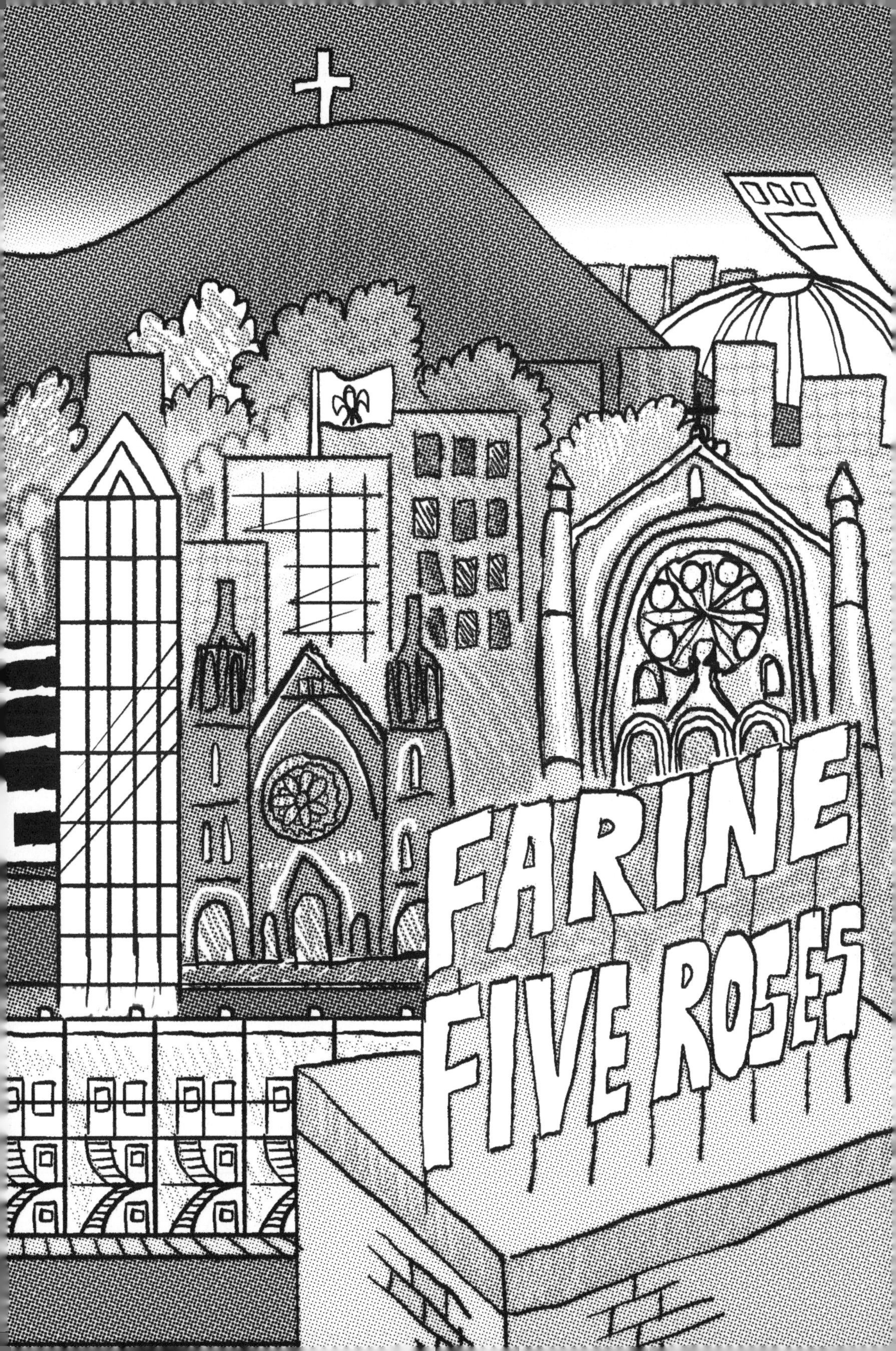
FARINE
FIVE ROSES

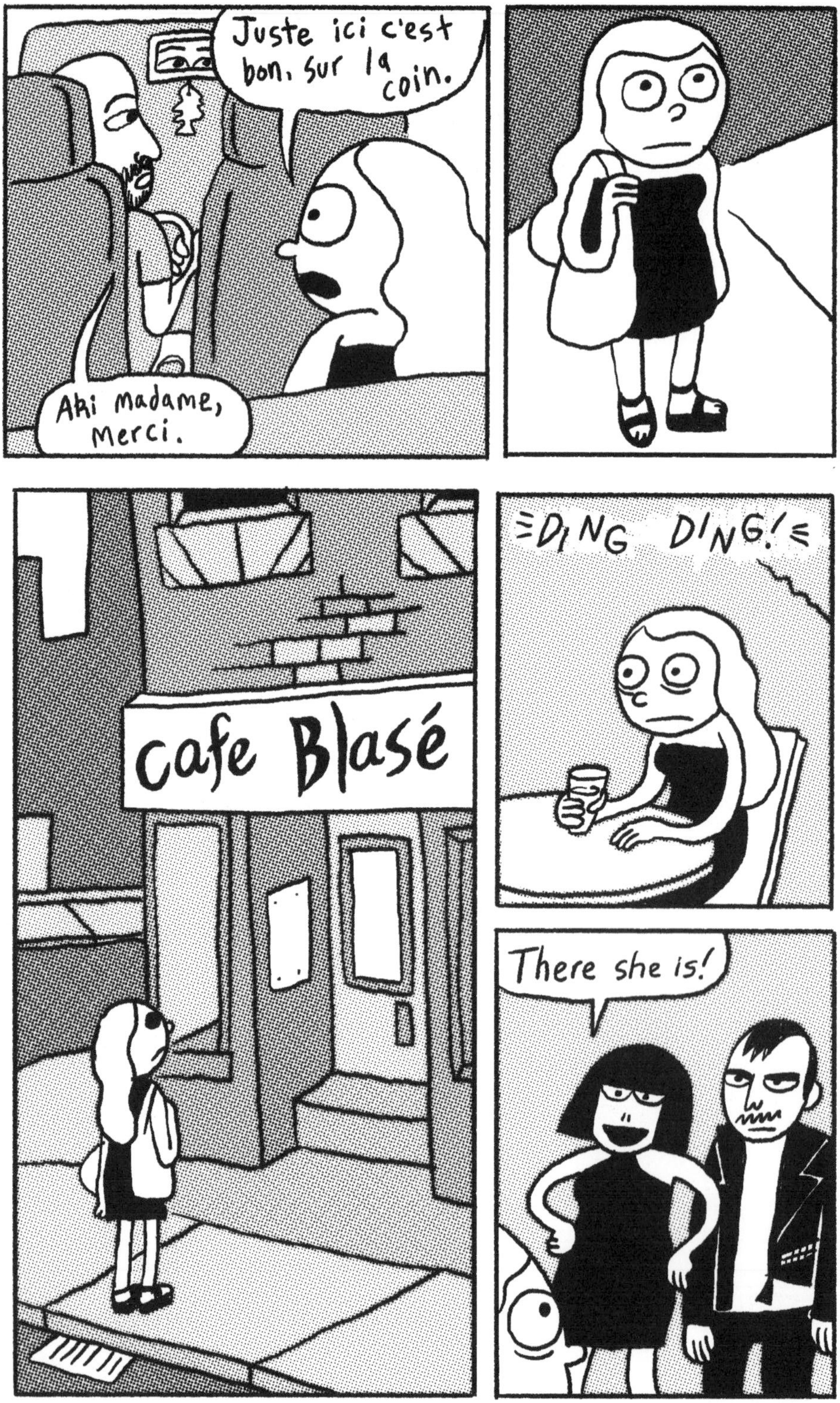
Juste ici c'est bon, sur la coin.
Aki madame, Merci.
cafe Blasé
DING DING!
There she is!

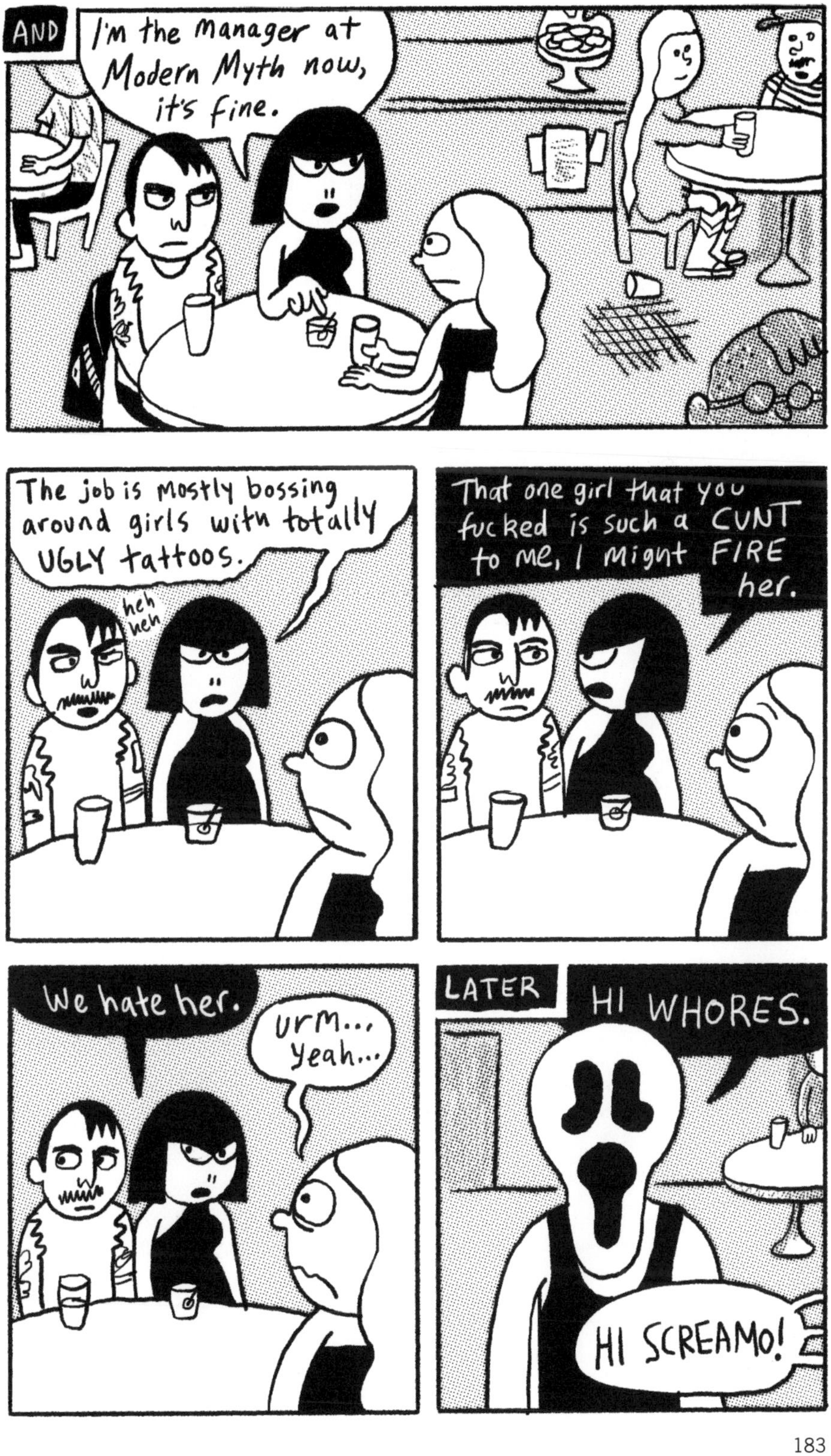
AND
I'm the manager at Modern Myth now, it's fine.
The job is mostly bossing around girls with totally UGLY tattoos.
heh heh
That one girl that you fucked is such a CUNT to me, I might FIRE her.
We hate her.
urm... yeah...
LATER
HI WHORES.
HI SCREAMO!

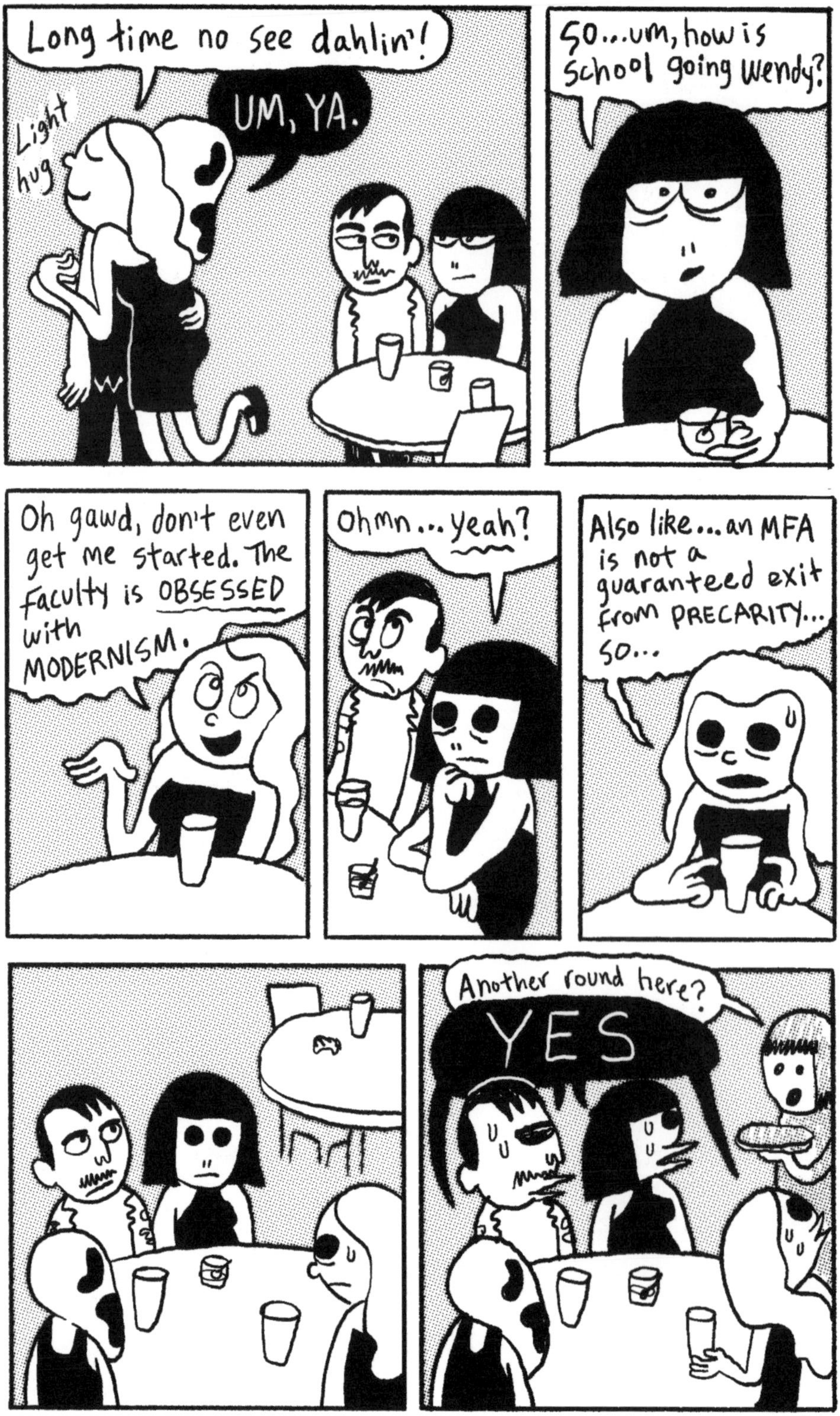
Long time no see dahlin'!
Light hug
UM, YA.
So...um, how is school going Wendy?
Oh gawd, don't even get me started. The faculty is OBSESSED with MODERNISM.
Ohmn... yeah?
Also like... an MFA is not a guaranteed exit from PRECARITY... so...
Another round here?
YES

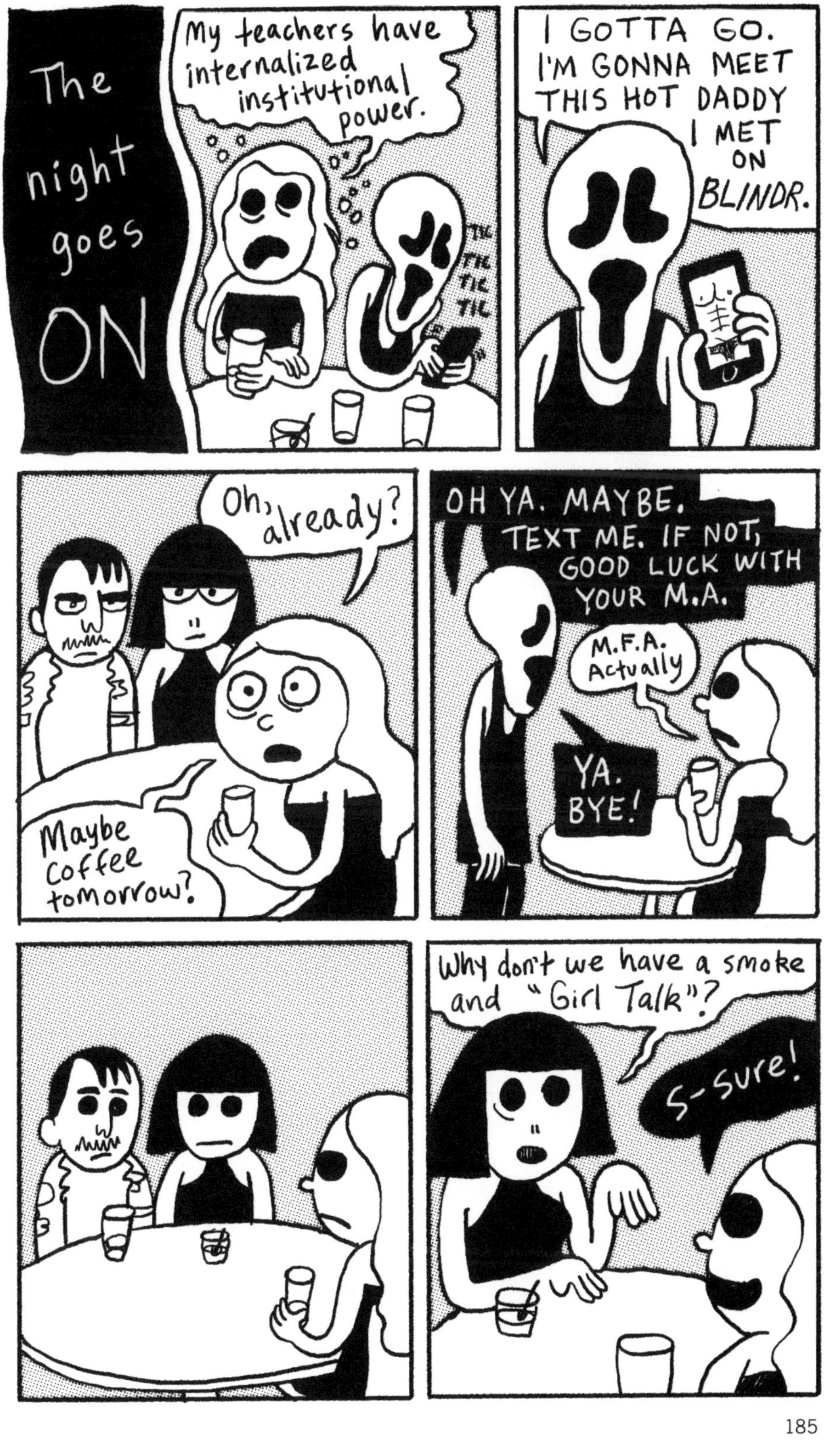
The night goes ON
My teachers have internalized institutional power.
TIC TIC TIC TIC
I GOTTA GO. I'M GONNA MEET THIS HOT DADDY I MET ON BLINDR.
Oh, already?
Maybe coffee tomorrow?
OH YA. MAYBE. TEXT ME. IF NOT, GOOD LUCK WITH YOUR M.A.
M.F.A. Actually
YA. BYE!
Why don't we have a smoke and "Girl Talk"?
S-Sure!

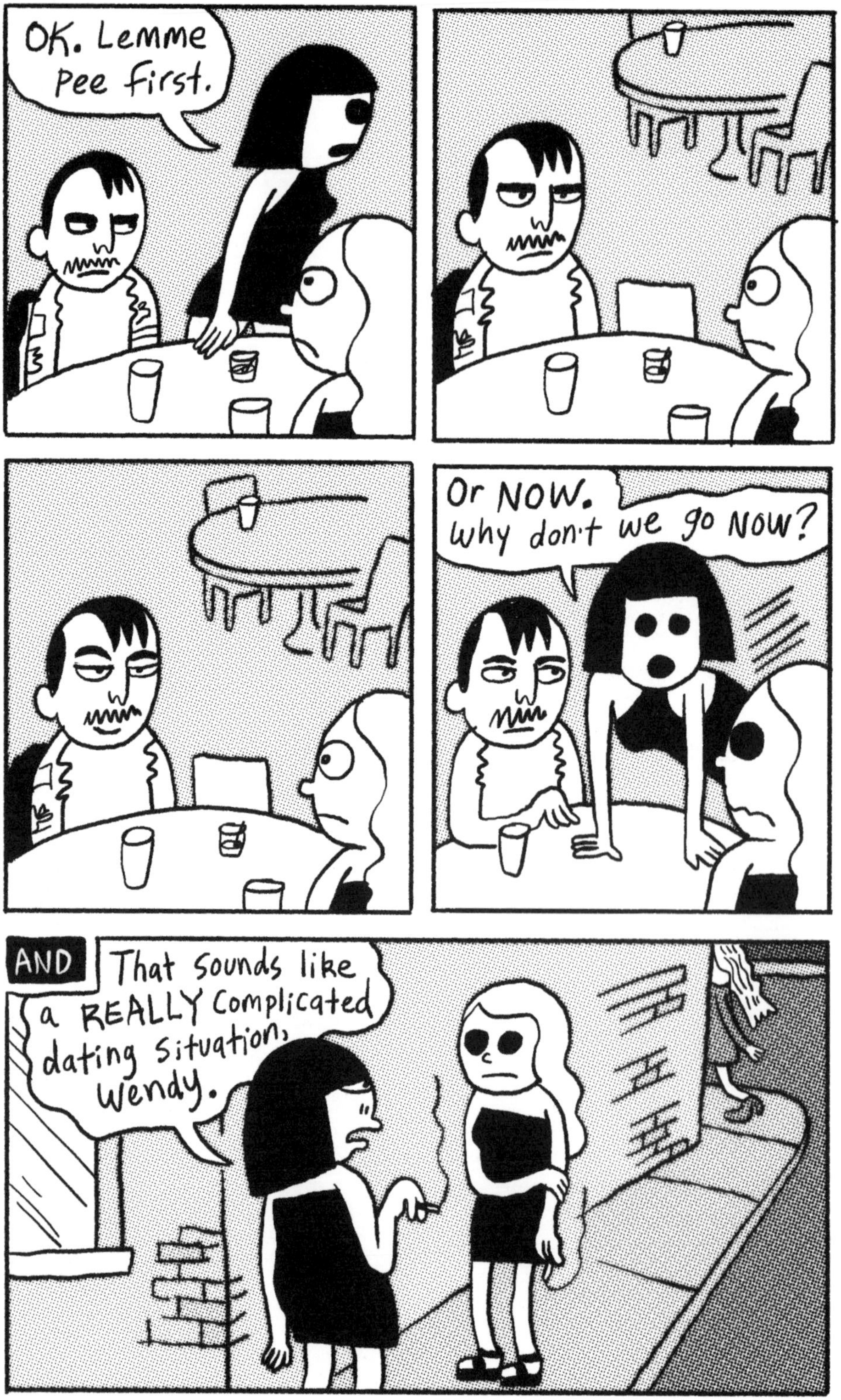
OK. Lemme pee first.
Or NOW. Why don't we go NOW?
AND
That sounds like a REALLY complicated dating situation, Wendy.

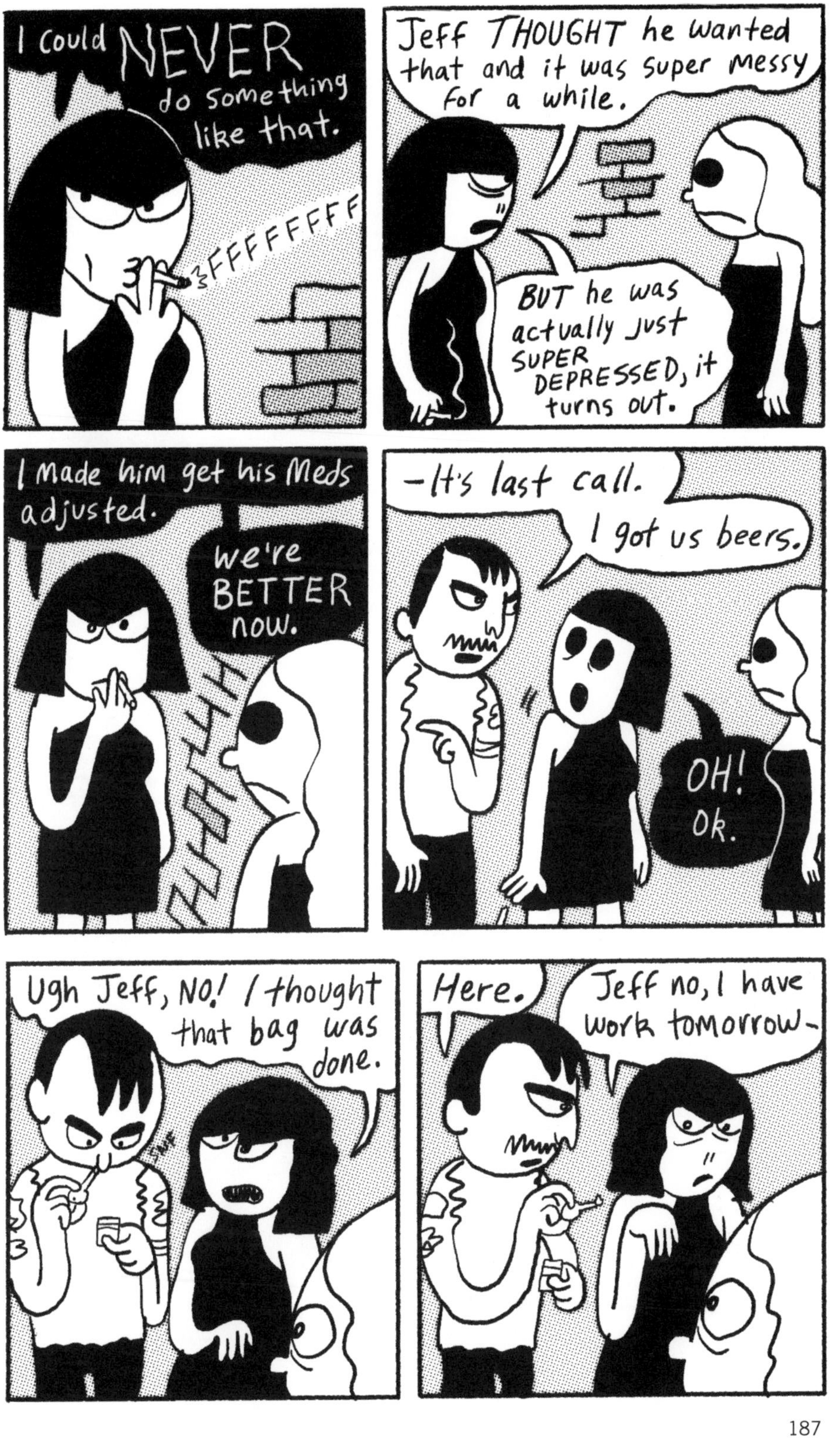
I could NEVER do something like that.
FFFFFFFF
Jeff THOUGHT he wanted that and it was super messy for a while.
BUT he was actually just SUPER DEPRESSED, it turns out.
I made him get his Meds adjusted.
We're BETTER now.
-It's last call.
I got us beers.
OH! Ok.
Ugh Jeff, NO! I thought that bag was done.
Here.
Jeff no, I have work tomorrow-

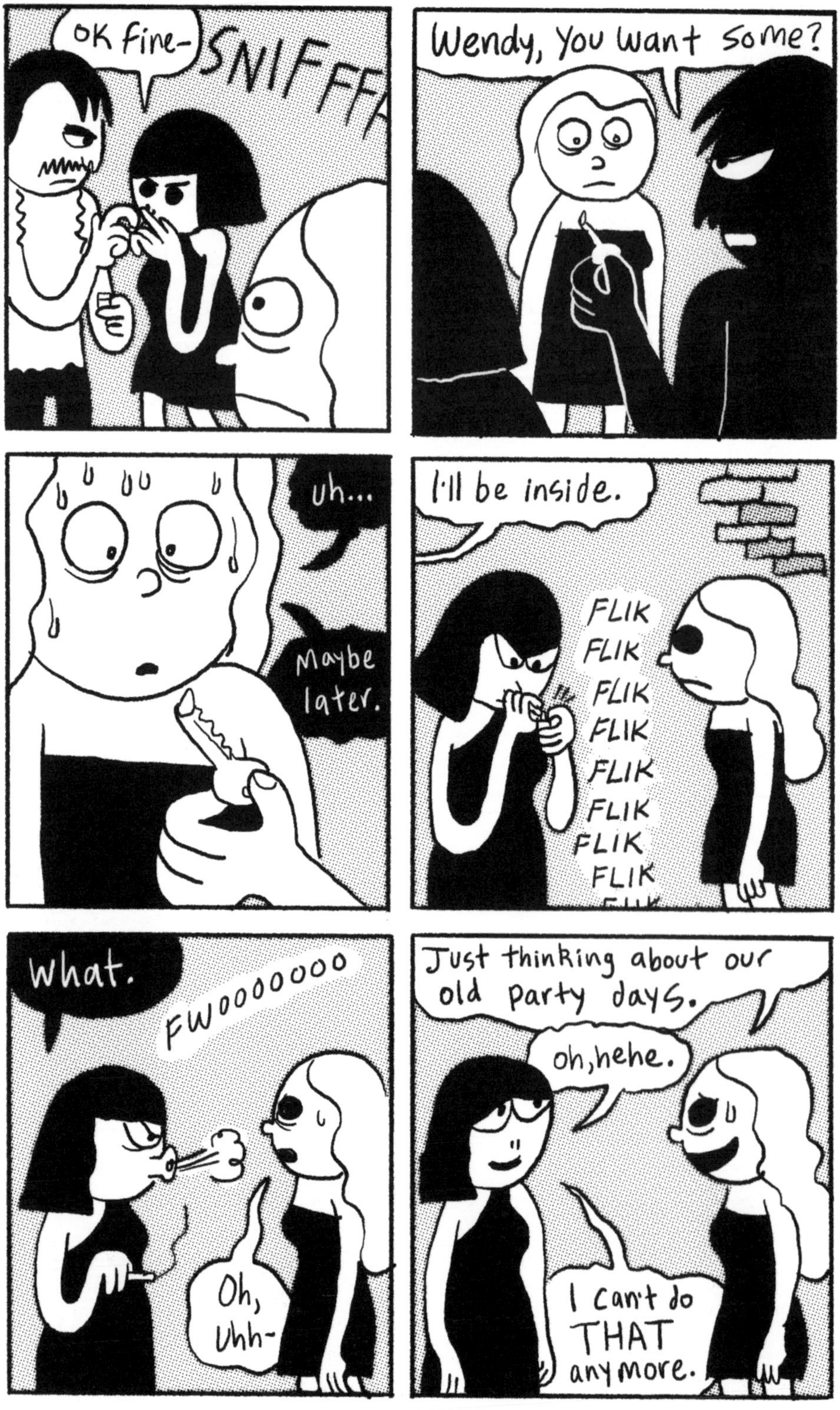

OK fine-
SNIFFFF
Wendy, You want some?
uh...
Maybe later.
I'll be inside.
FLIK
FLIK
FLIK
FLIK
FLIK
FLIK
FLIK
FLIK
What.
FWOOOOOOO
Oh, Uhh-
Just thinking about our old party days.
oh, hehe.
I can't do THAT anymore.

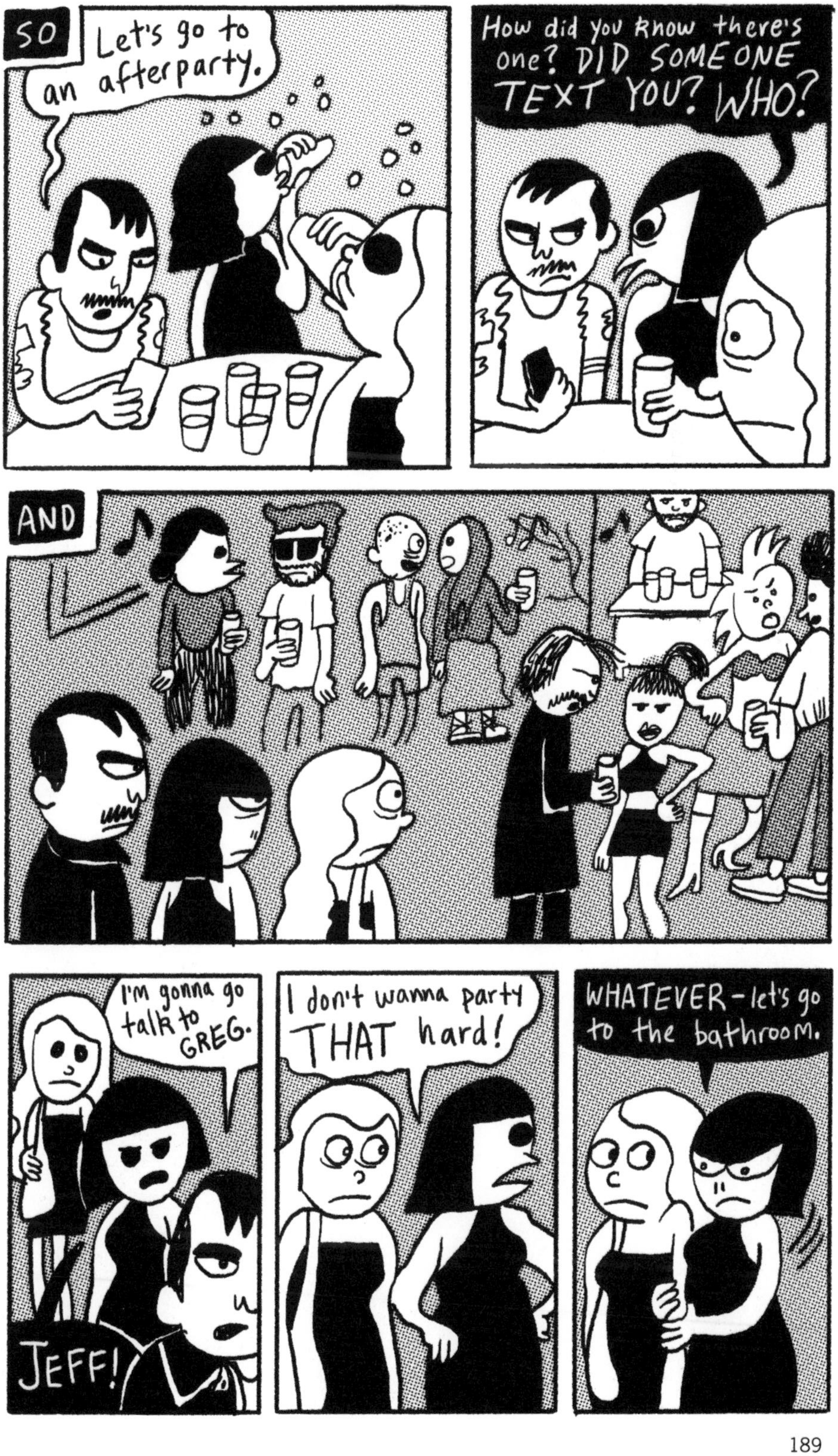
SO
Let's go to an afterparty.
How did you know there's one? DID SOMEONE TEXT YOU? WHO?
AND
I'm gonna go talk to GREG.
JEFF!
I don't wanna party THAT hard!
WHATEVER - let's go to the bathroom.

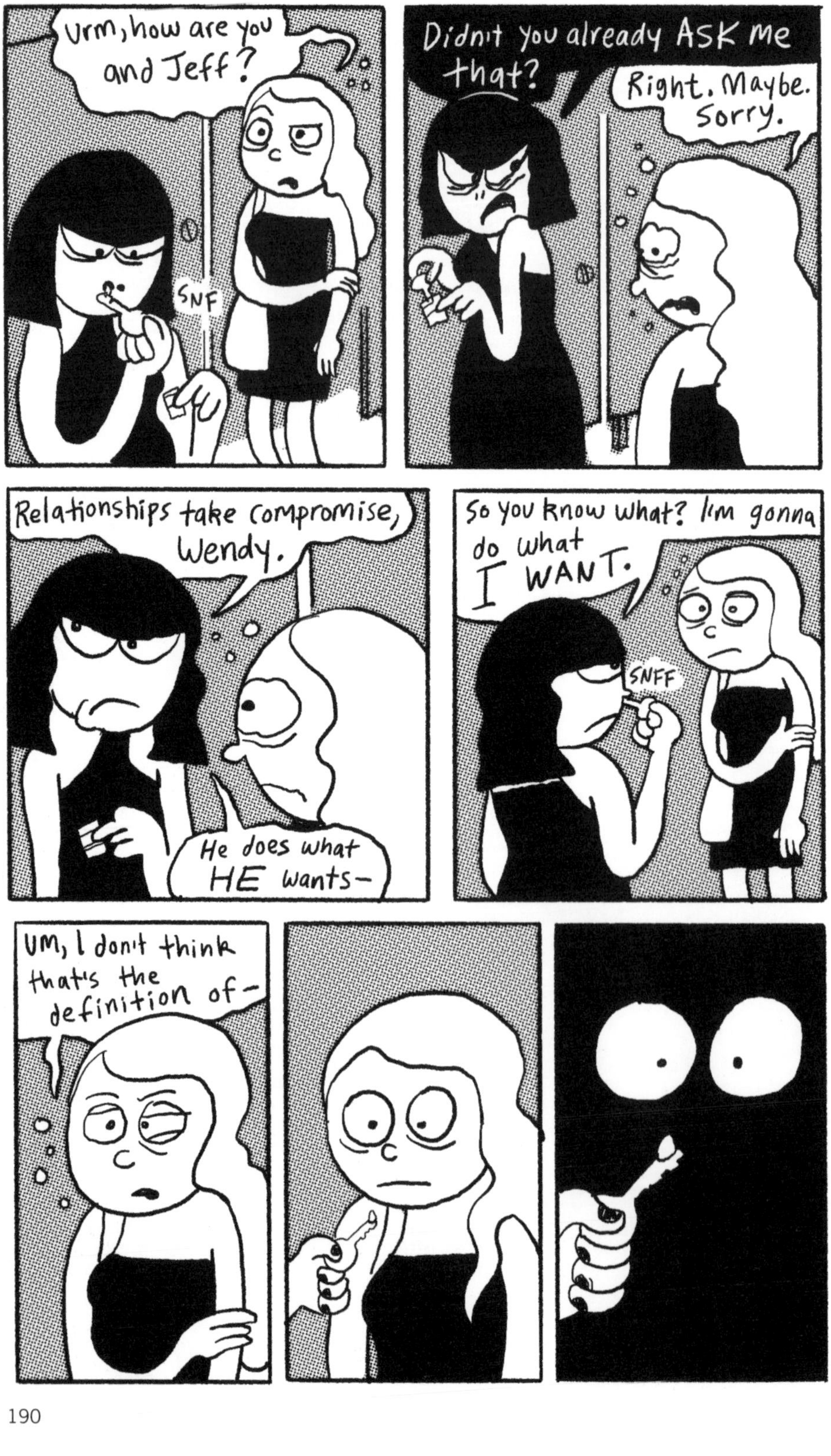

Urm, how are you and Jeff?
SNF
Didn't you already ASK me that?
Right. Maybe. Sorry.
Relationships take compromise, Wendy.
He does what HE wants-
So you know what? I'm gonna do what I WANT.
SNFF
Um, I don't think that's the definition of-

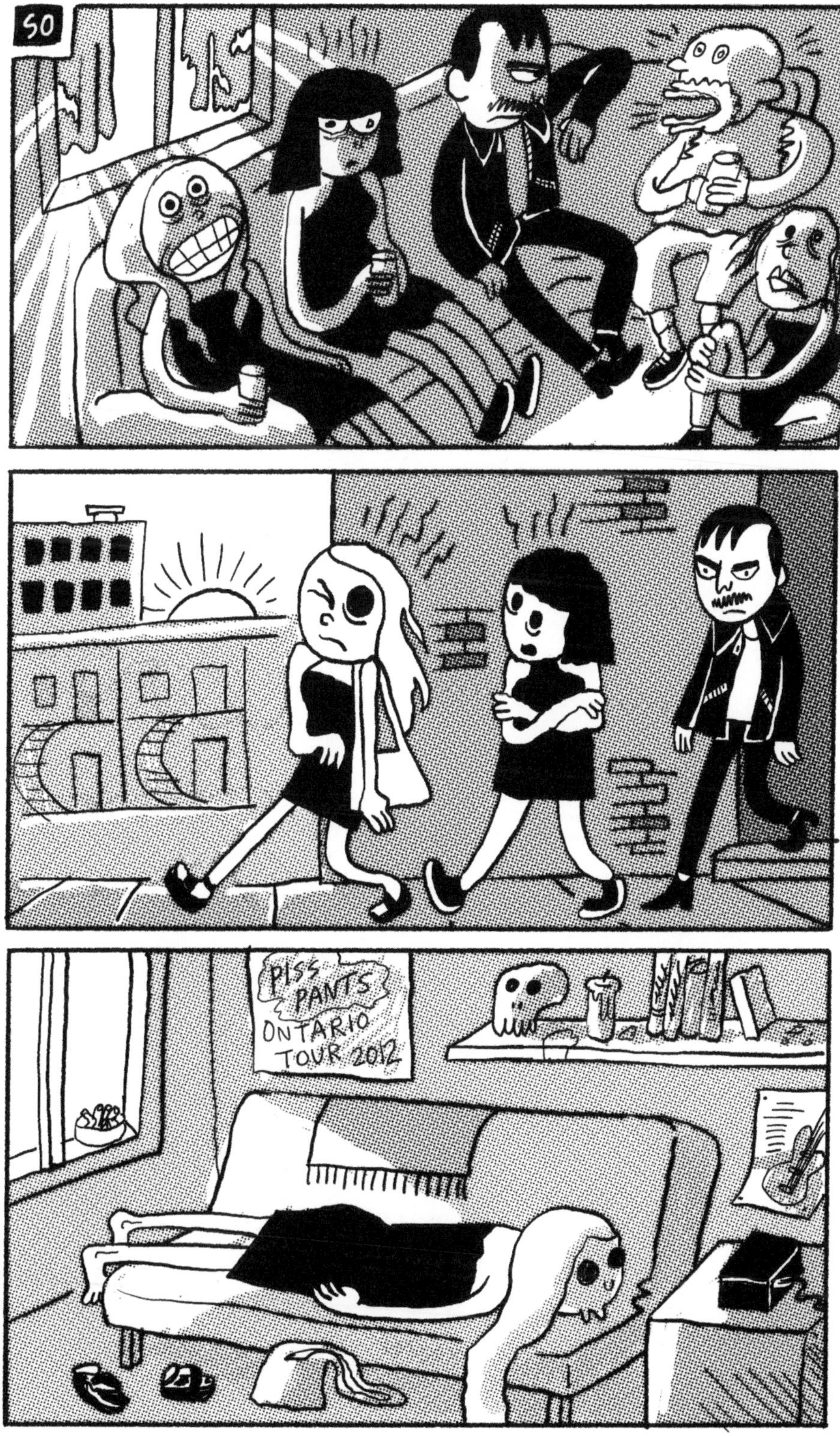
50
PISS PANTS
ONTARIO TOUR 2012

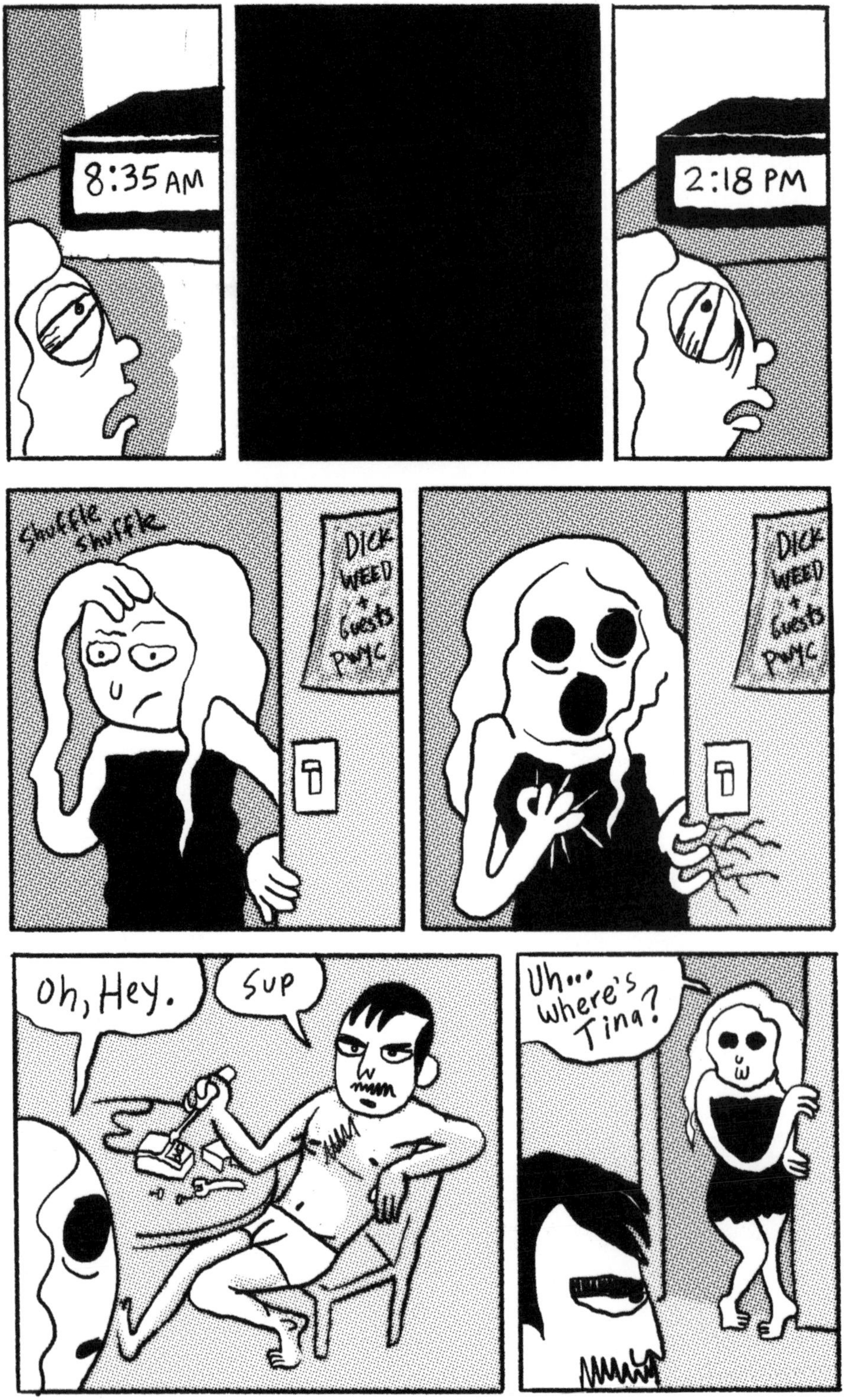
8:35 AM
2:18 PM
shuffle shuffle
DICK WEED + Guests PWYC
DICK WEED + Guests PWYC
Oh, Hey.
Sup
Uh... where's Tina?

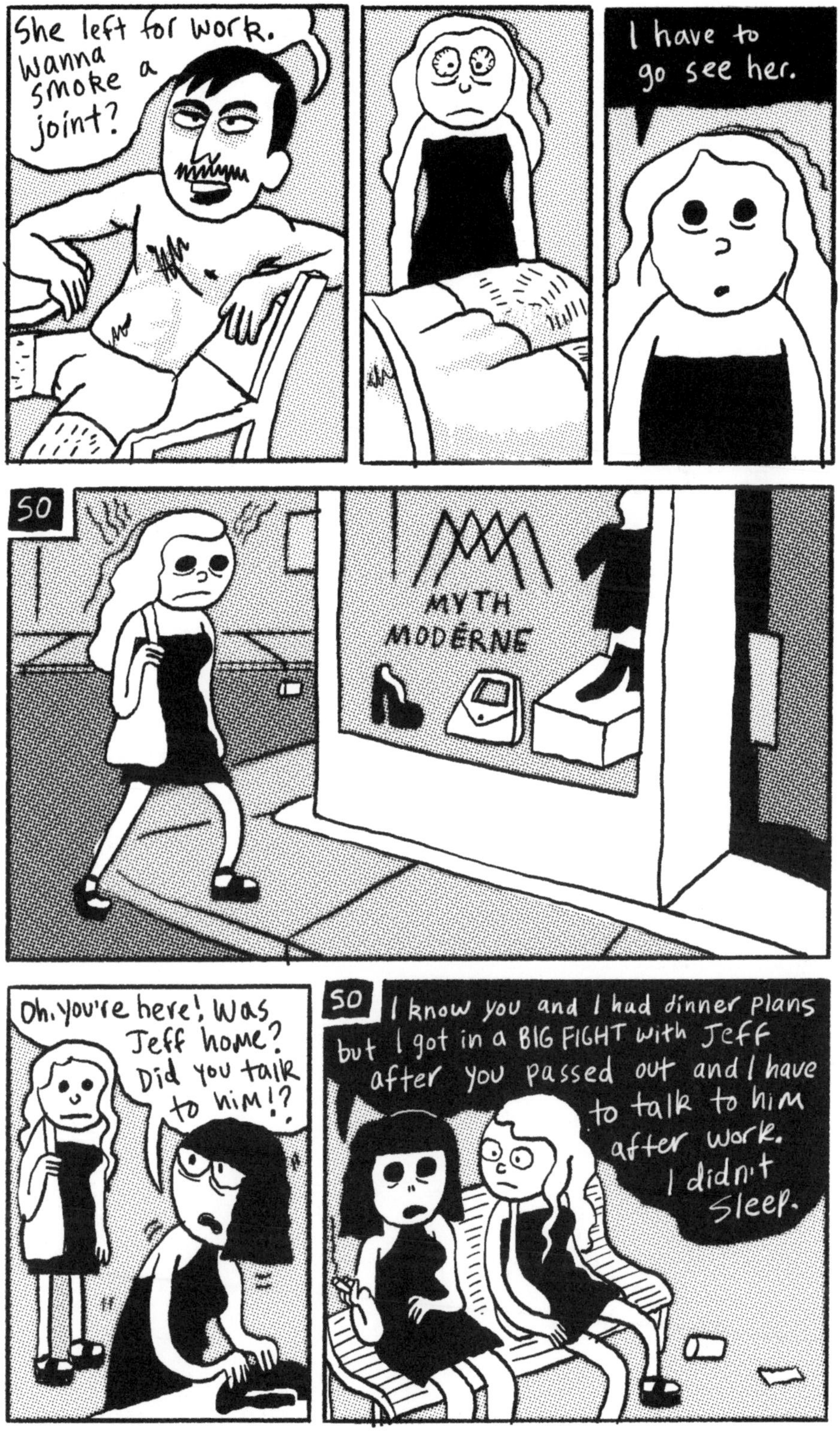
She left for work. Wanna smoke a joint?
I have to go see her.
SO
MYTH MODÉRNE
Oh, you're here! Was Jeff home? Did you talk to him!?
SO
I know you and I had dinner plans but I got in a BIG FIGHT with Jeff after you passed out and I have to talk to him after work. I didn't sleep.

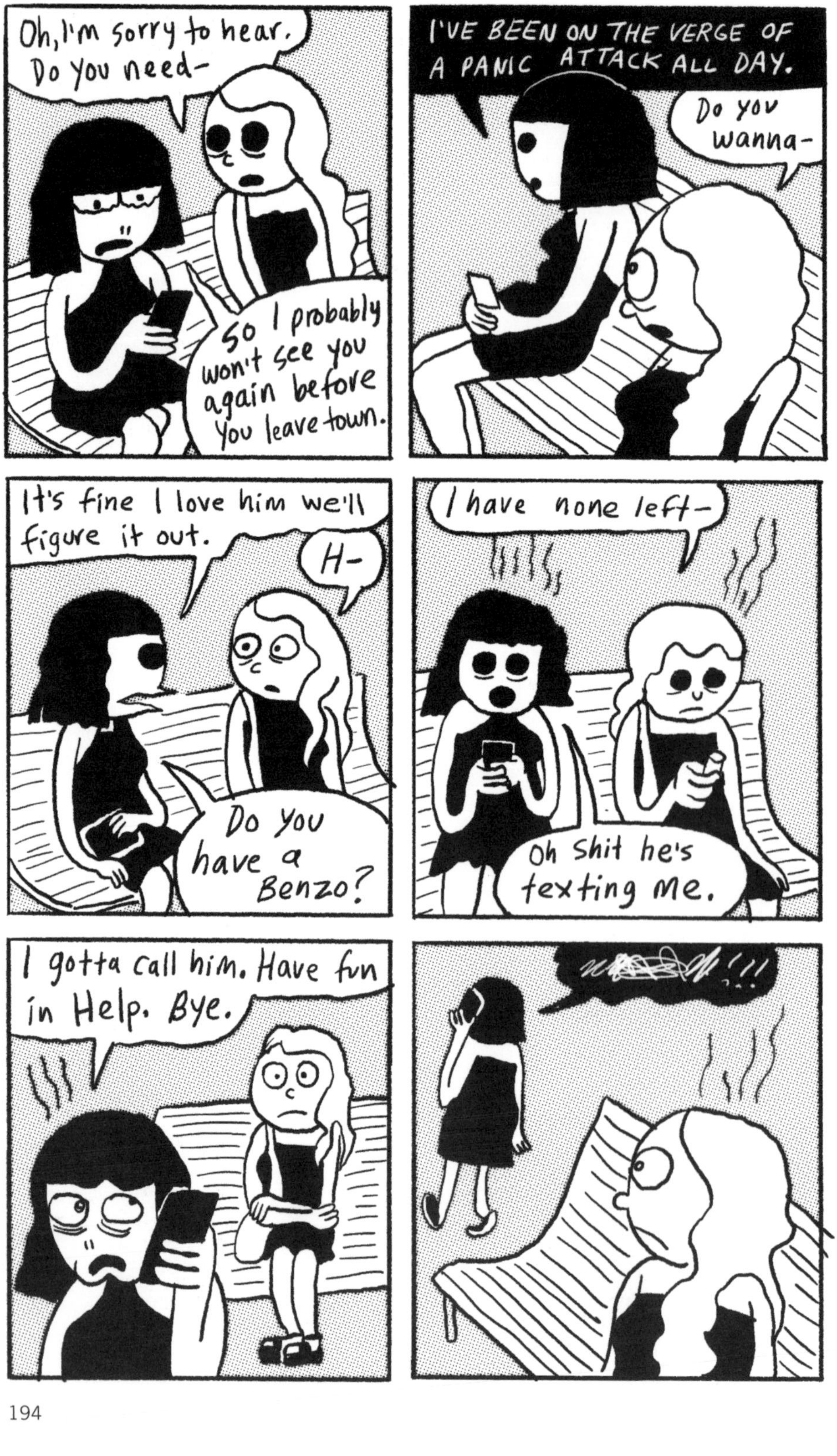
Oh, I'm sorry to hear. Do you need-
So I probably won't see you again before you leave town.
I'VE BEEN ON THE VERGE OF A PANIC ATTACK ALL DAY.
Do you wanna-
It's fine I love him we'll figure it out.
H-
Do you have a Benzo?
I have none left-
Oh shit he's texting me.
I gotta call him. Have fun in Help. Bye.
!!!

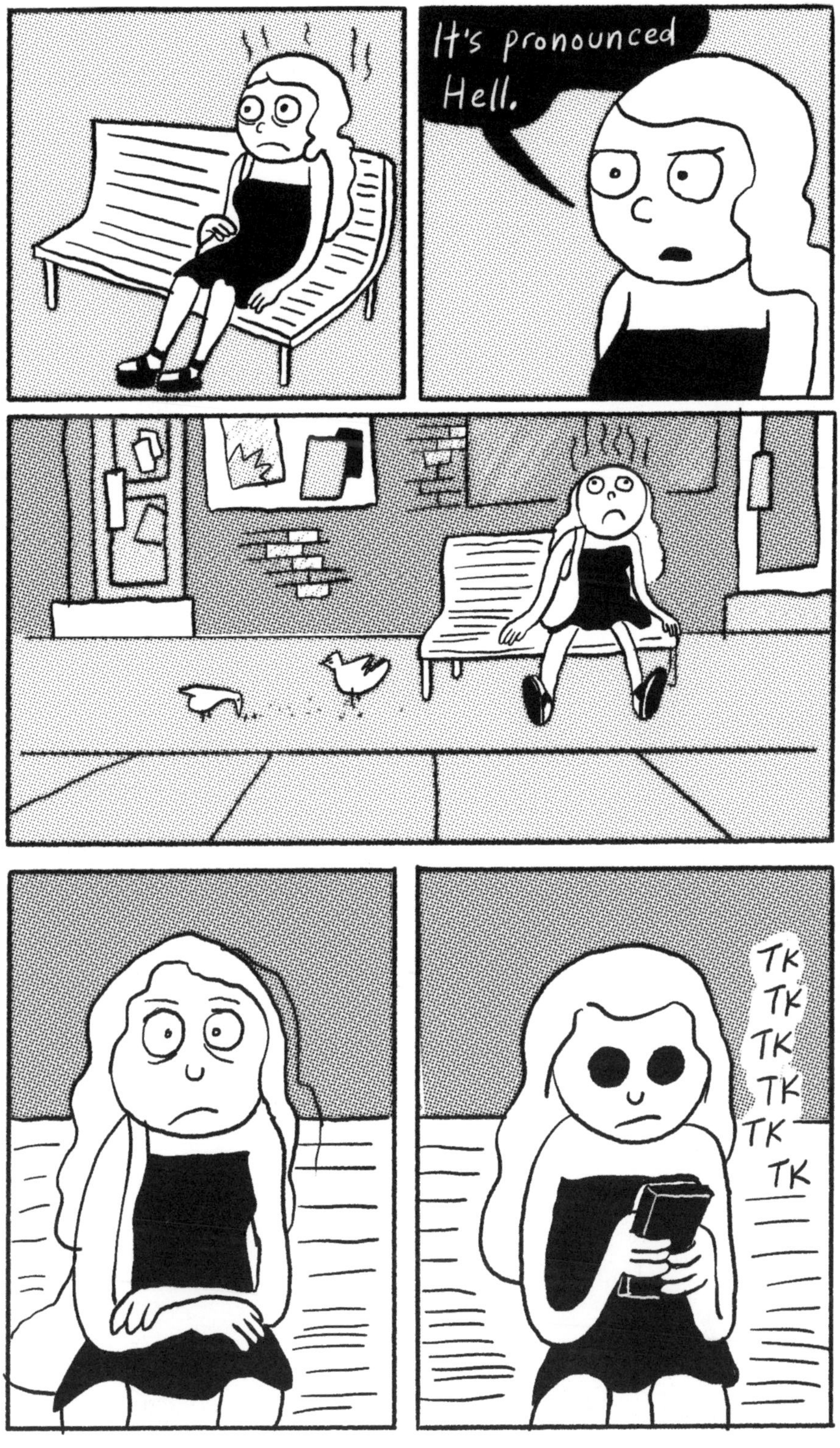

It's pronounced Hell.
TK TK TK TK TK TK

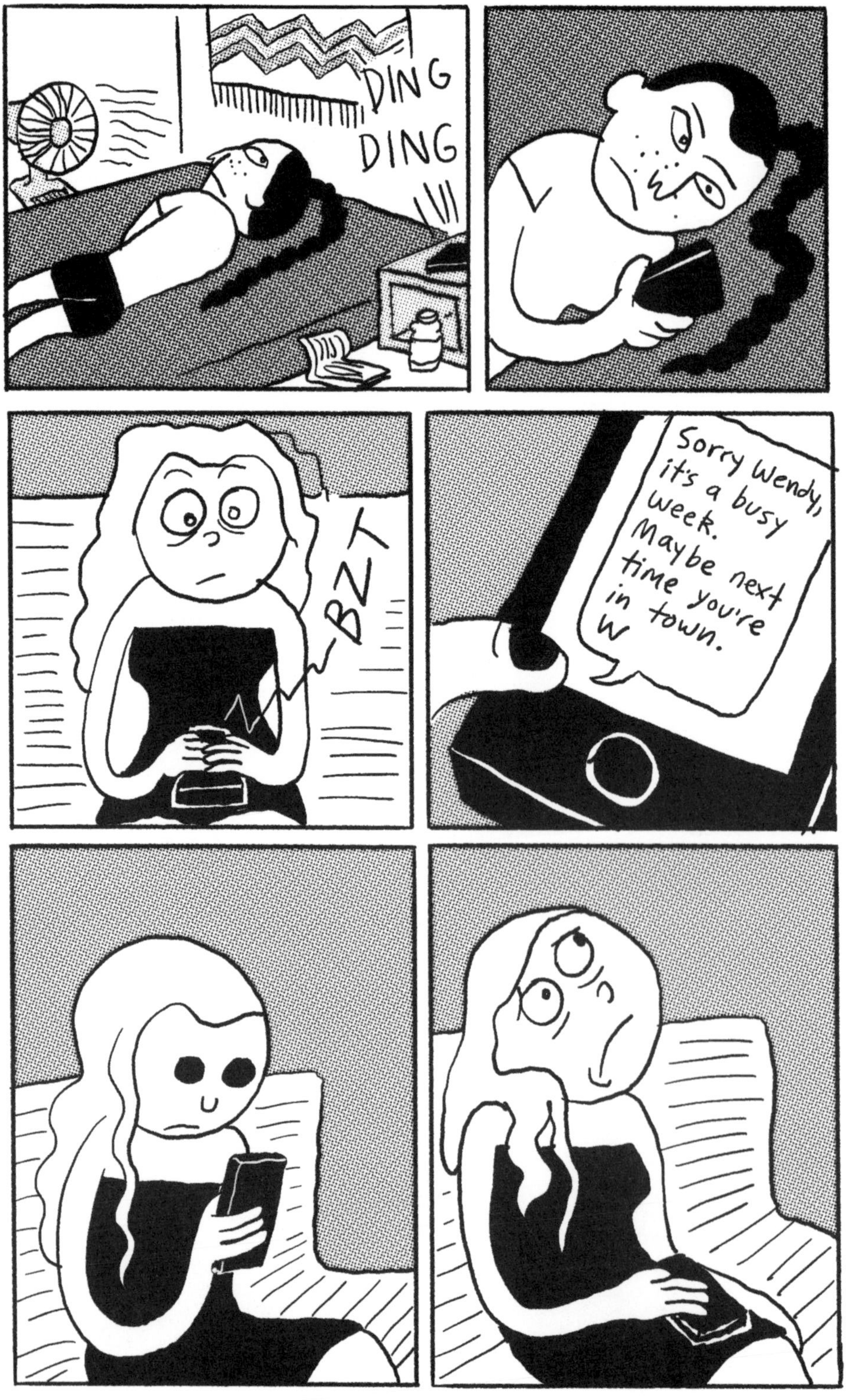
DING
DING
BZZT
Sorry Wendy, it's a busy week. Maybe next time you're in town.
W

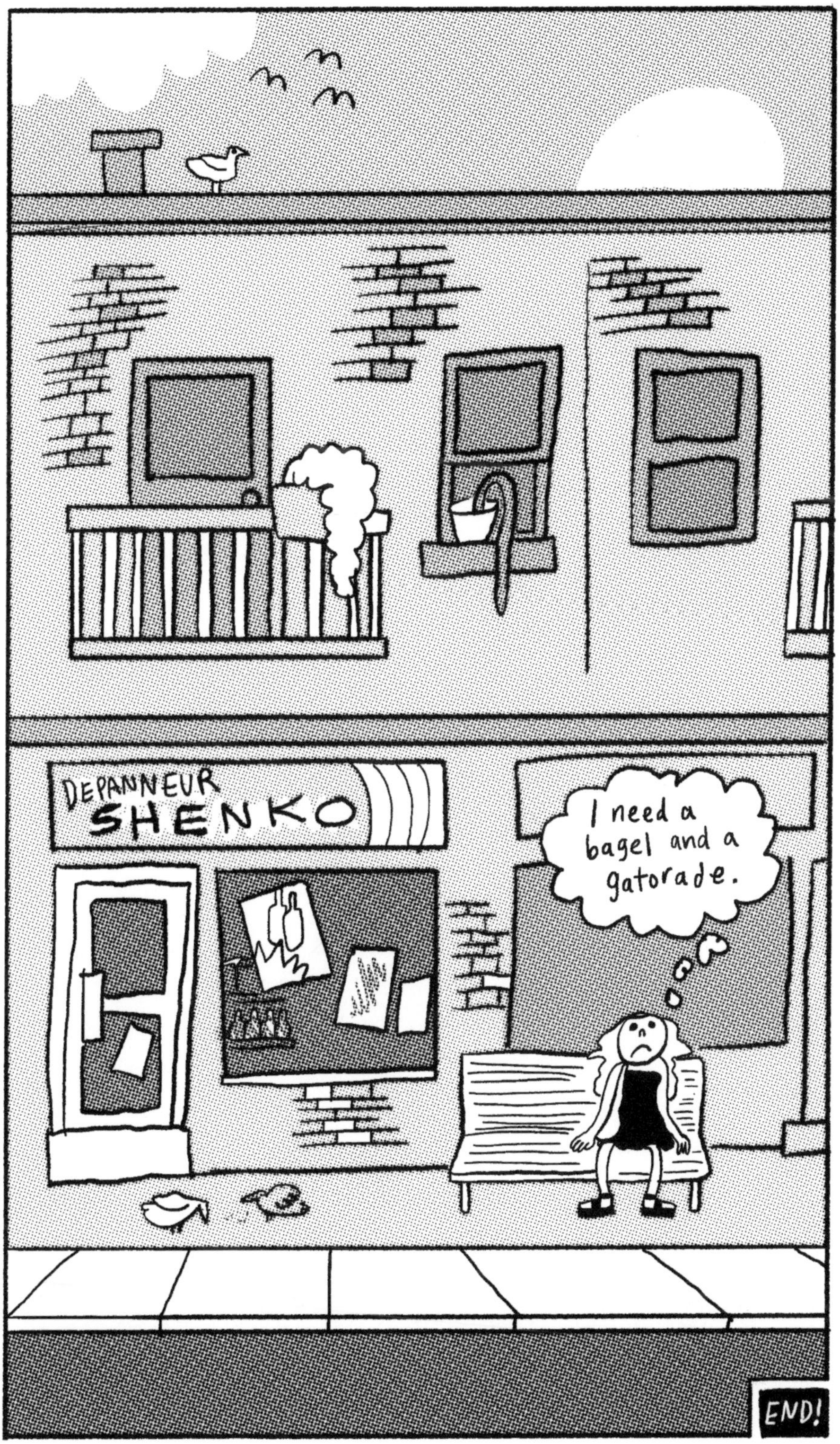
DEPANNEUR
SHENKO
I need a bagel and a gatorade.
END!

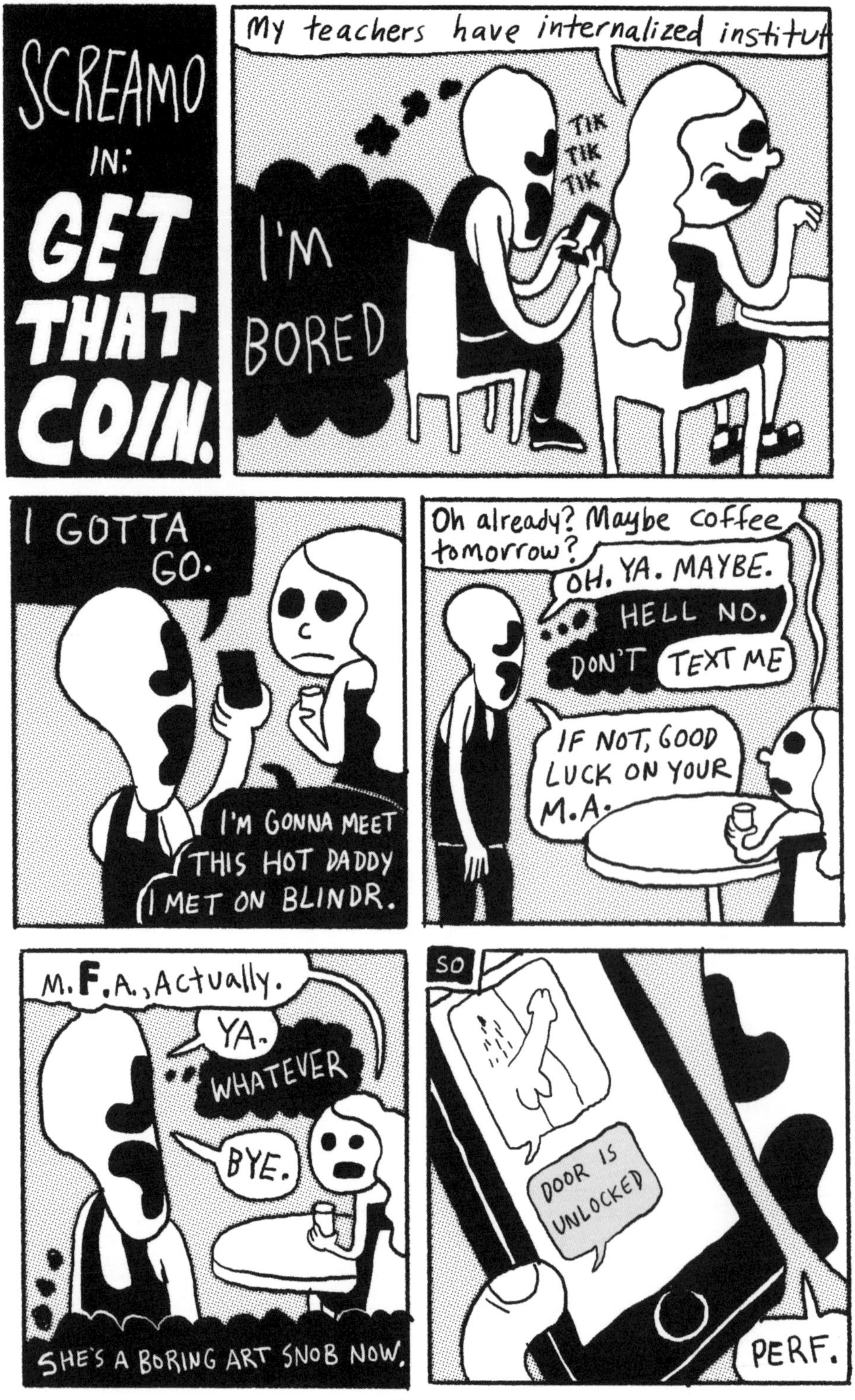
SCREAMO IN: GET THAT COIN.
My teachers have internalized institut
TIK TIK TIK
I'M BORED
I GOTTA GO.
I'M GONNA MEET THIS HOT DADDY I MET ON BLINDR.
Oh already? Maybe coffee tomorrow?
OH. YA. MAYBE.
HELL NO.
DON'T
TEXT ME
IF NOT, GOOD LUCK ON YOUR M.A.
M.F.A., Actually.
YA.
WHATEVER
BYE.
SHE'S A BORING ART SNOB NOW.
SO
DOOR IS UNLOCKED
PERF.

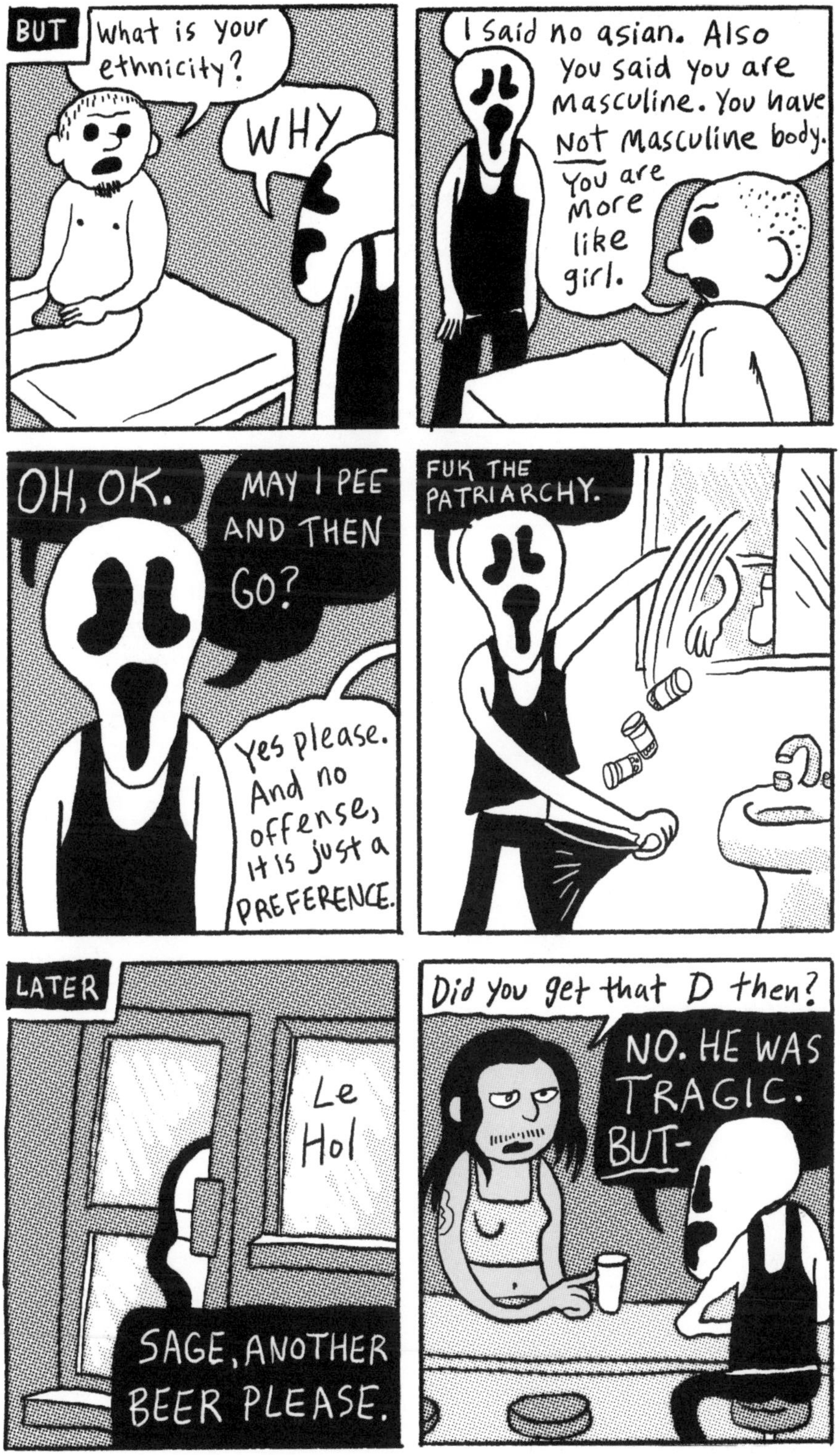
BUT
What is your ethnicity?
WHY
I said no asian. Also you said you are masculine. You have NOT masculine body.
You are more like girl.
OH, OK.
MAY I PEE AND THEN GO?
Yes please. And no offense, It is just a PREFERENCE.
FUK THE PATRIARCHY.
LATER
Le Hol
SAGE, ANOTHER BEER PLEASE.
Did you get that D then?
NO. HE WAS TRAGIC. BUT-

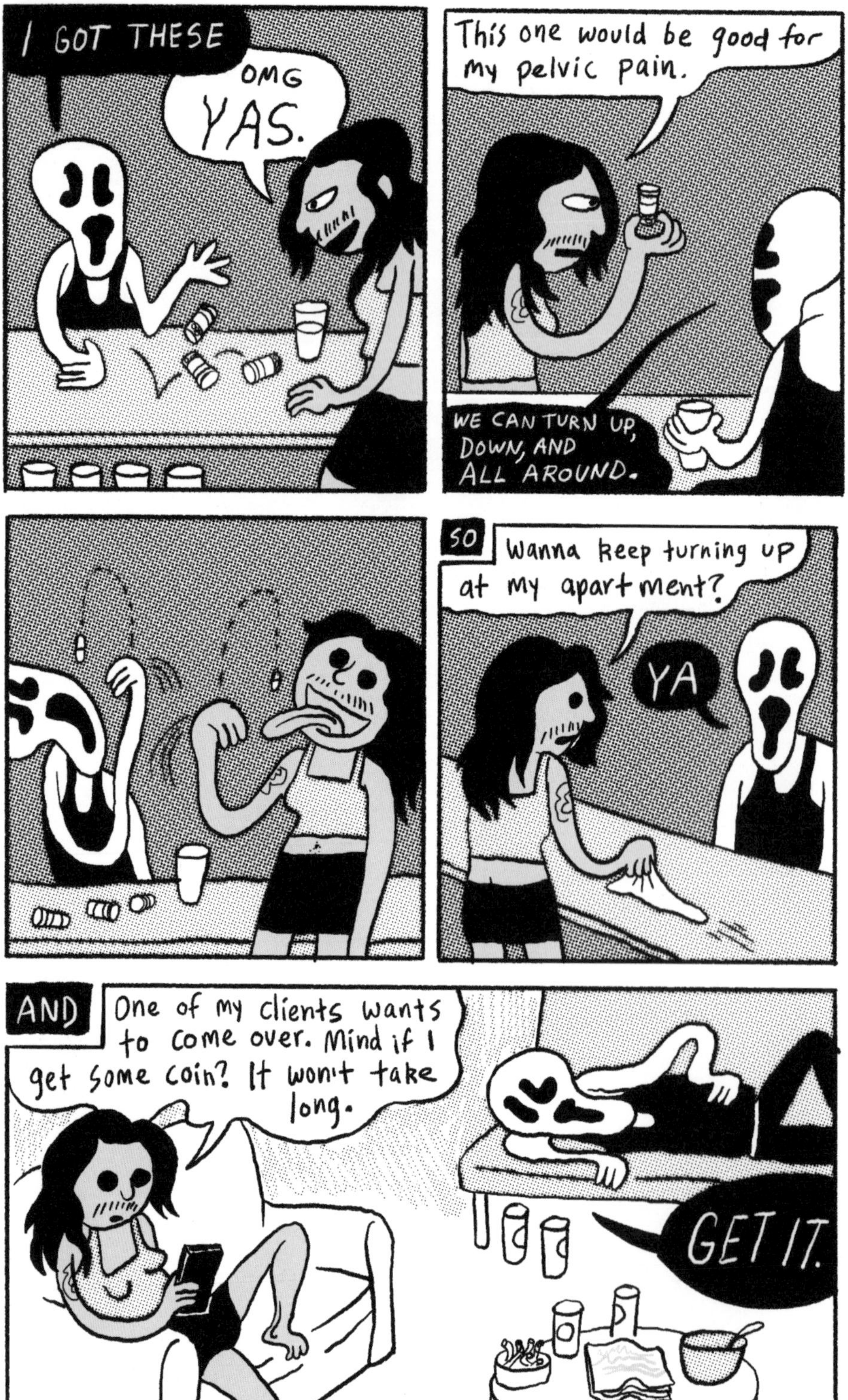
I GOT THESE
OMG YAS.
This one would be good for my pelvic pain.
WE CAN TURN UP, DOWN, AND ALL AROUND.
SO
Wanna keep turning up at my apartment?
YA
AND
One of my clients wants to come over. Mind if I get some coin? It won't take long.
GET IT.

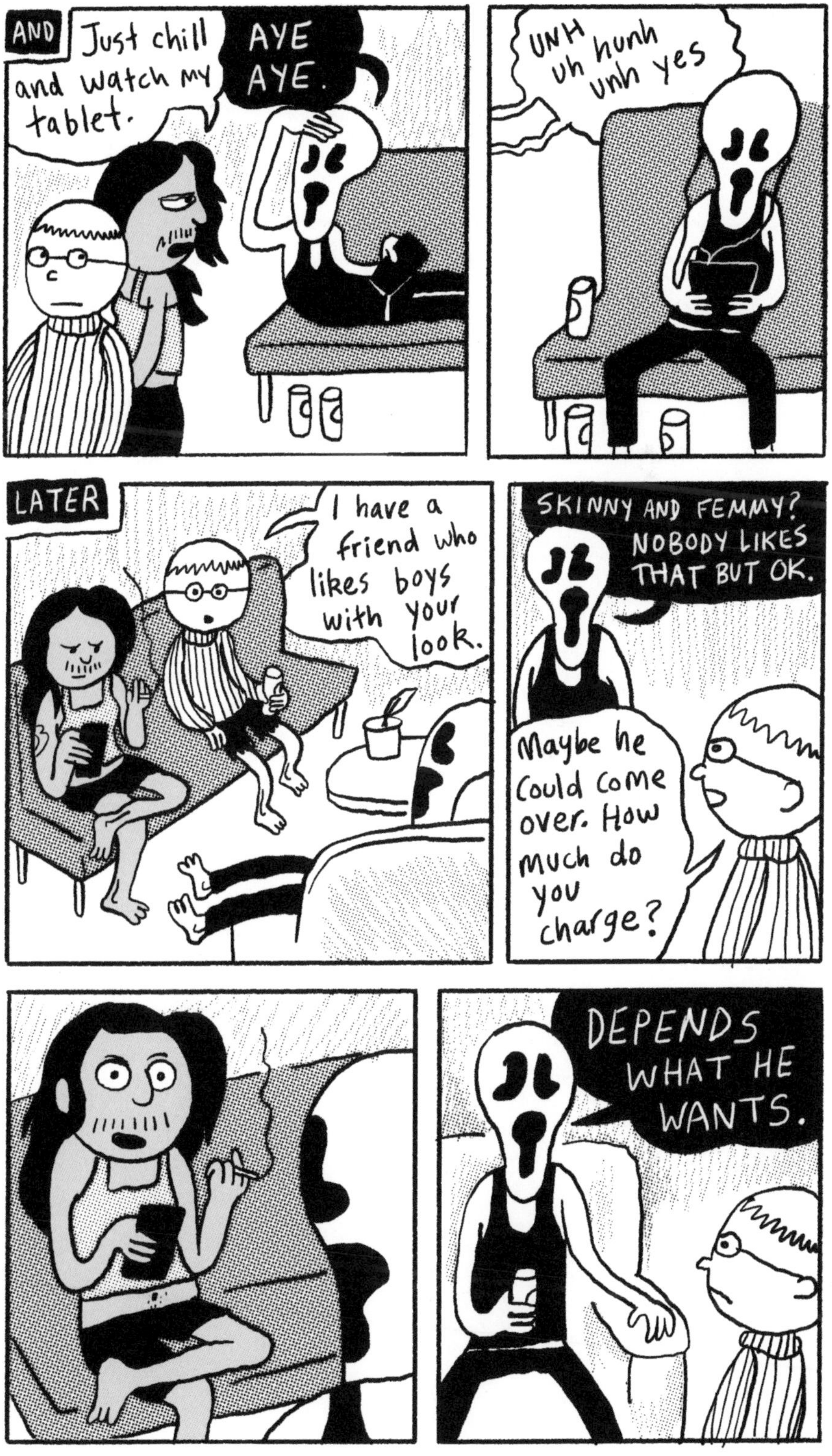
AND
Just chill and watch my tablet.
AYE AYE.
UNH uh hunh unh yes
LATER
I have a friend who likes boys with your look.
SKINNY AND FEMMY? NOBODY LIKES THAT BUT OK.
Maybe he could come over. How much do you charge?
DEPENDS WHAT HE WANTS.

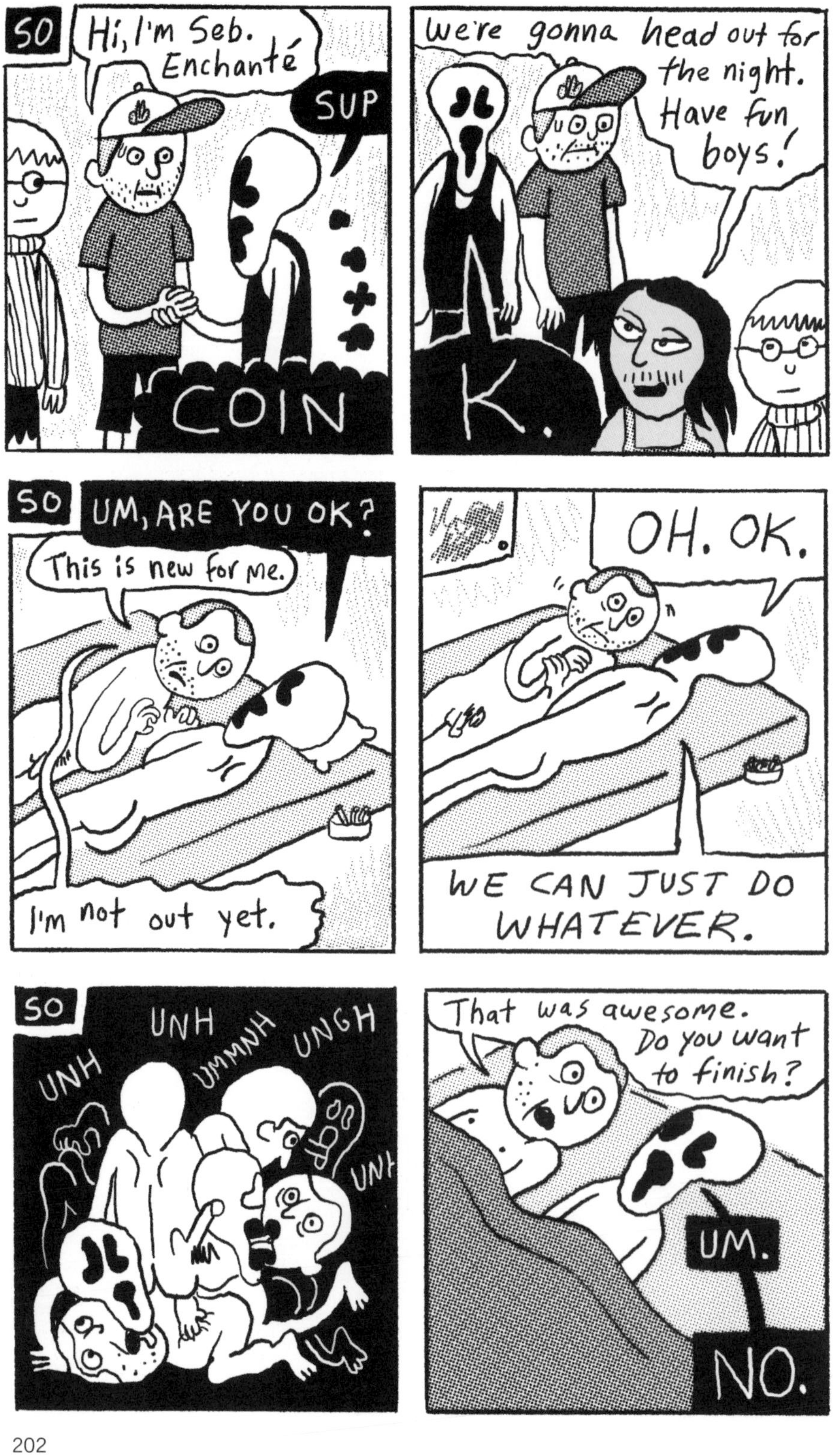
SO
Hi, I'm Seb. Enchanté
SUP
COIN
We're gonna head out for the night. Have fun boys!
K.
SO
UM, ARE YOU OK?
This is new for me.
I'm not out yet.
OH. OK.
WE CAN JUST DO WHATEVER.
SO
UNH
UNH
UMMNH
UNGH
That was awesome. Do you want to finish?
UM.
NO.

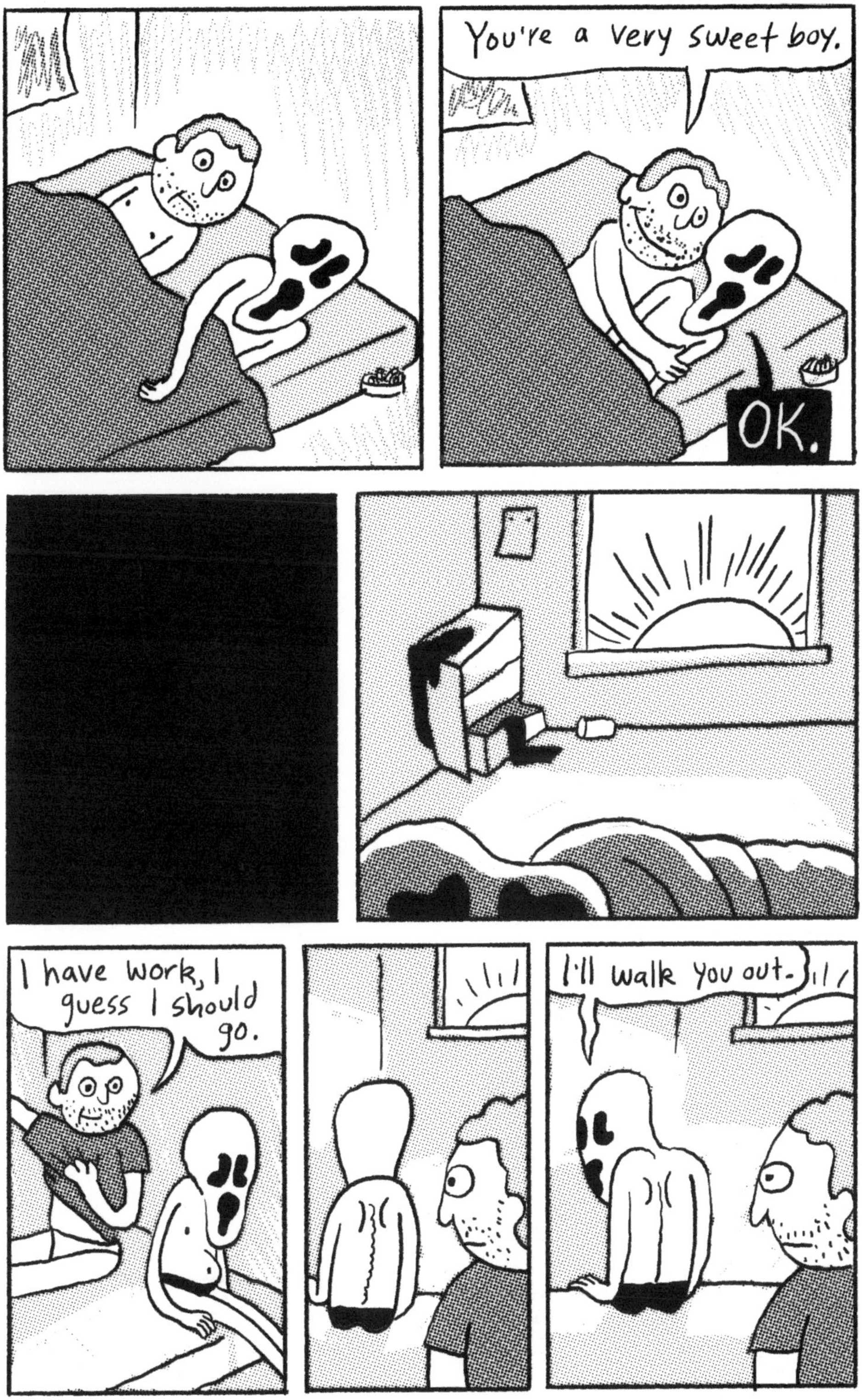
You're a very sweet boy.
OK.
I have work, I guess I should go.
I'll walk you out.

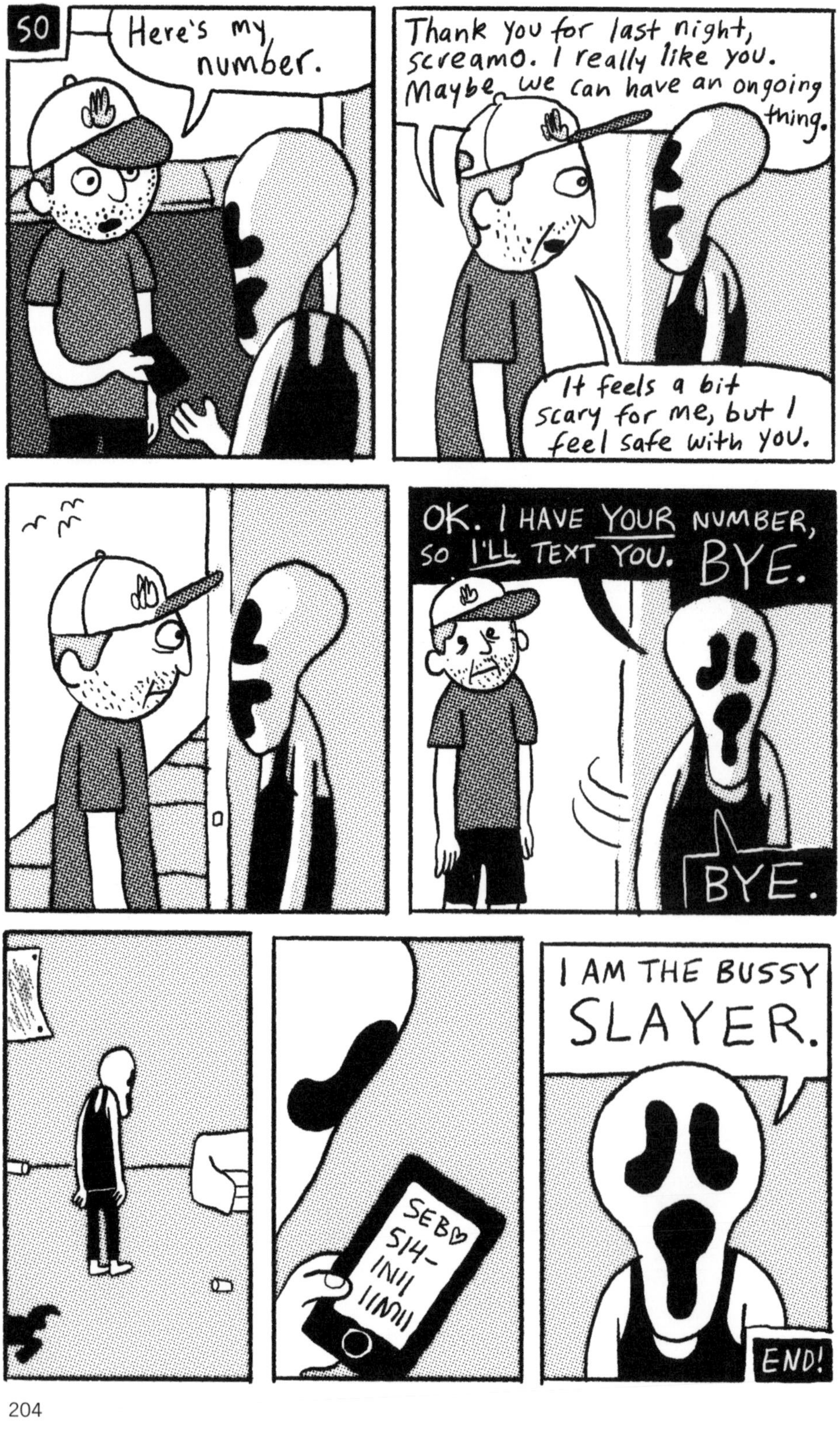
50
Here's my number.
Thank you for last night, screamo. I really like you. Maybe we can have an ongoing thing.
It feels a bit scary for me, but I feel safe with you.
OK. I HAVE YOUR NUMBER, SO I'LL TEXT YOU. BYE.
BYE.
SEB
514-
I AM THE BUSSY SLAYER.
END!

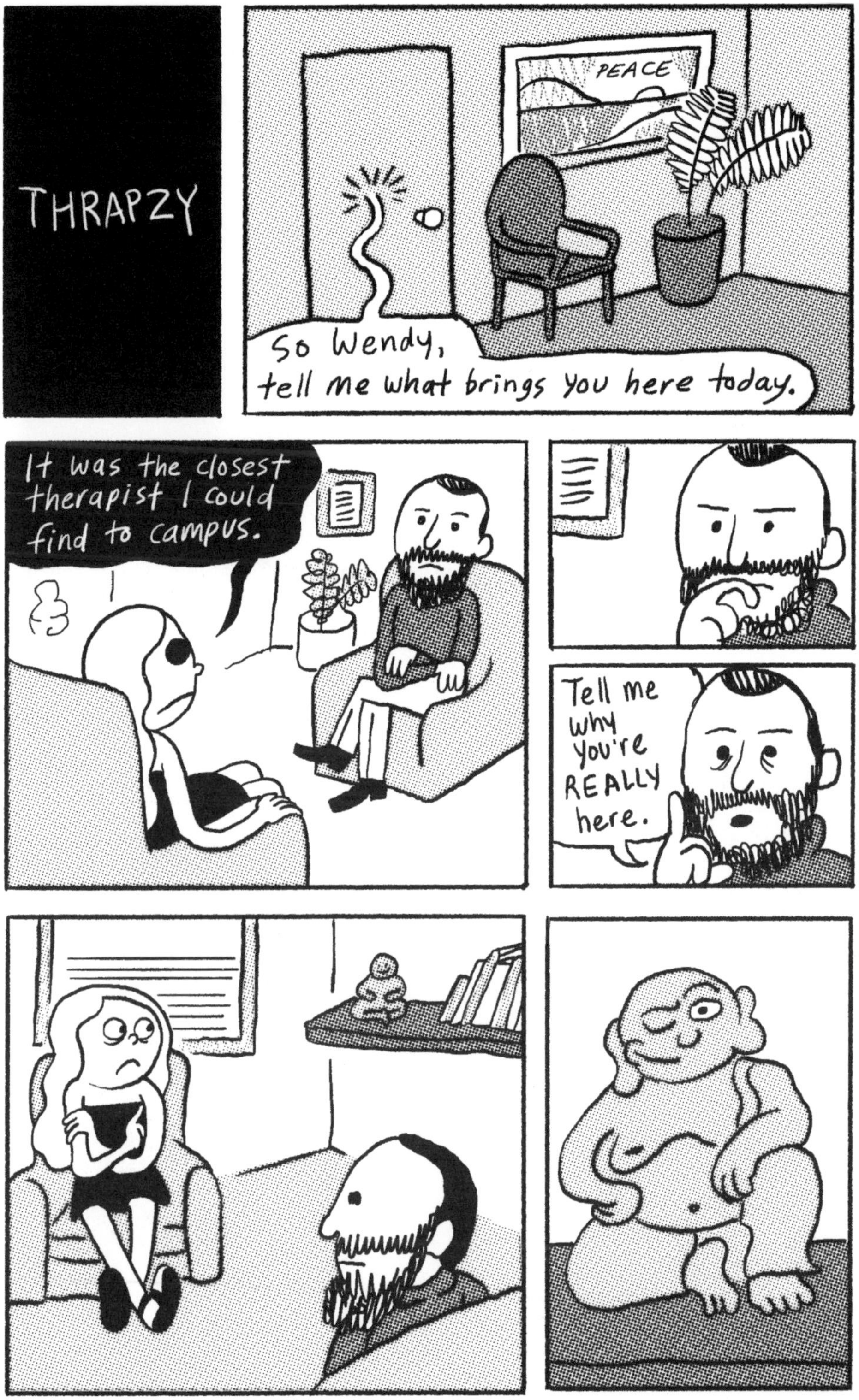
THRAPZY
PEACE
So Wendy, tell me what brings you here today.
It was the closest therapist I could find to campus.
Tell me why you're REALLY here.

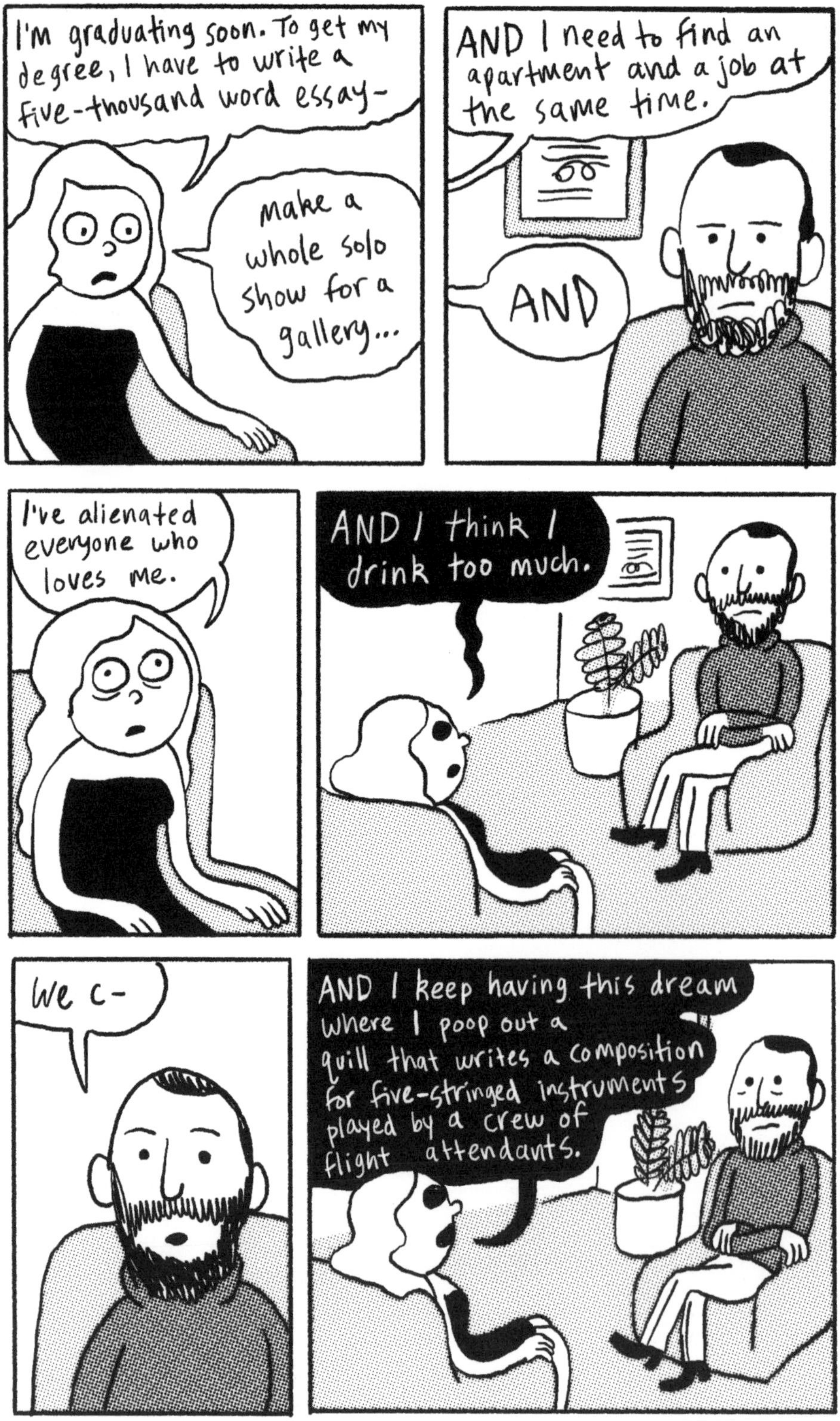

I'm graduating soon. To get my degree, I have to write a five-thousand word essay-
Make a whole solo show for a gallery...
AND I need to find an apartment and a job at the same time.
AND
I've alienated everyone who loves me.
AND I think I drink too much.
We c-
AND I keep having this dream where I poop out a quill that writes a composition for five-stringed instruments played by a crew of flight attendants.

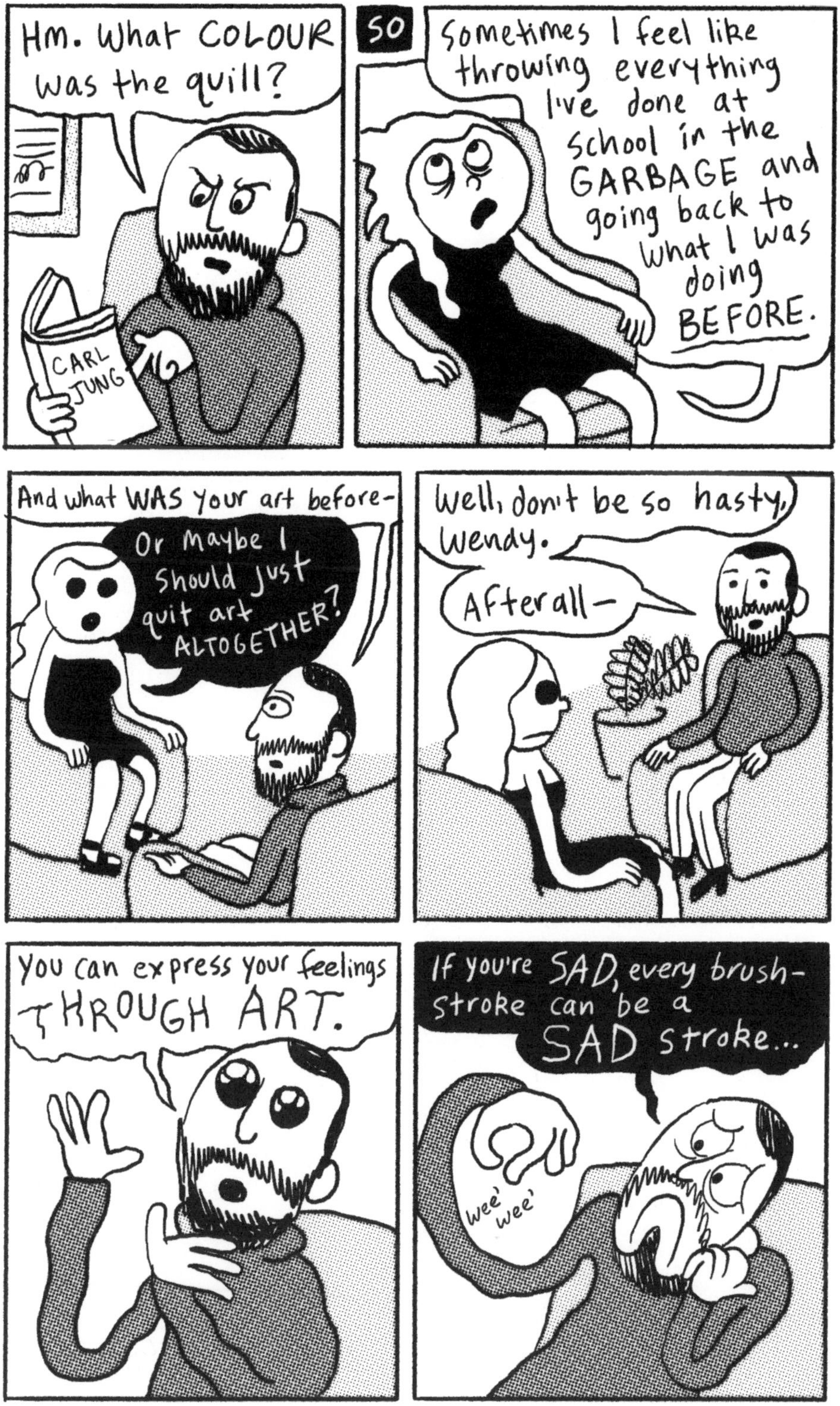
Hm. What COLOUR was the quill?
CARL JUNG
SO
Sometimes I feel like throwing everything I've done at school in the GARBAGE and going back to what I was doing BEFORE.
And what WAS your art before-
Or maybe I should just quit art ALTOGETHER?
Well, don't be so hasty, Wendy.
Afterall-
You can express your feelings THROUGH ART.
If you're SAD, every brush-stroke can be a SAD stroke...
wee' wee'

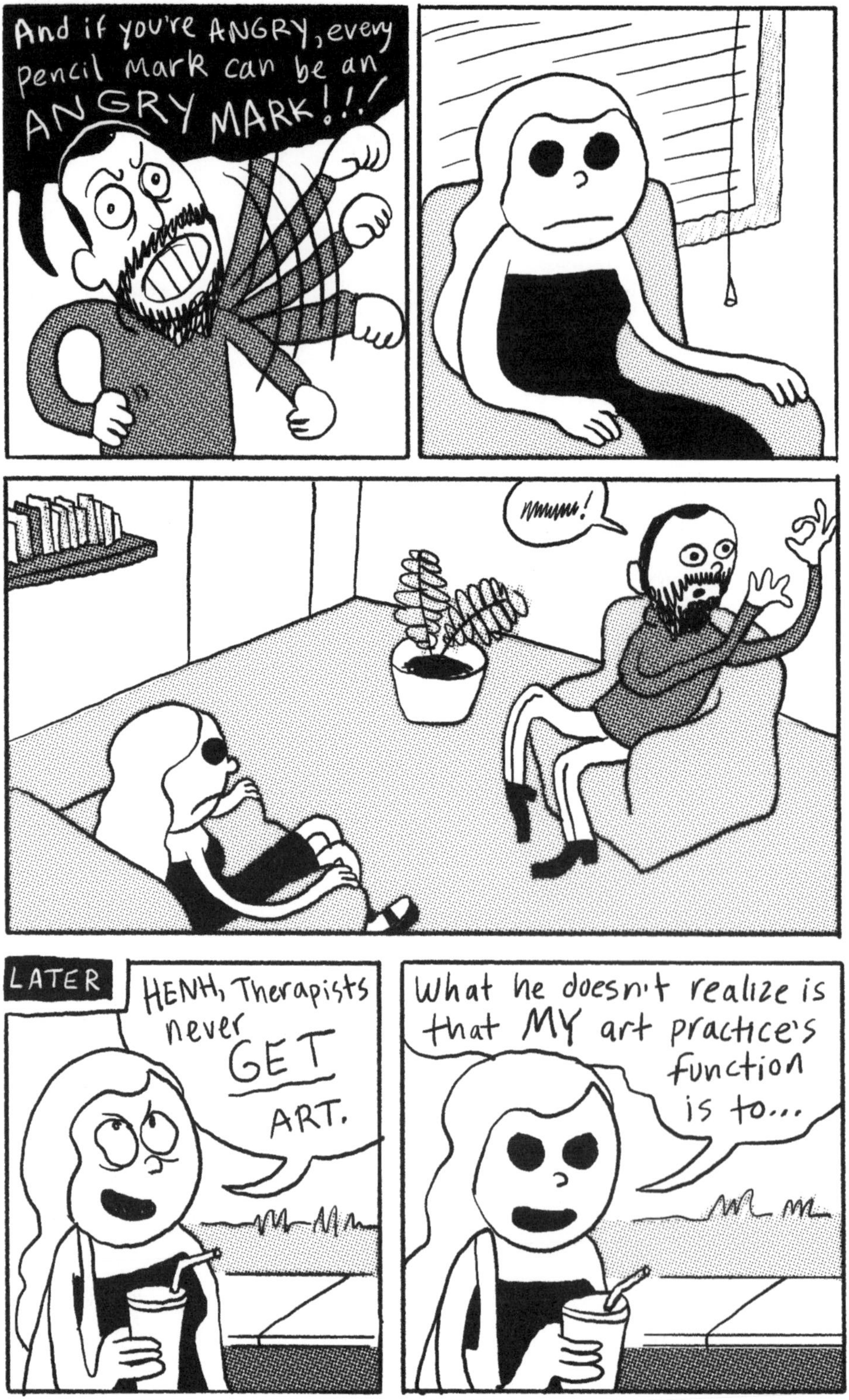
And if you're ANGRY, every pencil mark can be an ANGRY MARK!!!
mmm!
LATER
HENH, Therapists never GET ART.
What he doesn't realize is that MY art practice's function is to...

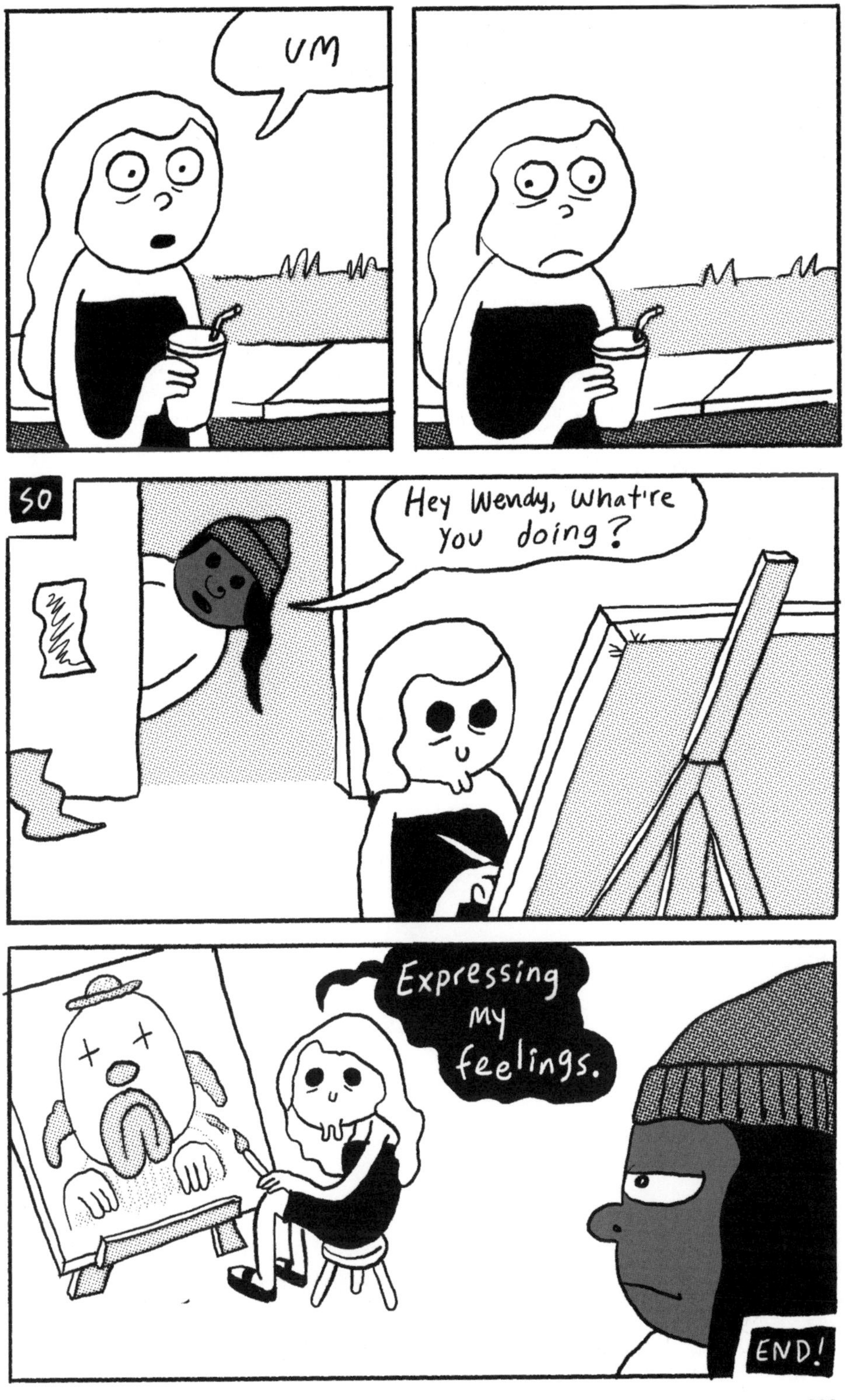
UM
SO
Hey Wendy, what're you doing?
Expressing my feelings.
END!

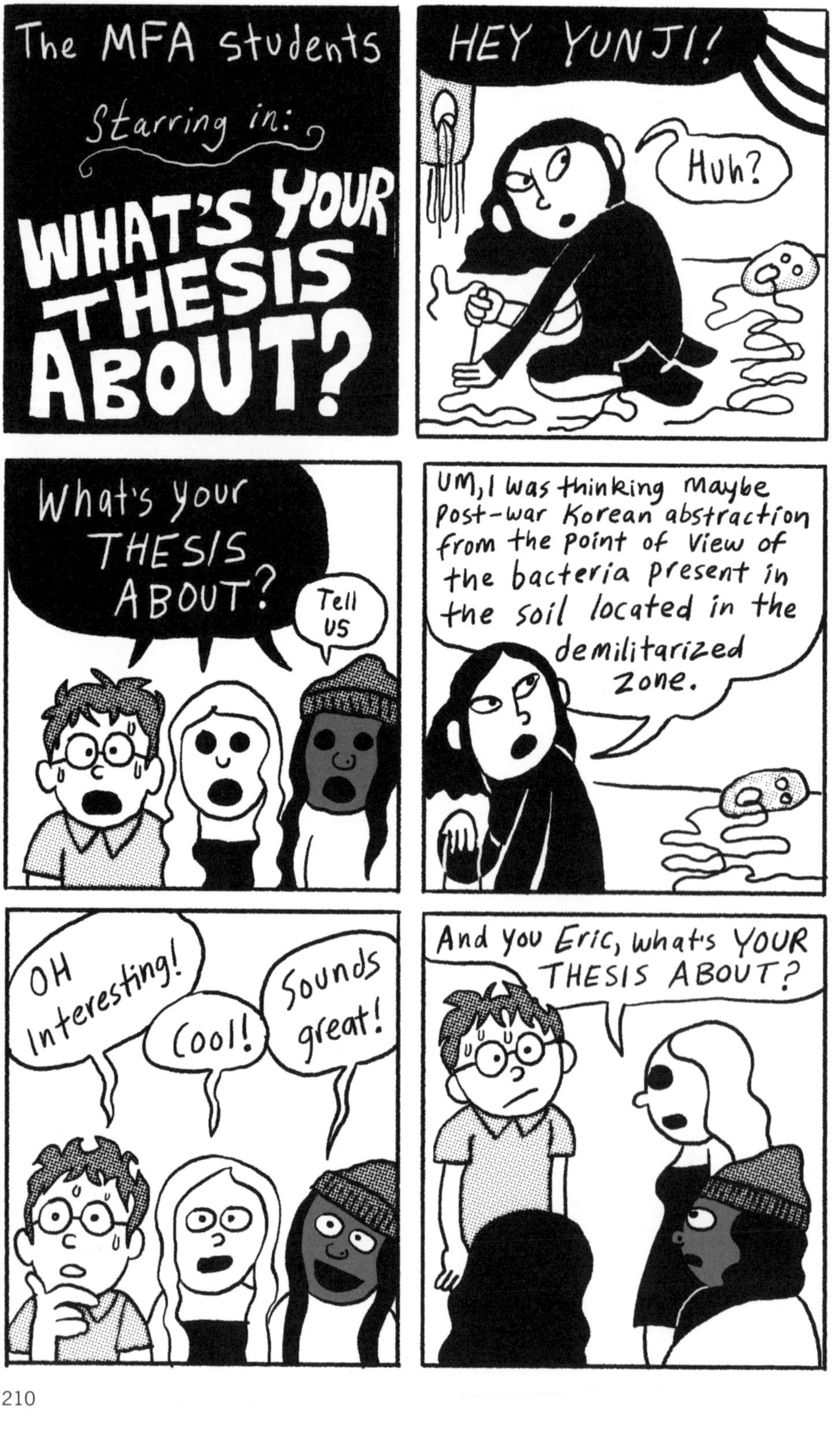
The MFA students
Starring in:
WHAT'S YOUR THESIS ABOUT?
HEY YUNJI!
Huh?
What's your THESIS ABOUT?
Tell us
UM, I was thinking maybe post-war Korean abstraction from the point of view of the bacteria present in the soil located in the demilitarized zone.
OH Interesting!
Cool!
Sounds great!
And you Eric, what's YOUR THESIS ABOUT?

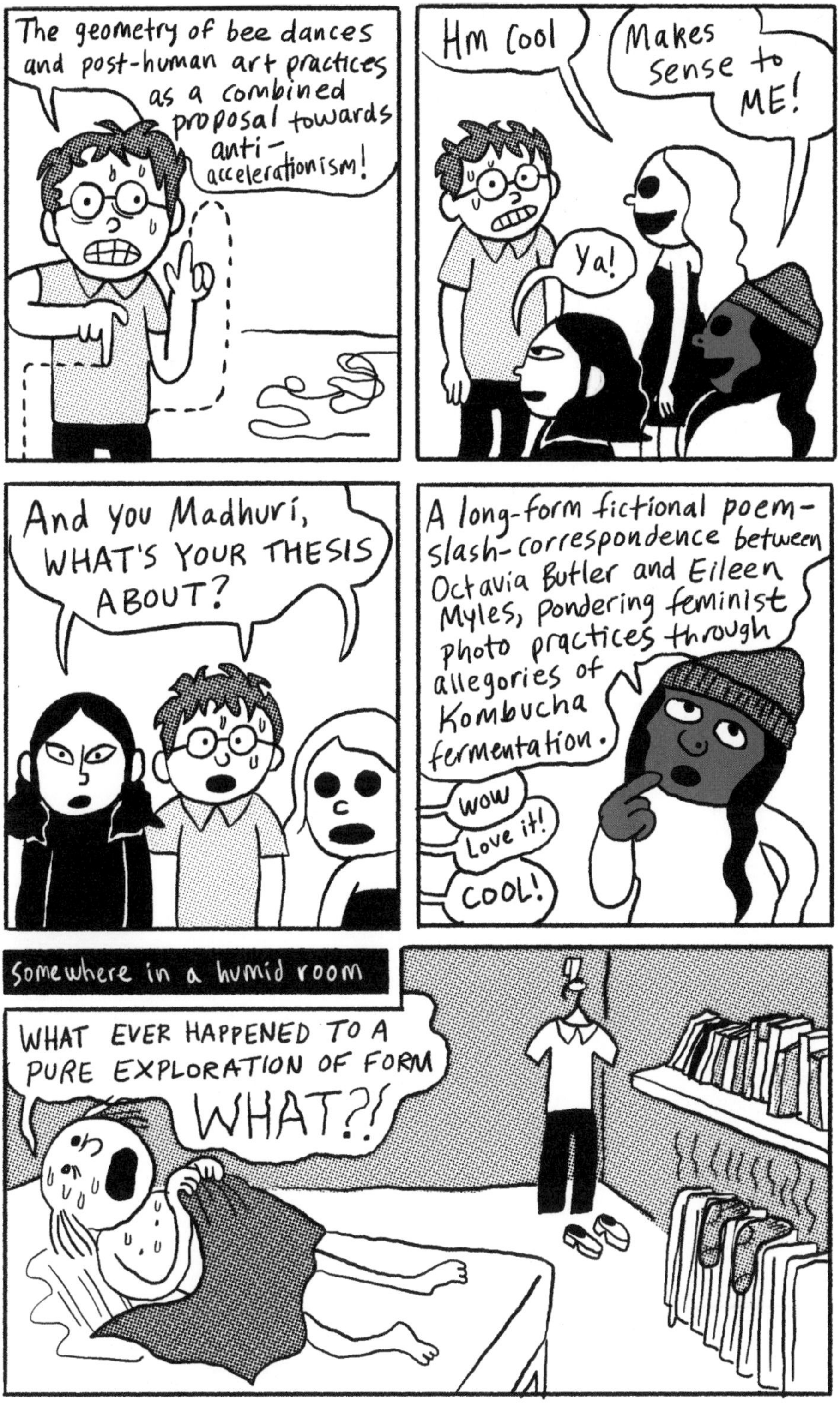
The geometry of bee dances and post-human art practices as a combined proposal towards anti-accelerationism!
Hm Cool
Makes sense to ME!
Ya!
And you Madhuri, WHAT'S YOUR THESIS ABOUT?
A long-form fictional poem-slash-correspondence between Octavia Butler and Eileen Myles, pondering feminist photo practices through allegories of Kombucha fermentation.
WOW
Love it!
COOL!
Somewhere in a humid room
WHAT EVER HAPPENED TO A PURE EXPLORATION OF FORM
WHAT?!

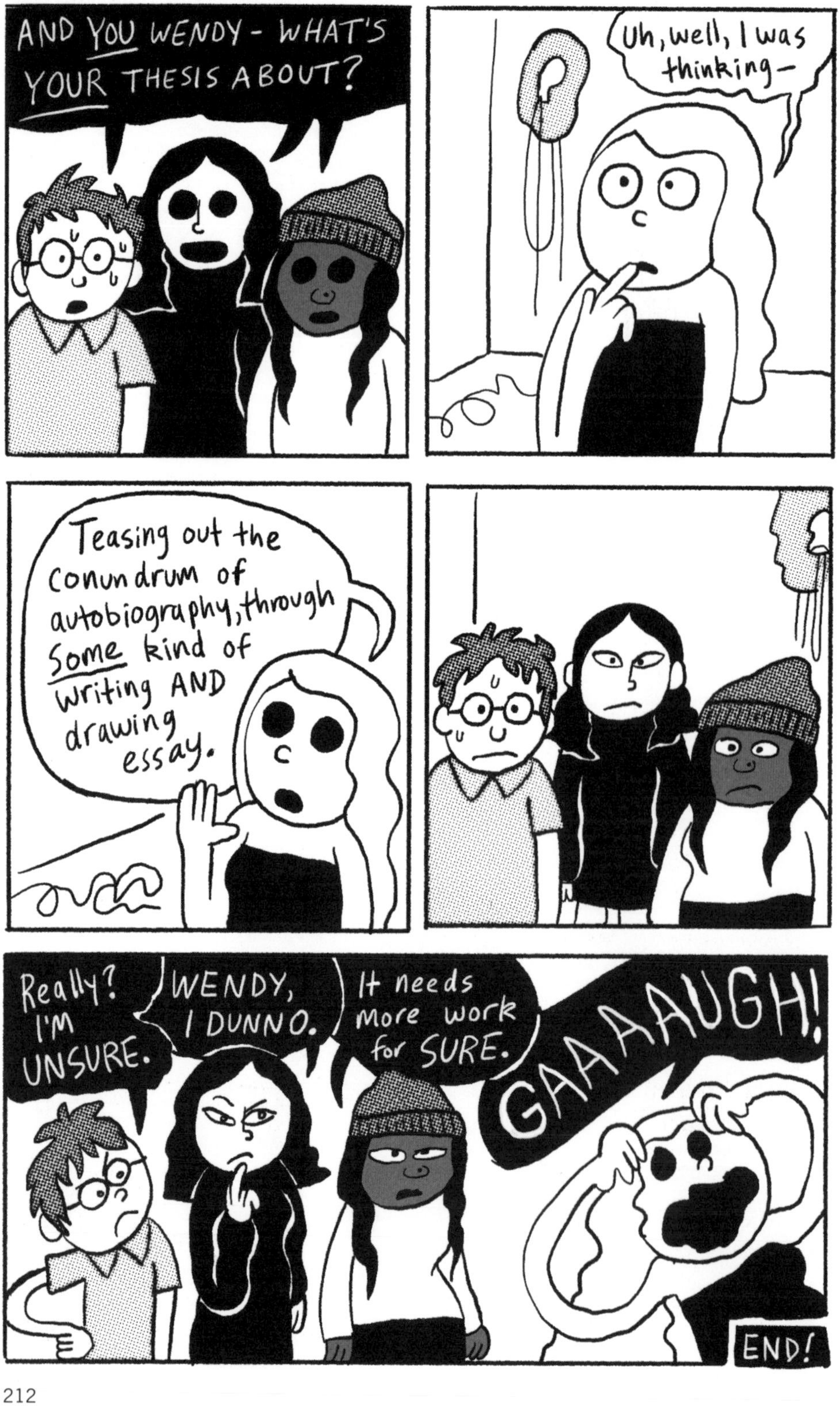

AND YOU WENDY - WHAT'S YOUR THESIS ABOUT?
Uh, well, I was thinking-
Teasing out the conundrum of autobiography, through some kind of writing AND drawing essay.
Really? I'M UNSURE.
WENDY, I DUNNO.
It needs more work for SURE.
GAAAAUGH!
END!

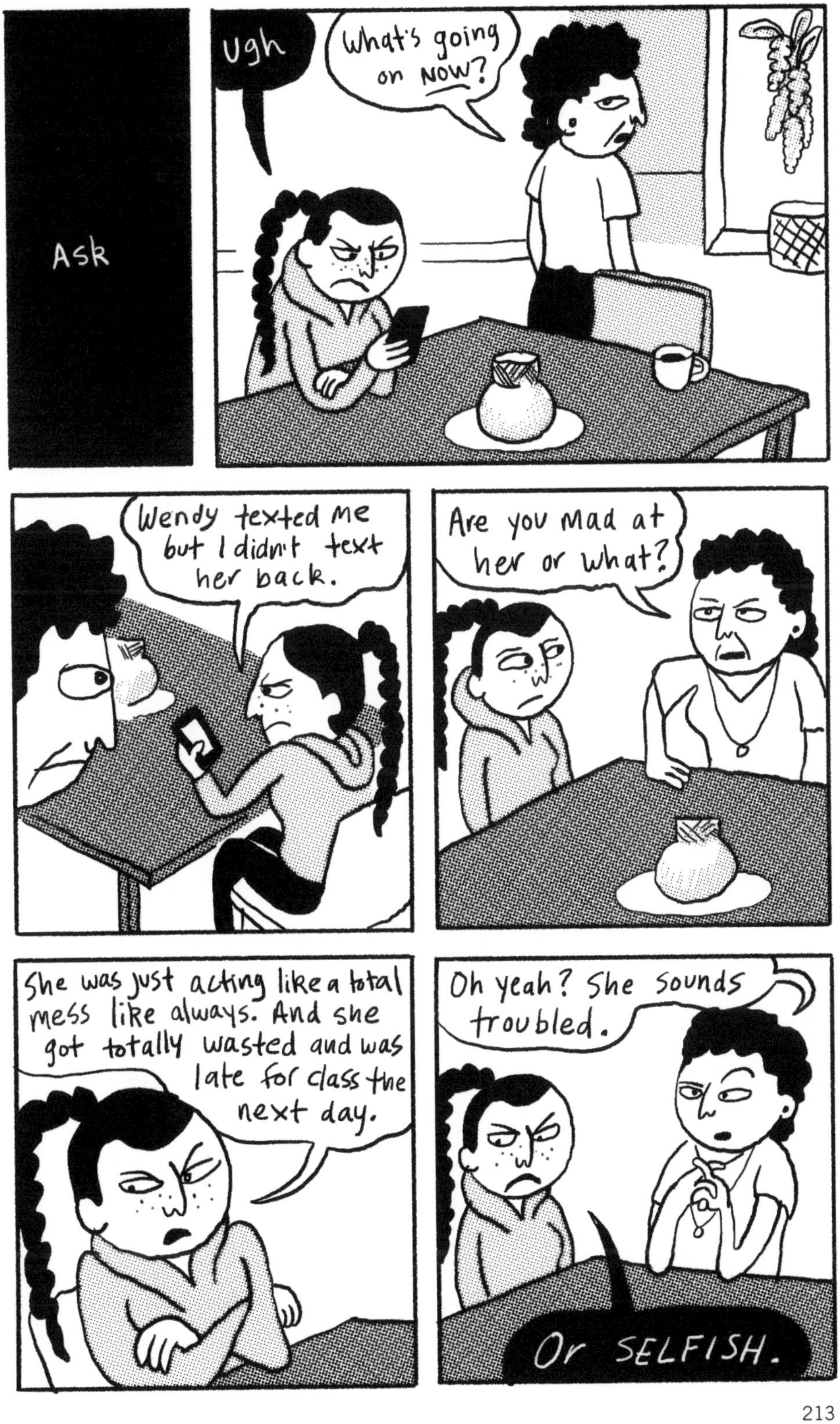

Ask
Ugh
What's going on NOW?
Wendy texted me but I didn't text her back.
Are you mad at her or what?
She was just acting like a total mess like always. And she got totally wasted and was late for class the next day.
Oh yeah? She sounds troubled.
Or SELFISH.

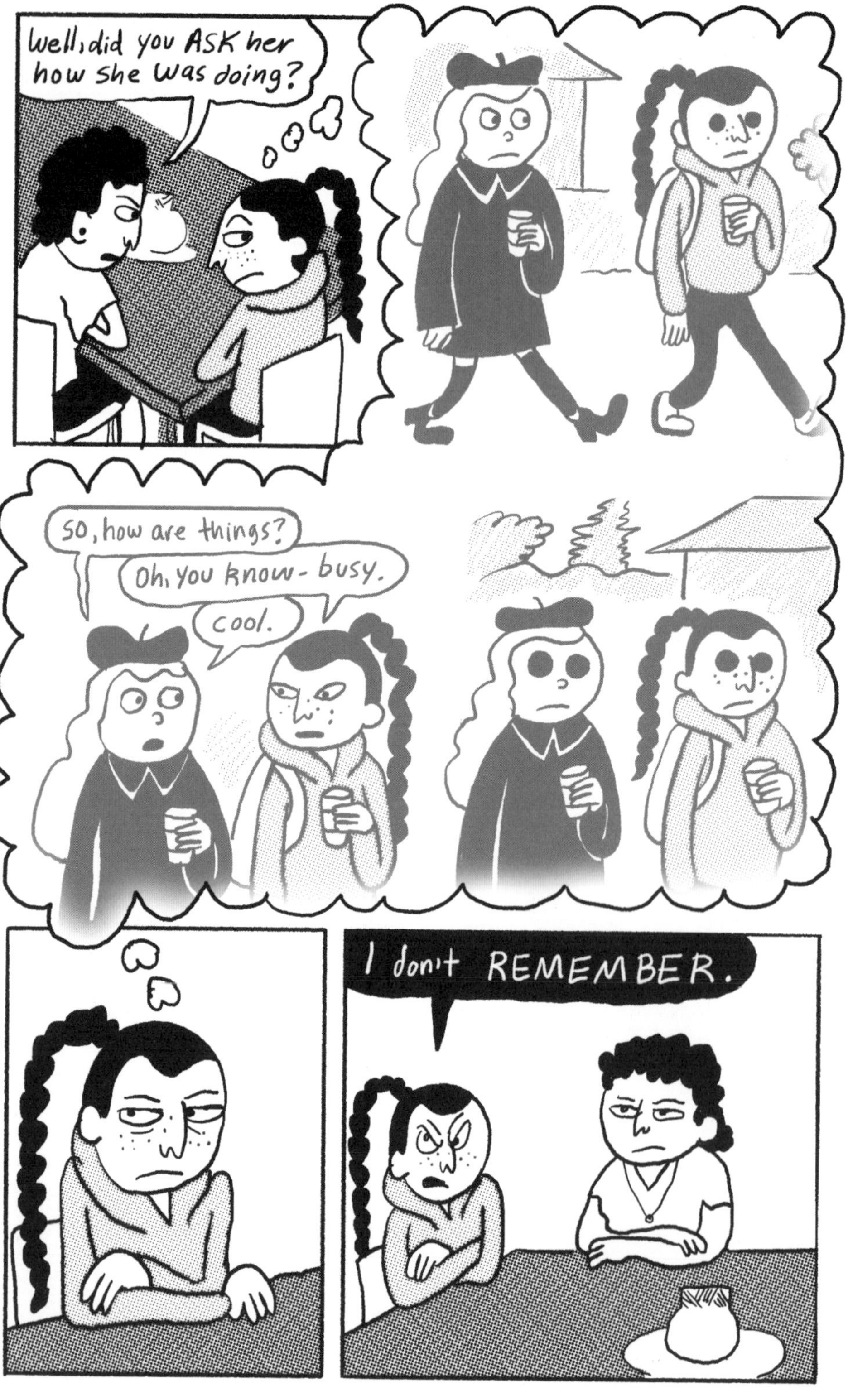

Well, did you ASK her how she was doing?
So, how are things?
Oh, you know - busy.
Cool.
I don't REMEMBER.

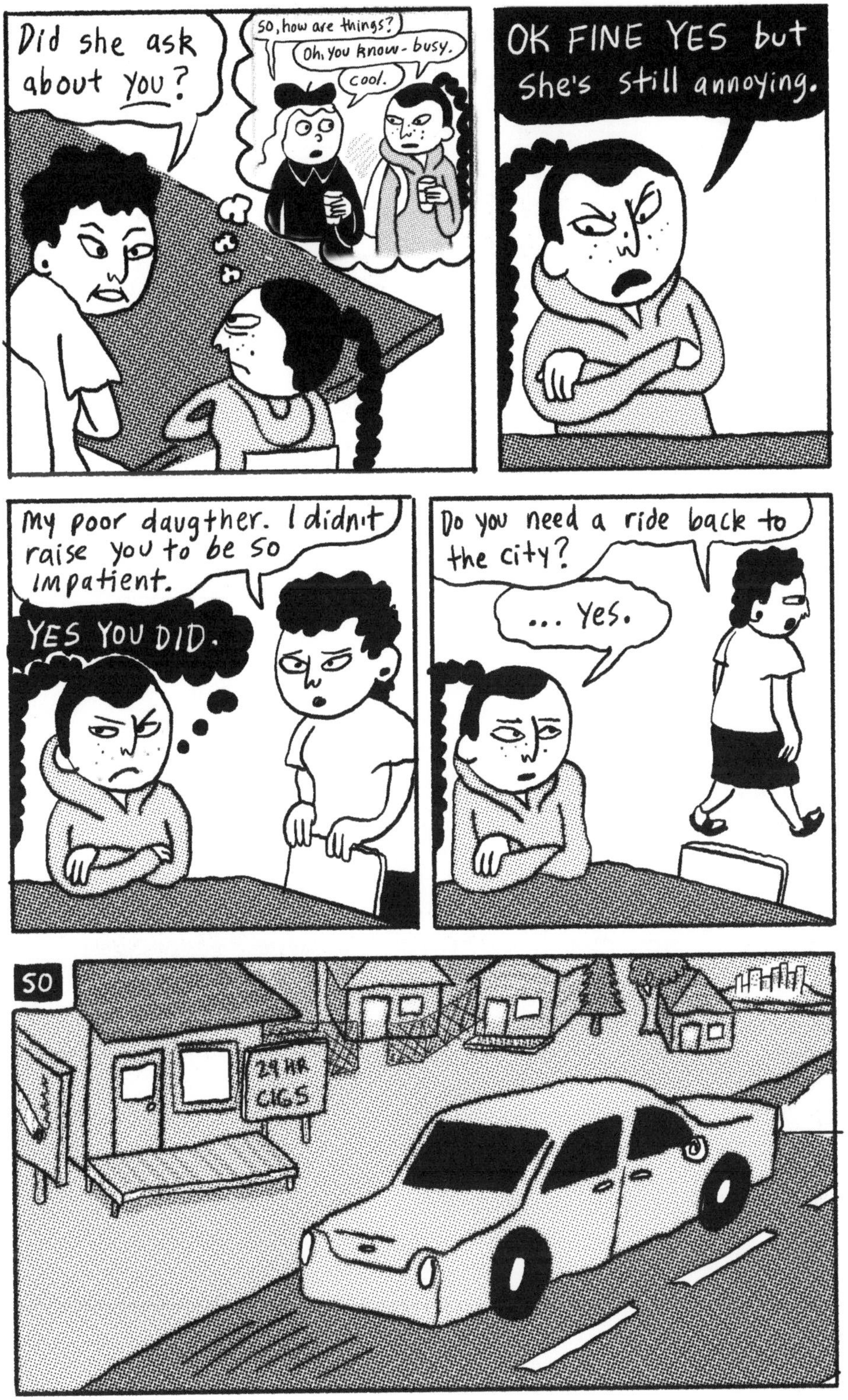

Did she ask about you?
So, how are things?
Oh, you know - busy.
Cool.
OK FINE YES but She's still annoying.
My poor daugther. I didn't raise you to be so impatient.
YES YOU DID.
Do you need a ride back to the city?
... Yes.
50
24 HR CIGS

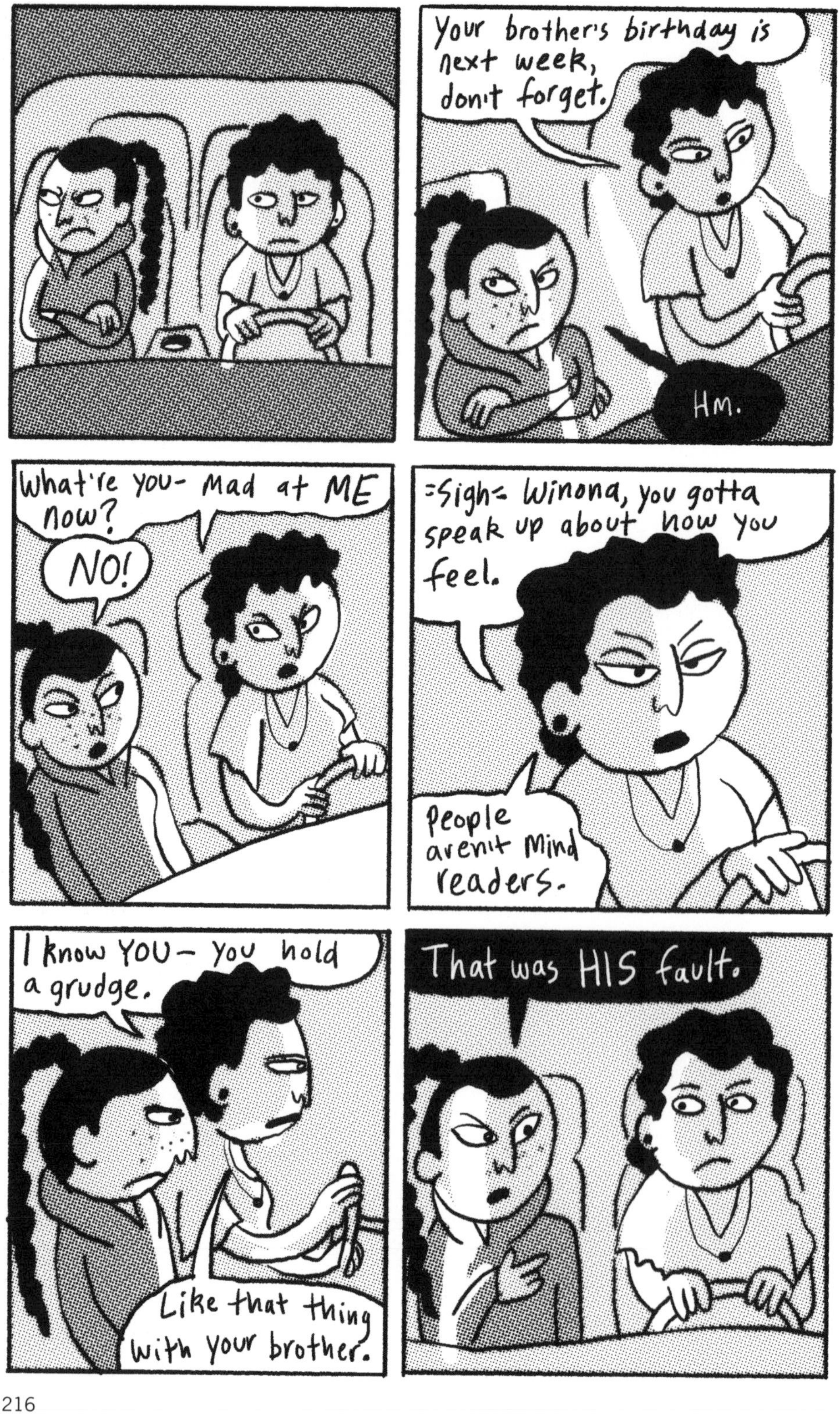
Your brother's birthday is next week, don't forget.
Hm.
What're you- mad at ME now?
NO!
=Sigh= Winona, you gotta speak up about how you feel.
People aren't mind readers.
I know YOU- you hold a grudge.
Like that thing with your brother.
That was HIS fault.

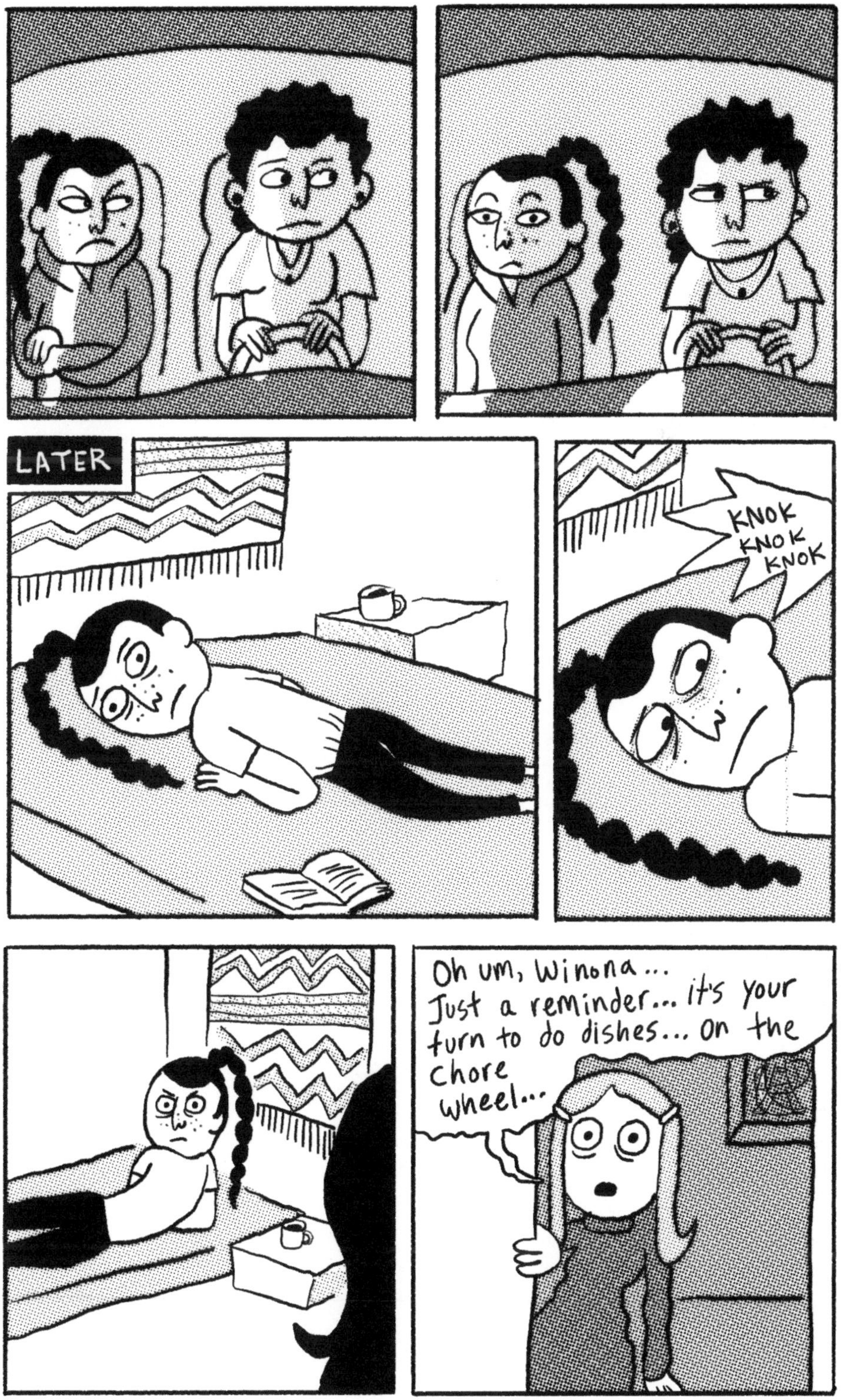
LATER
KNOK KNOK KNOK
Oh um, Winona...
Just a reminder... it's your turn to do dishes... on the chore wheel...

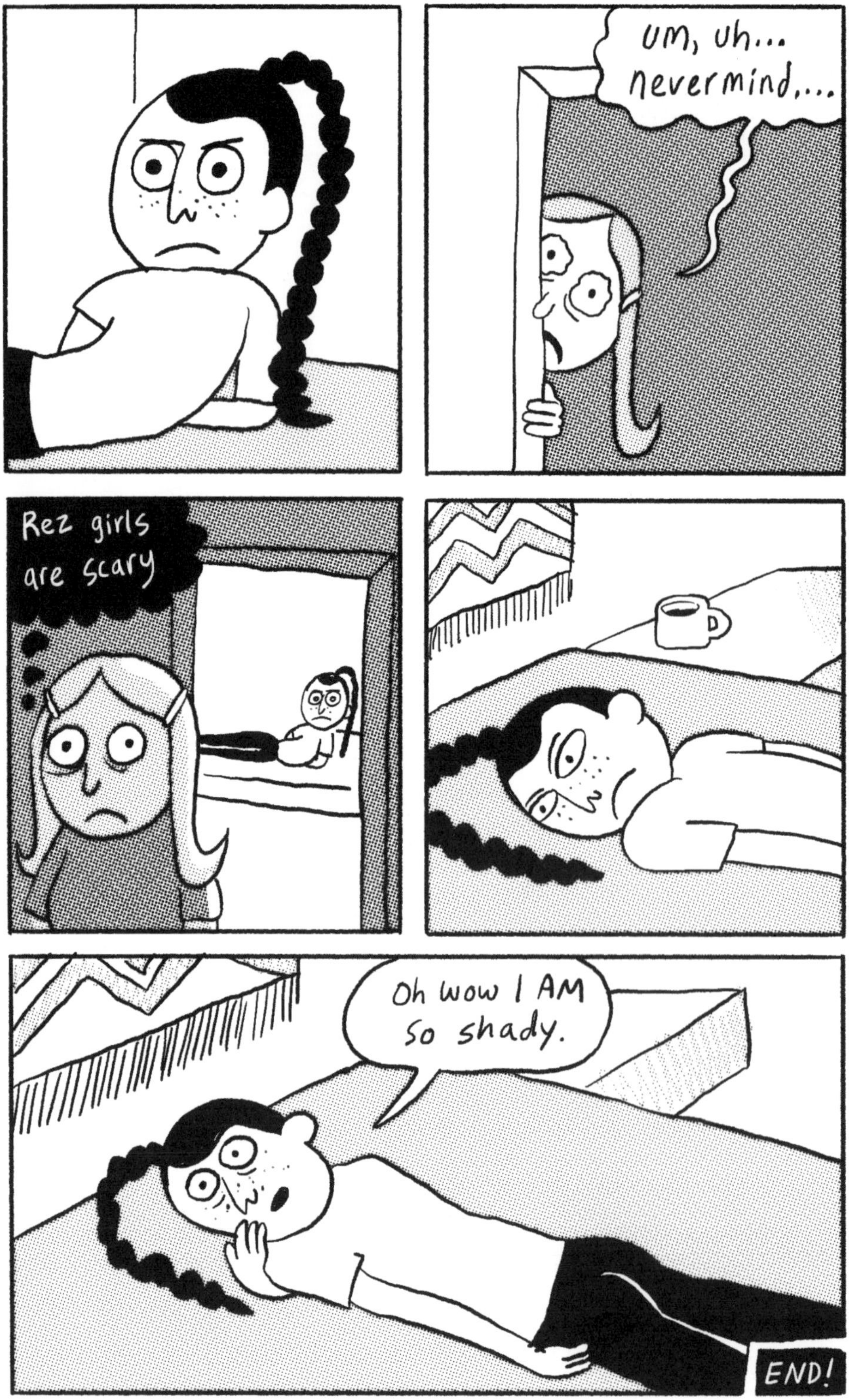
um, uh...
nevermind,....
Rez girls are scary
Oh wow I AM so shady.
END!

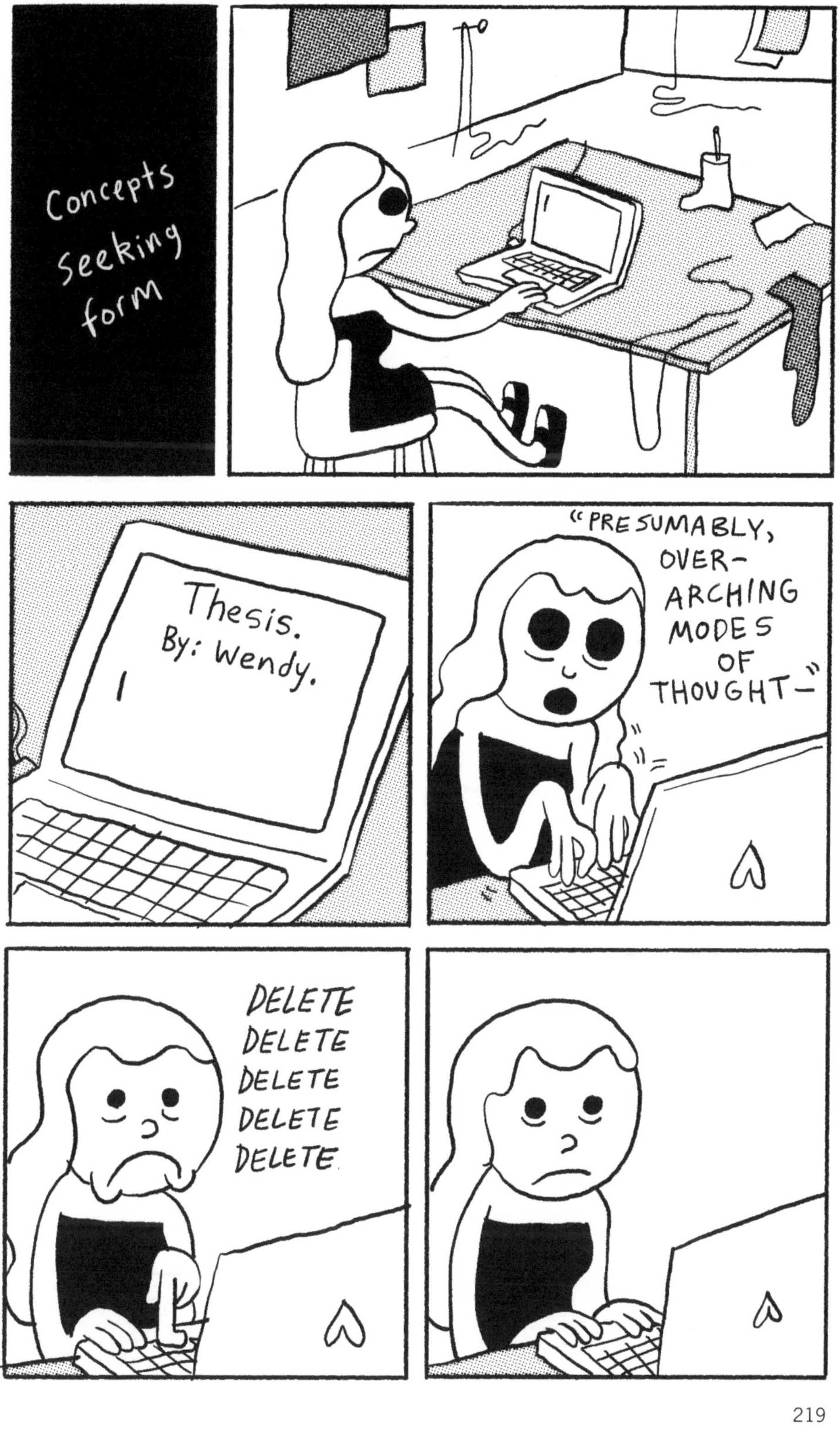
Concepts seeking form
Thesis.
By: Wendy.
"PRESUMABLY, OVER-ARCHING MODES OF THOUGHT—"
DELETE
DELETE
DELETE
DELETE
DELETE

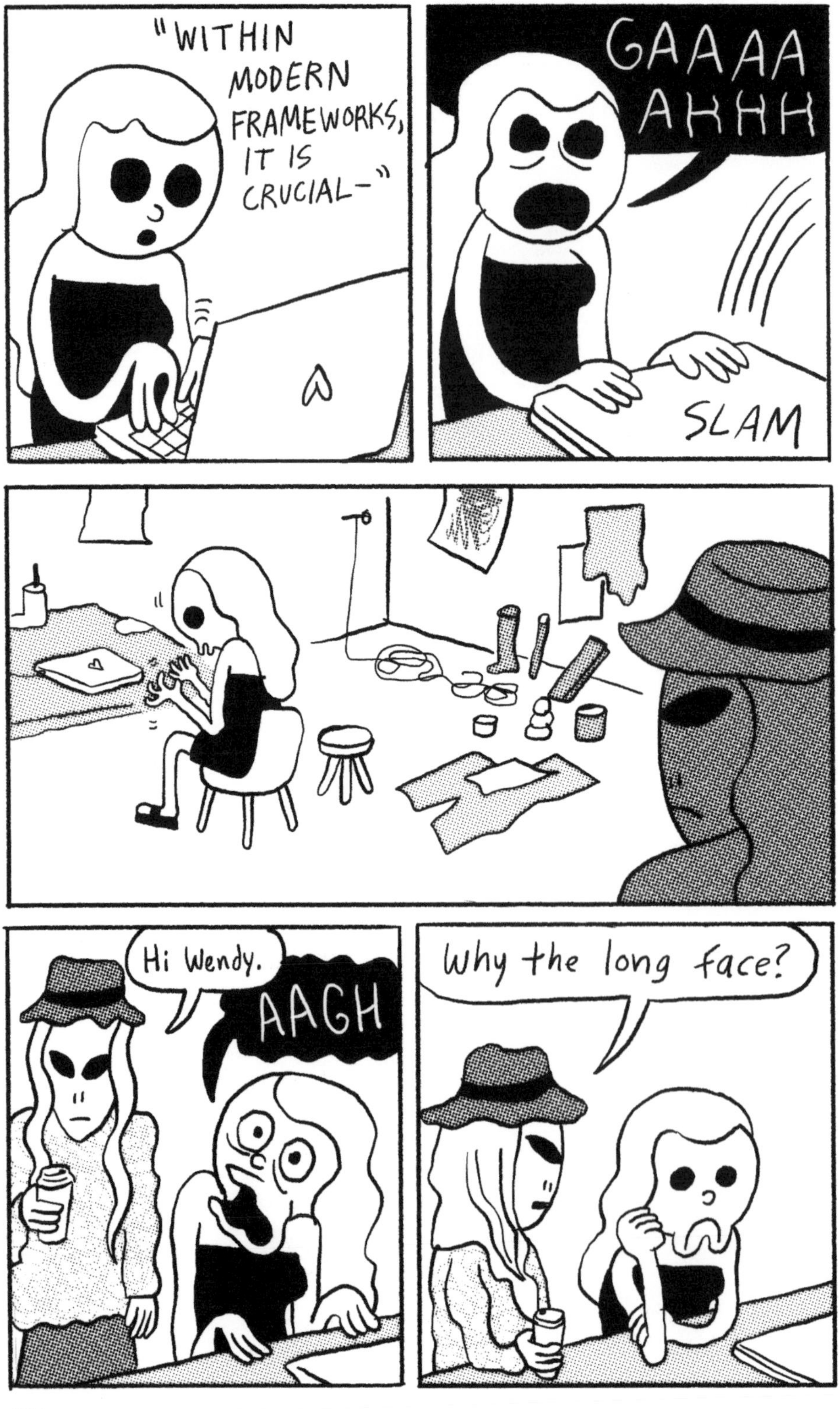
"WITHIN MODERN FRAMEWORKS, IT IS CRUCIAL-"
GAAAA AHHH
SLAM
Hi Wendy.
AAGH
Why the long face?

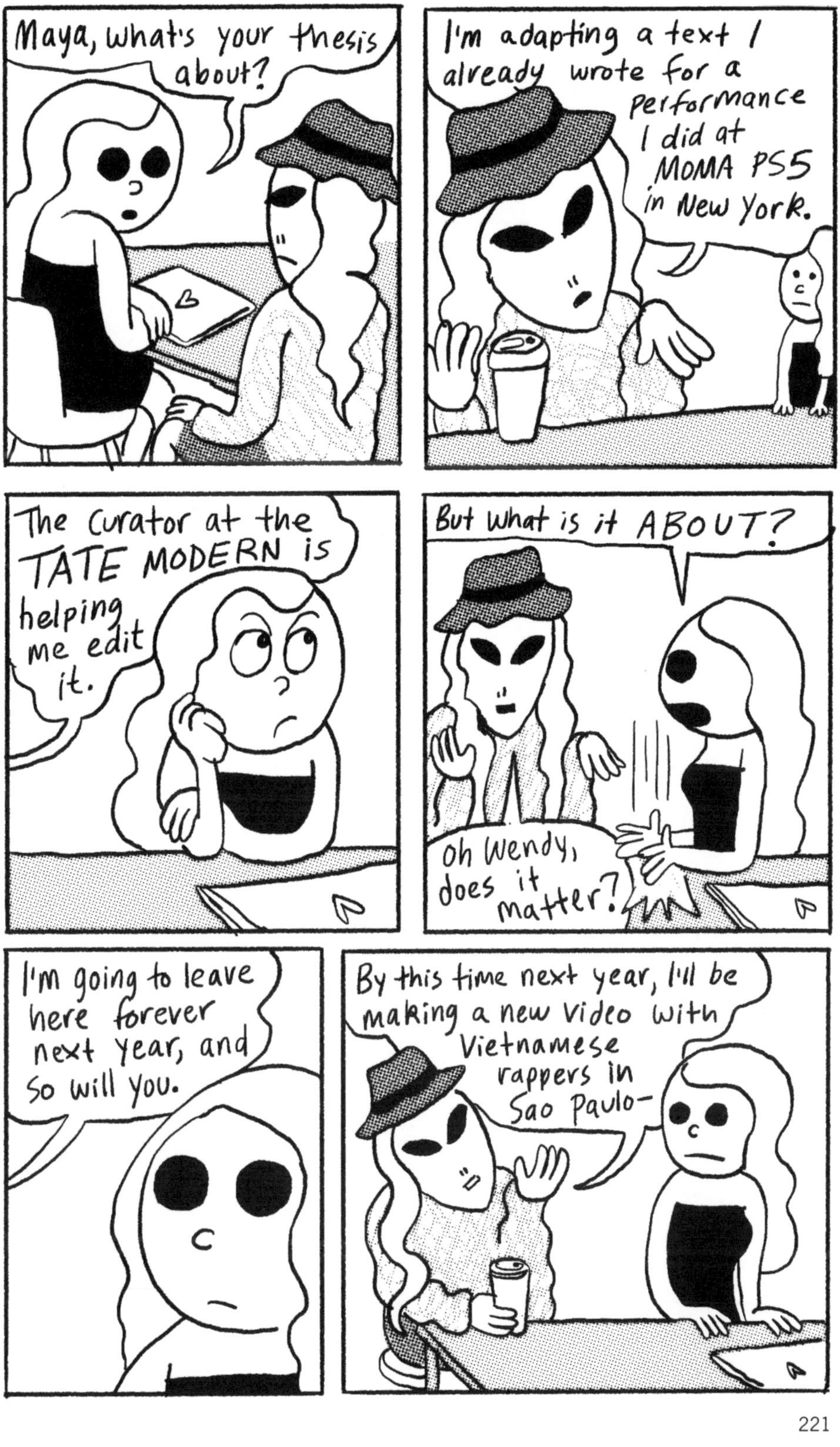
Maya, what's your thesis about?
I'm adapting a text I already wrote for a performance I did at MOMA PS5 in New York.
The curator at the TATE MODERN is helping me edit it.
But what is it ABOUT?
oh Wendy, does it matter?
I'm going to leave here forever next year, and so will you.
By this time next year, I'll be making a new video with Vietnamese rappers in Sao Paulo-

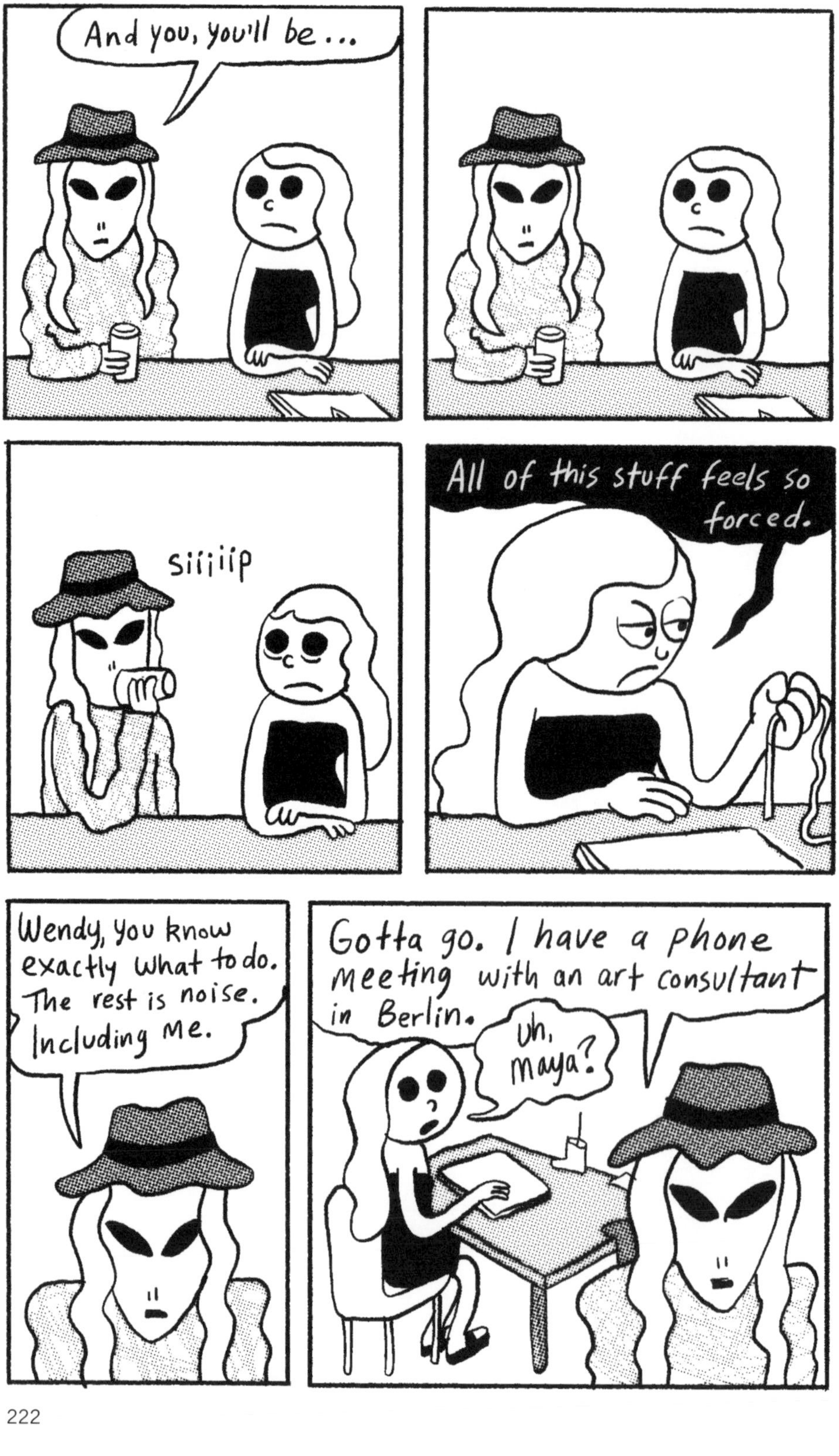

And you, you'll be...
siiiiip
All of this stuff feels so forced.
Wendy, you know exactly what to do. The rest is noise. Including me.
Gotta go. I have a phone meeting with an art consultant in Berlin.
Uh, Maya?

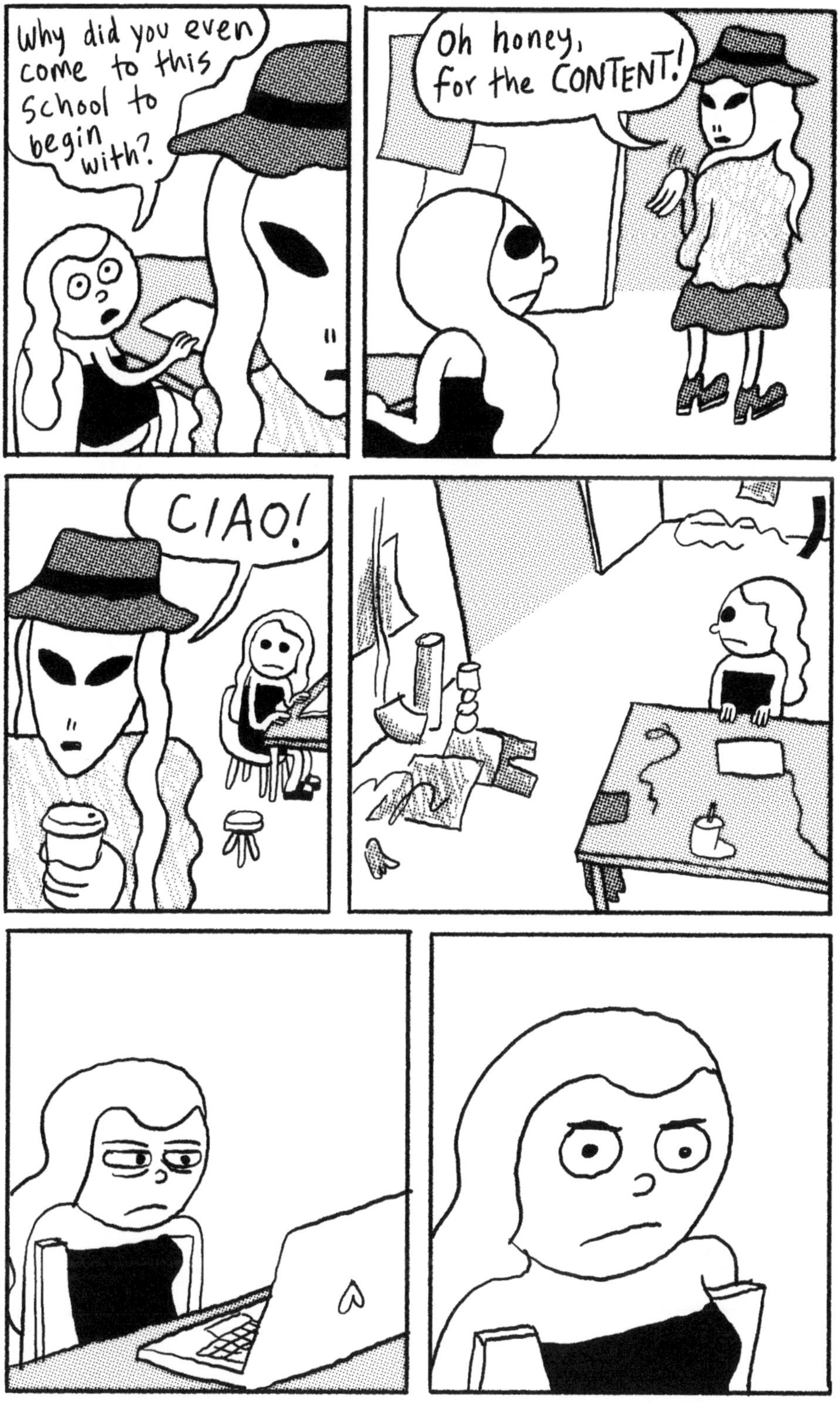
Why did you even come to this school to begin with?
Oh honey, for the CONTENT!
CIAO!

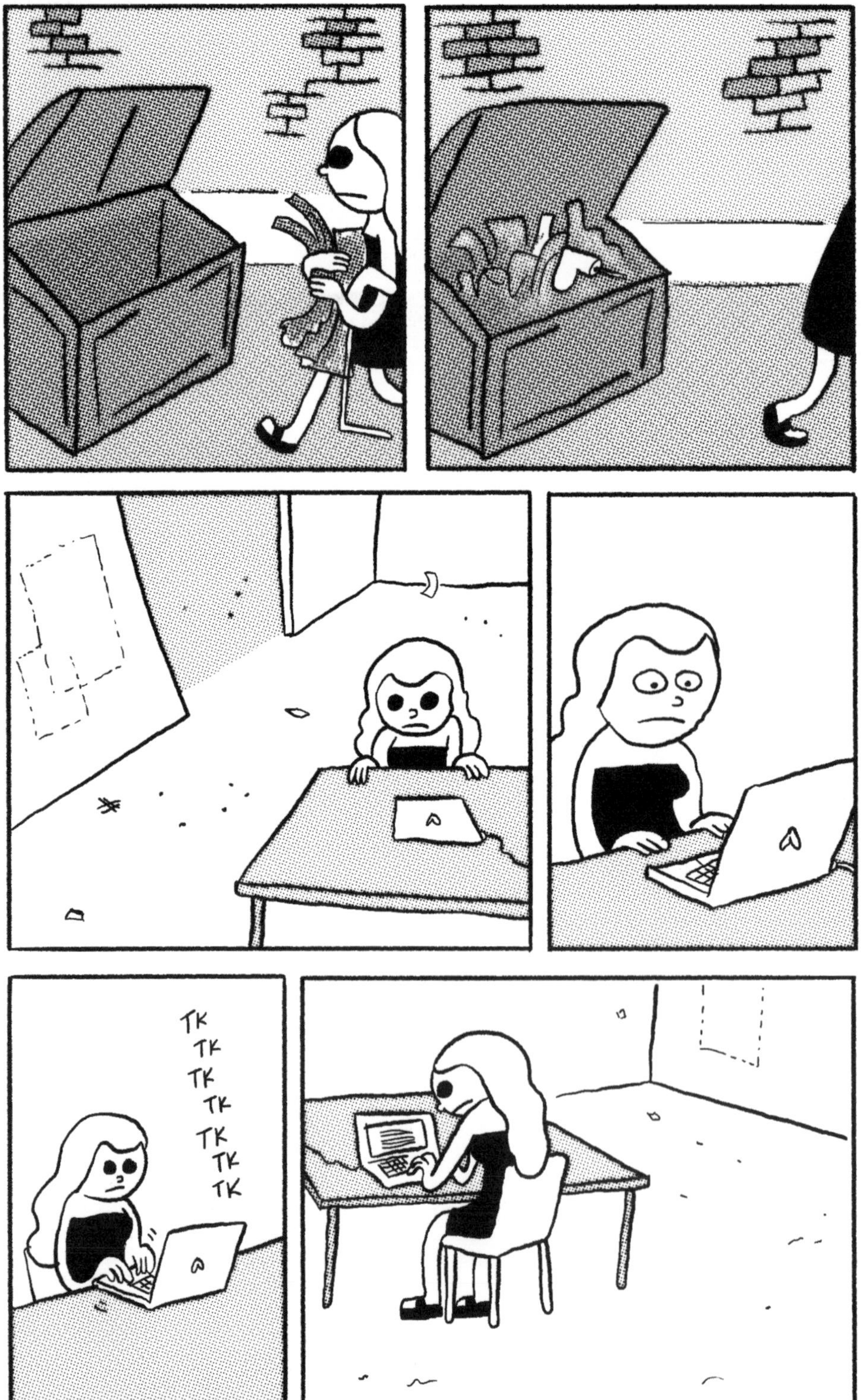
TK
TK
TK
TK
TK
TK
TK

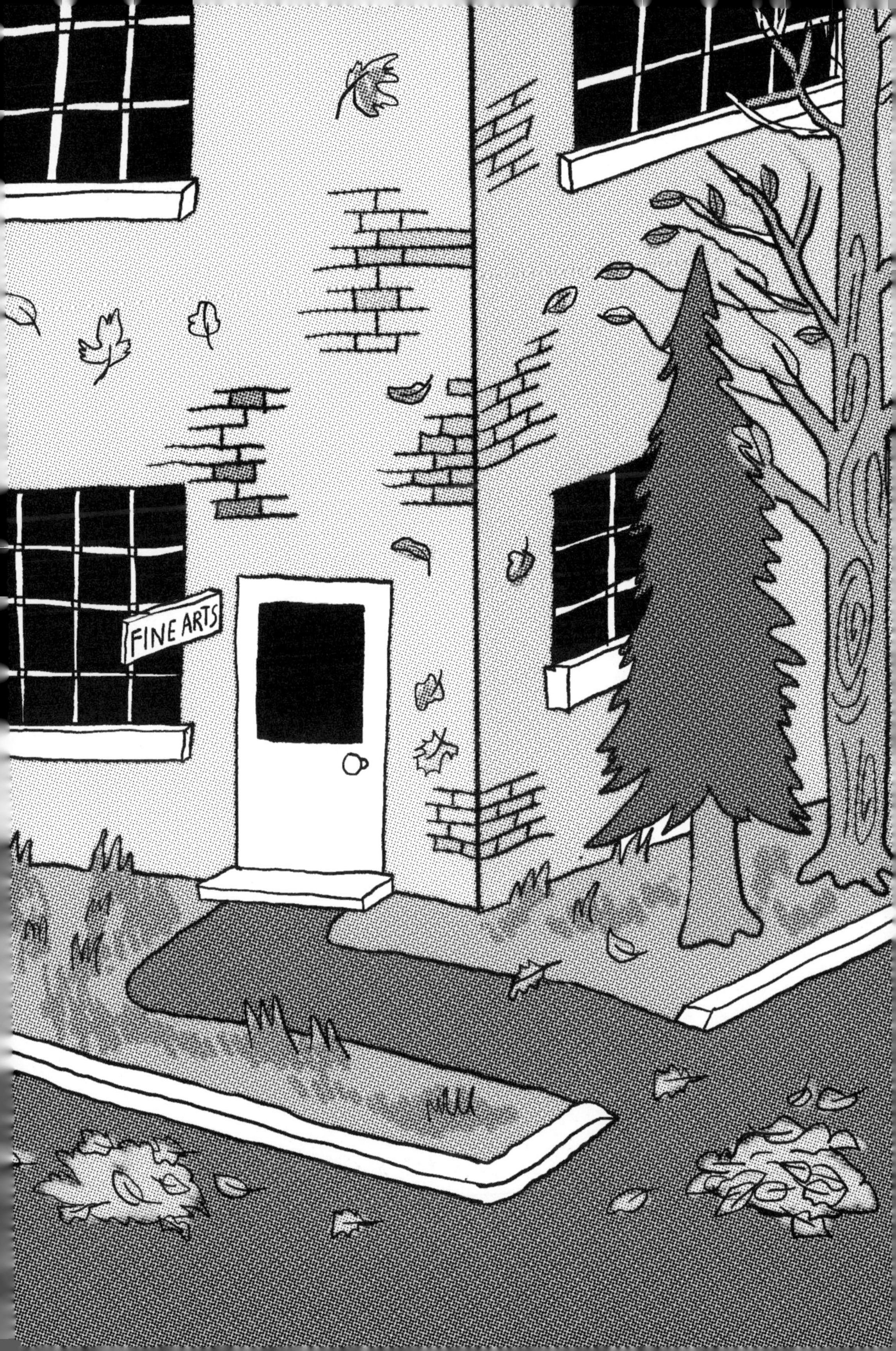
FINE ARTS

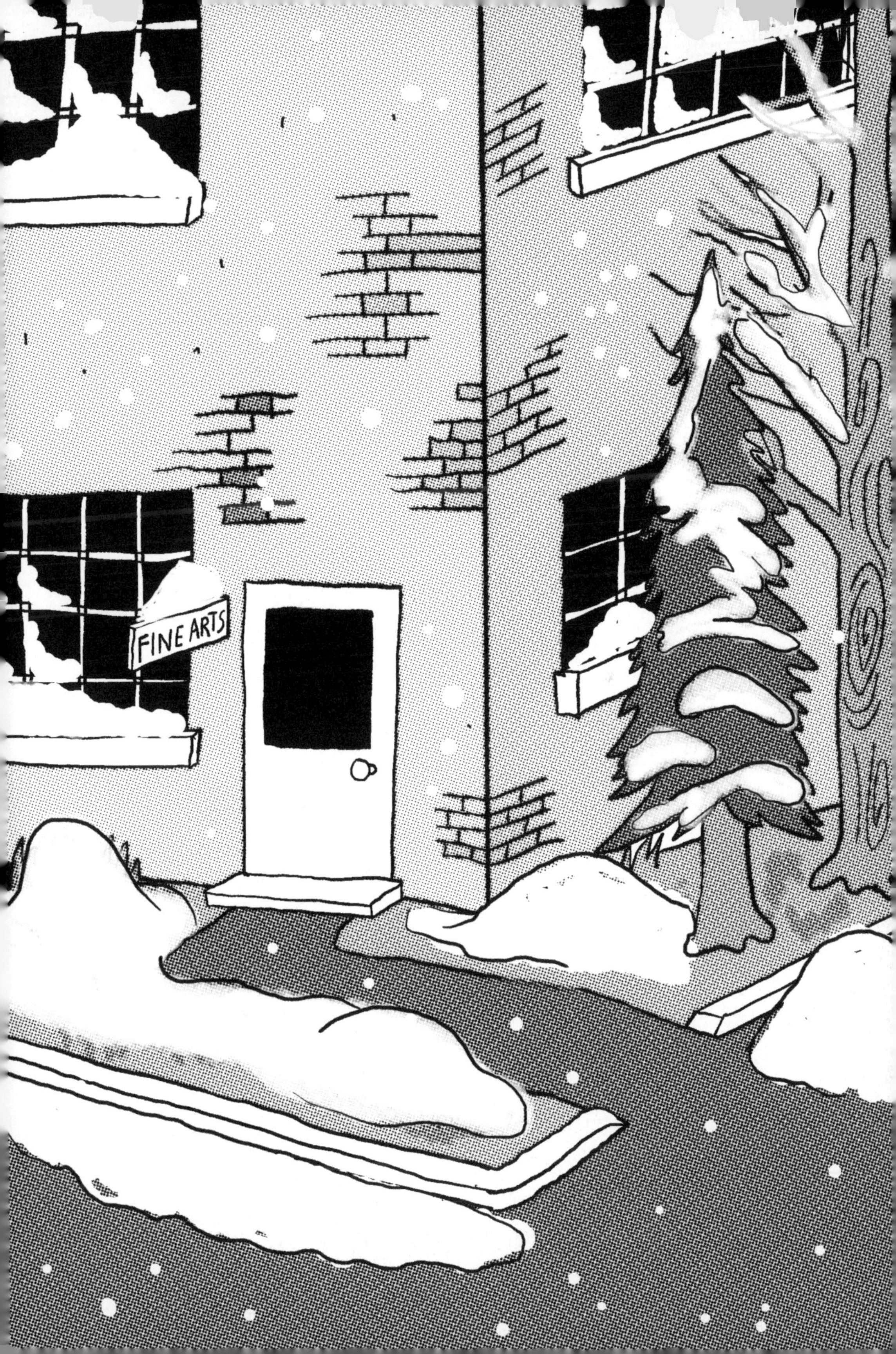
FINE ARTS

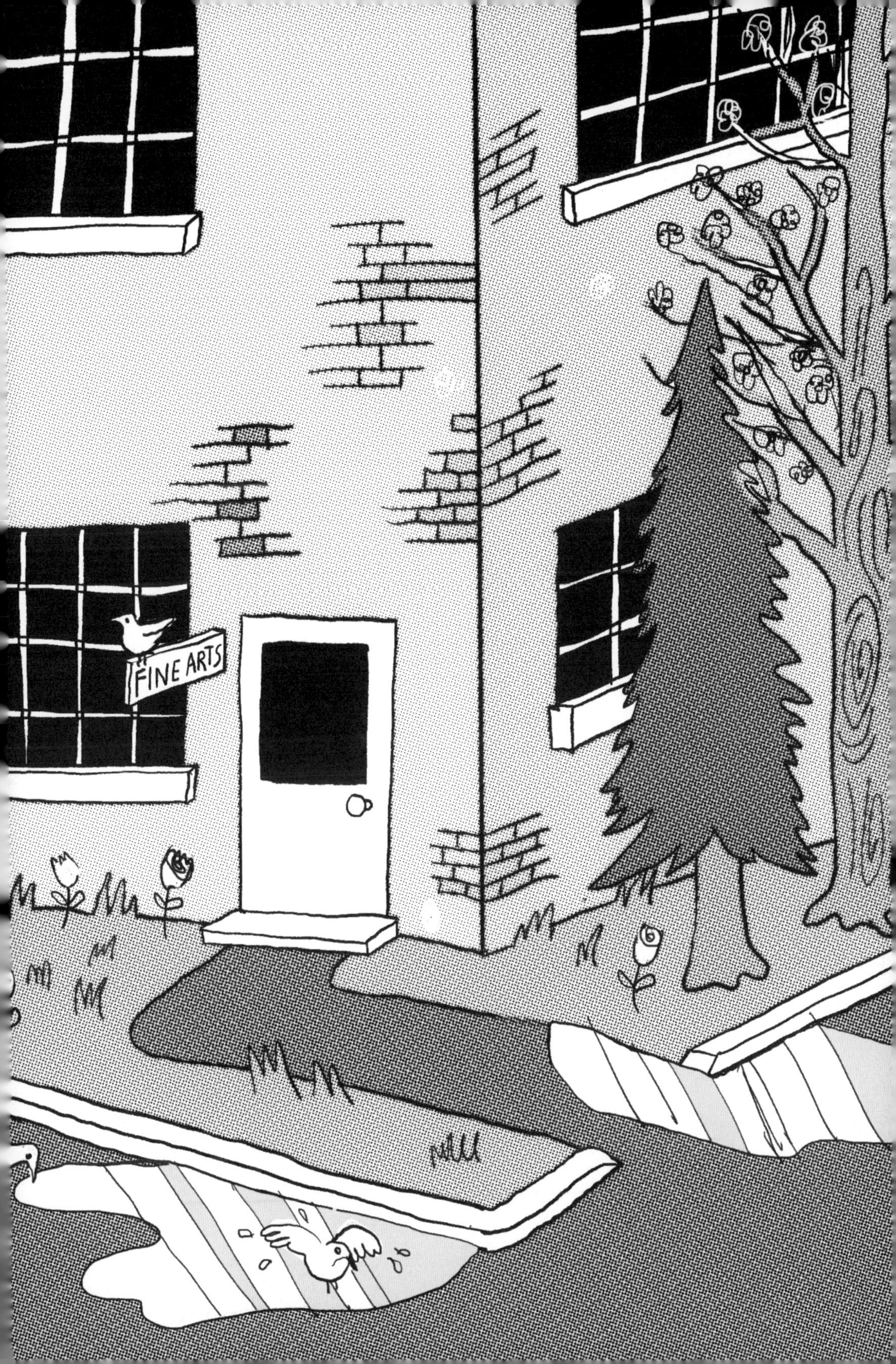
FINE ARTS

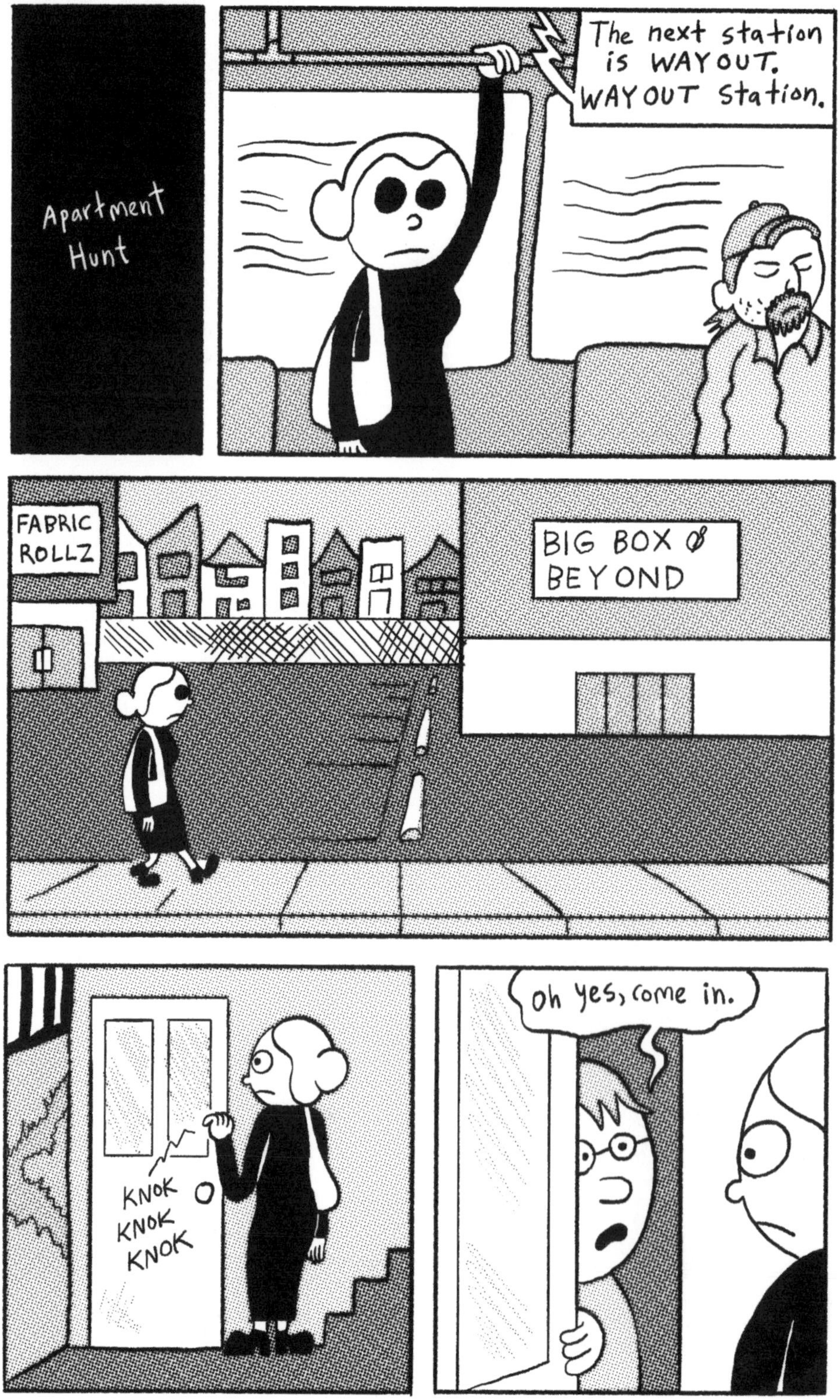
Apartment Hunt
The next station is WAYOUT. WAYOUT Station.
FABRIC ROLLZ
BIG BOX & BEYOND
KNOK KNOK KNOK
Oh yes, come in.

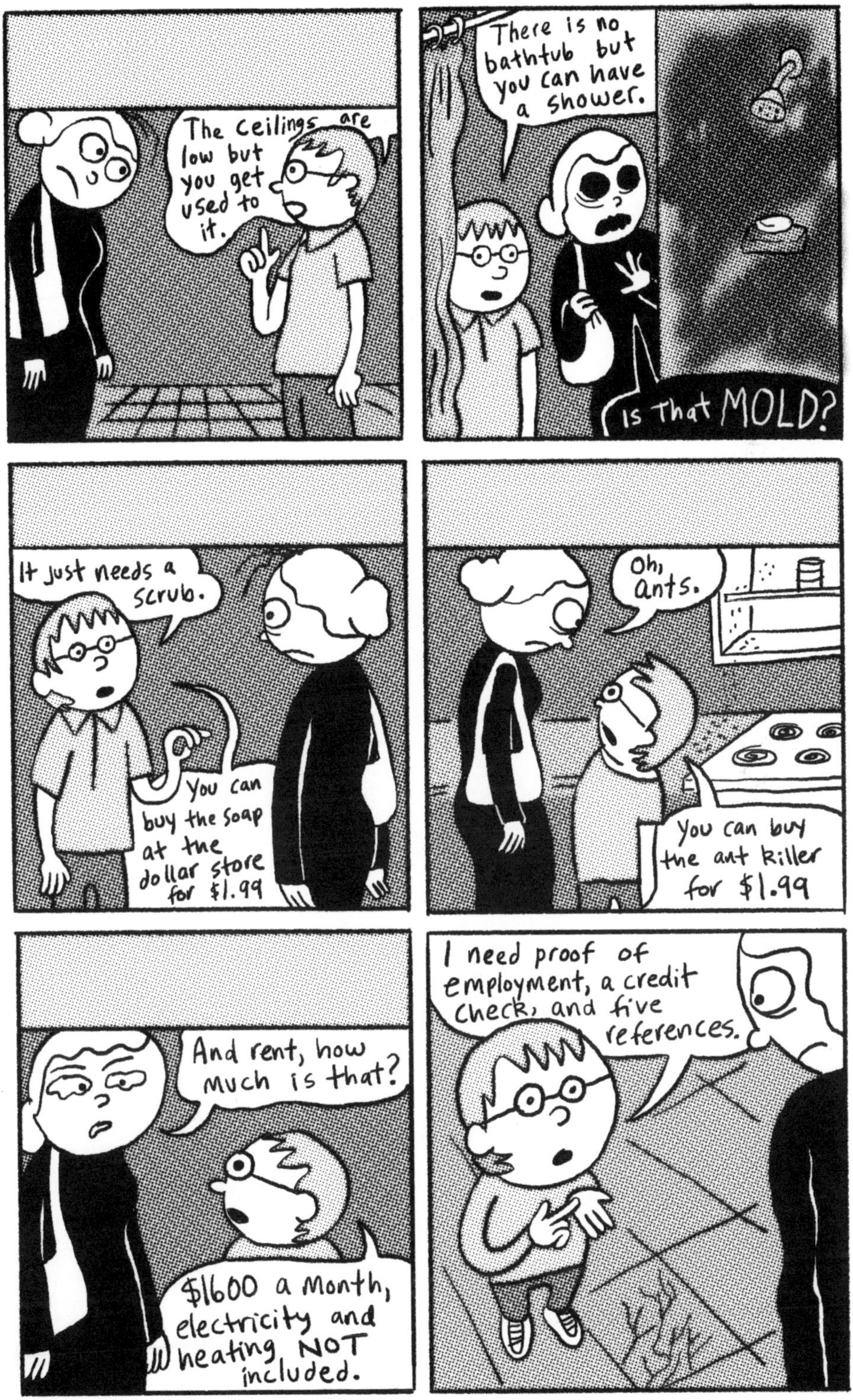
The ceilings are low but you get used to it.
There is no bathtub but you can have a shower.
Is That MOLD?
It just needs a scrub.
You can buy the soap at the dollar store for $1.99
Oh, ants.
You can buy the ant killer for $1.99
And rent, how much is that?
$1600 a Month, electricity and heating NOT included.
I need proof of employment, a credit check, and five references.

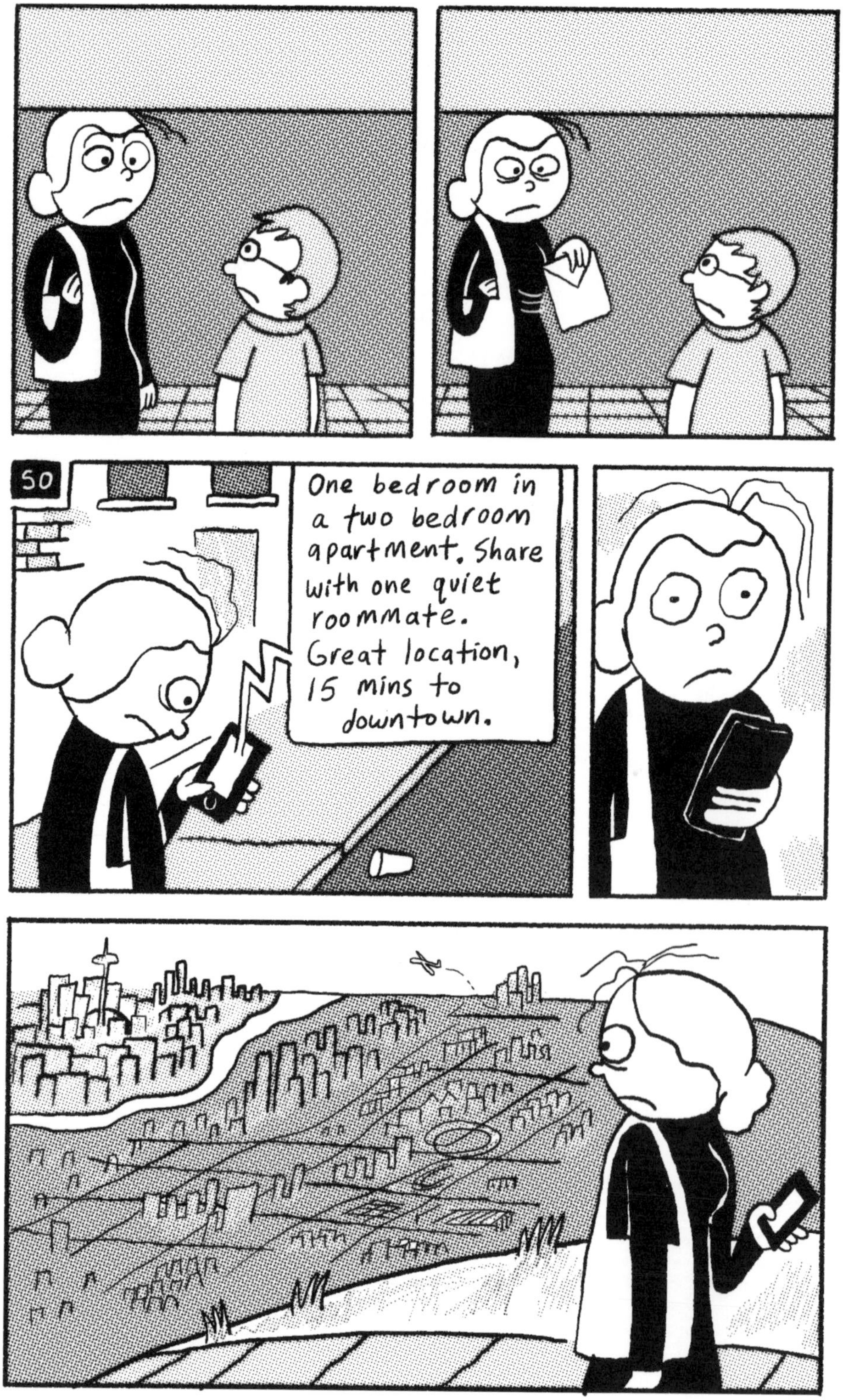
SO
One bedroom in a two bedroom apartment. Share with one quiet roommate. Great location, 15 mins to downtown.

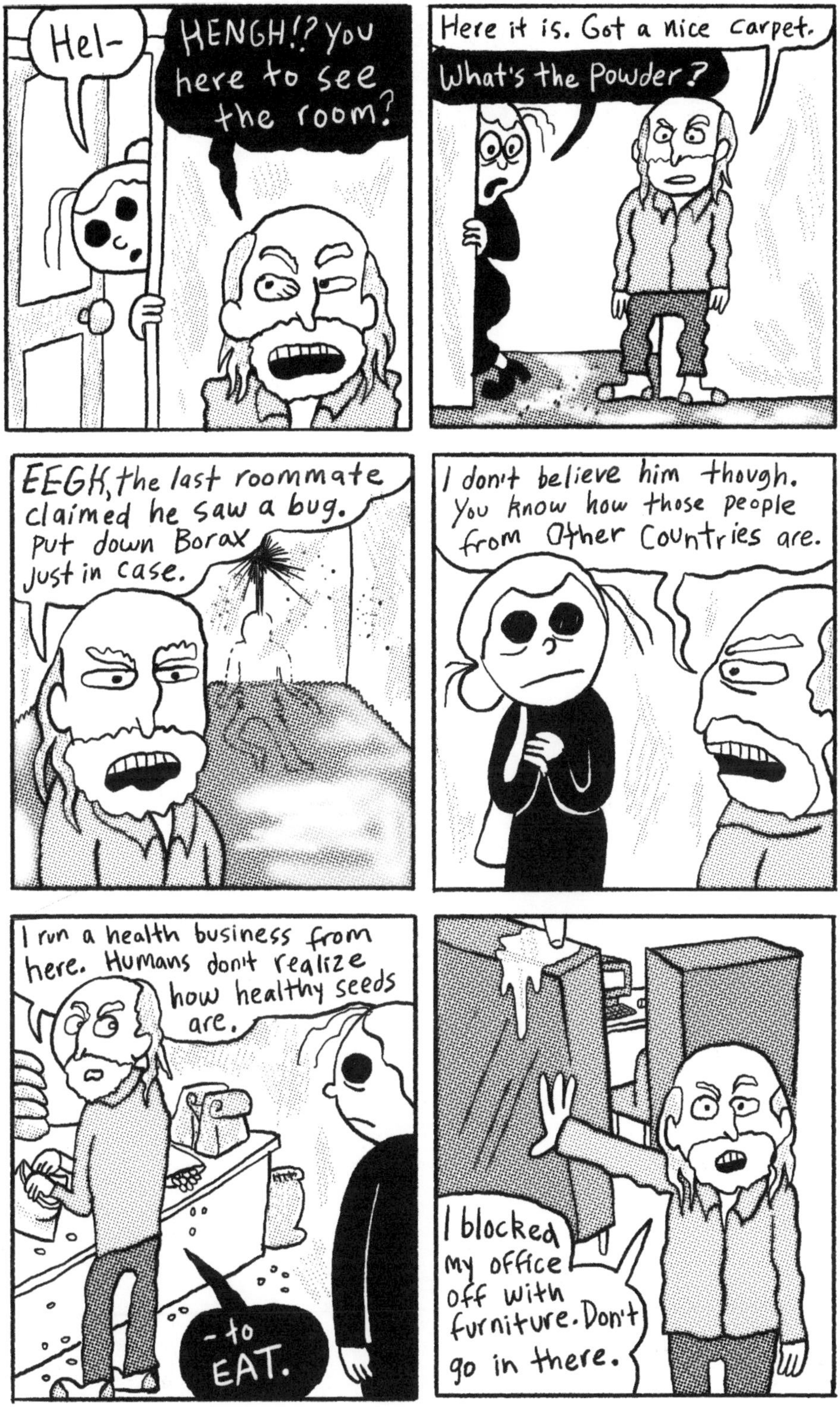
Hel-
HENGH!? you here to see the room?
Here it is. Got a nice carpet.
What's the Powder?
EEGH, the last roommate claimed he saw a bug. put down Borax just in case.
I don't believe him though. You know how those people from Other Countries are.
I run a health business from here. Humans don't realize how healthy seeds are.
-to EAT.
I blocked my office off with furniture. Don't go in there.

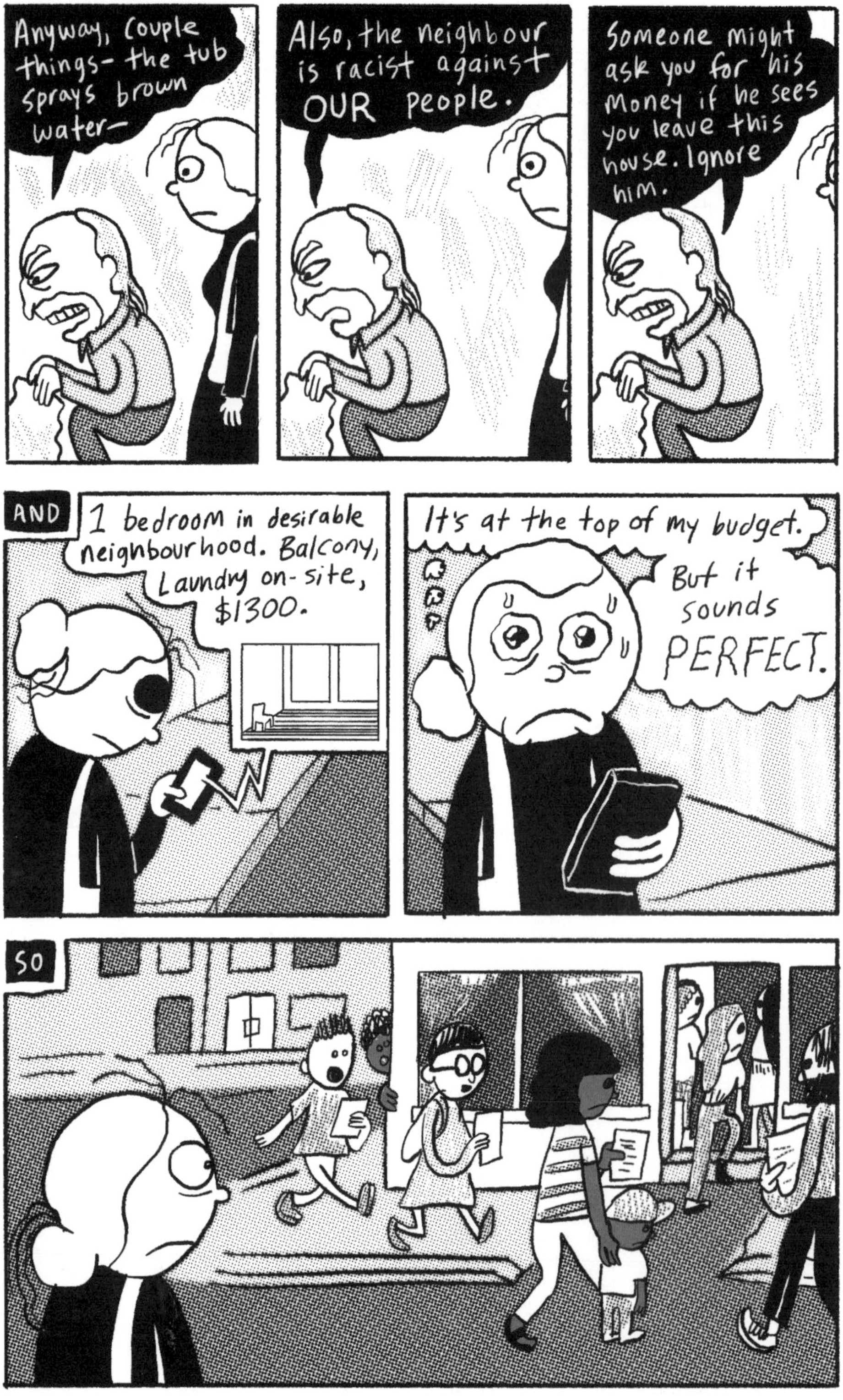
Anyway, Couple things- the tub sprays brown water-
Also, the neighbour is racist against OUR people.
Someone might ask you for his Money if he sees you leave this house. Ignore him.
AND
1 bedroom in desirable neighbourhood. Balcony, Laundry on-site, $1300.
It's at the top of my budget.
But it sounds PERFECT.
SO

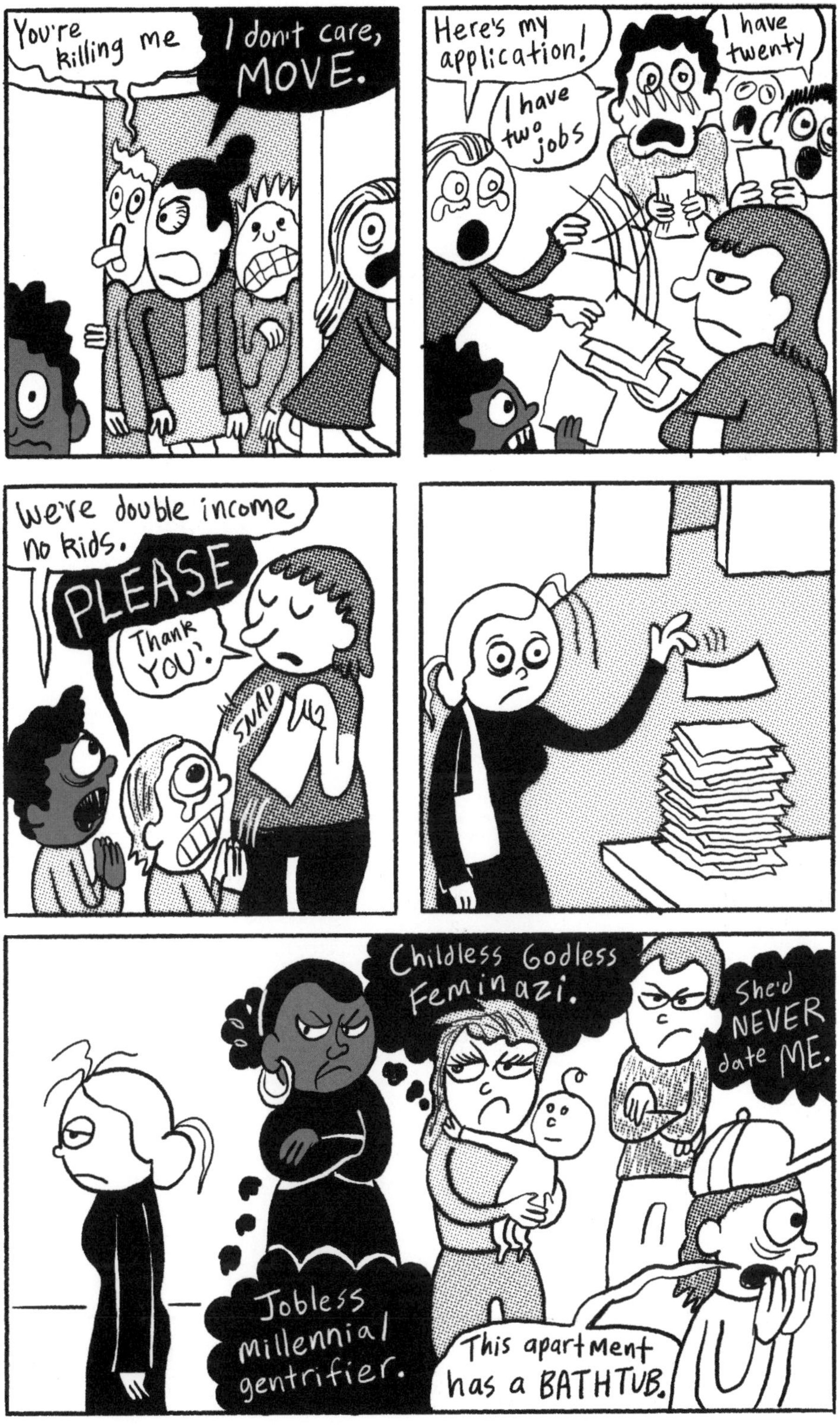
You're killing me
I don't care, MOVE.
Here's my application!
I have two jobs
I have twenty
We're double income no kids.
PLEASE
Thank YOU.
SNAP
Childless Godless Feminazi.
She'd NEVER date ME.
Jobless millennial gentrifier.
This apartment has a BATHTUB.

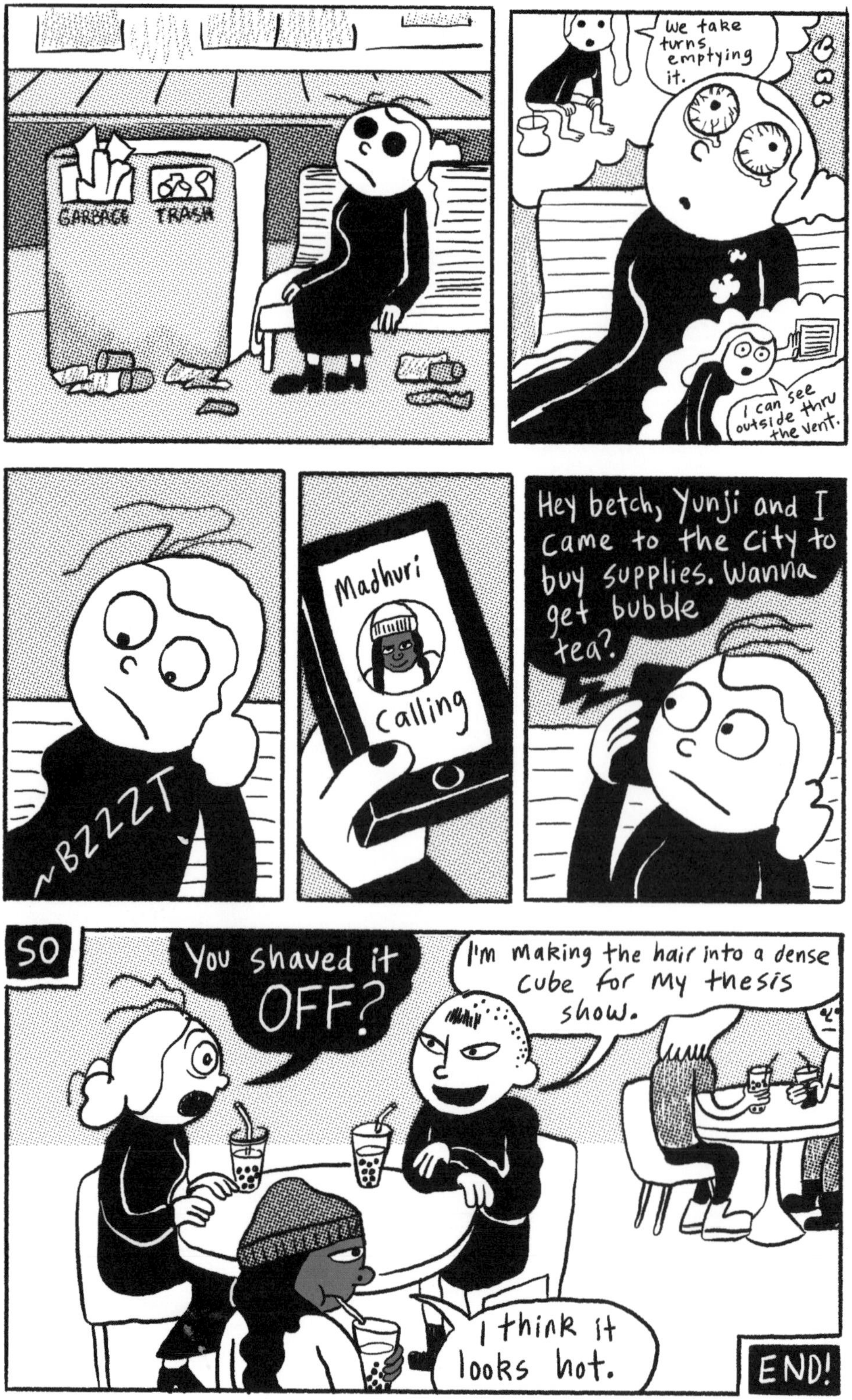

GARBAGE
TRASH
We take turns emptying it.
I can see outside thru the vent.
~BZZZT
Madhuri
Calling
Hey betch, Yunji and I came to the city to buy supplies. Wanna get bubble tea?
SO
You shaved it OFF?
I'm making the hair into a dense cube for my thesis show.
I think it looks hot.
END!

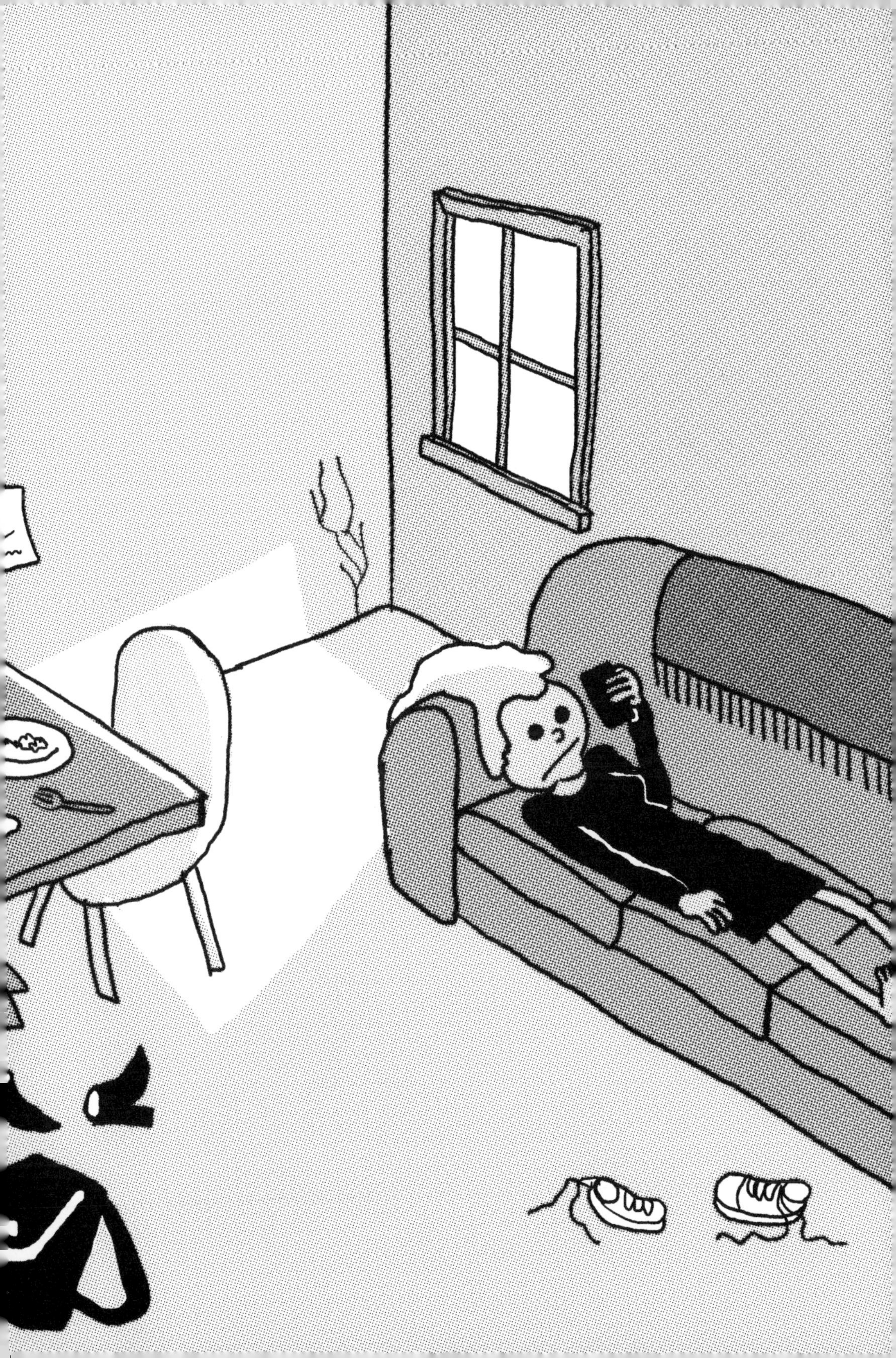

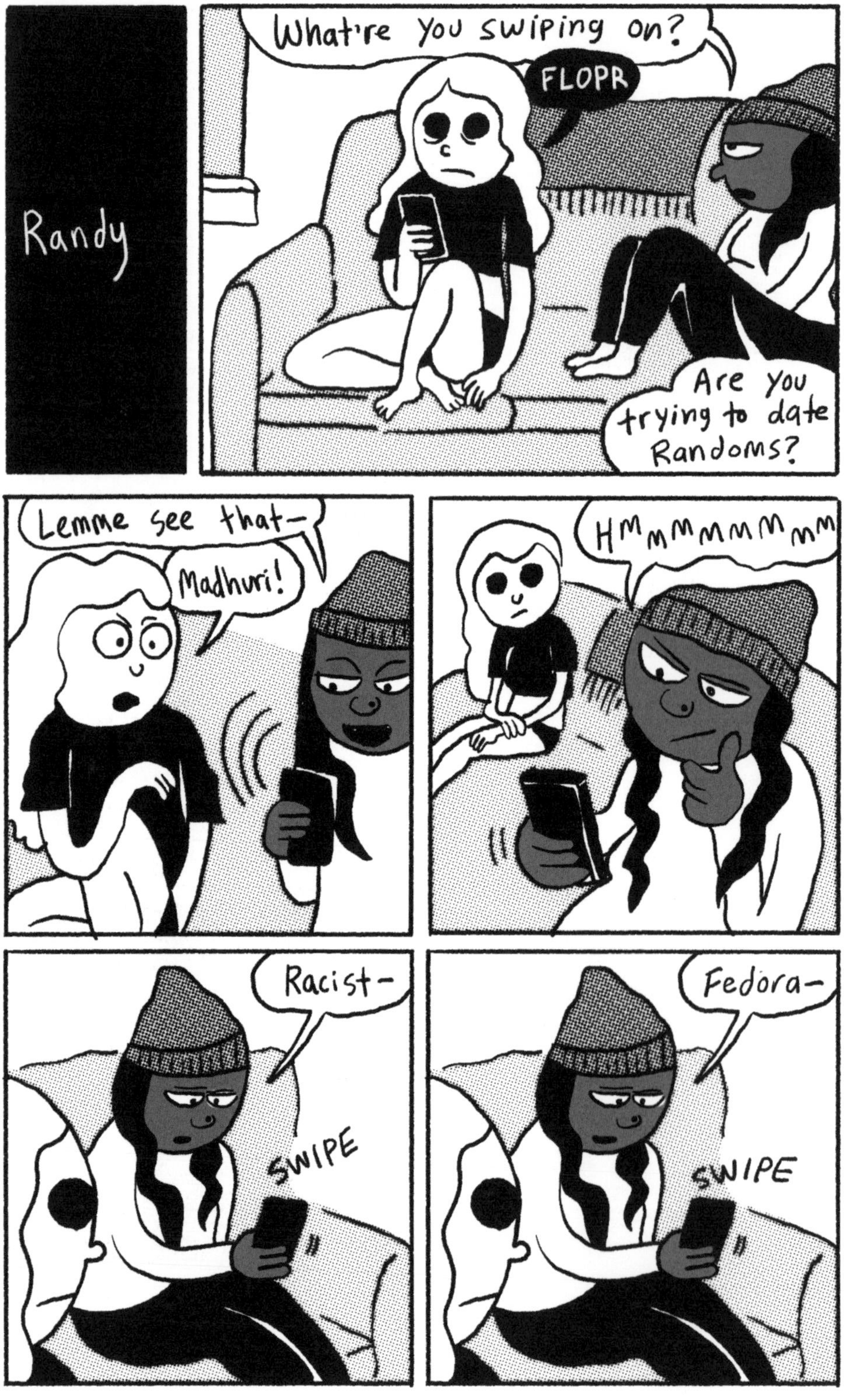
Randy
What're you swiping on?
FLOPR
Are you trying to date Randoms?
Lemme see that—
Madhuri!
HMMMMMMMMM
Racist—
SWIPE
Fedora—
SWIPE

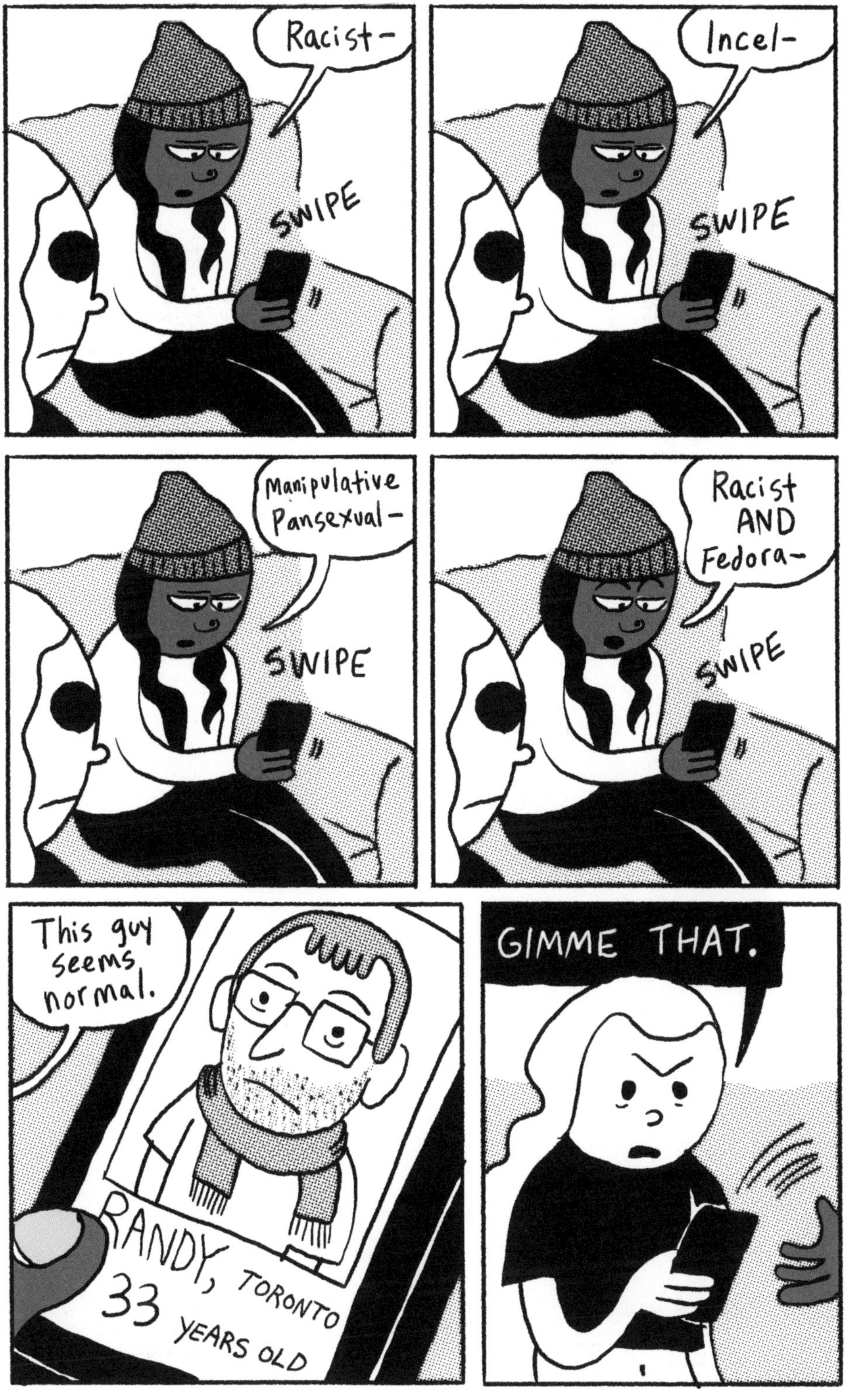
Racist-
SWIPE
Incel-
SWIPE
Manipulative Pansexual-
SWIPE
Racist AND Fedora-
SWIPE
This guy seems normal.
RANDY, TORONTO
33 YEARS OLD
GIMME THAT.

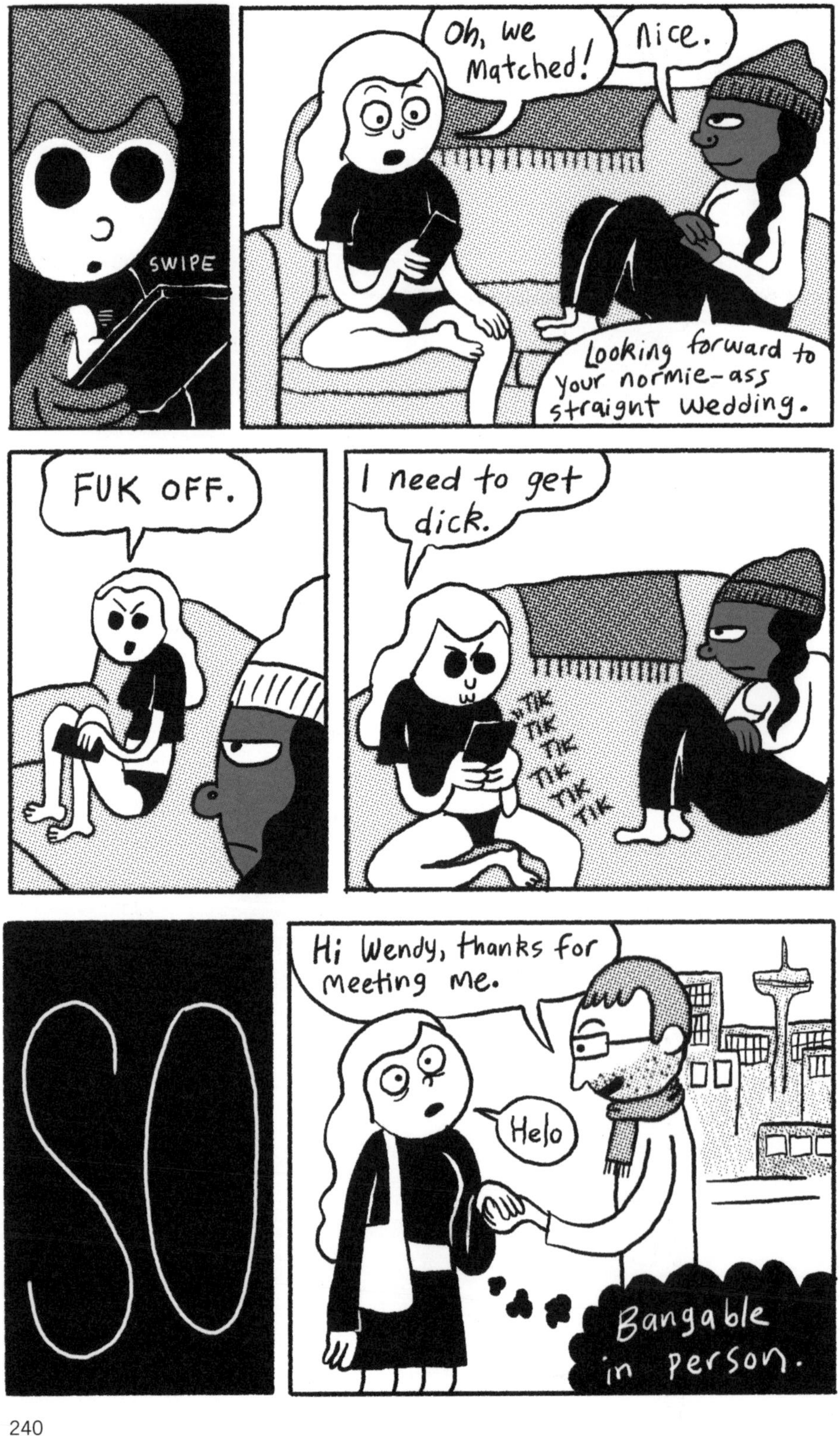
SWIPE
Oh, we Matched!
Nice.
Looking forward to your normie-ass straight wedding.
FUK OFF.
I need to get dick.
TIK TIK TIK TIK TIK TIK
SO
Hi Wendy, thanks for meeting me.
Helo
Bangable in person.

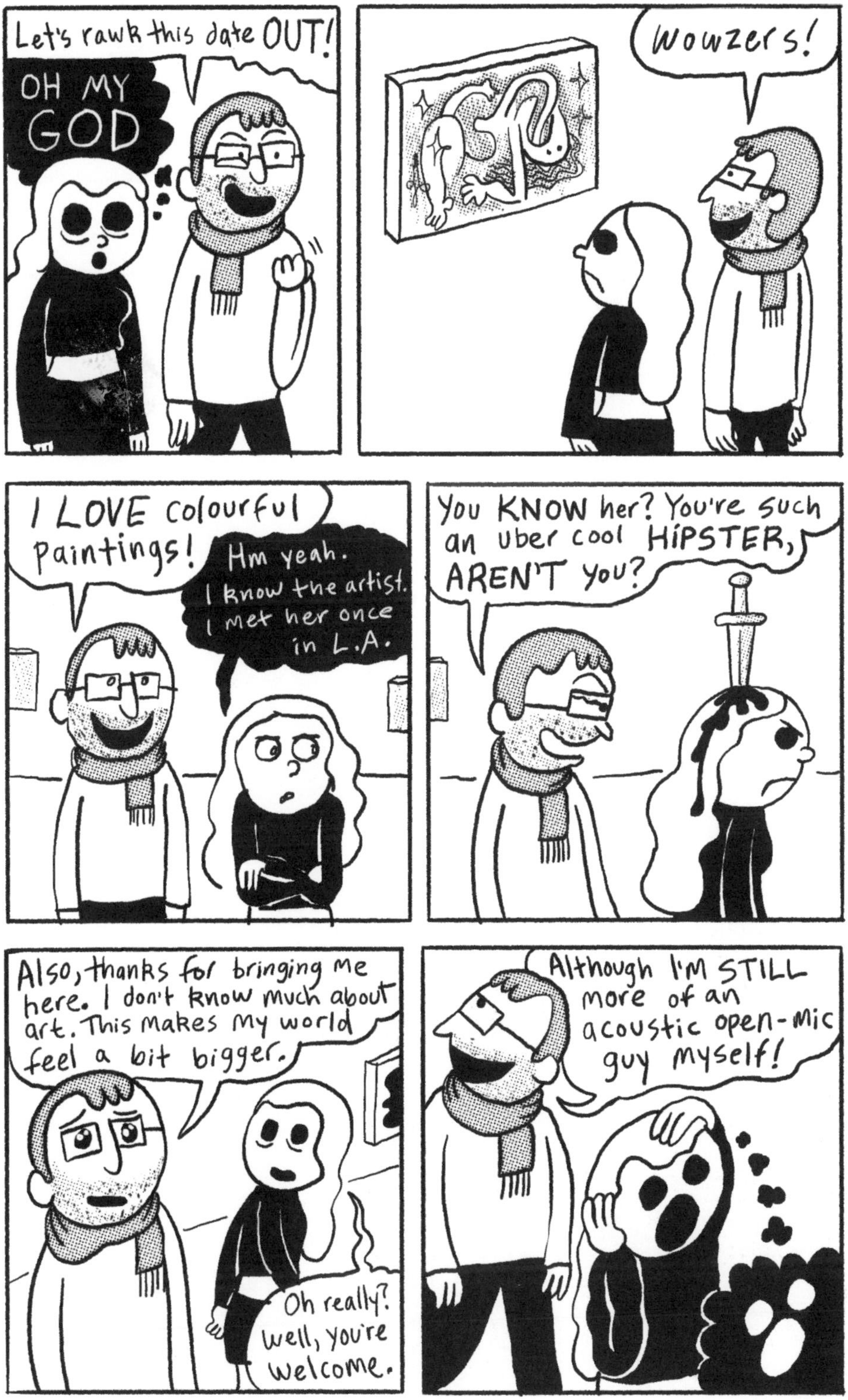
Let's rawk this date OUT!
OH MY GOD
Wowzers!
I LOVE colourful paintings!
Hm yeah. I know the artist. I met her once in L.A.
You KNOW her? You're such an uber cool HIPSTER, AREN'T you?
Also, thanks for bringing me here. I don't know much about art. This makes my world feel a bit bigger.
Oh really? Well, you're welcome.
Although I'M STILL more of an acoustic open-mic guy myself!

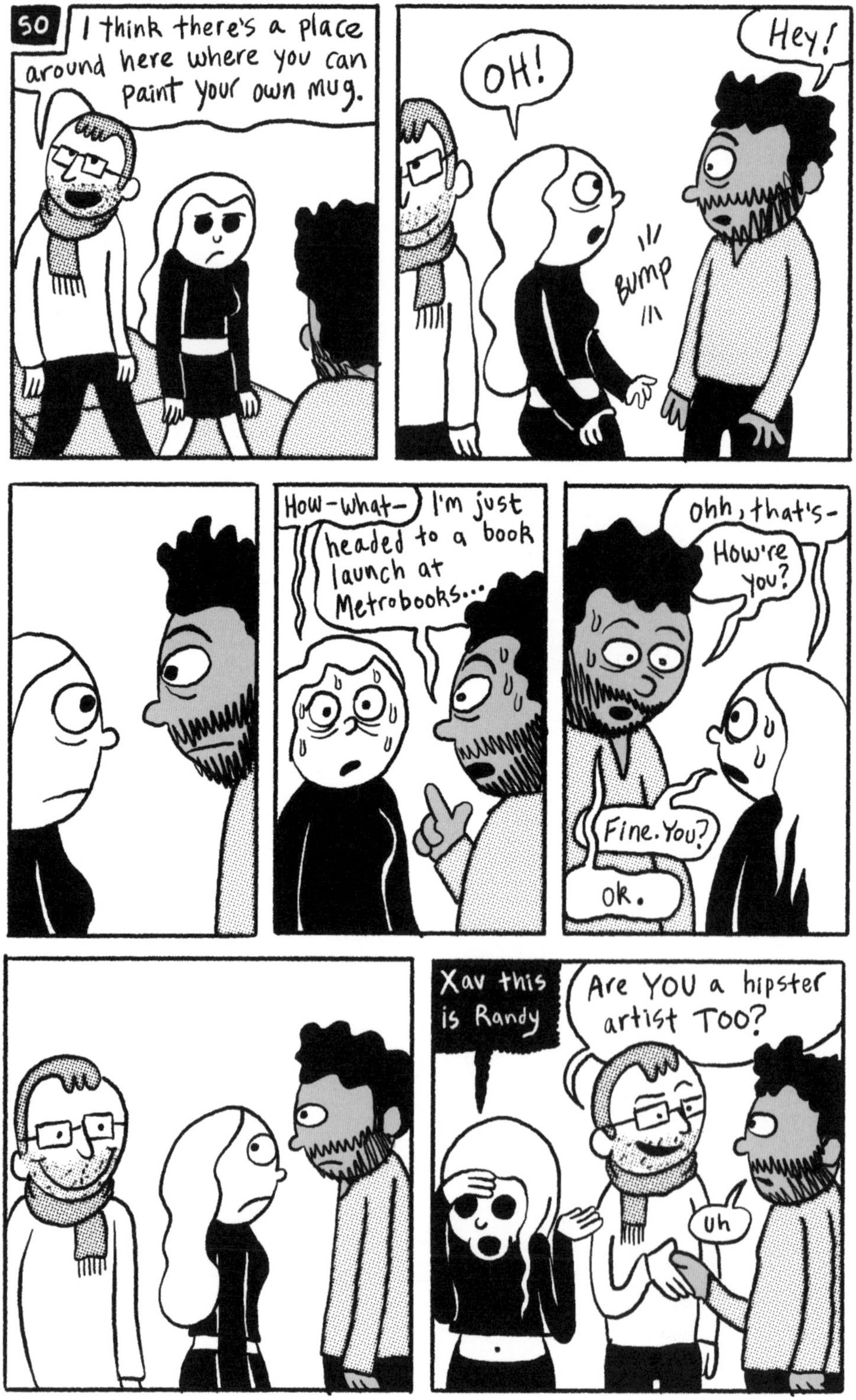
SO
I think there's a place around here where you can paint your own mug.
OH!
Hey!
BUMP
How-what-
I'm just headed to a book launch at Metrobooks...
Ohh, that's-
How're you?
Fine. You?
Ok.
Xav this is Randy
Are YOU a hipster artist TOO?
Uh

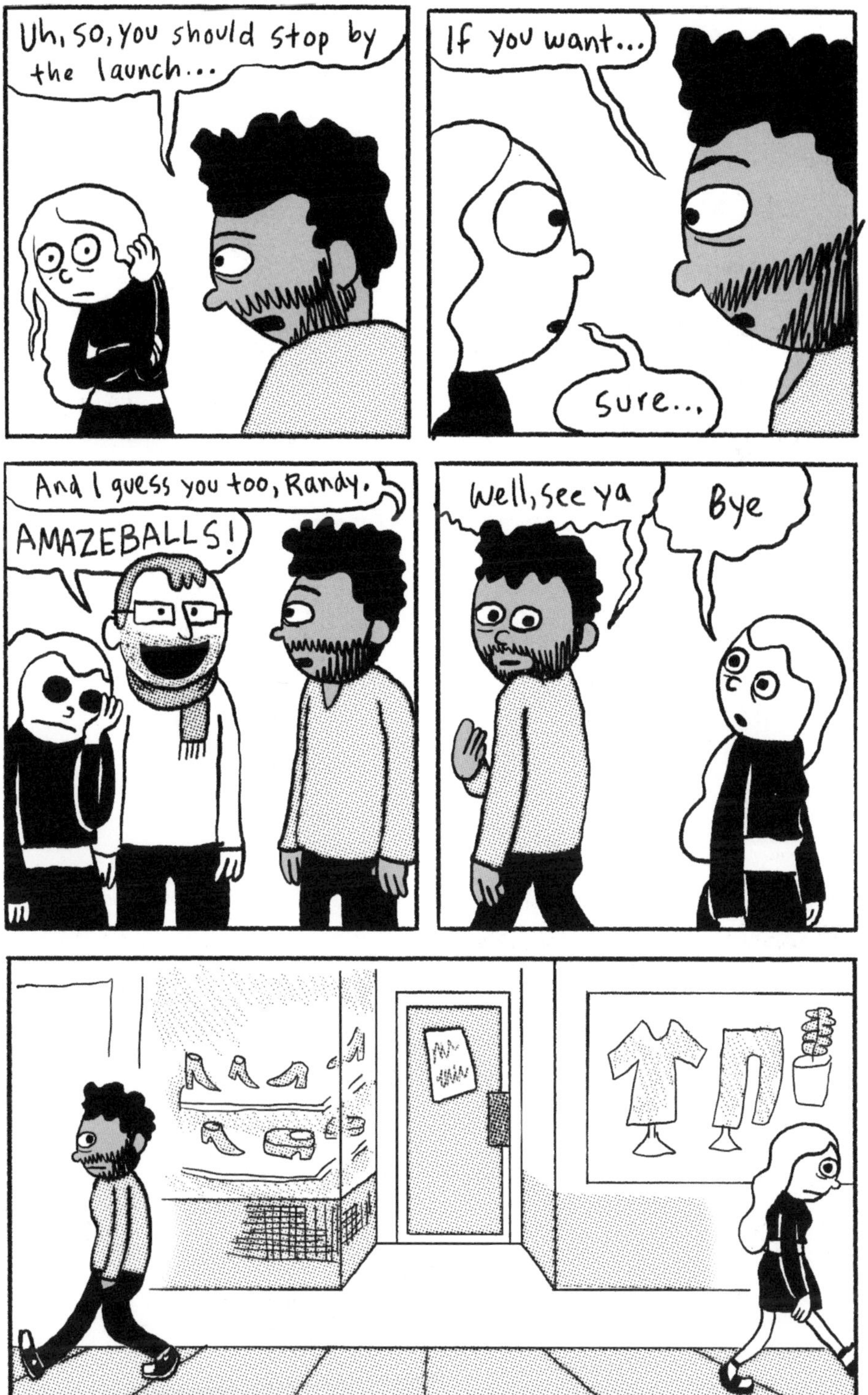
Uh, so, you should stop by the launch...
If you want...
Sure...
And I guess you too, Randy.
AMAZEBALLS!
Well, see ya
Bye

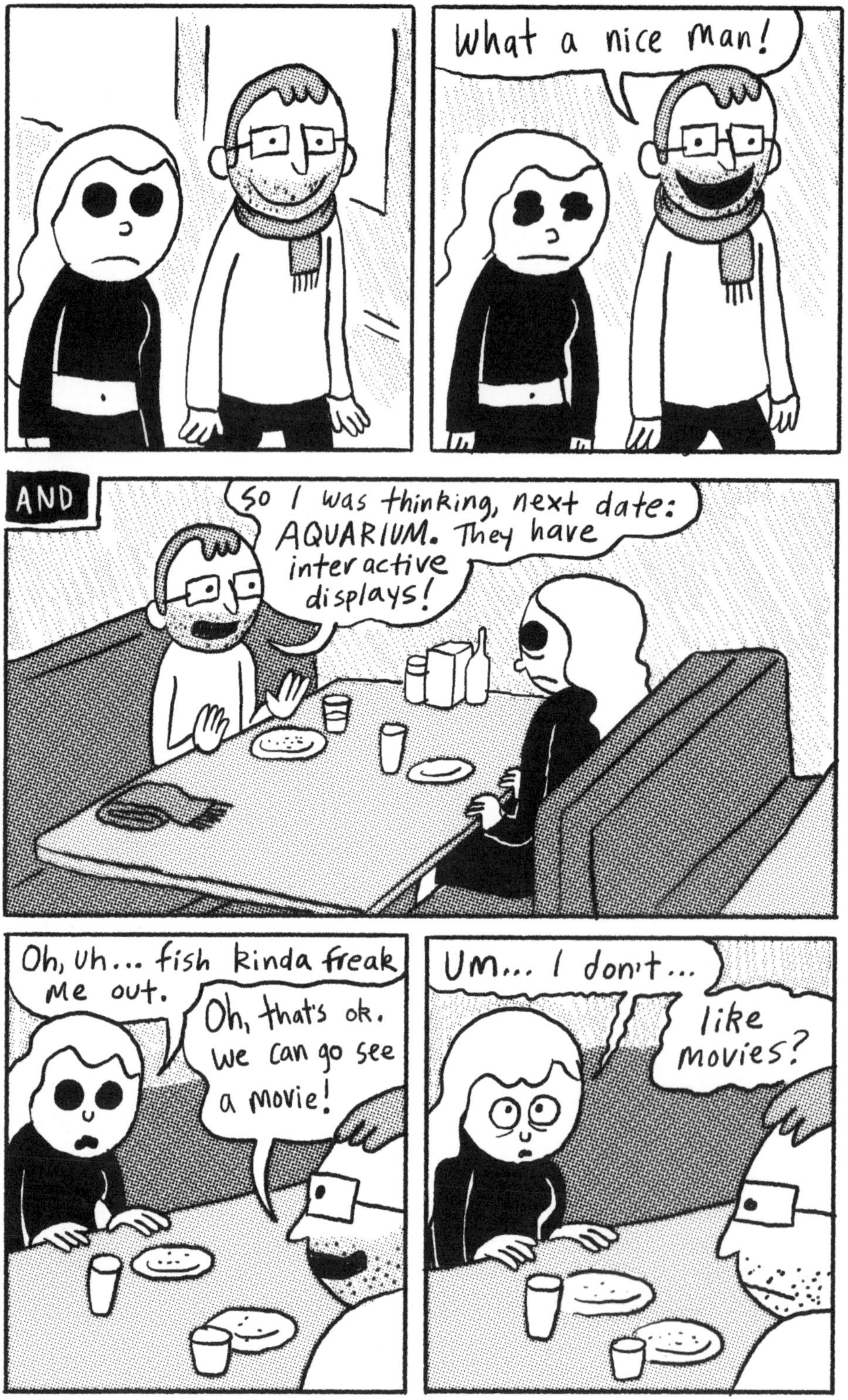
What a nice man!
AND
So I was thinking, next date: AQUARIUM. They have interactive displays!
Oh, uh... fish kinda freak me out.
Oh, that's ok. We can go see a movie!
Um... I don't...
like movies?

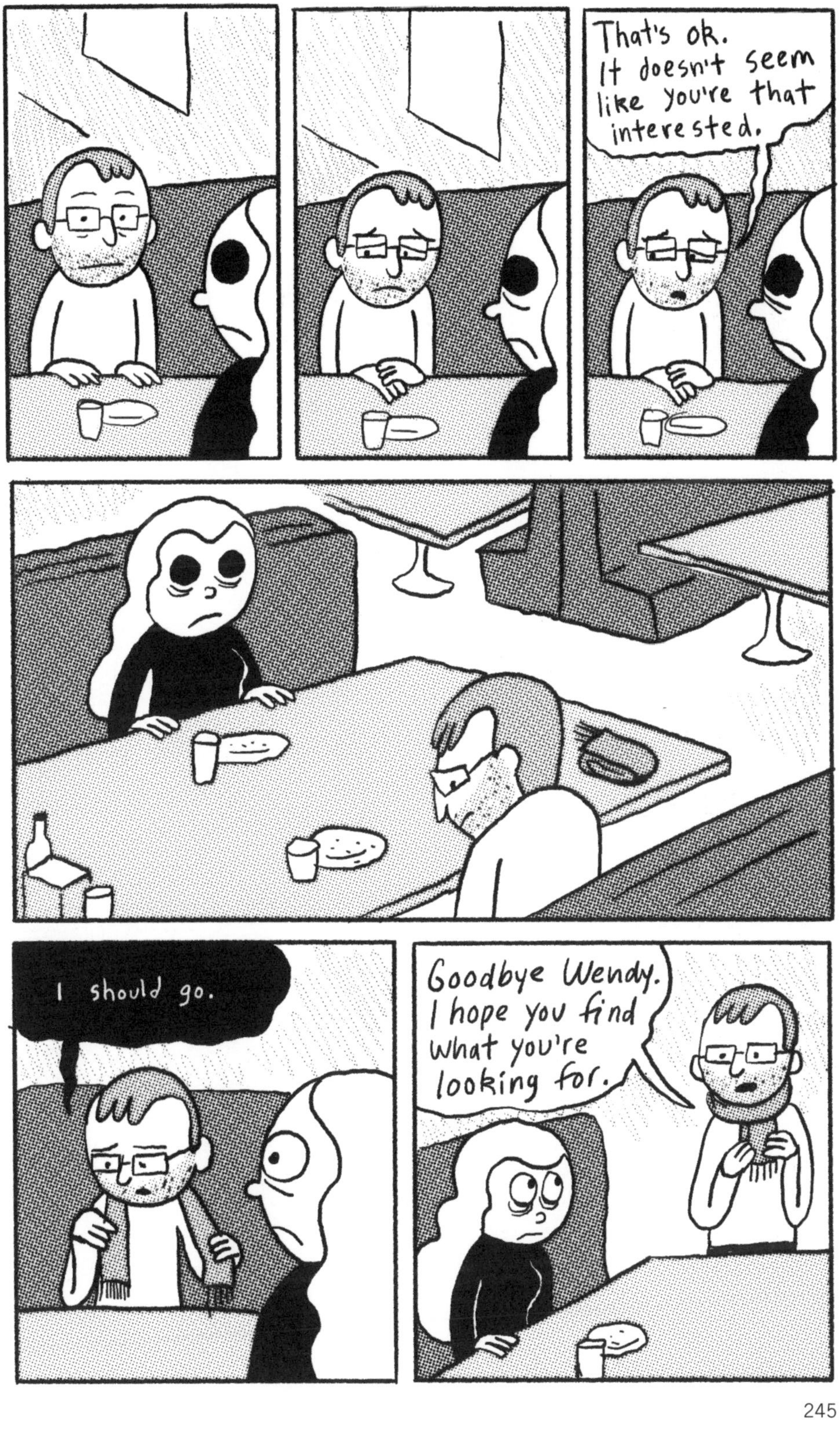
That's ok. It doesn't seem like you're that interested.
I should go.
Goodbye Wendy. I hope you find what you're looking for.

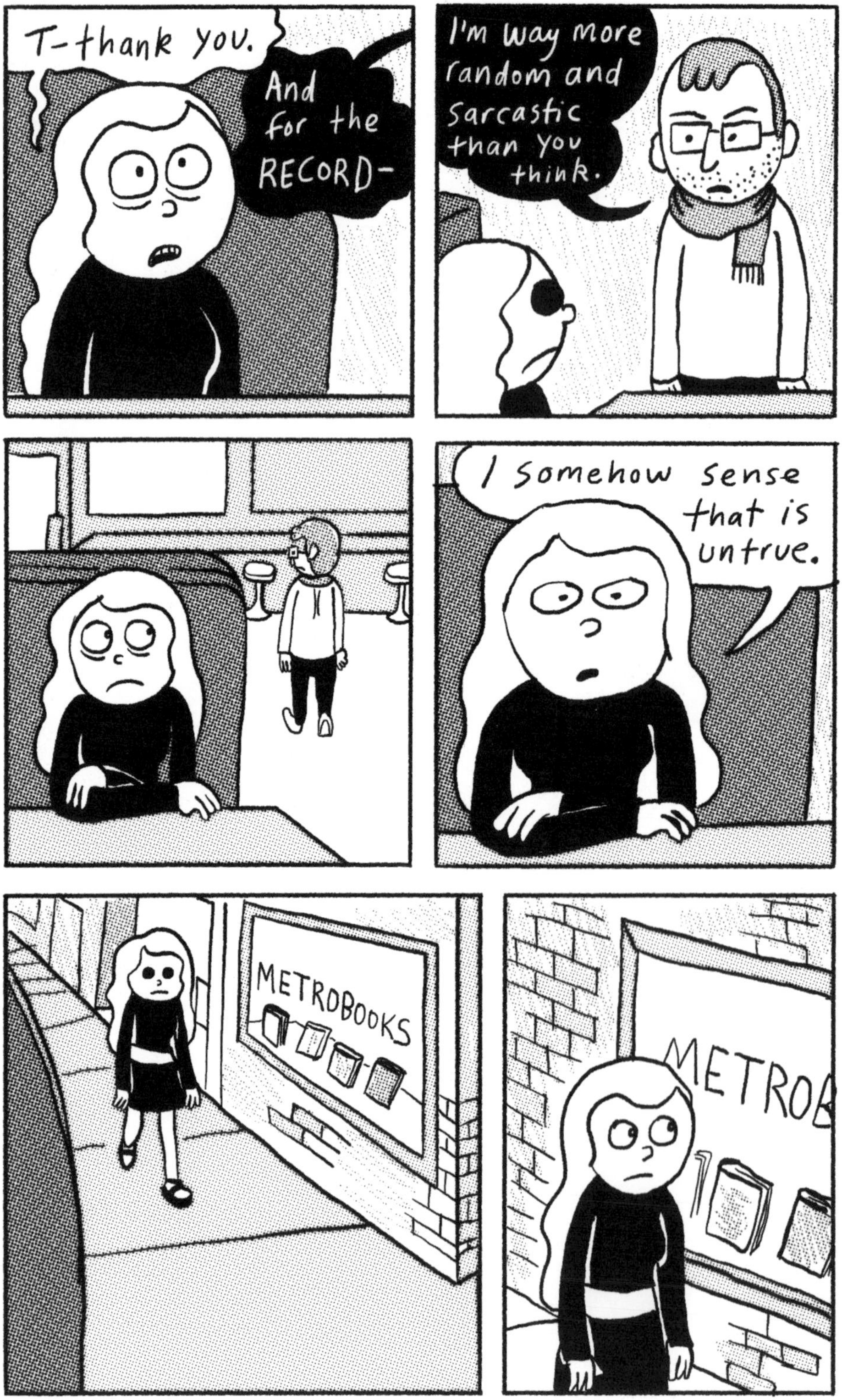
T-thank you.
And for the RECORD-
I'm way more random and sarcastic than you think.
I somehow sense that is untrue.
METROBOOKS
METROB

METROBOOKS
METROBOOKS
BOOKS

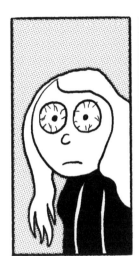

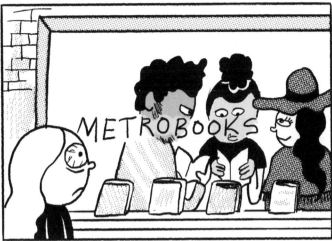

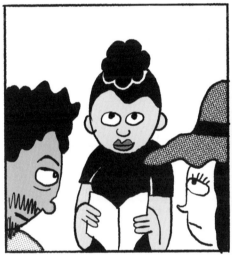

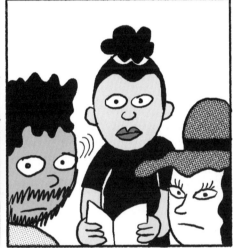

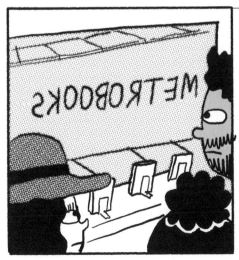

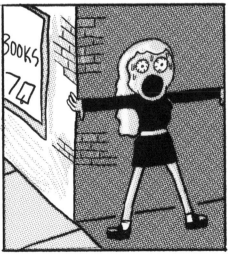

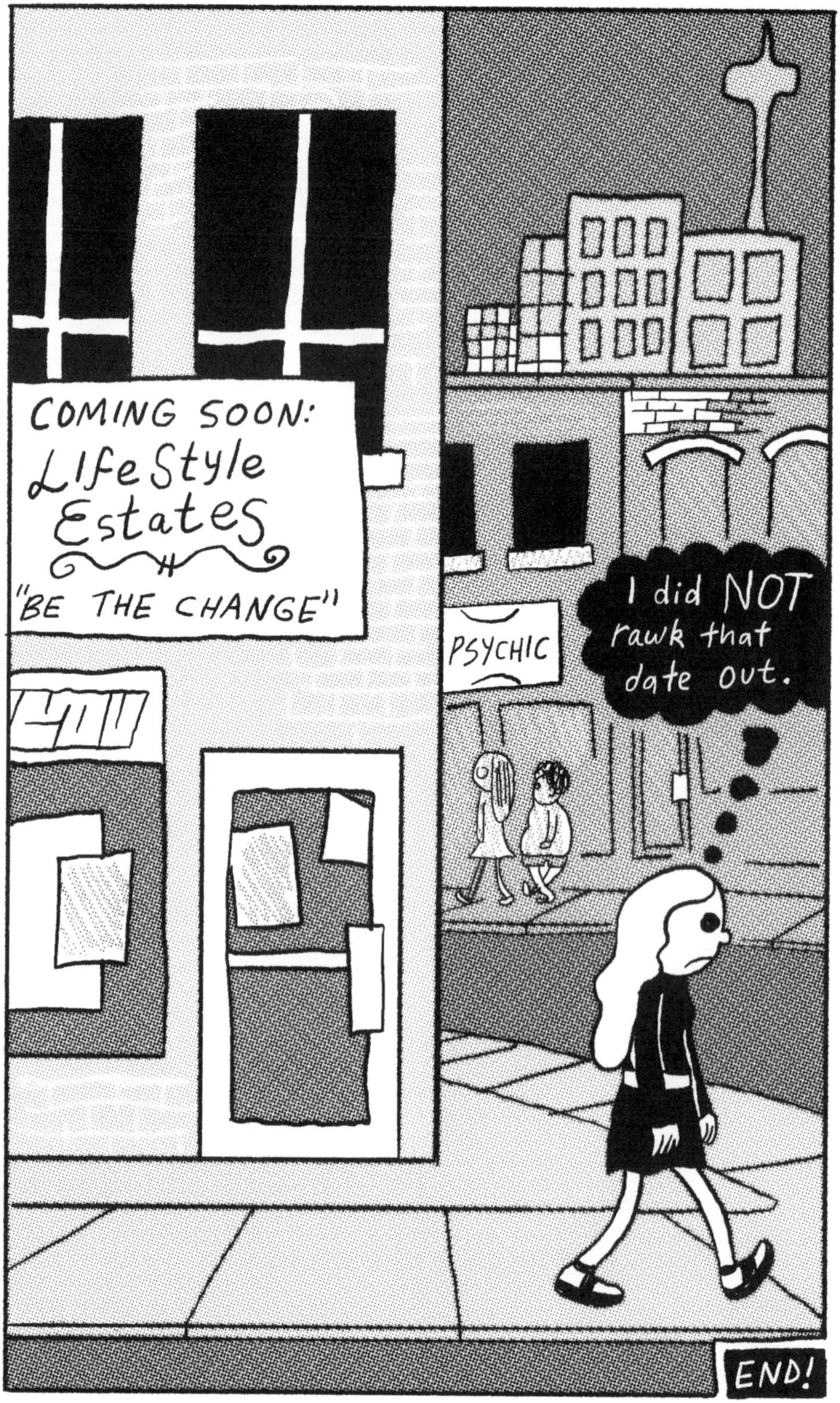
COMING SOON:
LifeStyle Estates
"BE THE CHANGE"
PSYCHIC
I did NOT rawk that date out.
END!

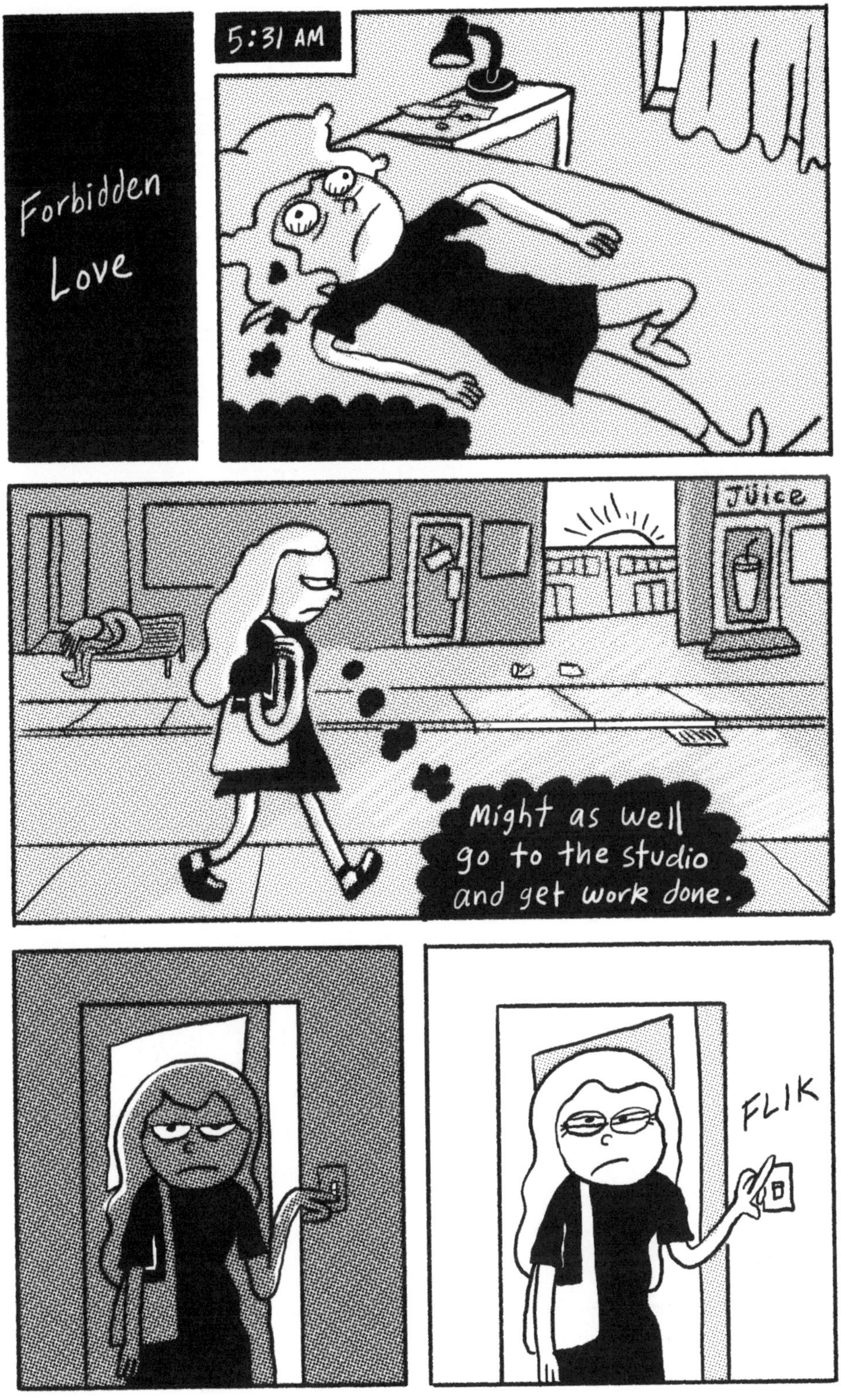
Forbidden Love
5:31 AM
JUICE
Might as well go to the studio and get work done.
FLIK

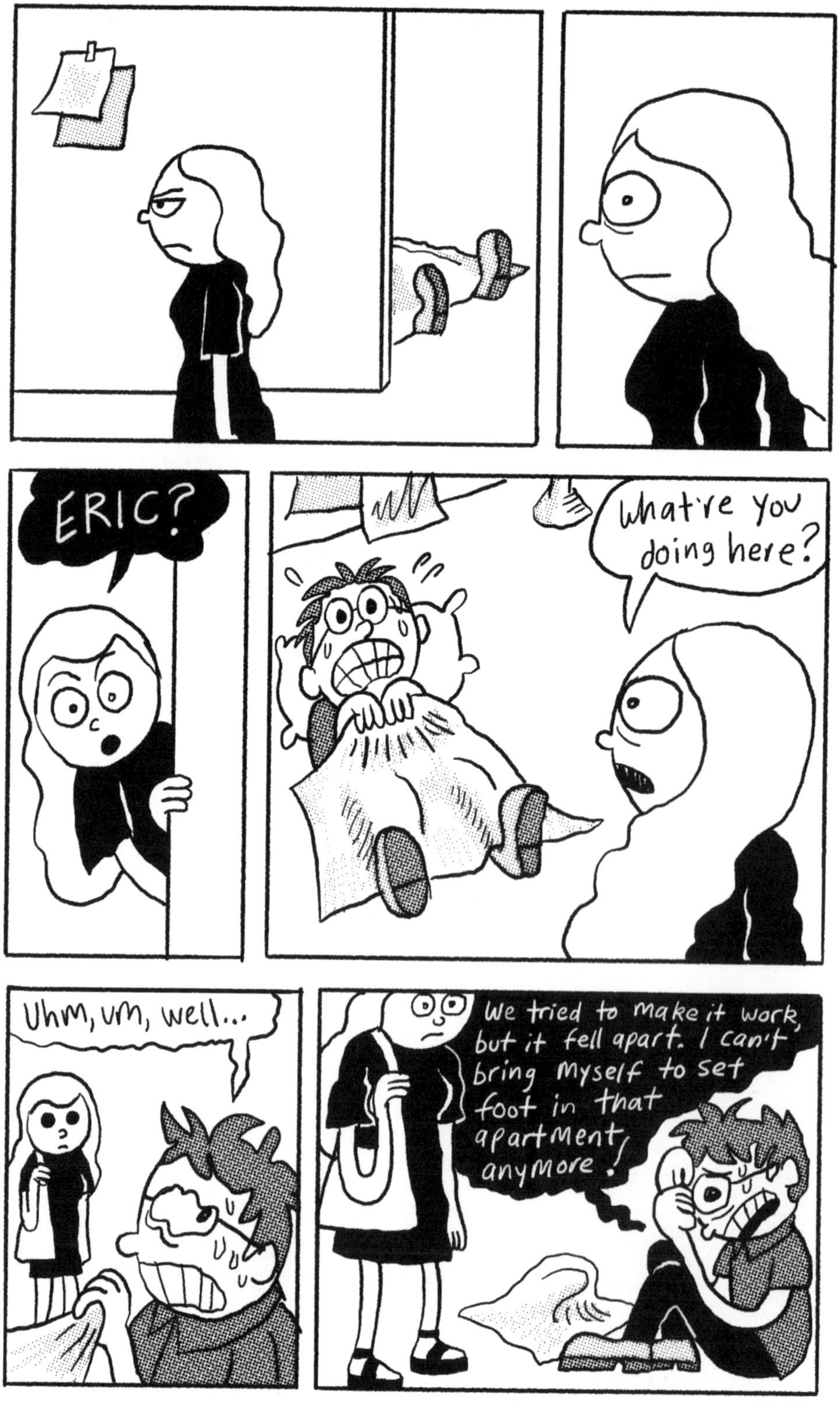
ERIC?
What're you doing here?
Uhm, um, well...
We tried to make it work, but it fell apart. I can't bring myself to set foot in that apartment anymore!

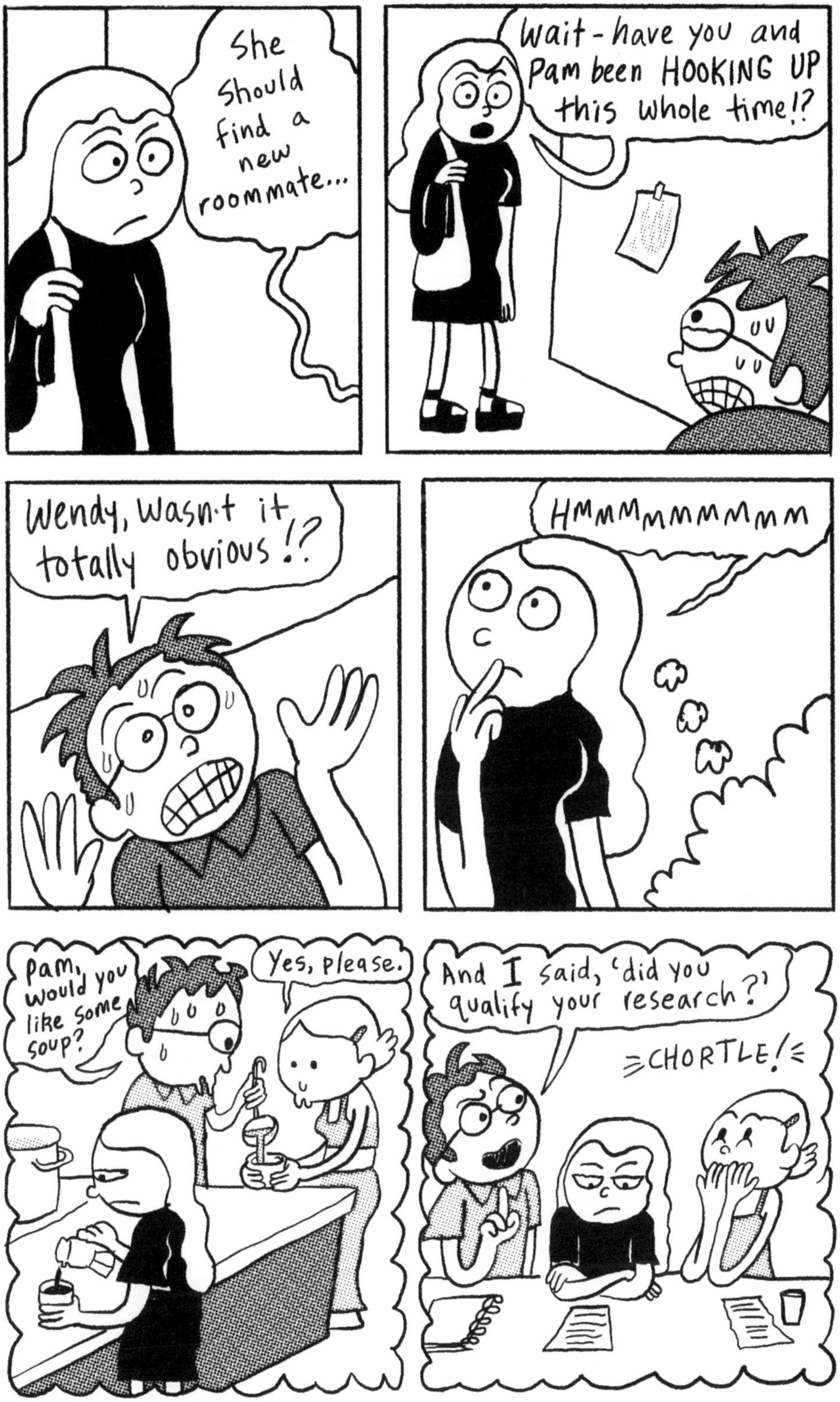
She Should find a new roommate...
Wait-have you and Pam been HOOKING UP this whole time!?
Wendy, Wasn't it totally obvious!?
HMMMMMMMMM
Pam, would you like some soup?
Yes, please.
And I said, 'did you qualify your research?'
CHORTLE!

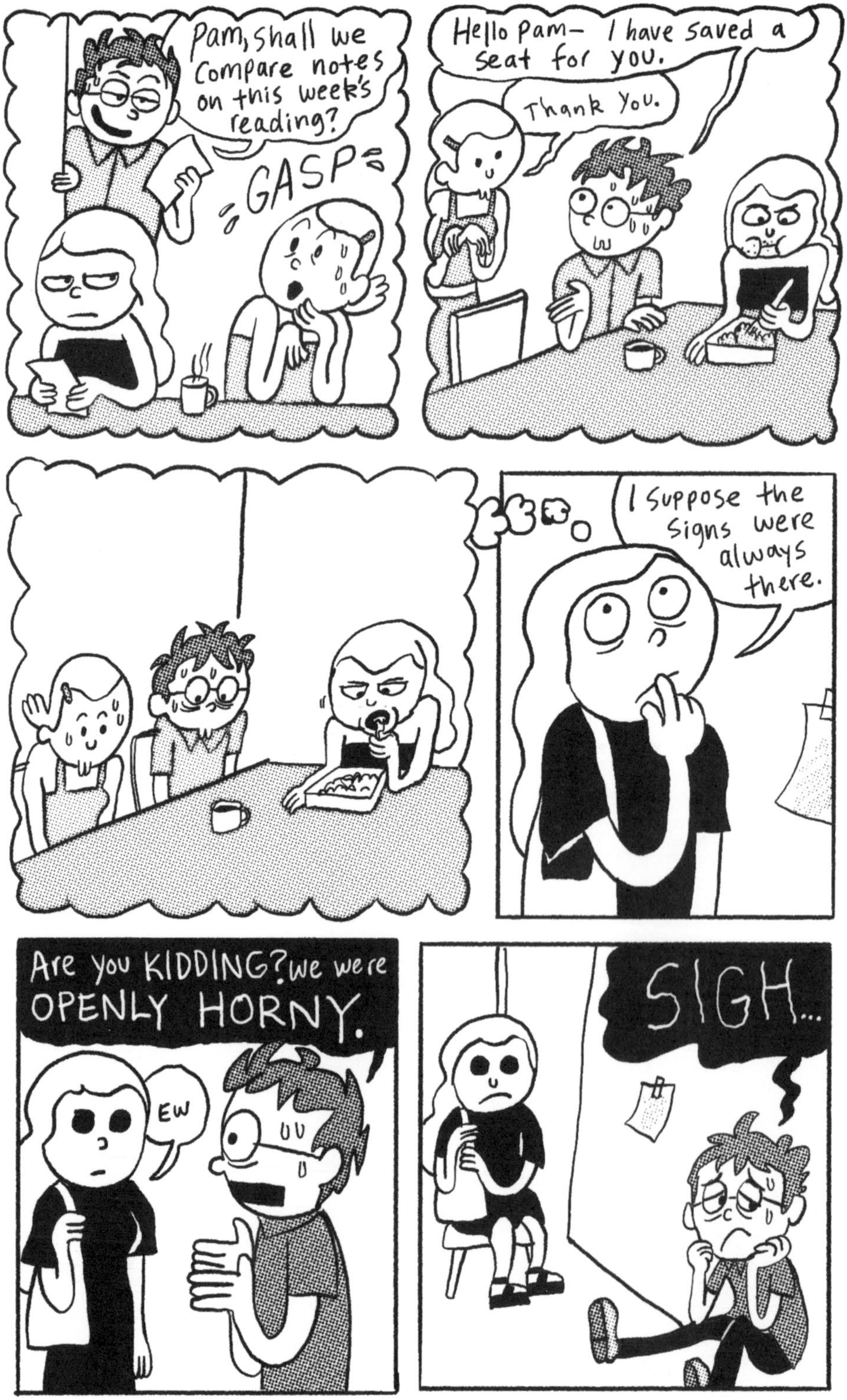
Pam, shall we compare notes on this week's reading?
GASP
Hello Pam— I have saved a seat for you.
Thank you.
I suppose the signs were always there.
Are you KIDDING? We were OPENLY HORNY.
EW
SIGH...

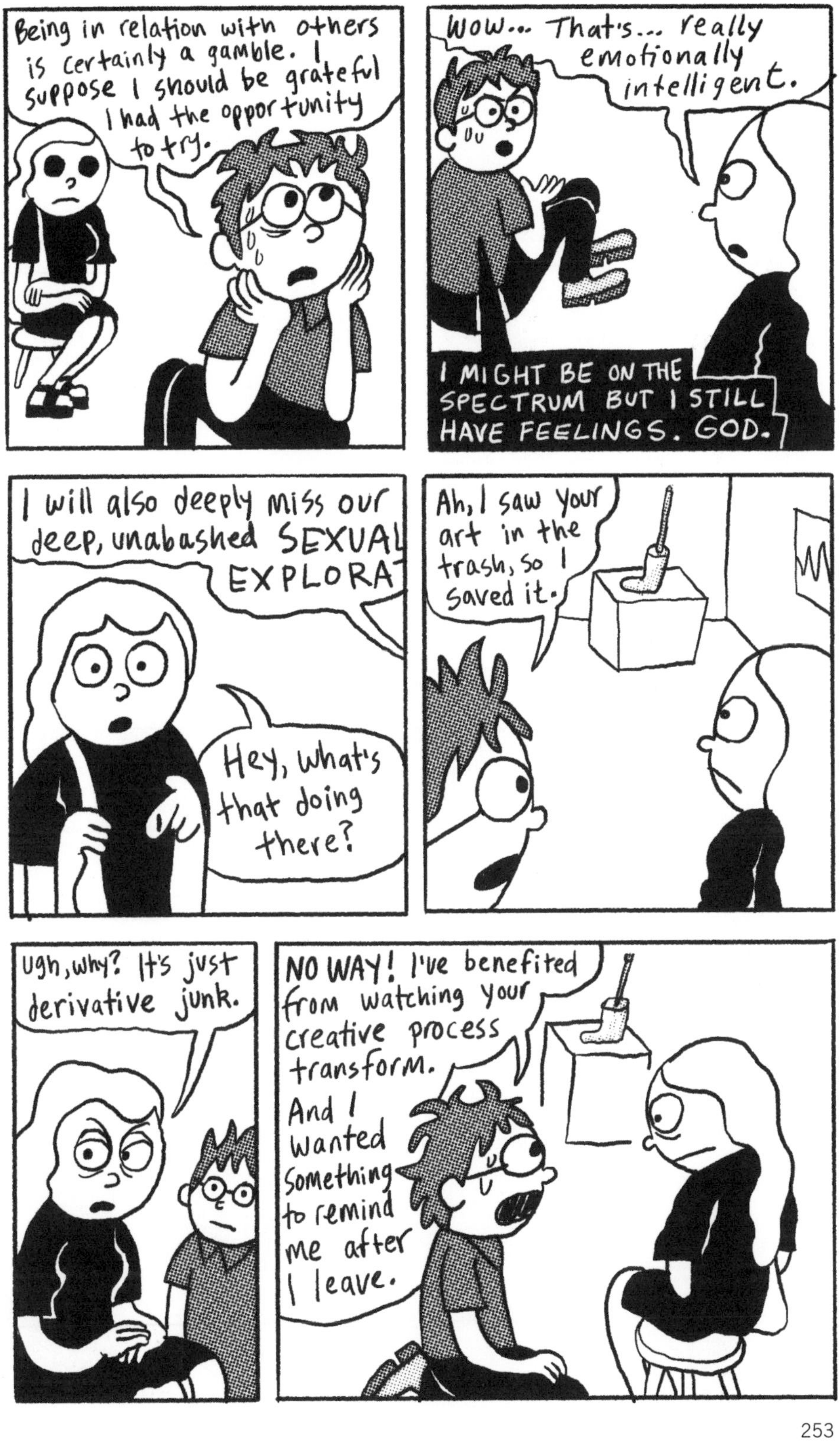
Being in relation with others is certainly a gamble. I suppose I should be grateful I had the opportunity to try.
Wow... That's... really emotionally intelligent.
I MIGHT BE ON THE SPECTRUM BUT I STILL HAVE FEELINGS. GOD.
I will also deeply miss our deep, unabashed SEXUAL EXPLORAT
Hey, what's that doing there?
Ah, I saw your art in the trash, so I saved it.
Ugh, why? It's just derivative junk.
NO WAY! I've benefited from watching your creative process transform.
And I wanted something to remind me after I leave.

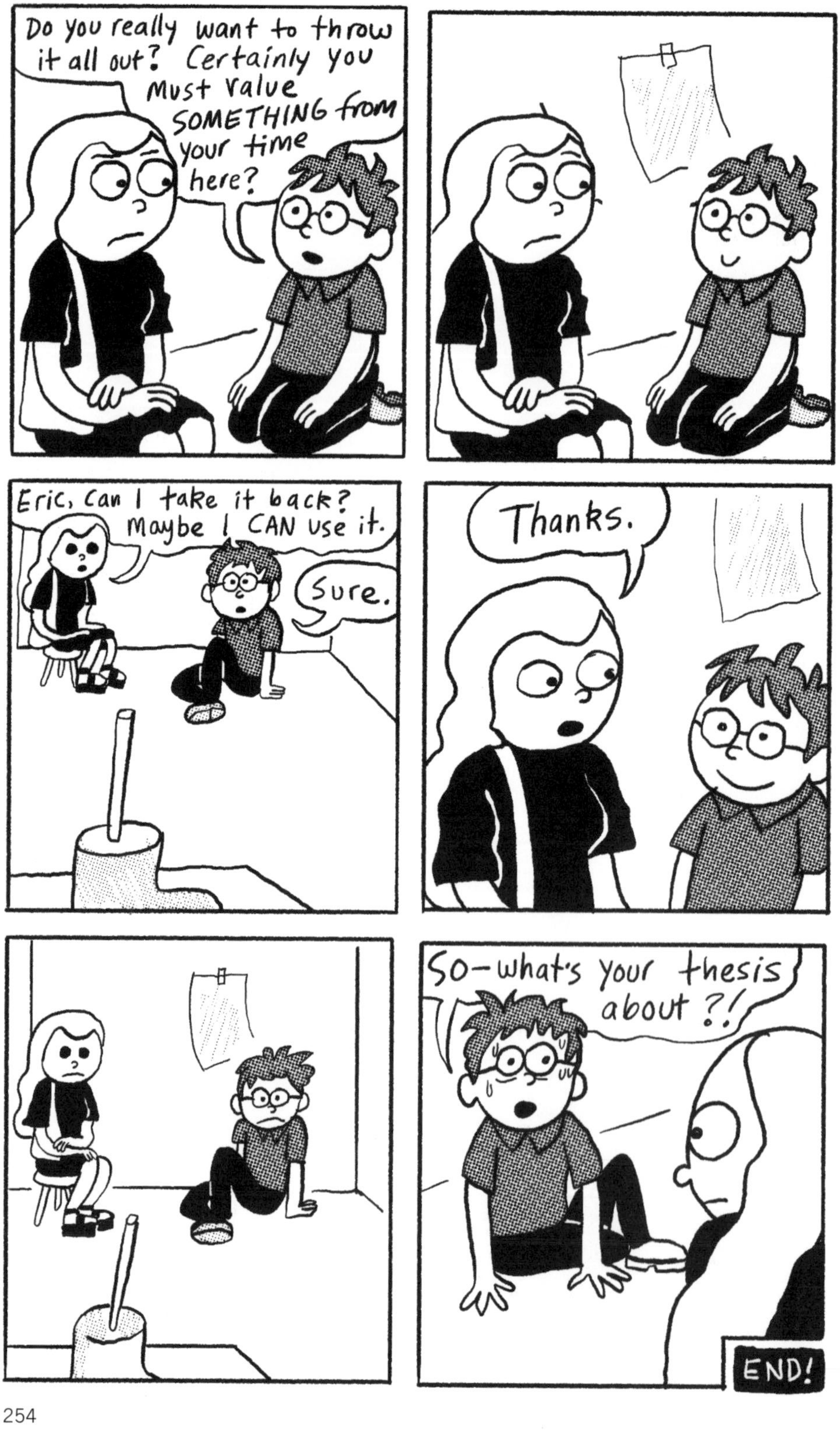
Do you really want to throw it all out? Certainly you must value SOMETHING from your time here?
Eric, can I take it back? Maybe I CAN use it.
Sure.
Thanks.
So—what's your thesis about?!
END!

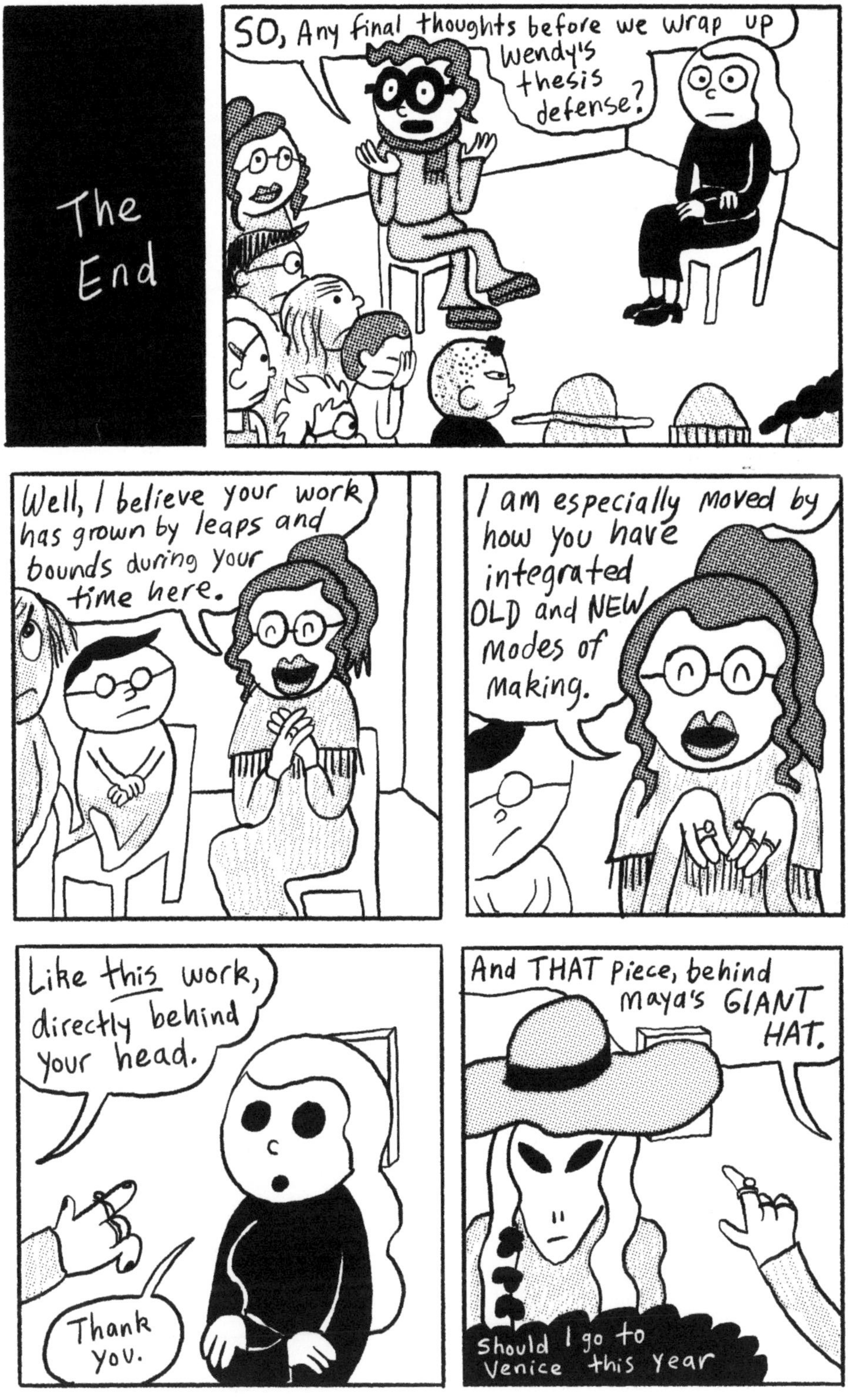
The End
SO, Any final thoughts before we wrap up Wendy's thesis defense?
Well, I believe your work has grown by leaps and bounds during your time here.
I am especially moved by how you have integrated OLD and NEW modes of making.
Like this work, directly behind your head.
Thank you.
And THAT piece, behind Maya's GIANT HAT.
Should I go to Venice this year

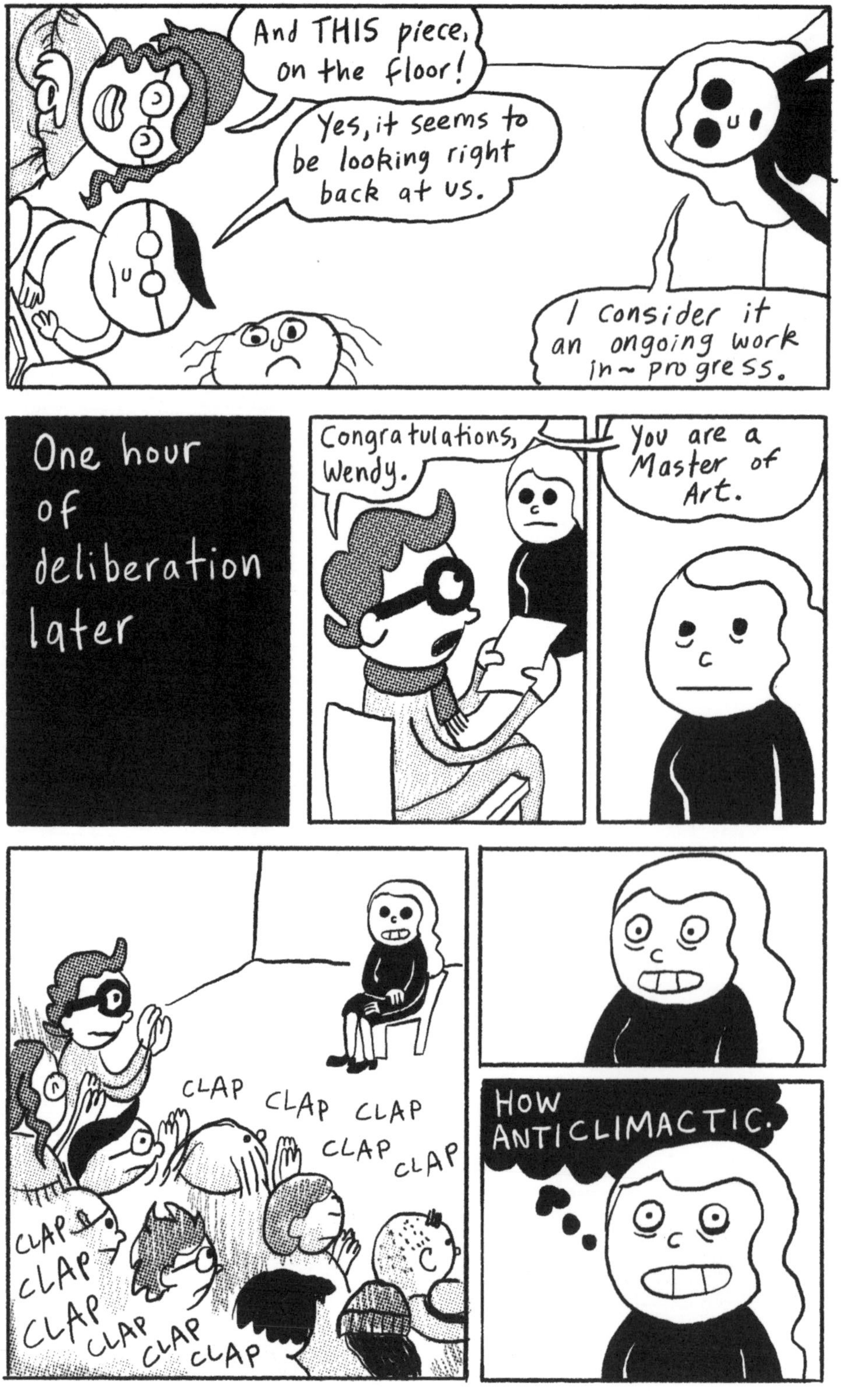

And THIS piece, on the floor!
Yes, it seems to be looking right back at us.
I consider it an ongoing work in~progress.
One hour of deliberation later
Congratulations, Wendy.
You are a Master of Art.
CLAP CLAP CLAP CLAP CLAP
CLAP CLAP CLAP CLAP CLAP CLAP
HOW ANTICLIMACTIC.

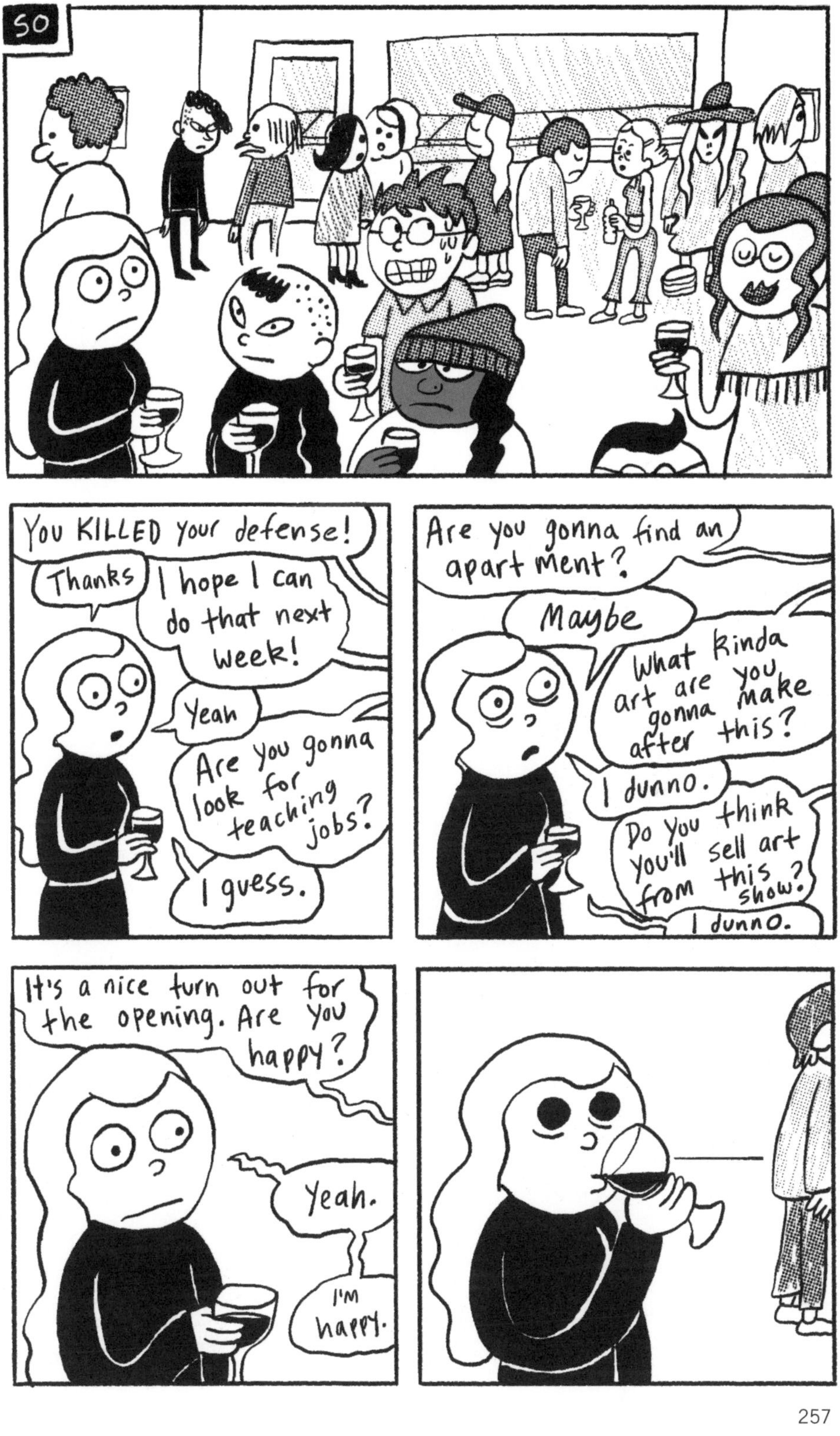

50
You KILLED your defense!
Thanks
I hope I can do that next week!
Yeah
Are you gonna look for teaching jobs?
I guess.
Are you gonna find an apartment?
Maybe
What kinda art are you gonna make after this?
I dunno.
Do you think you'll sell art from this show?
I dunno.
It's a nice turn out for the opening. Are you happy?
Yeah.
I'm happy.

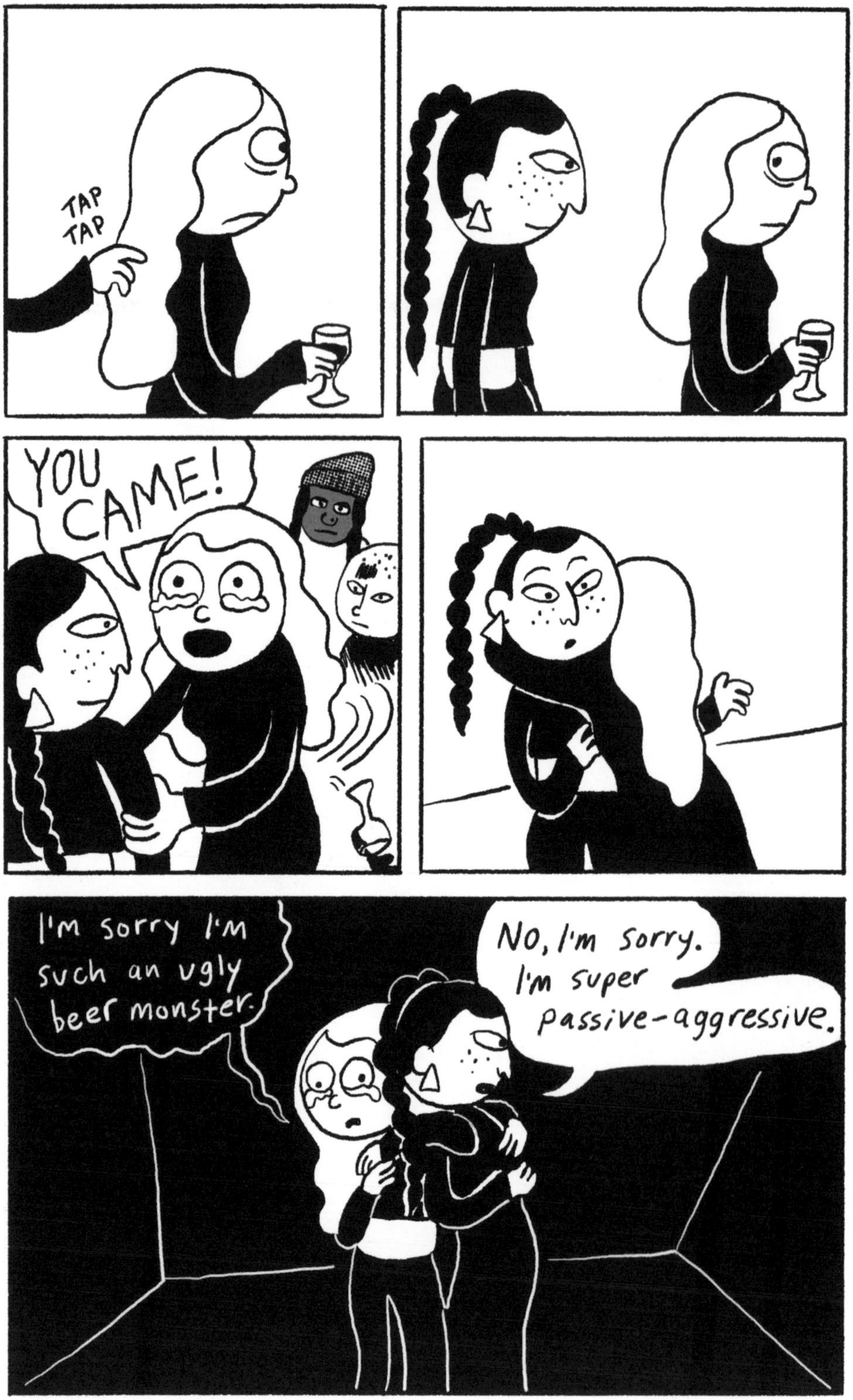
TAP
TAP
YOU CAME!
I'm sorry I'm such an ugly beer monster.
No, I'm sorry. I'm super passive-aggressive.

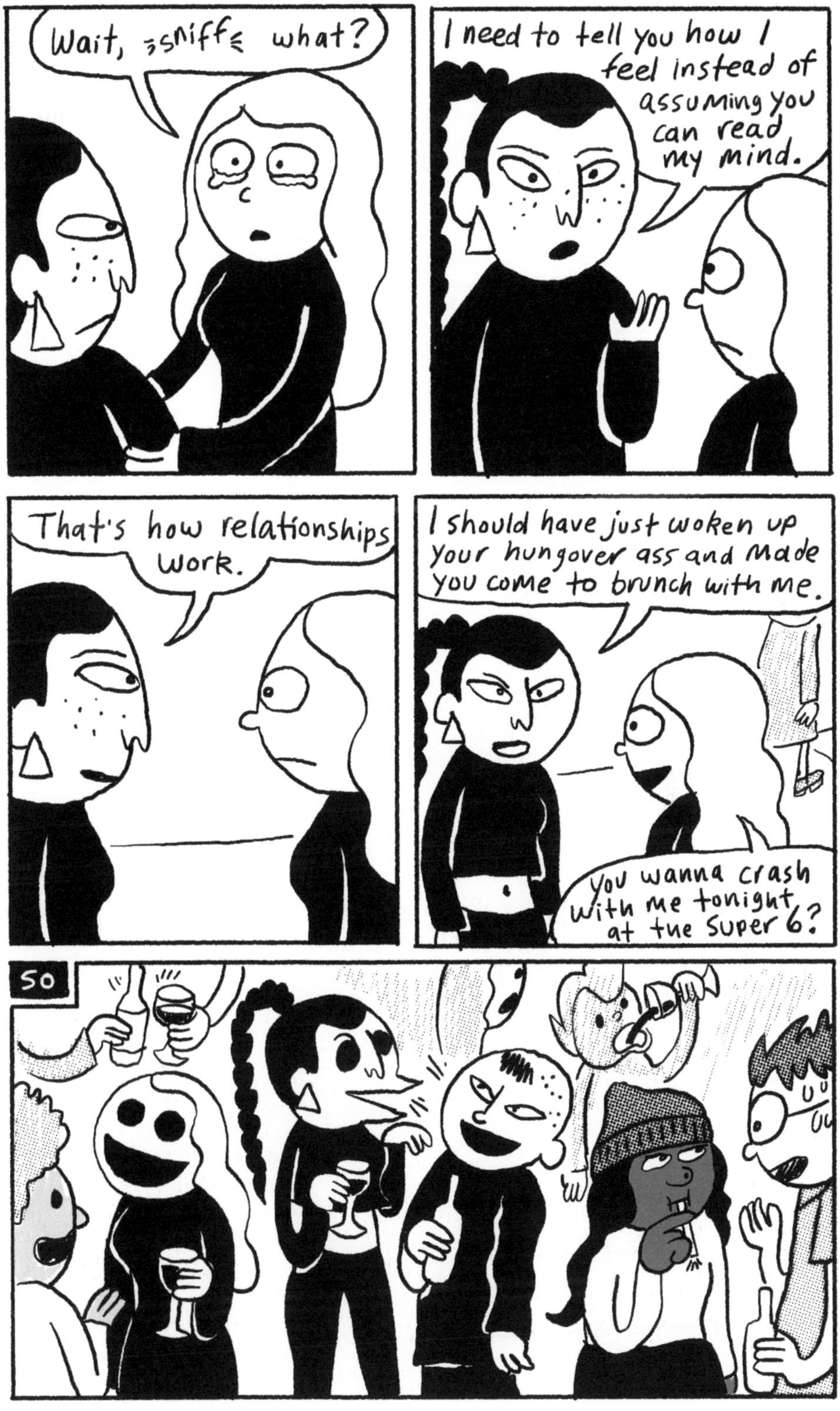
Wait, sniff what?
I need to tell you how I feel instead of assuming you can read my mind.
That's how relationships work.
I should have just woken up your hungover ass and made you come to brunch with me.
You wanna crash with me tonight at the Super 6?
SO

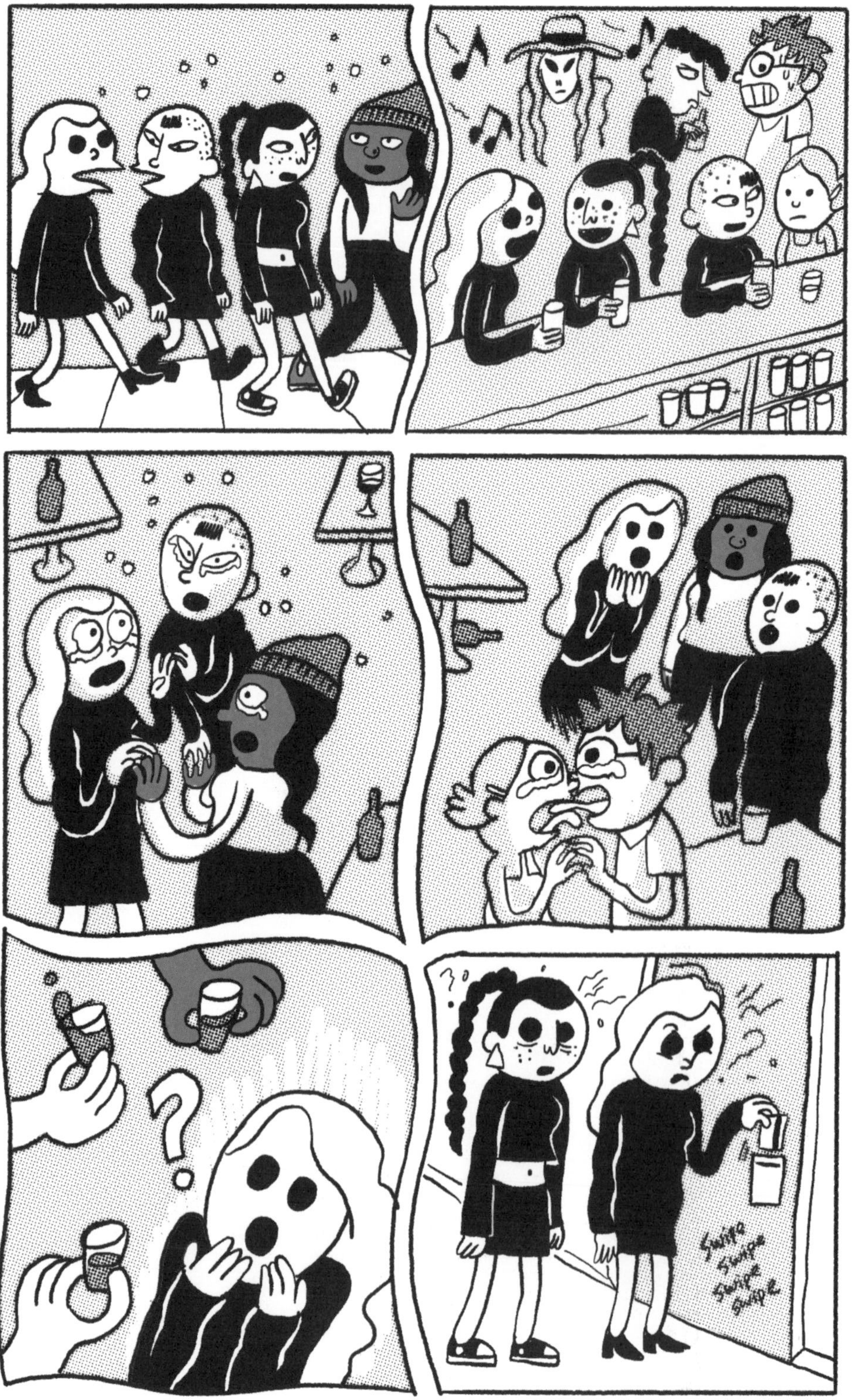
Swipe
Swipe
Swipe
Swipe

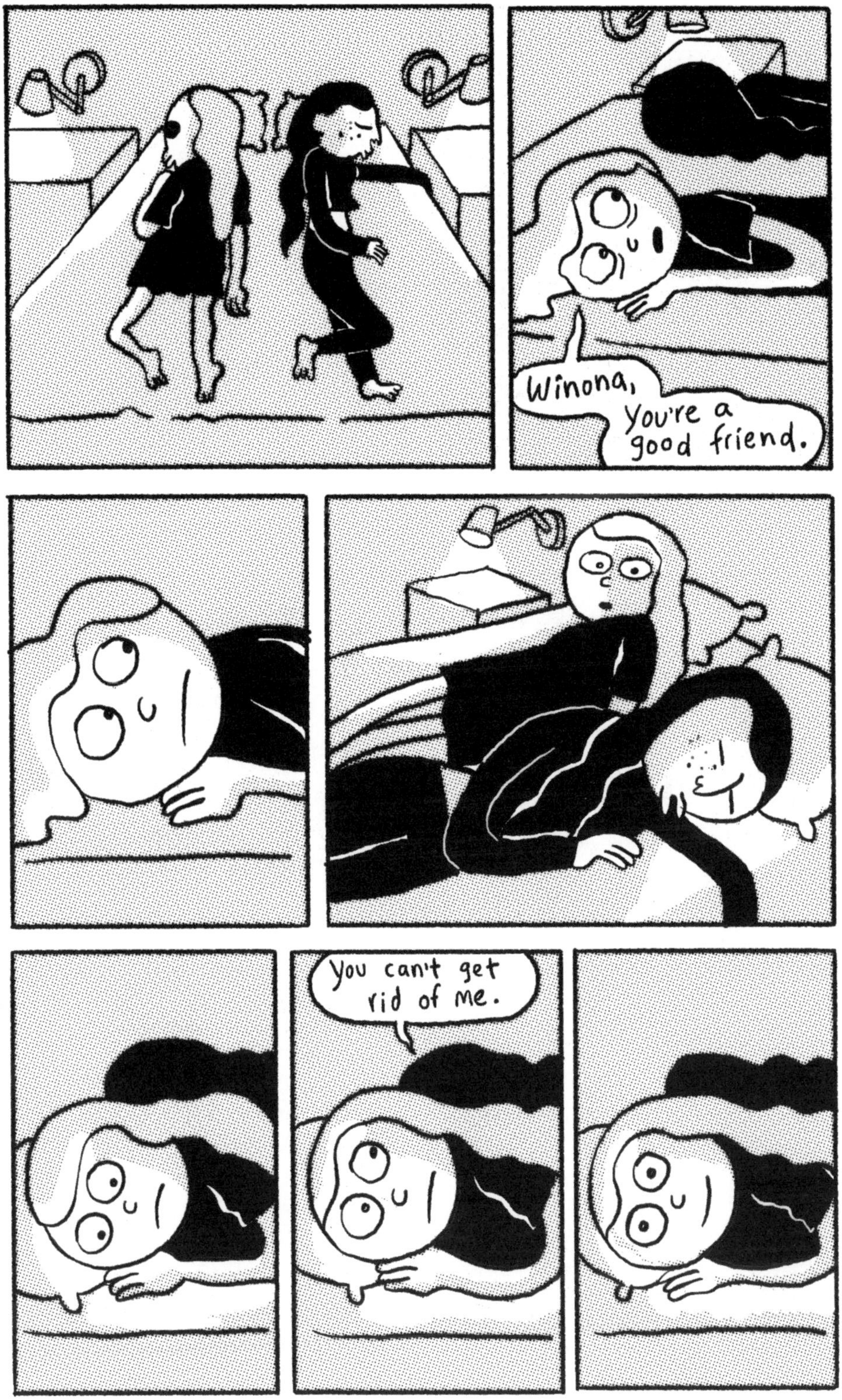
Winona, you're a good friend.
You can't get rid of me.

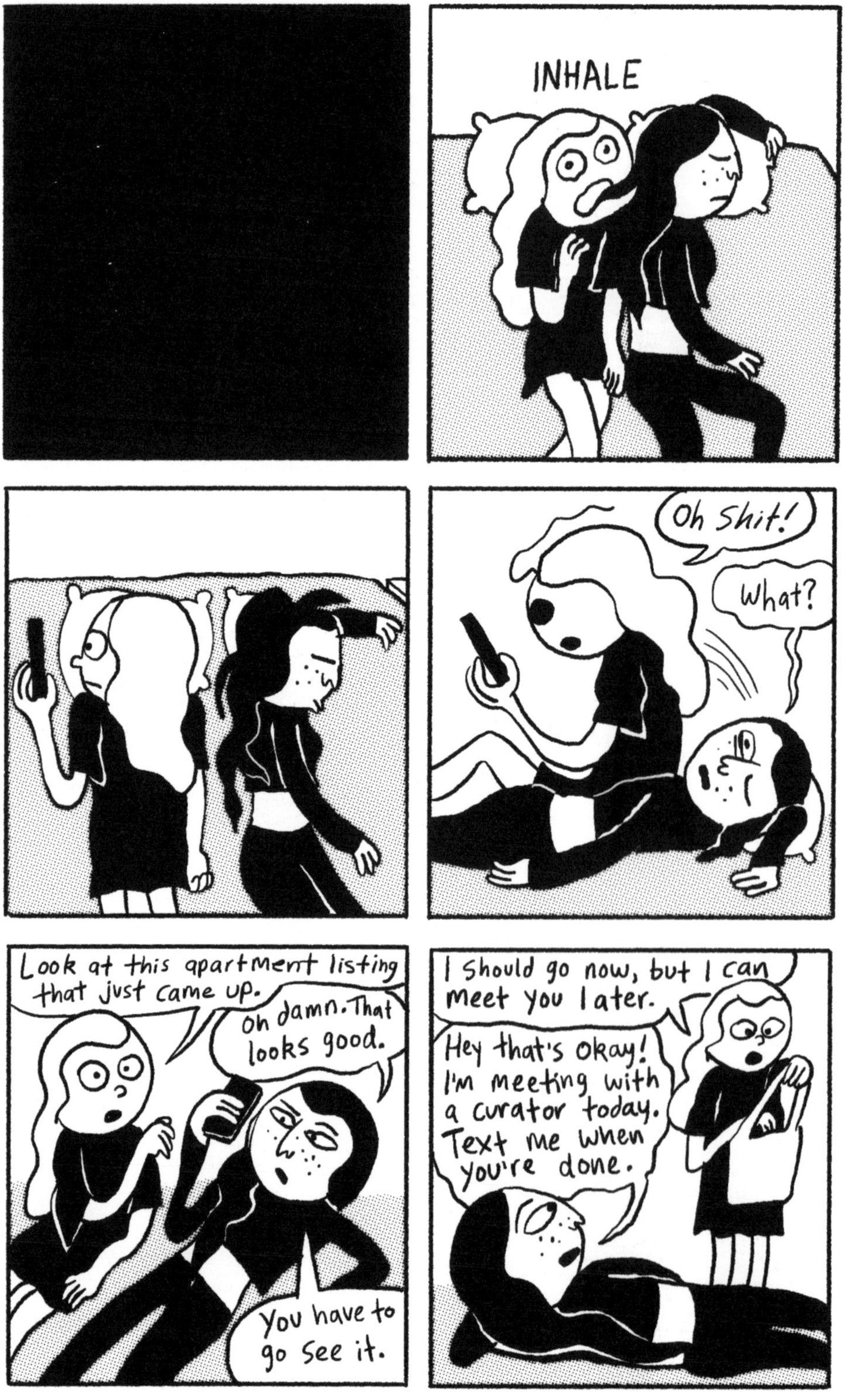
INHALE
Oh Shit!
What?
Look at this apartment listing that just came up.
Oh damn. That looks good.
You have to go see it.
I should go now, but I can meet you later.
Hey that's okay! I'm meeting with a curator today. Text me when you're done.

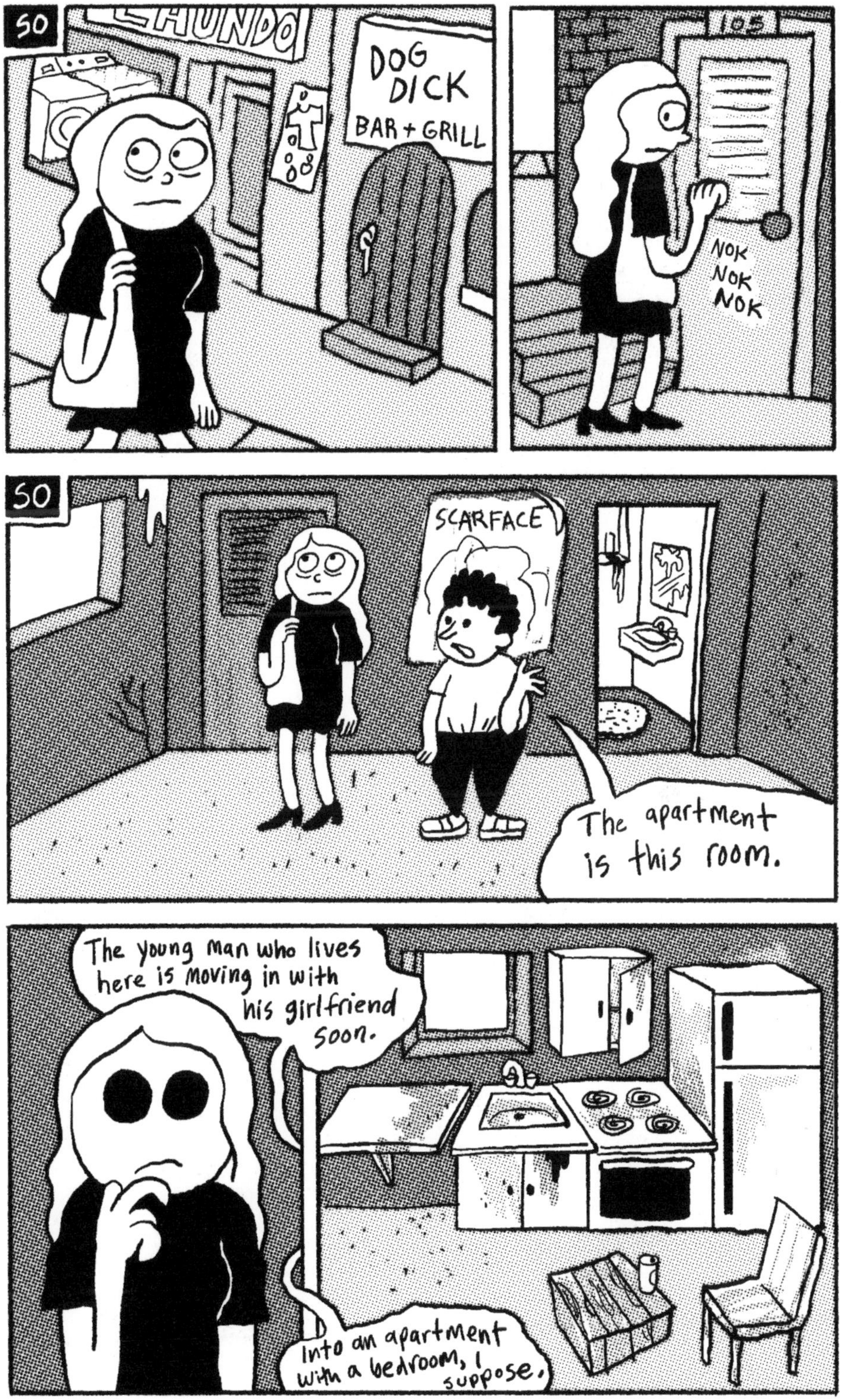
SO
LAUNDRO
DOG DICK
BAR + GRILL
105
NOK
NOK
NOK
SO
SCARFACE
The apartment is this room.
The young man who lives here is moving in with his girlfriend soon.
Into an apartment with a bedroom, I suppose.

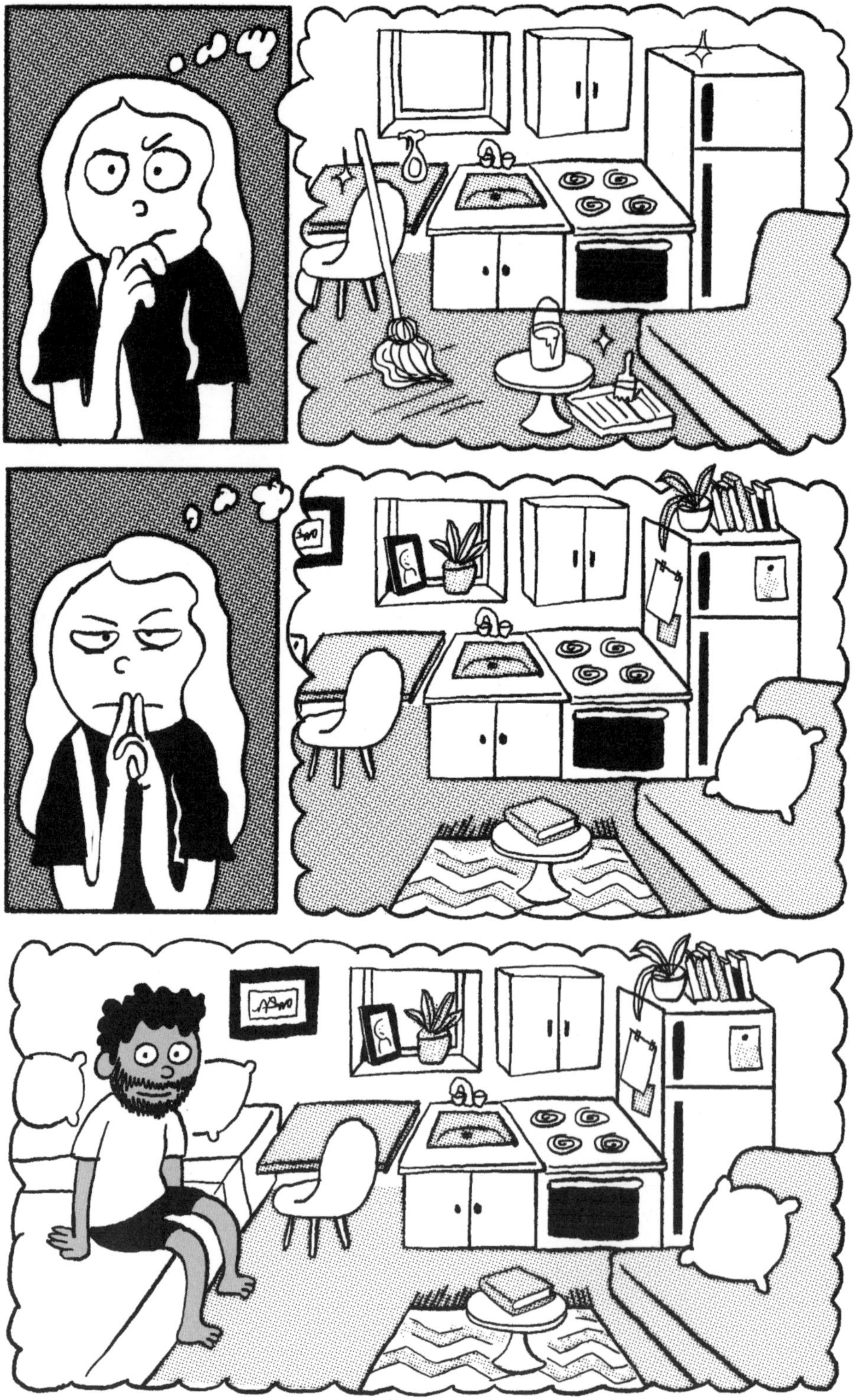

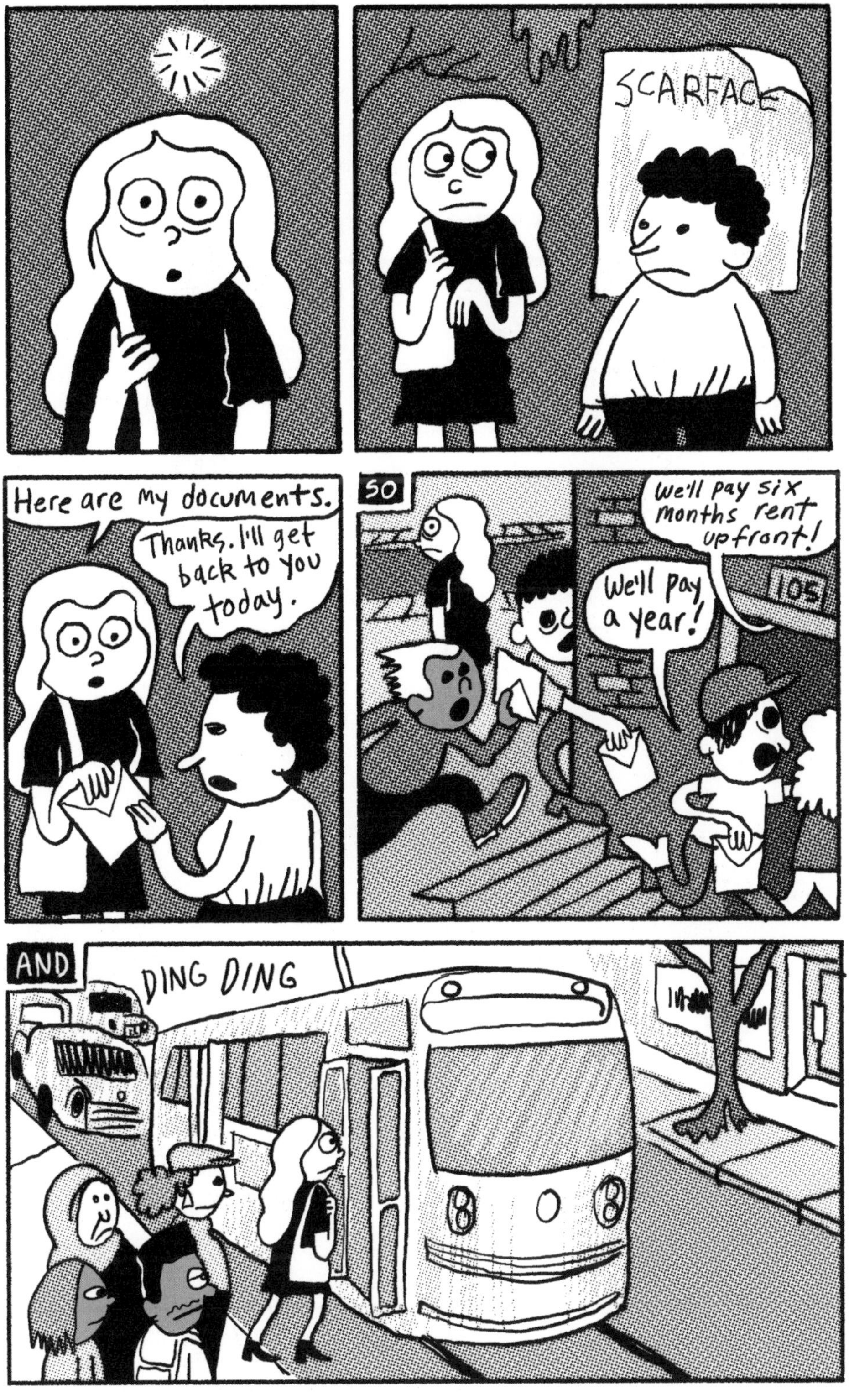
SCARFACE
Here are my documents.
Thanks. I'll get back to you today.
SO
We'll pay six months rent upfront!
We'll pay a year!
105
AND
DING DING

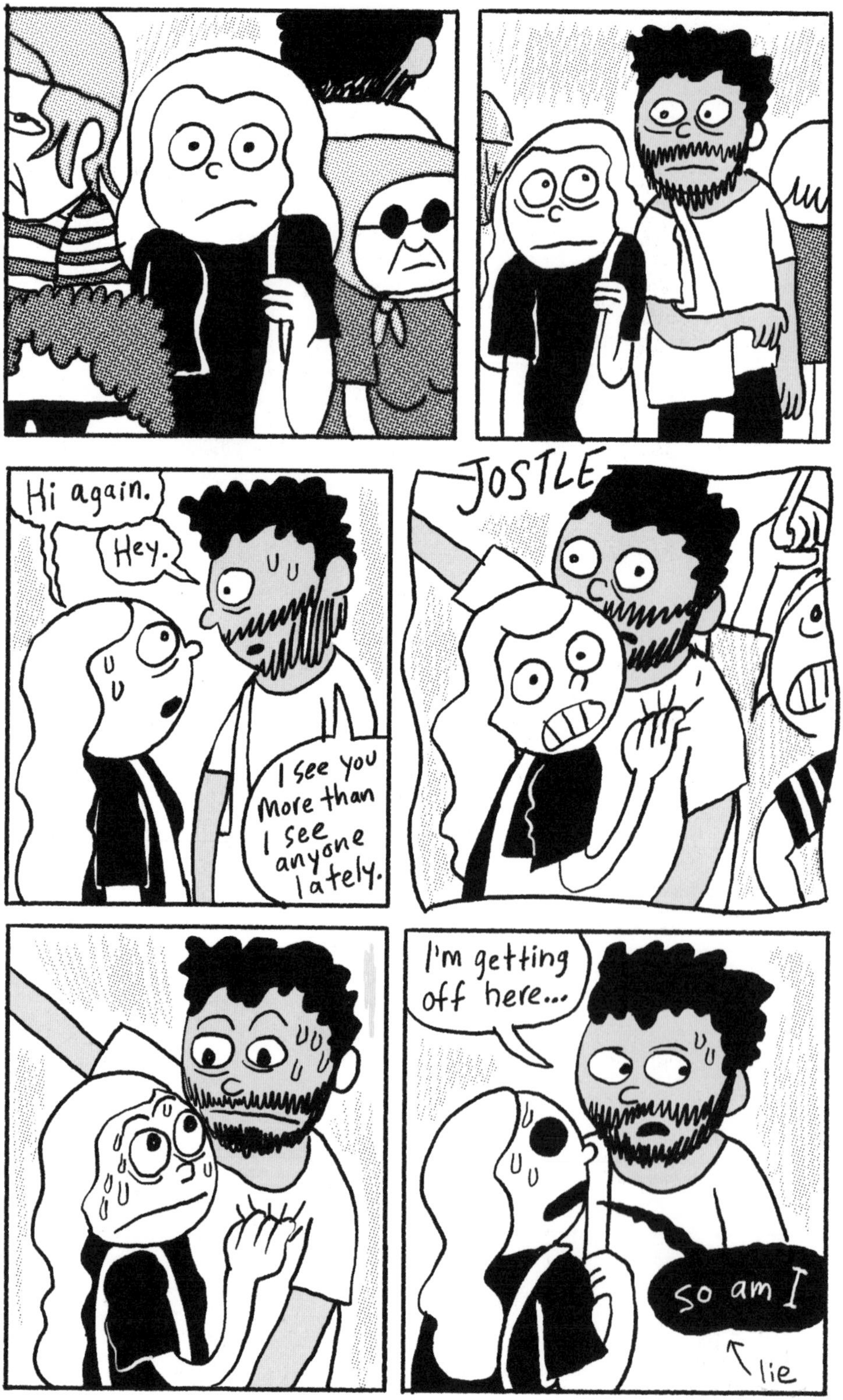
Hi again.
Hey.
I see you more than I see anyone lately.
JOSTLE
I'm getting off here...
so am I
lie

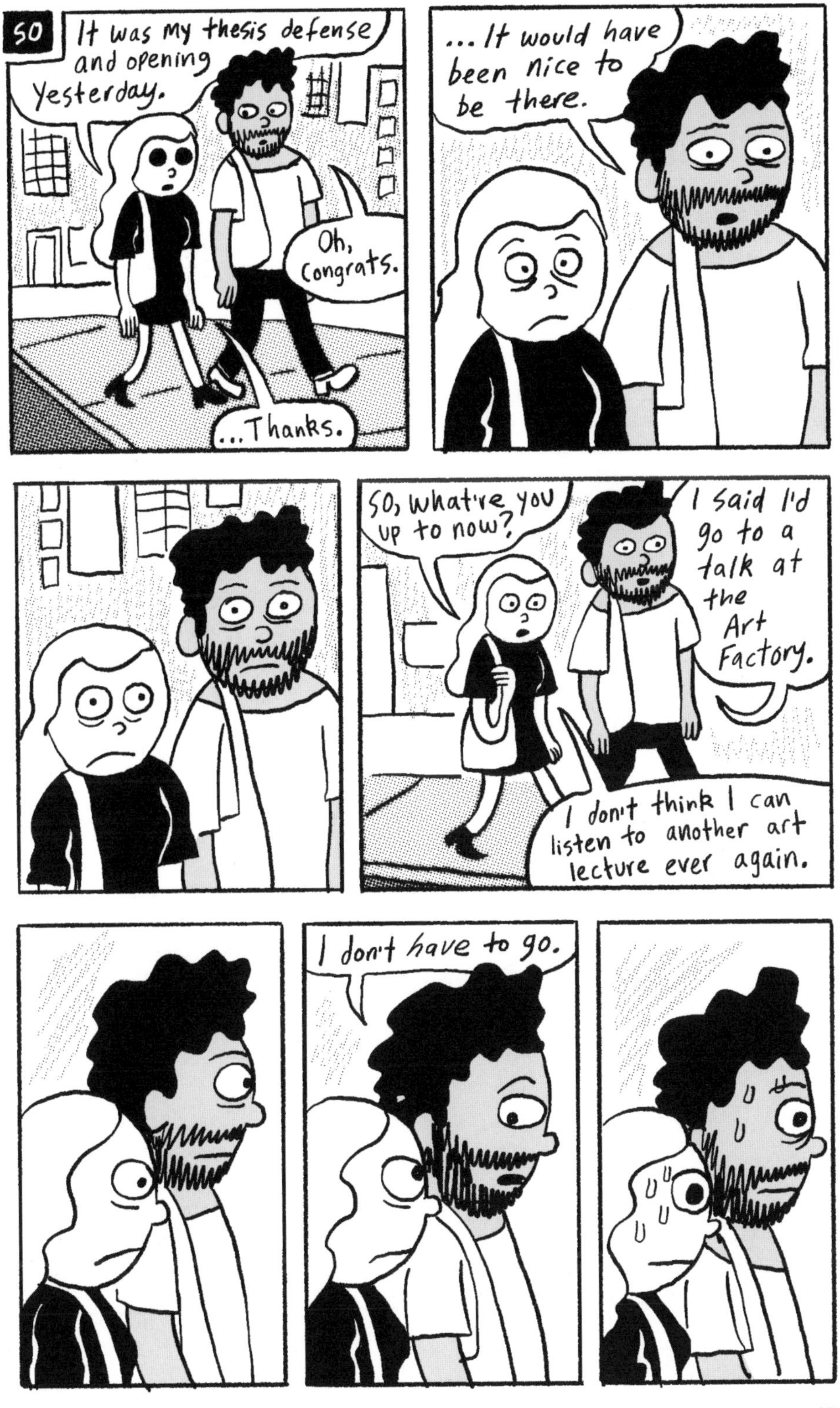

SO
It was my thesis defense and opening yesterday.
Oh, congrats.
...Thanks.
...It would have been nice to be there.
So, what're you up to now?
I said I'd go to a talk at the Art Factory.
I don't think I can listen to another art lecture ever again.
I don't have to go.

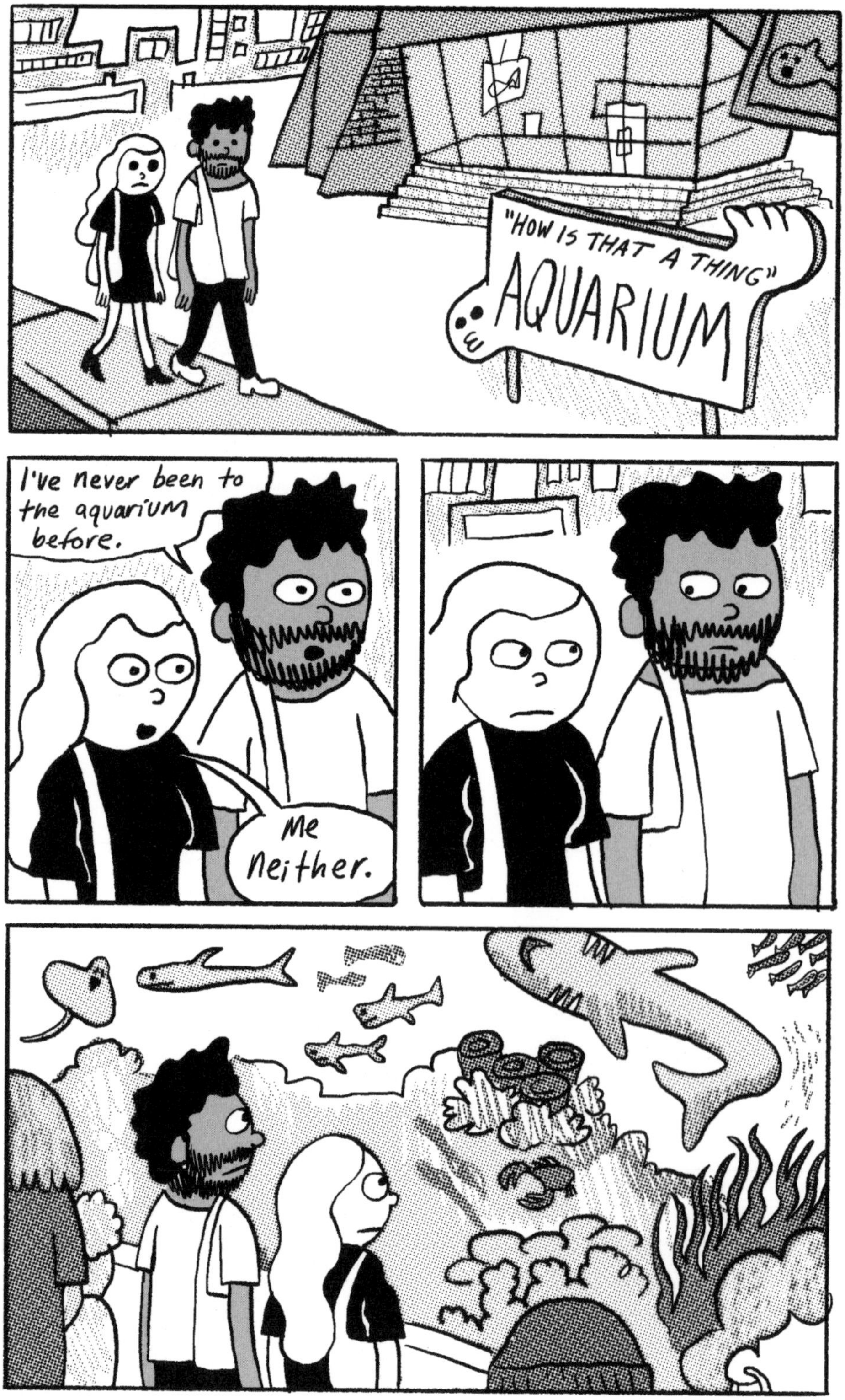
"HOW IS THAT A THING"
AQUARIUM
I've never been to the aquarium before.
Me neither.

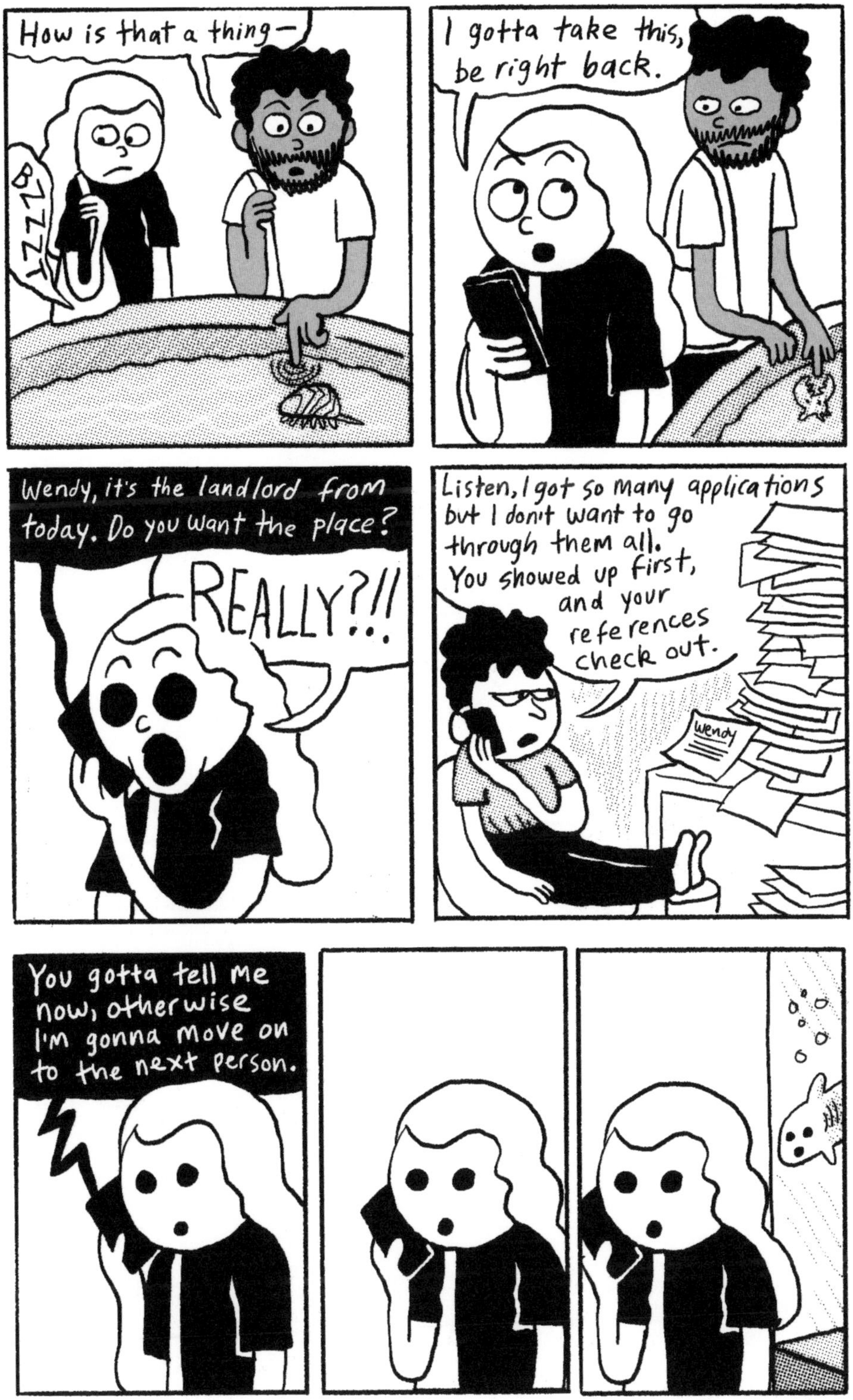
How is that a thing—
BZZZT
I gotta take this, be right back.
Wendy, it's the landlord from today. Do you want the place?
REALLY?!!
Listen, I got so many applications but I don't want to go through them all. You showed up first, and your references check out.
Wendy
You gotta tell me now, otherwise I'm gonna move on to the next person.

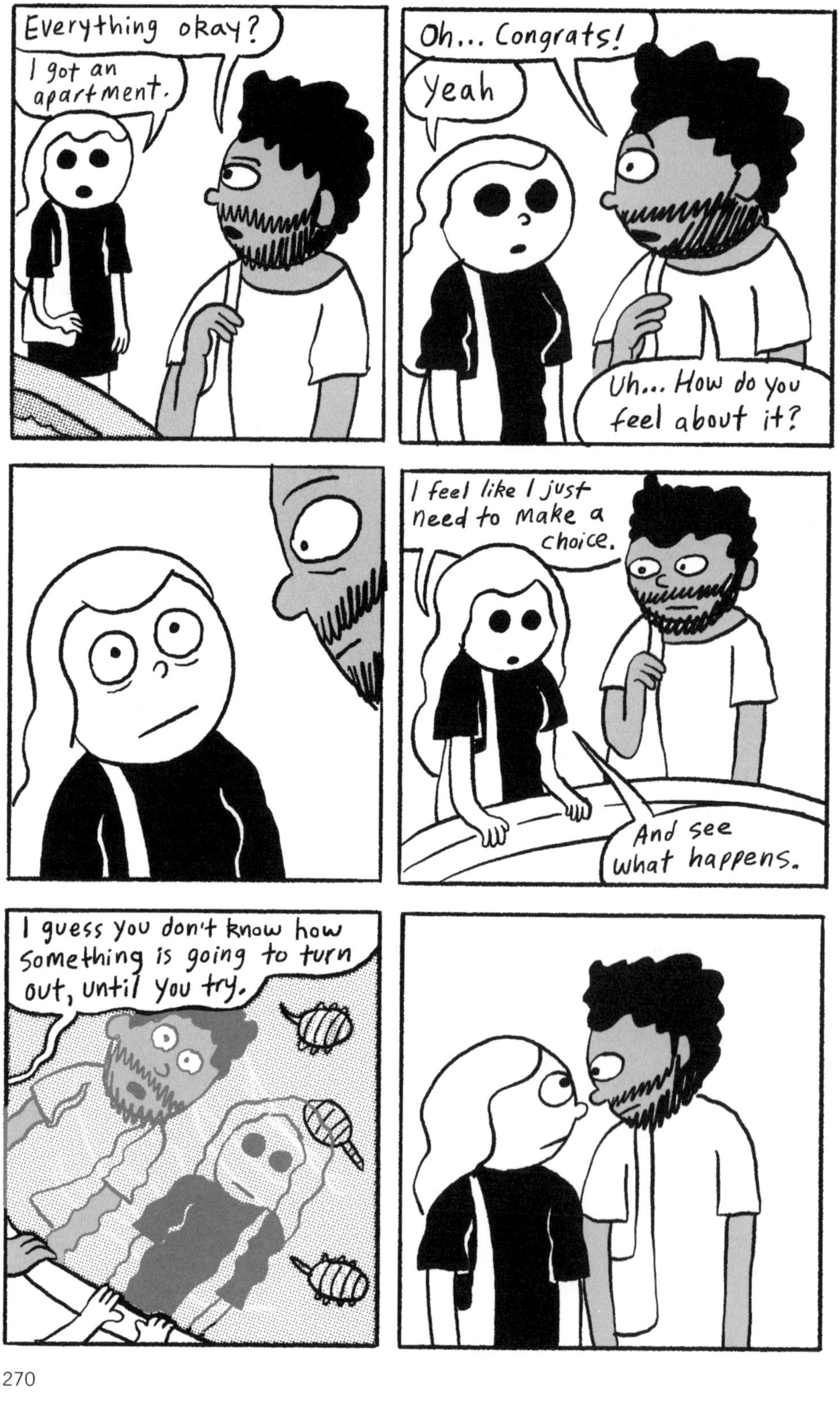
Everything okay?
I got an apartment.
Oh... Congrats!
Yeah
Uh... How do you feel about it?
I feel like I just need to make a choice.
And see what happens.
I guess you don't know how something is going to turn out, until you try.

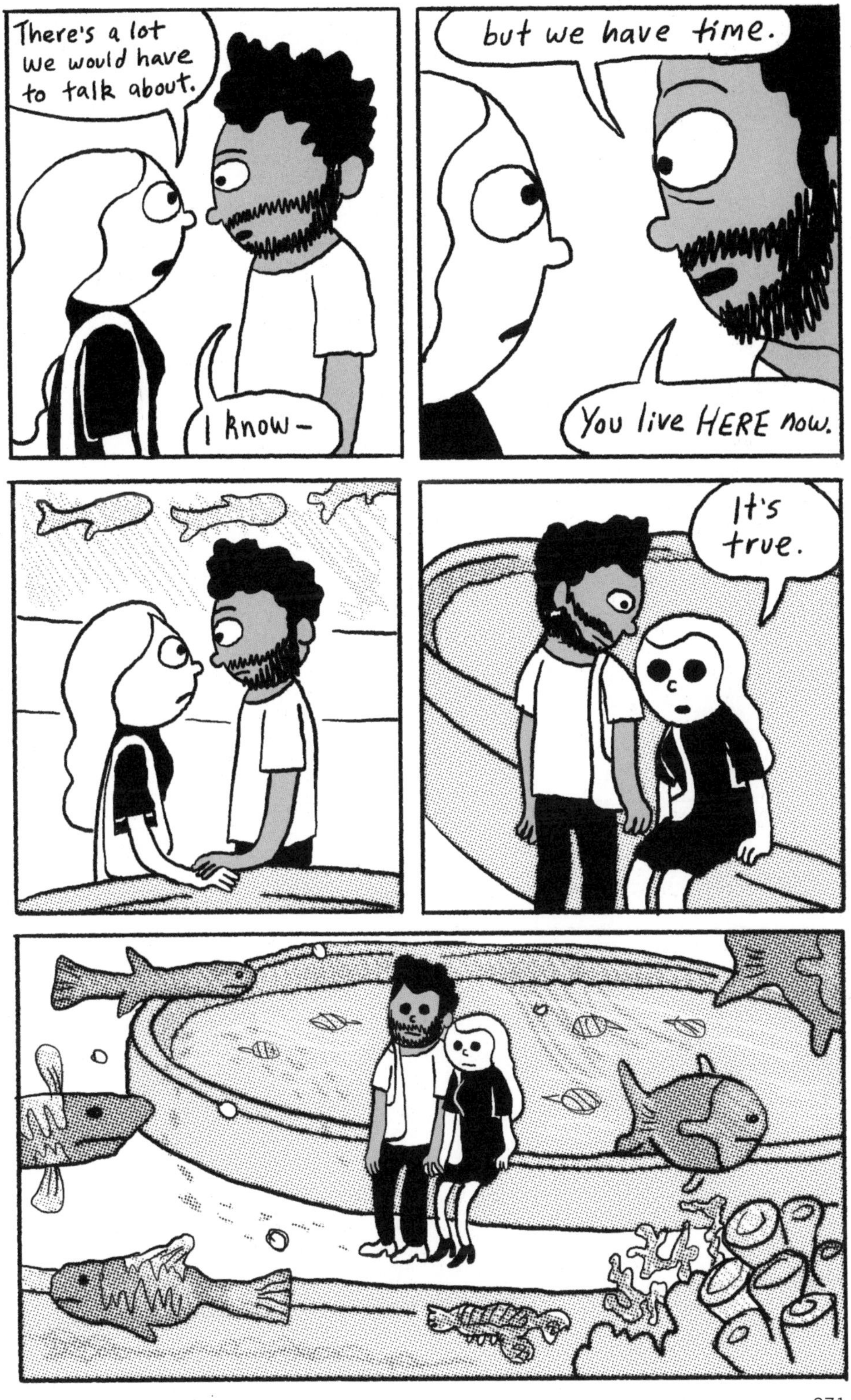
There's a lot we would have to talk about.
I know-
but we have time.
You live HERE now.
It's true.

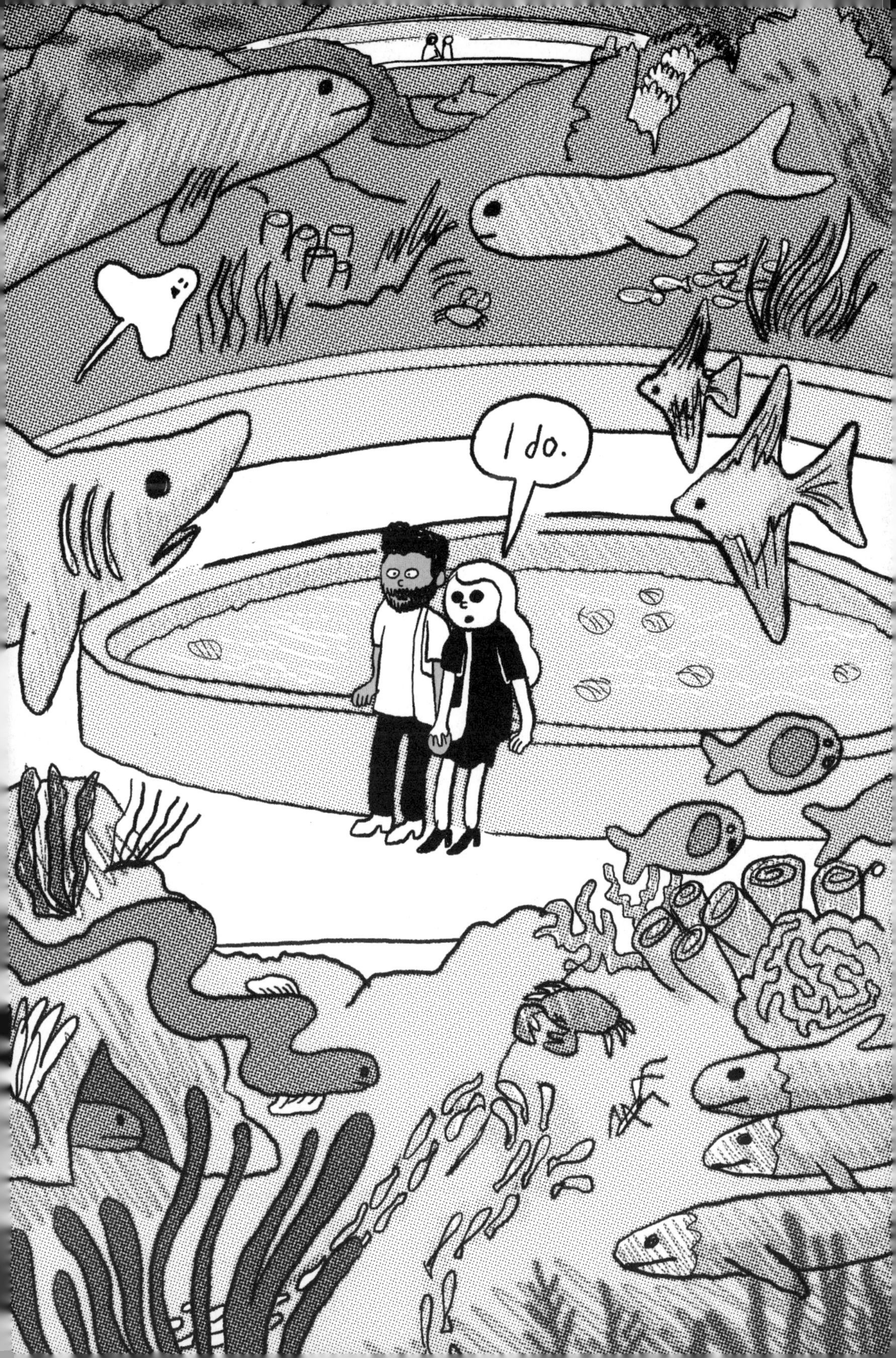
I do.

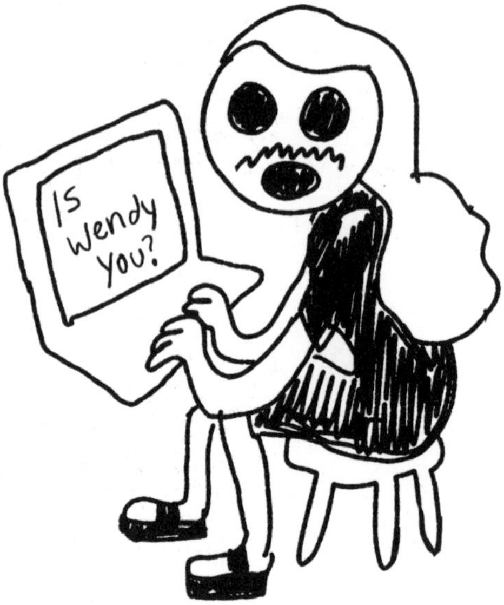
Is
Wendy
you?

WALTER SCOTT is an interdisciplinary artist working in comics, drawing, video, performance, and sculpture. His comic series *Wendy* chronicles the continuing misadventures of a young artist in a satirical imagining of the contemporary art world. *Wendy* has been published in two previous volumes and featured in *Canadian Art*, *Art in America*, and on the *New Yorker* website, and was selected for the 2016 edition of *Best American Comics*. Scott completed an MFA at the University of Guelph in 2018.